Neotropical
Wildlife Use and
Conservation

Neotropical Wildlife Use and Conservation

EDITED BY

John G. Robinson and Kent H. Redford

With Forty-Seven Contributors

THE UNIVERSITY OF CHICAGO PRESS

Chicago and London

The University of Chicago Press, Chicago 60637
The University of Chicago Press, Ltd., London

© 1991 by The University of Chicago
All rights reserved. Published 1991
Printed in the United States of America

00 99 98 97 96 95 94 93 92 91   5 4 3 2 1

Library of Congress Cataloging in Publication Data

Neotropical wildlife use and conservation / edited by John G. Robinson and Kent H. Redford,
with forty-seven contributors.
    p. cm.
    Includes bibliographical references and index.
    ISBN 0-226-72258-9.—ISBN 0-226-72259-7 (pbk.)
    1. Hunting—Latin America. 2. Wild animal collecting—Latin America. 3. Wildlife con-
servation—Latin America. 4. Wild animal trade—Latin America. 5. Wildlife management—Latin America. I. Robinson, John G. II. Redford, Kent Hubbard.
SK159.N46 1991
639.9'098—dc20   90-44430
                                                                               CIP

Contents

Part 3   Market Hunting and Collecting

Part 4   Wildlife Farming and Ranching

Part 5   Sport Hunting

Foreword

ALFRED L. GARDNER

Sport hunting, subsistence hunting, market rearing and hunting, commercial harvesting of wildlife? Are these legitimate activities in the neotropics, where the loss of humid tropical forests has become one of the greatest catastrophes of the twentieth century? Yes! is the clear, but qualified, answer. This is not to say that all opinions and conclusions contained in this book argue for or against these enterprises. Indiscriminate, opportunistic, and uncontrolled exploitation already has reduced many populations of economically important species to levels where the loss of critical habitat through forest conversion means extinction. Sustainable yield is not simply a "use it or lose it" philosophy without planning or control. Neglect, status quo attitudes, and continued ignorance of the dependence of local people on wildlife and other forest and river resources have contributed to the loss of biological diversity. Exploitation pressure often is claimed to be self-controlling because as acquisition costs approach or exceed the value of a resource, interest diminishes and efforts to acquire the resource drop. However, to assume that the greater time and rising cost of hunting increasingly scarcer animals will reduce exploitation pressure until the populations recover to harvestable levels is naive because the take is largely opportunistic and the conversion of forested land to agricultural use impedes or prevents that recovery.

As its title suggests, this book focuses on issues concerning subsistence and commercial uses of wildlife. The contributions explore diverse topics, including wildlife as food; the sport hunting of doves, ducks, and deer; commercialization through the sale of parrots, bush meat, turtle eggs, and the skins and hides of mammals, crocodilians, and lizards; and a relatively new enterprise—the management and domestication of wildlife for commercial purposes. Pertinent questions, interwoven throughout the book, hold these topics together: What kinds of wildlife are used? How heavy is that use? and What are the sustainable-use levels? The fundamental problem is, how do we maintain a biological community while continuing to use the resources that community provides? This book, the first of its kind to address these questions for the neotropics, reflects the concern of its contributors and editors for the conservation of biological diversity. That concern recognizes the human impact on wildlife resources and contains the hope that human needs can be met without further endangering the survival of other life forms on this planet.

Nearly 10 years ago I coauthored a report titled "Establecimiento de una Estación de Investigaciones Científicas en el Parque Nacional Yasuni de la República de Ecuador" with Dr. Angel Paucar M. This was one of several reports resulting from a cooperative agreement between the U.S. Fish and Wildlife Service and its Ecuadoran counterpart, the Programa Nacional Forestal of the Ministerio de Agricultura y Ganadería. Ecuador was interested in establishing, among other projects, a biological research facility in the Amazon lowlands.

Dr. Paucar, then head of the Sección de Vida Silvestre, and I pursued the idea of a biological research station. We conceived the plan for a research and training facility whose focus would be divided between the open inquiry of basic research in tropical biology and a more applied program of research directed toward the development of appropriate sustainable-yield technologies for the management of economically important native plants and animals. Although well aware of the acute need for basic research in tropical biology, we believed that it was at least as important to develop alternatives to more national parks as to reduce forest destruction. We wanted development options that protected biotic diversity while supporting basic human needs and contributing to the overall regional and national economy. Our choice was to establish a facility that would develop technologies and maintenance strategies for economically important plants and animals, strategies that used economic incentives to protect habitat.

In justifying our projected program for the research station, we emphasized the potential economic benefits from the sustained-yield management of large, diverse tracts of tropical humid forest for native biotic resources as an alternative to timber harvesting and the more traditional conversion of forested lands to various agricultural uses. An appropriate management technology would have other benefits: it would encourage ranchers to manage wildlife resources in remnant forests and wetlands as a cash crop instead of clearing and draining these habitats to enlarge their agricultural use, for example. Dr. Paucar had already conducted preliminary surveys on the kinds and estimated weights of wildlife consumed by Ecuadorans living in the eastern lowlands. We used those data with other information to estimate potential income from primates for biomedical research, some birds and mammals for meat, a few other mammals and crocodilians for meat and skins, and some turtle and fish resources for meat. We derived an estimated return per hectare that was exceeded only by the potential income from cutting merchantable timber or by mineral extraction. Timber cutting destroys the forest and is practical only where there is access to a sawmill. Mining (or oil extraction) is possible only where proven deposits and reserves are available and accessible and their removal is economically justified.

We were extremely conservative in calculating economic values for two reasons. First, potential income was based on tentative and difficult-to-support estimates of yield and market value; second, we were aware of the prevailing erroneous opinion that the "jungle" does not support much animal biomass of economic worth. To counter arguments that our projected revenues were exaggerated, we excluded other potential revenue sources from our calculations. Excluded sources were tourism, the pet trade, sport hunting, scientific interests, the tropical fish industry, butterflies, ornate insects, and other invertebrates. Also we did not include all meat resources (especially fish and turtles) and, perhaps most significantly, we did not consider any plant resources, which some botanists believe have the greatest economic potential. We became convinced that, given the realities of our economically driven society, species could be saved by cropping some individuals to justify saving the habitat, which ultimately is critical for *all* species, including those having little or no perceived economic value.

We anticipated problems and resistance to a program that would encourage the selective cropping of native species of plants and animals. The major emphasis in conservation was (and still is) on supporting and enlarging viable systems of protected wildlands (reserves, preserves, refuges, and national parks). Compliance with the Convention on International Trade in Endangered Species of Wild Flora and Fauna (CITES) made the taking of many economically important species illegal. Active programs that permit use of the native biota advocate captive rearing and propagation as the desired, if not only, alternative to harvesting these resources in the wild. We knew also that land tenure laws in Ecuador, typical of those in most Latin American countries, require that the land be improved (i.e., that the forest be removed) before a colonist can gain and hold title.

We reasoned as follows:

1. Given the conversion rate of tropical humid forests, the best system of protected wildlands has the potential of saving only token representatives of the native biota. A complementary program would be necessary for increased, broader protection.

2. Captive rearing and propagation programs are expensive, labor intensive, and adaptable only to a few species. Although useful for some species, these programs tend to operate on the premise that humans can outdo nature.

3. Rural and forest-dwelling people rely heavily on the full array of forest and river products as food, medicine, tools, and construction materials. Some of these products commonly are sold or bartered to acquire otherwise unattainable goods and services.

How safe will protected wildlands be when these people exhaust subsistence resources elsewhere? If a primary goal of governments is to use land in ways that sustain the populace while contributing to the economy, why must the rich, diverse, and valuable biota that characterize most tropical forests be destroyed as part of the developmental process when the same resources could be used to meet those economic needs on a sustainable basis? As an analogy, a monkey in the cooking pot might be worth thirty cents, whereas that same monkey sold on a legitimate international market may be worth $400.

Responses to our proposal varied from enthusiasm to apathy and hostility. I was not well prepared for the latter. The research station did not become a reality, probably due as much to the steep decline in the price of crude oil as to anything else.

My education began, and I soon became more aware of attitudes and thought processes in the scientific and conservation communities. Far from being new, our ideas about trying to augment protected wildland systems by using economic incentives to conserve additional habitat had been around for a long time. Nonetheless, some dominant personalities in the conservation community have adopted inflexible protectionist outlooks and strategies. Relatively few seemed willing to acknowledge the dependency of subsistence-level people on forest resources. Those who did sometimes had an unrealistic special faith that native people would not overexploit their resources no matter how their technology was altered by the addition of guns, axes, machetes, and motors. Years of field experience in Latin America had already taught me that governments tend to give low priority to the needs of subsistence-level people. These people usually are outside of the active economy and contribute little to cover the cost of the services available from their governments.

I had assumed that the subsistence dependency on forest and river resources by rural people in lesser developed countries was understood and widely known in the conservation community. On the contrary—a surprising number of people seemed only vaguely aware of this dependency or chose to think romantically of it as quaint. During one seminar on issues and perceptions in tropical conservation I commented that the numbers of doves, quail, and other larger birds killed annually in Mexico for food by men and boys using slingshots must number in the millions. The overwhelming response was that I was exaggerating or, if these figures could possibly be true, to ask how could the killing be stopped. My motive for making the comment was to point out some kinds of subsistence dependency on wildlife that are poorly understood and usually ignored and to stress that, if we are to plan wisely for the conservation of biological diversity, we must understand how biological resources are used. In other words, my purpose was not to stop the activity, but to understand it in terms that permitted integrating that usage and dependence into planning for responsible conservation programs.

With few exceptions, knowledge of subsistence dependency is still in the realm of folklore. Unfortunately, when scientists find what they believe to be "virgin" habitats, most of the important animal resources already have been exploited. We simply do not know what the carrying capacity is for most economically important species. To compound the problem, planners and decision makers come from increasingly urbanized societies in which they develop little or no empathy for or understanding of the complexities of tropical environments.

We already know a lot about some species such as primates. Unfortunately, we know little more about other groups than what the species look like. Research is necessary on three fronts. First, we must understand the natural history of the taxa we wish to use and the communities comprising them in order to plan cropping strategies that have the least negative effect. Some of this information already is available in the cultures of native peoples. Second, we need to develop suitable capture and cropping techniques and transfer that technology to the users. Finally, and perhaps most importantly, we must know the market. If cropping is for commercial purposes, we need to implement marketing methods, strategies, and controls to ensure the maximum return to the legitimate producer while protecting the market from illegal competition. We must remember, however, that while wildlife is the most conspicuous forest resource next to the trees themselves, it is only one component of an array of biological resources that figure in the economics of human societies.

Some of the sentiments, experiences, and opinions expressed here were included in a seminar given at the University of Florida in 1983. That seminar encouraged the editors to hold a lecture series at the University of Florida in 1987 to examine the uses of wildlife in the neotropics; this series became the basis for this book. For this and the opportunity to comment, I am genuinely grateful.

Preface

This volume focuses on the use and conservation of the large-bodied mammals, birds, and reptiles of the neotropics. The importance of these animals as components of their ecological systems, as sources of animal protein for subsistence hunters, and as resources exploited by commercial markets has not been appreciated until recently, since most of the large-bodied species are denizens of the forest, and little was known about their ecology or behavior. In contrast, in Asia and especially Africa, much more was known about many large-bodied wildlife species, because they live in open country, are easy to observe, and are important game species.

Until the second half of this century, what was known derived largely from the biological expeditions and collecting trips of the eighteenth and nineteenth centuries. South America was very much the "dark continent" with respect to our biological knowledge. Field ecology in the neotropics began slowly. William Beebe from the New York Zoological Society began traveling to Mexico, Trinidad, British Guiana, and Venezuela during the first decade of the century. The Barro Colorado Island Biological Laboratory, in what is now Panama, was established as a center of entomological and tropical disease research in 1923. The island became a center for neotropical ornithology through the work of Frank Chapman from the American Museum of Natural History. In the 1930s Robert Enders pioneered the study of mammalian natural history, and Clarence Ray Carpenter fathered field primatology on the island. Alexander Skutch went to Costa Rica in 1935 and helped establish Central America's tradition in tropical ornithology. Institutional involvement, however, was needed to provide the impetus for further development of the field. Barro Colorado Island came under the control of the Smithsonian Institution in 1946. In 1949, the New York Zoological Society established a permanent home for its itinerant Department of Tropical Research at Simla in the northern range of Trinidad. In 1963, the Organization for Tropical Studies (OTS) was founded and produced a generation of young field biologists interested in tropical systems.

As knowledge of tropical systems expanded, so did the concern with their conservation. The issue of tropical forest conversion came to the fore in the early 1970s and gained popular attention with the publication of Goodland and Irwin's "Amazon Jungle: Green Hell or Red Desert" in 1975. In the following years, there were numerous conferences, policy statements, reports, and recommendations: The U.S. National Academy of Sciences report on the conversion of tropical moist forests in 1980, the World Conservation Strategy in the same year, the U.S. Strategy Conference on Biological Diversity in 1981, the Office of Technological Assessment report to the U.S. Congress in 1987, to name a few.

Despite the increased knowledge and concern with neotropical ecosystems, little attention was paid to the large-bodied mammals, birds, and reptiles. Field research initially concentrated on the elegant interrelationships and biological peculiarities so evident in the tropics. The large species are more difficult to study: They occur at low densities and are frequently susceptible to human disturbance. Field studies of these species require both time and money. Conservationists, who in the palaeotropics were interested in the large, charismatic species, in the neotropics were more concerned with the loss of biological diversity, much of which resides in the flora and invertebrates.

Students of human systems in the tropics, however, recognized these large-bodied vertebrates as important sources of dietary protein for people. Anthropologists documented the reliance of both indigenous groups and colonists on wild game and other natural products. The preservation and protection of indigenous cultures requires the conservation of natural systems, particularly populations of game species. Sociologists and economists began to document the use of wildlife and wildlife products in local cultures and markets.

Wildlife biologists, especially nationals from tropical countries, also appreciated the importance of large-bodied species. Traditionally focused on game species in the temperate regions, wildlife managers in recent years have expanded their interests to encompass nongame and tropical species. With an appreciation of both biological conservation and the harvest of game species, wildlife biology can bridge differences among tropical ecologists, conservationists, and social scientists.

This volume therefore incorporates perspectives from a number of disciplines. All the chapters focus on large-bodied vertebrates and their conservation, which by definition involves an examination of use of wildlife by human populations. Some authors stress the need to conserve viable wildlife populations, others are more concerned with the depletion of natural resources, while still others concentrate on the welfare and rights of people who exploit wildlife populations. All recognize the incompleteness of their knowledge and the need to develop multidisciplinary approaches to these complex issues.

Most of the contributions to this volume derive from a seminar series at the University of Florida in the fall of 1987. We invited specialists and requested they address three issues: What is the importance of wildlife to people? What impact does the use of wildlife by people have on populations or the biological community? Is the present pattern of human use sustainable over the long term or could it be made so? Before they arrived, authors submitted a manuscript, which was then circulated to a small group of graduate students. The students critically examined and edited each manuscript and provided feedback to the speakers. The contributors and editors owe a great deal to these students for their diligence, constructiveness, and professionalism: Hector Arita-Watanabe, Ruth Buirkle, Peter Carlson, Peter Crawshaw, Gustavo Fonseca, Alejandro Grajal, Martha Groom, Phil Hall, Leslie Hay, Thia Hunter, Agustín Iriarte, Jeff Jorgenson, Rodrigo Medellín, Daniel Navarro, Claudio Padua, Dan Pearson, Peter Polshek, Andres Seijas, Jody Stallings, Phil Tanimoto, John Thorbjarnarson, Laurie Wilkins, and Petra Wood.

The authors not only had to address the initial set of questions and respond to the suggestions of the students, they also—on subsequent drafts—had to deal with the editors. The authors met these challenges with humor, diligence, and professionalism. We, the editors, must express our appreciation and gratitude. All the authors have agreed to join the editors in donating their royalties from this volume to provide scholarships for students from tropical countries working in wildlife conservation.

Any undertaking that involves complicated logistics, such as that involved in the production of this book, requires the help of a large number of people. Allyn Stearman, Herb Raffaele, and Susan Jacobson read through the whole manuscript and made innumerable comments. We thank them for their constructive criticism and help. We regularly turned to students and faculty in the Program for Studies in Tropical Conservation (PSTC) for assistance. Jody Stallings coordinated schedules of speakers who flew to Florida at regular intervals from locations throughout the Americas. Jeff Jorgenson, Agustín Iriarte, Rodrigo Medellín, and Peter Polshek helped with final translation, editing, and production of papers. Liz Mosier retyped a large number of manuscripts, collated the bibliographies, and inserted myriad changes and corrections. Funds to bring in speakers were provided by the International Programs office at the University of Florida, and we especially thank Ron Labisky and Hugh Popenoe for their personal support of this endeavor. Additional funds were provided by the Program for Studies in Tropical Conservation.

We thank our wives, Linda Cox and Pamela Shaw, who not only had to endure the gestation of this volume, but whose homes were periodically invaded during the seminar series by speakers and an increasingly rowdy group of faculty and students.

JOHN G. ROBINSON
KENT H. REDFORD

Part 1
Framing the
Issues

1

The Use and Conservation of Wildlife

JOHN G. ROBINSON AND KENT H. REDFORD

The use of wild animals by humans has been debated on both ethical and pragmatic levels. The ethical debate (Singer 1976; Callicot 1980; Nations 1988) in its simplest terms concerns whether humans should adopt a homocentric or a biocentric perspective: Do we, as human beings, have the right to use wildlife for our own purposes and benefits, or do wild species have inalienable rights of their own? In this book, we and most other authors agree that unless wildlife has some use to people, then wildlife will not be valued by people. If wildlife has no value, then wildlife and its habitat will be destroyed to make way for other land uses. That use of wildlife can be consumptive or nonconsumptive. People can value wildlife for commercial, recreational, scientific, esthetic, or spiritual reasons. But *people* must use and therefore value wildlife, otherwise wildlife will be lost.

The pragmatic debate is concerned with whether the use of wildlife furthers or hinders its conservation (Eltringham 1984; Geist 1988). It is perhaps brazen to link the words conservation and use, as we have done in the title of this book, but it is our opinion that wildlife has been, is, and will always be used by people, and those of us who advocate the conservation of wild species and biological communities must incorporate that use into our conservation strategies. It is unclear, however, what uses will further conservation. Are uses such as hunting for subsistence or exploitation for large commercial markets compatible with conservation? What about sport hunting? Does ecotourism benefit an area, or do the social, economic, and ecological changes associated with tourism ultimately destroy the resource? Even if some uses are conceivably compatible with conservation, the question of appropriate management remains. Can subsistence hunting be managed in the neotropics? Can large commercial enterprises exploiting wildlife be regulated? In a number of the contributions in this book, authors directly address these questions.

These debates concerning wildlife use should not be confused with debates concerning the economic justification of wildlife use (Prescott-Allen and

3

Prescott-Allen 1982; Ehrenfeld 1988; McNeely 1988; Robinson 1989). Accepting use as a means to conserve wildlife is not the same as providing economic justifications for conserving wildlife. We do equate value with use, but not all value can be measured using economic indices. To the extent that the use of wildlife brings animals or their products into the marketplace, wildlife will also have economic value. But economic value does not supersede other values; it augments them. Debates over the assignment of value to wildlife frequently confuse the terms use, value, and commerce. While it follows that if wildlife is used for some purpose it will have value, it does not follow that value will be economic value, or that once wildlife enters the commercial world, decisions concerning its conservation must be based solely on economic considerations. Value cannot be completely described in economic terms. Value transcends economics. While a number of authors in this book use dollars as one index of the importance of wildlife to people, few, if any, would argue that dollars completely measure the value of the wildlife.

Despite all the debate about conservation and use, there is a paucity of published data addressing these issues. Researchers seeking to conserve wildlife communities frequently prefer to channel their energy into resolving the real-world conflicts inherent in the human use of a natural resource. They rarely have the luxury of stepping back to place their work in a broader context. This is especially true in the neotropics, where there are a large number of active researchers and conservationists but little agreement on how and if people should use wildlife. We decided to provide these researchers with the opportunity to address the questions of use and conservation in the real situations with which they are familiar.

The volume focuses on the neotropical realm, which extends from Mexico to the tip of the South American continent. Contributors have worked in tropical lowland forests, deciduous woodlands, savannas, and high-altitude grasslands. The diversity of habitats included makes general conclusions difficult, but one pattern that emerges from the studies reported is that commercial and consumptive exploitation of species is not equally likely in all ecosystems. Highly seasonal ecosystems, with low species diversity, are more likely to contain large-bodied species with high densities and intrinsic rates of population increase. These are the species that have traditionally been exploited commercially. Capybara and caiman both occur in open savanna. Both have been exploited commercially, and both have the potential to be managed sustainably. Guanaco and vicuña are two species of the high-altitude grasslands that also have commercial importance. In contrast, the more species-diverse habitats, such as tropical forests, do not appear to contain single species with high enough densities and rates of population increase to be commercially exploited. Tropical forest species are more likely to have importance to subsistence hunters who harvest a diversity of species.

Five categories of wildlife use can be distinguished in this volume. Subsistence use is restricted to situations in which people hunt wildlife for their own consumption. Local market uses are those in which people exploit wildlife for sale in local markets, and capital investment in the process is minimal. Wildlife farming and ranching involves the raising of wildlife on private land. Sport hunting is a self-evident category. Commercial uses are distinguished from local market uses by their much larger scale and by their need for significant capital investment. Obviously the boundaries among categories are not clear. Many subsistence hunters augment their income by selling some of their kill. The animal products that market hunters sell in local markets might be used subsequently in large commercial enterprises. Nevertheless, the categories are useful because they reflect different patterns of wildlife use, and these differences have implications for the conservation and management of populations.

This volume is only a beginning. Our knowledge of the response of many species to harvest is still fragmentary. We know little, for instance, about the effect of hunting on peccary—yet the three species are arguably the most important game species in the neotropics. Our understanding of the effects of local, national, and international markets on wildlife populations is minimal. Whether local communities or national governments can regulate wildlife harvest remains an open question. In this volume we can do no more than frame the issues.

2

Subsistence and Commercial Uses of Wildlife in Latin America

KENT H. REDFORD AND JOHN G. ROBINSON

Humans have become increasingly dependent on domesticated plants and animals as sources of food. This dependency has led, particularly in the developed world, to ignoring the importance that wild species play in the nutrition of humans, particularly those in lesser developed countries. To many humans, wild species are not only sources of food but also serve a wide variety of other purposes. Four examples demonstrate the extent to which we rely on wild species: (1) The commercial trade in wild plants and animals has an estimated value of $5 billion (Hemley, 1988); (2) about 55,000 shipments containing wildlife valued at $800 million entered or departed the United States in 1984 (Jorgenson and Jorgenson, in press); (3) between 1976 and 1979, $90 million of wildlife products were exported from Buenos Aires, Argentina, annually (Mares and Ojeda 1984); and (4), in at least sixty-two countries wildlife and fish contribute at least 20% of the animal protein in the diets of the human inhabitants (Prescott-Allen and Prescott-Allen 1982).

It is our purpose to document the ways humans use the wildlife of Latin America, especially the tropical areas. While we define wildlife as nondomesticated vertebrates, our discussion in this paper excludes fish. Humans interact with wildlife in five major ways. They consume wildlife for food; harvest it for skins, leather, and other nonedible products (including ceremonial use); exploit it in the form of live animals for pets, zoos, and the biomedical trade; use it for sport hunting or tourism; and finally exploit it as a source of domesticated animals.

Wildlife for Food

Subsistence

In many parts of Latin America wildlife serves as a major source of food for local peoples. Various authors have calculated the contribution protein from game makes to the overall diet of various groups (cf. Ojasti, Fajardo, and Cova O. 1987). In parts of Amazonian Peru, wildlife provided all of the animal protein consumed by colonists (Pierret and Dourojeanni 1967), and in Nicaragua wildlife (mostly green turtle, *Chelonia mydas*) provided 98% of the meat and fish consumed by Miskito Indians (Nietschmann 1973). In contrast, wild fauna provided only 2% to 20% of the protein requirements of colonists living along the TransAmazon highway in Brazil (Smith 1976a).

A wide variety of wildlife is hunted for food (figs. 2.1 and 2.2) (Ayres et al., this volume; Mittermeier, this volume; Vickers, this volume). The bushnegroes of Suriname take at least twenty-seven species of mammals, twenty-four species of birds, three species of turtles, and two of lizards (Geijskes 1954), while the Maracá Indians of Colombia take at least fifty-one species of birds, including ten species of hummingbirds (Ruddle 1970). Hunters generally take more mammals than birds and more birds than reptiles (Redford and Robinson 1987). The most commonly taken mammals are listed in table 2.1 and the most commonly taken birds in table 2.2.

The numbers of animals taken by subsistence hunters can be very large. Over a period of less than a year the inhabitants of three Waorani villages in Ecuador killed 3,165 mammals, birds, and reptiles (Yost and Kelley 1983).

Figure 2.2. Yuqui Indian with macaw and toucan (Bolivia). (Photo, K. H. Redford.)

Figure 2.1. Kayapó Indians with capybara, paca, and kinkajou (Brazil). (Photo, K. H. Redford.)

TABLE 2.1
Mammals Most Important to Subsistence Hunters

Marsupialia	Primates	*Dasyprocta* spp.
Didelphis marsupialis	*Callicebus* spp.	*Myoprocta* spp.
Edentata	*Aotus* spp.	*Hydrochaeris*
Dasypus novemcinctus	*Cebus apella*	*hydrochaeris*
Dasypus spp.	*Cebus* spp. (non-tufted)	Perissodactyla
Priodontes maximus	*Alouatta* spp.	*Tapirus terrestris*
Tamandua tetradactyla	*Ateles* spp.	Artiodacyla
Myrmecophaga	*Lagothrix lagothricha*	*Tayassu pecari*
tridactyla	Lagomorpha	*T. tajacu*
Bradypus tridactylus	*Sylvilagus brasiliensis*	*Mazama* spp.
Choloepus hoffmanni	Rodentia	Carnivora
	Squirrels	*Nasua* spp.
	Agouti paca	*Potos flavus*

Source: Redford and Robinson 1986.

TABLE 2.2
Birds Most Important to Subsistence Hunters

Tinamidae	*Pipile pipile*	Columbidae
Tinamus spp.	*Nothocrax urutum*	Psittacidae
Crypturellus spp.	*Mitu* spp.	*Ara* spp.
Phalacrocoracidae	*Pauxi pauxi*	*Amazona* spp.
Phalacrocorax sp.	*Crax* spp.	Ramphastidae
Ardeidae	Phasianidae	*Pteroglossus flavirostris*
Anatidae	*Odontophorus gujanensis*	*Ramphastos* spp.
Cracidae	Psophiidae	*Selenidera reinwardtii*
Ortalis sp.	*Psophia* spp.	
Penelope spp.		

Source: Redford and Robinson 1987.

This total includes 562 woolly monkeys (*Lagothrix lagothricha*), 313 Cuvier's toucan (*Ramphastos cuvieri*), and 152 white-lipped peccary (*Tayassu pecari*). Certainly not all groups hunt at this intensity, but using average kill rates based on studies of colonist hunting (Redford and Robinson 1987), it is possible to calculate the number of birds and mammals killed in one year by the rural population of Amazonas state, Brazil (Redford and Robinson, unpubl. ms.). This 1,564,445-km^2 area supports a rural population of 573,885 (as of 1982) who, if they hunt at average levels, annually kill 2,824,662 mammals and 530,884 birds. If reptiles are included, the figure probably reaches 3.5 million vertebrates killed annually by people for food.

It is clear that as a general rule, wildlife is more important to Indian groups than to settlers of European descent (Redford and Robinson 1987). This results from a stronger hunting tradition by Indians, fewer domestic animals, and less access to packaged meat. To many Indian groups, wildlife and fish are the sole sources of meat. As the isolation of these indigenous groups diminishes, Indians are increasingly consuming tinned meat, which has higher prestige but requires cash to purchase and draws the hunter into a market economy and away from the "free" wildlife of the forests (cf. Paolisso and Sackett 1986).

Commerce

Until the arrival of the Europeans in South America in the early 1500s there appears to have been only a limited market for meat from wildlife, probably due to problems of transportation and storage. However, as early as the seventeenth century, Europeans established a commercial trade in meat of manatee (*Trichechus manatus* and *T. inunguis*). The meat was either dried or preserved in its own fat. Until the mid-1900s in the Amazon, the average annual catch of *T. inunguis* was at least several thousand animals. After that period the market increased, peaking in 1959, when a minimum of 6,500 animals were killed. The sale of manatee meat is now prohibited by law, but as with many traditionally exploited species, it is still available in local markets (Domning 1982).

Two other important commercialized sources of meat in the Amazon are caiman and river turtles (McGrath 1986). Caiman of several species, but principally of the genus *Caiman* have been and still are an important source of meat in some areas of the Amazon basin. In the Tocantins River drainage, caiman meat is an important element in the local diet, particularly for poor people. The current annual trade in meat is estimated to involve 21,500 to 32,000 individual caiman (McGrath 1986).

The first European to navigate the Amazon River found many Indian villages with hundreds of penned turtles (mostly *Podocnemis expansa*). Despite ferocious exploitation for meat and eggs (see following discussion), female *P. expansa* continued to gather near nesting beaches and be plentiful enough through the 1850s to impede river traffic on the Madeira (Coutinho 1868 in Smith 1974). *Podecnemis expansa* and several other species of freshwater turtles that were once commercially exploited are now rare. Though no longer extensively harvested, such river turtles are considered a delicacy and are still found in markets from Belize (Moll 1986) to Brazil (Johns 1987).

There has been much trade in the meat of chelonians besides river turtles. The giant tortoises of many oceanic islands, but particularly the Galapagos, were once an important source of meat. In the period between 1831 and 1868 over 13,000 giant tortoises were removed from the islands of the Galápagos to feed the crews of sailing vessels (Townsend 1925). During recent decades green turtle meat has been a very important commercial item (Milliken and Tolunaga 1987; Nietschmann 1973; Pritchard 1979).

Although no longer available on its former scale, game is still readily obtained in many local markets. Unlike the situation in Europe and the United States, game is usually cheaper than the meat of domestic animals. Carvalho (1981 in Seeger 1982) quotes prices in the Manaus market in which capybara was $2/kg and manatee was $1.35/kg while chicken was $3/kg and beef was $5.85/kg. A similar situation has been reported in other markets (Johns 1986;

Redford, unpubl. ms.) although this pattern may be reversed in areas where wild animals have been largely hunted out (Iñigo, pers. comm., 1989). Castro, Revilla, and Neville (1975–76) report the meat of twenty-four species of wild-life for sale in the markets of Iquitos, Peru, including six species of primates. They estimate that 11,000 primates were sold annually in this market and that the inhabitants of the Peruvian department of Loreto, which includes Iquitos, kill 370,000 monkeys annually for consumption and sale.

In many Latin American countries the sale of wildlife is prohibited. However, the legislation is widely ignored, and game is listed on restaurant menus from México to Argentina. In some cases it commands very high prices.

Capybara (*Hydrochaeris hydrochaeris*) meat is an important commercial item in certain parts of Latin America. In some regions of the Amazon Basin the meat of this species is consumed for subsistence, although in others it is not eaten because of its taste (cf. Becker 1981). There is a limited local market in fresh and salted capybara meat within the Amazon Basin (McGrath 1986). The only large commercial exploitation of capybara meat is in Venezuela, where it is eaten especially during the week of Lent. Over 90,000 animals were harvested for this trade in Venezuela in 1981 (Ojasti, this volume).

There is a special trade in wild game involving countries in the Southern Cone. There, meat from introduced species provides an important source of income. For example, between 1976 and 1979 Argentina exported 14 million kg of meat annually, almost all from exotic species. The axis deer (*Axis axis*), the blackbuck (*Antilope cervicapra*), and, of overwhelming importance, the European hare (*Lepus capensis*), accounted for 99.7% of the total (Mares and

TABLE 2.3
Faunal Exploitation in the Peruvian Amazon 1962–67

Animals	No. Individuals Exported
Live monkeys	183,664
Skins	
Caiman	
Melanosuchus niger	47,616
Caiman crocodilus	101,641
Mammals	
Hydrochaeris hydrochaeris	67,575
Lutra longicaudis	47,851
Pteronura brasiliensis	2,529
Felis pardalis	61,499
F. wiedii	9,565
Panthera onca	5,345
Tayassu tajacu	690,219
T. pecari	239,472
Mazama americana	169,775
Total	1,626,751

Sources: Grimwood 1968; Hvidberg-Hansen 1970a, 1970b, 1970c, 1970d; Smith 1979, 1981.

Ojeda 1984). The hare was originally exploited for its pelt, and thirty-four million were exported between 1941 and 1960. Currently, however, in Argentina the meat is more valuable, and at least six million hares are shot annually, with an average annual worth of $24 million (Jackson 1986). Both hares and rabbits are also harvested in Chile and exported to Europe (Iriarte and Jaksíc 1986).

Bird eggs are an important source of food in some areas (Cott 1954). For example, riverine Indians in Peru harvest the eggs of various species that nest on river beaches (Groom, pers. comm., 1988); greater rhea (*Rhea americana*) eggs are seasonally important to some Indian groups such as the Sirionó (Stearman, pers. comm., 1989); eggs of the black-bellied whistling-duck (*Dendrocygna autumnalis*) are harvested by local people in El Salvador (Benítez 1986), flamingo eggs are eaten locally (Campos 1986) and exported (Flamingo eggs smuggled into Chile 1986); and in the Caribbean, sea bird eggs are an important source of food for local people and to a limited extent the egg harvest has also been commercialized (Haynes 1987).

However, reptiles are the most important source of eggs. Eggs of lizards, the iguana (*Iguana iguana;* Werner, this volume; Parra L. 1986), and the tegu (*Tupinambis* sp.; Norman 1987, Fitzgerald, Chani, and Donadio, this volume) are frequently consumed by rural peoples of Latin America. In some areas such eggs have added worth as they are thought to have particular value as an aphrodisiac (Parra L. 1986).

Of the reptiles, turtles provide the most important source of eggs. Freshwater turtle eggs have been heavily exploited in the past for industrial and nutritional purposes. In the Amazon basin, the eggs of *Podocnemis expansa* were so abundant that an industry developed to process them. Oil from the eggs was used for cooking and lighting, and as early as the eighteenth century in Brazil, royal decree controlled the lucrative harvest. In 1719, 192,000 pounds of oil equaling about twenty-four million eggs was produced from the upper Amazon, as late as the 1860s at least forty-eight million eggs yearly were harvested to supply the industry (Smith 1974).

Sea turtle eggs are also an important source of food in many parts of Central America (cf. Cornelius et al., this volume). In Honduras the exploitation is an important source of income and so intense that virtually all nests of the olive ridley turtle have been found and harvested (Lagueux, this volume).

Wildlife for Nonedible Products

Leather

For millennia, humans have been using leather made from the skins of wild animals for clothing, armor, utensils, and decoration. To a limited extent this continues in Latin America, though in most cases manufactured goods have replaced such handmade items.

The earliest commercial exploitation of nonedible products from wildlife by Europeans involved leather. Of the taxa we are considering, perhaps the earliest exploited were the deer. In 1898, 75 metric tons of deer skins, representing about 54,000 animals (probably mostly *Mazama americana*), were exported from Belém (McGrath 1986). Between 1860 and 1879 over two million pampas deer (*Ozotoceros bezoarticus*) skins were exported from Buenos Aires (Jackson and Langguth 1987), and between 1900 and 1950 Costa Rica exported an estimated 832,000 white-tailed deer (*Odocoileus virginianus*) skins (Vaughan, this volume).

TABLE 2.4

Numbers of Wildlife Specimens Exported from Buenos Aires, Argentina, as Nonfood Items and Declared Port-of-export Values of Wildlife Products 1976–79 (in Millions of dollars)

Species	Total Numbers (% of Total)	Total Value (% of Total)
Gray fox	3,580,338	79.924
(*Dusicyon* spp.)	(16.6)	(32.60)
Red fox	32,121	0.764
(*Dusicyon culpaeus*)	(0.15)	(.30)
Puma	3,538	0.146
(*Felis concolor*)	(0.02)	(.06)
Pampas cat	78,239	1.865
(*F. colocolo*)	(0.40)	(.80)
Geoffroy's cat	341,558	8.695
(*F. geoffroyi*)	(1.60)	(3.60)
Skunks	784,974	5.543
(*Conepatus* spp.)	(3.60)	(2.30)
Vizcacha	341,451	1.212
(*Lagostomus maximus*)	(1.07)	(.50)
Nutria	8,981,596	113.027
(*Myocastor coypus*)	(41.70)	(46.10)
Capybara	79,526	0.838
(*Hydrochaeris hydrochaeris*)	(0.40)	(.40)
Peccaries	172,371	1.025
(All three spp.)	(0.80)	(2.30)
Guanaco (young)	223,610	5.617
(*Lama guanicoe*)	(1.04)	(.30)
Opossum	1,268,675	8.338
(*Didelphis* spp.)	(5.90)	(3.40)
Rheas	103,543	1.028
(*Rhea* and *Pterocnemia*)	(4.80)	(.40)
Boa	141,423	1.138
(*Epicrates*)	(6.60)	(.50)
Lizards	5,284,850	15.349
(*Tupinambis*)	(24.50)	(6.30)
Caimans	82,714	.567
(*Caiman*)	(0.40)	(.20)
Toads	3,772	—
(*Bufo*)	(0.02)	—
TOTAL	21,534,299	245.076

Source: Mares & Ojeda 1984.

From the 1930s to the early 1950s there was brief commercial use of manatee leather. Many skins were shipped from the Amazon to southern Brazil for use as machinery belts, hoses, gaskets, and glue. Though brief, this exploitation was intense, with at least 19,000 manatees taken in the Brazilian state of Amazonas alone (Domning 1982).

Most of the recent market for leather has been for luxury items such as purses, gloves, and expensive shoes and overcoats. The principal species involved in this trade are peccaries, capybara, and various reptiles, though there are some of minor commercial importance such as rheas (Cajal 1988).

Peccary leather has always been popular, particularly in Europe and Japan (Broad 1984; Hvidberg-Hansen 1970e). The trade involved many animals, with 2,013,006 collared peccary (*Tayassu tajacu*) skins and 848,364 white-lipped peccary (*T. pecari*) skins exported from Iquitos, Peru, between 1946 and 1966. Though less active now, the trade is still extensive; one German importer reported a yearly purchase of 36,000 peccary hides from Paraguay (Peccary skins seized, 1986).

Capybara are another source of high-quality leather. Between 1960 and 1969, 497,323 capybara skins were exported from the Brazilian Amazon (Smith 1981). Until recently, Argentina was the only Latin American country with an industry centering around the tanning of capybara skins and the production of finished goods.

At present, the most important wildlife in the leather industry are the reptiles: caiman lizards, tegu lizards, crocodilians, and to a lesser extent, sea turtles, snakes, and toads. The caiman lizard (*Dracaena guianensis*) is exploited at fairly low levels, with 278,046 skins exported from Latin America between 1980 and 1985 (Luxmoore 1988). Exploitation of the two species of tegu lizard (*Tupinambis teguixin* and *T. rufescens*) is considerably greater, with over 1,250,000 skins exported annually from Argentina alone (Fitzgerald, Chani, and Donadio, this volume). Sea turtle leather comes mostly from the olive ridley (*Lepidochelys olivacea*) and the green turtle (*Chelonia mydas*) and is second only to crocodilian leather in price. Between 1970 and 1986 Japan, the major consumer, imported over 650,000 kg of sea turtle leather. Approximately 70% of the total comes from Latin America and the Caribbean, and of this, about three-quarters comes from Ecuador (Milliken and Tokunaga 1987; Woody 1986).

Outnumbering these species in trade by severalfold are the crocodilians. During the peak of the trade in the 1950s and 1960s worldwide, five to ten million crocodilian skins were traded annually (Hemley, 1988). The extent of the trade is staggering: for example, in Venezuela during 1930 and 1931, 3,000 to 4,000 caiman skins were being sold daily, and between 1951 and 1980 Colombia legally exported 11,649,655 *Caiman sclerops* skins (Medem 1983).

Despite current legislation in many Latin American countries prohibiting such export, an estimated one million caiman skins still leave South America each year (Hemley, 1988). Between 1980 and 1984 there were 2,593,834 crocodilian skins recorded as exported from South America, but this should be considered as a minimum estimate of the animals actually killed for the trade. There were at least seven species involved, with *Caiman crocodilus* representing 91.8% of the identified skins (Villalba-Macias, in press).

Skins

Before the European conquest, wildlife skins were important locally with some peoples such as the Ono Indians, who relied exclusively on guanaco (*Lama guanicoe*) pelts for clothing and shelter (Miller 1980). However, just as the case with leather, Europeans brought large-scale commercialization of skins to Latin America. Both trades are directed at the luxury markets in Europe, Japan, and North America.

The skin trade has always focused on only a relatively few species. The earliest species to be exploited were pinnipeds (cf. Sielfeld K. 1983) and are therefore outside the scope of this review. Chinchillas (*Chinchilla* spp.) were heavily exploited in the late 1800s and early 1900s, with between seven and twenty-one million skins exported from Chile between 1828 and 1916. The trade in the Southern Cone then shifted to foxes and otters (Iriarte and Jaksic 1986). The trade in fox skins continues to be very important; Argentina exported 3,612,459 fox pelts (*Dusicyon* spp.) between 1976 and 1979. Other important furbearers were skunks (*Conepatus* spp.), opossums (*Didelphis* spp.), Geoffroy's cat (*Felis geoffroyi*), and especially nutria (*Myocastor coypus*). During one four-year period, the total value of exported furs was over $225 million (Mares and Ojeda 1984). As discussed previously, the trade in the skins of introduced European hare (*Lepus capensis*) and rabbit (*Oryctolagus cuniculus*) was once important but now has been largely replaced by a trade in the meat of these animals (Jackson 1986; Iriarte and Jaksíc 1986).

Two other species of southern South America have been heavily exploited: the guanaco (*Lama guanicoe*) and the vicuña (*Lama vicugna*). Indians of the Andes and Patagonia killed guanacos and vicuña for their skins. In an early example of wildlife management, the Incas captured vicuña in large numbers, killing the males and older females and releasing the younger females. The vicuña, and to a lesser extent the guanaco, are the only wild animals in Latin America whose wool is harvested (Rabinovich, Capurro, and Pessina, this volume). The wool of the vicuña is extremely fine and therefore quite valuable (Franklin 1982b). Young guanacos (chulengos) are also extensively harvested: in Argentina the legal harvest in 1979 consisted of over 86,000 individuals (Franklin and Fritz, this volume).

The trade in skins originating in the Amazon basin has been well documented (Doughty and Myers 1971; Grimwood 1968; McGrath 1986; Smith 1976a, 1981). This trade has concentrated on a few species: giant otter (*Pteronura brasiliensis*), river otter (*Lutra longicaudis*), jaguar (*Panthera onca*), and "ocelot" (*Felis pardalis* and much smaller numbers of *F. wiedii* and *F. tigrina*) (fig. 2.3). The trade in cat skins began with jaguars at the end of the last century. In the 1960s, apparently in response to overexploitation of jaguar and the

TABLE 2.5
Number of Pelts Exported from Chile, 1910–84

Taxon	Total
Chinchilla, *Chinchilla*	319,657*
Vizcacha, *Lagostomus*	1,032
Coypu, *Myocastor*	38,417
Rabbit, *Oryctolagus*	2,141,359
Hare, *Lepus*	1,929,412
Guanaco, *L. guanaco*	35,059
Vicuna, *L. vicugna*	3,299
Skunks, *Conepatus*	9,425
Otters, *Lutra*	38,263
Foxes, *Dusicyon*	315,659
Wild cats, *Felis*	2,952
Sea Lion	361,372
Unidentified	434,154
Total pelts	5,630,062

Source: Iriarte & Jaksíc 1986.
*Some live specimens included.

Figure 2.3. Ocelot skin (Brazil). (Photo, K. H. Redford.)

concommitant decrease in numbers, the cat trade shifted to smaller species (McMahan 1986).

The period between the end of the Second World War and the early 1970s was the "golden era" of the trade in skins originating from the Amazon Basin (McGrath 1986). Between 1960 and 1969, 23,900 giant otter skins were exported from the Peruvian and Brazilian Amazon (Smith 1981). In the 20 years beginning in 1946, the Amazon River port of Iquitos, Peru, exported 22,644 giant otter skins, 90,574 river otter skins, 12,704 jaguar skins, and 138,102 ocelot skins (Grimwood 1968).

This trade, though better documented in the Amazon Basin, was not confined to it. Nietschmann (1973) provides export figures for Nicaragua between 1966 and 1971, when 1,751 jaguar skins, 17,157 ocelot skins, and 21,473 margay (*Felis wiedii*) skins left the country.

The international trade in skins has greatly decreased due to legislation such as Argentina's law prohibiting the export and internal trade in nine species of cats (Argentina's trade ban, 1986). However, this has not stopped the killing of wildlife for skins: in 1982, 34,915 skins, 77% of which belonged to carnivores, were seized in Brazil (Duarte and Rebêlo 1985), and in 1986 over 6,000 carnivore skins were seized in Uruguay (Skins seized, 1986). Aranda (this volume) documents the small-scale, but active, trade in skins in southeastern México.

Feathers

Exploitation of feathers has long been an important part of wildlife utilization in some parts of the neotropics. Indigenous peoples have developed elaborate and sophisticated feather art that reached its pinnacle in the feather capes used by Aztec emperors (Haemig 1978). The feathers of birds such as the quetzal (*Pharomachrus mocinno*), the roseate spoonbill (*Ajaia ajaia*), and the macaws (*Ara* spp.) were highly prized for their decorative qualities. Their value was such that the Incas collected tribute in exotic bird feathers from their Amazonian Indian subjects (Baudin 1962 in Haemig 1978), and Indians in the southwestern United States traded a thousand kilometers south for young scarlet macaws (*Ara macao*) to raise for feathers (Hargrave 1970). Feathers are still important in the ceremonies of Indian groups in Latin America (cf. Delgado 1988), (fig. 2.4), though increasingly artifacts made from feathers are sold for the tourist trade (fig. 2.5) (Redford pers. obs., 1986; Seeger 1982).

Though currently out of fashion, feathers were once very important elements in the women's fashion trade. In 1886 an ornithologist in New York City identified the feathers from at least forty species of birds used for ladies' hats, and fashionable ladies wore dresses edged with marabou down or the heads of finches (Doughty 1975). An extensive trade in bird feathers originated in Latin America. One observer reported that 400,000 hummingbirds and 360,000 other birds were exported from southeastern Brazil (Guenther 1931 in Dean 1985); in the early 1900s Argentina exported over 60,000 kg of rhea feathers (Miller

Figure 2.4. Kayapó Indian with feather headdress (Brazil). (Photo, K. H. Redford.)

Figure 2.5. Artifacts made by Ko-fan Indians for tourist trade (Ecuador). (Photo, K. H. Redford.)

1914). The trade concentrated on egrets and herons. At the height of the feather frenzy, premium feathers went for $5 per plume or $28 per ounce in New York. Between 1899 and 1920 South America (principally Argentina, Brazil, and Venezuela) exported 15,000 kg of egret and heron feathers representing plumes from an estimated 12 to 15 million smaller species of birds and 3 to 4.5 million larger ones (Doughty 1975).

To a large extent the trade in feathers has disappeared. The exception is feathers from greater rheas and lesser rheas (*Pterocnemia pennata*). Dusters from the feathers of these birds are a common sight in Brazil, Bolivia, and Argentina. In some cases birds are shot just for their primary feathers (Stearman, unpubl. ms.), though there is also a market for the skins. Between 1976 and 1984, 7,745 kg of rhea feathers were exported from Argentina (Cajal 1988), and the domestic market probably represents many thousands of kilos more.

Other

Humans obtain several other nonedible products from wildlife. One of these is guano, or feces, for which colonial nesting seabirds have been the most important source. The famous guano islands off Peru exported over 20 million tons between 1848 and 1875 (Murphy 1981). With the development of chemical fertilizers, the industry decreased, although bird and bat guano are still harvested in small quantities (Haynes 1987). One of the markets for such guano is organic gardeners.

Another wildlife product is oil. Various species have been used as commercial sources of oil, including caiman, whose oil was mixed with kerosene and used to illuminate Brazilian towns (Pereira 1944); turtles, whose eggs were used to produce oil for lamps (Smith 1974); and manatees, whose oil was mixed with pitch to caulk boats (Smith 1981). Though on a much smaller scale, nestlings of the oilbird, *Steatornis caripensis,* have also been harvested and rendered for oil (cf. Ortiz-Crespo 1979).

The hard parts of wildlife carcasses have long served as raw material for handicrafts and tools. Bones of many species, ranging from curassow to deer, were split to become arrow points, the teeth of rodents like the agouti (*Dasyprocta*) were used to help in the manufacture of arrows, armadillo shells were fashioned into baskets and guitars, and bird beaks and claws were used in ornamentation. Many of these items, replaced by manufactured goods, have become important items in the tourist trade. Bones are used for other purposes as well; those of olive ridley turtles are used for bone meal (Woody 1986). In this category the most valuable item is tortoise or turtle shell. Originating mostly from green turtles and hawksbill turtles (*Eretmochelys imbricata*), the Latin American portion of this trade coming largely from the Caribbean, notably Panama and Cuba (Canin and Luxmoore 1985).

Wild animals have also been used for ritual and medicinal purposes. Tradi-

Figure 2.6. Animal products for sale in La Paz, Bolivia, markets. (Photo, K. H. Redford.)

tionally, many Indian groups have utilized certain species of animals for such purposes. During the ceremony of the singing souls, the Matses Indians hunt sloths, a species not usually taken at any other time (Romanoff, 1984). In order to perform another festival, the Kayapó Indians must kill a tapir which, tied with vines, is featured in a tug-of-war involving the entire village (Redford, pers. obs., 1986).

In many parts of Latin America the medicinal uses of wildlife continue (see fig. 2.6). In the market in Belém, Brazil, dried lizards of several species, the genitalia of dolphins, fox fur, and many other pieces of wild animals are sold for medicinal and magical purposes. Only rarely are wild animals from Latin America commercialized for such purposes, but in 1982 a shipment containing pills of unknown origin made from the tissue of little spotted cats (*Felis tigrina*) was sent to Hong Kong (Jorgenson and Jorgenson, in press).

Wildlife as Live Animals

Pets

Wild animals have been captured and kept as pets or in zoos for centuries. The Incas had a menagerie in Cuzco that contained adult anacondas, rheas, and caiman (Lathrap 1975), and the Aztec emperors had a menagerie stocked with birds, ocelots, jaguars, snakes, and even centipedes, which had been sent as tribute from subject peoples (Haemig 1978). Other Indian groups kept pets; in fact, there are probably few groups that did not. In a survey of four Kayapó villages, at least thirty-one species of animals were kept for pets, including five turtle species, sixteen parrot and macaw species, a lizard, and a spider (Redford and Posey, unpubl. ms.) (fig. 2.7).

Not only Indians keep wild animals as pets. The tradition of keeping pets is also ubiquitous among people of European descent. In the Brazilian city of Rio Branco, fifteen species of primates were kept as pets (Pereira 1987), and caged song birds and parrots are a common sight throughout Latin America. In Brazil finches are captured and sold by the hundreds of thousands. Of particular value are species valued for their song. A good singer can sell for over $3,000 (Levinson 1987).

There is a thriving export trade in wild animals for pets, particularly parrots. Between 1981 and 1986 the United States imported 703,000 parrots from the neotropics; this number represented at least 96 of the 141 species native to that area (Iñigo and Ramos, this volume; Jorgenson and Thomsen 1987; Thomsen and Brautigam, this volume). Not only does this trade involve large numbers of birds, it also involves large amounts of money. In the United States the annual retail turnover of parrots, both wild and captive-bred, is an estimated $300 million (Hemley, 1988).

Biomedical and Zoo Trade

Another important use of live animals is as experimental animals in the biomedical trade. Much of this trade originated from the Peruvian town of Iquitos, which exported 139,000 live primates between 1961 and 1965 (Grimwood 1968) and at least 91,662 in 1973 (Castro, Revilla, and Neville 1975–76). The most commonly exported monkeys were squirrel monkeys (*Saimiri*), followed by night monkeys (*Aotus*), marmosets of the genus *Saguinus,* and capuchin monkeys (*Cebus*) (Castro, Revilla, & Neville 1975–76; Jorgenson and Jorgenson, in press).

Much less important than the biomedical trade is the trade in animals for zoos. For example, between 1983 and 1984 the United States imported thirty-two giant anteaters (*Myrmecophaga tridactyla*), presumably for the zoo trade (Jorgenson and Jorgenson, in press). Though small in scale, the zoo trade frequently focuses on rare animals.

Figure 2.7. Kayapó Indians with parrot, parakeet, and peccary pets (Brazil). (Photo, K. H. Redford.)

Sport Hunting

Latin America, never a major destination of big game hunters, has long attracted bird hunters, who are particularly interested in doves. Eared doves (*Zenaida auriculata*) are important game birds in Brazil, and hunters kill hundreds of thousands for sport each year (Aguire 1976). But the most important species of dove is the white-winged dove (*Zenaida asiatica asiatica*). In the 1986–87 season, U.S. hunters shot approximately three million white-winged doves in northeastern México (Purdy, this volume; Smylie 1987). Hunters are offered hunting trips to Colombia with glowing promises such as "four, five or six hundred dove per day is not unusual" (Trek news, 1987).

In virtually all Latin American countries, bird hunting is a popular sport. In southern Brazil tinamous are managed for hunting, in Venezuela ducks are important game birds (Gómez-Dallmeier, this volume), and in Chile native species such as the caiquen (*Chloephaga picta*) and introduced species such as the European partridge are targets of hunters.

There is some sport hunting of larger animals. White-tailed deer hunting is a major sport in Costa Rica (Vaughan and Rodríguez, this volume), brocket deer and white-tailed deer are important game species in Venezuela, and collared peccary, deer, and big-horned sheep are commonly hunted in México.

Tourism

Wildlife tourism has not been as important in Latin America as it has in Africa; however, a growing number of people are taking trips specifically to look for wildlife. Increasingly, organizations are attempting to get schoolchildren interested in the animals of their own country, frequently focusing on a well-known species such as the golden lion tamarin (*Leontopithecus rosalia*) or the spectacled bear (*Tremarctos ornatus*).

International wildlife tourism has increased as well. The initial thrust was provided by bird watchers, some of whom are willing to pay large sums to be taken to remote locations such as Manu National Park in Peru (Groom, Podolsky, and Munn, this volume) or El Triunfo in Chiapas, Mexico. Increasingly, however, tourists interested in just seeing natural beauty are traveling to Latin America. The destination of many of these people is Central America, particularly Costa Rica, Mexico, and Belize, but many go to South America as well. In many cases, it is the wildlife that draws so many people to places such as the Galápagos, the Valdés Peninsula, and the Brazilian Pantanal.

Domestication

Wild animals have provided the stock from which domesticated animals originated. There are historical accounts of semidomestication by several Indian groups; for example, early accounts indicate that the Maya raised, and perhaps bred, ocellated turkeys (*Meleagris ocellata*), collared peccary, and white-tailed deer (Pohl and Feldman 1982), and the tribes of Patagonia captured guanacos for pets and food (Gilmore 1950).

Recently, there have been attempts to begin the domestication process of several wild species of Latin American animals, including the paca (*Agouti paca:* Smythe, this volume) and the capybara (Alho 1986). Other species have been proposed, including the red-footed and yellow-footed tortoises (*Geochelone denticulata* and *G. carbonaria:* Moskovits 1988) and the large caviomorph rodent *Kerodon* (Lacher 1979).

Conclusions

Wild animals have played a major role in the lives of the human inhabitants of Latin America. In many ways they now play fewer, less important roles. However, to many people, such as the millions that rely on subsistence hunting for food, wildlife continues to be very important. Wild animals are also important components of the medicinal, magical, and esthetic worlds of many local peoples.

It is clear that the old patterns of human-wildlife interactions cannot continue into the next century unless new ways of conserving, harvesting, and using wild animals are developed. Otherwise, most of Latin America will be deprived of its rich fauna.

Acknowledgments

For comments on the manuscript we would like to thank Jeff Jorgenson, Cynthia Lagueux, Eduardo Iñigo, and Agustín Iriarte.

3

The Outlook for Sustainable Harvests of Wildlife in Latin America

JAMES H. SHAW

Conservationists throughout the world realize that the primary threats to Latin America's wildlife are loss of pristine habitats, particularly tropical moist forests (Myers 1979, 1983, 1986), and unregulated harvests, mainly for commercial purposes (Ojeda and Mares 1982; Mares 1986). While both threats are immediate and real, they leave the impression that there is little role for sustained, regulated harvest of Latin American wildlife. Indeed, governments in many tropical nations seem to view wildlife management primarily as a matter of protecting animals from direct harvest (Dasmann 1987).

This paper attempts to present a broader, more analytical view of wildlife harvest in Latin America. It is based upon three premises. First, Latin Americans, like people elsewhere, are more likely to support conservation programs that offer them tangible incentives instead of legal prohibitions. Regulated game harvest is one such incentive. Second, the effects of harvest upon game populations are still poorly understood, especially in the tropics. Conditions in Latin America offer opportunities to measure these effects and to apply the results to hunted populations in that region and elsewhere. Third, regulated harvests may be complementary to, rather than incompatible with, traditional protection offered by national parks and reserves.

In many respects, the outlook for wildlife in much of Latin America is unfavorable. Human population growth, destruction of tropical forests, underregulated hunting and trapping, too few wildlife professionals, and too little funding for natural resource management together threaten the survival of many wild species. The neotropics feature some of the highest levels of species diversity on earth, making the stakes very high for wildlife conservation.

Wildlife in the United States was faring little better in 1900 than it is in Latin America today. That year Congress made interstate shipment of market-hunted wildlife a federal offense through passage of the Lacey Act. Market hunting had so depleted plume birds, waterfowl, and big game that some conservationists of the time were as alarmed about the future of North America's wildlife as their modern counterparts are about wildlife in Latin America. Habitat loss was extensive, with most tallgrass prairies broken by the plow and native forests exploited with no thought given to sustainable yields. The trends of the early twentieth century caused Hornaday (1913) to predict the extinction of the pronghorn (*Antilocapra americana*), the bighorn sheep (*Ovis canadensis*), and even the elk (*Cervus elaphus*).

Yet those extinctions failed to occur, thanks to a combination of widespread public support, effective legal protection, and reintroductions of wild animals into areas from which they had been extirpated. Sport hunters were required to purchase hunting licenses, thus providing sustainable funding for wildlife agencies. Abandonment of family farms, accelerated by the depression of the 1930s, led to increased urbanization and reversion of croplands to wildlife habitat. Gradually, as wildlife management became scientifically more sophisticated, techniques of habitat restoration appeared. Together these developments helped formerly depleted wildlife populations to recover. The white-tailed deer (*Odocoileus virginianus*), the most widespread and popular big game animal in the United States, increased by an estimated 25-fold between 1900 and 1975 (Trefethen 1975). The annual legal harvest of the species now exceeds the entire white-tailed deer population of 1900 by about fourfold (Hesselton and Hesselton 1982). Depletion and the threat of extinction were replaced by a widely accepted form of restrained and sustainable harvest.

Of course it would be folly to assume that Latin America's substantial problems in wildlife conservation could be solved merely by transplanting a system developed and used successfully in the United States. Numerous failures in economic development projects and in technical assistance in agriculture attest to the dangers of imposing foreign systems without considerable modification. Yet a review of both the successes and the shortcomings of wildlife management in the United States can undoubtedly aid in the management of wild species in Latin America. The necessary modifications, both biological and sociological, can be done by Latin Americans themselves. Above all, it is crucial that programs be sustainable, a key environmental consideration in developing nations.

Sustainable Exploitation of Wildlife

The simplest and most widely used tools for regulating wildlife harvests in North America have been hunting seasons and bag limits. These are empirical methods, often arbitrary and subject to the influences of tradition, politics, emotion, practical experience and, in a relatively minor way, scientific research (Hurst and Rosene 1985). Applied over areas the size of states or provinces, the resulting harvests are "sustainable" only in the sense that they generally prevent widespread overharvest. Seasons and bag limits can neither optimize nor maximize game harvests because both lack the biological precision and the administrative authority required for distributing hunting pressure and for monitoring the kill (Shaw 1985).

Practices regulating game harvests in the United States have changed little since they were first developed around the turn of the century. The utility of season and bag limits, though untested scientifically, gained broad acceptance by a large majority of sportsmen, conservationists, wildlife administrators, and commissioners. Such crude, imprecise tools can lead to only one of two outcomes: underharvest or overharvest. The fact that game generally persisted and in many cases actually increased shows that the former typically occurred.

The primary value of seasons and bag limits is thus more cultural than scientific. Those who actually do the harvesting accept and even embrace the importance of restraint. In this important way, sportsmen in the United States may be far ahead of their counterparts in agriculture, range management, and forestry (a key factor behind this progress is that modern hunters hunt for sport rather than for economic gain, a distinction with obvious implications for the management of wildlife in Latin America and elsewhere). The majority of sport hunters in North America implicitly accept the notion that it is better to underharvest than to overharvest.

Amid these cultural developments, biologists seeking to understand harvest and to predict its effects needed three things: conceptual models, analytical models, and empirical data. Conceptual models of game harvest furnish the broad framework for generating and testing hypotheses and represent a crucial first step. Wildlife biologists seem to accept implicitly either one of two conceptual models: the complete compensation model or the partial compensation model (Caughley 1985).

The complete compensation model contends that harvest has no real effect on a game population unless and until a certain threshold is reached. If harvest levels continue to exceed the threshold, the population is driven to extinction; if not, there is no measurable effect.

In contrast, the partial compensation model states that *any* level of harvesting affects the population, first by pushing it beneath unharvested levels and second by triggering density-dependent responses such as increased fecundity and survival of young, decreased natural mortality, or both.

Although these models are simple and straightforward conceptually, rigorous testing between the two is no easy task. Caughley (1985) evaluated what he considered to be two of the best studies of wildlife harvesting and found that neither could conclusively demonstrate which of the two models applied. Adequate testing between the two conceptual models must include at least three different harvesting levels continued for at least two generations of the game species under study. Moreover, field experiments should be kept simple, emphasizing the overall effects of harvest on the population as a whole rather than more complex effects on sexes or age classes. As biologists await results of such field experiments, they should note that Caughley (1985) evaluated thorough studies on the white-tailed deer (McCullough 1979), the Cape buffalo (*Syncerus caffer*) (Sinclair 1977), and the Himalayan thar (*Hermitragus jemlahicus*) (Caughley 1970) and concluded that the partial compensation model was the more appropriate.

Analytical models of game harvest use computer programming to analyze a particular game species under a specific set of circumstances. They can be divided into two broad groups: accounting models and stock-recruitment models (McCullough 1984). Accounting models rely upon age-specific estimates of fecundity and mortality to determine the effects of hunting mortality upon a particular population. Although accounting models are valuable in research and in teaching, they require extensive, detailed field data that are rarely available. If data are not available, they have to be simulated over assumed ranges of variation, greatly reducing their predictive value and thus their utility to managers. In addition, accounting models cannot simulate the many subtle ways in which parameters affect one another, further eroding their predictive abilities (McCullough 1984).

For better understanding the effects of harvest upon game populations, McCullough (1984) recommended use of stock-recruitment models, such as those he successfully developed for white-tailed deer on the George Reserve in Michigan (McCullough 1979). Stock-recruitment models require only a few high-order variables such as population size and actual harvest rather than the larger number of low-order variables like age-specific mortality and fecundity required for accounting models. Stock-recruitment models assume that the high-order variables accurately reflect the outcome of the more numerous effects of low-order variables. Obviously, the high-order variables are considerably easier to obtain from the field. They also offer far greater reliability as predictors and thus appeal more to managers.

Nonetheless, stock-recruitment models still need empirical data. These data should come from rigorously designed and executed field studies. In the United States, deeply entrenched beliefs and practices connected with sport hunting often present practical obstacles to the very experiments needed to understand the effects of harvest. Hunters still largely believe in free, unimpeded access to hunting areas. They oppose experiments largely because such efforts require unacceptable levels of control by wildlife management agencies. In addition, hunters in the United States are often reluctant to cooperate in experiments requiring deliberately high levels of harvest. Field studies on harvest in the United States usually rely upon special hunts.

Special hunts typically result from resident game populations that are deemed excessive on National Wildlife Refuges, state wildlife management areas, and in some cases on private land on which the owner holds a game breeder's license. Such hunts increase hunting opportunities while at the same time reducing local game populations to more desirable levels.

Special hunts also offer opportunities to measure the effects of harvest with far more precision than was previously possible. Access is usually tightly controlled, the number of hunters limited to a predetermined quota, and the resulting harvest carefully measured. When these tight controls are combined with accurate estimates of game populations and habitat carrying capacities, the special hunts furnish important new grist for the modeler's mill. As these empirical data help test and refine harvest models, managers can ensure more efficient harvests and often higher ones as well.

Key Differences between the United States and Latin America

A fundamental difference between Latin America and the United States is that the former is mostly tropical, whereas the latter is almost all temperate. Since most of what is known about harvesting wildlife comes from temperate regions, application of this knowledge to wild populations in tropical regions presents special challenges.

Game species in temperate zones typically reproduce in spring, when conditions of weather and food are most favorable. Sport hunting is done in fall, in part because young of year are by then independent of adults, so that the detrimental effects of hunting are minimized. Tropical species can reproduce year round, although there may be some synchrony of reproduction in regions with pronounced wet-dry seasons (Brokx 1984). Thus, in many portions of the tropics, there may be no seasonally advantageous time to hunt.

Latin America also differs from North America in terms of forms of government and the ways in which laws are enforced. The United States and Canada rely upon popular support, often beginning at the local level, to pass new laws or to modify old ones. Regulatory laws are usually changed only after extensive public hearings and other opportunities for public scrutiny. This process is cumbersome and at times slow, but despite some inevitable grumbling, it does sustain the support and cooperation of most citizens.

Although recent trends in South America have been toward increasing democratic rule, Latin America as a whole has a long tradition of government from the top down, much as it was during colonial times. This form of government presents practical problems for game management. Administration is often centralized and rigid. Enforcement of the numerous laws can be inconsistent, both in terms of which laws are enforced and which groups of people are involved. Culturally, this top down approach can disenfranchise local people, who then see game laws as oppressive rather than for the common good.

Another major difference between Latin America and the United States is reflected in the difference in human population densities and growth projections. Central America, together with Mexico, has nearly 150 million people and is already populated beyond the land's capacity to sustain current levels of exploitation. Populations are projected to increase at an average rate of about 2.6% annually, making them among the fastest growing human populations.

Meanwhile, populations in South America are growing at more than twice the rate of those in Canada and the United States (World Resources Institute 1987). Such high projections of population growth greatly limit the options available to wildlife managers.

Most of Latin America lacks both the numbers and the extent of protected areas that are common in many other regions. These areas include national parks and various types of equivalent reserves, all of which are supposed to function as habitat reserves protected from human disturbance. The International Union for Conservation of Nature and Natural Resources (IUCN), based in Switzerland, maintains high standards for official listing of such parks and reserves, making sure that they have adequate legal protection, sufficient de facto protection, and adequate area. By 1986, the IUCN listed more than 3,500 protected reserves worldwide, including 329 in the United States and Canada, 60 in México and Central America, and 267 in South America (World Resources Institute 1987). The land area protected in Mexico and Central America is less than 1% of the total and in South America is less than 3%, compared with 4.5% for the United States and Canada and an average of about 3.2% worldwide.

A high proportion of Latin American birds and mammals are internationally listed as threatened or endangered. Six percent of Canada's species of mammals and 2% of its native birds are listed as threatened, compared with 8% and 6% for native mammals and birds, respectively, in the United States. Latin American nations list between 10% and 16% of their native birds as threatened, at least twice the proportion listed by their Anglo-American neighbors. Between 7% and 15% of native mammals in Central America and Mexico are threatened, as are between 12% and 29% of the species of South American mammals (World Resources Institute 1987). Such comparisons, however, should be interpreted cautiously. Nations have different criteria for designating species as threatened and endangered, as well as different procedures for listings. In the absence of adequate survey data, many Latin American governments may list species merely reputed to be threatened, a practice that would inflate the final percentages.

Loss of habitat through encroachment by humans is not the only major threat to Latin American wildlife. A flourishing commercial trade in live animals and products from them contributes to the decline of some wild species. Most authorities on international trade in wildlife products (cf. Ehrlich and Ehrlich 1981; King 1978; Ojeda and Mares 1982) contend that the key to regulating trade lies with regulating imports into consumer nations. If demand can be reduced in the case of threatened species and virtually eliminated for the endangered ones, the prices paid for the products in the producing nations will decline. As prices fall, so presumably will hunting efforts, allowing populations to recover.

Garment manufacturers, for example, have long used spotted cats to satisfy customer demand. Conservationists became increasingly concerned about the effects of commercial harvest upon cats, noting that as a group, the felids reproduce very slowly and presumably cannot accommodate heavy harvests. The U.S. Endangered Species Act of 1969 sharply curbed imports of some of the larger spotted cats and began regulation of smaller ones. Four years later the Act was superseded by the expanded Endangered Species Act of 1973. By the mid-1970s the United States and Canada were among the signatories of an international treaty, the Convention on International Trade in Endangered Species (CITES). This Convention required export permits for species listed as "threatened" (appendix II) and both import and export permits for those listed as "endangered" (appendix I), a more serious category (Lyster 1985).

These new restrictions have apparently reduced trade in endangered species substantially. The United States legally imported 13,500 jaguar (*Panthera onca*) skins in 1968, the last year of unrestricted imports (King 1978). By 1979, all signatories to CITES, including the United States, traded a total of only fifty jaguar skins internationally (McMahan 1986).

Conclusions and Recommendations

Most game species in the United States have benefited from implementing a self-supporting system of regulated harvests. The advantages most commonly cited in support of such an arrangement are the recovery of formerly depleted big game (the most conspicuous change) and the importance of revenue provided through sales of hunting licenses and other "user-pay" sources (Jahn and Trefethen 1978; Shaw 1985). But there is another advantage of far greater long-term importance. Regulated hunting also furnishes important incentives to practice less intensive forms of land use. Sustainable harvest of wild game cannot be produced in extensive agricultural and forest monocultures. Wild game does not abound on lands suffering from chronic pollution or lands depleted by soil degradation. Indeed, the presence of healthy populations of wild game generally attests to healthy, sustainable land. Good land health is as critical in tropical regions as in temperate ones.

Although sustainable hunting can be implemented in Latin America, it will almost certainly have to exclude the most common forms of market or commercial hunting. The problem is not so much one of morality as one of sustainability. Other products of the land—including crops, livestock, timber, and pulpwood—are harvested commercially and, under proper practices, are sustainable. Wildlife, though, is regarded throughout most of the world as public property, or "commons." When commons are exploited for individual financial gain, they are typically overexploited (Hardin 1968, 1985), particularly as market demand accelerates, when new harvest technologies become available, or both. Latin American people who hunt wild animals commercially usually have little economic alternative (Ojeda and Mares 1982). Commercial pressure on native wildlife could thus be reduced and eventually eliminated through broader social and economic reforms. Difficult though they may be, such reforms may prove more effective than direct attempts to regulate commercial hunting.

As successful as it has been, wildlife management in the United States has encountered serious problems, in part because of its widespread acceptance. Traditional methods of restraining harvests, including seasons and bag limits, have such strong political support that they preclude many scientific discoveries that would result from increasing harvests experimentally and then monitoring their effects. Since popular acceptance of seasons and bag limits is not the rule in most of Latin America, this apparent drawback offers certain advantages.

An important player in improving wildlife management in Latin America will undoubtedly be the owner of large, private ranches. In Venezuela, for instance, hunting seasons are long and not rigidly enforced (Brokx 1984). Harvest on private lands is regulated de facto more by land owners than by governmental agencies. Thus if governmental agencies, conservation organizations, and wildlife biologists could work effectively with private landowners, they could experimentally regulate harvests. These experiments could, in turn, provide valuable new information about the effects of known levels of harvest upon neotropical game species. As these effects become better understood, they will provide a solid, scientifically supported basis for refining harvest regulations.

Table 3.1 lists six possible approaches to the sustainable harvest of Latin American wildlife. Improved regulation of the harvest is essential in all cases, though practices on private lands should be easier to enforce than those on land open to all.

Subsistence hunting presents special difficulties. Because of its traditions and the fact that it is practiced in remote areas, there is some question as to

TABLE 3.1
Approaches to the Sustainable Harvest of Wildlife in Latin America

Method	Comments
Subsistence hunting	Already in practice in de facto manner; Refinements could give exclusive rights in exchange for accepting harvest quotas.
Popular sport hunting	Much like U.S. system with license sales and fees used to pay for enforcement; would require wide acceptance and effective enforcement.
Sport hunting for foreigners (safari)	Could bring in important foreign currency; resentment by indigenous people and other nationals could pose problems.
Land tenure system for commercial uses	Similar to Canada's registered traplines; would require effective enforcement, including protection against poaching.
Commercial hunting preserves	Popular in the U.S.; an option on private land; intense but usually artificial; exotic game should be discouraged.
Wildlife ranching on private land	Could combine with livestock ranching; would need pilot projects; sales of meat or hides need regulation.

whether subsistence hunting can ever be adequately regulated. As with most forms of commercial hunting, subsistence hunting makes it difficult to sustain animal populations. Not only are indigenous people capable of hunting at rates too high for wild populations to sustain, they are also tempted to shift to even heavier levels of commercial hunting as markets become available (Redford and Robinson 1985). For subsistence hunters to accept harvest quotas would likely require that they be given exclusive hunting rights within certain areas—a difficult, though perhaps not impossible condition.

The second option in table 3.1, and the one most common in Anglo-America, is popular sport hunting requiring licenses and tags. These requirements already exist in some Latin American countries, though compliance is generally thought to be low (Brokx 1984). Obstacles in this case are more cultural than biological or legal. Demonstration areas on private ranches might, if publicized, help gain acceptance of the need to regulate harvest.

Some African nations have earned foreign exchange from safaris by wealthy foreign sportsmen (Dasmann, 1987; MacKinnon et al. 1986). Traditional safaris have occurred less frequently in recent years; however, they have been replaced to some extent by photographic safaris. One drawback is that local peoples grow to resent limitations upon their own activities that appear to be for the benefit of wealthy foreigners. In Latin America, the shortage of large, "charismatic" wild animals readily visible in grassland and savannas would also limit the utility of this approach.

Canadian authorities regulate fur harvest through a registered trapline system that grants individuals or families exclusive trapping rights on designated areas. Exclusive rights are granted for extended periods with the idea that people who count on the harvest income for many years will be careful not to harvest excessively in any given season. With appropriate modifications, such a land tenure system might have utility in Latin America, particularly in more remote regions.

Commercial hunting preserves enjoy popularity in parts of North America, though their value in conservation is usually marginal. Depending upon the demand as well as on the purchasing power and leisure time of enough citizens, such commercial operations could work on private land in Latin America. Commercial preserves should be limited only to the use of native species and should not provide an excuse for exotic introductions.

Wildlife ranching for carefully selected species has definite potential on private land in Latin America. Wild vertebrates that provide products could be integrated into livestock ranching where conditions permit. Game ranching has been practiced with some success in South Africa (Eltringham 1984; Fitter 1986; Mossman and Mossman 1976). Sufficient markets as well as effective transportation from field to market would be essential, particularly for perishable commodities.

There may be other approaches to sustainable use of wildlife in the neotropics, as well as an almost infinite number of ways to combine the six methods listed here. All would require popular support and increased regulation.

Promoting sustainable harvests of Latin American wildlife will cost money. To date, most efforts have been sponsored by foundations and other organizations outside of Latin America; these efforts need to be expanded and new sources tapped. New sources could include private venture capital to test the feasibility of various forms of commercial game ranching. Others might be derived from taxes imposed upon internationally traded products, ranging from timber to pelts and hides to live wild animals. Latin American foundations need to be developed to help sustain research and development (Mares 1982). Above all, revenue should be routinely derived from excise taxes placed upon development projects and earmarked for purchase of wildlife habitat to mitigate losses imposed by development. Because many of these projects are funded internationally, wealthier nations would be paying their share of the costs of conservation automatically.

Regulated, sustainable harvests of wildlife in Latin America could complement efforts to preserve biological diversity through systems of parks and reserves. Since harvests offer important incentives to maintain productive game habitat, regulated hunting areas along park or reserve boundaries could act as protective buffers. Studies of insular ecology (cf. Lovejoy et al. 1986; Wolf 1987) have shown that creation of national parks and reserves will not guarantee the long-term survival of all, or even most, of the wild species initially present. Increasingly, parks function as islands in a sea of intensive human activity and, like their counterparts in the oceans, may prove incapable of sustaining biotic diversity over the long term. Extinctions occur even in the best-protected parks, largely as a function of inadequate area, and lead to faunal collapse.

There are at least two ways of thwarting these area-induced extinctions. The most obvious approach is simply to create much larger parks and reserves. This option, though, is rarely realistic. The costs, both of additional acquisitions and of keeping land completely out of production, are usually too high, particularly in developing nations. In many cases farms and settlements outside of existing park or reserve boundaries preclude expansion.

Another possibility rests with creation of buffer zones around biological reserves. Although substantially less protected than the reserves themselves, buffer zones could combat faunal collapse by ensuring that boundaries are ecologically less abrupt. Rather than surrounding reserves with crop and forest monocultures incapable of sustaining wild animals, buffer zones might instead be comprised of small-scale, diverse farms, limited timber and firewood harvest zones, and low to moderate intensity grazing areas for livestock. They could also allow regulated hunting (MacKinnon et al. 1986). The effect would be similar to outright expansion of the reserves but without the economic and social costs.

Besides helping protect reserves against the loss of species, such buffer zones would also gain the support of local people. Following to some extent their own traditions, local people could seek game and other resources from within regulated buffer zones. They would come to regard the park or reserve as a protected breeding ground for game produced for their benefit, rather than just an area from which they were legally excluded.

Sustainable harvests of wild species should play a major role in Latin American conservation for several reasons. Regulated harvests have the potential of providing sustainable land use practices on private lands and on lands adjacent to parks and reserves. Conditions in Latin America may prove to be even more conducive to experimental manipulation than those in the United States, thus furnishing important findings on the effects of harvest on game abundance and allowing them to be adjusted to deal with tropical conditions. Finally, regulated harvests can be crucial in winning the support of local people for environmentally sound and sustainable practices.

Part 2
Subsistence Hunting

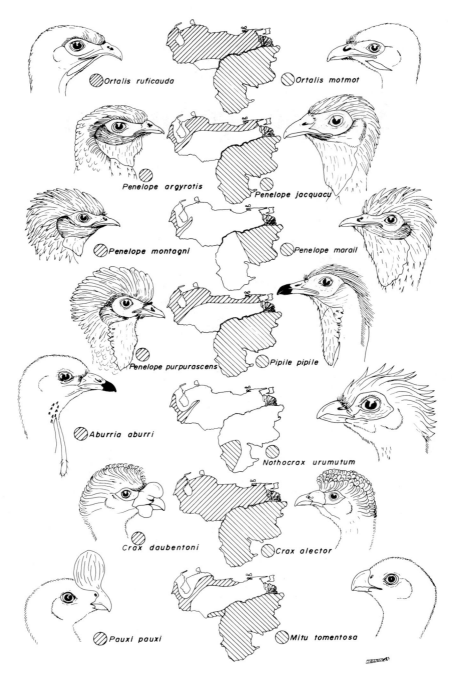

Figure 4.1. Members of the Family Cracidae that inhabit Venezuela and their distributions.

4

Human Impact on Populations of Chachalacas, Guans, and Curassows (Galliformes: Cracidae) in Venezuela

JOSÉ L. SILVA AND STUART D. STRAHL

The Family Cracidae (Aves: Galliformes) is composed of forty-nine species of large, neotropical forest-dwelling birds. Cracids range in size from the smaller chachalacas (genus *Ortalis:* 400 to 750 g) and medium-sized guans (genera *Penelope, Penelopina, Chaemepetes, Pipile, Aburria, Oreophasis:* 750 g to 2.5 kg) to the larger curassows (genera *Crax, Mitu, Pauxi, Nothocrax:* 2 to 3.5 kg). The family is distributed from north-central Mexico (with one species of chachalaca reaching southern Texas) through Central and South America to northern Uruguay and Argentina.

In Venezuela, the Cracidae are represented by fourteen species whose combined ranges cover most of the country (fig. 4.1). Most species are found in primary forests: lowland tropical forest (humid or deciduous), montane cloud forest, and riparian (gallery) forest. Except for chachalacas, most species are very selective with respect to a particular habitat. Cracids are strict frugivores, although some species (chachalacas and, to a lesser extent, the guans) also consume leaves and flowers. As large tropical forest frugivores, these species probably play an important role as seed dispersers for certain plant species (see Terborgh 1986). This aspect of their ecology has been largely neglected in the scientific literature (Strahl, in press).

The Cracidae are widely recognized as an important source of "bush meat" among campesino and indigenous populations, both in Venezuela (Hames 1979; Ruddle and Wilbert 1980; Amengual et al. 1981; Ojasti, Fajardo, and Cova O., 1983; Coppens 1983) and in the rest of Latin America (Pierret and Dourojeanni 1966, 1967; Lenselink 1972; Smith 1976b; Ayres and Ayres 1979; Redford and Robinson 1987). At nine locations in five South American countries, Ojasti, Fajardo, and Cova O. (1983) reported that when subsistence hunters ranked species groups by the percentages of total biomass, these birds occupied fourth and tenth places among indigenous peoples and colonists, respectively. Virtually all other studies list the Cracidae as the family contributing the most avian biomass extracted by hunters in the neotropics. In Venezuela, the importance of cracids as food was known for a few sites before this study but not quantitatively analyzed on a wide scale.

Little is known about the ecology of the fourteen cracid species in Venezuela. All appear on the official list of game birds, although hunting of *Aburria aburri, Pauxi pauxi,* and *Nothocrax urumutum* is totally prohibited. In the 1987 hunting season, the hunting schedule included eight species. However, according to interviews conducted by the Ministry of the Environment (MARNR), cracids are not a highly preferred game among sport hunters in Venezuela (Parra 1984; Gomez-Nuñez 1983, 1986).

Indigenous people also use Cracidae in the production of arms and ornaments. Curassow feathers are the only ones used in arrows by the Yanomami and Ye'kwana in southern Venezuela (Hames 1979). Along the Rio Caura, the Yanomami use curassow femurs to make arrowheads (pers. obs., 1986). Indians also use cracid feathers in bracelets, belts, headbands, and other ornaments for adornment, religious functions, and for sale to tourists. This appears to be the most important commercial use for the Cracidae in remote locations, although campesinos have also commercialized the meat in a few areas on a local scale.

Many authors have recognized the susceptibility of the Cracidae to human perturbations. Due to hunter preferences and the strict habitat requirements of the birds, populations of the larger species, such as the curassows and guans, are very susceptible to disturbance (Delacour and Amadon 1973). In Venezuela, as in most Latin American countries, illegal hunting pressures and habitat destruction are the principal factors affecting cracid populations. Both are quite widespread, extending into national parks and other protected areas. Subsistence hunting has been cited for the drastic reduction of fauna over much of the country (Amengual et al. 1981).

These factors, although their presence and effects are well known, have not been extensively studied in Venezuela. This paper presents quantitative data on the preference for the Cracidae as food in five locations in Venezuela and estimates the effects of hunting pressure on censused populations of eight cracid species.

Study Sites

The areas surveyed in this study included three sites north of the Orinoco River, Guatopo National Park in the states of Miranda and Guárico, Henri Pittier National Park in the state of Aragua, and Hato Jaguar in Yaracuy state; and two sites south of the River in Bolívar state, the Caura Forest Reserve and Canaima National Park (fig. 4.2).

In Guatopo National Park, censuses were performed in ecotone habitat between deciduous-humid late secondary and primary forest between 350 and 750 m. Cracid species known to occur in the Park included *Ortalis ruficauda, Pe-*

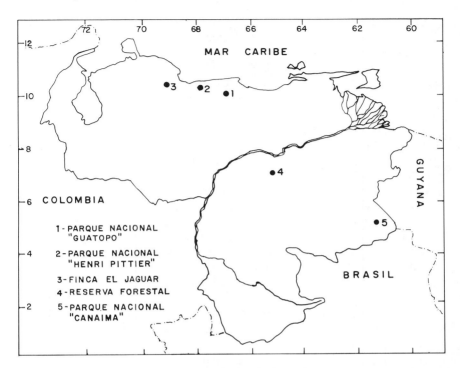

Figure 4.2. Map of Venezuela showing the study sites for the work.

nelope argyrotis, P. purpurascens, Crax daubentoni, and *P. pauxi.* Guatopo has a total area of 92,640 ha of mostly mountainous forest, but its borders have extensively deforested areas. These disturbances have been caused by campesinos from small towns and villages surrounding the park. Settlements are quite dense in the area, and illegal hunting occurs widely within and surrounding Guatopo. The economic activities of commerce and agriculture provide adequate employment and food supplies for most of the inhabitants, and this illegal hunting is for sport. Inhabitants hunt for sport on weekends, holidays, vacations, but not according to standard sport hunting regulations. These hunters may or may not eat their prey, and hunted animals are not their main source of food.

Henri Pittier National Park has an area of 107,800 ha. Censuses made in cloud forest between 1,140 and 1,490 m found only *P. argyrotis* and *P. pauxi.* In the lower extremes of elevation, *O. ruficauda, P. purpurascens,* and *C. daubentoni* were also found. A number of small towns and villages exist along and within the north-central boundary of the park. Inhabitants engage in commercial and tourist service activities, subsistence agriculture, and hunting. Roughly two-thirds of the hunters in the area are illegal sport hunters. One-third are subsistence hunters, who hunt on a regular (not spare time) basis and who rely on game as a major source of animal protein.

Hato Jaguar is an active cattle ranch of some 27,000 ha, 16,000 of which are covered by primary humid cloud forest. The remainder has been converted to grassland. Censuses were undertaken between 640 and 850 m, and cracid species in the area included *P. argyrotis, P. purpurascens,* and *P. pauxi.* In the lower areas of the ranch, *O. ruficauda* and *C. daubentoni* are also present. Small villages and other ranches are found nearby, but the area is only sparsely populated. Cattle ranching and agriculture are the principal activities in the region, and both illegal sport and subsistence hunting are fairly common.

The Caura Forest Reserve includes 4,804,000 ha of primary humid lowland forest in the Caura, Erebatu, and Nichare River drainages. Censuses were performed in the northern limits of the Reserve between 80 and 100 m, where *Ortalis motmot, Penelope jacquacu, Pipile pipile, Crax alector,* and *Mitu tomentosa* occur. *Penelope marail* is found in the forests to the south. Four villages are present within 20 km of the census site, with low population densities of campesino colonists. In the southern part of the reserve there are indigenous populations of Ye'kwana and Sanema Indians. Hoti Indians inhabit the northwest portion of the reserve. Campesinos and indigenous people alike engage in commercial and subsistence agriculture, hunting, and fishing. There is little or no economic development in the region, and plans for the management of the reserve are currently in litigation.

In Canaima National Park (3 million ha) we censused at 850 to 900 m in a primary humid forest fragment (22,820 ha), Taren Baurú, near San Ignacio de Yuruaní. This fragment is surrounded by the Gran Sabana and the extensive grassland which covers most of the region. Recent evidence suggests that the grassland is the result of centuries of repeated burning by the indigenous Pemón population for agriculture and hunting (Galan 1984). In Taren Baurú *O. motmot* and *P. jacquacu* were present. The towns of San Francisco de Yuruaní, San Ignacio de Yuruaní, and Santa Cruz de Mapaurí are located on the north, west, and southwest borders of the forest, respectively. These towns represent low population densities of transculturized Pemón Indians. There are no market or commercial activities, employment is low, and little imported food is available within the park.

Methods

Censuses of Cracid Populations

To census cracid populations at each study site, we used the variable-length transect of King (in Overton 1971). The formula described by this model for species density (D) is:

$$D = \frac{Z}{2\,\bar{x}\,\Sigma\,L}$$

where Z = the total number of individuals of a given species observed on all transects, $\bar{x}$ is the mean perpendicular distance of all sightings (xi) of that species from the transect, and ΣL is the sum of the lengths of the transects. The resulting measure of D represents a mean density from repeated samplings of the habitat, as the formula produces a density estimate independent of the number of transects, each of which can be considered as an independent sample. The results are expressed in individuals of each species per square kilometer. To convert this measure to a biomass estimate, we used the average weights of birds reported in Schaefer (1953), Delacour and Amadon (1973), and Hames (1979).

At each study site, we censused populations in two consecutive years along available trails and primitive roads. Table 4.1 presents total effort spent in censuses. We visited the Caura Forest Reserve site twice in the first year of the study because five species of Cracidae were in the area.

TABLE 4.1
Censusing Effort at Each of the Study Sites

Study Site	Localities Censused	Month/Year	No. of Transects	TL*
Guatopo	La Macanilla, El Lucero,	Sept. 1985	11	40.1
	Aguas Blancas y Sta. Crucita	June 1986	24	45.2
Heri Pittier	Rancho Grande	Aug. 1985	34	52.7
		Aug. 1986	13	28.0
El Jaguar	El Jaguar	July 1985	19	42.0
		Aug. 1986	22	69.1
El Caura	La Urbana —Pto. Cabello	June 1985	5	25.5
		Nov. 1985	14	147.7
		Nov. 1986	20	102.3
Canaima	Taren Baurú	Dec. 1985	5	15.1
		Dec. 1986	13	22.3
		Total	180	590.0

*TL = Total length of transects in kilometers.

When censuses were performed from roadways, we measured the perpendicular distance of each sighting (xi) from the edge of the roadway for arboreal species (e.g., *Penelope, Ortalis*). For terrestrial-arboreal species (e.g., *Crax, Pauxi*) we measured the perpendicular distance from the middle of the road. We did this because roads did not represent continuous habitat for arboreal species. A measure of $xi = 1.0$ m was recorded for birds flying across the transect and for arboreal species located on the edge of a roadway. Terrestrial species observed on roadways were assigned an xi = one-half of the width of the road.

For additional details on the census methodology and a more detailed examination of the results obtained, see Strahl and Silva (in press).

Interviews With Local Hunters

We interviewed residents in villages and towns within or bordering each study site to quantify the preference for cracids as food and to estimate hunting pressure in each region (see table 4.2 for localities). The interviews addressed seventeen questions in six categories.

1. Age and sex of hunter; number of years in residence in the region; size of family; means of subsistence; level of education.
2. Areas hunted; presence of cracids in these areas.
3. Acceptability of cracid meat to the hunter.
4. Number of cracids hunted in the previous two years. Did he hunt throughout the entire year?
5. Reasons for hunting; preferred methods of hunting.
6. Other species hunted in addition to cracids; human preference for cracids and mammalian game species; preference between cracids and domestic fowl; reasons for any preference.

We attempted to put the hunter at ease at the beginning of the interview by presenting ourselves as nongovernmental biologists interested in finding out about the habits of cracids in the region, with the aim of establishing a program for captive breeding. We also told the hunter that we were looking for people

TABLE 4.2
**Total Number of Hunter Interviews in Each Study Area
Between 1985 and 1986**

Study Site	Localities	No. of Hunters Interviewed
Guatopo	Santa Teresa, Altagracia de Orituco, San Francisco de Macaira, San Francisco de Yare, Ocumare del Tuy, La Colonia, Uverito, San Miguel, Orocollal y El Banco.	35
Henri Pittier	Ocumare de la Costa, Cuyagua, La Trilla, Aponte y Cumboto.	23
El Jaguar	El Jaguar, Cararapito y Gusanillal.	9
El Caura	La Urbana —Pto. Cabello Las Trincheras y Jabillal	32
Canaima	San Francisco de Yuruaní, San Ignacio de Yuruaní y Santa Cruz de Mapaurí.	48
	Total	147

with experience with the local fauna and attempted to create an atmosphere of trust between ourselves and the subject.

Questions to determine the number of individual cracids hunted were the most subjective. To avoid biases we asked the hunter to respond only if he could remember the rough number hunted. To evaluate the significance of his answer, we used the abundance of the species in the area, the type of hunter, the areas where he hunted, and whether he hunted all year as subjective criteria. For the other questions, we did not expect major inaccuracies due to the simplicity of their content.

We based our evaluation of interview success at each study location on the percentage of hunters that collaborated with the work (interviews made/interviews attempted $\times$ 100) and on our subjective impressions of the veracity of the responses.

We quantified the preference for Cracidae as food by determining the percentage of the hunters that (1) found cracid flesh palatable, (2) preferred the Cracidae over domestic fowl, and (3) preferred to hunt and eat cracid flesh over the flesh of mammalian game. Preferences were scaled as none, low, and high based on the above percentages, which we calculated for each study location using all interviews from 1985 and 1986. We assumed that a significant tendency was shown when the percentage involved was significantly greater than 50% according to a test of proportions (Yamane 1969).

Hunting pressure was measured directly as the number and biomass of cracids taken per active hunter per year at each study site.

Results

The percentage of hunters who participated in the interviews was 95.5%, and the veracity of data collected was considered generally to be high. The fact that nearly all hunters interviewed were quite open and frank regarding their illegal activities, including those that hunted within the confines of the national parks, can be taken as subjective evidence of the veracity of the data. From the interview guide, only question 4 needed verification, and of all of the interviews conducted, only three from Caura and one from Canaima were rejected due to the exaggerated number of birds reportedly taken. Even so, we emphasize that the data we present in calculating hunting pressure should be considered as estimates due to inherent imprecision on the part of the hunters and the constraints of the interviewing techniques.

Cracid Population Densities

The population density estimates for Cracidae in each study area are presented in table 4.3. These are comparable on a gross level between years and areas, as the formula used for D was independent of sampling effort. However,

TABLE 4.3
Population Densities Expressed as Birds/km^2 and kg/km^2
of the Cracidae at Each Study Site

Study Site	Species	Month/Year		Z*	X*	Birds/km^2	kg/km^2
Guatopo	*Penelope argyrotis*	Sept.	1985	2	7.0	4	3
		June	1986	8	8.4	11	9
	Penelope purpurascens	Sept.	1985	39	13.7	36	57
		June	1986	23	8.9	29	46
	Ortalis ruficauda	Sept.	1985	6	9.8	7	4
		June	1986	13	11.8	12	7
Henri Pittier	*Penelope argyrotis*	Aug.	1985	11	5.7	18	15
		Aug.	1986	2	5.6	6	5
	Pauxi pauxi	Aug.	1985	2	12.5	2	7
		Aug.	1986	0	0.0	0	0
El Jaguar	*Penelope argyrotis*	July	1985	2	3.0	8	7
		Aug.	1986	5	11.0	3	2
	Penelope purpurascens	July	1985	38	15.2	30	47
		Aug.	1986	43	10.9	29	46
	Pauxi pauxi	July	1985	4	6.0	8	26
		Aug.	1986	0	0.0	0	0
El Caura	*Ortalis motmot*	June	1985	4	5.8	14	6
		Nov.	1985	29	8.6	11	5
		Nov.	1986	19	10.9	9	4
	Penelope jacquacu	June	1985	10	6.9	28	41
		Nov.	1985	100	12.1	28	41
		Nov.	1986	33	18.3	9	13
	Pipile pipile	June	1985	0	0.0	0	0
		Nov.	1985	2	10.5	1	2
		Nov.	1986	3	20.0	1	2
	Crax alector	June	1985	5	7.0	14	54
		Nov.	1985	21	7.0	10	39
		Nov.	1986	23	14.5	8	31
	Mitu tomentosa	June	1985	2	21.0	2	5
		Nov.	1985	0	0.0	0	0
		Nov.	1986	0	0.0	0	0
Canaima	*Ortalis motmot*	Dec.	1985	0	0.0	0	0
		Dec.	1986	2	15.0	3	1
	Penelope jacquacu	Dec.	1985	4	16.5	8	12
		Dec.	1986	5	20.8	5	7

*Z = total number of birds registered; X = mean perpendicular distance.

because of differences in habitat use and species characteristics, detectability almost certainly varied.

Comparing population densities among species north of the Orinoco River, we found that *P. purpurascens* had similar densities in Guatopo and Hato Jaguar. *P. argyrotis* had the highest density in Henri Pittier in 1985 and in Guatopo in 1986. With the exception of *P. argyrotis* in Guatopo, population densities of both species decreased from 1985 to 1986 in all sites. In 1985, *P. pauxi* showed a higher density at Hato Jaguar than at Henri Pittier. No bird of this species was seen at either site in 1986.

South of the Orinoco in the Caura Reserve, the recorded densities of *O. motmot*, *P. jacquacu*, and *C. alector* decreased over the 2.5 years of the study. *P. jacquacu* showed the most drastic reduction. *P. pipile* and *M. tomentosa* had very low densities, comparable to those of *Pauxi* and representing the lowest calculated densities of all species. In Canaima, densities of *O. motmot* and *P. jacquacu* were lower than those of the two species at Caura.

Human Preference for Cracid Meat

In all study areas, the Cracidae were used as a source of food by the campesino or indigenous populations. However, the preference for cracids as food changed with locality (table 4.4).

TABLE 4.4
Preference for the Cracidae as Food at Each Study Area

| Study Site | Palatability | Preferred Cracids Over: | |
		Domestic Fowl*	Mammals*
Guatopo	77.1	37.1	5.7
Henri Pittier	100.0	73.9	34.8
El Jaguar	77.8	11.1	33.3
El Caura	100.0	56.3	6.3
Canaima	100.0	37.5	25.0

*Percentage of those interviewed who preferred to eat and hunt cracids over domestic fowl and over mammals, respectively.

In Guatopo, the majority of hunters found cracid flesh palatable, but the preference for cracids as food was generally low. This was probably because only the border of the park is subject to hunting pressure, and in these localities, only *O. ruficauda* is abundant among hunted Cracidae. The meat of chachalacas is exceedingly tough, and the bird is small. Even so, the relationship of cost of ammunition to quantity of meat obtained encouraged the hunters to look for larger mammalian prey, and hunting pressure is therefore higher on the mammal community. There was a significant preference for mammals over the Cracidae. Mammal meat was considered to be more tender and have better taste.

In Henri Pittier, the preference for cracids as food was high. All hunters found cracid flesh palatable, and a significant majority preferred these species over domestic fowl. Although there was a tendency to prefer mammals over cracids, the difference was not significant.

At Hato Jaguar, cracids were the preferred food of a minority of respondents although this was only significant when compared with domestic fowl. This and the low hunting pressure on the Cracidae (see following discussion) indicate that the preference for cracids as food is low in the region.

In both Caura and Canaima, despite the fact that most hunters preferred mammals only slightly over Cracidae, all hunters found cracids palatable, and there was no clear preference between cracids and domestic fowl. In addition, there was an extremely high hunting pressure on the Cracidae in both areas, as discussed in the following section.

Hunting Pressure

Hunting pressure on each species by study site is listed in table 4.5. Comparing the study areas, we found the highest hunting pressure in Caura and Canaima, where most hunting was for subsistence. Hunting pressure was far lower at sites north of the Orinoco, in both numbers and biomass of birds taken. *C. alector* was the most commonly taken of all cracids in Caura, and *P. jacquacu* was the species most harvested in Canaima. At the sites north of the Orinoco, *O. ruficauda* and *P. purpurascens* were the most frequently hunted species.

Information on hunting pressure cannot be directly related to population densities at all of the sites. The hunting data for Guatopo and Henri Pittier derives from the villages and towns bordering the parks. In Henri Pittier, some hunting occurred in the interior of the park as well, including the census area. In Guatopo, there is no hunting in the region censused due to the daily vigilance of park guards in that region. At both Jaguar and Canaima, hunting occurred in the censused region as well as the surrounding region. In Caura, the informants hunted in a variety of locations up to 100 km from the census sites, and the hunting pressure figures represent a vast region but also include the census area.

TABLE 4.5
Hunting Pressure on Each Species of the Family Cracidae at Each Study Site

Study Site	Species	Birds/Hunter/Yr	Kg/Hunter/Yr
Guatopo	*Ortalis ruficauda*	8.0	4.7
	Penelope purpurascens	0.22	0.35
Henri Pittier	*Ortalis ruficauda*	1.8	1.1
	Penelope argyrotis	1.3	1.1
	Penelope purpurascens	1.7	2.7
	Crax daubentoni	0.67	1.8
	Pauxi pauxi	0.22	0.73
Hato Jaguar	*Ortalis ruficauda*	6.0	3.5
	Penelope argyrotis	1.0	0.81
	Penelope purpurascens	3.2	5.0
	Crax daubentoni	0.60	1.6
	Pauxi pauxi	0.20	0.65
Caura Forest Reserve	*Ortalis motmot*	0.76	0.34
	Penelope jacquacu	1.9	2.8
	Pipile pipile	4.2	6.5
	Crax alector	10.3	39.8
	Mitu tomentosa	2.4	5.9
Canaima	*Ortalis motmot*	6.1	2.8
	Penelope jacquacu	12.6	18.3

Discussion

Effects of Hunting on Cracidae Populations

To explain differences in population densities between study sites, a number of potential causal factors must be considered, both ecological and those related to human disturbance. Of the ecological factors, habitat preference by cracid species will be discussed. Among human causal factors, hunting pressure is the most important, as habitat destruction within the census areas was generally low or nonexistent. For a more detailed discussion of cracid densities and the factors affecting them, see Strahl and Silva (in press).

According to Schaefer (1953) and Delacour and Amadon (1973), *P. argyrotis* occurs in higher densities in cloud forest between 900 and 1,500 m elevation. We therefore expected that population densities of *P. argyrotis* would be the highest in Henri Pittier, lower in Jaguar, and lowest in Guatopo. This was the observed order of densities found in 1985, but the order in 1986 was Guatopo, Henri Pittier, and Jaguar (table 4.3). The high density in Guatopo is even more surprising because the habitat is partly secondary. The observed increase in density in 1986 could be real, since there is no perturbation in the census area.

P. purpurascens occurs in higher densities in primary rain forest (Delacour and Amadon 1973; De Schaunsee and Phelps 1978), although it also occurs in ecotone habitats (Hilty and Brown 1986). We expected that densities of this species should be similar at Guatopo and Jaguar, with possibly a tendency toward higher densities at Jaguar, which was more humid. Our data show densities were similar at the two sites but slightly higher in Guatopo in 1985.

The habitat of *P. pauxi* is cloud forest between 500 and 2,200 m, with higher densities normally occurring from 1,000 to 1,500 m (Schaefer 1953; De Schaunsee and Phelps 1978). In 1985 (the only year during which this species was observed in either location), *P. pauxi* showed a higher density in Jaguar than in Henri Pittier, contrary to what was expected.

The differences between expected and observed density measures might be explained by selective population reduction in some areas. Hunting pressure seems to have reduced population densities of certain species in Henri Pittier and Jaguar. The preference for cracids as food in these two areas is not directly related to hunting pressure. In Jaguar, more cracids are hunted per hunter than in Henri Pittier (table 4.5), even though cracids are not a preferred food item (table 4.4). We believe that the suboptimal habitat at Jaguar also affected densities of *P. argyrotis* and *P. pauxi*. The absence of hunting pressure in the censused areas of Guatopo explains to a large degree why species densities are high at this site despite the marginal or suboptimal nature of the habitat for the species involved.

In our census area, *O. ruficauda* was only present in Guatopo. *Crax dauben-*

toni was not censused but is present in the lowland regions of Guatopo, Jaguar, and Henri Pittier. Although *O. ruficauda* is the most hunted cracid, it is still abundant along the borders of Guatopo, Henri Pittier, and Jaguar. Hunting pressure in the past has probably reduced *C. daubentoni* population on the study sites. This species is extirpated or rare in some localities along the boundaries of Guatopo, and it is rare in Henri Pittier and Jaguar.

We censused all the Cracidae in Caura and Canaima within their preferred habitats, except for *P. pipile* and *M. tomentosa*. *P. pipile* and *M. tomentosa* prefer riparian vegetation within the primary humid forest, and the low observed densities reflect this. In the census area of Caura, hunting pressure appears to be the major determining factor for reducing cracid densities over the 2-year period, especially in the cases of *O. motmot*, *P. jacquacu*, and *C. alector.* In this region, the preference for cracids produces a high hunting pressure on them. Furthermore, in the census region, hunting pressure increased dramatically from 1985 to 1986. This was associated with logging exploration and the paving of the access road.

In Canaima Park, the high levels of hunting pressure in Taren Baurú have undoubtedly diminished the population densities of both *O. motmot* and *P. jacquacu*. While densities did not change much over the census period, they are no doubt a product of long-term sustained hunting in the area, and annual differences in density with such low levels would be extremely difficult to detect. In this region, all game species are rare. The high hunting pressure in the area can be explained by the preference for cracids as food and the Adventist religion of a large percentage of the Pemón Indians in the region, which permits the hunting of only birds and deer among the higher vertebrates. The future of the remnant cracid populations in Taren Baurú is uncertain: This forest fragment is surrounded by savanna, which is partially burned each year. Hunting pressure is heavy, and present population densities are quite low.

Campesino Versus Indigenous Impact on Cracidae Populations in the Neotropics

Anthropologists and biologists have documented the use of wildlife by campesinos and indigenous populations in various locations in the neotropics. While studies have dissimilar data bases and means of analysis, it is possible to examine the use of cracids as a food source. Redford and Robinson (1987), reviewed the patterns of use of wild game by campesino colonists and indigenous populations and found the following with regard to the Cracidae:

1. The harvest of cracids, both by number and by weight, exceeded that of all other avian families. *Penelope* was the most hunted genus among avian genera.
2. Mammals as a whole were harvested more commonly than cracids; however,

cracids as a group were harvested more frequently than any mammalian order except for primates and rodents.

From these data one can readily appreciate the magnitude with which the Cracidae are hunted and their relatively high importance and preference as a source of bush meat for both campesino and indigenous populations in the neotropics. In turn, campesinos and indigenous people affect cracid densities but in different ways.

Latin American campesinos are generally characterized as sedentary, hunting with shotguns along cleared paths, and they exert a lower pressure of extraction on avian communities than do indigenous peoples (Ojasti 1984; Redford and Robinson 1987). This can be explained because campesinos in general prefer mammalian game (see Redford and Robinson 1987), hunt in previously disturbed areas, and have alternative sources of food. This influences the potential impact of their hunting on cracid populations. In the short term, during the settlement process, the campesinos' efficient hunting techniques also reduce local cracid densities, in spite of their preference for larger mammalian game and their sedentary nature. In the longer term, reductions of low natural densities of Cracidae and their slow population recovery rates (see following discussion) can lead to local extinctions in the face of sustained hunting pressure. This process appears to be in progress in our study areas of Henri Pittier and Hato Jaguar.

Indigenous peoples are much less sedentary than campesinos, usually hunt with bow, blowgun, or shotgun, and often use a rotational system of site use. Compared to colonists these groups take more Cracidae on a per capita annual basis (Redford and Robinson 1987), which initially suggests that they should have a heavier impact on cracid populations. However, while hunting by Indians may reduce cracid densities in the short term, the rotating system of use of hunting areas, and in some areas, cultural limitations on the number of individuals hunted over a given period, allows recovery of harvested populations. This system is lacking in campesino hunting methods, which usually deplete cracid populations rapidly. A clear example of this is the extinction of the Cracidae in nonprotected areas in Venezuela, where there is much campesino hunting. In contrast, many of the more remote areas of the country, especially south of the Orinoco River, have been subjected to centuries of hunting by Indians and still contain relatively viable cracid populations. Densities of indigenous hunters are usually far lower than those of campesinos, which no doubt contributes to these results.

The introduction of the shotgun and "acculturation" of indigenous groups, frequently associated with missionary activity, increases the efficiency and sedentary nature of their hunting practices. In Toki, Venezuela, the introduction of the shotgun to the Ye'kwana increased hunting efficiency and seriously affected populations of arboreal and volant species (Hames 1979). As a direct consequence, the Ye'kwana extracted roughly six times more individuals of these species than the resident Yanomami, who hunted with blowgun and bow. Despite this, the rotational system of the Ye'kwana did not reduce cracid population densities irreversibly, as witnessed by the fact that the hunters first acquired shotguns before 1930 and still hunt in the same areas.

On the other hand, the Yanomami community and other indigenous peoples that hunt with traditional methods will probably not reduce cracid communities to dangerous levels, provided that they continue to use rotational systems and remain at low population densities themselves. This extraction is usually noncommercial, based on food needs, and is to some extent balanced as part of the trophic system of their environment.

Management and Conservation of Cracid Populations

The fact that the Cracidae are important prey species for campesinos and indigenous populations argues for an effective management plan for these species. It is probable that sustained-yield harvesting of cracids is not possible in areas of high-level continuous hunting. A simple verbal model illustrates this conclusion. Let us begin with some generous assumptions regarding cracid species:

1. Seventy-five percent of pairs annually have one successful nest, a liberal estimate by Skutch (in Buckley et al. 1985).

2. Clutch size in successful nests is two (Delacour and Amadon 1973).

3. In areas where species are not hunted, natural annual survivorship is 0.8 at all ages.

4. Sexual maturity is reached at an age of three years (based on the larger Cracidae in captivity: J. Estudillo, pers. commun., 1987).

These figures for nesting success and survivorship are quite high for large neotropical forest birds (Skutch in Buckley et al. 1985). Nevertheless, these conservative assumptions predict that:

1. Each pair will produce 1.5 offspring per year, giving a per adult recruitment rate of 0.75 young/yr/adult.

2. Survivorship curves predict that roughly 51% of young will survive to age of first breeding.

3. The average adult must produce 2.4 offspring to replace itself in the population, and this will require slightly more than three breeding seasons.

4. It will require at least 6 years of life for the average cracid to replace itself in the population.

Under the somewhat limited conditions of this model, the recovery rate of a cracid population, even without hunting, must be relatively slow. It is not surprising, therefore, that populations of these species in nature have consistently shown the inability to maintain themselves under continuous hunting, especially in combination with habitat destruction and forest fragmentation. However, in extensive areas of forest with limited local hunting, it may be more probable that the long-term consequences of this type of human disturbance might be minimized.

Human impact on the Cracidae may have irreversible long-term effects on the biology of neotropical forest ecosystems. Along with the reduction or local extinction of population densities of these species, we may expect a reduction in seed dispersal of various plant species and perhaps the elimination of a vital link in the trophic system of large frugivores and their predators. For these reasons, among others, we must develop an effective management plan for this family in the neotropics, using and expanding the available data base on their biology. This must begin not just with "lifeboat" projects on endangered species but with in-depth research on related congeners as well (Strahl, in press).

The development of management programs necessarily implies the previous regional investigation of species population parameters, reproductive ecology, and dietary habits. These programs must be developed on a regional basis, since population parameters of species change with habitat and region. At the same time, the development of robust statistical models, which predict harvest rates and a sustained yield, are needed. In this way, bag limits by species will be set. These models should be tested regionally using new data each year. Periodic monitoring of regional populations must examine population dynamics and test models of hunting regulations. In addition to the standard sport hunting regulations, methods to regulate subsistence hunting must be developed.

Illegal hunting is a significant problem throughout Latin America. Hunting regulations are largely ignored throughout the region (Ojasti 1984). A primary reason for this is the lack of vigilance and enforcement of the laws. To increase enforcement of the laws, national programs in environmental education and improvements in rural standards of living are required. Educational programs must encompass several levels, including training of personnel in enforcement agencies such as the National Guard, environmental awareness campaigns for rural populations, and the education of the general public. These programs should emphasize rational use of wildlife coupled with general information on management and protection of key species and protected areas. However, we cannot expect rural populations living on a subsistence level, as many campesinos and transculturized indigenous peoples do, to accept and abide by hunting regulations unless alternate sources of work, food, and funds are provided.

These programs would require substantial funding. Latin American governments have traditionally lacked the financial resources necessary to implement such broad-scale measures for wildlife study and management, especially in the face of the social, economic, and educational problems that face many neotropical countries. For this reason, we suggest that private institutions and scientific organizations work closely with the government, both financially and logistically, to arrive at effective solutions to management and conservation problems for the Cracidae and other important faunal groups.

Acknowledgments

We would like to express our thanks to the organization and staff of Fundación para la Defensa de la Naturaleza (FUDENA) and Wildlife Conservation International (a division of the New York Zoological Society) for the extensive financial and logistic aid that these two organizations have given this project. We also thank the following Venezuelan Institutions for their cooperation and participation: the Ministry of the Environment and Renewable Natural Resources (MARNR) for permitting us to use vegetation and radar maps of our study sites; the National Institute of Parks (INPARQUES) for allowing us the use of park facilities at Henri Pittier and Guatopo and for donating maps of these parks to the project; Electrificacion de Caroni (EDELCA) for logistic support and lodging in Canaima National Park; Tranarg, C.A., for the donation of aerial photographs of the Caura Reserve; and the Venezuelan National Guard for logistic aid. We also thank Sr. Mauricio Delaudier of Hato Jaguar, who offered his logistic aid and hospitality. Finally, we wish to thank all of the people who gave us aid in the field and in Caracas during the study, who are too numerous to name here. Finally, thanks to Hernan Castellanos, who prepared the figures for this text.

5

Hunting Yields and Game Composition Over Ten Years in an Amazon Indian Territory

WILLIAM T. VICKERS

Wildlife plays an extremely important role in the lives of the indigenous people of the Amazon Basin. First, wild animals provide significant amounts of calories and essential nutrients such as proteins and fats to the Indian diet (Dufour 1983; Flowers 1983; Yost and Kelley 1983). Animal products also contribute to the material culture as tools, ornaments, and raw materials (Aspelin 1975; Steward 1948). Finally, animals are inextricably woven into the native world view, mythology, religion, symbolism, art, and also serve totemic functions in the social organization of many Amazonian groups (Goldman 1963; Reichel-Dolmatoff 1971; Roe 1982; Wagley 1977).

This chapter focuses on a native Amazonian community in Ecuador where wild animals are used primarily to meet the subsistence needs of local people. The purpose here is to present long-term data on hunting activities and yields and to evaluate the effects of this subsistence hunting on local animal populations. The analysis to be presented suggests that, when given traditional native conditions of low human population density, dispersed settlements, and a subsistence economy, most of the game species utilized by Amazonian Indian communities can be hunted on a sustainable basis.

Regrettably, such "native conditions" no longer exist in many areas of the neotropics, where a plethora of development-related pressures are modifying both the physical and human landscapes. Hence, the final section of this chapter will focus on resource conservation and its relationship to the civil and economic rights of native people. While some observers see continued native hunting as a threat to wildlife survival, I argue that conservation policies must recognize certain residential and foraging rights of indigenous peoples while encouraging and promoting their participation in wildlife conservation and management programs.

The Research Setting

This chapter focuses on a native Siona-Secoya community of the Aguarico River in northeastern Ecuador (figs. 5.1, 5.2). In 1973 the site on the Aguarico known as "Shushufindi" (or "San Pablo") began to be settled by Siona and Secoya immigrants from a community on the Cuyabeno River (40 km to the northeast). Over the next few years, more people arrived, and Shushufindi grew into a seminucleated, semidispersed "village." By the late 1970s, the central portion of the village began to decline as people moved short distances up or down river. By 1984–85, only two or three households remained at the former center of the settlement (M. Cipolletti, pers. comm., 1985). Hence, in a period of about 12 years, a village had flourished and then apparently dissipated. Such

Figure 5.1 Siona and Secoya hunters sharpening spears. Bamboo-tipped spears are a traditional weapon for hunting terrestrial game such as peccaries and tapirs. Since the 1950s, the shotgun has replaced both the spear and blowgun in most hunting. Most of these shotguns are single shot 16 gauge. Factory manufactured shells are expensive, so all hunters reload the plastic shell casings with primers, shot, and gunpowder purchased from river traders. (Photo, William Vickers.)

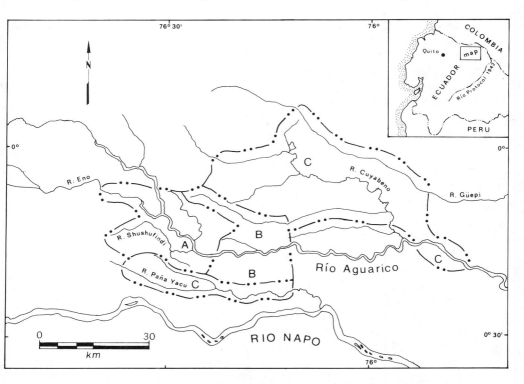

Figure 5.2 Areas hunted by Siona-Secoya Indians from the Shushufindi settlement (A) in north-eastern Ecuador during 1973–82. Ninety-three percent of the hunting sample occurred within a 1,150-km^2 territory around the settlement (areas A and B). A 590-km^2 core area (A) was hunted on a daily basis, while slightly more distant areas (B) were hunted in all months of the year. Even more distant areas (C) were visited by Shushufindi's hunters intermittently or seasonally but were also hunted by Siona Indians from the Cuyabeno River and Lowland Quichua Indians from the lower Aguarico and Napo rivers. Land to the west of the core area (on both sides of the Aguarico) is traditional Kofán Indian territory, although it was increasingly penetrated by non-Indian colonists during the study period.

settlement movements are characteristic of most Amazonian peoples, and various hypotheses have been proposed to account for them, including game depletion (reviewed in Hames and Vickers 1983). In this study, however, the movements covered short distances and all of the new house sites along the Aguarico River fell within the existing hunting territory that the people had been exploiting since their arrival in the area in 1973.

The landscape in the study area has a mean elevation of 250 m with mild relief. The dominant vegetation is "tropical wet forest" (Holdridge et al. 1971) interspersed with some seasonally flooded swamp forest. The Aguarico is a white water river that carries substantial loads of Andean sediments, especially during the rainy season of April through July. The river is swift and the channel narrow, so little of the silt is deposited in the area inhabited by the Siona-Secoya. The soils in the region are relatively good by *terra firme* standards (due to ancient alluvial depositions), although not uniformly so (Vickers 1983).

Siona-Secoya hunters in this area focused more on the terrestrial, arboreal, and volant species of the forest rather than the aquatic species of the rivers (except for fish, which are not discussed here). Lands above the floodplain are cultivated, but not beaches or seasonally flooded areas. Hence the subsistence economy was the type that anthropologists term *terra firme* rather than *várzea*, which is characterized as intensive cropping in floodplains and more emphasis on hunting aquatic species (Meggers 1971; Roosevelt 1980).

Methods

Sampling and Data Collection

The total sample is a record of 863 man-days of hunting spanning 10 years (with observations recorded in 1973, 1974, 1975, 1979, 1980, and 1981–82). The universe from which this sample is drawn consists of the total hunting activities (regardless of location) of the Siona-Secoya population under study (fig. 5.3). I estimate that this universe totals about 22,881 man-days of hunting from 1973 through 1982 (based on the known numbers of hunters and their frequency of hunting). Hence, the record of 863 man-days of hunting represents a sample of about 3.77% of the 10-year universe and about 6.65% of the estimated 12,979 man-days of hunting during the 6 years in which observations were recorded.

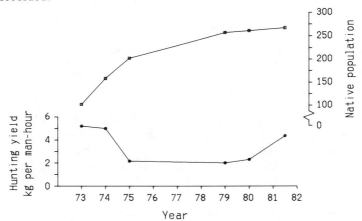

Figure 5.3. Hunting yields and native population in the 1,150-km² Shushufindi territory from 1973 to 1981–82. The yields are mean live weight per man-hour of hunting per year. Population is mean annual value for persons present within the territory. It is adjusted for births, deaths, immigration, emigration, and time spent outside the area.

The data in the record come from both direct observations of hunting and posthunt interviews based on a structured questionnaire that was designed to elicit information on hunting yields, location, time expenditure, participants, and other factors (Vickers 1980, 1988). The sampling strategy was to record as many hunts as possible by accompanying or interviewing hunters whenever there was an opportunity to do so. The main limitation on sampling was the dispersed nature of the community (i.e., it was physically impossible to visit or monitor all households on a daily basis). I collected data when I accompanied or interviewed hunters as I moved about within the community and territory or as people from more distant households visited the part of the settlement where I lived. To expand coverage, I trained two native assistants to administer the hunting questionnaire; cross-checks showed that they did so accurately and reliably. Any attempt to randomize observations from these possibilities would have reduced the number of cases recorded, which I judged to be undesirable.

This sample of 863 man-days of hunting is among the most extensive ever recorded in a native Amazonian community. As a study of ecological dynamics, its representativeness is enhanced by the fact that the data span 10 years (with observations in 6 years), thus giving a perspective on hunting through time and avoiding the problem of generalizing from a set of observations in a single year.

Definition of the Hunting Territory

Most anthropological studies of Amazonian hunting have given little or no attention to the definition of territories or catchment areas from which animals are "harvested" or "cropped." Such information is very important to an understanding of hunting dynamics as well as for assessing the impact of hunting on prey populations. Throughout the present study an attempt has been made to track Siona-Secoya hunters through time and space, and this concern prompted me to ask questions that elicited their perceptions of the environment, including toponyms, habitat variations, and the names of streams and hunting trails that run through the forest. The Siona-Secoya divide their environs into many areas that are associated with natural or humanmade features of the landscape. Hence a returning hunter has no difficulty communicating the location of a kill to his fellow villagers; indeed, this is a normal part of the customary "retelling" of the hunt.

With Shushufindi as the departure point, there were more than twenty named areas or locations within "striking distance" of Siona-Secoya hunters. Since the present chapter is not intended as an analysis of microhabitats, these smaller areas are grouped into broader classifications based on distance and frequency of use. Figure 5.2 depicts the entire range hunted by the Siona-Secoya from Shushufindi from 1973 to 1982, along with three use classifications (labeled A, B, and C). A "core" area of 590 km^2 (fig. 5.2, area A) around the confluence of the Shushufindi and Aguarico rivers surrounded the area of greatest settlement and was easily accessible to all hunters (most of it could be reached in a half-day or less of travel by foot, canoe, or both). This area received the greatest pressure, involving some hunting on a daily basis. Overall, the core area was the focus of 80.65% of the hunting man-days in the recorded sample.

Slightly more distant areas totaling 560 km² (fig. 5.2, area B) were hunted regularly (in all months of the year) and involved 12.28% of the man-days in the hunting sample. Portions of these "intermediate" areas might be hunted in a single day (departing from and returning to Shushufindi), but hunting in them often involved overnight stays in camps.

Finally, much more extensive areas of approximately 1,350 km² (fig. 5.2, areas C) were hunted on an intermittent and seasonal basis and always involved considerable travel. Such "expedition hunts" involved 7.07% of the hunting man-days in the sample. These latter areas were also hunted by Siona Indians residing on the Cuyabeno River and Lowland Quichua Indians from the lower Aguarico and Napo Rivers.

For this chapter, I have chosen to base the analysis on hunting activities and yields in the study community's area of exclusive (or near-exclusive) use, or "territory." This territory covers, 1,150 km² and consists of both the "core" and "intermediate" areas just described (fig. 5.2, areas A and B). Several considerations have influenced this decision. First, this 1,150-km² territory was hunted on a regular basis from the beginning of the study, almost exclusively by local Siona-Secoya residents (interpretation would be difficult if animal populations were also being impacted by hunters who were not part of the study). Second, hunting in this territory constituted 92.93% of the hunting effort recorded for the study community, so this frame of reference provides good insights into overall hunting conditions from the perspective of the human consumers. Finally, the sizes of both this territory and the resident human population correspond closely to the aboriginal conditions along the Aguarico River reported by eighteenth-century Jesuit missionaries (Vickers 1983). Indeed, the mean native population density within the territory for all observed years was 0.2 persons per square kilometer, or the same as both the aboriginal estimate for the lowland tropical forest habitat of Amazonia (Denevan 1976) and the Encabellado ancestors of the Siona-Secoya (Steward 1949). Hence, the focus on hunting dynamics and game conditions within the 1,150-km² territory is relevant to an understanding of both the aboriginal and modern adaptations of the Siona-Secoya.

Settlement Dynamics within the Hunting Territory

As noted earlier, in 1973–74 most of the arriving Siona and Secoya immigrants constructed houses in or near the village of Shushufindi (later known as San Pablo). At this time there were also a number of "detached" houses and small clusters of houses at other sites along the Aguarico and Eno rivers. All of these were located within the 590-km² core area (fig. 5.2, area A), were considered to be a part of the native community and were included in this study from its inception. And from the beginning, the hunters of this community took game throughout the entire range depicted in figure 5.2 (i.e., in area A, B, and C), although they hunted most heavily in the 590-km² core area (A).

By the late 1970s, a dozen predominantly Siona households had departed the village of Shushufindi and moved upriver to new sites along the Aguarico River. These were short moves of 1 to 6 km, and all of the new house sites remained within the boundaries of the core hunting area. In the same period fourteen Secoya families constructed new houses downriver from Shushufindi at distances ranging from 2 to 18 km. Ten of these new houses were located in the "intermediate" portion of the hunting territory (fig. 5.2, areas B). Most of these families, however, split their time between their older and newer houses and therefore maintained a form of dual residence.

My purpose in discussing these details is to show that Siona-Secoya settlement is a very complex issue. While there is some degree of continuity in settlements or villages, considerable flux occurs on a short-term basis as visitors come and go and as people participate in foraging expeditions. It occurs on a longer-term basis as entire households "join" or "split" from settlements, but such events may involve short or long distances and may be full-time or part-time.

To deal with this complexity, I kept a log of the activities and comings and goings of people (based on observations as well as the general flow of information in the community). Hence such factors as the "mean annual population" for specific areas can be defined with a fair degree of precision and give a more accurate index of the human presence than does a static listing of "residents" (who may or may not be present at any given time).

Preferred and Less-preferred Species

The kill data that follow are presented in numbers of kills per 100 man-hours of hunting per year. This gives a standard kill rate per unit of hunting effort and is suitable for graphical representation. To present information on the variability of kill rates within the hunting sample for each year, the values for ± 1 standard deviation (SD) are also indicated on the figures that follow (when the annual sample is divided into subsamples of 100 hours). Because this subdivision "pseudoreplicates" the sample (Hurlbert 1984), these standard deviations are presented as descriptors of the variation in annual hunting yields and not as statistics.

For "preferred" game species (i.e., those that a hunter will almost always attempt to kill upon encountering them), the kill rates should be directly proportional to animal population densities in the area, because kill rates are a function of encounter rates, which in turn are a function of the densities of the animals. Most of the area hunted by the Siona-Secoya in this study is relatively homogeneous and undisturbed tropical rainforest where preferred species such as tapir, peccaries, woolly and howler monkeys, the curassow, and guans are widely distributed. This is not to suggest that animals always appear randomly, for there are seasons, microhabitats, or both in which the appearance of certain species is predictable (e.g., November and December, when river turtles lay their eggs on river beaches and April and May, when woolly monkey troops congregate around fruiting trees [cf. Yost and Kelley 1983]). Such conditions, however, are not typical of most hunts throughout the year.

For "less-preferred" species (i.e., those that a hunter may pass up when encountered), the kill rates are not reliable indices to population densities, but they do indicate the animals' presence in the area. The decision to kill or pass up a less-preferred game type is often based on considerations such as the presence or absence of more preferred game types (or the expectation of their presence or absence), the cost of ammunition, or both. Hence the interpretations of the observed kill rates for less-preferred animals must also consider the overall hunting yields in the same time period (fig. 5.3). The data presented here suggest that when overall yields are high, kills of less-preferred game tend to go down, and when yields are lower, kills of less-preferred animals tend to go up.

In general, the Siona-Secoya prefer game animals that are the larger species of their types (e.g., large ungulates such as tapir and peccaries, large primates such as woolly and howler monkeys, and large birds such as the curassow and guans). The less-preferred tend to be the smaller species (e.g., ungulates such as deer, primates such as the monk saki and the squirrel monkey, and birds such as parrots and toucans). Most rodents, edentates, and reptiles are also less preferred than the larger ungulates, primates, and birds.

These preferences are operationalized as hunters encounter animals and make decisions about which to pursue and are manifested in the differential kill rates of various species (table 5.1), which often do not reflect the relative population structures reported for animal communities in the neotropics (cf. Eisenberg, O'Connell, and August 1979; Eisenberg 1980). For example, the Siona-Secoya killed both white-lipped and collared peccaries about four times more

TABLE 5.1
**Number of Hunting Kills and Mean Kill Rates
in the 1,150-km² Shushufindi Territory 1973–82**

Common Name	Scientific Name	Number Killed	N per 100 Man-hours
1. Woolly monkey	*Lagothrix lagothricha*	295	4.802
2. White-lipped peccary	*Tayassu pecari*	206	3.353
3. Collared peccary	*Tayassu tajacu*	182	2.962
4. Salvin's curassow	*Mitu salvini*	95	1.546
5. Blue-throated piping guan	*Pipile pipile*	82	1.335
6. Agouti	*Dasyprocta* sp.	49	0.798
7. Spix's guan	*Penelope jacquacu*	43	0.700
8. Howler monkey	*Alouatta seniculus*	42	0.684
9. Paca	*Agouti paca*	40	0.651
10. Gray-winged trumpeter	*Psophia crepitans*	36	0.586
11. Tapir	*Tapirus terrestris*	26	0.432

TABLE 5.1 (*continued*)

Common Name	Scientific Name	Number Killed	N per 100 Man-hours
12. Greater long-nosed armadillo	*Dasypus kappleri*	18	0.293
13. Great tinamou	*Tinamus major*	16	0.260
14. Cuvier's toucan	*Ramphastos cuvieri*	14	0.228
15. Red squirrel	*Sciurus igniventris*	13	0.212
16. Coatimundi	*Nasua nasua*	12	0.195
17. Spectacled caiman	*Caiman sclerops*	12	0.195
18. Ocelot[a]	*Felis pardalis*	11	0.179
19. Scarlet macaw	*Ara macao*	11	0.179
20. Brocket deer	*Mazama americana*	9	0.146
21. Tortoise	*Geochelone denticulata*	7	0.114
22. Common long-nosed armadillo	*Dasypus novemcinctus*	5	0.081
23. Dusky titi	*Callicebus moloch*	5	0.081
24. Many-banded aracari	*Pteroglossus pluricinctus*	5	0.081
25. Mealy parrot	*Amazona farinosa*	5	0.081
26. River turtle	*Podocnemis unifilis*	5	0.081
27. White-lipped, black-mantled tamarin	*Saguinus nigricollis*	5	0.081
28. Black caiman	*Melanosuchus niger*	4	0.065
29. Capuchin monkey[b]	*Cebus albifrons*	4	0.065
30. Deer	*Mazama* sp.?	4	0.065
31. Jaguar[a]	*Panthera onca*	4	0.065
32. Undulated tinamou	*Crypturellus undulatus*	4	0.065
33. Acouchi	*Myoprocta* sp.	3	0.049
34. Cacique bird	*Cacicus* sp.	3	0.049
35. Capybara	*Hydrochaeris hydrochaeris*	3	0.049
36. Monk saki	*Pithecia monachus*	3	0.049
37. Squirrel monkey	*Saimiri sciureus*	3	0.049
38. Blue-and-yellow macaw	*Ara ararauna*	2	0.033
39. Oropendola	*Gymnostinops* sp.	2	0.033
40. Small birds	unidentified	2	0.033
41. Snowy egret[c]	*Egretta thula*	2	0.033
42. White-necked heron	*Ardea cocoi*	2	0.033
43. Black-headed parrot	*Pionites melanocephala*	1	0.016
44. Hoatzin	*Opisthocomus hoazin*	1	0.016
45. Lettered aracari	*Pteroglossus inscriptus*	1	0.016
46. Otter[a]	*Lutra* sp.	1	0.016
47. Puma[a]	*Felis concolor*	1	0.016
48. Red and green macaw	*Ara chloroptera*	1	0.016
Total kills		1,300	
Mean kills per 100 man-hours of hunting			21.160
Mean kills per man-day of hunting			1.621

Note: Sample represents 802 man-days of hunting, totaling 6,143.74 man-hours.

[a]Taken for pelt; not eaten.

[b]Taken for use as bait in ocelot trap; not eaten.

[c]Taken for feathers; not eaten.

frequently than agoutis (table 5.1), although it is extremely unlikely that peccary densities are higher. Hunters also express their preferences verbally. While there are minor variations in individual preferences, as well as cultural influences on how certain animals are perceived, the suggested guideline that Siona-Secoya hunters most prefer the larger ungulates, primates, and birds is useful in interpreting the differential kill rates among various animals.

Sustainability and Depletion

One of the concerns of this volume is whether human use of wildlife resources is "sustainable." A related concept is that of "depletion" (i.e., if an animal population is being "depleted," one expects that its harvest will not be "sustainable"). Eltringham (1984:38) defines sustainable yields as those that "do not exceed the capacity of the population to replace them." Depletion may be said to occur when any of the following conditions exists (J. G. Robinson, pers. comm., 1987): (1) A species becomes locally extinct; or (2) its population is so reduced that it is likely to become extinct due to genetic or reproductive factors; or (3) its population is so reduced that it no longer constitutes a significant resource for humans.

The third condition is the most relevant to this study because the major indicator of game conditions is the observed kill rate made by Siona-Secoya hunters. When the kill rate of a preferred game animal drops, I assume that this reflects a decline in the available numbers of that species. This may be due to the impact of hunting, population movements, or other factors that may reduce populations (e.g., climatic variation, habitat destruction, food scarcity, morbidity, nonhuman predation, demographic cycles, and pollution). However, this study does not have quantitative measures for all such factors, so some qualitative judgments are required. I assume that most observed declines in the kill rates of preferred species result from the impact of native hunting (in the case of *Tayassu pecari*, herd movement is suggested). This is because hunting was the most apparent factor observed (i.e., little or no evidence of animal morbidity, mortality due to pollution, or climatic variation was observed).

Considerable colonization and subsequent deforestation did occur in the upper Aguarico Basin along the Quito-Lago Agrio-Coca road, but this zone's center was 65 km northwest of the study area. By 1980, several colonist "precooperatives" and an African palm company had staked land claims along or within the western fringes of the Siona-Secoya hunting territory, but a small amount of forest (less than 5%) was cleared by 1982, when the study ended. Colonist hunting did not appear to have a significant influence on the results of this study because most of the land claimants had not yet established full residence in the area, and those that I interviewed did not possess shotguns or other hunting weapons.

No attempt is made in this chapter to estimate the maximum sustainable yield (MSY), since for wild game populations this task is difficult or "impossible to calculate accurately . . . from theoretical formulations" (Eltringham 1984:46). However, some general principles from the theory of sustained-yield harvesting are useful in interpreting the kill rate trends observed in this study. One is that when wild populations are at carrying capacity they are "nonproductive" because recruitment is balanced by mortality. When a population is made "productive" by cropping, its "density would be about halved and the impression of superabundance would be less striking" (Eltringham 1984:52–53). Hence an initial decline in the numbers of a species (or, indirectly, its kill rates) does not, by itself, constitute depletion. As a population begins to be harvested, some decline in numbers (or kill rates) is to be expected. If the initial decline is followed by relatively stable kill rates over several years the observed pattern is consistent with that to be expected from "sustainable" cropping, since "the maximum sustainable yield is that which holds an otherwise expanding population steady" (Eltringham 1984:46). If, however, the observed kill rates show a steady decline through time, one might expect that the capacity of the population to replace its losses has been exceeded and that such kills are not sustainable.

Results

Ungulates

The most frequently killed ungulates at Shushufindi were the white-lipped peccary (*Tayassu pecari*) and the collared peccary (*T. tajacu*; fig. 5.4). Both are

Figure 5.4. Collared peccary (*Tayassu tajacu*), one of the most important game species of many indigenous groups in the Amazon. (Photo, John Robinson.)

highly prized because of their large body sizes. Figure 5.5 presents the observed annual kill rates for these species. White-lipped kills fluctuated over a wider range of values than collared peccary kills and reflect the former's tendency to form large, migratory herds (cf. Kiltie 1980; Kiltie and Terborgh 1983). White-lipped kill rates are high when one or more herds are in the vicinity of a native settlement and low when they are not. Collared peccaries form

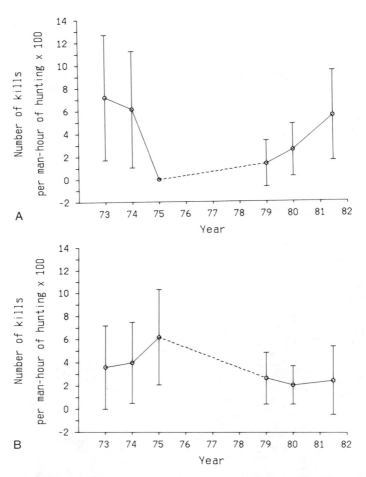

Figure 5.5. A, *Tayassu pecari* kill rates from 1973 to 1981–82. The vertical bars represent ± 1 standard deviation (when the hunting sample for one year is divided into subsamples of 100 man-hours each). When no kills are recorded, as in 1975, the standard deviation is zero and no bars are drawn. White-lipped peccary kill rates fluctuate greatly and appear to reflect the movements of herds within or through the hunting territory rather than continuous local interactions between hunters and prey. B, Collared peccary (*Tayassu tajacu*) kill rates rise during the 1973–75 period and are slightly lower and more stable in 1979–82.

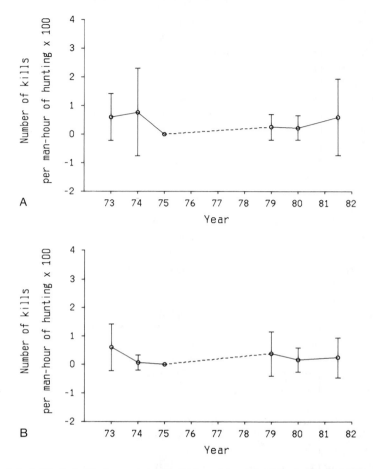

Figure 5.6. A, The tapir (*Tapirus terrestris*) is the largest ungulate of the Amazon rainforest and the most desired game animal for the Siona-Secoya. Its kill rates were low, but stable, throughout the study. B, Deer (Cervidae) kill rates are also low and stable. A traditional belief that deer are demons may have limited their desirability to some hunters (see text).

smaller groups with smaller home ranges. At Shushufindi, the kill rates suggest that the collared peccary population was growing during the initial years of settlement, followed by lower, but steady, kill rates during 1979–82. Both peccary patterns suggest sustainable harvests at the observed levels of human density and predation.

The tapir (*Tapirus terrestris*) is the largest terrestrial mammal in Amazonia and the most prized game animal for the Siona-Secoya. Tapirs tend to occur solitarily (except for females with offspring). The tapir had low, but steady, kill rates within the Shushufindi area (fig. 5.6A). The kill rate in the 1981–82 period was about the same as that of 1973, the first year of the settlement.

Figure 5.6B presents the kill rates for deer (Cervidae). These are quite similar to those of the tapir. Deer, however, are far smaller than the tapir and were traditionally considered to be demons and therefore tabooed as food. This taboo has partially eased in recent years, perhaps due to increased Siona-Secoya interaction with missionaries and others who consume deer meat and who pronounce the "silliness" of the taboo. The adoption of shotguns may also have made deer kills easier. Regardless, many hunters still express a distaste for them. Were deer more preferred, they might have been killed more frequently. The observed rates for tapir and deer appear stable, with no indication of decline through time.

Primates

Primates are an important category of game for the Siona-Secoya and were traditionally taken with blowguns and poisoned darts (as Yost and Kelley, 1983, have described for the Waorani of Ecuador). Today they are taken primarily with shotguns. The woolly monkey (*Lagothrix lagotricha*) was the most frequently killed primate species, which may reflect its population density, the ease of making multiple kills once a troop is located, or both. The resistance of the *Lagothrix* population to depletion appears good when the 1,150-km^2 territory is the frame of reference (fig. 5.7A). But when one takes the more constricted frame of reference of the 590-km^2 core area around the village of Shushufindi, there is clear suggestion of local depletion through time (fig. 5.7B). Of all the prey species discussed here, *Lagothrix* appears to be one of the two that are most susceptible to depletion. These results suggest that the hunting of woolly monkeys may be sustainable only when native population densities are low and/or settlement locations are shifting or hunting territories are relatively extensive (i.e., the prevailing "native conditions" in the 1,150-km^2 territory described here).

Howler monkey (*Alouatta seniculus*) kill rates were quite stable through time (fig. 5.8A) but showed a slight rise toward the end of the study. This suggests that natural reproduction or immigration was sufficient to replace hunting kills of this species. Like *Lagothrix, Alouatta* is a preferred game species, but it was always killed at lower rates. Groups are smaller than those of *Lagothrix,* and overall population density in the area may be lower, as evidenced by the much higher kill rates for the latter (Yost and Kelley, 1983, also report higher kills of *Lagothrix* among the Waorani Indians of eastern Ecuador). However, behavioral differences may affect the relative ease of locating and killing these species, such as *Alouatta's* habit of hiding high in the forest canopy when disturbed (Hernández-Camacho and Cooper 1976:54).

The spider monkey (*Ateles belzebuth*) is also considered an edible species, but it was not found in the Shushufindi area. According to native informants, the nearest location with this species was on the southern bank of the Napo

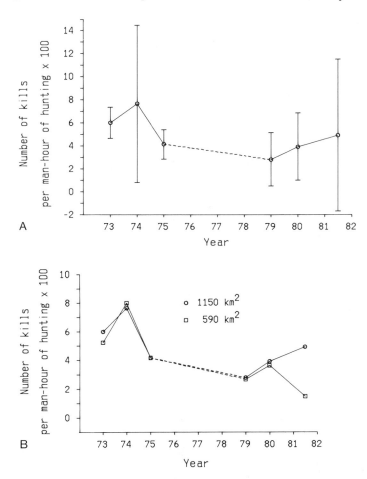

Figure 5.7. A, The woolly monkey (*Lagothrix lagotricha*) was the most frequently killed primate in this study. Its yields appear sustainable when the 1,150-km² territory is the frame of reference. B, Depletion is suggested for woolly monkeys when observations are limited to the 590-km² core area.

River, about 25 km to the south. This may be because *Lagothrix* and *Ateles* tend to occur in mutually exclusive areas (Hernández-Camacho and Cooper 1976:63).

Primates other than *Lagothrix* and *Alouatta* were generally ignored by the Siona-Secoya hunters in this study. These are all smaller species of such genera as *Cebus, Pithecia, Saimiri, Saguinus, Callicebus,* and *Cebuella.* Even when such smaller primate groups are combined (fig. 5.8B), the resulting kill rates are no higher than those recorded for *Alouatta* (fig. 5.8A). Given these low kill rates, it is unlikely that the populations of these genera were threatened by

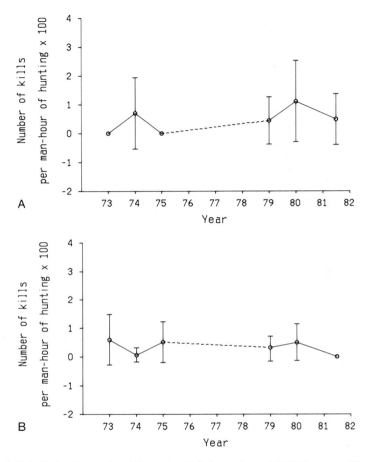

Figure 5.8. A, the howler monkey (*Alouatta seniculus*) was always taken at low rates. The rising kill rates toward the end of the study suggest a slightly increasing population. B, Smaller primates such as *Cebus, Pithecia, Saimiri, Saguinus, Callicebus,* and *Cebuella* were taken very infrequently, so it is useless to present long-term graphs of kill rates for each species (most values would be zero). When all kills of these genera are combined, the rate remains low. Most hunters ignored these smaller primates because the little meat they provided was not considered worth the cost of a shotgun shell.

Siona-Secoya hunters. Had more hunters used blowguns instead of shotguns, kills of these smaller primates might have been higher (i.e., hunters were reluctant to expend shotgun shells on very small animals).

Rodents

Rodents are sometimes thought to be of great importance to Amazonian hunters because their populations are said to have high reproductive potentials and therefore survive despite hunting pressure (e.g., Ross 1978). Some species are also believed to thrive around settlements because of the increased food availability in native gardens. Observations indicate significant rodent populations in the study area. Their kill rates, however, were low. Hunters tended to ignore rodents unless larger and more preferred game animals were not encountered. Hence rodents served as a less-preferred reserve category that could be relied upon when required.

Capybara (*Hydrochaeris hydrochaeris*), the largest Amazonian rodent, was present but was disdained by most hunters in this study because they perceived it as having a "foul taste." This is an exception to the suggested "rule" that the larger animals of a type are most preferred. Only three capybara kills were recorded in the entire study. This low rate of hunting should have no significant impact on the capybara population.

The paca (*Agouti paca*) and agouti (*Dasyprocta* sp.) were the most frequently killed rodents. Agouti kill rates (fig. 5.9A) are instructive because they tend to be low in the years of highest overall hunting yields and rise when overall hunting yields are lower. Hence the relationship of *Dasyprocta* kill rates to overall yields is inverse. The same relationship is shown for squirrels (Sciuridae) in figure 5.9B.

Paca kill rates (fig. 5.9C) appear anomalous because they are at zero in the 1973–75 hunting sample but rise steadily in the 1979 through 1981–82 period. This is the type of growth in rodent kill rates we might expect to see if overall hunting yields were declining steadily, which they were not (fig. 5.3). My interpretation of this apparent anomaly is based on the rather specialized nature of paca hunting. The Siona-Secoya hunt them by paddling their canoes along stream banks in the twilight and evening hours, when pacas emerge from their resting places to drink and forage. They are relatively vulnerable and, when encountered, may be easily speared, shot, or chased down by dogs. From 1973 to 1975, paca were present at Shushufindi, but the hunting record indicates that almost no one was hunting them. At some point thereafter, overall yields must have been lower and the paca hunting began. People had enjoyed hunting paca on the Cuyabeno River, and now they had "rediscovered" this sport on the Aguarico and Shushufindi Rivers and their smaller tributaries. The popularity of this specialized activity continued into the 1980–82 period, even as kills of other rodents were declining.

The acouchi (*Myoprocta* sp.), a small rodent, was taken rarely. Only three kills were recorded in the hunting sample. This species was taken primarily by children or adolescents who set small traps in gardens.

None of the rodent populations at Shushufindi appear to have been significantly affected by native predation. Declining kills of agoutis and squirrels toward the end of the study reflect the fact that people were getting ample meat from more preferred species.

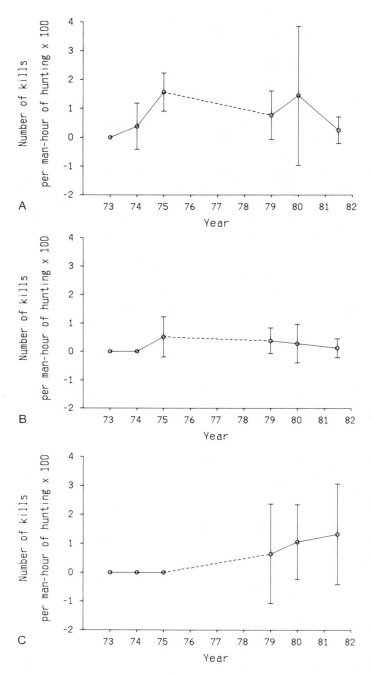

Figure 5.9. A, Agouti (*Dasyprocta* sp.) kill rates tend to be low in years with high overall yields (by weight) and higher in years with lower yields (cf. fig. 5.3). Similar inverse relationships to overall yields are observed in the kill patterns of several of the less preferred species (cf. figs. 5.9B, 5.10A, 5.10B, 5.11A). This suggests that hunters increase their kills of less preferred game when more preferred, and generally larger, game are not encountered. B, Squirrel (Sciuridae) kill rates also appear inverse to overall yields. C, Paca (*Agouti paca*) kill rates are at zero in the 1973–75 period and then rise steadily in the 1979–82 period. This unusual pattern is interpreted in terms of specialized hunting techniques and historical circumstances (see text).

Edentates

The principal edentates taken by the Siona-Secoya are the greater long-nosed armadillo (*Dasypus kappleri*) and the common long-nosed armadillo (*D. novemcinctus*). Anteaters and sloths are tabooed as food and never appeared in the hunting record. One sloth was captured and temporarily kept as a household pet.

In most cases, armadillo hunting involved locating burrows and digging them out. Hence, this nocturnal animal was usually taken in daylight hours. On several occasions, hunters expressed knowledge of burrow locations before they attempted kills and stated that they had waited until the meat was needed. Figure 5.10 presents kill rates for *Dasypus kappleri* and *D. novemcinctus* from

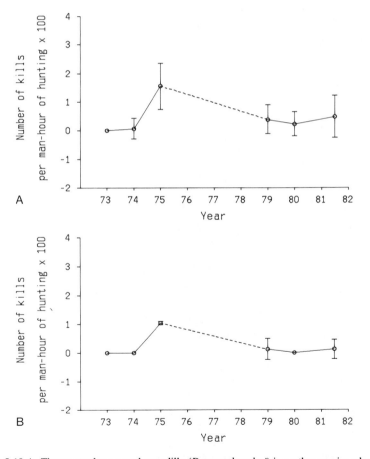

Figure 5.10 A, The greater long-nosed armadillo (*Dasypus kappleri*) is another species whose kill rates suggest an inverse relationship to overall yields, although the observed pattern is not a "perfect" one (e.g., kills in 1981–82 increase rather than decrease). B, The kill pattern for the common long-nosed armadillo (*Dasypus novemcinctus*) is very similar to that of the greater long-nosed armadillo.

1973 to 1981–82. As shown, the rates of hunting armadillos were generally low, but there are peaks for both species in 1975. This appears to be a response to the generally lower overall yields of that year (i.e., armadillos, like rodents, are a somewhat less-preferred game category that may be used as a reserve).

Reptiles

Reptiles present a complex picture in terms of distribution, habits, and the hunting techniques employed to take them. Both caimans (Crocodilidae) and river turtles (*Podocnemis expansa* and *P. unifilis*) are aquatic and may achieve local abundance in specific habitats and/or seasons within the Aguarico River Basin. Tortoises (*Geochelone denticulata*) are generally found individually, traversing the forest floor. The 1,150-km² area around Shushufindi does not have particularly favored habitats for caimans or river turtles, so they were taken infrequently (fig. 5.11). More favorable areas for hunting them include the distant oxbow lakes of the upper Cuyabeno River for caimans and, for turtles, the beaches of the Cuyabeno and lower Aguarico rivers during the turtle egg-laying season of November and December.

Caiman hunting around Shushufindi was a nocturnal activity in which hunters employed canoes and flashlights (torches were used originally). A person at the rear of the canoe paddles as silently as possible, while another at the prow searches for caimans and harpoons or shoots them. At times, caimans were taken in daylight hours, especially when they were sunning on river beaches. Such kills were used only for food (the Siona-Secoya in this study were not involved in the marketing of hides).

As figure 5.11A indicates, no caiman kills were recorded in the first 2 years at Shushufindi. In 1975 about one caiman was taken for every 100 man-hours of hunting, and the rates declined thereafter. Since caimans are not a highly preferred game type, the declining kill rates probably reflect a decline in hunting them. Hence, the caiman rates can be interpreted in the same way as the agouti, squirrel, and armadillo rates discussed earlier (i.e., as kills of preferred species increase, those of less preferred species tend to decrease).

Podocnemis unifilis appeared to be rare at Shushufindi and was infrequently captured there (fig. 5.11B). The larger *Podocnemis expansa* never appeared in the hunting sample but was reported as present on the lower Aguarico. Both of these species probably are depleted and threatened with future extinction in the Aguarico and its tributaries. This is most likely due to commercial exploitation by non-Indians rather than subsistence hunting by natives. Siona Indians residing on the Cuyabeno report that Colombian residents of the Putumayo River come to the area in large numbers during November and December to exploit turtles and their nests, which has sharply reduced the numbers of nests observed in recent seasons.

The common land tortoise (*Geochelone denticulata*) was taken at very low, but stable, rates (fig. 5.11C). Tortoises were captured by hand and carried back

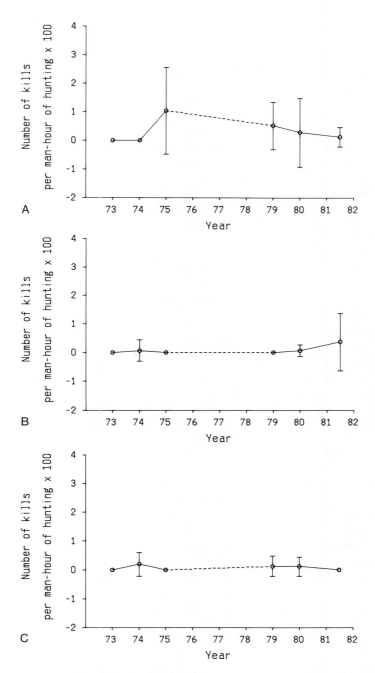

Figure 5.11. A, Caimans (Crocodilidae) are yet another prey type whose kill rate pattern suggests an inverse relationship to overall yields (by weight). B, The Shushufindi territory did not present favorable nesting beaches for the common river turtle (*Podocnemis unifilis*), so it was captured infrequently there. C, The common land tortoise (*Geochelone denticulata*) was also captured infrequently. This low rate of use probably reflects a low preference by hunters rather than tortoise densities.

to the household, where they were kept alive until needed for a meal. The harvest of tortoises appears sustainable under the observed conditions of human density and predation.

Birds

The Siona-Secoya classify many birds as edible, but only a few species are taken regularly. The most preferred species is the curassow (*Mitu salvini*), a large, turkeylike bird of the forest understory. As figure 5.12A shows, there is strong suggestion of depletion of the curassow population in the 1,150-km² territory around Shushufindi (as evidenced by the steady decline in kill rates from 1974 to 1981–82). This is the strongest evidence of depletion for any species hunted by the Siona-Secoya during the study.

The trumpeter (*Psophia crepitans*) is a large ground-dwelling bird that is also favored by native hunters. Its kill rates (fig. 5.12B) show a slight decline if one compares the 1973–75 period with the 1979–82 period, but this is a pattern that could be expected in the sustainable harvesting of a productive population that formerly was at carrying capacity. However, when observations are limited to the smaller 590-km² core area around the village of Shushufindi (fig. 5.2, area A) depletion is suggested (fig. 5.12C).

Figure 5.13 presents the kill rates for the blue-throated piping guan (*Pipile pipile*) and Spix's guan (*Penelope jacquacu*). Both show initial declines in their kill rates, after which the values appear more stable from year to year. This suggests that these populations were somewhat reduced but not depleted. Reproduction or immigration appears to have been adequate to maintain guan populations at intermediate levels, so their yields appear sustainable at the observed levels of human density and predation.

Other birds taken for food include parrots and macaws (Psittacidae), toucans (Ramphastidae), tinamous (*Tinamus* and *Crypturellus*), the speckled chachalaca (*Ortalis guttata*), quail (Phasianidae), doves and pigeons (Columbidae), an oropendola (Icteridae, *Gymnostinops* sp.), and two caciques (Icteridae, *Cacicus* spp.). All of these were taken very infrequently in the study area because their relatively small body sizes were not considered worth the cost of a shotgun shell. Graphs would show kill rates of zero for most species in most years, so it is unlikely that Siona-Secoya hunting has a significant impact on the populations of these birds. Such smaller birds may have been killed more frequently in the past, when the blowgun was the weapon of choice for taking avian species (cf. Yost and Kelley, 1983, for the many birds taken by the blowgun-hunting Waorani Indians of eastern Ecuador).

It should be noted that some small birds are occasionally hunted for their feathers, including tanagers (Emberizidae) and cotingas (Cotingidae). The previously mentioned macaws, parrots, toucans, and curassows also provide feathers for native crafts. At the time of this study, such animal products were primarily used for traditional domestic purposes, such as the making of fire fans

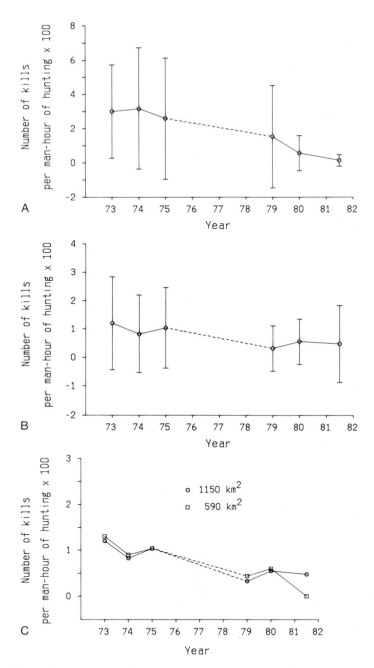

Figure 5.12. A, Curassow (*Mitu salvini*) kill rates decline steadily after 1974 and suggest depletion of this large bird's population in the 1,150-km² Shushufindi territory. B, Trumpeter (*Psophia
crepitans*) kill rates are about 50% lower in the 1979–82 period than in the 1973–75 period, but
such a pattern could be consistent with sustained yield harvesting of the population. C, When
observations are limited to the 590-km² core area, depletion of the trumpeter population is clearly
suggested.

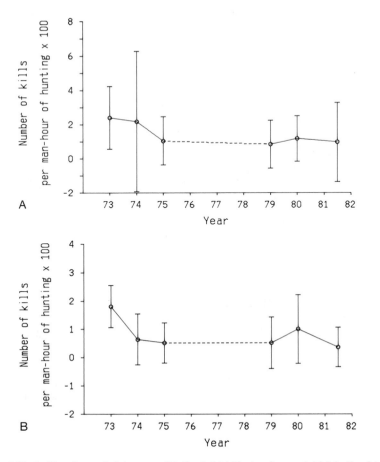

Figure 5.13. A, Blue-throated piping guan (*Pipile pipile*) kill rates show an initial decline followed by stable values in the 1979–82 period. Such a pattern suggests a sustainable harvest at the observed levels of human density and predation. B, The pattern for Spix's guan (*Penelope jacquacu*) is very similar to that of *Pipile pipile*.

from curassow feathers. There was no regular "artifact trade" among the Siona-Secoya involving feathers, but on a few rare occasions a woman or two were observed selling feathered necklaces to visitors. The women of Dureno, a Kofán village 50 km to the northwest, appeared to be substantially involved in such trade.

Discussion

From the perspective of conservation the depletion of even one animal species is of concern if that species' survival is everywhere threatened. However, to the native hunter the more immediate concern is the availability of game near his settlement. From the latter perspective, the Siona-Secoya along the Aguarico present a picture of a human population living well within the faunal resources offered by their environment. At the level of the 1,150-km^2 territory, clear-cut evidence for the depletion of animal species through native hunting is indicated only for the curassow (*Mitu salvini*). When observations are restricted to the smaller 590-km^2 core area around the Shushufindi village site (see also Vickers 1988), depletion is also indicated for the woolly monkey (*Lagothrix lagotricha*) and the trumpeter bird (*Psophia crepitans*). So, even within the more tightly defined local area, the observed kill rates for most of the game species hunted by the Siona-Secoya do not suggest depletion (including all of the ungulates, rodents, and edentates, all but one of the primates, and all but two of the birds).

This study also reveals the great selectivity of Siona-Secoya hunters (see Lee, 1979, for similar findings among the !Kung San, a foraging people of Namibia and Botswana). Indeed, most of the 100 or more species defined as "edible" by the Siona-Secoya were taken so rarely that they did not appear in the hunting record or appeared so infrequently that it is impossible to construct meaningful long-term graphs of their kill rates. Such selectivity in making kills is yet another indication that the Siona-Secoya in this study were not hard pressed in their search for meat.

In a preliminary paper (1980) based on the observations from 1973 through August 1979, I reported a decline in the kills of larger species (e.g., white-lipped and collared peccaries, woolly and howler monkeys, the curassow, and guans) and an increase in the kills of smaller animals (e.g., the agouti, squirrels, and toucans), and I took this as evidence of depletion of the preferred large game. Now that the hunting data extend over 10 years, it is evident that this interpretation was premature and overly simplistic. The notable rise in the white-lipped peccary kill rates in 1980 and 1981–82, along with the more modest rises in tapir and collared peccary rates in 1981–82, appear to have provided sufficient meat so that hunters reduced their kill rates for a number of smaller game. This suggests that Amazonian game availability results from a far more complex set of phenomena than is often assumed by anthropologists, who have tended to propose that game depletion around native settlements is a broad-based and linear process through time (cf. Vickers 1988).

Because of the debates among anthropologists about the dynamics of native adaptation, it is important to emphasize that the human densities reported here are about the same as the estimated mean for aboriginal inhabitants of the lowland forest habitat of Amazonia (i.e., around 0.2 persons per square kilometer [Denevan 1976]). Hence, I believe that this study can inform our understanding of traditional native adaptations in this portion of the Amazon Basin. The most obvious deviation from aboriginal conditions is the fact that the shotgun has replaced the blowgun and spear in most hunting. If anything, this would be expected to accelerate any tendencies toward depleting the preferred game spe-cies, since the shotgun is a more efficient weapon in hunting them (Hames 1979; Yost and Kelley 1983).

The Issue of Conservation

As mentioned earlier, such "native" or "near-native" conditions no longer prevail in many areas of Amazonia. Even the Shushufindi area has now been invaded by oil companies, agribusiness concerns, and non-Indian colonists, whose combined modifications of the environment pose a far greater threat to fauna than does the subsistence hunting of native people. For many natural scientists and conservationists, the issue is not so much one of debates about aboriginal adaptation as it is one of developing strategies and policies to save neotropical flora and fauna from extinction.

In this altered context native foraging is sometimes viewed as one of the threats to animal survival, especially when people engage in commercial hunt-ing (cf. Redford and Robinson 1985). One question is whether native people should be subjected to the same hunting rules and regulations as other citizens, including those that pertain to access to ecological reserves. I am concerned about the protection of Amazonia's natural environments and resources but also about the land, civil, and economic rights of indigenous people, who have le-gitimate claims to traditional territories. Native people are "acculturated" in varying degrees, but we cannot assume that this will negate their rights to re-sources within traditional homelands. Indeed, many native groups are becom-ing increasingly sophisticated and organized in pressing their claims through formal legal actions and other means. Yet if unrestricted hunting and other de-velopments lead to the extinction of fauna no one will benefit, least of all native people.

The International Union for Conservation of Nature and Natural Resources (IUCN) has studied the various terminologies and legal statuses of protected areas throughout the world (Eilers 1985). It proposes that all such protected areas be classified into ten basic types:

   I.   Scientific Reserves/Strict Nature Reserves
   II. National Parks/Provincial Parks
   III. Natural Monuments/Natural Landmarks
   IV. Nature Conservation Reserves/Managed Nature Reserves/
        Wildlife Sanctuaries
   V.   Protected Landscapes
   VI. Resource Reserves (Interim Conservation Unit)
   VII. Anthropological Reserves/Natural Biotic Areas
   VIII. Multiple Use Management Areas/Managed Resource Areas
   IX. Biosphere Reserves
   X.   World Heritage Sites (Natural)

Eilers, an anthropologist, has evaluated the rationales and criteria for these various categories in terms of their possible significance for native peoples (1985). He concludes:

None of these . . . (excepting, perhaps, Category I) really restricts native people's claims to ancestral rights.

In some cases indigenous groups would benefit from the fact they . . . inhabit protected areas (Categories IV, V, VIII, IX) by finding more . . . acceptance for their . . . cultural (and nature preserving) contribution to their country. Successful integration will depend on . . . the system of zoning. . . . In all systems with clearcut functional zones (Categories II, VIII, IX) is the chance to control integral native territories.

As conceived by UNESCO's "Man and the Biosphere" program, *biosphere reserves* will have a system of zones, including *natural* or *core* areas, *manipulative* or *buffer* areas, *reclamation* or *restoration* areas, and *stable cultural* areas. Biosphere reserves may incorporate existing protected areas within their boundaries, and the economic activities of traditional communities are to be included in the planning and management of these reserves. National parks, multiple use, and managed resource areas have similar zoning systems that may provide avenues for recognizing and protecting the rights of indigenous populations.

Of course, these modalities will not be employed to benefit native people unless politicians, scientists, administrators, and other decision makers accept the premise that the indigenous presence is necessary, appropriate, and just. In my view, the most effective strategies for conservation will be those that include native people rather than those that simply attempt to outlaw hunting or block native access to protected areas (many of which are superimposed on native settlements and hunting territories). Insofar as native people view such regulations as arbitrarily imposed and against their interests, they will violate them, and effective enforcement will be extremely difficult. The intelligent approach is to enlist native cooperation and provide ongoing incentives and support to nurture and maintain it. As national parks and ecological reserves are established, the residential rights of natives within those areas should be protected. Foraging rights for subsistence purposes should be protected but with limitations on the hunting of animals judged to be endangered. Strong incentives and enforcement will be needed to discourage commercial hunting, which is a grave threat in some areas. Strictures on the hunting of endangered species and commercial hunting will be successful only if native people understand and accept them. The greatest understanding and acceptance will occur when native individuals are incorporated into park management systems as rangers, assistants, or administrators.

This approach has already been implemented in several Ecuadorian situations. Both lowland Quichua and Kofán Indians are working to protect the Cayambe-Coca Ecological Reserve (some as paid rangers and some as unpaid, but very enthusiastic, volunteers). Likewise, Siona Indians are cooperating in the protection of the Cuyabeno Wildlife Reserve (Coello Hinojosa and Nations 1987). In these examples, the native people remain in traditional homelands that have been incorporated into reserves, which they now help to protect.

Although the defense of such areas is not airtight, field observations lead me to believe that resident natives do a better job of controlling violations than many city-born employees who are posted to remote locations. Native people are not only willing to defend reserves, they also have among them very bright people who are excellent "natural" ecologists and who respond to conservationist education and training, especially when they are treated with respect and their individual and communal interests are recognized and dealt with fairly. Such people may offer the best hope for effective conservation programs in many areas of Amazonia. They will not require large salaries, but they will require a clear legal status and reliable administrative support from the state.

My appeal to anyone working in the areas of indigenous rights or environmental conservation is the following. First, promote the establishment of parks, reserves, and land holdings of sufficient size to allow the survival of flora, fauna, *and* native people. Second, capitalize on the wisdom and expertise of native people by employing them as rangers and volunteers to defend such areas from unauthorized depredation and settlement. Third, enlist the cooperation of native people in the protection of endangered species. They will respond if the proper protection of their lands and their hunting rights for nonendangered species are guaranteed and supported.

All of this will require appropriate educational programs and competence and responsibility on the part of scientists and government officials. Experience convinces me that failures are much more likely to occur on the bureaucratic, or "civilized," side, rather than on the native, or "savage," side.

Acknowledgments

My research among the Siona-Secoya has been supported by the Henry L. and Grace Doherty Charitable Foundation, the National Institute of Mental Health, the Florida International University Foundation, Inc., Cultural Survival, Inc., and the Latin American and Caribbean Center and College of Arts and Sciences of Florida International University. Affiliations with Ecuadorian institutions were provided by the *Instituto Nacional de Antropología e Historia* and the *Instituto Nacional de Colonización de la Región Amazónica Ecuatoriana*. Analysis of the data during a sabbatical was supported by the School of American Research, Santa Fe, New Mexico, and a Resident Scholar Fellowship from the National Endowment for the Humanities. I thank all of the Siona and Secoya people who cooperated in making this fieldwork possible, especially E. Piaguaje and J. Lucitande, who were research assistants. I thank J. Yost for logistical support during certain periods of the research and L. Hay-Smith, P. Tanimoto, and A. Iriarte for comments on the manuscript. C. Canaday assisted in the identification of birds.

6

On the Track of the Road: Changes in Subsistence Hunting in a Brazilian Amazonian Village

J. Marcio Ayres, Deborah de Magalhães Lima, Eduardo de Souza Martins, and José Luis K. Barreiros

The use of wild animals as a food source among indigenous peoples varies with biological factors such as the presence and density of different species and cultural factors such as the method of hunting (Redford and Robinson 1987). Changes in characteristics of game populations or in local traditions can affect the use of wild animals, but usually these changes occur over such a long time period that they are difficult to detect. The Brazilian Amazon, however, offers a unique opportunity to investigate the factors affecting wildlife use, because changes are occurring very rapidly.

This paper deals with changes in game yields and diet in a small village in the southern part of the Brazilian Amazon before and after the arrival of the first road to connect the community to the rest of the country.

Study Area and Methods

Aripuanã, with an area of 98,631 km², is the largest county of Mato Grosso State, but until 1980, with 0.14 inhabitant per square kilometer, it had the smallest human population density in that state (FIBGE 1983). The country is located in the northwestern part of Mato Grosso State and thus contains elements of Amazonian fauna (fig. 6.1). The vegetation varies from tall primary forests in the north to open savannas (cerrados) in the south.

The village of Dardanelos (Aripuanã in the official charts), the county capital, is located at 10°10'S and 59°27'W (fig. 6.1), 203 m above sea level, on the right bank of Rio Aripuanã, a tributary of Rio Madeira, just above the two largest falls. The village is located about 800 km north of Cuiabá, the capital of Mato Grosso State and over 900 km south of the city of Manaus in the state of Amazonas.

The predominant vegetation in the area is primary upland forests (*matas de terra firme*) and narrow stretches of partially flooded forests (*igapó*) along the principal rivers (for a better description of the vegetation, see Ayres 1981). The

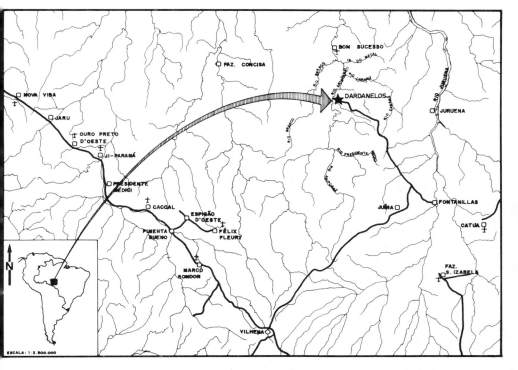

Figure 6.1. Map of the study area showing the town of Dardanelos and the connecting road to Vilhena, a village on the Cuiaba–Porto Velho road.

vegetation is therefore not typical of central Amazonia, but the fauna is Amazonian. The climate is tropical monsoon, Amg according to the classification of Koppen, with a dry summer and a rainy winter season. Annual average rainfall is around 2,100 mm and average temperature $25.5 \pm 1.5°C$.

Early Brazilian settlements in the area of Dardanelos, dating from late last century, were established by rubber collectors coming from the north and northeast of Brazil and later by gold and diamond prospectors. There were approximately eighty inhabitants in 1970. The population increased after 1973, when a colonization project, the Nucleus of Humboldt, was established in the area by the Government of Mato Grosso and the Instituto Nacional de Pesquisas de Amazônia (INPA) (Arnaud and Cortez 1976). Because of this project and the construction of the road (MT-170) money circulation in the village increased. In May 1978, when the first part of this research was carried out, there were 638 inhabitants in Dardanelos (Ayres and Ayres 1979).

Until 1978, Dardanelos was basically an isolated village. Access by river was difficult; falls and rapids downstream make navigation possible only for small canoes. The main access to the village before building of the road was by airplane. Food and other imported goods were more expensive than in most other areas of the country. Agriculture was restricted to small plantations of manioc, maize, rice, and beans. The population relied on the extraction of natural resources such as rubber, oil (*Copaifera* sp.), Brazil nuts, fish, and wild game. Unlike most other Amazonian towns, fishing in Dardanelos is not important because the numerous falls along Rio Aripuanã prevents the upstream migration of the larger characids (see Goulding 1980). Until July 1978, the total area which had been cleared of forest did not exceed 300 to 400 ha.

In the second half of 1978, the completion of road MT-170 linked Dardanelos to BR-364 (the Cuiabá–Porto Velho road) and thus to the rest of the country. The road brought settlers, speculators, colonization enterprises, cattle ranching, and agricultural projects to the region. Most immigrants were from the southern and central parts of Brazil. Land increased in value, and land disputes were common. The community rapidly changed from a noncapitalist to a precapitalist stage, using the categories defined by Forewaker (1981), and the economy of the area became incorporated into that of the rest of Brazil.

We collected data on the use of wildlife and the population of hunters during two periods and interviewed the entire population of the village on both occasions. The first survey was in May 1978, just before the arrival of the road. Results of this survey were published in Ayres and Ayres (1979). The second was conducted in May 1980, 1½ years after the arrival of the road. On both occasions we collected general informaticn about the interviewee and his or her family, recorded the identity of all game captured during the first 4 months of the year, and noted what the family had eaten at their last two meals. The questionnaire was given to all households in Dardanelos. We checked information through interviews at school. In addition, JMA accompanied hunters at the beginning of the study. The trips totaled 110 km along twelve hunting trails. All interviews were done in May so that results would not be affected by seasonal changes in food availability and hunting methods (for a description of hunting methods see Ayres and Ayres 1979).

Sources for body weights of animals are described in Ayres and Ayres (1979), and the same data were used for comparison purposes in 1980. Because larger game are easier to remember, the method of data collection biases the list toward large-bodied animals such as the tapir (*Tapirus terrestris*), the white-lipped peccary (*Tayassu pecari*), or the deer (*Mazama* sp.). In addition, the harvest of protected species such as the giant otter, the jaguar, and some small cats, which are taken illegally for the skin trade, would not be detected using interviews.

The statistical methods employed are described in more detail by Sokal and Rohlf (1969) using computer programs developed by Ayres and Ayres (1987).

Results

Changes in the Human Population

From May 1978, the time of the first survey, until May 1980, the time of the second, the human population of Dardanelos increased by 54.5% (from 638 to

986 inhabitants) (table 6.1) There was no significant difference in the relative growth of different sex or age classes in the population.

Ability to hunt is probably related to the cultural background of the hunters. Amazonian people are probably more familiar with the environment and its fauna than people born in other areas of Brazil. Accordingly, we recorded the birth place of each inhabitant in order to document changes in the composition of the population (table 6.2). In 1978 almost 35% of the inhabitants of Darda-

TABLE 6.1
**Distribution of the Population in Dardanelos in
1978 and 1980, by Sex and Age Classes**

| | Total Population | | | | Hunters | |
| | 1978 | | 1980 | | 1978 | 1980 |
Age Class	M	F	M	F	M	M
0–9	110	144	188	202	0	0
10–19	71	53	120	94	3	0
20–29	51	48	55	72	19	2
30–39	39	36	66	61	15	11
40–49	31	12	47	27	6	8
50–59	17	12	19	11	4	1
60–69	6	8	12	8	0	1
> 70	0	0	3	1	0	0
Total	325	313	510	476	47	23

TABLE 6.2
Origin of Population and Hunters of Dardanelos in May 1978 and 1980

| | 1978 | | 1980 | |
Birth Place	Total Number	Hunters (N)	Total Number	Hunters (N)
Mato Grosso State				
Dardanelos	123	—	31	—
Aripuana (County)	96	12	221	2
Other	99	1	230	4
Subtotal	318	13	482	6
Other areas of Brazil				
North	231	23	284	10
Northeast	44	5	71	2
East	13	1	48	2
South	16	1	79	1
Other	16	1	22	—
Subtotal	320	31	504	15
Total	638	44	986	21

Note: Division of Brazil according to great regions follows FIBGE (1980).

nelos were born in Aripuanã county. In 1980 this proportion had fallen to nearly 25%. People coming from eastern Brazil represented 2% of the 1978 population. By 1980 this percentage had doubled. An even greater increase was detected in those inhabitants coming from southern Brazil, representing 2.5% in 1978 and 8% in 1980.

When data were grouped by Brazilian regions there was an increase in people coming from the southern and, to a lesser extent, the eastern part of the country [DM(b)($=$ 0.158; $p >$ 0.01]. If data are grouped into the totals for Mato Grosso State and other regions of Brazil, no differences in these proportions are detected ($\chi^2 =$ 0.143; Correction of Yates $=$ 0.107; $p >$ 0.05). This indicates that despite the differences found in the origin of the population according to regions within Brazil, those from the north still account for most of the population in Dardanelos.

Changes in the Origin and Number of Hunters

Despite the increase in total population, the total number of hunters decreased by half, from forty-four individuals in 1978 to twenty-one in 1980 (table 6.2). In 1978 almost 80% of the hunters came either from the northern region or from the Aripuanã region. Two years later only 66.7% came from these regions. These differences are not statistically significant whether these data are grouped by Brazilian regions [Kolmogorov-Smirnov test; DM(b) $=$ 0.103; $p >$ 0.05] or within the state of Mato Grosso [DM(b) $=$ 0.59; $p <$ 0.05].

Most hunters during both surveys were at least 20 years old, but the modal class in both samples was 30 to 39 years old (table 6.1). A Kolmogorov-Smirnov test indicates that there was a significant change in the proportions of age classes [DM(b) $=$ 0.35; $p =$ 0.05] with displacement to the older classes in 1980. The most striking change was in the class of 20- to 29-year-old hunters, which decreased from nineteen to two individuals, probably because of changes in activities within the village and/or migration with less input of new hunters from the lower age classes.

In 1978, of the sixty people who were employed and had to work on average forty hours weekly in their jobs (32.4% of the town's population), only five were hunters. Of the fifty-six non-wage earners (21.4%), such as those in small businesses, subsistence, and mining, twelve were hunters. The bulk of the hunters, however, was from the seventy temporary workers (37.8%) (freelance laborers) in the village, of which twenty-seven hunted. In 1980, while there was a decrease on the proportions of temporary (to 18.4%) and permanent (to 13.8%) workers and an increase in the proportions of non-wage earners (to 58.6%), there was little change in the distribution of hunters among employment classes.

A very striking feature of hunting in Dardanelos is that very few hunters accounted for most of the game killed in both periods. In 1978 only four hunters together captured more than 47% of the total weight of game for the village. In 1980 it was even more striking. Only two individuals killed over 58% of the total game taken (table 6.3). These hunters live almost entirely from selling game in the village.

TABLE 6.3
**Performance of Hunters According to Weight of Game Taken
per Hunter in Aripuanã in 1978 and 1980**

Weight of Game (kg)	Number of Hunters		Percent Contribution	
	1978	1980	1978	1980
0–99	27	13	12.26	7.71
100–299	9	4	19.82	16.56
300–499	4	2	20.17	17.58
500–999	2	1	16.07	14.73
1,000–2,000	2	1	31.32	43.85
Total	44	21	100.0	100.0

Note: The table represents the total amount hunted in the first 4 months of each year (1978 and 1980).

Game Captured

In the first 4 months of 1978, the total amount of game killed by hunters in the forests surrounding Dardanelos was about 8,850 kg. During this period, 338 white-lipped peccaries (*Tayassu pecari*) represented nearly 70% of the total weight of game killed. Other important species included the tapir (*Tapirus terrestris*), the collared peccary (*Tayassu tajacu*), and the brocket deer (*Mazama* sp.). During this period the most hunted primate species was the woolly monkey (*Lagothrix lagothricha*). The thirty-five individuals killed represented only 2.5% of the total game weight captured. A total of fifteen species of mammals, nine species of birds, and two reptiles were recorded.

In 1980 the total amount of game harvested was 30.7% of the game taken during the same time period in 1978. White-lipped peccaries, were again the most consumed species, and represented a similar percentage of total game weight harvested in that year, but the total number of captures was down to 44.3% of the 1978 harvest. The total number of tapirs killed was very similar to the number killed in 1978, and their importance as the percentage of total game harvested in that year doubled. No monkeys appeared in the 1980 list, and the total number of species used as a food source was reduced to six mammal and two bird species. The number of kills increased for only two mammal groups: the agouti (*Dasyprocta* sp.), from seven to twelve individuals, and the paca (*Agouti paca*), from two to four (table 6.4).

TABLE 6.4
**Game Killed in Dardanelos (R. Aripuana) from January to April 1978
and January to April 1980**

	Body Weight (kg)	1978		1980	
Species		Number of Individuals	% Weight	Number of Individuals	% Weight
Mammals					
Tayassu pecari	18.0	338	68.69	148	72.79
Tapirus terrestris	110.0	9	11.18	8	23.90
Tayassu tajacu	12.0	70	9.47	1	0.32
Mazama sp.	23.5	12	3.12	2	1.28
Lagothrix lagothricha	6.3	35	2.48	—	—
Dasypus kappleri	9.5	7	0.75	—	—
Felis concolor	23.0	1	0.26	—	—
Chiropotes albinasus	2.8	8	0.25	—	—
Dasypus novemcinctus	2.5	7	0.20	—	—
Dasyprocta sp.	2.5	7	0.20	12	0.80
Agouti paca	6.7	2	0.15	4	0.73
Nasua nasua	3.0	1	—	—	—
Cebus albifrons	2.7	1	—	—	—
Callicebus moloch	0.7	1	—	—	—
Callithrix argentata	0.4	1	—	—	—
Reptiles					
Platemys platicephala	0.5	1	—	—	—
Podocnemis unifilis	4.0	2	—	—	—
Birds					
Mitu mitu	3.2	40	1.45	—	—
Penelope sp.	2.0	33	0.75	3	0.16
Cairina moschata	3.5	8	0.32	—	—
Ara macao and A.ararauna	1.0	14	0.16	1	0.02
Pipile cujubi	3.2	6	0.22	—	—
Psophia viridis	2.0	4	0.09	—	—
Phalacrocorax olivaceus	1.8	4	0.08	—	—
Amazona sp.	0.5	1	—	—	—
Butorides striatus	0.2	1	—	—	—
Total		582		179	

Note: See Ayres and Ayres (1979) for body weight sources.

Diet and Domestic Animals

To examine the relative contribution of game in the diet of people in Dardanelos, during household interviews we asked what had been eaten in the two
previous meals. These data measure the number of times different types of meat
were mentioned (table 6.5). The comparison between consumption of animal
protein between 1978 and 1980 reveals a change in diet composition that is
probably related to changes in subsistence strategies. As expected from the data
on kills, the contribution of game to the diet of the human population in Dardanelos decreased considerably. The main source of meat in 1978 was canned
or dried meat (34% of meals) followed by game (20%). The frequency of these

TABLE 6.5
Number of Times Meat of Different Types Was Reported as Eaten during Two Meal Samples in One Day of May 1978 and 1980 (Two Meals per Individual)

Type of Meat	1978		1980	
	Frequency	%	Frequency	%
Domestic or Processed				
Dried beef	392	30.69	165	8.37
Canned meat	38	3.01	142	7.20
Pork	—	—	48	2.42
Beef (fresh)	144	11.32	619	31.39
Chicken	42	3.29	123	6.24
Subtotal	616	48.31	1,097	55.62
Wild meat				
White-lipped pecary	173	13.52	36	1.83
Collared pecary	18	1.41	—	—
Tapir	26	2.04	8	0.40
Deer	24	1.88	—	—
Armadillo	5	0.39	—	—
Agouti	—	—	3	0.15
Curassow	—	—	12	0.61
Subtotal	246	19.24	59	2.99
Fish	162	12.70	154	7.81
No information	—	—	21	1.07
Meals without meat	252	19.75	641	32.51
Totals	1,276	100.0	1,972	100.0

two top meat types declined in 1980. Canned or dried meat was consumed 2.2 times less frequently and game a remarkable 6.4 times less frequently. Fresh beef increased in consumption 2.8 times, appearing in 31% of meals, and was the most common type of meat. Even though its consumption declined, canned or dried meat was the second most consumed meat (16% of meals) in 1980 (fig. 6.2). The number of meals without any type of meat increased by 50% (fig. 6.3).

An inventory of backyard domestic animals used for food in 1978 and 1980 showed an increase from 691 to 1,466 animals (chicken, ducks, pigs, turkeys, and sheep). This increase in the number of domestic animals was proportionally greater than the growth of the human population (χ^2 with Yates correction = 22.0; $p < 0.01$). Chickens represented the highest percentage, with over 85% of the total number of backyard animals in both years. The only difference in 1980 was that turkeys were replaced by sheep.

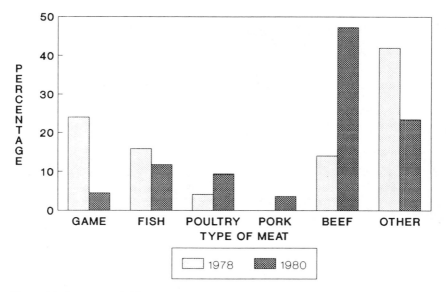

Figure 6.2. Proportion of different sources of animal protein in the diet in 1978 and 1980, based on meals that included meat.

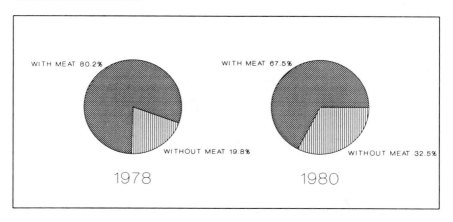

Figure 6.3. Percentage of meals with and without meat in 1978 and 1980.

Discussion and Conclusions

This study detected a significant decrease in game yields in a small village in southern Amazonia. There are several hypotheses to explain this decline. We discuss the following: (1) reduction in densities of wildlife because of habitat disturbance by deforestation or human hunting pressure; (2) change in human population structure leading to emigration of more active and experienced hunters and migration of inexperienced settlers from other areas of Brazil; and (3) cultural and economic changes affecting food preferences or subsistence activities.

Little can be said about the first hypothesis, as this study did not systematically measure wildlife densities. Among the data that do exist on mammal densities in the neotropics, it is clear that in different areas certain species such as peccaries, agoutis, deer and monkeys occur at different densities (Eisenberg 1979; Emmons 1987). These differences are probably related to soil quality and hydrological regime, vegetation structure, presence of potential competitors, and human hunting pressure (Emmons 1984).

An indirect mode of estimating wildlife depletion is by habitat alternation. Analysis of Landsat imagery from a quadrant of 18.150 km^2 around Dardanelos in 1978 shows that deforestation covered an area of 16.8 km^2 immediately around the village. By 1980, over three times as much forest had been cleared around the village and along the road. The photographs used for these estimates have a maximal resolution of 30 m for each point, and small crops and clearings could not be included (Brazilian Institute for Forest Development [IBDF] 1980, 1982). Two considerations indicate that this clearing did not by itself reduce game yields. First, most medium- to large-scale clearing took place on the right bank of Rio Aripuanã around the village, while the left bank of Rio Aripuanã was the most frequently hunted area. Second, during both sample years, JMA carried out a study on the socioecology of primates on the left bank of Rio Aripuanã, where there was no deforestation. Significant changes in the primate populations were not detected (see Ayres 1981).

The reduction in game yields could also have been a consequence of hunting pressure. The data show, however, that the number of hunters in the population decreased (table 6.2). The presence of game in meals also decreased significantly, whereas the presence of fresh beef and other domestic meat became more frequent (table 6.5). In 1978 a wider range of game was taken, including a number of small-bodied prey species. In 1980 fewer species were taken overall, and large-bodied species comprised a higher proportion (table 6.4). The comparison of these data indicates that hunting had become a commercial activity in 1980. The concentration of the game takes by a small number of hunters support this (table 6.3).

The second hypothesis is related to the population changes brought by the road. People born in the Aripuanã region, especially those between 16 and 30 years of age, emigrated to other areas, particularly to the newly discovered gold mines around Rio Branco (a tributary of Aripuanã). This loss of potential hunters could have been an important factor causing the decrease of game yield in Dardanelos. The road brought a number of gold prospectors from other areas of southern Amazonia who took with them a number of villagers as laborers. As most of the game was taken by only a few individuals, the emigration of one key hunter could have played an important part in the observed reduction.

The road also increased immigration, attracting families from other regions of Brazil. The population increase between 1978 and 1980 mostly resulted from immigrants coming from the southern and eastern parts of the country. As hunting involves knowledge of the local forest and its fauna, not readily obtainable by the newcomers, the decrease in game yields may have been caused by poor hunting success.

The third, and perhaps most important, hypothesis that might explain the change in game yields in Dardanelos involves cultural and economic changes. Political decisions may lead to important economic implications that affect subsistence patterns. Before the arrival of the road, the local mayor donated a number of plots of land to the villagers as a possible strategy against concentration of land by large entrepreneurs. To secure their property, many of these small land holders invested more time taking care of their plots and plantations. Before the road there was apparently no great concern about land property, and land had mainly a subsistence use. When the road arrived, the local people quickly learned that land value was associated with crops and that its possession could only be secured by continuous use. Because of this, local people devoted more time to their lands and probably less to hunting.

Due to the large number of falls and rapids, fishing has never been important in Dardanelos, and red meat was the preferred source of animal protein in both surveys. With the road, fresh beef became more available and the population increased its consumption of it. Because hunting is essentially an unreliable means of obtaining meat, it is likely that given the opportunity to purchase fresh beef, the population preferred to do so.

The arrival of the road and the consequent integration of the village into the national economy brought considerable sociocultural change, including changes in diet composition. Our data suggest that cultural and economic factors played a more important role in changing game yields than actual reduction of animal densities. This, however, does not mean that wildlife was unaffected by human-caused environmental disturbance. Despite the fact that hunting became less important for human subsistence, the integration of Dardanelos into the national market economy by the road brought other threats to the regional wildlife, including logging, cattle ranching, mining, and large-scale agriculture.

Acknowledgments

This research was supported by the National Institute for Amazonian Research (INPA/MCT). We thank Mr. Antonio Martins from Museu Goeldi (CNPq) for figure 6.1.

7

Hunting and Its Effect on Wild Primate Populations in Suriname

RUSSELL A. MITTERMEIER

At present, there are some 233 living species of nonhuman primates, of which 80 occur in the neotropical region. The International Union for Conservation of Nature and Natural Resources (IUCN) already considers approximately half of these to be under some threat, and fully 45 species worldwide are listed as endangered, 10 of them from the neotropical region (IUCN 1988). Eight species occur in the small South American country of Suriname, the second of the three Guianas in size and population (163,265 km²; 377,000 inhabitants; fig. 7.1) and a former Dutch colony that became independent in 1975. The species

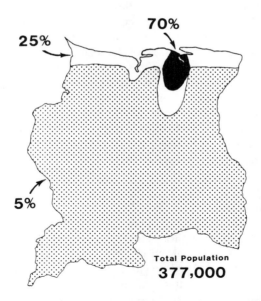

Figure 7.1. Distribution of Suriname's human population. Note that the vast interior is largely uninhabited. (Drawing by S. D. Nash).

occurring in Suriname are the golden-handed tamarin (*Saguinus midas midas*), the Guianan squirrel monkey (*Saimiri sciureus sciureus*), the Guianan or white-faced saki (*Pithecia pithecia pithecia*), the northern bearded saki (*Chiropotes satanas chiropotes*), the tufted capuchin (*Cebus apella apella*), the weeper capuchin (*Cebus nigrivittatus*), the red howler monkey (*Aloujatta seniculus seniculus*), and the black spider monkey (*Ateles paniscus paniscus*) (Mittermeier and van Roosmalen 1981; Baal et al. 1988).

The main threats to primate populations can be divided into three major categories: habitat destruction in its many forms, hunting of primates for food and other purposes, and live capture for export to foreign markets or a local pet trade. The effects of these forms of exploitation differ considerably from area to area and from species to species, depending on the extent of forest habitat available, the degree and kind of human activity in the area in question, the proximity of commercial animal dealers that serve local or foreign markets, and the size and desirability of different species as food items (Mittermeier 1977; Mittermeier 1987; Mittermeier and Coimbra-Filho 1977; Mittermeier and Cheney 1986; Mittermeier et al. 1986).

Habitat destruction is by far the most significant threat to the survival of nonhuman primate populations in most parts of the world, but in a few countries like Suriname it is still only a minor factor. Habitat destruction and alteration has taken place in the coastal region of the country for a long time (fig. 7.2), but the primate species occurring there are very adaptable, have had little difficulty coping with the changes that have taken place, and are still abundant in many areas. The vast interior of the country, covering about 80% of the land area, is still largely undisturbed, with only a few scattered Amerindian and Bushnegro communities along some of the major rivers. Slash and burn agriculture is common in the vicinity of these communities, but human populations are still so low that fallow periods are long. Indeed, some of the smaller primate species (e.g., *Saguinus m. midas*) may actually benefit from the mosaic of different forest types and edges that are created by this form of agriculture. Timber extraction and geological exploration destroyed small areas of habitat in the interior, especially in the 1960s and 1970s, and some clear-cutting of forest for charcoal production took place in the northern part of the interior and the southern part of the coastal region as well in the 1970s. However, during the 1980s, these activities largely ceased in the interior, and the forest has now reclaimed most of the cleared land.

The most damaging habitat destruction thus far carried out in Suriname was the damming of the Suriname River for the production of hydroelectric power. This project, which was completed in 1964, resulted in the flooding of 2,250 km² of rainforest in the northeastern part of Suriname (Walsh and Gannon 1967) and the destruction of large tracts of primate habitat. A similar project was initiated in the Kabalebo River area in western Suriname in the 1970s, but was stopped because of lack of funds.

Figure 7.2. The major zones of Suriname. (Drawing by S. D. Nash).

Live capture of primates for export has never been of much importance in Suriname. Individuals were occasionally shipped out by several dealers primarily interested in bird and reptile export, but the primate trade never approached the proportions that it reached in neighboring Guyana or in the major exporting centers in Peru and Colombia before the institution of import bans in the 1970s.

Live capture to serve a local pet market also has little effect. During 15 months in Suriname, only eighty-four primates were seen being kept as pets. The majority of these (45.2%) were *Cebus apella,* but all seven other species were represented in small numbers as well (table 7.1) Capture of infants as pets is usually a by-product of meat hunting. If a hunter happens to see a female with an infant, he often shoots at her in preference to other group members. Frequently the infant is also killed by the fall or by stray shot, but if it survives the hunter has both a source of meat and a pet that he can sell in town or keep for himself. In any case, the local pet trade has little effect even when one takes into account the losses during capture and from inadequate care in captivity.

TABLE 7.1
Primates Being Kept as Pets in Areas Investigated in Suriname and
French Guiana (April–June 1975; January 1976–March 1977)

Species	N	%
Saguinus midas	9	(10.7)
Saimiri sciureus	8	(9.5)
Pithecia pithecia	4	(4.8)
Chiropotes satanas	3	(3.6)
Cebus apella	38	(45.2)
Alouatta seniculus	4	(4.8)
Ateles paniscus	15	(17.9)
Total	84	

By far the most important factor contributing to the disappearance of primate populations in Suriname is hunting, mainly as a source of food for populations living in the interior. Elsewhere (1987), I have reviewed the effects of hunting on primate populations worldwide. In this paper, I focus on the effects of primate hunting in Suriname, its impact on the different primate species occurring there, and its significance for the future of primate populations in that country.

Information on the ecology and behavior of Suriname monkeys will not be reviewed here but can be found in Mittermeier (1981, 1982, 1983), Mittermeier and van Roosmalen (1980), Mittermeier et al. (1983), Buchanan, Mittermeier, and van Roosmalen (1981), van Roosmalen, Mittermeier, and Milton (1981), Fleagle, Mittermeier, and Skopek (1981), and van Roosmalen (1985). Suriname's nature protection systems and conservation laws are covered in Schulz, Mittermeier, and Reichart (1977) and Baal, Mittermeier, and van Roosmalen (1988).

Importance of Primates in the Diet of Surinamese People

The importance of hunting primates differs from area to area, depending on local hunting traditions, tastes, and taboos and the availability of other protein sources. Furthermore, several species are infrequently hunted, whereas others may be subject to intense local hunting pressure. The larger species, *Ateles, Alouatta, Chiropotes,* and the two *Cebus,* are usually hunted, and *Pithecia,* though a smaller animal, is also popular. All these species are hunted by some, if not all, of the hunters in any given village. On the other hand, the two smallest species, *Saguinus* and *Saimiri,* are little persecuted, in part because of local taboos and in part because these small animals barely recompense the hunter for the cost of his shotgun shell.

Several kinds of data were gathered to determine the importance of primates in the diet of the human inhabitants of Suriname during a study conducted from March 1975 to February 1977 (Mittermeier 1977). First, forty-two interviews were conducted with Javanese farmers, Bushnegroes from four different tribes, and Amerindians from five indigenous groups. Second, data were gathered on the number of animals brought into field camps or villages over certain time periods. These data are based on freshly killed animals brought in by hunters and were recorded by myself or other dependable observers in the camp or village during the period in question (table 7.2). Finally, kitchen middens were examined in several Bushnegro and Amerindian camps and villages and their contents recorded (table 7.3). Midden skull counts gave a reasonably accurate measure of the larger animals eaten in the past few years but were biased against smaller mammals and birds, the remains of which were rapidly destroyed in the middens.

TABLE 7.2
Average Body Mass and Number of Mammal, Bird, and Reptile Specimens Taken by Four Hunting Groups in Suriname

Species	Average Body Mass (kg)	Suralco Field Crew[a]	Tirio Indian[b]	Carib Indian[c]	Bushnegro, Amerindian, Hindustani[d]
Mammals					
Primates					
Pithecia pithecia	1.9	2	4	1	—
Chiropotes satanas	3.0	3	8	—	7
Cebus apella	3.7	7	50	3	—
Cebus nigrivittatus	3.5	1	8	—	—
Alouatta seniculus	7.0	1	56	2	5
Ateles paniscus	7.8	8	11	2	—
Saguinus midas	0.5	—	5	—	—
Saimiri sciureus	0.7	—	1	1	—
Total primates		22	143	9	12
Nonprimates					
Dasyprocta sp.	4.2	4	26	1	3
Agouti paca	8.3	2	15	—	1
Dasypus novemcinctus	9.7	4	10	—	—
Mazama spp.	15.0	1	7	5	—
Tayassu spp.	21.4	4	19	17	23
Nasua nasua	3.4	—	3	—	—
Tapirus terrestris	171.9	—	4	3	—
Myoprocta exilis	1.5	—	2	—	—
Bradypus tridactylus	3.8	—	9	—	—
Tamandua tetradactyla	8.0	—	1	—	1
Hydrochaeris hydrochaeris	15.0	—	—	3	—
Coendu prehensilis	3.6	—	—	1	—
Felis yagouaroundi	7.5	—	—	1	—
Potos flavus	3.0	—	—	1	—
Total nonprimates		15	96	32	28
Total mammals		37	239	41	40

(*continued*)

TABLE 7.2 *continued*

Species	Average Body Mass (kg)	Suralco Field Crew[a]	Tirio Indian[b]	Carib Indian[c]	Bushnegro, Amerindian, Hindustani[d]
Birds					
Crax alector	3.5	33	23	—	47
Penelope marail	1.1	13	43	—	6
Tinamus sp.	1.5	1	—	—	5
Ara spp.	1.6	2	7	—	1
Odontophorus gujanensis	0.5	—	9	—	—
Psophia crepitans	1.5	—	58	—	—
Ramphastos spp.	0.6	—	12	—	—
Total birds		49	152	—	59
Reptiles					
Geochelone spp.	4.4	18	33	—	17
Phrynops sp.	3.0	—	2	—	—
Iguana iguana	5.0	—	—	1	—
Tupinambis nigropunctatus	3.0	—	—	1	—
Total Reptiles		18	35	2	17
Total		104	426	43	116

[a]Number of animals of each species brought into the geological field camp between February and April 1976.

[b]Number of animals of each species brought into the village of Alalapadoe in March 1972 (from Lenselink 1972).

[c]Number of animals captured and brought into the village of Bigi Poika between February and May 1975 (from Van der Staalj 1975).

[d]Number of animals found during brief visits to six camps and villages in the interior from September 1976 to February 1977 (data from my own records and from M. G. M. van Roosmalen, N. Duplaix, L. Haarman, and A. Hassel).

TABLE 7.3
**Average Body Mass and Number of Mammal, Bird, and Reptile Specimens
Taken in the Entire Sipaliwini-Pouso Tirio Area in Suriname**

Species	Average Body Mass (kg)	Tirio Indian[a]	Sipaliwini-Pouso Tirio[b]	Bushnegro, Amerindian Hindustani[c]
Mammals				
Primates				
Pithecia pithecia	1.9	—	—	2
Chiropotes satanas	3.0	1	10	6
Cebus spp.	3.6	3	9	5
Alouatta seniculus	7.0	21	35	9
Ateles paniscus	7.8	4	20	20
Total primates		29	74	42

(continued)

TABLE 7.3 *continued*

Species	Average Body Mass (kg)	Tirio Indian[a]	Sipaliwini-Pouso Tirio[b]	Bushnegro, Amerindian Hindustani[c]
Nonprimates				
Dasyprocta sp.	4.2	1	3	5
Agouti paca	8.3	1	—	1
Dasypus novemcinctus	9.7	—	1	1
Mazama spp.	15.0	4	1	2
Tayassu spp.	21.4	230	18	110
Nasua nasua	3.4	—	—	1
Tapirus terrestris	171.9	8	—	3
Hydrochaeris hydrochaeris	15.0	1	—	—
Cerdocyon thous	6.0	—	1	1
Panthera onca	29.5	—	—	1
Priodontes giganteus	40.0	—	—	1
Odocoileus virginianus	28.3	1	—	—
Total nonprimates		246	24	126
Total mammals		275	98	168
Birds				
Crax alector	3.5	1	—	4
Penelope marail	1.1	1	4	3
Ara spp.	1.6	3	3	3
Total birds		5	7	10
Reptiles				
Geochelone spp.	4.4	227	67	171
Phrynops spp.	3.0	—	1	—
Caiman crocodilus	7.9	4	1	2
Podocnemis unifilis	5.6	5	—	—
Total reptiles		236	69	173
Total		516	174	351

[a]Number of animals found in kitchen middens in the village of Pouso Tirio.

[b]Number of animals eaten by Tirio Indians at two hunting camps along the Sipaliwini-Pouso Tirio trail near the Suriname-Brazil border.

[c]Number of remains found in kitchen middens surrounding the Sipaliwini airstrip.

Interview Results

The interviews indicated that most rural Surinamers do eat monkeys. Of forty-two people interviewed, thirty-four (81%) said that they ate one or more of the eight Suriname species. The four most popular species were *Chiropotes, Alouatta, Cebus nigrivittatus,* and *Cebus apella,* closely followed by *Ateles* and *Pithecia. Chiropotes* and *Alouatta* were eaten by all of the interviewees that said they would eat monkeys, *Cebus nigrivittatus* by 96.7%, *Cebus apella* by 94.1%, and *Ateles* and *Pithecia* by 86.7%. *Saimiri* and *Saguinus,* on the other hand, were far less popular. *Saimiri* was eaten by only 61.8% and *Saguinus* by only 32.4% (fig. 7.3).

Most of the interviewees indicated preferences for certain species. Although *Pithecia* was not eaten by everyone, many of those who did eat it had a very high opinion of its meat. It was cited as the favorite species by 26.7%. *Cebus apella* was also highly considered and cited as the favorite by 26.5%. *Ateles* was preferred by 13.3%, *Chiropotes* by 10%, *Alouatta* by 8.8%, and *Cebus nigrivittatus* by 3.3%. No one considered *Saguinus* or *Saimiri* a favorite species (fig. 7.4).

The people who ate no monkeys at all gave several reasons for avoiding the animals. Two people said that monkeys were their *trefu* (i.e., it was taboo for them to eat monkeys), others said monkeys gave them stomachaches or made them vomit, and one claimed he would not eat them because their sexual behavior was like that of humans.

The people who ate at least some monkeys also had personal biases or *trefus* against certain species. *Saguinus* was usually considered a last resort even by those who ate all eight species. It was considered too small by some, too pretty by others, and several people said that they considered it crazy because it sometimes fell out of trees. *Saguinus* was also taboo for twins or people with twin offspring. *Saimiri* was also considered a last resort by those who said they

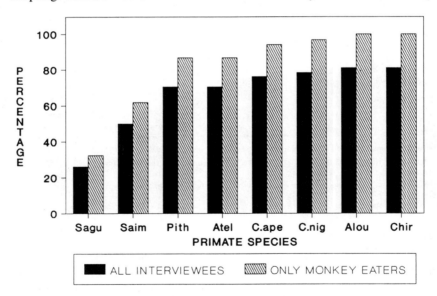

Figure 7.3. Percentage of interviewees who report eating different primate species (Sagu = *Saguinus midas;* Saim = *Saimiri sciureus;* Pith = *Pithecia pithecia;* Atel = *Ateles paniscus;* C. ape = *Cebus apella;* C. nig = *Cebus nigrivittatus;* Alou = *Alouatta seniculus;* Chir = *Chiropotes satanas*). Percentages calculated for all interviewees (black bars) and for those interviewees who report eating monkeys (hatched bars).

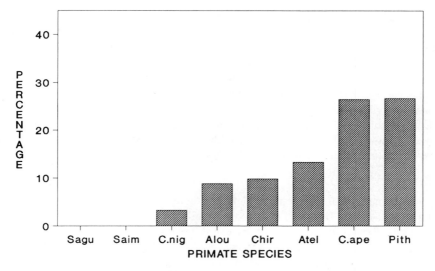

Figure 7.4. Percentages of interviewees who prefer the meat of different species. Percentages calculated for those interviewees who report eating monkeys.

would eat it, while those who did not eat it usually thought it too small. One person considered *Saimiri* part of a twin *trefu*. No one gave a reason for not eating *Pithecia*, but I imagine that it was also considered too small by most of those not eating it. The two *Cebus* species were usually popular, but a few Bushnegroes who ate only one or two monkeys would not eat them for unspecified reasons. Like *Saimiri, Cebus apella* was also considered part of a twin *trefu* by one person. *Chiropotes* and *Alouatta* were eaten by all those who ate monkeys. Everyone seemed to like *Chiropotes,* but several complained that *Alouatta* either smelled too much or that its botflies were repulsive. *Ateles* caused strong reactions in a number of people. Although some Bushnegroes and Amerindians considered it their favorite species, others were disgusted at the thought of eating it. Several Bushnegroes said they would not touch it because its skin was black like a man's; others thought it looked too human or that it cradles its infant like a woman. A few simply complained about its smell or taste or said that it gave them a stomachache.

First-hand Information from Field Camps and Villages

Data on freshly killed animals brought into field camps and villages indicated that *Alouatta* (sixty-four specimens) and *Cebus apella* (sixty-one specimens) were the most heavily hunted monkeys, probably because both are abundant and conspicuous and high on the list of preferred species. *Ateles* (twenty-one specimens) and *Chiropotes* (eighteen specimens) are less commonly shot, and rarer species like *Cebus nigrivitattus* (nine specimens) and

Pithecia (seven specimens), though popular, are far more difficult to find. Finally, *Saguinus* (five specimens) and *Saimiri* (one specimen), though both quite abundant, are as indicated by the interviews, of little interest as food items.

In Suriname, monkeys and most other game animals are usually hunted with shotguns (generally 16-gauge). Bushnegroes hunt almost exclusively with shotguns and use bows and arrows only for fishing. Amerindians also hunt largely with shotguns, which are becoming available even in the more remote villages in Suriname. Some Amerindians still hunt monkeys with bow and arrow. However, as noted by Lenselink (1972) in Alalapadoe, most hunters just stay home when shotgun shells are not available.

Kitchen Midden Data

Examination of kitchen middens in field camps and villages in the Sipaliwini-Pouso Tirio area (Suriname-Brazil border) resulted in findings similar to the first-hand observations discussed previously (tables 7.2 and 7.3). *Alouatta seniculus* (sixty-five specimens) was again the most abundant species, followed in this case by *Ateles* (forty-four specimens). *Chiropotes* (seventeen specimens) was in essentially the same position as in the first-hand observations. The two *Cebus* species (seventeen specimens), combined here because of the difficulty in distinguishing them from fragmentary remains, were comparatively rare in the kitchen midden sample but still comprise a substantial portion of the monkeys found. *Pithecia* (two specimens) was, as usual, quite rare, and *Saguinas* and *Saimiri* were not represented. However, the skulls of these last three are quite fragile and thus unlikely to survive intact in kitchen middens for any length of time.

The Importance of Monkeys in the Total Game Intake

Monkeys are definitely an important source of protein for people living in the Suriname bush. At a SURALCO (Suriname Aluminum Company) geological exploration camp in the previously unexplored Lely Mountains, 21.2% of the game animals taken over a 3-month period in 1976 were monkeys, and they accounted for 22.7% of the total game biomass. At the Tirio Indian Village of Alalapadoe, monkeys accounted for 33.6% of the total number of game animals taken (fig. 7.5) and 28.5% of the biomass over a 7-month period (Lenselink 1972). At the Carib Indian village of Bigi Poika, monkeys comprised 20.9% of the animals taken (excluding birds) and 3.9% of the total biomass over a 3-month period (van der Staaij 1975). On the basis of kitchen midden remains, monkeys accounted for 13.9% of the number and 6.7% of the biomass of game animals eaten over an undetermined period (probably 1 to 3 years) in the Sipaliwini-Pouso Tirio area (table 7.3).

In all areas investigated, nonprimate mammals made up the bulk of the game diet, followed by monkeys, forest tortoises, or birds (data on the dietary importance of fish were not collected during this study). The most important mam-

Figure 7.5. Tirio hunter holding recently killed tufted capuchin monkey (*Cebus apella*). (Photo, Mark Plotkin).

mals were the collared and white-lipped peccaries (*Tayassu tajacu, Tayassu pecari*), which, when locally abundant as in the Sipaliwini-Pouso Tirio area, can by themselves account for more than 50% of the forest-based protein diet. Other frequently eaten mammals include agoutis (*Dasyprocta* sp.), pacas (*Agouti paca*), armadillos (*Dasypus* spp. and others), deer (*Odocoileus virginianus, Mazama* spp.), and several other species listed in the tables. Because of their size, tapirs (*Tapirus terrestris*) can contribute a lot to the game biomass, but they occur at comparatively low densities and are therefore not as commonly shot as many other species. The tortoises, *Geochelone denticulata* and *Geochelone carbonaria,* are often very abundant and can be a very important source of protein. They have the added advantage that they can be kept alive for months with virtually no care. The most heavily hunted birds are the cracid genera *Crax* and *Penelope*. *Crax* is especially important because it is large (up to 4 kg) and very common in undisturbed forest. When field crews opened up new tracts of forest in the Lely Mountains in 1976, *Crax* was the most frequently taken game animal.

Monkey Hunting for Other Purposes

Monkeys are sometimes hunted for purposes other than human consumption. In Brazilian Amazonia, for example, monkey carcasses are occasionally used as fish or turtle bait or to bait traps for spotted cats (Mittermeier and Coimbra-Filho 1977). This can be a serious drain on populations of larger, slow-breeding species like *Ateles*. In Suriname, however, monkeys are rarely or never used as bait.

As in other parts of Amazonia, the long, bushy tails of *Chiropotes* and *Pithecia* are sometimes used as dusters by local people, and various parts of the anatomy of several species are used to make Amerindian ornaments. The Tirio Indians, for example, make a dancing ornament called *makui* (the Tirio name for *Saguinus*) from macaw feathers and a *Saguinus* tail. They also make a comb from woven rope and an *Ateles* forearm bone. The Akurios people use *Ateles* bones to make the points of fish and bird arrows and the handle of an agouti tooth drill. Teeth of *Cebus apella* and *Ateles* are used to make necklaces, and an *Alouatta* hyoid with seeds inside is employed as a baby rattle (Geijskes 1954). The *Alouatta* hyoid also had medicinal use. Some Surinamers believe that drinking from it can cure stuttering (P. Teunissen, pers. comm., 1976). In addition, I found several with strings attached to them hanging in an uninhabited Tirio camp but was unable to determine their function.

As in the case of live capture for pets, use of monkey parts to make ornaments and other items is usually a by-product of hunting for food.

Conclusions

The Long-term Effects of Concentrated Hunting

The available information indicates that as long as human populations are low, hunting pressure is not too heavy, and large tracts of undisturbed forest are available to buffer and resupply the area of concentrated activity, populations of primates and other forest animals can readily bounce back in the face of exploitation. Temporary field camps in the interior (such as those operated by the Suriname Aluminum Company, SURALCO; the Airport Maintenance Service, LVD; and the Geological and Meteorological Services, GMD) apparently have little long-term effect, even though hunters may extract several thousand animals over the course of a few years. For example, the SURALCO field crew that operated on the Brownsberg plateau in the middle to late 1960s hunted heavily in the area (H. Parker, pers. comm., 1976). However, Brownsberg was evacuated in 1969 and is now a nature park where most rain forest mammals and birds are quite abundant.

Hunting pressure was also heavy in the Lely Mountains, where a SURALCO crew operated from 1973 to the end of 1976. Nonetheless, when I visited the area in February and March, 1976, I found commonly hunted species like *Alouatta* and *Cebus apella* close to the main camp and the airstrip.

However, field crews are usually small (ten to forty men), and their game intake moderate because the companies they work for supply them with at least some food. On the other hand, larger, sedentary villages may crop game at a rate that exceeds the sustained yield level. Data from the Tirio Indian village of Alalapadoe supports this contention. The population of Alalapadoe was 450 in 1972, and far more animals were taken per month at Alalapadoe than by the SURALCO crew at Lely. At the time of Lenselink's study (1972), game was still abundant around Alalapadoe. Since the latter part of 1975, however, almost no game has been shot in the vicinity of this village (N. C. Keulemans, pers. comm., 1976), and many of the inhabitants have started to move to a new site about 100 km away.

In 1986, I visited the village of Kwamalasamoetoe, where most of the Tirio Indians from Alalapadoe had moved in the late 1970s, and the situation there was largely the same. Within at least a 5-km radius of the village in all directions, the only primate species I was able to see was *Saguinas midas*. In 1975, I noted the same situation in the vicinity of Saul in the interior of French Guiana; the only primate found close to this gold mining town was *S. midas* (Mittermeier, Bailey, and Coimbra-Filho 1977).

The Tirios apparently used to live in small, dispersed groups that had minimal effect on local game populations. However, with increasing missionary influence, they began to concentrate in villages like Alalapadoe. The apparent result is that continued hunting in the vicinity of these permanent villages results in local extermination or decimation of most game species. Missions will have to introduce domestic animals to make up for the disappearance of game animals; otherwise, the tribes will periodically move to new hunting sites, break down into traditional groups, or simply suffer from protein deficiency.

As long as human populations remain small and the surrounding areas of undisturbed rain forest remain large, primates and other animals should be able to bounce back after depleted areas are abandoned. In other words, although serious local depletion can occur as a result of hunting, if one considers the entire interior of Suriname, primate hunting at current levels is probably sustainable. However, if the human population increases far beyond current levels, the likely result would be the eventual disappearance of all but the most adaptable species.

The Outlook for Primate Conservation in Suriname

Although habitat destruction is taking place in Suriname and hunting poses a threat to some of the more vulnerable species such as *Ateles* and *Chiropotes,* the overall outlook for primate conservation in the country is excellent. Both habitat destruction and hunting are still far less significant than in almost any other South American country, and a number of protective measures have been instituted on behalf of these animals. The 1954 game law and the 1970 game resolution provided official protection for all primates except *Cebus apella,* which was listed as a game species. New legislation has now been proposed that would bring the two small species, *Saguinus* and *Saimiri,* into a pet category, and would place the other larger primates into a game species category. However, in the more densely populated Northern Zone of the country (fig. 7.2), hunting would be closed throughout the year, meaning that all six larger monkeys would be fully protected there. In the sparsely populated Southern Zone of the country, hunting would be open throughout the year. Although this situation is less than ideal in terms of primate protection, it is realistic and reflects the fact that primates remain an important part of the diet of local people in the interior and that control of hunting in the interior is very difficult. In any case, protective legislation does prevent transport of smoked or frozen monkey meat from field camps and villages to markets in town, a once common practice and a much more serious threat than subsistence hunting.

The major long-term threat to Suriname monkeys is eventual development of the interior. However, given the current policies of the Suriname government, exploitation of the interior on the scale of what is currently taking place in areas like Brazilian Amazonia is still years away, if in fact it ever occurs. Indeed, Suriname is one of the few countries in the world that is both fortunate enough to still possess major tropical forest wilderness areas and wise enough to realize that maintaining them intact for the future is a sound development strategy.

In addition, Suriname already has a system of parks and reserves equal to or superior to that of many neotropical countries. Nine nature reserves and one nature park established as of 1983 cover 5,825 km², or 3.53%, of the country, and if one includes additional areas that are being proposed or are already in the process of being created, the total increases to 23,563 km², or 14.28%, of the country (fig. 7.6; Baal, Mittermeier, and Van Roosmalen 1988). In summary, the excellent nature protection system and the undisturbed state of most of the interior of Suriname make that country one of the best remaining areas on earth for the conservation of rainforest primates and other species. Even though primate hunting can take a serious toll at the local level, the low human population and the large areas of undisturbed forest habitat mitigate the effects of hunting and prevent it from posing a serious threat to any of the eight species found in that country. Indeed, given current trends, Suriname is likely to remain a major stronghold for primates and rain forests for many years to come.

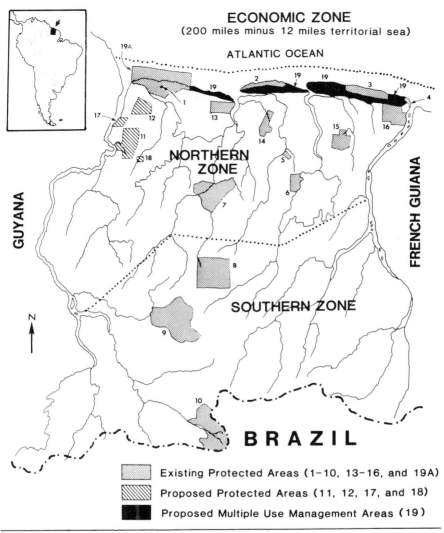

ECONOMIC ZONE
(200 miles minus 12 miles territorial sea)

ATLANTIC OCEAN

NORTHERN ZONE

SOUTHERN ZONE

GUYANA

FRENCH GUIANA

N

BRAZIL

Existing Protected Areas (1–10, 13–16, and 19A)

Proposed Protected Areas (11, 12, 17, and 18)

Proposed Multiple Use Management Areas (19)

1 Hertenrits NR (100 ha)
2 Coppename monding NR (12,000 ha)
3 Wia-wia NR (36,000 ha)
4 Galibi NR (4,000 ha)
5 Brinck-heuvel NR (6,000 ha)
6 Brownsberg NP (8,400 ha)
7 Raleighvallen/Voltzberg NR (78,170 ha)
8 Tafelberg NR (140,000 ha)
9 Eilerts de Haan NR (220,000 ha)
10 Sipaliwini NR (100,000 ha)
11 Kaboeri NR (68,000 ha proposed)

12 Nani NR (54,000 ha proposed)
13 Peruvia NR (31,000 ha)
14 Boven Coesewijne NR (27,000ha)
15 Copi NR (28,000 ha)
16 Wanekreek NR (45,000 ha)
17 Mac Clemen BR (6,000 ha proposed)
18 Snake Creek BR (4,000 ha proposed)
19 Bijzonder BG Estuariene Zone (310,000 ha,
    of which 120,400 ha is already protected)
19A Bigi Pan BG (68,300 ha, includes
    adjacent sea area)

NR = Nature Reserve   NP = Nature Park   BR = Forest Reserve   BG = Multiple Use Management Area

Figure 7.6. Existing protected areas in Suriname (1–10), together with new protected areas that have been proposed or are in the process of being created (11–18). The boundary between the Northern Zone and the Southern zone is also indicated.

Part 3

Market Hunting and Collecting

8

Management of Olive Ridley Sea Turtles (*Lepidochelys olivacea*) Nesting at Playas Nancite and Ostional, Costa Rica

STEPHEN E. CORNELIUS, MARIO ALVARADO ULLOA, JUAN CARLOS CASTRO, MERCEDES MATA DEL VALLE, AND DOUGLAS C. ROBINSON

In 1970 Richard and Hughes (1972) discovered the synchronous emergence of thousands of olive ridley turtles (*Lepidochelys olivacea* Eschscholtz, 1829) at Playas Nancite and Ostional on the Pacific coast of Costa Rica. This spectacular phenomenon has generated interest and outright awe among the general public and the scientific community as one of the most impressive examples of mass reproductive activity in the animal kingdom.

The behavior of mass nesting (*arribada*) occurs at a few sites in Mexico (Cliffton, Cornejo, and Felger 1982), Nicaragua (Paredes 1983), Panamá (Cornelius 1982), and India (Kar 1980). The Costa Rican assemblages are the largest in Latin America; as a result, Nancite and Ostional are considered two of the most important olive ridley nesting sites in the world (Bjorndal 1982). Nevertheless, the value of the beach as a source of recruitment to regional olive ridley populations has been questioned because hatchling emergence seems to be markedly below the production potential (Robinson 1983). This is reportedly because many nests are destroyed by nesting turtles (Hughes and Richard 1974). Turtles are known to dig into incubating nests at other tropical rookeries. At some this is considered an irregular occurrence and of little importance in determining recruitment to the adult population (Fowler 1979); at others it is felt to cause significant loss (Fretay and Lescure 1979).

Though not actively captured for food or industry along the Pacific coast of Central America (Cornelius 1982), regionwide declines of olive ridley populations are evident (Cliffton, Cornejo, and Felger 1982). Incidental capture in fishery operations and perturbation to nesting beaches by shoreline development have contributed to reductions in populations of this species (Cornelius 1982), but the principal factors have been large-scale commercial fishing of turtles in Mexico and Ecuador, which includes turtles dispersing from Central America after nesting (Green and Ortiz-Crespo 1982; Cliffton, Cornejo, and Felger et al. 1982; Cornelius and Robinsin 1986) and uncontrolled harvest of eggs on Central American nesting beaches (Cornelius 1982; Cruz and Espinal

1985; López and Cornelius 1985; Morales 1985; Moreira and Benítez 1985; Rosales 1985). In several countries, collecting turtle eggs has been a lucrative activity of local and regional importance for many years (Cornelius 1982; Minarik 1985). Many legislative efforts in the region have attempted to regulate this activity, either through total bans or through establishment of egg-collecting seasons, but none have been very effective (Cornelius 1982).

The purpose of this study was (1) to evaluate nest survival and hatching success at two mass nesting sites for olive ridleys in Costa Rica (Nancite, where no egg collecting occurs, and Ostional, where eggs are extensively utilized); (2) to examine the temporal and spatial parameters that influence reproductive success at both sites; and (3) to devise an active management plan that would improve recruitment to both populations, perhaps assist restoration of other populations, and benefit the human residents of Ostional.

Study Area

Playa Nancite is located in northwest Guanacaste Province along the northeastern edge of the Gulf de Papagayo (fig. 8.1) and has been fully protected within Santa Rosa National Park since 1971. Its physical isolation has probably never allowed large-scale human use of turtles or their eggs. The beach is approximately 1,050 m long and bounded by shear-faced rock headlands. The northern 300 m is covered by button mangrove trees (*Conocarpus erecta*) that extend seaward to the high-water spring-tide line (HWST). The beach is unvegetated in the central 500 m and reaches its greatest width in front of an estuary dominated by red mangrove (*Rhizophora mangle*). The estuary receives runoff from a small watershed and is separated from the sea throughout most of the year by a sand bar. Heavy rains cause the estuary to open at the center of the beach and sometimes at the northern end. Unshaded habitat available for nesting varies from 13,000 to 22,000 m², depending on whether the beach is in an erosional or accretional phase (Cornelius and Robinson 1985). An additional 8,500 m² is available for nesting beneath hibiscus (*Hibiscus tileaceus*), brazilwood (*Haematoxylon brasiletto*), and madrone (*Gliricidia sepium*) trees on the beach.

Playa Ostional is located approximately 100 km south of Nancite between Cabo Velas and Punta Guiones on the Nicoya Peninsula and was declared a National Wildlife Refuge in 1983. The beach is slightly smaller (880 m) and less well defined than Nancite. Boundaries of the principal nesting area are a rocky outcrop to the south and the mouth of Ostional Estuary to the north. Nesting habitat actually extends several kilometers north and south of the main beach, but these areas are not normally used during arribadas. The beach is about 35 m wide throughout its length, with the nesting area totaling approximately 28,000 m². There is very little shaded nesting habitat available because a dense thicket of spiny terrestrial bromeliad (*Bromelia pinguin*), columnar

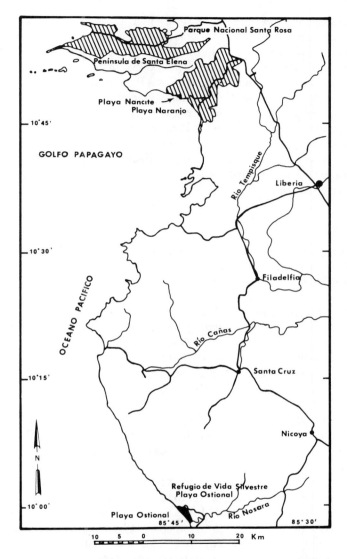

Figure 8.1. Location of Playa Nancite, Parque Nacional Santa Rosa, and Playa Ostional, Refugio de Vida Silvestre, in northwest Costa Rica.

cacti, and wooden fences constructed by the residents effectively prevent most turtles from reaching a narrow stand of hibiscus located on the landward border of the beach. The watershed is larger than Nancite's, and the estuary is open to the sea during most of the year, except for a period of 2 to 4 months during the dry season.

The easy access to Ostional, the severe human poverty of the area, and especially the large, regular supply of a high-demand product has encouraged uncontrolled exploitation of tens of thousands of nests by residents of this and neighboring communities, despite the illegality of the activity. Ostional has been the major source of turtle eggs in Costa Rica for at least the past 30 years, and the few attempts made to halt exploitation at Ostional during the past 15 years have failed (Cornelius and Robinson 1985). Residents have long advocated legalization of subsistence and commercial use of turtle eggs. Controlled, legal harvest of olive ridley eggs has been discussed as a management option at Ostional by the scientific community (Pritchard 1984a, 1984b; Cornelius 1985); however, the legal and scientific bases to support use of the egg resource at Ostional have been absent.

Methods

The study principally focused on Nancite, where nests were monitored between 1981 and 1984. A complementary study was carried out at Playa Ostional in 1984.

The size of the arribada was estimated from counts made every 2 to 3 hours during the night in 100-m² quadrats of the total number of turtles: (1) the number present, (2) the number preparing nest cavities, and (3) the number laying. The number of quadrats sampled at Nancite ranged from six to seventeen, depending upon the width of the beach during a given arribada. At Ostional, three sample quadrats were always used. (See Cornelius and Robinson [1982] for a detailed description of the technique.)

Each beach was divided into sections in order to quantify the effect of nest location in determining its fate. The Nancite study site was divided into nine sections of 100 m each and one section of 150 m (fig. 8.2), identified consecutively from the south to the north end as sections 1 to 10, respectively. Sections 6, 7, and 10 fronted the estuary mouths. The beach was further divided into a low-beach zone (the littoral portion covered by the high tide), unvegetated mid-beach zone (the supralittoral portion located between the average reach of the high tide during a tidal cycle and the vegetation line), and the shaded beach zone (portions of mid- and high-beach covered by woody vegetation). At Ostional the beach was divided into three sections of approximately 290 m each (fig. 8.3). Section 3 was adjacent to the estuary mouth.

The scheduling of nest marking to represent without bias the spatial and temporal distribution of nesting turtles was difficult because it required a reasonably accurate estimate of how many turtles would arrive during a particular night and how they would disperse along the beach. A prescribed number of nests for marking was established as a goal for each arribada in which the activity was to occur. We marked nests at random during each of the first three or four nights of the arribada by walking the length of the beach and searching

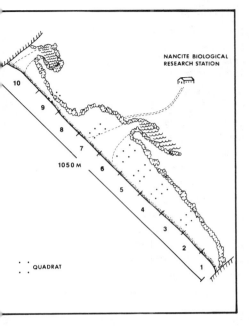

Figure 8.2. Location of census quadrats and
beach divisions at Playa Nancite.

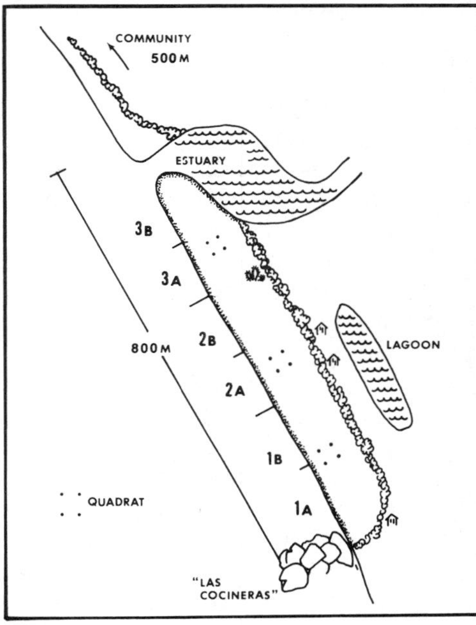

Figure 8.3. Location of census quadrats and
beach divisions at Playa Ostional.

for turtles that were dropping eggs. The marking occurred at various times
throughout a given night in order to approximate the time and space distribution
of the nesting activity. Their correlation was measured by comparing estimates
of nesting turtles based on quadrat counts to number of marked nests in each
section or sections represented by that quadrat.

We marked individual study nests with a 40-cm-long plastic ribbon placed
within the nest before the turtle had finished nesting and with a section of flexible garden hose attached to a 40-cm-long wooden stake, which was buried 1 m
north or south of the nest. Both ribbon and stake were numbered. Nests were
monitored each morning during the incubation period. In 1983 and 1984 each
nest site was checked to see if it had been washed during the previous tidal
cycle.

The appearance of the ribbon on the beach surface during or immediately
following an arribada was interpreted as evidence of the nest having been destroyed by other turtles. If the ribbon was found at any other time, it was assumed the nest was destroyed by predation or erosion from tidal or estuary
action, depending upon the associated signs. Nests that completed the incubation period undisturbed by erosion, turtles, or predation were called *term* nests.
The average clutch size was estimated from data gathered in previous studies of

turtles in oviposition. Average clutch size for Nancite nests was 99.6 eggs (SD = 17.0; n = 115; Cornelius and Robinson 1985) and for Ostional, 107.4 (SD = 17.4; n = 66; Alvarado 1985).

At day 45 of incubation, nest sites were covered in situ by a hardware cloth cage. Each site was then examined several times daily to collect emergent neonates. When 2 days had passed consecutively with no additional neonates appearing, or if none had been collected by day 55, the nest was excavated, dead and live neonates were counted, and the condition of the unhatched eggs was recorded. Because of the density of nests during arribadas, marked nests were often located a few centimeters from other nests laid during the same or other arribadas, and thus determination of clutch size during excavation was unreliable.

During the quadrat censuses, we also recorded the number of turtles that had reached at least the nest construction stage and had destroyed a previously deposited nest. Annual estimates of the rate of nest destruction by turtles based on quadrat data closely reflected the estimates derived from marked-nest data (Cornelius and Robinson 1985). These data also provided a more precise estimate of the variation in turtle-related nest loss during an arribada, between arribadas within a season, and between seasons than could be acquired from the marked-nest data alone.

The location of successful but unmarked nests was identified by measuring the distance from the berm separating the low- and midbeach zones to the point of neonate emergence.

All statistical tests and confidence limits are given at the 95% level of significance unless otherwise indicated.

Factors Limiting Hatching Success at Nancite

At Nancite there were fourteen arribadas during the peak nesting months of August to November in 1981–84—four for each year except 1983, when only two occurred (fig. 8.4). Arribadas averaged 55,400 ± 15,500 nesting turtles and ranged from 20,000 to 110,000.

A total of 541 nests were marked during the eight arribadas in August and September: 1981 (138 nests), 1982 (176), 1983 (157), and 1984 (70). Of these, 119 markers were lost during the study, leaving 422 nests for which fates were determined (fig. 8.5). One hundred and fifty-five study nests (36.7%) were disturbed before completion of the incubation period. A total of twenty-three study nests (5.5%) were destroyed by high tides or the opening of the estuary. The impact of erosion on nest survivorship varied among years. Nearly 30% of the study nests were washed away in 1984; however, only 6% were thus destroyed in 1981, and none were lost in either 1982 or 1983.

Because hatching from one arribada normally did not occur before another mass nesting occurred, a large proportion of the nests was often destroyed by

Figure 8.4. Olive ridley arribada at Playa Nancite. Note dug-up eggs distributed over the beach. (Photo, Stephen Cornelius).

subsequent arribadas. Turtles destroyed seventy-two study nests, twenty-five (5.9%) during the same arribada in which the nests were marked and forty-seven (11.1%) during the next mass survival, normally 28 to 30 days later (fig. 8.6).

The relative importance of turtles digging up nests of others was directly related to number and size of the arribadas. In years of very large arribadas, as in 1981, when approximately 340,000 nestings occurred during the study period, turtles destroyed 22.5% of the marked nests. This estimate is comparable to data from the sample quadrats, which indicate turtles destroyed 25% of nests. During the 1982 study season, when 200,000 nestings occurred, the nest loss to turtles was estimated at 23.6% and 19.3%, based on marked-nest and quadrat data, respectively. In 1983, a year in which only two relatively small arribadas of approximately 25,000 turtles each occurred during the study period, the proportion of nests lost to nesting turtles decreased to 6.5% and 10.3%, based on marked-nest and quadrat data, respectively. The number of nests increased to 184,000 in 1984, and marked-nest and quadrat count data concurred with nest loss estimates of 13.6% and 13.7%, respectively.

Based on quadrat data, rates of nest destruction by turtles increased with each successive night of an arribada. The average percentage of females encountering a nest on the first night of thirteen peak nesting season arribadas during 1981–84 was 11.4 (no data were taken on one opening night). This rate of nest destruction increased to 17.4% on fourteen second nights, 22.7% on fourteen third nights, 32.1% on nine fourth nights, and 34.7% on four fifth nights.

118

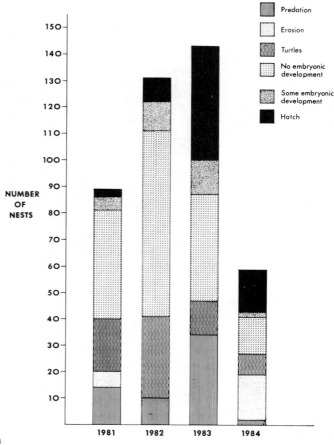

Predation

Erosion

Turtles

No embryonic development

Some embryonic development

Hatch

NUMBER OF NESTS

150
140
130
120
110
100
90
80
70
60
50
40
30
20
10

1981   1982   1983   1984

Figure 8.5. Fates of marked nests at Playa Nancite (1981–84).

PLAYA NANCITE

The rate of nest destruction by turtles based on quadrat data increased also with each arribada over the season. Approximately 11.4% (unweighted mean) of the females nesting during two August arribadas (1981, 1982) encountered a previous nest. This increased to 17.8% for four September arribadas (1981–84), to 23.9% for four October arribadas (1981–84), and 24.7% for three November arribadas (1981, 1982, 1984).

Natural predation of study nests fluctuated widely during the study period. Twenty-five percent were depredated in 1983, whereas only 3.4% of the study nests were excavated by mammalian predators during 1984. The weighted average for the entire study was 14.2%. Coatis (*Nasua narica*) were the most visible and numerous mammalian egg predators, followed in importance by raccoons (*Procyon lotor*) and coyotes (*Canis latrans*).

Predation, erosion, and nesting turtles collectively destroyed 155 of 422 study nests (36.7%) before the eggs could complete incubation. In 165 of the

Figure 8.6. Nesting turtle destroying a nest that had been laid earlier in the arribada. (Photo, Stephen Cornelius).

surviving 267 nests (61.8%) there was no apparent embryonic development or the embryo perished very early during the incubation period. Hatchability of nests deposited during peak season arribadas at Nancite varied among years. In 1981 and 1982, 83.7% and 77.8% of term nests, respectively, showed no sign of embryonic development. Another 10.3% and 12.2% of these nests in 1981 and 1982, respectively, contained some eggs with unhatched moribund embryos at various stages of development but no successful hatching. Hatching rate was much higher in 1983, with nearly 45.3% of the term nests or 30.9% of all study nests producing at least one hatchling. This improved hatching rate continued in 1984, with neonate turtles appearing in 50.0% of the term nests and 27.1% of all nests.

Spatial Distribution of Successful Nests at Nancite

Disturbed and failed nests were not distributed randomly over the beach. Nearly 34% of the study nests located in sections 8, 9, and 10 during 1981–84 (fig. 8.7) were depredated. Nearly 60% of the nests in section 9, which was totally covered by button mangrove trees, were lost to coatis, raccoons, and coyotes. In contrast, less than 8% of the study nests in the open, mid 400 m of the beach were disturbed. Predation rates were strongly linked to vegetative cover ($\chi^2 = 56.6$, d.f. = 6, $p < .0001$). The relation between predation and

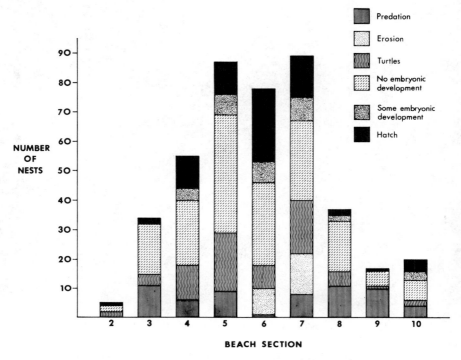

Figure 8.7. Fates of marked nests at Playa Nancite (1981–84) by beach section locations.

vegetation was even more obvious when nest fates were analyzed in relation to vertical beach zone (fig. 8.8). Less than 7% of the 1983 and 1984 nests located in the open low- and midbeach zones were depredated, whereas over 72% of those located in vegetated mid- and high-beach zones were lost to predators ($\chi^2 = 85.8$, d.f. $= 6, p < .0001$).

Study nests lost to erosion occurred only where the estuary broke through to the sea. Fourteen percent of the nests located in sections 6 and 7 were washed away by the estuary, the majority in 1984.

Disturbance of nests during arribadas tended to be greater in the central 400 m of the beach than at its northern and southern extremes. Vertically, disturbance was greater in the midbeach zone than in the low or high zones. The differences were not statistically significant, however ($p < .10$).

The percentage of nests surviving the incubation period intact varied along the beach from a low of 35.3 in section 9 to a high of 76.9 in section 6. Nest survival in the low-beach zone (81.5%) and in the unvegetated midbeach zone (71.1%) was better than nests in the vegetated mid- and high-beach zones (25.0%; $\chi^2 = 28.4$; d.f. $= 1; p < .001$). Again these differences were due to variation in predation pressure.

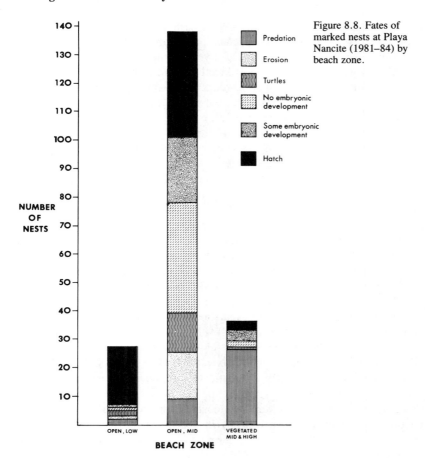

Figure 8.8. Fates of marked nests at Playa Nancite (1981–84) by beach zone.

Nests that survived erosion, predation, and disruption by adult turtles and hatched were located primarily in one of two well-delineated areas. The first was midbeach of sections 6, 7, and 10 in front of the estuary. Over 46% of the term nests were located in these sections, but they accounted for 60% of the total number of hatched nests ($F = 16.9$, d.f. $= 1,2$, $p < .001$). Hatching success was particularly high in section 6, where 41.6% of the term nests produced neonate turtles. This compared to only 22.2% in the remainder of the beach.

The second area of Nancite that consistently produced successful nests was a narrow band running the length of the beach and coinciding with the low beach–midbeach berm. The width of the band varied annually and sometimes within a nesting season, depending upon whether the beach was eroding or expanding. For example, in 1981 and 1982, when the whole beach was narrow, the productive band was 3 to 5 m wide and positioned on the low-beach side of the berm, whereas during the following 2 years, when Nancite had broadened considerably, it was wider and extended well onto the midbeach platform.

Hatching success in this area appeared to be positively associated with the frequency and extent that the nest area (but not necessarily the clutch of eggs) was washed by incoming tides. In 1983, the sites of thirty-one study nests that did not hatch were washed an average of 4.5 days (SD = 4.5) during incubation, while the sites of thirty successful nests were washed twice as often (x = 9.3 days; SD = 4.9; t = 3.73; p < .001). In 1984 only three of thirty-two study nests sites were wave-washed. Surf reached one of these on 19 days during incubation, yet it and the other two produced neonate turtles.

The positive influence of wave washing was also apparent when hatch rate was evaluated with respect to beach zone. Of the nests marked in 1983 and 1984 that survived to the end of the incubation period, 95% of those in the low beach produced neonates. In comparison, only 36.4% of the term nests in the unvegetated midbeach zone and 33.3% of those in the vegetated zones hatched (χ^2 = 23.7, d.f. = 4, p < .0001). In 1983, successful nests averaged 5.0 m (SD = 11.7) from the berm, while unsuccessful nests averaged 8.2 m (SD = 7.9). The differences are not statistically significant because of the very good overall hatch rate of nests in front of the estuary regardless of proximity to the berm. In 1984, the sixteen successful nests were located on average 12.8 m (SD = 8.5) from the berm, while sixteen unsuccessful nests were located on average 19.5 m (SD = 8.0), a statistically significant difference (t = 8.9; d.f. = 30; p < .001).

Unmarked successful nests were also located along the berm and on the midbeach platform in front of the estuary. In 1983, hatchlings from 264 nests emerged only 2.9 ± 0.9 m above the berm. Average site of emergence was on the landward side of the berm only in sections 6 (8.2 ± 2.1 m; n = 93), 7 (6.4 ± 3.9 m; n = 33), and 10 (8.2 ± 3.5 m; n = 4). In sections distant from the estuary, the average site of hatchling emergence ranged from directly at the berm to 2.9 m below. No emerging hatchlings were located beyond 5 m on the landward side of the berm in these sections.

In 1984, the beach had broadened, and a two-tiered, midbeach platform developed. As a result, the average site of hatchling emergence from 1,318 unmarked nests was 11.5 ± 0.5 m above the new berm (which had developed between the low-beach zone and the lower of the two midbeach platforms) and ranged from 10 m below this division to 42 m above it. Hatchlings emerged farther inland in sections 6 and 7 (x = 12.9 ± 1.3 m; n = 420) than elsewhere on the beach (x = 10.9 ± 1.2 m; n = 898; t = 51.4; p < .001). Few successful nests were found on the upper (older) platform except in the sections in front of the estuary.

Factors Limiting Hatching Success at Ostional

We recorded five arribadas at Ostional during the peak nesting months of August to December in 1984. The total number of nesting females was estimated for three arribadas: 74,900 in August, 130,000 in September, and 47,200 in December. There was no arribada during the incubation period for nests deposited in December.

We marked 202 nests during the August arribada and 60 during that in December. Forty-six nest markers were lost, forty-three from the August arribada and three from the December arribada. Humans dug up nine and seven nests from August and December, respectively, and we have excluded them from the data analysis, which leaves 150 nests from August and 50 nests from December for which fates were determined (fig. 8.9).

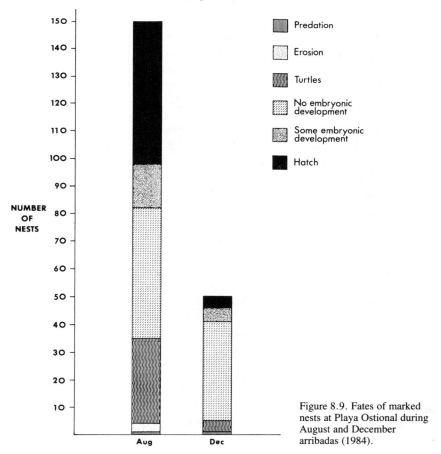

Figure 8.9. Fates of marked nests at Playa Ostional during August and December arribadas (1984).

There was no significant difference in the number of nests that completed the incubation term from the August and December arribadas (χ^2 = 5.9, d.f. = 3, p > .90). A total of forty study nests (20.0%) were destroyed before the end of incubation. The majority of these were disturbed by nesting turtles, sixteen nests marked during the arribada and nineteen nests during the subsequent arribada. Three study nests were lost when the estuary broke through and eroded portions of the beach during heavy September rains. No study nests were lost to natural vertebrate predators, which are rare at Ostional, but two were dug up by feral dogs.

As at Nancite, the proportion of nests destroyed by turtles increased with each successive night of an arribada and was related to total size of the arribada. Quadrat counts indicated that between 50.0% and 69.5% of the turtles nesting during the fourth and fifth nights destroyed a nest made previously, whereas between 12.2% and 30.0% of the turtles nesting during the first three nights of the arribada disturbed an earlier nest. Twenty-two percent of the turtles that reached the stage of nest cavity construction during the August arribada had disturbed a previous nest. This value rose to 44% during the larger September arribada and returned to 22% during the small December arribada.

A total of 115 study nests from the August arribada (76.6%) and 45 (90.0%) from the December arribada escaped predation, erosion, and digging turtles and completed the incubation period intact. Of these (both months together), 83 (51.9%, or 41.5% of the total) revealed no evidence of embryonic development. An additional 21 nests (13.1%, or 10.5% of the total) revealed some moribund embryos in middle to late stage of development. Fifty-six nests (35.0%, or 28.0% of the total) produced hatchlings. August nests had a significantly higher hatching rate than did December nests (χ^2 = 22.8; d.f. = 2; p < .0001).

Spatial Distribution of Successful Nests at Ostional

The proportion of August nests destroyed by turtles or predators were equally distributed in all zones (p > .90), while a higher than expected loss due to erosion was recorded in section 3 (χ^2 = 22.4; d.f. = 6; p < .001; fig. 8.10). Factors limiting nest survival were not associated with any particular portion of the beach for the December-marked nests (χ^2 = .44; d.f. = 4; p > .75).

As at Nancite, a higher proportion of nests hatched near to the estuary mouth (section 3) than elsewhere on the beach. This was true for both the August (χ^2 = 9.5; d.f. = 4; p < .05) and December-marked nests (χ^2 = 23.3; d.f. = 4; p < .0001).

There were many successful nests on the midbeach platform, in contrast to the Nancite pattern of little hatching in the midbeach area except near the estuary. Nevertheless, there was an indication that proximity to the high tide line may be related to high nesting success areas at Ostional. Sites of fifty-three

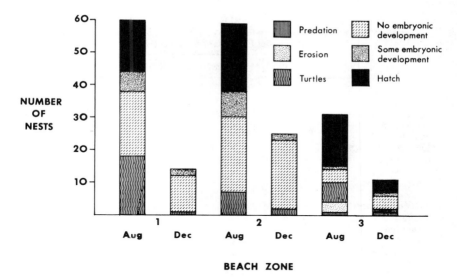

Figure 8.10. Fates of marked nests at Playa Ostional (August and December 1984) by beach zone (Sections 1–3).

successful study nests from August averaged 14.7 ± to 2.7 m inland of the berm, whereas 62 unsuccessful nests averaged 16.1 ± 2.5 m from this division ($t = 7.73; p < .001$).

Nests did not appear to have been harmed by occasional high tide washing. Of twelve study nests that received tidal washings for 1 to 24 days during the incubation period, only two did not hatch and these were washed very infrequently. Another nest was washed continuously for 6 to 11 days during each trimester of development, yet it produced turtles.

Emergence Success of Study Area Nests and Hatchling Production?

Nancite

A total of 1,624 emergent turtles, plus 163 live but nonemerged neonates, was collected from seventy-one successful nests (table 8.1) at Nancite. Mean number of neonates per nest was 25.2 ± 6.0 and ranged from 1 to 93. Variation in number of neonates emerging from successful nests among years was not significant ($F = 0.75$; d.f. $= 3,67$). Hatching success ranged from 0.8% to 10.0% for all study nests ($x = 4.2\%$) and 1.5% to 14.6% for term nests ($x = 6.7\%$). The total estimated number of neonate turtles produced from August through November ranged from 270,000 in 1981 to 518,000 in 1983. Total production for the 4 years was estimated to be 1.45 million turtles.

TABLE 8.1
Hatchling Emergence from Successful Study Area Nests and Estimates of Neonate
Production at Playa Nancite, 1981–1984

	1981	1982	1983	1984	Combined
Number of nests with fates determined	93	131	139	59	422
Number of term nests	50	90	95	32	267
Number of nests where neonates:					
Emerged unassisted	2	9	38	9	58
Recovered alive in nest	1	0	5	7	13
Recovered dead in nest	0	0	0	2	2
Number of neonates:					
Emerged unassisted	77	195	1244	108	1624
Recovered alive in nest	0	0	139	24	163
Recovered dead in nest	0	3	68	16	87
Total live neonates	77	195	1383	132	1787
Percent of term nests with live neonates	6.0	10.0	45.3	50.0	26.6
Mean hatching % of term nests	1.5	2.2	14.6	4.1	6.7
Mean hatching % of all nests	0.8	1.5	10.0	2.2	4.2
Mean hatching from successful nests	25.7 ± 62.8	22.7 ± 9.8	32.2 ± 8.8	8.2 ± 5.6	25.2 ± 6.0
n	3	9	43	16	71
Range	3–53	3–47	1–93	1–38	1–93
Total nests deposited in August–November					
Arribadas	340,000	200,000	52,000	185,000	777,000
Neonates produced	270,000	299,000	518,000	405,000	1,452,000

Note: Hatching percent based on mean clutch size of 99.6 ± 3.1 ($n = 115$).

Ostional

A total of 1,212 emergent neonates were recovered from thirty-eight nests marked in the two Ostional arribadas (table 8.2) Some, or all, neonates from seventeen additional nests emerged outside the respective wire cylinder and escaped capture. These nests were included with the thirty-eight nests to calculate the percentage of producing nests in an arribada but were not used to calculate the within-nest hatching percent or the mean number of hatchlings from successful nests.

Thirty-five nests from the August arribada with accurate collection data averaged 33.5 ± 9.5 hatchlings and ranged from 1 to 108 per nest. December nests, though only three had good collection data, produced 15.7 ± 7.0 neo-nates (range = 10 to 22), significantly fewer than August (t = 6.1; d.f. = 36; p < .0001). Percent hatch for all August study nests was 8.3% (132 nests), whereas for those nests that survived to term it was 11.2% (97 nests). Hatch rate for all December study nests was 0.9% (49 nests) and 1.0% for term nests (44 nests). Approximately 665,000 turtles were produced from the August arribada compared to only 45,000 from the December nesting.

Extrapolating data from study nests in 1984 as Ostional and Nancite, we estimate that 2.4 million olive ridley hatchlings emerged from the August and September arribadas at Ostional, or about 860/m², compared to only 135,000, or about 5/m², for the same period at Nancite (table 8.3).

TABLE 8.2
Hatchling Emergence from Successful Study Area Nests and Estimates of Neonate Production at Playa Ostional, 1984

	ARRIBADA OF MARKING		
	August	December	Combined
Number of nests with fates determined	150	50	200
Number of term nests	115	45	160
Number of nests where neonates:			
Emerged unassisted	50	4	54
Recovered alive in nest	2	0	2
Recovered dead in nest	1	0	1
Number of neonates:			
Emerged unassisted	1,165	47	1,212
Recovered alive in nest	2	0	7
Recovered dead in nest	2	0	2
Total live neonates	1,172	47	1,219
Percent of term nests with live neonates	45.2	8.9	35.0
Mean hatching percent of term nests	11.2	1.0	8.0
Number of nests with complete hatch data	97	44	141
Mean hatching percent of all nests	8.3	0.9	6.3
Number of nests with complete hatch data	132	49	181
Mean hatchlings from successful nests	33.5 ± 9.6	15.7 ± 7.0	32.1 ± 9.4
Number of nests with complete hatch data	35	3	38
Range	1–108	10–22	1–108
Total nests deposited in August and December arribadas	74,900	47,200	122,100
Neonates produced	665,100	45,000	710,200

Note: Hatching percent based on mean clutch size of 107.4 ± 4.2 (n = 66). Some or all neonates escaped from seventeen marked nests in August and one marked nest in December before being tabulated. These nests were not considered in calculations of within nest hatching percent and mean clutch size though they were used to calculate percent of nests that were successful.

TABLE 8.3
Comparison of Neonate Production Estimates of the August and September 1984
Arribadas at Playas Nancite and Ostional

	Nancite	Ostional
Total number of nestings	60,300	207,900
Percent of nests that hatched	27.1	34.6
Number of nests that hatched	16,341	71,933
Mean clutch size	99.5	107.4
Number of eggs in successful nests	1,625,959	7,725,647
Percent hatch of successful nests	8.3	31.2
Number of neonates produced	134,955	2,410,402

Appraisal of Nesting Success

The degree of correlation between the distribution of study nests and nesting distribution at Nancite varied among years in its statistical significance. For example, in 1981 the relationship was not as close ($r = .458; n = 6; p < .36$) as it was in 1982 ($r = .635; n = 6; p < .17$), or 1983 ($r = .561; n = 6; p < .25$; or 1984 ($r = .923; n = 6; p < .10$). There was no statistical correlation between location of study nests and actual nesting distribution at Ostional for the August ($r = .614; n = 3; p > .40$), and December ($r = -.31; n = 3; p > .60$) arribadas. Though unfortunate, we believe that this discordance does not qualify the general conclusions presented below.

Nest loss to wild vertebrate predators was much higher at Nancite than at Ostional because of the wilderness nature of the site. Feral dogs and pigs at Ostional did not have the same degree of impact as did the large populations of raccoons, coatis, and coyotes at Nancite. However, other sources of nest failure, such as erosion and nesting by other turtles, did not vary greatly between beaches. A greater percentage of arribada nests at Ostional (80%) survived intact to the end of the incubation period than at Nancite (63%; $\chi^2 = 34.1$; d.f. $= 2; p < .0001$). The percentage of these nests that hatched was not significantly different at the two beaches ($\chi^2 = 4.47$, d.f. $= 2; p < .90$), but the number of hatchlings produced from the successful nests was clearly higher at Ostional than at Nancite ($t = 10.1$; d.f. $= 107; p < .0001$). To eliminate the bias of marked annual fluctuations in nest survival and hatching success evident at Nancite and seasonal differences apparent at Ostional, we evaluated only the August and September data sets for 1984. More Ostional nests completed the incubation period ($\chi^2 = 38.4$; d.f. $= 2; p < .0001$); an equal percentage of term nests hatched at both beaches ($\chi^2 = 1.1$; d.f. $= 2; p > .44$); and more hatchlings were produced per successful nests at Ostional ($t = 18.9$; d.f. $= 49; p < .0001$). The difference between the number of hatchlings produced at Nancite and Ostional in August and September of 1984 (table 8.3) was the result of several factors. Ostional had 3.5 times as many nests deposited during the period, an 8% larger mean clutch, 7.5% more nests surviving until the end of incubation, and four times more neonates emerging from successful nests than did Nancite.

The difference in the production of turtles might partly be a consequence of the human excavation of large numbers of eggs. Most of the extraction at Ostional occurs during the first two nights of the arribada, and this possibly improves the hatching rate of nests deposited on subsequent nights. This argument assumes that when a turtle makes contact with a previously laid nest, not only is the first nest destroyed, as has been shown to be the case by Fowler (1979) with green turtle nests, but the hatching success of the second is diminished because of contamination of the nest media by broken eggs and/or microorganism growth.

There may be important differences in the physical characteristics of the two beaches. Turtles may be less crowded at Ostional. The beach is wider and turtles have the option of spreading to adjacent beaches, although this generally does not happen. Steep headlands keep the turtles on a finite beach at Nancite. Consequently, destruction of nests by turtles in the long term might be less at Ostional.

Another difference is that microorganism contamination of the nest media may be less extensive at Ostional. There is little reason to believe that arribadas have been present at the two beaches for the same period of time. Residents claim that large arribadas began at Ostional less than 30 years ago. Confirmation of this is difficult, and it is not possible to determine when mass nesting began at Nancite, where there has never been a permanent human settlement. If turtles have been arriving at Ostional for fewer years than at Nancite a consequence might be less extensive microorganism contamination of the nest media at the former.

An unexpectedly large percentage of nests that survived intact to the end of the incubation period at both beaches did not produce any turtles (75% Nancite; 52% Ostional). This may be a general characteristic of olive ridley arribada nesting or perhaps a local characteristic of the Nancite and Ostional beaches. Though the causative mechanism has yet to be established, it seems certain that soil microorganisms, especially fungi, are involved. Many strains of fungi and bacteria have been isolated from decaying nests and nest media (Cornelius and Robinson 1982; Mo, pers. comm., 1986), but it is not clear what is their mode of disturbance, if any (e.g., arresting embryonic development by interrupting gas exchange, upsetting water balance within the eggs, causing accumulation of metabolic waste products to toxic levels within the clutch). It is also possible that eggs do not develop because of other factors (such as high infertility rates) and that the decaying nest contents simply provide a favorable culture medium for microflora and fauna that are independent of embryonic success.

Ghost crabs (*Ocypode* spp.) have been reported to eat turtle eggs at nesting beaches around the world (Hirth and Carr 1970; Hughes 1974; Hill and Green

1971; Fowler 1979; Stancyk 1982). They may play a key role in the destruction of nests at Nancite and Ostional by tunneling into a clutch and breaking open a few eggs. The crab's burrow could provide a pathway for insects to lay their eggs in the nest. In fact, flies (*Asyndetus* sp.) have been captured from crab burrows and beetles (*Trox* sp.) have been found in turtle nests. Larvae of both insects may feed on the contents of broken turtle eggs or destroy eggs directly, thus providing a proper media for the establishment and growth of fungi and bacteria on the egg mass. As the nest deteriorates from the activities of crabs, insect larvae, fungi, and bacteria, the odor of rotting eggs probably attracts mammalian predators, especially coatis. If this scenario is accurate, attempts to control populations of coatis, raccoons, and coyotes or protection of natural nests from mammalian predation will not be effective, as many of the predated nests are already in some stage of decomposition. Protection of individual nests from mammalian predation would increase the production of olive ridleys hatchlings at Nancite only after crab and microorganism populations are reduced.

Successful nests were associated spatially with the small estuaries at Nancite and Ostional. Sand in these areas was usually deposited at the end of the wet season, when the estuary mouth closed. Compared to the remainder of the nesting beach, the media of these nests presumably have a greatly reduced level of organic matter, lower microorganism populations, fewer crabs, and perhaps a sand particle size more suitable for proper egg incubation. There is an obvious trade-off to nesting in an uncontaminated section adjacent to an estuary. Most, or all, nests deposited here during any 2-month period between July and October were washed away with the opening of the estuary. Most turtle production from the area near the estuary consequently resulted from nests deposited between April and June and in November.

Sea turtle nests located near the HWST line are often doomed because of sea water infiltration, beach erosion, or both (Mrosovsky 1983a, 1983b). Obviously, if a nest is so poorly situated that it becomes totally submerged at frequent and regular intervals or if it is subject to storm tide erosion, it will be lost. However, many nests at Nancite, and to a lesser degree at Ostional, appear advantaged by a seaward site. Indeed, we conclude that the farther inland an olive ridley nest is located on an intensively used arribada beach, the less likely it is to hatch. The narrow band of successful nests along the low beach was obviously associated with the reach of the average high tide. Hatching success trailed off quickly below the berm and was virtually nonexistent above it (except in front of the estuary). If soil organisms are pathogenic to turtle eggs and if they are relatively intolerant to salt water intrusion of the nest media, then occasional tidal washing of sand above the nest would exclude these microorganisms from the low-beach/midbeach interface and permit proper embryonic development.

Spatial and temporal correlates of nest success at both Nancite and Ostional are complex, and analysis is confounded by the large proportion of nests that fail for reasons not related to erosion, predation, or nesting turtles. It seems unlikely that the population of olive ridleys nesting at Nancite can be maintained by local recruitment for many more years given the poor neonate production rate. The number of little turtles leaving Nancite each year is equivalent to the annual reproductive effort of no more than 8,000 females (assuming four major arribadas of 55,000 females each, two nests per female, and 6.7% hatching success). If 5% of these reach sexual maturity, then annual recruitment to the Nancite population would be fewer than 15,000 turtles of both sexes. Though the estimated rate is slightly better for Ostional, it too seems to be much below the minimum required to maintain the population at current levels. The long-term survivability of the arribada nesting strategy at a given site, in the absence of active management of nests, is questionable (Robinson 1983).

Management Options

Playa Nancite

Because olive ridleys have been depleted elsewhere in their east Pacific range, the large populations nesting at Nancite deserve active management. Data presented herein suggest that nest management at Nancite is feasible and could substantially increase the number of neonates produced at this beach, if that were determined to be desirable. In addition, nest and/or hatchling transplant operations using the excess eggs could help recuperate depleted rookeries elsewhere. It is neither logistically practical nor sociopolitically desirable to encourage the commercial exploitation of eggs at Nancite as we propose for Ostional.

The principal management activity at Nancite concerns nests located in the midbeach platform that are doomed to failure. Nests located in front of the estuary and along the high tide line should be left to incubate under natural conditions. Though it is clear that nest predation by mammals is restricted almost entirely to sections beneath woody vegetation, protecting nests located here would probably not be worthwhile without first reducing microorganism populations in the nest media. Attempts to significantly reduce or eliminate predation is not recommended, since Santa Rosa Park was established to protect the biodiversity of the area, not just to conserve sea turtles. Some species seasonally depend on sea turtle eggs for a substantial portion of their diet, and the predator-prey interactions at Nancite should not be upset by overprotection of turtle nests.

If turtles return to nest at their natal beaches, management to raise recruitment into the adult population brings with it the risk of exacerbating the current problem of too many nests being deposited in too small an area. Accordingly, nest density should be reduced by transplanting nests to corrals either on Nancite or to nearby Naranjo beach in the park and then transporting the hatchlings to other beaches in Costa Rica, or even to rookeries elsewhere in the region that are in need of restoration. A more complex option would be to transplant eggs, instead of neonates, directly to these sites from Nancite. Investigations of the genetic variability of olive ridleys in the east Pacific would be a prerequisite to this activity. The plan would have the additional advantage of possibly improving the success rate of nests remaining in situ and, perhaps in the long-term, reducing the Nancite population to a level that is stable and appropriate for the available space.

Ostional

Our data support the need for experimental management of olive ridley nests at Ostional. An immediate objective should be to motivate local interest in conserving the resource by providing the necessary scientific criteria for a sustained cash and subsistence-based use. Equally important should be the exploitation of the resource for direct conservation purposes, either to manipulate an increase in hatchling production, theoretically raising recruitment to the Ostional nesting population, and/or to exploit the excess eggs to restore other populations.

The management guidelines to achieve the objective of sustained use have three basic considerations: legal, biological-ecological, and socioeconomic. Strict and close coordination among them is necessary if the guidelines are to be successful. Furthermore, it is essential to base the guidelines on solid scientific information and to have the flexibility to respond rapidly to changing socioeconomic realities and additional demographic and ecological knowledge.

Legal authority to manage Ostional for sustained use of eggs was partially provided in 1984, when the beach was declared a National Wildlife Refuge under the jurisdiction of the Wildlife Directorate. In 1987, the Agricultural Production Law reformed the statute that universally prohibited egg use, permitting commercialization of olive ridley eggs only at Ostional and only after the community had formed an economic development association. A research-based management plan justifying and regulating such use was required.

The new law stipulates that net revenues from the sale of eggs be distributed between the community (80%) and the Ministry of Agriculture (20%). Expenses relating to egg removal and distribution would be subtracted before the revenues are divided. The unique legal right to harvest eggs is vested in members of the Ostional Association, who must use their portion for community development activities. An anomaly of the statute requires the government portion to be managed by the Aquaculture and Fisheries Department, a different entity than the one with management responsibility for the refuge. There is, therefore, no guarantee that government revenues will be available to meet management and research needs at Ostional. A priority for the future should be to identify clearly the management authority for Ostional, require it to enforce harvest guidelines, and guarantee the investment of funds in refuge research and management activities. These activities should include construction of facilities, hiring of biologists and guards, and implementation of reasonable conservation/management projects aimed at maintaining or improving the hatchling production rate. Without this requirement, an important conservation argument for permitting the commercial use of the resource is seriously weakened.

Available data allow us to establish the time and location of eggs for harvest, transplant, or manipulation in situ to improve hatching and recruitment rates. The basic objective should be to use nests that have a low expectation of success, either because they will be destroyed by later nesting turtles or beach erosion or because there is a high probability that embryonic development will be impaired due to physical and biological characteristics of the nest site.

Our data suggest that egg extraction from May through December should be restricted to the first 24 hours after an arribada commences (defined by the presence of more than 200 turtles on the beach), with no defined quota of nests permitted. Eventually it may be possible to identify more precisely when harvesting is most appropriate during a given arribada. It should also be possible to determine if certain arribadas during the season could be harvested more heavily than others.

Hatching success is probably not constant throughout the season because of variation in egg viability (Chaves 1986), fluctuations in levels of microorganism populations (Mo, pers. comm., 1986), and changes in the physical characteristics of the nest media (Ackerman 1980). For example, Ostional residents claim that hatching success declines drastically in December with near-zero production of neonates during the dry season. Our data support this. If it can be clearly substantiated that the nest media are too hot and dessicated for successful embryo development between January and May, then higher egg use could be encouraged during this season. Innovative manipulations such as occasional moistening of portions of the beach, artificial shading, or both might also improve hatchling production during this period.

Nest taking could be restricted to areas of the beach in which hatching appears to have the least chance of success, particularly the midbeach platform away from the estuary. This, and similar spacially based harvest rules, however, would be considerably more difficult to enforce than temporally based guidelines. Their implementation should only occur in the future after surrounding communities have accepted the Ostional community's unique right to the resource.

Both commercial and subsistence use should be restricted to nests of olive ridley turtles. The occasional nests of Pacific greens (*Chelonia mydas agassizi*) and leatherbacks (*Dermochelys coriacea*) are easily distinguished from olive ridleys by a larger area of disturbed beach. Their eggs should not be collected or manipulated. Additionally, all harvesting should be confined to the principal nesting beach (880 m), since solitary nests of olive ridleys appear to have a high chance of success if not dug up by humans (Cornelius 1976; Acuña 1983; Castro 1986).

From the socioeconomic viewpoint, the few data available suggest that there is little danger to the nesting population inherent in permitting egg harvests at current levels. Uncontrolled exploitation of large arribadas in the past has probably removed less than 15% of the total nests (Cornelius and Robinson 1982). During peak season arribadas, the number of egg collectors never approaches the number of turtles on the beach. Supply is simply much greater than the capacity to harvest. Certain harvesting traditions appear to guarantee adherence to the biologically based guidelines. For example, residents usually collect nests during the first and final night of major arribadas, when turtle densities are low. During the intervening nights the number of local egg collectors declines because it is too uncomfortable to collect eggs when sixty or more turtles occupy each 100 m^2 of beach. The importance of the arribada as a social event diminishes after the first night, further reducing the number of people collecting eggs. It is possible that a higher percentage of nests are collected during smaller off season arribadas but, as mentioned earlier, few if any of these nests appear to hatch anyway.

Poaching of nests of all species at other beaches in Costa Rica could be reduced if the price of Ostional eggs were kept below contraband eggs and if they were available wherever illegal eggs are normally sold. Therefore, we strongly urge a wide distribution of Ostional eggs, clearly identified as originating from this beach, throughout Costa Rica, targeted at locales where there is an existing demand. No foreign export of the eggs should be permitted. Whether a low price can be best maintained by the community assuming responsibility for distribution, instead of relying on intermediaries and traditional networks, must be carefully analyzed.

This preliminary management policy addresses the following realities: (1) enforcement capabilities are currently inadequate; (2) spatially based harvest regulations would be difficult to implement under present conditions; (3) temporally based guidelines are easily regulated and have the advantage of being socially acceptable, since they are compatible to the traditional harvest schedule. These recommendations, and any subsequent ones, should be subject to regular and critical revaluation by the refuge administration and their scientific advisors. With expanded financial and personnel resources (which hopefully will be provided for by the government's share of the egg sale proceeds and outside funding), additional research on the spatial and temporal aspects of mass nesting productivity can be conducted. In addition, a consistent methodology to monitor the status of the adult nesting population can be established and management techniques can be developed. Results of this research will surely modify the pragmatic approach of the initial management plan and provide it with a more technical base.

Acknowledgments

This study would not have been possible without the kind assistance of many people not directly concerned with the project. Specifically, we thank F. Cortéz, Head of Research, National Park Service, and E. López, Director of the Wildlife Department, for providing permits to work at Nancite and Ostional, respectively; Santa Rosa Park Administrators F. Chávez, S. Marín, and F. Picado for logistical assistance at Nancite; and F. Valverde and V. Varela for preparing the drawings. The University of Costa Rica was instrumental in providing logistical support for work at Ostional. We also thank the community of Ostional for their cooperation and understanding of the study's importance. Early drafts of the manuscript benefited from critical comments by D. Duffy, J. Frazier, and N. Mrosovsky. This study was financed by the Office of Endangered Species, U.S. Fish and Wildlife Service, from 1980 through 1984 and by the World Wildlife Fund–U.S. in 1982 and 1984. To these organizations and specifically to J. Woody (USFWS), D. Bowman (USFWS), C. Freese (WWF-US), and N. Hammond (WWF-US) we express our sincere appreciation for their active support.

9

Economic Analysis of Sea Turtle Eggs in a Coastal Community on the Pacific Coast of Honduras

CYNTHIA J. LAGUEUX

Throughout history, turtle eggs have been collected by coastal residents of the tropical and subtropical regions of the world. Turtle eggs are regarded as aphrodisiacs and prized for their medicinal value. They supply a source of protein for people and domestic animals, primarily pigs (Cornelius and Robinson 1982) and also provide a means to purchase other goods through the generation of income. Although turtle eggs are not part of the international market, on a local or regional level, their benefits may be significant.

Nesting of the olive ridley (*Lepidochelys olivacea*) sea turtle on the Pacific coast of Honduras was first documented in 1947 (Carr 1948). For over 40 years the eggs of this species have been providing economic, social, and cultural benefits to this area. To date none of these benefits have been described or quantified. The importance of identifying the current market value of wildlife resources and the direct and indirect employment related to these resources is vital for their conservation and rational use. This importance was emphasized by Woody (1986) in an analysis of Mexico's legal harvest program of adult olive ridley turtles and the clandestine egg trade.

To identify the economic importance of sea turtle eggs to local residents, I conducted preliminary work on the Pacific coast of Honduras in 1982, 1983, and 1984 (Minarik [Lagueux] 1985). I followed this with an in-depth study in 1987. This chapter will explore the economic importance of olive ridley sea turtle eggs to local residents, the impact of harvesting on the resource, and the sustainability of the current levels of exploitation on the Pacific coast of Honduras. This analysis is part of a larger work in progress.

I calculated the amount of income generated through the sale of eggs and the cost of living per household in the community of Punta Ratón and determined economic importance by the percent of egg income generated in relation to cost of living. The impact of harvesting on the resource will be treated from a historical perspective and discussed in terms of current knowledge on sea turtle biology.

136

Study Area

The study area is located on the Pacific coast of Honduras within the Gulf of Fonseca, Central America (fig. 9.1). The southwest end of the Gulf opens up to the Pacific ocean. The north, northeast, and east coastlines of the Gulf are Honduran territory. The west and southern coastlines border El Salvador and Nicaragua, respectively. The majority of the coastline and islands within the Gulf of Fonseca are within Honduran territory, although the jurisdiction of one island, Isla Meanguera, still is in dispute with El Salvador. The Honduran coastline is composed of relatively long stretches of sand beach and mangrove swamps dissected by estuaries. Mean vertical tide range is 2.4 m (U.S. Department of Commerce 1986). The Gulf is dominated by the presence of Isla del Tigre, an inactive volcanic island.

Detailed economic data on egg sales were collected in the community of Punta Ratón. Punta Ratón lies on the eastern coastline of the Gulf of Fonseca, approximately 30 km north of the Nicaraguan border in Honduras. The sand beach at Punta Ratón extends for 6 km. An additional 2.7 km of sand beach

Figure 9.1. Map of the Gulf of Fonseca and the community of Punta Ratón.

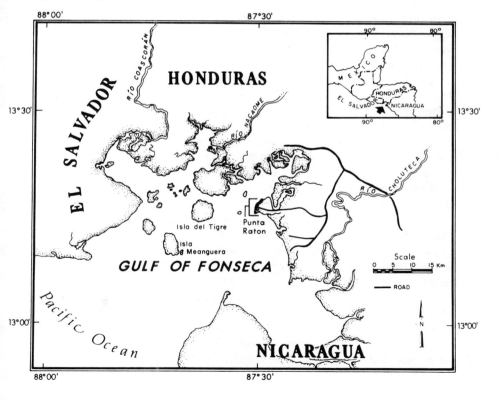

extends into the Gulf from the point but is exposed only at ebb tide. The north extent of the beach at Punta Ratón is dissected by the estuary Los Barrancones and the south end by another estuary, referred to locally as Vuelta de los Viejos. Most of the nesting activity occurs along a 1-km stretch of beach on the north side of the point and also on the 2.7-km extension of shoal when it is not inundated.

Punta Ratón is a community of ninety-three households. Most of the houses are located on either side of a dirt road that runs perpendicular to the waterline (1.5 km south of estuary Los Barrancones) and within 0.5 km, on the north side, of the point. The point is located approximately 3 km south of the road.

Methods

Intensive field work was conducted from July through December 1987. At the start of the field season, I interviewed at least one member of each household at Punta Ratón to determine the number of egg clutches collected per household and corresponding egg prices before I arrived at the study area. These preliminary interviews also enabled me to reestablish rapport with the community. By my definition a household is comprised of only permanent residents in the home. I did not include individuals present only during the nesting season who consider themselves residents of another community. Demographic data describing the composition of the households were collected by surveying a random sample of the households at the end of the nesting season.

Aided by a student assistant, Ramón Zuniga, or local residents I obtained data on the collection of eggs during nightly beach surveys throughout the study at Punta Ratón (fig. 9.2). I interviewed egg collectors at the time of egg collection or as soon as possible thereafter and recorded the following data: date, time and location of oviposition, number of eggs deposited, name of egg collector, name of egg buyer, and the price at which the buyer purchased the eggs from the collector. If an egg collector did not know the current price of eggs or did not know to whom he would sell the eggs, I used prices reported from the same night or prices reported from nights bracketing the night in question.

Five households in Punta Ratón were selected for an in-depth study of the cost of living. I defined cost of living as the monetary amount expended per household per day to meet subsistence needs without assessing the quality of that subsistence. These five households were selected based on the criteria that at least one member within the household participated in egg collection and on the willingness of the members within the household to be interviewed. Households that were selected varied in the number of household members and ages of the children. Not all of the households included an adult male. Each household was surveyed every 10 days throughout the 5-month study. A 10-day interval avoided biases that occur between days of the week. The total number of

Figure 9.2. Author interviewing an egg collector at Punta Ratón.

interviews conducted for each household varied: thirteen interviews for two households, twelve interviews for another two households, and eleven interviews for the fifth household. The following data were recorded at each interview: (1) the quantity of each item purchased on that day (midnight to midnight) and, for food items the number of meals supplied by this quantity, (2) the cost of the item, (3) the income or food generating activities pursued and which family members that participated in the activity, (4) the amount of time involved in the activity (not always available), (5) the gross and net income generated, (6) the debts incurred, and (7) any gifts given or received in meeting social obligations for the same period. Interviews occurred as late as possible during the day of the scheduled interview, or as soon as possible the following day. The purchased items were categorized as prepared and unprepared food, medicine, clothes, and miscellaneous.

Recorded interviews were conducted with key informants, including the original residents of Punta Ratón. Qualitative information on the levels of exploitation over the years is used to develop a historical perspective from this information.

Results

The study period comprised 147 nights. Nesting data were collected on 96% of these nights. A total of 742 recorded egg clutches were laid at Punta Ratón from May through 8 December 1987 (fig. 9.3). Of this total, 91 (12.3%) of the clutches were collected, transported, and reburied in a protected area. The majority of these clutches (n = 89) were collected during the Honduran government project (G. Cruz, pers. comm. 1987). The remaining 651 egg clutches, which averaged 98 eggs per nest for a total of 63,798 eggs, were collected and sold from Punta Ratón for the 1987 season.

Turtle eggs are sold by the *mano* (hand), which is equivalent to six eggs. Egg prices almost quadruple from the season low of $0.08 per egg (early September) to season highs of $0.31 per egg at the onset (May) and close (December) of the nesting season (fig. 9.4.). As in classic supply and demand economics, the price per egg is lowest (early September) when the largest number of eggs is available in the market.

Egg collectors earned at least $10,000 through the sale of turtle eggs from the beach at Punta Ratón. Throughout the study period, I identified at least 224 egg collectors at Punta Ratón. Of these, 34 (15.2%) were identified as nonresidents of the Punta Ratón community. They represented seven other communities. Egg collectors from La Colonia represent 41% (n = 14) of the non-Punta Ratón residents. La Colonia is a community located 10 km inland from Punta Ratón. Non-Punta Ratón residents earned $2,320.53 from turtle eggs collected at Punta Ratón.

The community of Punta Ratón was comprised of ninety-three households,

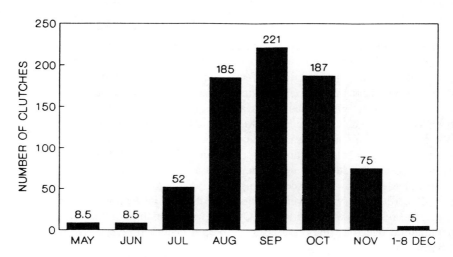

Figure 9.3. Number of clutches laid by *Lepidochelys olivacea* at Punta Ratón in 1987.

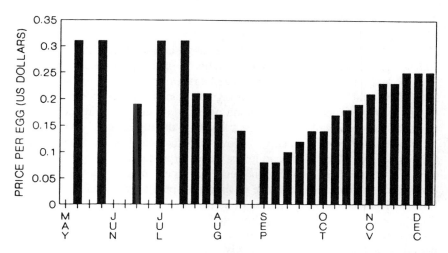

Figure 9.4. Olive ridley (*Lepidochelys olivacea*) sea turtle egg prices at Punta Ratón throughout the 1987 nesting season.

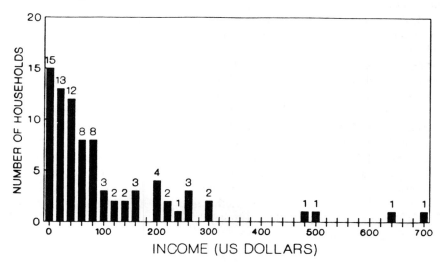

Figure 9.5. Egg collector income through the sale of olive ridley (*Lepidochelys olivacea*) eggs from Punta Ratón in 1987.

of which 88.2% (n = 82) of the households had at least one member of the household participating in turtle egg collection. Of these eighty-two households, 81.7% (n = 67) earned income from turtle eggs. The total earned was $7,680.30 (76.8% of total). The amount of income earned by different households is illustrated in 20-dollar increments in figure 9.5. Fifteen households (18.3%) had members who searched for turtle eggs but derived no income from this resource during the 1987 study period. The total amount of income earned by the residents of Punta Ratón through the sale of turtle eggs ranged from $3.75 to $684.56 per household. The median is $40.70 and the average is $93.66 earned per household. A large majority of the households (80%) earn $160 or less per year from selling turtle eggs. Four of the households earned 23% of the total income generated through the sale of turtle eggs.

The average expenditure per person per day in Punta Ratón was calculated from the five household case studies. Items in the unprepared food category were purchased most frequently, followed by medicinal items. The majority (82.5%) of the unprepared food items were not produced in Punta Ratón. On the average, people in Punta Ratón spend $1 per person per day to meet subsistence needs. As there is an average of six people per household in Punta Ratón, this equals a total cash expenditure of $6 per household per day. If the assumption that expenditures from July through November are similar from December through June, then expenditures for a household of six is $2,190 for a 1-year period. If net income is approximately equal to net expenditure, then income from sea turtle eggs accounts for 4.3% of the yearly expenditure for the average household.

Qualitative historical information on the nesting abundance of the olive ridley sea turtle in this region is, fortunately, still available from informants. Interviewees relate stories of 200 to 300 turtles nesting along the full length of beach at Punta Ratón in one night. During this period, *cayuco* (dugout canoes) loads of turtle eggs were transported to El Salvador. Carr (1948) reports that during his study nearly 100% of the olive ridley eggs laid were collected by Salvadorans and transported to El Salvador. At this time there was not a market for sea turtle eggs in Honduras. According to informants this extensive removal of eggs had been going on at least 20 years before Carr's visit in the 1940s (Carr, pers. comm. 1985). During the 1960s, Pritchard (1979:709) reports from the same location that every night there were more egg collectors than turtles on the beach. Surveys of all potential nesting beaches in the Gulf of Fonseca conducted every 2 weeks in 1987 verifies that nearly 100% of the turtle eggs laid are still being collected and have been collected for some time, primarily for the Honduran market.

Discussion

For the past 40 years nearly 100% of the olive ridley eggs laid on the Pacific coast of Honduras have been collected and sold in El Salvador or Honduras. It is apparent that the turtle population cannot withstand this level of exploitation without experiencing detrimental effects. In fact, it is rather perplexing why olive ridley nesting still occurs on these beaches.

Although the olive ridley is considered to be one of the most abundant sea turtles in the world (Carr 1952; Cornelius and Robinson 1981), its reproductive stages are the least understood of the eight species of sea turtles (Cornelius 1976; Nietschmann 1975). Studies of the green turtle (*Chelonia mydas*) indicate that, once mature, sea turtles probably return to their natal beach to nest and never nest anywhere else (Carr, Carr and Meylan 1978). If this is true for the olive ridley, the nesting population in the Gulf of Fonseca has been on a steady decline; probably since the 1920s and certainly since the 1940s. If there has been little to no recruitment into the population during this period, which to date has been the case, then the forecast for the olive ridley population nesting in the Gulf of Fonseca is pessimistic.

The majority of egg collection is carried out by residents of the local community. Widespread demand for turtle eggs is apparent from the large number of individuals that participate in this activity. Although the majority of households earn at least some income through this activity, only a very few earn a substantial amount of their yearly expenditure by selling turtle eggs. For these few households it is evident that sea turtle eggs provide a vehicle to obtain money by which other goods can then be purchased. The purchase price of eggs varies throughout the season. The highest prices per egg being received at the beginning and end of the reproductive season.

It is imperative to protect a substantial number of clutches against exploitation and to allow eggs to incubate and hatch in situ to provide for future generations. If this is not done, nesting activity will continue to decline, and the remaining reproductive effort will be divided among an ever increasing human coastal population. Unless an improved conservation effort is made, which assures recruitment into the turtle population, both the olive ridley sea turtle in the Gulf of Fonseca and the economic benefit that human populations derive from collecting eggs will be known as a historical occurrence.

Acknowledgments

First and foremost, I would like to extend to the people of Punta Ratón my deepest gratitude for their trust, honesty, and patience in answering my many queries. Also, I would like to thank the many individuals throughout the Gulf of Fonseca, in the market places of Choluteca, San Lorenzo, Jícaro Galán, Nacaome, Tegucigalpa, and Comayagüela, without whose information this study would not have been possible. A special thanks to Hernan for his unfailing dependability. Doña Angelita kept me content with her comida tipica and cerveza fría. L. Gomez provided accommodations at Punta Ratón. S. "Pilar" Thorn, B. Myton, and Amparo opened up their homes to me. The following people have offered invaluable advice since inception of the study: K. Redford, J. Mortimer, J. Robinson, and M. Schmink. I am grateful to J. Mortimer and L. Campos for their editorial guidance. The ARTP study group led me through an understanding of the other side. I would like to thank the Honduran Department of Renewable Natural Resources and Peace Corps/Honduras for their assistance. Financial support was provided by World Wildlife Fund project No. 6245, U.S. Fish and Wildlife Service, and the Vining Davis Grant from the University of Florida. This is contribution No. 35 from The Program for Studies in Tropical Conservation.

10

Effects of Hunting on the Reproduction of the Paraguayan Caiman (*Caiman yacare*) in the Pantanal of Mato Grosso, Brazil

PETER G. CRAWSHAW, JR.

With the worldwide decline of many crocodilian species with commercial value, the (legal and illegal) international trade of crocodilian hides and products has focused increasingly on the more abundant but less valuable *Caiman crocodilus* and *C. yacare* (Medem 1983; Magnusson 1984; Brazaitis, pers. comm., 1986; Brazaitis and King 1984; King 1986). This situation has led countries such as Venezuela (Blohm 1973; Rivero Blanco 1985) and Brazil (Crawshaw and Schaller 1980; Brazaitis 1986a) to develop management plans that incorporate ranching and farming of the species, following the examples of many other countries throughout the world (Brazaitis 1986b; Luxmoore et al. 1985).

Hides of the Paraguayan caiman (*C. yacare*) (fig. 10.1) make up three-quarters of the caiman skin market (*Caiman* spp., *Melanosuchus*). The majority of these animals are taken illegally from Brazil (Brazaitis, pers. comm., 1986) and exported from Paraguay and Bolivia (King, pers. comm., 1986). As a result, the Brazilian Institute for Forest Development (IBDF, now IBAMA) has been pressured, regionally and internationally, to implement harvest management schemes of caimans in the Pantanal of Mato Grosso, where the highest populations occur in Brazil.

From 1978 through 1983, I collected data on the reproductive biology of *C. yacare* in two areas of the Pantanal (Crawshaw 1987). The study encompassed three nesting seasons (1979–81) in Poconé, in northern Pantanal, and another three (1981–83) in Miranda, in the south. Although the areas are about 400 km apart, environmental factors were similar in both. The main difference between them was that Poconé caimans had been intensively hunted until 1974, while no hunting had occurred in Miranda.

This difference in the recent history of hunting pressure on caiman populations between the two areas allowed me to gain insights into breeding strategies used by populations under different hunting regimes. This paper focuses on the

Figure 10.1. Paraguayan caiman (*Caiman yacare*) in the Pantanal. (Photo, K. H. Redford.)

effects of hunting on the nest-guarding behavior of females from the two areas and the relation of nest guarding to individual reproductive success in the two populations. Assuming that females guarding nests on land were more vulnerable to hunters, did female nest attendance differ between the two areas? If so, how did this difference affect nesting and, ultimately, reproductive success between the two populations? And lastly, how can the findings of this study be incorporated into the management of the species in the Pantanal?

Study Areas

The Pantanal of Mato Grosso is located in the states of Mato Grosso and Mato Grosso do Sul in southwest Brazil. It covers an area of approximately 140,000 km² of the upper basin of the Paraguay river, roughly between 16° and 22° latitude south and 55° and 58° longitude west (IBGE 1977). The terrain is flat to undulating (rarely exceeding 100 m above mean sea level) and contains extensive savannas dotted with palm trees, open woodlands, riparian forests, and islands of semideciduous forest of various sizes. There are many slow flowing streams and shallow ponds clogged with water hyacinth (*Eichhornia*).

The climate is seasonal, being hot and humid for most of the year, with temperatures climbing over 40°C. From June through August, however, cold winds from the south can lower temperatures to 0°C. Most of the average annual precipitation of 1,200 mm in the Pantanal falls between the months of December and February. This concentration of the rains causes an annual flooding season from early January through March, when the Paraguay river and its tributaries overflow and cover large tracks of land. In May, the waters start to recede, and by October or November only scattered ponds remain.

Poconé

The town of Poconé lies at the extreme north of the Pantanal, 100 km south of the city of Cuiabá, the capital of Mato Grosso state. Nesting ecology was studied along the Bento Gomes river (16°15′ S, 56°30′W). The Bento Gomes is a small river, no more than 30 m wide, bordered by a mosaic of gallery forests, thickets, pastures, and cerrado (Crawshaw and Schaller 1980).

Miranda

Miranda is a small town at the southern border of the Pantanal, about 200 km west of Campo Grande, the capital of Mato Grosso do Sul state. Studies were conducted from July 1980 through February 1983 in the Miranda Estancia ranch (19°57′ S, 56°25′ W), which is located 5 km north of Miranda. Observations on caiman nesting ecology were made in the surrounding areas of the Corcunda Lake at one of the ranch's outposts, where the research base was established. The lake is long (4.5 km) and narrow (50 to 200 m), and it marks the transition from the high ground to low-lying areas subject to annual flooding. It is bordered on its east side by a continuous block of semideciduous forest and by savannas, thickets, and gallery forest on the west side.

Methods

During the nesting season, I searched for caiman nests along the banks of the Bento Gomes river (in Poconé) and Corcunda Lake (in Miranda) and surrounding areas. In addition, I paid local people to report the location of other nests. During the first visit to a nest, I gathered information on presence and behavior of the female, type of habitat, material used in nest construction, distance from water (permanent or flood water), dimensions of the nest and egg chamber, number and measurements of the eggs, temperature within the egg chamber and at the surface of the nest, and other pertinent data. When revisiting nests, I noted presence and behavior of the female, status of the nest (intact, depredated, flooded), and temperature outside and within the egg chamber for most nests. The frequency of my visits depended on the ease of access and proximity to hatching.

Nesting success was expressed as the proportion of nests in which at least some eggs hatched. Hatching success was calculated as the proportion of eggs that hatched in successful nests. The probability of hatching was defined as the product of nesting and hatching success (Hall and Johnson 1987).

The fate of some nests had to be assessed after the nesting season had ended. In these instances, a nest was judged to have been successful, depredated, or flooded by its general appearance.

Results

Between 1979 and 1983, 160 *C. yacare* nests were found, 92 in Poconé and 68 in Miranda. Of these, 5 had been totally depredated when found, and 6 had no eggs. The remaining 149 active nests (with eggs) provided information on nest, egg, embryos, and clutch size, ecological requirements, predation and survival rates for the two areas (Crawshaw 1987). Certain aspects of the analysis rely more heavily on data from the 1979 and 1980 nesting seasons in Poconé, which were studied more intensively.

The reproductive season started with courtship in late August, in the early dry season, and ended in mid-April, toward the end of the wet season. Male contribution to reproduction terminated with copulation. Females selected secluded, shaded sites, and built mound nests in which they deposited an average of thirty eggs. The incubation period, as estimated from embryo growth (Crawshaw 1987), was about 65 days, during which the 24-cm embryos grew at a rate of approximately 0.37 cm/day.

Nest Attendance and Female Behavior Toward Potential Predators

There was a significant difference in female nest attendance between the two areas ($z = 16.6$, $p < 0.0001$, $n = 834$; binomial test of proportions using normal approximation; Ott 1984). In Poconé, which was hunted until 1974, females were present on 54 out of 437 (12.3%) visits to 82 active nests. By contrast, females were present on 237 of 397 (60%) visits to 49 nests in Miranda, which had not been hunted. Seven females out of twenty (35.0%) present on the first visit to nests in Poconé fled at my arrival. In Miranda, eight of forty-seven (17.0%) fled. The behavior of those that remained at the nest was classified as aggressive (38.5% in Poconé; 69.2% in Miranda) or passive (65.5% in Poconé; 30.8% in Miranda). Female aggressiveness included behaviors such as the female positioning herself between the nest and intruder, laying over the nest, hissing, or lunging toward the intruder. In one instance, an attacking female in Miranda had to be diverted with a pole at less than 1 m from the observer, which suggests that attacks may not always be "ritualized bluffs" (Neill 1971). Aggressive females attended the nests more consistently (present on 79% of 269 visits to thirty-one nests, both areas pooled), whereas passive females tended to abandon the nest after my first or second visit (34% of 88 visits to twenty nests). However, most females in Poconé (including those never seen during daytime visits) made nightly visits. This was evident from the tracks on and around the nests.

Some females decreased nest attendance after being disturbed by humans, while others completely abandoned the nest during daytime hours. For instance, there was a decrease from 21% to 6.4% in female presence from the first to the third visit to nests in 1979 (table 10.1) Therefore, predation rates may have been affected somewhat in that even the passive presence of a female

TABLE 10.1
Percentage of Females Present at Nests in the First Three Visits to
Caiman yacare Nests (*N* = 134) in the Pantanal

| Area and Year | N | Visits | | | % Change |
		1st	2d	3d	
Poconé					
1979	43	21.0	8.1	6.4	−69.5
1980	18	28.0	23.5	11.7	−58.2
1981[a]	18	28.0	—	—	—
Miranda					
1981	11	91.0	91.0	62.5	−31.3
1982	28	60.7	60.7	69.2	+14.0
1983	16	56.2	33.0	42.8	−23.8

[a]Nests were visited only twice, once in midseason and once at the end of the season.

at the nest may decrease chances of predation (Deitz and Hines 1980). This was not always the case: six nests in Miranda at which the females had been passively present during my visits were partially preyed upon. Given the difference in behavior displayed by individual females toward humans, I surmised that aggressive females were more likely to drive away natural predators.

Nest fates in Poconé and Miranda are depicted in figures 10.2 and 10.3. Figure 10.4 provides a comparison of nest fates between areas and the results for the two areas combined.

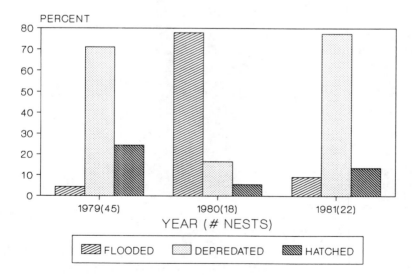

Figure 10.2. Fate of caiman nests in Poconé, 1979–81.

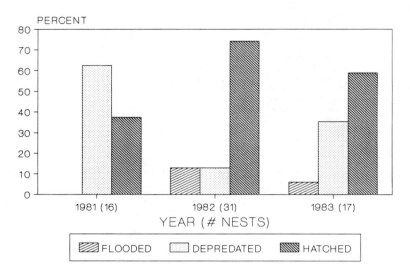

Figure 10.3. Fate of caiman nests in Miranda, 1981–83.

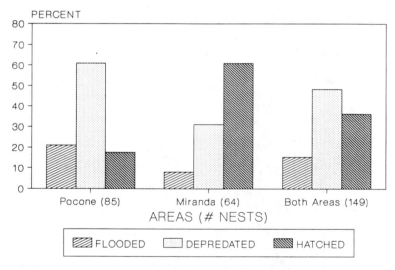

Figure 10.4. Caiman nest fates in Pocone and Miranda, 1979–83, and combined for the two areas.

Nesting and Hatching Success

Overall, nesting success (nests in which at least some eggs hatched) was three times greater ($z = 5.9$, $p < 0.001$) in Miranda than in Poconé (table 10.2). Accordingly, the probability of hatching (nesting success × hatching success) was also three times higher in Miranda, since there was no significant difference between hatching success rates between the two areas ($z = 2$, $p > 0.05$).

Sixty-five nests of known fate, at which the female was present during the first observer visit (twenty-one in Poconé, forty-four in Miranda) were used to test whether female behavior affected nest fate. There was a positive relationship between the behavior of females toward observers (aggressive or passive)

TABLE 10.2
**Reproductive Success of *Caiman yacare* in Poconé
and Miranda, Pantanal**

Area and Year	N	A	B	A × B	C
Poconé					
1979	45	0.24	0.80	0.19	5.7
1980	18	0.06	0.73	0.04	1.2
1981	<u>22</u>	0.14	0.90	0.13	3.9
1979–81	85	0.18	0.82	0.15	4.5
Miranda					
1981	16	0.38	0.79	0.30	9.0
1982	31	0.74	0.82	0.61	18.3
1983	<u>17</u>	0.59	0.65	0.38	11.4
1981–83	64	0.61	0.76	0.76	13.8
Both Areas	149	0.36	0.79	0.28	8.4

Note: A = nesting success; B = hatching success; A × B = probability of hatching; C = recruitment [$n \times 30 \times (A \times B) \div n$].

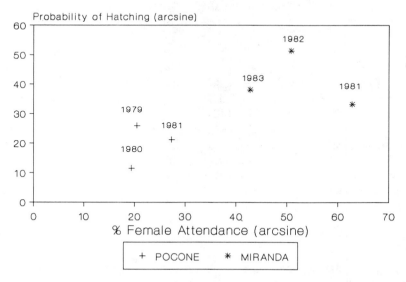

Figure 10.5. Probability of hatching as related to female attendance during the study period in the two areas (both measures were arcsine transformed).

and the fate of the nest (failure or success) ($\chi^2 = 7.91$, d.f. $= 2$, $p < 0.05$, Pearson's coefficient of contingency $= 0.327$). Although the two-by-two tests for the preceding value were not statistically significant, the individual associations that contributed most to the positive relationship were female aggressiveness and hatching success ($\chi^2 = 2.05$, $p > 0.05$), and female aggressiveness and lack of predation ($\chi^2 = 1.94$, $p > 0.05$). Given this trend, one could expect the contingency relationships to attain greater value as the sample size increased. The same seems to be true for the relationship between female attendance and probability of hatching by season and by area (fig. 10.5), which approached significance ($r^2 = 0.54$, $p = 0.096$, d.f. $= 5$).

Female behavior had no significant effect on nest fate between the two areas ($\chi^2 = 8.56$, d.f. $= 5$, $p > 0.1$; $n = 65$).

Nest Failure

Natural predation was the most important factor affecting egg survivorship in the two areas (figs. 10.2, 10.3, 10.4), with the exception of the 1980 season in Poconé, for which flooding induced the greatest loss. In 1979, only ten out of forty-four nests (22.7%) in Poconé escaped predation. Six nests (7%) in Poconé and five nests (7%) in Miranda were already totally destroyed when found; another two (2.3%) were partially depredated in Poconé and eight (11.4%) in Miranda. Recurrent predation on individual nests was apparent, as I recorded sixty-five instances of predation on fifty-three nests in Poconé and forty-two on twenty-seven nests in Miranda. Eight nests in Poconé and four in Miranda were rebuilt by the females after partial predation, and some eggs from three nests in Poconé and from nine nests in Miranda hatched after partial predation.

Recruitment

Assuming no embryo mortality during incubation, each nesting C. yacare female would produce a mean of thirty young per nesting season. However, using the results shown in table 10.2, the actual mean production (number of nests × mean number of eggs per nest [= 30] × probability of hatching/ number of nesting females [= number of nests]) ranged from as low as 1.2 young per nesting female in Poconé 1980 to 18.3 young/female in Miranda 1982. Mean production (all years combined) in Poconé was 4.5 young/nesting female/year and 13.8 in Miranda. The combined average for the two areas was 8.4 young/female/year.

Discussion

In crocodilians, most parental care is restricted to females, although in some species, males can also help in some aspects of caring for the eggs and young (Alvarez del Toro 1969; Garrick and Lang 1977; Lang et al. 1986). Generally, it is the female that selects a secluded site, constructs the nest, protects it against predators, frees the young at hatching time, carries the hatchlings to water, and remains with them for at least several months (Deitz 1979; Lang, Whitaker, and Andrews 1986).

In this study, there was a marked difference in the frequency of female *C. yacare* nest attendance between the two areas (fig. 10.5). Given the fact that Poconé females had been exposed to intense hunting until recently, it is likely that they had learned to avoid humans by decreasing time guarding the nest and away from the safety of water. The observed difference in the proportion of nest attendance between areas would thus be a response of the females to such a selective pressure. No difference was found in the type and intensity of behaviors displayed by aggressive females in both areas. This evidence suggests that aggressive females in Poconé may have had little or no previous contact with hunters.

The fact that Poconé females were more prone to decrease or interrupt nest attendance after being disturbed (table 10.1) had a marked effect on egg survivorship. Although hatching success was similar in the two areas, the probability of hatching in Miranda, once mortality factors were accounted for, was three times higher than at Poconé (table 10.2, fig. 10.5). The number of hatchlings per nesting female ranged from 1.2 in the Poconé 1980 season to 18.3 in Miranda 1982 (table 10.2).

Data on the nesting of *Caiman yacare* in the Pantanal suggest an intricate relationship among ecological and environmental variables that play important roles in caiman reproduction. Hunting and predation pressure, the distance of the nest from standing water, and vegetation cover, are interrelated factors that can affect the degree of parental care of females. They reduce nest attendance and thereby influence reproductive success by allowing increased nest predation (Crawshaw 1987). These results indicate that to successfully manage caiman populations for commercial harvesting, two models of exploitation must be considered. On a more intensive farming model, eggs can be collected from nests in the wild early in the nesting season and incubated in artificial hatcheries. Heavy losses from natural predation would be avoided. Hatchlings could then be reared in captive conditions to an age of commercial size. On the other hand, for a more extensive ranching model, disturbance of females at the nest should be kept to a minimum to allow adequate nest protection against predators. Alternatively, additional protection to the eggs, such as wire mesh cages over the nest, could prove useful against natural predation. The potential increase in survival of animals to a commercial size class would then allow the harvest of a fraction of the population. Further research for a cost/benefit analysis of these methods in different areas of the Pantanal will provide a basis for rational exploitation of the species in Brazil.

11

The Effect of Hunting on Tapirs in Belize

José Manuel V. Fragoso

Tapirs (family Tapiridae) are becoming increasingly rare throughout their range in the forests of southeast Asia and neotropical South and Central America (IUCN. 1982). All four species (*Tapirus bairdii, T. terrestris, T. pinchaque,* and *T. indicus*) are considered endangered by the International Union for the Conservation of Nature and Natural Resources (IUCN 1982). Baird's tapir (*T. bairdii*) (fig. 11.1) has been extirpated in El Salvador and is extremely rare in Mexico and throughout its remaining range (IUCN 1982). Habitat destruction and overhunting are generally blamed for declining populations (Leopold 1959; Terwilliger 1978; Williams and Petrides 1980; IUCN 1982; Janzen 1983a), but

Figure 11.1. Baird's tapir (*Tapirus bairdii*) in Belize. (Photo, José Fragoso.)

the exact influence of different human activities is unknown. This study examined the impact of hunting on tapir (*T. bairdii*) populations and describes tapir habitats in Belize, Central America.

In 1977 approximately 80% of Belize's land area was covered by wild vegetation (Frost 1977). Seventy-four percent of Belize is still covered by closed broadleaf forest (Hartshorn et al. 1984). With 150,000 people, Belize has one of the lowest population densities in the world (Hartshorn et al. 1984).

During a preliminary study in 1982, few signs of tapirs were encountered in areas distant from bodies of water (Fragoso 1983). Terwilliger (1978) also found that Baird's tapir is closely associated with open water. These observations led to the selection of study sites adjacent to rivers.

Methods

Densities of tapirs and tapir habitats were examined at two locations: the Macal River, located in the Chiquibul Forest Reserve (a 1,849-km² area) in the Cayo District, and the Rio Grande Forest, in the Toledo District (fig. 11.2). The Chiquibul area is uninhabited by humans, and the forest is relatively undisturbed, though it has been selectively logged for a few tree species for over 50 years (Johnson and Chaffy 1972). Hunting and farming are not permitted in the reserve. The nearest permanent community was located on the opposite side of the Maya Mountains, 26 km from the study site. Within the reserve, a 10-km length of the Macal river and adjacent strips of land (60 ha) were selected for intensive study (fig. 11.2). Tapirs were censused during June, and the vegetation was sampled in July and August 1985.

The second study site, with dimensions similar to those described for the Macal river site, was located along the Rio Grande river. The forest here extends from the Mexican to the Guatemalan border, but farms and towns are interspersed through the area. The Rio Grande site was selected because it was located 2 km downriver from an Indian village whose inhabitants hunt and practice shifting cultivation (farms known as *milpas*) within the 60-ha study site. Within the 60-ha study area there were only three active and numerous fallow milpas. None was larger than a hectare. Like the Macal site, Rio Grande has been selectively logged (D. O. Lewis, pers. comm., 1985, a former Belizean-British government official). At Rio Grande, tapirs were censused in September and the vegetation examined in October and November 1985.

To census tapirs, each 10-km length of river was canoed fourteen times— eight times during the day and six at night. Night searches were conducted using a miner's headlamp. This method proved very effective, as light reflects from tapir's eyes and this type of light does not seem to unduly disturb tapirs (Terwilliger 1978; Fragoso 1983). For each observation I noted the hour, number of individuals, presence of young, sex (when possible), and location. I also recorded the time I started and finished each transect, the total elapsed time,

Figure 11.2. The study sites at
Macal River and the Río Grande,
Belize.

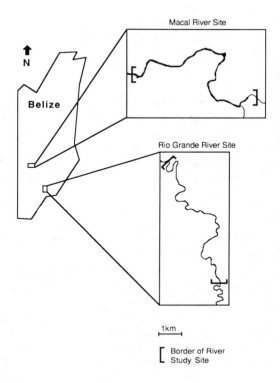

and the rate of travel. The location of each sighting was flagged so that vegetation data could be collected at a later date.

Normally two observers were in the canoe. On one occasion there were four. We recognized individual tapirs by physical features such as skin spotting, scars, size, and the presence of offspring. Only individual tapirs that could be positively identified during transects were included in the population estimate, which is therefore an estimate of the minimum number known in the area.

Another independent estimate of tapir density was made by examining the density of tapir trails. This was accomplished by randomly locating three 530-m-long transect lines on each side of the rivers (six transects at each study site) and counting all tapir trails that crossed the line. The transect began at the water line at a right angle from the water's edge. The transect continued inland for a distance of 30 m before turning upstream at a right angle for 500 m. Occasionally, because of meanders, we encountered the river. When this happened, the transect continued at a 90° angle from the water's edge. Tapir trails were easily recognized. They often appeared as wide plantless paths, with compacted soil, tapir tracks, and cropped plants evident along the trails (fig. 11.3).

We saw no tapirs at Rio Grande. To estimate tapir abundance at this site from the number of trails encountered, I used the equation $D = (M/T)G$, in which D

is the relative abundance at Rio Grande, *M* is the tapirs observed at Macal, *T* is the number of tapir trails at Macal, and *G* is the number of trails at Rio Grande. As differences in tapir abundance may be due to habitat and vegetation characteristics, I examined and compared the vegetation of both study sites. To collect vegetation data and note the frequency of plants cropped by tapirs, the trail transect lines were used minus the first 30 m. Quadrats 25 m² in area were located at 50-m intervals along the 500-m-long transect line. In each quadrat we recorded the presence of tapir-cropped plants, maximum canopy height, and percent leaf cover, along with the diversity and abundance of the different plant life forms (trees, saplings, herbs, vines, cane, grasses, shrubs, ferns, palms) in various size classes, and the percent leaf cover at a 50-cm height. We collected data on forty-eight vegetation variables. These plant criteria were selected for

Figure 11.3. Well-delineated tapir trail at the edge of a river. (Photo, José Fragoso.)

analysis rather than species composition because identification to species was not possible for most plants, and tapirs also select food plants based on their physiognomy (Terwilliger 1978; Janzen 1982; Kamstra 1983).

To survey the vegetation at the sites where tapirs were seen ("tapir quadrats," nineteen previously flagged sites) a 25-m² quadrat was centered at the site of observation. When tapirs were seen in the water, the quadrat was located where the animal walked onto land. Habitat use was determined by considering the frequency of tapir encounters and browsed plants in different habitats.

We used TWINSPAN, a multivariate statistical method, to classify habitats (Hill 1979). Classification was based on the similarity of the measured plant variables in the 120 quadrats distributed throughout the two study areas (60 quadrats at each site) and the 19 tapir quadrats. Similar quadrats were grouped together. TWINSPAN also listed the most important variables in order of importance when segregating quadrats. These variables were used to draw representative diagrams of the habitats. Only eight habitats were identified to maintain adequate sample sizes within each habitat for other statistical tests (e.g., tapir abundance).

Results

At Macal, where no hunting occurred, the river transects averaged 4 hours and 28 minutes per transect (speed = 2.2 km per hour). We observed tapirs twenty-two times, equaling 1.6 observations per 10 km of river. A minimum of eight tapirs frequent this area (table 11.1).

At Rio Grande, where hunting occurred, transects averaged 3 hours and 31 minutes (speed = 2.9 km/hr). No tapirs were seen here. An estimate of two tapirs per 10 km of river was obtained by extrapolating from tapir trail occurrence (table 11.1). This figure is supported by a local farmer, who reported that two tapirs were regularly seen in the study area.

The difference in numbers of tapirs between the hunted (Rio Grande) and unhunted (Macal) areas is statistically significant (χ^2 = 5.5, d.f. = 1, $p < .025$), as is the difference between the number of trails (χ^2 = 45, d.f. = 1, $p < .01$). Local people always stated that they did not hunt tapirs,

TABLE 11.1
Tapir and Tapir Trail Abundances in Two Areas

Site	Total Tapir Sightings	Tapirs per 10 km of River	No. of Trails per 2,180 m
Macal River (not hunted)	22	8	114
Rio Grande (hunted)	0	2*	27

*Estimated, not seen.

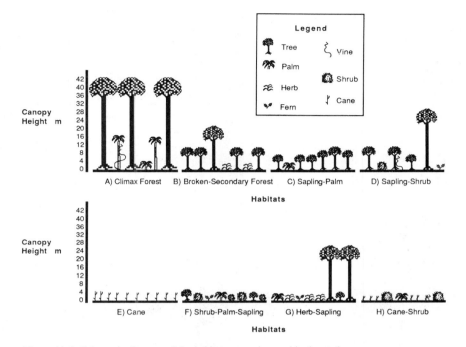

Figure 11.4. Schematic diagram of the habitat categories used in the study.

but hunters were encountered seven times during the Rio Grande river transects. Local authorities report that villagers do kill tapirs (D. O. Lewis, pers. comm., 1985; C. Wright, pers. comm. 1985 [local scientist]), and Walton (1984) found a dead tapir (shot) at Rio Grande.

Eight habitats were classified using TWINSPAN and the vegetation data from both study sites. Figure 11.4 shows the plant variables important in identifying the habitats. The climax forest habitat consists of quadrats located in unlogged-primary forest. The broken-secondary, sapling-palm, and sapling-shrub habitats probably developed after selective logging, since the canopy of these habitats was heterogeneous in height and cover. Many habitats occurred at both sites in approximately comparable proportions (table 11.2).

Tapirs were sighted most often ($n = 14$) in the four floodplain habitats that covered 55% of Macal and 23% of Rio Grande. The second greatest number of tapir sightings ($n = 5$) occurred in the logged forest that covered 34% of Macal and 66% of Rio Grande. No tapirs were seen in the unlogged climax forest, although it covered 10% of the Macal and 13% of the Rio Grande sites.

A comparison between tapir abundance in logged and unlogged forests revealed that tapirs avoided the latter (table 11.2). This occurred even though 12% of the study sites were covered by unlogged forests. Furthermore, none of

TABLE 11.2
Percent Area Covered by Eight Habitats in Three Vegetation Communities, Percent Tapir Encounters, and Percent of Quadrats with Cropped Plants in Each Habitat

Vegetation Community	Habitat	Macal River (%)	Rio Grande (%)	Tapir Sightings (%)	Quadrats Cropped (%)
Unlogged	Climax	10	13	0	0
Logged	Broken-secondary	30	25	16	30
	Sapling-palm	3	27	5	0
	Sapling-shrub	1	12	5	0
Floodplain	Cane	13	5	6	30
	Shrub-palm-sapling	30	15	47	35
	Herb-sapling	6	0	11	4
	Cane-shrub	6	3	0	0

*Note:*These data are only from the Macal River site, as tapirs and cropped plants were not observed at Rio Grande.

the quadrats located in this forest type contained tapir-cropped plants. Logged forests covered 47% of the study areas and 26% of the tapir sightings ($n = 5$) occurred in this habitat type. The most preferred vegetation community, that of the floodplain, covered 42% of the study areas, yet 74% of the tapir encounters ($n = 14$) occurred there.

Discussion

Differences in animal populations could result from differences in the availability of suitable habitat. This study found that good tapir habitat occurred at both study sites, yet no tapirs were seen at Rio Grande. The scarcity of tapirs at Rio Grande cannot be attributed to habitat (or vegetation) differences between the two sites.

Neither could selective logging account for the scarcity of tapirs at Rio Grande. Since both study sites were selectively logged at similar intensities (C. Requena, pers. comm. Barrow Lumber Co., and D. O. Lewis, pers. comm., 1985), it is unlikely that logging would negatively impact populations in only one area. In this study tapirs preferred floodplain and selectively logged forest. These two habitats also contained the greatest density of preferred tapir food plants (Fragoso 1987). No tapirs or tapir-cropped plants were seen in unlogged forests. Thus, there is little support for the hypothesis that selective logging has a negative impact on tapir populations.

Few studies have explored the effects of selective logging on tropical forest mammals. Most of those studies focused on primates (e.g., Chivers 1974; Johns 1983, 1986). Selective logging for a few species of trees at the harvesting intensity typical in the Chiquibul Forest, Belize (Johnson and Chaffy 1972) benefits tapirs. Selective logging mimics natural tree falls by creating gaps in the forest canopy. These gaps and clear soil areas permit the growth of colonizing plant species (Chivers 1974; Crawley 1983). Tapirs feed preferentially on new growth of these plant species (Fragoso 1987). These plant types were most abundant in structurally heterogeneous and recently disturbed plant communities (Fragoso 1987).

A seasonal change between sampling periods may have influenced the sighting of tapirs in the two study sites. This possibility was addressed by comparing the density of tapir trails, which presumably remain for long periods of time (Eisenberg and Thorington 1973; Terwilliger 1978; Eisenberg 1981). Significantly more trails were found at Macal, indicating that seasonal differences were probably not responsible for the absence of tapirs at Río Grande.

In human-occupied areas, low densities of wildlife may result from diseases transmitted by domestic animals. No dead tapirs were encountered during this study, nor had local people encountered bodies of tapirs that had not been shot. Thus, it is unlikely that disease was responsible for the scarcity of tapirs at Rio Grande.

Perhaps changing cultivation practices at Rio Grande negatively affected the tapir population. Evidence from a previous study conducted near the Macal study site discounts this hypothesis (Fragoso 1983; Kamstra 1983). Fragoso (1983) and Kamstra (1983) reported that tapirs frequently visited and fed in active and fallow milpas. Furthermore, tapirs greatly preferred weeds growing in milpas to vegetation in nearby forest. Conflict does develop between tapirs and farmers because tapirs feed on some crop species (Fragoso 1983). As a result, farmers will shoot tapirs but usually only after informing the Belize Forestry Department of the problem (O. Rosado, pers. comm., 1982, Belize Forestry Dept.). Farmers also kill tapirs illegally before crops are browsed as a preventive measure (D. O. Lewis pers. comm., 1985; A. C. S. Wright, pers. comm., 1985).

Tapirs were once common at Rio Grande (D. O. Lewis and A. C. S. Wright, pers. comm., 1985). Tapir densities decreased soon after humans moved into the area. With the growth of a town near Rio Grande, tapirs became exceedingly rare (D. O. Lewis and A. C. S. Wright, pers. comm., 1985). This study did not document hunting of tapirs at Rio Grande, but there is evidence that tapirs are commonly killed. At least three tapirs were killed by humans at Rio Grande in the 4-year period before this study (D. O. Lewis, pers. comm., 1985). In addition, Walton (1984) found the body of a shot tapir within the Rio Grande study site. During this study hunters were encountered many times jacklighting wildlife along the river (Fragoso 1987). Data collected from a nearby area before people knew of the tapirs' protected status indicates that overhunting can explain tapir population declines (Kamstra 1983).

The major difference between the Macal and the Rio Grande study sites therefore was human presence in the latter. Hunting is the most parsimonious explanation for the rarity of tapirs at Rio Grande. Hunting is probably also the reason for the decline of tapir populations in areas of the Stann Creek Valley, Belize (Fragoso 1983).

In Belize, tapirs are probably threatened more by hunting than by habitat destruction. Tapirs probably disappear from an area before the destruction of suitable habitat. This pattern undoubtedly occurs in other areas of their range (Leopold 1959; Terwilliger 1978). My observations are supported by Emmons' (1984) study of South American mammal densities. She found very low densities of large mammals in forest near centers of human activity and attributed it to hunting.

Although tapirs are totally protected from hunting, they can be killed legally if they are destroying crops or become dangerous to humans (Belize Wildlife Ordinance, 1981). Meat from legally killed tapirs can be sold; thus one can occasionally find tapir meat at local markets (Fragoso 1983; D. O. Lewis, pers. comm., 1985). This regulation probably allows tapirs to be illegally killed by market hunters, which results in overhunting in some areas. Tapirs remain common in Belize because they are not a preferred meat species (Frost 1977; Fragoso 1983). Only one ethnic group, the Garifuna, eats tapir meat (Fragoso 1983), and this group inhabits only a few places in Belize (Hartshorn et al. 1984). In countries where tapirs are preferred as meat, they have become rare (Mexico, Leopold 1959; Peru, some areas, Dourojeanni 1978; Panama, Terwilliger 1978; Costa Rica, Janzen 1983; Brazil, some areas, Emmons 1984).

Acknowledgments

This study would have been very difficult without the support of Dr. James Bendell, my academic supervisor. Peter Quinby was extremely helpful with the multivariate statistical analysis and Dan Pearson with the diagrams. Jean Huffman, Michele Williamson, and Adib Bejos were helpful in the field and in town. This project could not have been completed without the support of the Belize Forestry Department and Department of Archaeology, in particular, Henry Flowers, O. Rosado, and Winnel Branchi. The study was financially supported by World Wildlife Fund–Canada; the Zoology Department, University of Toronto; and from an NSERC grant to Dr. James Bendell.

12

Mammalian Densities at Protected Versus Hunted Sites in Central Panama

WILLIAM E. GLANZ

The mammal community on Barro Colorado Island, Panama (BCI), has been extensively studied and presents several interesting puzzles to those working on neotropical mammals. The island was created in 1914 during the construction of the Panama Canal and has been protected as a forest reserve since 1923. Since 1946 it has been managed by the Smithsonian Institution (Leigh 1982). Enders (1935), Eisenberg and Thorington (1973), and Glanz (1982) review the history and species composition of the mammalian fauna of BCI. Many mammals are easily observed on BCI, especially howler monkeys (*Alouatta palliata*), agoutis (*Dasyprocta punctata*), and coatis (*Nasua narica*), and appear to be more abundant there than in other Panamanian forests. A recent survey (Glanz, in press) confirms that density estimates of these and some other species are high on BCI in comparison to those published for certain other neotropical sites. All such comparisons, however, involve sites geographically distant from BCI, with major differences in habitats sampled and mammal species present at each site. From 1977 to 1986 I censused mammals on BCI at roughly 2-year intervals (Glanz 1982; in press). During three of these sampling intervals, I was able to obtain census data from four other sites within 30 km of BCI. In this paper I compare mammal densities on BCI with the densities at these four nearby mainland sites.

Various theories have been offered to explain high mammalian densities on BCI. Most have focused on features related to the isolation of the island by water gaps and the subsequent extinction of large predators there (see Glanz, in press, for review of theories). BCI, being only 15 km^2 in area, is presumably too small to maintain viable populations of jaguars, pumas, and harpy eagles. Their extinctions, according to this "predation hypothesis," have permitted various prey species to increase to abnormally high densities (Terborgh and Winter 1980). This hypothesis thus would predict consistently lower densities of prey species at mainland sites than on BCI. Mammalian species not preferred by these predators, however, should be similar among sites.

In this paper, I will evaluate this predation hypothesis and compare it to another that predicts mammalian densities from levels of human disturbance. BCI is probably the best-protected forest reserve in the neotropics, with a large, full-time staff of game wardens who can rapidly patrol the perimeter of the island using high-speed motorboats. During the past 20 years, the wardens have been very successful in preventing poaching, logging, and other forms of human disturbance on BCI. If such protection from human disturbance is primarily responsible for high mammalian abundance on BCI, then densities of mammal species vulnerable to human disturbance should be inversely correlated with the intensity of these disruptive activities at the Panamanian sites I have surveyed. The four mainland sites I studied included two that were intensively hunted, and two that had been protected from hunting for several years before my censuses and that were less accessible to casual human visitors than the two intensively hunted sites. If protection from hunting by humans is the primary cause of high mammalian densities on BCI, then densities at the two protected mainland sites should be higher than those at the intensively hunted sites and should approach the levels observed on BCI.

Both hypotheses outlined previously thus predict lower mammalian densities at mainland sites than on BCI; the predation hypothesis, however, does not predict specific differences among mainland sites, while the human disturbance–hunting hypothesis predicts higher densities at the protected sites than at the hunted sites. It is possible that large predators and human hunting may both have significant impacts on the mainland mammal communities. To separate such effects, I compared the magnitudes of density differences between hunted-mainland, protected-mainland, and protected-island (BCI) sites. It is also likely that different mammal species may show contrasting responses to these two mortality agents. To detect such patterns, I distinguished certain common species or groups of ecologically similar species and compared their density responses separately.

Census Methods

My colleagues and I have conducted systematic censuses of mammals on BCI since 1977 (Glanz, 1982; in press). Results reported here are from trail transect censuses, in which an observer walks a measured length of trail at a designated speed (1 km/hr for diurnal censuses), and records all mammals sighted or otherwise detected (see Glanz 1982). Although I measured distances from the animal to observer and trail, to derive more precise density estimates for each species (see Robinette, Loveless, and Jones 1974), I report data here only in terms of sightings per kilometer for each species. This approach allows easier comparisons between sites (Emmons 1984) but assumes that for a given species detectability is similar between sites.

Censuses were conducted at mainland sites during two separate time periods: 1977–78 for the Pipeline Road and Paraíso sites, and 1982–84 for the Gigante and Peña Blanca sites. Insufficient time, inadequate trails, or a lack of transportation to the sites prevented mainland censuses at other times when BCI was censused. Because mammalian densities on BCI vary considerably between years and these fluctuations can often be related to climatic influences on available foods (Glanz 1982; in press), I here restrict comparisons between sites to data collected in the same years. These are 1977–78 for BCI versus the Pipeline Road and Paraíso sites and 1982–84 for BCI versus Gigante and Peña Blanca.

Results reported here are from diurnal censuses only; almost all were conducted between 6:30 A.M. and 11 A.M., but due to transportation problems, several censuses on Gigante and Peña Blance were not completed until well after 11 A.M. Sighting rates in tables 12.2 to 12.4 are expressed as sightings/km; for social species (primates, coatis, peccaries) one group constitutes one sighting. See Glanz (1982) for additional details of census methods.

Site Descriptions

The vegetation of BCI has been described by Croat (1978) and Foster and Brokaw (1982). The island falls within the tropical moist forest life zone of Holdridge (1967), but Foster and Brokaw (1982) note the semideciduous nature of its forest, with peak leaf fall occurring during the dry season from January to April. Approximately half of BCI is young mature forest about 100 years old, 20 to 30 m in canopy height; the other half is older, undisturbed forest, at least 400 years old and averaging 30 to 40 m in height (Foster and Brokaw 1982). The young mature forest is often more uniform in canopy height and general physiognomy, with fewer large treefall gaps than the older forest, but the boundary between the two forest types is often difficult to determine. From 1980 to 1986 my assistants and I censused mammals along nine trail transect routes that together totaled 20 km in length. Of this trail distance, 66% was classified as young mature forest and 34% as old forest. Each route was censused at least five times per census period, giving at least 100 km of trail transects sampled per period. In 1977–78 fewer (six) routes were censused more often, but other transects were sampled intermittently, resulting in 314 km of trail censuses, with about 70% in young mature forest.

In 1977 and 1978 a heavily disturbed secondary forest near the town of Paraíso, 30 km Southeast of BCI, was censused during a study of two squirrel species (Glanz 1984). The vegetation along 7.2 km of trails and dirt roads censused was classified as 29% very young (less than 20 years old) successional forest, 19% grassy open woodland, 28% deciduous forest, and 22% moist forest. Most of the vegetational disturbance resulted from maintenance activities for the adjacent Panama Canal. During twenty-one visits to the area and 86 km of trail censuses, we encountered hunters or recent evidence of hunting eight times. One hunter questioned was from Paraíso, the other was from Balboa, an urban area near Panama City. Table 12.1 compares this and the other mainland sites to BCI.

A second area, the Pipeline Road reserve, was sampled less frequently in 1977–78. A 2.3-km census route along the Rio Limbo was sampled three times and an adjacent 1-km route was sampled once. In addition, 6 km of trail censuses were accumulated on two visits to the Río Agua Salud and Frijoles Road areas, 6 km northwest of the Limbo site. All of these routes are from 4 km to 10 km east of BCI. The Limbo site has been described by Karr (1971 and 1982) as mature (older than 100 years) moist forest with 20 to 35 m canopy. Karr (1982) notes that the vegetation there "is similar to the forest on Barro Colorado Island in structure, species composition, and number of lianas, but with more understory palms and perhaps more epiphytes than on Barro Colorado." The Río Agua Salud is very similar, but with steeper topography, while half the 3 km of census route on the Frijoles road consists of young, successional forest.

TABLE 12.1
General Characteristics of Sites Censused for Mammals

Barro Colorado Island (BCI)
    Reserve established in 1923; well protected from poachers.
    66% of trails censused in young mature forest (100 years old) and 34% in older mature forest
        (200–400 years old).
    Isolated from mainland by water gaps of at least 400 m.

Paraíso
    Forest and grassland area at Gaillard Cut of Panama Canal, 30 km southeast of BCI.
    Not protected; frequent hunting and other human activities.
    29% young successional forest (< 20 years old); 19% grassland; 28% dry forest; 22% moist,
        young mature forest (60 years old).
    Border by Canal; open habitats disturbed by maintenance operations of Canal and town of
        Paraiso.

Pipeline Road
    Forest reserve 4 to 10 km east of BIC.
    Not protected from hunting until after this study.
    Most trails in mature forest (> 100 years old); one trail in young, successional forest (20 to 40
        years).
    Agriculture areas 2 to 3 km away; road provides access for vehicles from southeast.

Gigante
    Forested peninsula on mainland south of BCI; 0.5 km from BCI at closest point.
    Protected from hunting since 1980; poaching uncommon.
    20% in very young forest (< 20 years old); remainder mature forest (60 to 400 years old).

Peña Blanca
    Forested peninsula on mainland west of BCI; 0.4 km from BCI at closest point.
    Protected from hunting since 1980; poaching rare.
    30% trails in very young forest (< 20 years old); remainder in mature forest (60 to 400 years
        old).
    Border areas of shifting croplands and pastures.

Hunters were encountered on three of the five visits to these sites, and recent evidence of hunting (shotgun shells and carcasses) was noted on the other two trips. Of two hunting groups encountered, both were from rural areas adjacent to the reserve and had walked to the site, but evidence of urban hunters (camp and target shooting sites with auto tracks, packaged food wrappers, and abandoned carcasses) were also found. Since my visits there, the entire Pipeline Road reserve has been included in the Soberania National Park, and protection from unregulated hunting has improved (J. Karr, pers. comm.).

Several mainland peninsulas near BCI were incorporated into the Barro Colorado National Monument in 1980, and during 1982–84 I sampled two of these: Gigante to the south and Peña Blanca to the west of BCI (table 12.1). Both areas abut regions settled by humans, and protection from poaching is not absolute. Nevertheless, the monument's wardens have been effective in deterring poachers, particularly on Peña Blanca (P. Acosta and A. Rodriguez, pers. comms.). In twenty census sessions (72 km) I noted possible but not conclusive evidence of hunting (dog and human tracks) twice, both on Gigante. Both areas were heavily hunted before achieving protected status in 1980. The vegetation on both peninsulas is similar to that on BCI (which is only 0.4 to 3 km away), but certain areas show substantial recent disturbance by agricultural activities of humans. About 20% of the 6.7 km of our census trails on Gigante was in very young forest with canopy height less than 15 m, and approximately 30% of 5.5 km of trails on Peña Blanca was in similar habitat. The remainder of both areas was mature forest, similar to the "young mature" or "old" forest types on BCI (see table 12.1). DeSteven and Putz (1984) and Sork (1987) provide additional data on the vegetation and seed predation rates at the Gigante site.

Results

Sighting rates of diurnal mammals on BCI in 1977–78 (Glanz 1982) are compared in table 12.2 with those from Pipeline Road and Paraíso. Total sighting rates at the Pipeline Road sites are extremely low (only 7% of the rates on BCI), with most of this difference being due to higher abundance of agoutis (*Dasyprocta*), squirrels (*Sciurus*), and howler monkeys (*Alouatta*) on BCI. All mammals seen were very wary and ran from me, unlike the relatively tame individuals frequently encountered on BCI. The only agouti seen at Limbo was shot by a concealed hunter seconds after it ran from me. No terrestrial mammals larger than that agouti (such as deer, peccaries, and tapirs) were seen, although all are present on BCI.

Larger mammals were similarly rare at Paraíso (table 12.2), but three small arboreal species, the squirrels *Sciurus granatensis* and *S. variegatoides* and the tamarin *Saguinus oedipus,* were relatively common. Most agoutis encountered were identified only by their alarm bark as they fled through the undergrowth. We noted three temporary platforms built by hunters near fruiting fig and

TABLE 12.2
Census Results for Diurnal Mammals in 1977–78, Comparing Sighting Rates
(Sightings/Km) on Barro Colorado and Two Unprotected Sites

	BCI	Pipeline Road	Paraíso
Primates			
Alouatta[a]	0.56	0.07	0
Ateles[a]	0.05	0	0
Cebus	0.10	0.07	0
Saguinus[a]	0.03	0	0.21
Xenarthrans			
Bradypus and *Choloepus*	0.06	0	0.01
Tamandua	0.08	0.07	p
Rodents			
Sciurus	2.51	0.07	2.16
Dasyprocta	3.26	0.14	0.10
Carnivores			
Nasua[a]	0.22	0.07	0.03
Eira	0.01	0	0
Ungulates			
Tapirus	0.01	0	0
Tayassu	0.09	0	0
Mazama	0.04	0	0
Odocoileus	0.01	0	0
Total Sighting Rate	7.04	0.49	2.51
Total km Censused	314	14	86

[a]Sightings of groups.

p = Present in area, not recorded on censuses.

mango trees, and two hunters interviewed said they were hunting specifically for agoutis. As at Pipeline Road, no deer or peccaries were seen.

Results from mammalian surveys of Gigante and Peña Blanca during the wet season of 1982 (July to November) are compared with concurrent data from BCI in table 12.3. Significant populations of howler monkeys, white-faced monkeys (*Cebus capucinus*), and agoutis were found, and total sighting rates on Gigante were 48% and on Peña Blanca, 55% of BCI levels. Too few kilometers of trail were censused for statistical comparisons, though, and more extensive sampling effort was undertaken in the 1983–84 dry season (December to February).

Results for 1983–84 are presented in table 12.4. They confirm the high primate abundances noted in 1982 but reveal that *Cebus* and *Saguinus* occurred at higher densities on the two mainland areas, while *Alouatta* was more common on BCI. Total primate sighting rates were slightly higher on the mainland peninsulas. Squirrels and agoutis were frequently encountered at both sites but were much more common at Peña Blanca. Collared peccaries (*Tayassu tajacu*) were sighted at Gigante, brocket deer (*Mazama americana*) at Peña Blanca, and white-tailed deer (*Odocoileus virginianus*) at both sites.

TABLE 12.3
**Census Results for Diurnal Mammals in 1982, Comparing Sighting Rates
on Barro Colorado and Two Protected Sites**

	BCI	Gigante	Peña Blanca
Alouatta[a]	0.81	0.76	0.83
Cebus[a]	0.21	0.35	0.17
Saginus[a]	0.03	0.18	0.17
Sciurus	1.20	0.18	0.17
Dasyprocta	1.35	0.41	1.00
Nasua[a]	0.35	0.06	0
Eira	0.29	0.06	0
All ungulates	0.19	0	0
Total Sighting Rate[b]	4.22	2.05	2.33
Total km Censused	168	17	6

[a]Sightings of groups; [b] Includes other taxa for BCI (see table 12.2).

TABLE 12.4
**Census Results for Diurnal Mammals in 1983–84, Comparing Sighting Rates
on Barro Colorado and Two Protected Sites**

	BCI	Gigante	Peña Blanca
Alouatta[a]	0.84	0.56	0.59
Cebus[a]	0.33	0.63	0.56
Saguinus[a]	0.02	0.11	0.14
Tamandua	0.10	p	0.09
Sciurus	1.05	0.26[b]	0.73
Dasyprocta	2.26	0.30[b]	1.14[b]
Nasua[a]	0.18	0.07	0.09
Eira	p	p	0.05
Tayassu[a]	0.36	0.15	0
Mazama	0.15	0	0.05
Odocoileus	p	0.04	0.05
Total sighting rate[c]	5.24	2.12	3.49
Total km Censused	98	27	22

Note: Taxonomic order, units and symbols as in tables 12.2 and 12.3. p = Present in area, not recorded on census.
[a]Sightings of groups.
[b]Different from BCI, $p < .05$ (U-test).
[c]Includes additional species for BCI; see table 12.2.

These comparisons were tested by calculating sighting rates for each census on each 1 to 4 km census route, and comparing these figures for Gigante ($n = 8$) and Peña Blanca ($n = 8$) against those for BCI ($n = 45$) using the Mann-Whitney U test. Differences between BCI and either peninsula were insignificant ($p > .05$) for each of the three primate species, although trends ($p < .10$) were observed for tamarins to be more common on the mainland and howler monkeys to be more abundant on BCI. Sighting rates for all primates combined were insignificantly different ($p > .05$). Squirrels (only one species, *Sciurus granatensis,* present at these sites) were significantly lower ($p < .05$) at Gigante than on BCI, and agoutis were significantly lower at both sites than on BCI ($p < .05$). All comparisons of other species between these sites were statistically insignificant, but high variances in sighting rates between trail segments at each site could easily have masked real density differences among sites. Sighting rates of all species combined (total sighting rate) were significantly lower on Gigante than on BCI but not on Peña Blanca in comparison to BCI.

Discussion

In all of these comparisons of total mammal sighting rates on BCI versus mainland sites, those on BCI are higher. For example, the extremely low sighting rates on the Pipeline Road censuses in 1977–78 provide a dramatic contrast with those on BCI during the same period. These results seem to support both the predation hypothesis and the human disturbance hypothesis outlined previously. Nevertheless, if the data on responses of individual species are examined closely, they show a far greater impact of unregulated hunting on most mammalian populations than that caused by large predators in this region.

Quantitative data on predator populations from these sites are inadequate at present. Both jaguars and harpy eagles have been reported from the Pipeline Road area, but verified records are extremely rare. The other sites discussed here are visited very infrequently by birders and other naturalists, and thus confirmed records are lacking. If large predators are more likely to have survived in large areas of contiguous forest, then Paraíso, where the forest is very fragmented, and BCI, due to its small island size, should have few such predators. Both the Pipeline Road reserve and the Gigante–Peña Blanca region, however, included or abutted large areas of forest until very recently (U.S. Army Map Service, 1968, and personal observations through 1980). Since 1982, cutting and grazing have been evident southeast of the Peña Blanca peninsula, but the Gigante region is still adjacent to larger forested areas and Pipeline Road is included in the large, protected Soberania National Park. Thus, the predation hypothesis would predict lowest densities of prey species used by large predators at both Pipeline Road and Gigante. Peña Blanca, which was recently separated from Gigante by about 1 km of disturbed forest and may still exchange predators with that site, should have similar or slightly higher prey abundance, and both BCI and Paraíso should have highest densities of mammalian prey. Although two sites (Pipeline Road and BCI) do have total mammal sighting rates as predicted by this predation hypothesis, the total rates at the other mainland sites do not confirm these predictions. Similarly, species sighting rates for jaguar prey (agoutis, peccaries, deer) or prey of harpy eagles (primates) show no obvious support for this hypothesis.

If, however, the mainland sites are ranked by their levels of human disturbance, as indicated by percent visits with evidence of hunting, then a clearer
pattern emerges. The Pipeline Road area, with highest frequency of hunting,
showed the lowest mammal sighting rate relative to BCI (7% of BCI rate).
Paraíso, also frequently hunted, had the next higher relative sighting rate (36%
of BCI). Of the two recently protected sites, Gigante had more evidence of
occasional poaching and had a slightly higher relative sighting rate (49% of BCI
in 1982, 39% in 1983–84), with Peña Blanca next (55% of BCI in 1982 and
64% in 1983–84). If BCI is included in this comparison (with lowest levels of
poaching and consistently the highest sighting rates), then the Spearman rank
correlation coefficient is significant ($R_s = 1.0, p = .01$).

If one examines apparent densities of only those species desirable to hunters,
an even more dramatic pattern emerges. Most hunters interviewed indicated
that they sought agoutis and ungulates when hunting during the day, switching
to pacas at night. The sighting rates of agoutis correlate precisely with degree
of protection ($R_s = 1.0$). Furthermore, peccaries and deer were not encountered at either of the two frequently hunted areas. These data strongly suggest
that unregulated hunting can greatly reduce population densities of preferred
game species such as agoutis, peccaries, and deer.

Tables 12.2 to 12.4 also suggest other, less desirable mammal species can be
affected by unregulated hunting. The low primate numbers at Pipeline Road
probably reflect the fact that the two species most commonly found in mature
forest, the howler monkey and the white-faced monkey, make easy targets due
to their bold behavior. The more wary, scrub-dwelling tamarins at Paraíso seem
to have withstood hunting pressure better, although their small size might also
make them less desirable as food to hunters than the other two species. No
hunters interviewed, however, actively sought any of these primates. In contrast, primates were much more numerous at the protected sites. In comparison
to the primate community on BCI, which is dominated by *Alouatta,* the primates of Gigante and Peña Blanca were more equitably distributed among *Alouatta, Cebus,* and *Saguinus.* The latter two, however, were more common in
younger successional forests, which were more widespread there than on BCI.
Differences between the primate communities of BCI and the two protected
mainland sites thus are probably related to habitat differences among sites, but
other factors, including those related to island effects, may also be contributing
to the dominance of *Alouatta* on BCI (see Eisenberg 1979).

Other mammal species not preferred by hunters may still be shot if they are
bold or slow moving. I have found armadillo, anteater, and coati carcasses at
Pipeline Road, Paraíso, and a nearby forested site that were likely unretrieved
hunter kills. All were on or near trails or roads, and many may have been left
by the wealthier, urban hunters willing to waste ammunition on undesirable
species. Although these patterns suggest an impact on certain uncommon, nongame species, the data presented here, with low sample sizes and variable sight-

ing rates, cannot be used to test for depressed densities of these rarer species.

Although comparison of hunted versus protected sites provides the greatest differences in mammal sighting rates, the two protected mainland sites, Gigante and Peña Blanca, still have significantly lower sighting rates of agoutis than on BCI, and Gigante is significantly lower for squirrels. Two explanations for the agouti results are possible: either (1) hunting before 1980 depressed agouti numbers so much that they had not recovered fully by 1982–84 (and current poaching may continue to affect them on Gigante) or (2) agouti numbers on BCI are "abnormally" high due to the absence of jaguars and pumas there. The greater density of agoutis on Peña Blanca than on Gigante provides some support for the first idea in that Gigante is closer to a likely source of hunters, the rural community of Las Pavas 3 km away, and less of its perimeter can be patrolled by wardens in boats. The second idea is supported by recent studies of jaguar ranging and feeding behavior by Schaller and Vasconcelos (1978), Schaller and Crawshaw (1980), Rabinowitz (1986), and Emmons (1987). All found jaguar to be generalized, solitary hunters that take prey over a range of sizes from armadillos to ungulates but that preferentially take large rodents like agoutis and capybaras when they are abundant. Emmons (1987) argues that jaguars may have a major effect on agouti and paca numbers because of the low reproductive rates of these prey in conjunction with jaguar preference for them. Thus, either hypothesis or both could help explain elevated agouti densities on BCI.

In contrast, neither of the two hypotheses appears to explain the high squirrel densities on BCI relative to Gigante. Squirrels are neither preferred game nor easy targets for hunters, and large predators are unlikely to have an impact on them. Smaller predators, such as ocelots (*Felis pardalis*), the ornate hawk-eagle (*Spizaetus ornatus*), and the black hawk-eagle (*Spizaetus tyrannus,*) are present on BCI and known to prey on squirrels. The distribution and abundance of the red-tailed squirrel (*Sciurus granatensis*), is strongly correlated with the availability of certain nutlike fruits, particularly palm nuts (Glanz et al. 1982; Glanz, 1984). The high densities of this species on BCI and Peña Blanca may be more related to food supplies. Conversely, the lower densities on Gigante and extremely low numbers at Pipeline Road should result from lower availability of preferred food trees. These predictions remain to be tested.

In summary, this comparison of mammal abundances at several sites in central Panama may provide some support for Emmons' (1987) theory that large felid predators can limit prey populations of some large rodents such as agoutis. The more dramatic differences between densities at the Panamanian sites in this study, however, are more easily attributed to impacts of hunting by humans. Data from BCI and the two protected peninsulas nearby contrast sharply with that from unprotected sites, and lack of protection appears to affect preferred game species more than other factors. Further anecdotal support for this effect can be seen recently in the Pipeline Road area (J. Karr, pers. comm.). Before

1980, access to the Pipeline Road was unrestricted, and rural, subsistence hunters and recreational hunters used the area. Since the region was placed within the Soberanía National Park, access by road has been severely restricted, but some rural hunters may still be entering on foot. Mammal numbers have increased greatly since establishment of the park, but this increase has not been quantified. I attempted to census two of our 1977 routes in 1982 and 1984, but both were very overgrown and difficult to find. Clearly, more censuses of both this area and the two protected peninsulas near BCI are needed to further assess how well tropical mammal populations can respond to protection. Nevertheless, the quantitative census data from this study strongly indicate that the abundance of mammals at BCI, Gigante, and Peña Blanca, in comparison to other forested sites in central Panama, results more from their protection from unregulated hunting than from the presence or absence of certain predators.

Acknowledgments

My mammalian census work in Panama has been supported by a Smithsonian Postdoctoral Fellowship; a series of grants from the Environmental Sciences Program, Smithsonian Tropical Research Institute; and a grant from the American Philosophical Society. I gratefully thank my field assistants involved in the censuses: Jeff Brokaw and Dan Glanz (1977–78); Mickey Marcus (1982–84); Alan Goldizen (1982); and Bill Johnson (1983–84).

13

Wild Mammal Skin Trade in Chiapas, Mexico

MARCELO ARANDA

Trade in wildlife and wildlife products was a severe problem in Mexico before the 1952 enactment of the Federal Hunting Law, which prohibited all such trade. Subsequently, the incidence of trade was reduced but never entirely eliminated; hunting and the sale of wildlife products continue to be widespread throughout Mexico (Leopold 1965).

The southern Mexican state of Chiapas contains abundant and diverse faunal resources distributed in highland and humid lowland habitats. This combined with severe socioeconomic problems produces an active commerce in live specimens, skins, and meat of a variety of mammal species.

The two most populous towns of the region are San Cristóbal de las Casas and Comitán. They comprise the centers of commercial activity for the Chiapan highlands and lowlands and the Mexico-Guatemala border region. Mammal skins and leather products are the most frequently available items. The skins, raw or tanned, are usually sold whole. Mounted animals are occasionally found. Leather products include purses, pouches, belts, masks, and toys. Skins are generally sold at craft shops in San Cristóbal de las Casas and at leather shops in Comitán (fig. 13.1). Despite their illegality, all wildlife products are openly displayed and sold.

Methods

I visited thirty-two stores in San Cristóbal de las Casas between July 1985 and February 1987 and sixteen stores in Comitán between September 1986 and February 1987. All skins were counted and identified to species, and quantities at each location were compared between months to determine the rate of turnover. Occasionally, the retail price of each skin was recorded.

174

Figure 13.1. Ocelot
(*Felis pardalis*) skins hanging
in a leather and boot store
in Comitán, Chiapas. (Photo,
John Robinson.)

Results

A total of 235 skins were found in sixteen of thirty-two stores in San Cristóbal de las Casas and ten of sixteen stores in Comitán. This total consisted of twenty-five species of wild mammals from five orders (table 13.1). Species represented by five or more skins were considered dominant elements in this trade (table 13.2). Combined totals in this category included 185 skins of eleven species making up 81% of the total 235 skins traded. Five species of carnivores contributed 92 skins, or 48% of the total. Of these, 57% were comprised of two species of felids, *Felis wiedii* and *F. pardalis*.

In San Cristóbal de las Casas, 180 mammal skins of twenty-four species were traded during the 18-month study (table 13.2). Five or more skins were recorded from ten species (eight families), totaling 149 skins.

In Comitán, 55 mammal skins of fifteen species were traded during the 6 months. Five or more skins were recorded from 4 species, totaling 36 skins (table 13.2).

TABLE 13.1
Mammalian Species Found for Sale in San Cristóbal de las Casas and Comitán.

Primates
  Alouatta pigra
  Ateles geoffroyi
Edentata
  Dasypus novemcinctus
  Tamandua mexicana
Lagomorpha
  Sylvilagus floridanus
Rodentia
  Sciurus aureogaster
  Orthogeomys sp.
  Agouti paca
Carnivora
  Canis latrans
  Urocyon cinereoargenteus
  Procyon lotor

Carnivores (*continued*)
  Nasua nasua
  Potos flavus
  Conepatus mesoleucus
  Mustela frenata
  Eira barbara
  Lutra longicaudus
  Panthera onca
  Felis concolor
  F. pardalis
  F. wiedii
  F. yagouaroundi
Artiodactyla
  Tayassu tajacu
  Odocoileus virginianus

TABLE 13.2
Frequency of Mammalian Skins for Sale in San Cristóbal de las Casas and Comitán

Taxon	San Cristóbal de las Casas (*N*)	Comitán (*N*)	Total (*N*)	Total (%)
Rodentia			31	
Sciurus aureogaster[a]	26		26	14.1
Agouti paca[a]	5		5	2.7
Edentata			15	
Dasypus novemcinctus[a]	15		15	8.1
Primates			6	
Alouatta pigra[b]	6		6	3.2
Carnivora	62	27	89	
Felis weidii[b]	24	16	40	21.6
F. pardalis[b]	6	6	12	6.5
Uroeyon cinereoargenteus[a]	18		18	9.7
Potos flavus[c]	14		14	7.6
Lutra longicaudis[b]		5	5	2.7
Artiodactyla	35	9	44	
Odocoileus virginianus[a]	24	9	33	17.8
Mazama americana[a]	11	—	11	5.9
Total	149	36	185	

[a]Hunting permitted.
[b]Hunting prohibited in all Mexico.
[c]Hunting prohibited in Chiapas.

Discussion

The results of this study clearly reveal the continuing significance of hunting to the Chiapan economy and to existing wildlife populations. Trade in skins and other wildlife products occurs throughout the year. It is conducted publicly with little or no concern for its illegality.

Mexico's General Hunting Law provides a means of regulating the taking of and trade in wildlife throughout the country. Nationwide hunting prohibitions are in effect for *F. pardalis, F. wiedii, Alouatta pigra,* and *Lutra longicaudus. Potos flavus* is afforded protection only within Chiapas. The remaining six species in table 13.2 can be hunted for all or part of the year (SEDUE 1983). The retail value of the various species of skins available ranges widely (table 13.3).

The source area for most of the eleven dominant species sold in San Cristóbal de las Casas and Comitán is the extensive humid lowland forests of the Selva Lacandona. Six of these species (*Sciurus aureogaster, Odocoileus virginianus, Dasypus novemcinctus, Mazama americana, Alouatta pigra,* and *Agouti paca*) are hunted mainly for meat, although a sizable market exists for their skins. The remaining five are hunted almost solely for their skins. The poorly known margay (*F. weidii*) is the most commonly traded to the skin trade of Chiapas (table 13.2).

Hunting for local markets is less intensive than subsistence hunting in the region. Nevertheless, rare protected species, particularly the felids, come under serious hunting pressure. Enforcement of existing hunting regulations is extremely lax, which leads to widespread disregard for the law in Chiapas and throughout Mexico. Wildlife populations are rapidly declining. Strict control of commercial hunting and trade in wildlife products is an important first step in slowing down the process.

TABLE 13.3
Retail Prices of Wildlife Products

Species	Price (U.S.$)	Product
Panthera onca	200	Skin
Felis pardalis	50–90	Skin
Lutra longicaudis	25–90	Skin
Canis latrans	20	Skin
Felis concolor	15	Skin
Felis weidii	5–10	Skin
Tayassu tajacu	5	Skin
Potos flavus	3	Skin
Alouatta pigra	2	Skin
Odocoileus virginianus	1.5–6	Skin
Procyon lotor	1.5	Skin
Dasypus novemcinctus	0.6	Carapace
Sciurus aureogaster	0.2	Skin

Note: Exchange rate at time = 1,000 pesos = 1 U.S.$

Part 4

Wildlife Farming and Ranching

14

The Rational Use of Green Iguanas

DAGMAR I. WERNER

In recent decades, rural development in the tropics has been invariably linked with deforestation. Forest has been cleared mainly for large government-supported development projects or for subsistence farming by campesinos (Heckadon 1982, 1983; Nations and Komer 1983a, 1983b; Caufield 1985; Uhl and Parker 1986). In Panama, farmers typically slash and burn 2 to 3 ha of forest to cultivate crops such as corn, rice, or yucca. Three years after deforestation, the thin acidic soil is degraded and can no longer support the campesino family. The land is then sold to cattle ranchers, and the campesinos move on to slash and burn a new piece of forest. By this process, 50% of the virgin forest in Panama has been cut in the past 40 years (Heckadon 1982). Figures for other tropical countries are equally alarming (Nations and Komer 1983a). Soil erosion caused by overgrazing and cattle trampling renders areas entirely infertile within 15 to 20 years after deforestation.

Protein shortage for local consumption must be included among the complex social and economic problems associated with slash and burn agriculture and the subsequent changes in land use. If cattle are raised, the meat is mainly for export and is inaccessible or too expensive for campesinos to buy (Mares 1986). Farmers who live in romote areas usually have little or no access to beef because the lack of refrigeration and transportation makes raising cattle unfeasible. Small game animals such as armadillos, deer, agouti, paca, iguanas, and others, which are much better suited for local consumption, are disappearing with the forest. Game animals that could survive in the remnant tree stands along river benches and creeks suffer from increased hunting pressure and have become locally extinct in most rural areas in Central America.

This chapter reports on research undertaken by the Iguana Management Project (IMP) at the Smithsonian Tropical Research Institute and the Pro Iguana Verde Foundation, Panama, to determine whether iguana populations can be restored to their natural habitat for rational and profitable management (Werner and Rand 1986). If restoration is successful, rural poor could continue to exploit this valuable protein source. Concomitantly, extinction of the species would be prevented and tropical forest on which the species depends could be protected and reestablished.

The Importance of the Iguana

The green iguana (*Iguana iguana*) has been a source of protein for humans for over 7,000 years (Cooke 1981). Many rural poor still depend on the iguana for protein (Fitch, Henderson, and Hillis 1982). Iguana meat and eggs are considered to be aphrodisiacs and delicacies in many areas. Iguana is consumed in all countries of its distribution. In Panama, an estimated 70% of the population would consume iguana meat and eggs if available. Exact data on the extent of consumption in other countries are lacking. The importance of iguana is evident, however, in the concern expressed about their dwindling numbers and the consequent protein shortage for those social and ethnic groups who depend on this protein source (Hirth 1963; Tovar 1969; Fitch and Henderson 1977; Ruiz and Rand 1981; Fitch, Henderson, and Hillis 1982). In most countries where it occurs, the green iguana has been declared an endangered species (Fuller and Swift 1985).

Iguana Management

Objectives

The research on iguana management aims at developing the scientific and technical basis for conserving and increasing iguana numbers in order to provide protein and income from iguana meat and eggs for campesinos. Management schemes examined include raising iguanas to harvestable size in confined conditions, management of wild populations, or combinations of captive rearing and management in wild areas. Management of free-living iguana populations requires tropical forest, the natural habitat of the species. One of the objectives of this project is to investigate whether reforestation with native multiple-purpose trees for iguana management might be a viable means to provide campesinos with needed tree products (timber, fuel wood, fruits), in addition to providing a medium for producing animal protein. The research also explores possibilities of maximizing the overall productivity of small farming systems (Stoney 1987; Werner 1987; Werner and Rey 1987).

Biological Feasibility

To assess the feasibility of iguana management, biological, cultural/social, and economic factors must be considered.

The biological feasibility of iguana management depends on demographic, reproductive, and nutritional characteristics of the species. The research explores how these characteristics can be used to develop techniques that increase reproductive output, survivorship, growth rate, and densities of iguana populations.

I. iguana is distributed from southern Mexico to Brazil and Paraguay, including some islands near the continent and in the Carribean (Etheridge 1982); (fig. 14.1). This prolific herbivore occurs in a diversity of tropical and subtropical forest habitats (Fitch, Henderson, and Hillis 1982). Males may reach 6 kg in weight but normally weigh no more than 4 kg (Swanson 1950; Mueller 1972). Females are smaller and typically weigh 1.5 to 2.5 kg (Rand 1984). Iguanas live in trees, where they feed on plant material (Henderson 1974; Hirth 1963) that is otherwise not exploited by domestic animals or humans. They rely on their camouflage to escape predation.

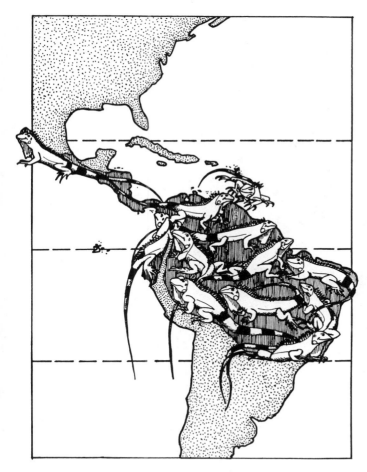

Figure 14.1. Geographical distribution of the green iguana.

Reptiles, because they are ectothermic, differ from birds and mammals in their metabolism and energy requirements. The daily metabolic cost of free existence for an active lizard is only 3% that of an equal-sized bird and 6% of an equal-sized mammal (Nagy 1982). Metabolic rates at 37°C of reptiles are only 10% to 20% of birds or mammals (Bennett and Dawson 1976). One of the consequences of this difference is that growth is relatively slow. A wild iguana grows about nine times slower than a domestic chicken. To grow to a 3 kg size, a wild iguana uses as much food as a chicken but needs three years instead of four months. Growth can be enhanced through management techniques and genetic selection, but it will never approach that of birds or mammals (fig. 14.2).

Figure 14.2. Three age classes of iguanas, a hatchling, a 1-year-old and a 3-year-old are shown by Dagmar Werner at the research facilities in Summit Gardens.
(Photo, C. Hansen.)

In the wild, iguanas display a distinct yearly breeding cycle. Mating and egg deposition are timed so that the hatchlings emerge with the onset of the rainy season (Rand and Greene 1982). In Panama, males establish territories, which may be as small as 5 m in diameter, in October (Dugan 1982), select highly visible display spots, and may mate with four and possibly more females. Females may mate with more than one male. Small males are nonterritorial but occasionally are successful in stealing copulations from females (Dugan 1982). One clutch of eggs is laid at the beginning of the dry season. Clutch size increases linearly with body size (Rand 1984). A female may lay between six (Werner, unpubl. data) and seventy eggs per clutch (Mueller 1972); average clutch size is forty-one eggs, or about 30% of the female's weight before laying (Rand 1984). Nest sites that offer adequate incubation conditions may be limited, and females may compete for nesting spots (Rand 1968; Rand and Rand 1978). The eggs are buried in the ground, where they incubate for about 90 days (Rand 1972; Bock, unpubl. man.). Annual hatching success is highly variable, ranging from virtually zero to above 80% (Rand and Robinson 1969; Rand and Dugan 1980). Success averages about 40% to 50% (Bock, unpubl. man.). Hatchlings emerge at the beginning of the rainy season, and the mortality rate is high. In the wild, only from 2.6% (Harris 1982) to about 5% (Van Devender 1982) of the hatchlings survive their first year. Survivorship at later ages is probably higher, but field data are entirely lacking. Iguanas are long lived, having an estimated maximum life expectancy of 7 to 10 years (Mueller 1972; Zug and Rand 1987).

With these biological characteristics, management of existing wild populations is obviously difficult. First, iguana numbers are severely reduced at the present time. Even if existing protection laws were observed, iguana numbers would recover at a very slow pace, or possibly not at all. Second, recruitment into the population would be highly variable because of unpredictable hatching success. If one goal of management is to harvest a defined number of adults every year, it will be necessary to ensure recruitment of a constant number of young into the population. This would result in the desired number of adults after 3 years.

Predictability of recruitment could be increased if eggs from wild females could be collected from natural nests and incubated under controlled conditions. The eggs could also be obtained from a captive reproductive colony. To bypass the high mortality rate of young during early ages, hatchlings could be raised in captivity until they reach harvestable size or to an age (size) having a low mortality rate and then be released into existing tree stands to grow to harvestable size. The carrying capacity of these tree stands could be increased if feeding stations, thermoregulation spots, and hiding places were provided.

Iguanas would be released only in those farms that still provide some trees (in their backyard or along rivers or creeks). Stands of trees near settlements in Panama are now scarce. The number and size of management areas could be increased by planting trees for iguana habitat. These trees would provide the farmer with other benefits at the same time (fuel wood, timber, fruits, water, and soil protection).

Management designs must be carefully considered. Eggs can be obtained from a wild or a captive colony. They might be collected from wild or from artificial nests and be incubated under natural or artificial conditions. Hatchlings may be released immediately after emergence or be raised for later release. They may also be raised until harvestable size in captivity. If hatchlings are raised and released, feeding stations and other management techniques may or may not be installed in the release areas, and reforestation may or may not be undertaken.

Many of these combinations are unfeasible, either biologically or logistically. Collection of egg clutches from wild nests is unfeasible. Excavation of the eggs out of the deep and often complex burrows (Hirth 1963; Mueller 1972; Rand and Dugan 1983) is extremely time consuming and finding the clutch is not certain. Moreover, this procedure would destroy the nest sites, which are used year after year by the females (Rand and Dugan 1983; Bock 1984; Bock, Rand, and Burghardt 1985). Eggs must therefore be obtained from artificial structures that make collection easy and do not destroy natural tunnels. Natural incubation of collected clutches would be absurd, because the eggs are being collected in order to incubate them under controlled conditions. Figure 14.3 lists potentially feasible management designs. The research undertaken in the IMP examined the feasibility of these management designs. Three key questions were: how to maximize reproductive output, how to make iguana numbers predictable, and how to increase survivorship. These biological characteristics

REPROD. COLONY	WILD								CAPTIVE							
NESTS	ARTIFICIAL								ARTIFICIAL							
INCUBATION	ARTIFICIAL								ARTIFICIAL							
HATCHL RAISING, 9MO	−				+				−				+			
FEEDING STATIONS	−		+		−		+		−		+		−		+	
REFORESTATION	−	+	−	+	−	+	−	+	−	+	−	+	−	+	−	+
CAPT RAIS FOR HARV	---															+

Figure 14.3. Potentially feasible iguana management models. Research in the IMP focuses on assessing the biological, social, and economic feasibility of these models.

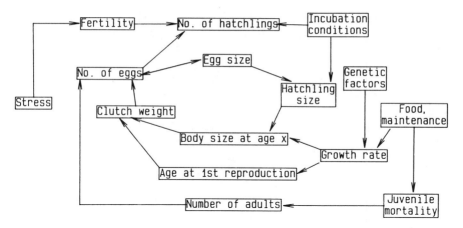

Figure 14.4. Biological variables and their interrelation (*arrows*). See text for implications of the interrelations for management.

are interrelated (fig. 14.4). Research was carried out on wild as well as on captive-reared iguanas.

Maximizing Reproductive Output

Experience shows that captive reproduction of reptiles is not easy. To my knowledge, no existing reptile management operation produces all of its own young. All crocodile and turtle operations collect eggs or young from the wild because of low reproductive rate, low fertility, or high hatching failure of captive-produced eggs.

An attempt to use gravid adult iguanas captured from the wild as reproductive stock in captivity failed. Of 120 captured females, 40 had died by three months after capture or had developed infections, most likely a result of stress (Werner, unpubl. data). All but 15 wild captured females were released back into the wild. Of these 15 individuals, 8 (53%) produced infertile clutches the following year. Five others (33.3%) developed fungus infections. By comparison, iguanas hatched in captivity from both wild-collected and captive-laid eggs developed no diseases, produced only 7.5% infertile eggs (of a total of 6,771 eggs), and only 2 out of 249 captive-raised females developed fungus infections (in 1987).

I systematically investigated the conditions that maximized the reproductive output of individuals in captive colonies. A variety of cage designs were tested for maintaining the reproductive stock of adults. Small cages, (1 m²), were used to house three or four females with one male (four adults/m²). In the medium-sized cages (33 m²), fourteen females were housed with four males (0.6 adults/m²). The largest cage was 750 m² and housed 100 adults (0.13 adults/m²). Growth rate and clutch size were similar in all three cage designs, but fertility was lowest in the 33-m^2 cages (72% compared with above 95% in the very small and very large cages). Material costs per individual iguana were similar for the small and medium cages and about twice as high for the very large cage. Obviously the large cage, which has the lowest population density of iguanas, is least feasible because of the high material costs per animal.

Group size for adult colonies is certainly important. No fighting occurred in the one male–three or four female cages, whereas fighting among males in the two larger cages was over ten times more frequent than observed in wild males. Optical barriers installed in these cages reduced the number of injuries inflicted by fighting, but so far it has been impossible to eliminate injuries entirely. The high frequency of chases and fights most likely influenced the relatively low fertility in the medium-sized cages.

In captivity, the ratio of breeding males should be kept as low as possible. A low socionomic sex ratio minimizes the amount of food necessary to produce a determined number of eggs and lowers fighting frequency. Enough males, however, must be present to guarantee female fertilization. A sex ratio of one male to four females resulted in virtually 100% fertility in most of our forty-five cages housing reproductive groups.

Experiments indicate that age at first reproduction is a function of size and thus growth rate. Twelve females (originating from ten mothers) were kept on a high-quality diet during their first 7 months of life. Twelve sisters of these females were kept on a low-quality diet for the same time span. After 7 months, both groups were fed the same diet. The females given the low-quality diet were 32% lighter than their sisters. Six of twelve females raised on the high-quality diet reproduced in their second year, whereas only one given the low-quality diet did so.

Reproductive output may be maximized by offering iguanas conditions in captivity that enhance natural growth rates. Growth rate of wild juvenile iguanas from Central Panama is 0.23 mm/day (Rand and Greene 1982). Our captive rearing experiments clearly show that growth rate is influenced by the maintenance and feeding regime to which the animals are exposed. A balanced nutrition that provides the reptiles with necessary elements is also vital for healthy animals. Increased growth rates of captive hatchlings to 1 year of age are reflected by the steeper slope of gain in snout-vent length in Figure 14.5. The initial growth rate of 0.19 mm/day in 1983 increased to 0.29 mm/day in 1985. This 52% increase in growth rate, as measured by body length, corresponds to a doubling of weight. The iguanas born in 1985 had attained the same size at an age of 2 years as those born in 1983 at an age of 3 years. In the first year (1983), only leaves and fruits were offered to the iguanas. In 1984, this diet was supplemented with boiled rice and rice germ. In 1985, meat and bone meal and fish meal were added as protein sources. In 1986, a diet was formulated on the basis of 20% protein, 4% fiber, 0.6% phosphorus, and 1.2% calcium. In addition, 25% of the vitamin and mineral ration used for chicken feed

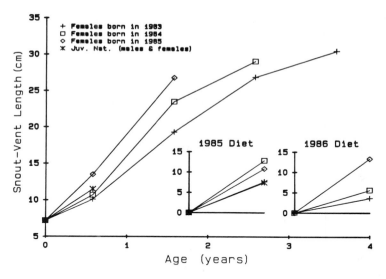

Figure 14.5. Growth of iguanas born in successive years in captivity. All iguanas were kept in the same 100-m² cage. Population composition changed, and densities were higher in progressive years. In 1983, the cage housed sixty hatchlings and five older iguanas. In 1987, sixty hatchlings and fifty-four older iguanas were kept in the cage. Improvements in maintenance and food quality are reflected by the increasing gain in snout-vent length of equal age classes in progressing years. The slope for growth of wild iguanas is known only for hatchlings (Rand and Greene 1982). Of nineteen females born in 1983, only three reproduced in their second year, whereas eight out of fifteen females born in 1984 laid eggs in their second year. After first reproduction, growth slopes level off.

was added to the mix. The food was supplemented with bean and mustard leaves in addition to fruits of the season (mango, bananas, pumpkin, melon). Cage designs were improved by providing more thermoregulation areas and creating visual obstacles and hiding places.

Many benefits result from fast growth:

1. Faster growth rates reduce maintenance (energy, food) costs because the time span between birth and harvest is shorter.

2. If survivorship in the wild is a function of size, which is likely, then a large juvenile of a certain age has a better chance of survival after release than a small juvenile iguana. This reduces the number of juveniles necessary to recruit harvestable adults, thus lowering costs.

3. Adult size is probably influenced by growth rates at early ages. Fast-growing iguanas probably reach a larger final size than slow-growing ones. This results in a double benefit: Iguanas are cheaper to maintain, because metabolic costs (food consumption) decrease with increasing body weight according to the equation: cal/day $= 53.5$ body weight (for herbivorous lizards (Nagy 1982). In addition, a smaller number of hatchlings has to be reared to produce one unit of meat.

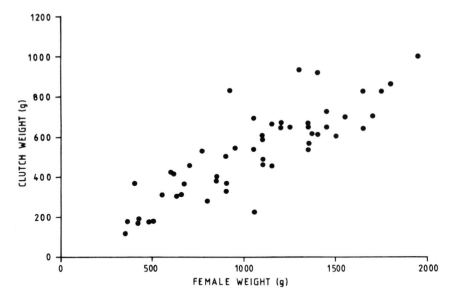

Figure 14.6. Relationship between female weight (after laying) and clutch weight for iguanas from the wild. For regression equation, see text.

4. Clutch size is a function of body size. Larger females will lay eggs earlier or they will lay larger clutches (see following discussion).

Clutch size increases with body size in wild iguanas (Rand 1984), as confirmed by our studies on females from Central Panama (Soberania National Park) and Western Panama (Chiriqui Province). The relationship corresponds to the function $y = 54.04 + 0.45x$ (y = clutch weight, x = female weight after laying, $r^2 = 0.72$, $p < 0.001$). Clutch weight varies greatly for a given body weight (fig. 14.6), which may reflect feeding conditions before and during egg production or variability in the reproductive strategies of individuals in the population.

Egg weight varies between females. The smallest eggs from fifty-three clutches of wild females weighed 11.9 g, whereas the largest weighed 21.3 g ($x = 15.9$ g, S.D. $= 2.2$ g). Hatchling weight depends on egg weight according to the function $y = 2.64 - 0.64 x$; ($r^2 = 0.60$, $p < 0.001$). Growth rate is not related to hatchling size (one-way ANOVA, $p > 0.05$, $n = 170$ hatchlings from ten females), and small hatchlings remain smaller throughout their development. If egg size is genetically determined, it may be desirable to select for large eggs at the cost of fewer hatchlings per female. Hatchlings from large eggs will reach harvestable size earlier than those from small eggs. If hatchlings are to be released into the wild, larger ones may be at an advantage if survivorship is positively related to body size.

Making Iguana Numbers Predictable

Ensuring the collection of the required number of eggs is a fundamental requirement for sustainable production of iguanas. In the wild, females often congregate in communal nest sites and compete for nesting spots. Finding eggs from wild nests is nearly impossible, and digging destroys the nest sites. Ages of the encountered eggs and the mother producing them are always unknown. Studies on the effect of incubation conditions on hatching rate and hatchling quality are therefore difficult or impossible to carry out, as is genetic selection for desired traits.

Constructing an artificial nest that simulated a natural tunnel entrance leading to a closed chamber resolved these problems (Werner and Miller 1984). Almost all captive females (294 out of 318) presented with these nests preferred laying their eggs in the artificial nests rather than digging their own. The eggs were collected in minutes and by comparing female weight before and after laying, more than 90% of the clutches could be attributed to their respective mothers.

The nesting season falls in the early dry season, which is January to March in Panama (Rand 1968). Hatching occurs at the beginning of the rainy season (Rand and Greene 1982), when fresh vegetation is sprouting. The exact onset of the rainy season, however, can not be predicted (Dietrich, Windsor, and Tunne 1982), and eggs may drown in their nest chambers (Bock, unpubl. man.). Another reason for egg mortality is nest predation (Rand and Robinson 1969).

To increase hatching success (fig. 14.7), I designed a seminatural incubation

Figure 14.7. Shells of iguana eggs are pliable and permeable to water. Optimizing incubation temperature and substrate moisture resulted in 95% hatching success. Hatchlings are born with a yolk reserve that supplies them with energy for their first 7 days of life. (Photo, Dagmar Werner.)

system (Werner 1988). Styrofoam boxes lowered into the ground served as incubators. They were filled with moist incubation substrate and provided incubation temperatures similar to those found in natural nests. A hatching success of 95% was achieved using this design, double that in the wild. Although iguana eggs are tolerant of a relatively wide spectrum of incubation conditions, temperatures below 27°C and above 33°C result in hatching failure (see also Licht and Moberly 1965). Hatchling quality (measured by snout-vent length, tail length, and weight) depend on incubation conditions (Werner 1988; Werner and Paton, unpubl. ms.). Hatchling weight may vary by over 15% under different incubation regimes. This difference was maintained proportionally during the first 2 years of development and probably will continue (Werner, unpubl. data). The growth period required to reach a specified size will differ by the same percentage as the difference between sizes resulting from different incubation conditions. Optimum incubation conditions are vital to achieving not only a high hatching rate, but also large hatchlings.

Maximizing Survivorship in Captivity

Survivorship in wild populations appears to be mainly a function of predation pressure and food and water availability. If body size is positively related to survivorship in the wild, fast growth will enhance survivorship. Survivorship in captivity was maximized by excluding predation by keeping iguanas in cages and meeting the iguanas' essential needs, such as a balanced diet, thermoregulation areas, and adequate social settings.

Survivorship in the 0- to 1-year age class is 95% in captivity, more than twenty times greater than in wild populations. The mortality rate of juvenile iguanas older than 1 year is virtually zero. In adult iguanas, there were three causes of death: (1) fighting males killing each other during the mating season (1.5%); (2) males in the multiple-male cages harrassing females to death by copulating (2%); and (3) females failing to deposit their eggs (2%). Male harrassment can be prevented by separating females from males after mating has taken place. Experiments to induce laying with oxytocin injections were unsuccessful in the captive iguanas.

Raising hatchlings in captivity to harvestable size at age 3 implies 5% mortality during the first year, 0% during the second year, and 4% during the third year. For a reproductive colony, the mortality rate remains at 4% during subsequent years (data only until 4 years of age) until the iguanas die of old age.

Optimum cage size and design depend on animal performance (growth, reproduction, etc.) and cage construction costs. Four years of experiments enabled us to increase densities of the youngest age class (through 7 months of age) from one to sixty individuals per square meter without loss in growth rate. This increase of individuals per holding space was achieved by optimizing thermoregulation areas, hiding areas, and food accessibility. High densities result in proportionally lower raising costs.

No difference in growth rate was observed in group sizes of twenty and forty hatchlings at equal space per individual (Alcedo and Saucedo 1987). We also have no evidence that larger group size (up to 500 0- to 7-month-old juveniles) affects growth rate, but the research is not yet concluded.

Green iguanas are extremely sensitive to social changes. Individuals that were removed from their group and placed into a foreign group either died (probably social stress) or at best lost 2 to 3 months of growth. This was true for all iguanas older than 2 to 3 months.

Green iguana hatchlings show a natural tendency for grouping (Burghardt, Greene, and Rand 1977). They recognize and prefer to group with their kin (Werner et al. 1987). We are investigating whether hatchling growth rate might be higher in kin groups compared to groups in which offspring from various mothers are mixed.

Maximizing Survivorship after Release into the Wild

A crucial consideration in assessing the feasibility of management of iguanas is the survivorship of captive-raised iguanas in the wild. To compare the survivorship of captive-raised iguanas with estimates for their wild counterparts, wild survivorship was assumed as follows: 50% hatching success, 4% survivorship during the first year, 40% and 70% for the following 2 years, and 90% for all subsequent years until they die at age 10. If survivorship of captive-reared iguanas after release is equal to natural survivorship, then a 45.2-fold greater number of iguanas results from captive management (controlled incubation produces a 2- and captive raising a 22.6-fold increase) than would result from a natural cohort. If survivorship of the captive-reared iguanas after release is lower, then a corresponding lower number of yearlings and adults will be produced. Raising hatchlings in captivity becomes increasingly less feasible as survivorship after release decreases.

Experiments to identify the survivorship of released iguanas began in December 1985. Since then, 7,000 captive-bred and-raised iguanas have been released in backyards in the interior of Panama. To assess the optimum age, size, and time of year for release, the animals were released at three ages: 7, 9, and 10 months old. Minimum survivorship data from regular censuses revealed that 1 year after these juveniles were released, 50% of them were still in the release areas. Survivorship is most likely above 60% and thus higher than in natural conditions. This indicates that captive raising has little or no detrimental effect on iguana survivorship in the wild or that mortality of natural populations varies with habitat and/or environmental conditions during a particular year. The apparently higher survivorship of captive-reared iguanas might also be a consequence of their larger than natural size at release and possibly better physical conditions. Alternate explanations are that mortality was overestimated in field studies (Harris 1982; Van Devender 1982), that hatching success in the wild was underestimated, or that survivorship may simply be higher in the agricultural areas where the iguanas were released because natural predators are less diverse and abundant.

To identify whether site fidelity, population density, and growth rate of released iguanas can be increased by making the food supply predictable, experimental feeding stations (fig. 14.8) were installed where iguanas were released. Stations were placed at 10-m, 20-m, and 40-m intervals at the edges of the 10- to 25m wide gallery forest and in the back yards of farm houses where iguanas were released. Control areas without feeding stations were also monitored. The feeding stations offered high-quality food supplements. The results indicate that the feeding stations increase iguana densities more than fourfold compared to natural densities. In the release areas with feeding stations, some 200 3-year-old iguanas per hectare were found. The highest density of adult iguanas in the wild reported was forty-five adults per hectare (Dugan 1982). Site fidelity is high. Iguanas released at 30-m distances in back yards of houses were found next to the same house in 90% of the sightings. Of 600 released juveniles that were sighted more than once in 159 censuses during 1½ years following the release, only one iguana was seen farther away than 10 m from the spot where it was usually seen. Site fidelity seems to be independent of the feeding stations, as iguanas in areas without feeding stations were as sessile as those living in areas with feeding stations.

Figure 14.8. Feeding stations installed in the experimental iguana repopulation areas attract captive-raised but also wild iguanas. The low-cost, high-protein food supplements enhance iguana growth and also affect a much higher than natural population density in the experimental areas. As many as 119 iguanas may visit one feeding station placed in the backyard of a farmhouse on a single day. (Photo, Dagmar Werner.)

Habitat management

To increase habitat for iguanas, native trees can be planted that support iguana populations. Iguanas use a great variety of high-quality lumber, firewood, and fruit trees. These can be planted along existing live fence post rows to serve as shelter belts as well as iguana habitat. This design results in a short-term income from iguana harvesting and firewood (5 years after planting), mid-term income from harvesting fruits for human consumption, and long-term income from high-quality lumber (10 to 40 years). In addition, the trees will protect soil and water resources (Stoney 1987; Werner 1987). Forest plantations can be adapted to include other wildlife species as soon as compatible management schemes have been developed.

In summary, all management models indicated in figure 14.3 are biologically feasible, at least according to the present state of research. Obviously, research is not yet concluded, and aspects not yet examined may indicate the greater biological feasibility of one specific model.

Economic Feasibility

Iguanas can be managed mainly for eggs or for meat. If iguanas are raised for their eggs, a reproductive stock must be kept that produces the desired number of eggs. Only females that die need to be replaced. If iguanas are raised for meat, they should be harvested at age 3 or whenever they have attained the desired size.

If iguanas are to be managed for eggs in the wild, one half of the eggs collected in artificial nests can be consumed or sold; the other half must be incubated and the hatchlings released to assure the same number of offspring as under natural conditions. An alternative is to collect 90% of the eggs and raise 10% of the hatchlings to 1 year of age for release. If iguanas are to be managed for meat in the wild, a defined number of adults must be harvested (e.g., all iguanas of age class 3) and be replaced by a corresponding number of juveniles raised in captivity. Iguanas can be permanently marked by hot branding, allowing the determination of age class. In either case, a desired number of eggs and adults for harvest must be replaced by a defined number of young.

The management techniques developed thus far are simple to understand and to implement. The artificial nest can be constructed of low-cost material, for instance of rocks, wood, branches, or any other solid material that can be shaped to the necessary dimensions. The food supplements are locally available and consist of the same basic ingredients as concentrates produced for chicken, cattle, or other domestic animals. Depending on the extent to which the benefit-cost ratio of iguana management can be improved, meat production may become cheaper than that of chicken, rabbits, or cattle.

Benefit-cost calculations presented here are very preliminary, because only fixed costs are taken into account. These are costs for cage, artificial nest, and incubation material, food, and other material costs. Benefits from optimizing variables, such as growth rate, clutch size, egg size, survivorship after release, location of and distance between feeding stations, food composition for captive animals and feeding stations, carrying capacity, and harvestibility are not included in the estimates because relevant research is not concluded. How these and other factors interrelate and determine feasibility of iguana management is illustrated in figure 14.9. Long-term benefits from forest products and soil conservation are also not considered.

Three models were selected to illustrate the economic implications of different designs (fig. 14.10). For ease of comparison, each model assumes the production of 100 iguanas that will be harvested when they are 3 years old. They will have produced one clutch of thirty eggs before harvesting. All models assume that eggs are collected from artificial nests and are incubated artificially, that hatchlings are raised during 9 months in 1-m³ cages at a density of sixty individuals/cage or less, and that food costs are those incurring presently for food purchased from a local feed company (if iguana management reaches a commercial stage, food costs will be some 20% lower). For comparison, it is assumed that half of the food in captivity and at feeding stations could be provided from farm products (fruits, leftover food from meals, leaves from crop plants and so on); however, availability of these food items varies from case to case and seasonally.

The value of time invested was not included in the economic estimates because this varies considerably depending on who does the work. Tending iguanas does not require more work than tending chickens.

For wild populations I assumed that only 50% of the clutches can be col-

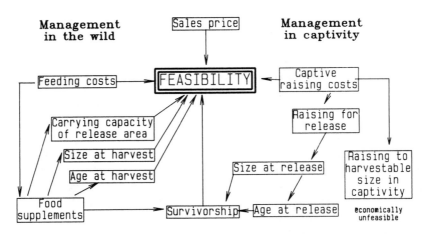

Figure 14.9. Interrelationships of variables influencing economic feasibility of iguana management. Details are only indicated for management designs in which hatchlings are raised for release into the wild.

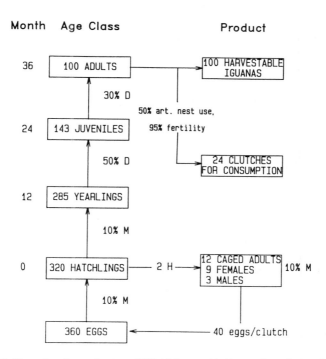

Figure 14.10. Flow chart for production of 100 adults sustained by captive colony and with feeding stations installed in the management area. Numbers per age class are indicated as well as mortality (M) and disappearance after release (D). Hatchlings (H) are produced from captive stock. Age at hatching is zero; the column "months" indicates months after hatching.

lected because only half of the female population may use the artificial nests. For captive colonies I assumed that all clutches can be collected. Mortality in captivity is assumed to be about twice that encountered in the research because campesinos have less experience and may not prove to be as fastidious as research personnel. I assumed that egg, hatchling, yearling (age class 1 to 2) and juvenile (age class 2 to 3) mortality are each 10% for captive iguanas. Disappearance rates for released iguanas are assumed to be 50% for yearlings and 30% for juveniles.

Food consumption data for caged iguanas were derived from measurements. Food consumption of wild iguanas is estimated from the amount of food eaten in the release areas, divided by the estimated number of individuals present. Consumption of supplemental food in the wild is roughly one-third of that in captivity.

The benefit-cost ratios were calculated for both low sale prices ($3 for one 3-kg iguana and $0.10 per egg) and high prices ($4 per iguana and $0.15 per egg). The low sale price corresponds to the average a campesino is willing to pay. Sale prices in the cities are higher and can reach $25 for a female with eggs on the black market in Panama City. Depending on accessibility to transportation and local differences in the value of iguana products, the real cost-benefit ratio will differ.

Model 1. Production of 100 adults raised in captivity

A negligible area (less than 100 m²) is needed. Low mortality in captivity requires a relatively low number of eggs and hatchlings and accordingly lower cage costs compared with models in which iguana hatchlings are raised and released. A major investment in cages, however, is needed to maintain the iguanas in captivity until harvest. Food costs per individual iguana are three times higher than those for released iguanas; overall feeding costs, however, are less costly than that because mortality is considerably lower in captivity than in wild populations.

The model proves quite unfeasible with a ratio of benefit-cost of around 0.5 and 0.7 at low and high sale prices, respectively. In other words, for each dollar the farmer invests he gets a return of only 50 and 70 cents, respectively. Assuming that the farmer can provide one-half of the food without cost from his farm, the ratios increase to 0.8 and 1.1, respectively. Feasibility can be increased if egg size, growth rate, and other biological factors are improved, but high cage and food costs will almost certainly keep this model at the margin of economic feasibility.

Model 2. Production of 100 adults, no feeding stations, sustained by wild reproductive colony

A relatively large forested area (2.2 ha) is needed for this management model. Cage and food costs are restricted to those for hatchlings. Because eggs are collected from wild iguanas, there is also no cost from captive maintenance of a reproductive stock.

The benefit-cost ratios are 2.2 and 3.0 for low and high sale prices, respectively. The model is economically feasible. The return to the farmer is twice what he invests in raising the hatchlings for low sale prices, and three times for high sale prices. If the farmer can provide half of the food for hatchlings from his farm, the benefit-cost ratio increases to 3.0 and 4.1, respectively.

An important assumption of this model is that the relatively large forest area constitutes no cost to the farmer. Most farmers do not have this much forest left. An area of one-quarter to one-half hectare of forest exists around most farm houses. This is the minimum needed to sustain an iguana population. A small area of land will not change the benefit-cost ratio, but it will decrease the number of iguanas produced, which might affect the marketing of the iguanas. In addition, capture of these iguanas may be difficult. Because no food is provided for them, they will remain in the tree tops and probably become very shy. Capture may be disruptive and the iguanas may leave the area because of disturbance.

Model 3. Production of 100 adults, with feeding stations, sustained by a captive reproductive colony (fig. 14.10)

The forest area required for this model is one-fourth of that required for model 2. Costs are considerably higher than in model 2 because of the cage and food costs for the reproductive stock and the costs of providing food supplement to the released iguanas.

The benefit-cost ratio is around 0.7 and close to 1.0 for low and high sale prices, respectively. The farmer invests as much or more into raising iguanas than he gains from selling them. If half of the food is provided from farm products at no cost, the ratios increase to 1.1 and 1.6. The model has high potential for feasibility because of a number of factors. A relatively large number of iguanas can be kept in a relatively small area. Moreover, iguanas will be tame and much easier to capture than in model 2. With food supplements, iguana growth will likely be faster, and mortality rates and disappearance will be drastically lower than in model 2. Calculations assumed equal growth rates and mortality rates. The model provides great potential for improvement. Selection for optimum egg size, growth rate, and other desired traits is possible because young are recruited from a captive reproductive stock. Costs for food supplements for released iguanas can be drastically economized by eliminating elements that the iguanas can obtain without cost from the trees (e.g., fiber).

Social and Cultural Feasibility

The green iguana is a traditional protein source throughout its range from Mexico to Paraguay (Fitch, Henderson, and Hillis 1982; Ruiz and Rand 1981). Because the decline in iguana numbers is a recent development, the tradition of eating this reptile is still alive. In areas where the reptile has gone locally extinct, people feel and lament its loss and are eager to see it back. However, reintroduction of the green iguana into areas of its former range requires accompanying education projects. The present attitude toward wildlife is to hunt whatever can be hunted, without concern for the recruitment of young animals. A campesino will hunt the very last iguana using the argument that if he does not take it somebody else will. A wildlife management project thus must be accompanied by education programs to change people's attitudes. The campesinos must learn that enough young have to be recruited to maintain the population.

To ensure acceptance of the management idea, educators in Panama have worked at the grassroots level. They generally live for 6 to 12 months in the community to establish working relationships with the campesinos and their representatives. Later the educators work on an extension basis. Farmers were found to be more than willing to accept new ideas and methods. They are raising iguanas in their backyards, attending their feeding stations, and assisting in collecting eggs from the artificial nests. They also participate in egg incubation and help us to census released iguanas (Borrell 1986; Chapin 1986; Cohn 1987).

While cooperation in the experimental villages has been high, it must be recognized that the farmers can make no investment other than the time they use to attend their iguanas. A crucial point in iguana management implementation will be reached once the economic feasibility of management designs has been firmly determined. At that time, educational methods must focus on the future benefits the farmer can expect from making an investment now. In the present experimental stage, this type of argument has not been presented to the farmers because the collection of data to determine the economic feasibility of the designs depends on the campesinos' cooperation.

Although acceptance of the iguana management idea is high, habits and ingrained practices are hard to overcome. For instance, many families already pay high prices for fuel wood and other tree products (a live fence post, which is a branch of about 3 cm diameter, is sold for 10 cents!), and farmers understand the advantages of having trees in their pasture. Nevertheless, few farmers are eager to take advantage of the technical assistance and materials to plant trees the IMP forester offers for free.

There are some land tenure limitations to iguana management. Probably 30% of the campesinos in Panama are employees of large landholders and do not own any land. Unless these people are given exclusive access to the resources, iguana management would only benefit the large landowner. Other campesinos own very small pieces of land and are reluctant to plant trees on it. The already small area barely supports the campesino family.

In addition, poor campesinos frequently do not have the money to pay for the initial investments of materials and iguana food. The same farmers usually live in remote areas without access to transportation. Selling the animals would be difficult in such a situation.

Obviously, different management designs must respond to different social and economic settings. Management of wild populations for egg collection might be an adequate design for poor campesinos in remote locations. Management of iguanas in release areas providing food supplements might be feasible for farmers that have access to transportation and hence to food supplements and cash income.

Acknowledgments

The support from the W. Alton Jones Foundation and the James Smithson Society for the research in the Iguana Management Project is highly appreciated. We are thankful to the Inter-American Foundation for their support of the education and implementation projects. We acknowledge the cooperation of the National Institute for Renewable Natural Resources of Panama and the Municipality of Panama. Many Panamanian students and assistants have contributed to the knowledge gathered about iguana biology and management. Lindie Nelson provided the calculations concerning the economic feasibility of iguana management. The cooperation of Panamanian campesinos, especially Don Diego González and the Group 24 de Julio and their representatives, was invaluable to the project. I owe special thanks to Daisy Rey, Yara Cerrud, Armando Batista, and all other Pro Iguana Verde and IMP personnel for their dedication and untiring help. John Robinson, Kent Redford, and their graduate students provided very helpful discussions and criticism of the manuscript. Brian Bock and Stanley Rand also contributed helpful comments.

15

Steps toward Domesticating the Paca (*Agouti* = *Cuniculus paca*) and Prospects for the Future

NICHOLAS SMYTHE

Given the serious setbacks of the green revolution and the dawning awareness of the minor role of 'food from the sea', it is apparent that ordinary agricultural practices must provide most of the food for the growing human population. One would think therefore that much money and expertise ought to be devoted to developing new, reliable, efficient sources of animal protein particularly by development of new forms. [Frankel and Soulé 1981]

Most of the species that are traditionally thought of as domestic have been domesticated since prehistoric times, yet they constitute a very small percentage of the species from which, when given the opportunity, humans derive high-quality protein. Most traditional domestic species do not thrive in the areas of the world where burgeoning populations create a growing need for new sources of protein. If those new sources are to be from wild species, it is logical to consider animals already adapted to the specific environments as the most promising candidates, especially those that are already esteemed as sources of meat.

As in any kind of exploration, there can be no guarantee of success but, as in other explorations, the only way to absolutely guarantee failure is to abandon ship before embarkation. It is surprising, therefore, to encounter statements in the literature such as:

We believe that this type of project [the "semi-domestication" of wild animals] is destined to fail. The [neotropical, lowland game animals] have been little investigated either in the wild or in captivity. The scientific literature says very little about their behavior, social necessities, or illnesses. Moreover, such animals have the characteristics of wild things and in many cases are neither manageable nor breed well in the presence of man. (Terborgh et al. 1986; translation from the original Spanish of this and other quotations from the same paper are by N. Smythe)

Terborgh, Emmons, and Freese (1986) and Emmons (1987) rejected the paca (*Agouti = Cuniculus paca*) as an animal that, in spite of its highly desirable meat, exhibits other characteristics that disqualify it as a prospective source of captive-grown protein. Under natural conditions, pacas are monogamous, territorial, aggressive toward unfamiliar conspecifics and other species, and have a low reproductive rate (Collett 1981; Leopold 1959; Smythe 1983).

The idea of raising pacas for meat is not new. Throughout neotropical America, young pacas are commonly collected from the wild and raised in private households. But they seldom breed. Because of the high esteem in which the meat is held, efforts have been organized by various institutions in several countries to raise pacas in captivity. All have failed or have met with very limited success. The principal impediment to these efforts is the social intolerance and aggressive nature of the animals. Most attempts have involved raising them singly or paired or, occasionally, placing them in groups; in groups, however, aggression and infanticide become serious problems (e.g., Matamoros 1982a, 1982b; Matamoros and Pashov 1986; Lander 1974).

The need for new sources of meat exists, and the desire to raise pacas as one means of helping to satisfy this need also exists. But, unless the natural social behavior of the animals can be changed, it is unlikely that paca raising will become anything more than casual. This report documents progress toward the goal of artificially altering the social behavior of captive-raised pacas as an essential early step in the process of their domestication.

Terborgh, Emmons, and Freese (1986) further state: "we view the concept of raising wild animals in captivity as well intentioned but without adequate biological basis." The rationale offered for this statement is that the wild animals in question do not behave, feed, or reproduce like domestic animals. If it is assumed that the behavioral and ecological characteristics of a given wild animal are fixed and unvariable, then one might conclude that its domestication would be impossible. But the same logic dictates that domestication of any wild species could never have occurred!

In spite of our ignorance of the actual process of domestication, we know that the wild antecedents of domestic species must have exhibited two essential prerequisites: first, they must have had something to offer, whether it was the performance of work, or hair, hide, meat, or other edible products, or a combination of these. Second, and more important, they must have been amenable to some degree of human handling, even if only when very young. If individuals could never be handled, it is unlikely that further steps in the process of domestication would ever have occurred, no matter how desirable the species' other qualities. But, if the behavior of a species that normally reacts aggressively to intra- and interspecific contacts could be ameliorated, subsequent steps in the process of domestication, such as control of reproduction and diet, would be greatly facilitated.

So, before the process of domesticating any new species is seriously embarked upon, the extent to which the "natural" behavior can be manipulated in order to change it for human ends must be investigated. Can the natural social behavior of a species such as the paca (monogamy, social intolerance and, aggressiveness) be altered, or are these characteristics fixed and immutable? Is there an adequate biological basis for believing that social development can be artificially manipulated to produce adults with an altered social organization? A brief examination of the literature indicates that patterns of social organization may not be as rigid as some assume.

Lott (1984) lists over 150 species of vertebrates whose social systems may vary, apparently in response to differing ecological conditions. Twenty-eight of these may switch from monogamy to polygyny under special circumstances, and other species may switch from territoriality to other forms of social grouping. Galef (1970) and Nikoletsias and Lore (1981), by changing the conditions under which laboratory rats were reared, demonstrated that ease of handling could be improved and intraspecific aggression levels reduced. Clark and Galef (1980, 1981) showed that gerbils (*Meriones unguiculatus*), which normally live in burrows, actually benefited—as measured by rates of growth and maturation and level of stress (as indicated by adrenal gland development—when they were denied such retreats.

Social behavior and adaptation to captivity can, therefore, be modified by environmental conditions. The literature of ethology documents cases where social behavior can be even more radically altered through a process of early learning or *imprinting* (Lorenz 1935) in which some animals can be taught to behave socially toward a totally inappropriate partner such as a different species or even an inanimate object.

This suggests the possibility that characteristics that make an animal like the paca unsuitable for captive breeding could be experimentally altered. Imprinting is said to occur in most traditional domestic animals (Kilgour 1985), and some form of rapid, early learning during a critical period has probably been important, if not essential, in the process of their domestication.

Imprinting has not been described in pacas, but an imprinting-like process does occur in another caviomorph rodent, the guinea pig (*Cavia* sp.) (Hess 1959; Shipley 1963; Sluckin 1968). Most of the animals in which rapid, early learning during a critical period occurs are precocial, as are all the caviomorphs. Matamoros (1982a) reports that pacas, if removed from parental influence early enough, become very tame. Tame pacas may exhibit some of the characteristics of imprinting, such as persistent following and sexual overtures toward inappropriate partners (D. H. Janzen, pers. comm., 1984; pers. obs.). This behavior is well known to indigenous people throughout the neotropical forests, who often keep very tame pacas that they obtain shortly after birth or by removing near-term embryos from freshly killed females and raising them. Such animals are usually kept solitarily and, even when in pairs, seldom reproduce. They will persistently follow humans and, given the opportunity, seek out human company. These patterns may persist for at least 5 years, even if the tame animal is returned to the company of other pacas and denied human contact (pers. obs.).

Only very young pacas can be tamed: if an animal is captured at an age of more than about 40 days, it never becomes tame. It growls and attempts to bite if restricted or panics and crashes into the walls of its cage if approached. The existence of an early critical period in the learning of social recognition is thus indicated, and the possibility of manipulating the development of social behavior of pacas by taking advantage of this pheomenon is suggested.

In a case of classic imprinting, a young animal becomes fixated on a single object. When this object is not a member of its own species, the subject's later recognition of social partners may be drastically altered, sometimes to the extent that it can no longer function in an intraspecific social situation such as courtship and breeding (Lorenz 1935; Scott 1953). This would, of course, be undesirable in an animal that is to be bred in captivity. But if an animal is susceptible to the learning of social recognition during a critical period, it is probably also susceptible to the learning of other characteristics of its environment during that same period. The purpose of the study described here was to test the possibility that recently born pacas would learn the characteristics of an artificial environment during a critical period and become accustomed to these characteristics as though they were "natural." The objective was to teach young animals to live in social groups and to be tolerant of human handling. If the learning of such behavior is the result of an imprinting-like process, then, since the capacity to learn (rather than the characteristics learned) is genetic, the young born to animals living in social groups should learn and adopt the behavior of their parents without the necessity of special training.

The tendency among people who keep wild animals in captivity is to attempt to duplicate, within the cage, the conditions that those animals favor in the wild. This is followed by most people who keep pacas and is also generally advocated by those who offer advice on their captive breeding (Matamoros and Pashov 1986; de la Espriella, n.d.). While such a practice may increase the probability of breeding in animals unaccustomed to captivity, it is unlikely to facilitate the process of domestication.

When permitted to live under wild conditions, most traditional domestic species quickly become feral. In attempting to domesticate a species, it would thus seem more advisable to deny the animals their "natural" surroundings, especially when such characteristics as burrowing or cryptic behavior make them more difficult to observe and manage, and to raise them under conditions that are convenient to their keeper. Some may not breed under such conditions, but those that do are thus the founders of a new stock; artificial selection for desirable characteristics will already have begun.

Methods

In 1983 a series of cages was constructed on a peninsula to the immediate west of Barro Colorado Island in Panama. Beginning in 1984 pacas were purchased throughout the country from people who had been keeping them in captivity for varying periods of time. These animals were the "founders" of the new colony. They were all past the age of the probable critical learning period, so no attempt was made to alter their social behavior. Since their most important purpose was to produce young, they were housed, in pairs, in cages that duplicated as nearly as practical the conditions of the wild. Each cage was equipped with a pond large enough for the occupants to fully immerse themselves and with at least one retreat with two access holes for each member of the pair (Smythe 1987).

An attempt was made to determine the complete history of each founder, although this was seldom successful. Owners often confused one individual with another and misidentified the sex of individuals. One animal, a female delivered by postmortem caesarean section by a hunter, was extremely tame and possibly human-imprinted.

Females were paired with males as near as their own age as could be judged. Pairs were observed each of four evenings, for 2 hours after formation, and examined each morning for signs of mate-inflicted injury. In the event of obvious noncompatibility, the male was removed from the cage and a different male introduced.

Artificial Socialization

The young animals in the colony have been raised following different regimes:

1. Of the founding animals, three males and three females were immature when obtained. They and the first paca born in the colony, which was removed from its parents at 2 months of age, were raised in "traditional" cages, similar to those of the breeding founders.

2. The next three young born (two females, one male) were left with their mothers for approximately 30 days and then removed and placed together in a 2- by 5-m concrete-floored cage, which contained a pond and a shelter with an entrance too large for one animal to defend. These three animals were initially caught and handled every day so that they could be weighed and the females checked for opening of the vaginal membrane (Weir 1974). The animals resisted being caught and became increasingly adept at avoiding it. When they began to suffer minor injuries such as lesions and sprained muscles during their efforts to avoid capture, the daily handling was stopped.

3. The next three born (two males, one female) were removed from their mothers at between 15 and 30 days and raised in small (1- by 0.5-m) cages in which they could be caught without being able to injure themselves. They were

handled and bottle-fed every day for 6 weeks in an attempt to tame them, and then they were released, together, into a cage identical to that of group 2.

4. The next eight (three males, five females) were removed from their mothers at between 1 and 14 days of birth. They were fed human infant formula (soya based) and solid food. They were handled every day for at least 2 hours and either carried in a canvas bag by the handler or housed in 1- by 1-m wire cages with plywood floors, which were kept within sight of the handler, as much as possible, day and night.

5. Neonates that were significantly underweight, or obviously sickly, were left with their parents to avoid any stress that might result from the imprinting process.

6. All subsequent, healthy young ($n = 22$) born to the founder females, with three special exceptions, were treated as follows: as soon as they were born, they were separated from their mothers during the night (when pacas are naturally active) and returned to them during the day. They were bottle fed and handled for 2 hours each morning and evening. Handling consisted of merely being held on a folded towel on the lap of the handler, who occasionally stroked them or offered them the bottle or pieces of food. They were permitted to sleep. Whenever possible each was handled with others born at approximately the same time so that each became accustomed to artificial siblings. During the night, when they were away from the mother but not actually being handled, the young pacas were housed in bare, 1- by 2-m, concrete-floored cages in groups made up of all those born within approximately 1 month of each other. A plate containing an artificial solid food diet was placed in the cage from the first day.

At the age of 1 month, each animal was kept in the 1- by 2-m cage during the day and not returned to its mother. It was joined by the younger animals each night. As subsequent animals reached 1 month of age, they were also moved into the same cage so that a group was formed. The females and one male from the group were then moved to a 2- by 5-m concrete-floored cage with a pond in which they could immerse themselves but which contained no other structure or any retreat in which they could hide. Members of these groups were weighed at least once per week.

7. Young ($n = 15$) born to animals that were themselves born in the colony and were living in the artificial groups were not subjected to special handling procedures aside from regular weighing. They were permitted to learn their social behavior from the other members of the group. As they reached the age of 2 to 3 months, they were separated from the parental group and placed in groups of their own.

Diet

A detailed study on the nutritional needs of pacas has yet to be done. We developed a diet consisting of conveniently obtained items that was accepted by

TABLE 15.1
The Diet and the Approximate Cost per Animal

	Daily (g)	Yearly (kg)	Cost/kg (U.S.$)	Cost/yr (U.S.$)
Soya meal	20	7.3	.48	3.50
Wheat bran	50	18.25	.17	3.10
Rice polishings	50	18.25	.21	3.83
Commercial rabbit food	40	14.6	.44	6.42
Dry maize	50	18.25	.29	5.29
Vitamin/mineral supplement	0.5	0.183	24.5	4.48
Total cost/animal/year				26.62

the animals and that maintained consistent weight gain in maturing animals. Pacas are primarily frugivorous in the wild (Eisenberg and Thorington 1973; Collett 1981); however, a diet of fruit is not suitable for captive animals because of seasonal scarcity and because it is difficult to guarantee adequate proportions of essential nutrients.

Pacas can be induced to eat a variety of foods by mixing small proportions of novel food with foods that they accept and then gradually increasing the proportion of the former. In this way a number of experimental diets have been tried in the colony. Table 15.1 details the diet presently in use. This diet is supplemented with leaves, chiefly those of *Byrsonima crassifolia* and *Ficus yoponensis,* throughout the year. It is used as a supplement when fruit is abundant and as the main diet when fruit is unavailable. Pieces of *B. crassifolia* branches of 2 cm to about 15 cm thick are regularly supplied to the animals for them to gnaw. They also receive whatever fruit is available from the surrounding forest and nearby abandoned settlements. Pacas, like most frugivorous mammals, are very fond of bananas. In this project they were never fed bananas except when it was necessary to administer oral medicine, which was mixed with small quantities of mashed banana.

Health

No catastrophic health problems have occurred so far nor, except for endoparasites, has any contagion affected the colony. The pacas, particularly in the early stages, frequently bit one another. These bites were occasionally serious, requiring as many as twenty sutures to close them. But all have healed with remarkable rapidity, and none has become infected with screwworm (*Cochliamyia* sp.; locally common in traditional domestic animals). Ticks (*Amblyonna* spp.) are seasonally abundant in the area of the cages, but otherwise healthy pacas do not become hosts. The same is true of botfly larvae (*Dermatobia* spp.), which commonly develop in local howler monkeys and domestic animals.

Endoparasitic nematodes, chiefly *Ascaris* sp., *Strongyloides* sp., and *Ancylostoma* sp., have been found in the animals since fecal analysis began shortly after the colony was started. Various commercial preparations have been used to combat this problem, and infection has been diminished but not completely eradicated, perhaps because there are wild pacas around the cages that act as a reservoir from which the captives are reinfected. Some commercial antihelminthics appear to cause more or less serious side effects in pacas; others appear to be ineffectual in deparasitization. The best compromise seems to be the products containing membendazole, administered at a dosage of 40 mg/kg body weight each of three consecutive days. The treatment is repeated after 15 days.

Results

The first offspring was born in February 1985. Between that time and 30 June 1988, another forty-six young have been born to twelve founder pairs and fifteen to animals that were themselves born in the colony. All litters have been single births, and the sex ratio has been thirty-four males to twenty-eight females. Young have been born in every month of the year, although there is a seasonal peak (fig. 15.1) in March through May that coincides with the beginning of the local season of fruit abundance. Neonatal weights of forty-eight young (fig. 15.2) varied between 535 and 900 g, the average being 708.1 g.

Of the founder females that have produced four or more young, one has had seven, two, six, and three, four. The intervals between these births have averaged 186.7 days and are generally around 162 or 186 days. The youngest female born in the colony to have produced an offspring herself did so at the age of 390 days.

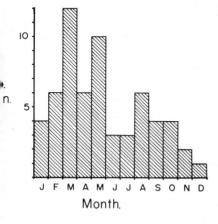

Figure 15.1. The number of young born in each month.

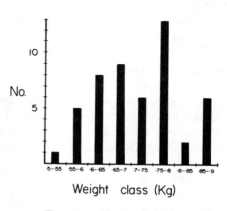

Figure 15.2. The weights of forty-eight neonates divided into 50-g classes.

Results of Artificial Socialization Procedures

The results of treatment 1 are that the animals nearly revert to the wild state, becoming shy and impossible to handle unless restrained in a net or special handling box. They will not tolerate a strange conspecific introduced into the cage, and they may show considerable aggression toward their mates. However, two of the pairs are among the best breeding pairs in the colony, one of them having produced seven young and the other six.

The animals in treatments 2 and 3 are somewhat easier to handle than those subject to treatment 1, but it is still not possible to hold them for physical examination or for such treatments as taking vaginal swabs without some form of physical restraint. They show considerably less aggression toward one another than those of group 1, although individuals occasionally bite and wound one another. It has been possible to introduce extra females into groups subject to these treatments. Animals in treatment 3 can be weighed regularly by gently moving toward them in such a way that they climb onto the platform of the scale.

The surviving animals of treatment 4 become tame and very easy to handle. They are unaggressive toward other group members, and there is evidence that their sexual behavior is normal. They show, however, a greater susceptibility to illness than any others, and three of them died in their first month. They have also, on the average, gained weight more slowly than the members of the previous groups.

The animals in treatment 6 remain tame and easy to handle, although there are individual differences in their tolerance to handling. The most tolerant will not bite aggressively even if a finger is forced into their mouth. They exist in social groups without friction, except for an occasional threat of one to another when all are eating from the same container (fig. 15.3). There are individual differences here too, and some group members occasionally bite others. Each actively seeks contact with the others rather than remaining isolated, so group members sleep in a heap. Perhaps the most significant manifestation of changed behavior is that animals, males or females, can be interchanged between groups. They gain weight rapidly, although there is still a plateau in their weight curves for a short period after they are removed from their parents (fig. 15.4).

The young born into the social groups (treatment 7) are generally accepted by the other members. Two nonmother females attacked newborn pacas in their groups, and one of them succeeded in killing one. After these females were separated from their groups, there were no further problems.

Females often show interest in a group member that is about to give birth and eagerly lick up prebirth fluids as they are expelled. In several instances nonmother females have eaten placentae or have shared them with the mother.

Young pacas in the group treat all members as though they were their parents, rubbing over all of them and nursing indiscriminately from the females,

Figure 15.3. A group of five young female pacas with a male. These normally aggressively asocial animals have learned gregariousness from parents that were trained to live in artificial social groups. (Photo, Nicholas Smythe.)

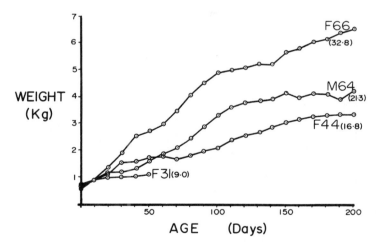

Figure 15.4. Typical rates of growth for animals raised under different regimes. F31 was separated from her parents at 9 days, fed the "traditional" high-fruit diet, kept in a cage with a retreat to hide in and not treated against endoparasites. F 44 was removed from her parents at 29 days, kept in a small cage for a further 6 weeks and handled every day, then moved to a larger cage. She was fed an artificial, high-protein diet and treated for endoparasites when removed from the parents. M64 was removed from parents at night from day 1, and returned to them during the day. He was fed the artificial diet from day 1, was permanently separated from the parents at day 29, and treated against endoparasites during week 1. F66 was left with her parents and offered the artificial diet from day 1. The numbers in parentheses represent the average weight, in grams per day, gained by each animal.

even attempting to nurse from, and being tolerated by, females that have not yet given birth. Adult group members frequently groom whatever youngster is closest to them.

In one instance a day-old baby delivered by caesarian section was fostered to a female that had delivered normally in another group. The odor of the foster mother was transferred to the strange baby by holding it and rubbing it over her while she was distracted. When she accepted it, the foster baby was also accepted into her group.

When these animals were separated from their parental groups and placed in a new group, they showed individual differences in willingness to tolerate strangers. Most accepted unfamiliar group members willingly, but some growled and avoided contact for several days before accepting the others. Most are easily handled, but the same ones that are socially reluctant may try to avoid the handler. None bite, and none panic when approached. There may be mild bickering at the food dish, but there is no fighting.

The animals in this group are not yet (30 June 1988) sexually mature. Males began showing sexual interest (sniffing of the vagina, enurination, mounting with pelvic thrusts) in the females at the age of 3 to 4 months. One female began apparently normal cycling of vaginal perforation at 2 months and the others at 4 to 5 months.

Discussion

The methods of raising young pacas described in treatment 6 are successful in their objective of producing an adult that is manageable and more socially tolerant than normal. Mason (1984) lists four criteria that differentiate domestic from wild animals: (1) the breeding is under human control; (2) a useful product is supplied; (3) the animals are tame; and (4) they have been selected away from the wild type. These pacas fulfill three of these criteria. But the methods are labor intensive and would obviously be uneconomical if it was necessary to repeat them with every animal born. The results of treatment 6 indicate, however, that changed social behavior will be adopted by subsequent generations without intensive infant handling.

As the number of pacas bred in captivity increases, opportunities to select for desirable characteristics will similarly increase, and a truly domesticated stock may be developed within a few generations. Whether or not this will happen depends on a number of factors, the most important of which is the prospect of economic feasibility. What is the probability that paca raising could be economically feasible?

It is possible to calculate the cost of feeding the animals in the present project (table 15.1) and, since the cost of food should be the major recurring expense for people involved in the next stage of domestication, to use this cost to make some predictions. It should be borne in mind that the food used in the present project is purchased retail and in relatively small quantities. A campesino raising pacas should be able to reduce the costs of food by growing it himself or supplementing the diet with food gathered from the forest.

The cost of producing paca meat, in terms of feeding, can be calculated as follows: the cost of producing a young animal is

$$T \times N \times C,$$

where

T = the time (in months) during which the reproductive unit (the parents) must be supported between litters.

N = the size of the reproductive unit per young born (1 [the mother] + the number of males per female in the group, all divided by the number of young per litter)

C = the cost ($US)/mo of feeding an animal.

It costs an additional $t \times C$ to raise an animal to maturity, where

t = the time (mo) during which young must be supported before reaching slaughtering weight.

So each animal at maturity costs: $(TNC) + (tC) = (TN + t)C$.

$$\text{The cost per kilo of meat} = \frac{(TN + t)C}{w} \qquad (1)$$

where

w = the weight of meat.

The present cost of keeping each animal = $26.62 per year, or $2.22/mo (table 15.1).

At the reproductive rate of one young/female/year (Terborgh et al 1986), the costs would be as follows: It is necessary to maintain two adults (since breeders, in traditional raising, are maintained in pairs) for 12 months, at a cost of $2.22/month, to produce each offspring. If each young animal requires 18 months to reach a weight of 6 kg, this entails the further expenditure of $39.96 before slaughtering, for a total of $93.24 per animal, or $15.54/kg live animal weight. If the carcass is 65% useable meat (3.9 kg), this would have cost $23.90 per kg to produce. This is expensive meat by even the most lavish "gourmet" standards and supports the conclusion of Terborgh, Emmons, and Freese (1986).

It is obvious that decreasing any factor in the top line of the equation results in a lower cost per unit weight produced. Thus, keeping pacas in polygynous groups of one male per five females, the number of adults necessary to produce one young is decreased from 2 to 1.2. The shortest interbirth interval in the colony, until now, has been 160 days, or 5.3 months, so each young paca, at this rate, would cost $5.3 \times 1.2 \times 2.22 = \$14.12$, at birth. Figure 15.4 shows that the rate of growth can vary widely; those born early in the project and raised according to the traditional methods gained weight slowly, reaching 6 kg in about 18 months. As diet and parasite control have improved, the rate of growth has increased, and the fastest-growing animals in the present colony reach 6 kg in just over 5 months. It would seem probable that selection could result in faster-growing pacas. Five months of growth requires a further expenditure of $11 for each, to give a total of $25.12. This is $4.19/kg ($1.90/lb) live animal weight, or $6.44/kg for the 3.9 kg of meat. Still very expensive meat, but not ridiculously expensive as a "gourmet" item. This figure is achievable using the methods presently employed.

What are the prospects for further economic improvement? The cost of food could be considerably reduced by a number of methods. The ultimate economic feasibility of paca raising will depend on two factors: first, the capital expenditure necessary to build adequate cages and, second, the reproductive rate. The present groups of pacas are kept in concrete and wire netting cages. Such cages might be practical in a commercial operation but would be beyond the resources of subsistence farmers.

There is a possibility that pacas could be kept without cages. This can not be adequately tested at the present site because there are wild pacas around the cage that would attack and possibly kill any that were released (pers. obs.). However, members of the artificial groups have walked out of their cages during daylight on several occasions when doors were inadvertently left open and have voluntarily returned. There are considerable differences in manageability between individuals, but the tamest can be released and will forage for a while before returning to their cages. One individual was regularly taken for walks in the forest. Since these were all first-generation captives, it appears probable that selection could result in animals that would live around human dwellings without being caged.

Terborgh, Emmons, and Freese (1986) state:

there is another disadvantage that is insurmountable because it is genetically programmed into each species. We refer to the low reproductive rate which is a characteristic of most wild animals. Reproduction is so slow that the possibility of profitable rearing is excluded. On the other hand, domestic animals have been subjected to intensive selection to increase their reproductive rates to the maximum. Domestic rabbits can give birth to 4–6 young every 6 months, but the paca only one per year.

The reproductive rate of the regular breeders in the present colony is a little better than two per year. What is the reproductive potential? It is not possible to answer this question at the present time, but indications are that the present rate is below the potential. All the births in the present colony have been single. Collett (1981) found only single fetuses in forty-two pregnant females. Matamoros (1982b) reports one litter of twins out of thirty-one births. I (Smythe

1987) observed seventeen female: young associations on Barro Colorado Island, three of which involved twins. A pair of twins (both male) was recently live-trapped near the colony. The previous owner of one of the founder females in the colony asserts that the animal is from a litter of captive-born triplets. So the possibility of multiple births exists. The extent to which the reproductive rate can be increased, however, is unknown, and its determination depends on further research.

In a group of five females with one male, if the reproductive rate of females could be raised to two per litter, the number of parents per young would be reduced to 0.6. If the young take 4 months to reach 6 kg and the time between litters could be reduced to 4 months and the cost of food reduced by 50%, the final cost per kilogram live weight would be $1.99. Since the average selling cost of beef in Amazonia is presently about $2.45/kg live weight (Buschbacher 1987), and paca meat, when available, universally sells for more than beef, the proposal of the paca as an economically feasible domestic animal appears reasonable.

Kyle (1987) compares the meat production of Venezuelan capybara (*Hydrochaeris hydrochaeris*) with cattle production and concludes that a female capybara produces 60 kg of meat per year, as compared to 40 kg per cow. Although strict comparison is not valid, since capybaras and cattle are "ranched" and pacas would be "farmed," it is possible to use similar calculation methods to compare the potential yield of meat from pacas. During the 4.5 years required for a steer to reach slaughtering weight, a female paca would produce, at the present rate, ten young with a total weight of 60 kg, or about 14 kg/year. If the meat is 65% of the carcass, the yield would be about 9 kg/year. This is far below the yield from capybara or cattle, but a campesino keeping a single group of one male and five females could expect to produce 45 kg/year, which compares favorably with one steer. He could also eat paca meat at shorter intervals without the necessity of refrigeration, rather than wait 4.5 years for his beef. Paca meat is far more popular than that of capybara, and pacas can be kept in areas that are unsuitable for capybaras. The keeping of cattle in the humid lowlands of the tropics is a major cause of deforestation. Paca keeping would encourage the preservation of forest and provide a source of high-quality protein.

Epilogue

The foregoing was written in July 1988. As of 15 April 1990, 117 pacas have been born in the colony. Sixty-seven are male with forty-nine female. All births have been single, although one female aborted a pair of premature fetuses. Sixty-six young have been born to the founders. As mentioned earlier, the first twenty-two of these were trained to live in social groups. The remainder have been left with their parents, handled once per day for weighing, and, when they reach the age of 1 month, placed in an already formed social group of youngsters born of the artificially socialized animals (from treatment 6). There have been thirty-four "second-generation" young born to the treatment 6 animals, and sixteen third-generation from the second. The third-generation animals remain very social and are easily handled.

One of the advantages of denying refuges to the pacas is that their behavior can be more easily monitored. A total of twenty complete copulations have been observed, permitting the calculation of a gestation period averaging 155 days (138 to 173 days). A large (about 13- by 3-cm) copulatory plug is formed at copulation, but its presence is not easy to detect. Two or 3 days after copulation the plug is expelled. It is sometimes expelled very slowly and eaten by the female as it emerges. Occasionally the entire plug is expelled, and it can be collected before it is eaten.

The cycling of vaginal aperture does not appear to be closely related to the reproductive state of a female. It varies from one to another, is not regular in a given individual, and sometimes occurs in pregnant females, although in such a case the opening is less and may be accompanied by a mucous discharge.

As artificial social groups mature and begin to produce young of their own, they are given to people in Panama who are willing to follow the methods developed in this project. These people then become members of a National Paca Breeding Cooperative. The young produced in the groups remain the property of the cooperative and are used to form new groups and will be distributed according to the wishes of the cooperative members. Four groups have been distributed so far. Each is on a rural farm where sufficient fruit and leaves are grown to make the cost of feeding the pacas negligible during the season of fruit abundance (May through September) and very low during the remainder of the year.

Acknowledgments

This project was supported by a grant from the W. Alton Jones Foundation. The tireless dedication of the site manager, Lic. Ofelina Brown, her contribution to discussions and suggestions for improving the methods, have contributed greatly to the project's success. I thank E. G. Leigh, Jr., for critically reading a manuscript.

16

An Analysis of the Spectacled Caiman (*Caiman crocodilus*) Harvest Program in Venezuela

JOHN B. THORBJARNARSON

As with most crocodilians, the spectacled caiman (*Caiman crocodilus*) has been subjected to a great deal of commercial exploitation, primarily for its hide. This exploitation has decimated populations of crocodilians worldwide, especially among the true crocodiles, which have the most commercially valuable hide, and has left a number of species on the verge of extinction (Groombridge 1982). The spectacled caiman (fig. 16.1) is the most widely distributed and ecologically adaptable of the New World crocodilians, and substantial populations remain in many parts of the species range. Because its hide is considered inferior to that of the larger crocodilians, commercial caiman hunting did not begin until the 1950s, when wild stocks of many of the other species had been reduced below harvestable levels. Due to the scarcity of more commercially valuable species, as well as international regulations banning their trade, caiman presently supply the majority of crocodilian hides on the world market

Figure 16.1. Spectacled caiman (*Caiman crocodilus*) in the llanos of Venezuela. (Photo, John Robinson.)

(Hemley and Caldwell 1986). In Venezuela, uncontrolled harvests during the 1960s reduced caiman population levels, and a total ban on commercial exploitation was imposed in 1972. During the 1970s caiman populations quickly recovered, especially in the central llanos savanna region where they became locally abundant. In 1982, an experimental caiman harvest began; its aim was to achieve sustainable use and manage caiman as a valuable natural resource.

The objectives of this paper are to examine the Venezuelan caiman harvest from an economic and biological viewpoint. Data on population ecology and the value of caiman meat and hides are used to answer two principal questions: (1) Is the present level of harvest sustainable? and (2) What are the economic benefits of the harvest? I discuss the feasibility of using this harvest program as a conservation tool and its applicability to other Latin American countries.

Ecology of Caiman in the Llanos

Numerous studies have dealt with aspects of the ecology and behavior of the spectacled caiman, and information on population ecology is available from Mexico (Alvarez del Toro 1974); Venezuela (Staton and Dixon 1975, 1977; Gorzula 1978; Ayarzaguena 1983); Suriname (Ouboter and Nanhoe 1984); and Brazil (Crawshaw and Schaller 1980; Crawshaw 1987). Much of what is known about the behavior and ecology of the spectacled caiman has been summarized in recent reviews by Medem (1981, 1983) and Gorzula and Seijas (1989).

The ecology of the caiman has been particularly well studied in the Llanos region of Venezuela (Rivero-Blanco 1974; Staton and Dixon 1975, 1977; Marcellini 1979; Seijas and Ramos 1980; Ayarzaguena 1983; Thorbjarnarson, unpubl. ms.) and Colombia (Medem 1981). The Llanos is a large, low-lying savanna region that comprises much of the northern and western sections of the Orinoco river drainage basin in Venezuela and Colombia. Within Venezuela, some 252,530 km² of the states of Apure, Barinas, Portuguesa, Cojedes, and Guarico form the heart of the llanos habitat. The llanos are characterized by a hyperseasonal climate with well-defined wet (May to November) and dry (December to April) seasons. Total precipitation is only 1,500 to 2,000 mm annually, but the extreme seasonality, low-lying topography, and relatively water-impermeable soil combine to cause widespread flooding from June to October. During the extended dry season, aquatic habitat is reduced to a few small lagoons, streams (caños), or rivers. In many parts of the llanos, reduced wetlands habitat during the dry season results in extremely dense concentrations of caiman. Reported dry season concentrations of 50 to 300 ha are not unusual (Staton and Dixon 1975; Marcellini 1979; Ayarzaguena 1983; Woodward and David 1985). The stressful dry season conditions virtually stop somatic growth in caiman of all size and sex categories and result in high mortality, especially among the smaller size classes (Staton and Dixon 1975; pers. obs.).

The spectacled caiman is a small- to medium-sized species with a maximum reported length of 2.5 m (1.8 m in females) (Brazaitis 1973; Medem 1981). Despite a relatively slow growth rate (Gorzula 1978; Ayarzaguena 1983), females in the wild may reach sexual maturity in as little as 4 years (ca. 60 cm snout-vent length [SVL]). This is in contrast to larger species of crocodilians, which may require 10 years or more to attain maturity. Smaller individuals principally consume small aquatic or terrestrial invertebrates (mostly insects), and larger caiman feed more on vertebrate prey (Staton and Dixon 1975; Ayarzaguena 1983). Nevertheless, two of the principal prey items of Llanos caiman over 40 cm SVL are freshwater snails (*Pomacea*) and crabs (*Dilocarcinus*) (Ayarzaguena 1983; Thorbjarnarson, unpubl. data).

In the llanos, patterns of movement and habitat use by the caiman are closely tied to the annual flooding regime. Caiman disperse from dense dry season concentrations in May with the arrival of the first significant rains. Adult males establish territories in more deeply flooded *estero* habitats, and it is here that most courtship and mating takes place during the months of June and July. Adult females begin nesting in late July, and the peak period of oviposition is in mid to late August. Caiman construct nests from a mixture of live or dead vegetation scraped together with soil and shaped into a mound approximately 40 cm high and 110 cm in diameter. Nests are located in a variety of raised microhabitats to minimize the probability of flooding mortality. An average of twenty to thirty eggs are laid in a hole dug into the top of the nest mound, then covered up and left to incubate. The duration of incubation is temperature dependent and may last from 70 to 90 days. The females generally remain in the vicinity of the nest, which they open to free the young at the end of the incubation period (October to November). The young caiman hatch toward the end of the wet season and, if they are to survive, must find permanent water habitats for the duration of the dry season. In this respect the female plays a crucial role by leading the young, sometimes over several kilometers of open savanna, to permanent water sites. By December, the dry season concentrations of caiman form again (Ayarzaguena 1983; Thorbjarnarson, unpubl. data). Although the female is aggressively protective of the young, first-year mortality from predation, cannibalism, and desiccation is extremely high (Staton and Dixon 1975; Ayarzaguena 1983). Mortality likely remains high for the first few years of life, then decreases in the subadult and adult age classes. Nevertheless, during the stressful dry season, mortality of larger individuals may be significant.

Caiman are remarkably adaptable in terms of habitat requirements and have been reported from virtually every major class of low-altitude wetlands in the neotropics (Gorzula and Seijas 1989). Habitats frequently include humanmade or altered habitats such as reservoirs and borrow pits, and in certain locations breeding populations can even be found in urban environments. In the Venezuelan llanos, caiman populations have greatly expanded over the last 50 years. Early explorers to the llanos (Gumilla 1741; Humboldt 1860; Paez 1862) universally commented on the abundance of crocodiles and made only fleeting references to caiman (locally referred to as *babas*). Before the beginning of this century, most permanent water habitats in the llanos were rivers or caños, both of which were principally the habitat of Orinoco crocodiles. With the virtual extirpation of crocodiles (see following discussion), the caños and rivers provided a great deal of new dry season habitat for the caiman. Settlement of the llanos was also accompanied by the construction of borrow pits along roads and the use of windmills or damming of caños to provide dry season drinking water for cattle. The result of these activities was to greatly expand the amount of dry season wetland habitat in the llanos and has greatly benefited the caiman populations.

Crocodilian Management Schemes

Of the twenty-two currently recognized crocodilian species, seventeen are listed by the International Union for Conservation of Nature and Natural Resources (IUCN) as endangered (12), threatened (1), or vulnerable (4) (Groombridge 1982). The worldwide decimation of crocodilian populations has been fueled primarily by the demand for reptile leather products, but habitat destruction, avarice, and fear have also contributed. Current management programs for crocodilians have stressed the ecological and economic importance of crocodilians as rationales for their conservation. These programs may be classified as either *recovery* programs for endangered species that are based on the unqualified protection of wild populations or *utilization* programs, which are designed to manage nonendangered species as a renewable natural resource.

Recovery programs are nonconsumptive and are designed to protect wild animals and speed population recovery. Recovery is allowed to occur naturally, by enforcing regulations protecting animals in the wild, or is speeded by reintroduction or restocking programs. However, due to the low esteem given to crocodilians in most parts of the world and the economic incentives for killing them, recovery programs must be backed by strong enforcement of protective legislation if they are to succeed. The limited ability of many developing countries to provide effective protection frequently limits the usefulness of these programs.

Utilization management schemes can be classified into two basic types: (1) captive propagation and rearing (farming) or (2) sustained-yield harvest. Within this latter category, animals may be taken from the population when young and reared in captivity to slaughtering size (ranching), or commercial-sized animals may be cropped directly from wild populations. Farming operations are operational or planned in no fewer than fifty-three countries worldwide (Luxmoore et. al 1985). Successful ranching and cropping management programs are also found in a number of countries such as Papua New Guinea, Zimbabwe, and the United States (Child 1987; Hines and Abercrombie 1987; Hollands 1987; Joanen and McNease 1987).

Crocodilian farming is currently being practiced on a worldwide basis. Luxmoore et al. (1985) report existing or planned farms in fifty-three countries, although only a small fraction of these are functional. The majority of farming operations are rearing crocodiles or alligators to produce the more valuable "classic" crocodilian hides (as opposed to the less valuable caiman skins). Similarly, ranching management programs are becoming widespread for classic skin species. The most successful of these programs are in Papua New Guinea (for estuarine and New Guinea crocodiles) and in Zimbabwe (Nile crocodile). Because ranching operations do not have to maintain a breeding population of adults, they have fewer overhead costs than do true farms, where the young are captively produced (Magnusson 1984). Ranching may also be seen as preferable from a conservation standpoint, as it fosters an economic tie to the preservation of wild crocodilian populations and their habitat. However, to trade internationally under the regulations of the Convention on International Trade in Endangered Species of Wild Fauna and Flora (CITES), crocodilian populations in the country of origin must be placed in the less restrictive Appendix II category. Transfer of a species from Appendix I (endangered species not allowed in commercial trade) to Appendix II, in practice, must be based on the presence of an operational management program and data indicating the nonendangered status of the populations in the country proposing the transfer. However, under the rules of CITES, trade restrictions on Appendix I species are lessened if the animals are captively produced. So in situations where natural populations are depleted, and no active management program is under way, farming is the only alternative for economic utilization.

The wild harvest of commercial-sized animals is perhaps the most broadly applicable type of management for crocodilians. There is no cost overhead associated with captive propagation or rearing animals in captivity and a sustained-yield harvest creates a direct economic link to the conservation of wild populations and their habitat. The direct cropping of wild populations may be the only economical method to manage species like *Caiman* that do not produce the more valuable classic hides (Magnusson 1984). Furthermore, in most countries, hunting has more of a cultural basis (from subsistence hunting or past commercial exploitation) than does farming or ranching crocodilians.

If not managed correctly, the direct harvest of wild animals may rapidly deplete or extirpate natural populations. This has been the principal lesson from the last 60 years of overexploitation of crocodilian stocks. However, this harvest was "managed" by the reptile leather industry with short-term economic gain as the principal objective. The modern approach to harvest management would replace that philosophy with one of long-term sustainable yields to provide economic benefits in perpetuity. Over the next 20 years, much of the battle to conserve crocodilian populations will be in convincing governments and the reptile leather industry of the benefits of this type of management.

Crocodilian conservation in Venezuela presents a microcosm of the problems facing wildlife managers around the world today. Of the country's five native species of crocodilians, two are nonexploitable (due to extremely low population densities and heavily ossified skin; (*Paleosuchus trigonatus* and *P. palpebrosus*); two are severely endangered crocodiles (*Crocodylus acutus* and *C. intermedius*); and one, the spectacled caiman, is abundant throughout much of the country. Recovery programs for the two crocodiles are being developed by the Venezuelan government and nongovernmental organizations. Since 1983, management for the caiman has been based on the cropping of adult males from wild populations. This caiman management program is unique in Latin America and holds much potential for conservation based on sustained utilization. The following section describes this management program and examines both economic and biological aspects of its implementation.

Venezuelan Caiman Management Program

World trade in crocodilian skins has declined from the peak period of the 1950s and early 1960s, when 5 to 10 million skins a year were traded, to the present annual volume of some 1.5 million skins (Inskipp and Wells 1979; Hemley and Caldwell 1986). During this time, the species in trade have also changed drastically from a predominance of classic skins to an increasing volume of caiman. Presently, the genus *Caiman* supplies some two-thirds of the crocodilian hides in trade worldwide (Hemley and Caldwell 1986). Although large numbers of caiman were exported from northern South America during the late 1950s and 1960s (see below), the majority of the skins today originate from southern Brazil and Bolivia and are shipped illegally to these or other Latin American countries (F. W. King, pers. comm., 1989). To address this problem, CITES is working with the Brazilian, Bolivian, and Paraguayan governments to develop a regional management plan for caiman in central South America (F. W. King, pers. comm., 1989).

At present, the only Latin American country that has a functional management program for caiman is Venezuela. This program began in 1983 and is based on the harvest of adult males on private lands in the Llanos. The program, despite implementation problems, has been an overall success and continues to evolve and improve. The Venezuelan government, with the aid of Venezuelan and international nongovernmental organizations, has demonstrated a commitment to tying species conservation to rational commercial exploitation. Ultimately, it is hoped that this program can serve as a model for *Caiman* exploitation in other Latin American countries.

History of Commercial Crocodilian Hunting in Venezuela and Colombia

Owing to the greater value of their hides, the first crocodilians hunted commercially in South America were the two species of crocodile: the American crocodile, *Crocodylus acutus,* and the Orinoco crocodile, *C. intermedius.* In

Venezuela and neighboring Colombia, hunting for American crocodiles along the coast began in 1928. Two years later intensive hunting for Orinoco crocodiles began in the inland Llanos savanna region (Medem 1981, 1983). French and German companies organized and equipped local fisherman and campesinos into groups of professional *caimaneros* (Medem 1981). The salted skins were exported mostly to Europe for tanning and manufacture into fine leather products.

Crocodile hunting was a major commercial activity while the resource lasted. The official export records grossly underestimate the true export figures, but it is estimated that some 700,000 to 800,000 American crocodile skins were exported from Colombia alone during the period 1928 to 1959 (Medem 1981). At least twice that many Orinoco crocodile hides were exported from Venezuela and Colombia during roughly the same period (Thorbjarnarson 1987); however, beginning in the mid-1930s both species of crocodiles became scarce in many of the more accessible areas. Hunting continued into the 1950s, but the caimaneros were forced to hunt in increasingly remote regions and devise new techniques for catching the dwindling number of crocodiles (Medem 1981, 1983). Although some sporadic poaching still occurs in Venezuela and Colombia, the widespread commercial hunting of crocodiles effectively died out during the 1950s.

When the crocodiles became harder and harder to obtain, the reptile leather industry began exploiting other species. In the late 1940s and 1950s, the bulk of the South American trade shifted to two crocodilians not found in Venezuela: the black caiman (*Melanosuchus niger*) and the broad-snouted caiman (*Caiman latirostris*) (Medem 1981, 1983). When these species were similarly overexploited, the reptile leather industry turned more and more to the spectacled caiman. Caiman were the least sought after species owing to the presence of heavy ossifications in the ventral scales. These ventral ossifications result in a stiff, nonpliable skin that has prominent surface pitting (King and Brazaitis 1971). Because of these ventral ossifications only a small lateral strip, or "flank," the skin from the proximal half of the legs, and the skin from along the lateral surface of the tail are normally taken from caiman for commercial use.

In Colombia, commercial caiman hunting began in the Río Magdalena drainage in 1951; when these caiman became scarce, hunting switched to other rivers such as the Atrato and the Acandi (Medem 1981). Hunting in Venezuela is reported to have started around 1960 (Medem 1983), although it is known that some exports began as early as 1958 (Rivero-Blanco 1974). One source cited by Medem (1983) stated that 2.6 million caiman hides were exported from Venezuela between 1965 and 1969. Official Venezuelan export figures for the period 1960 to 1971 were only 311,400 (Medem 1983), and Rivero-Blanco (1974) cites official export figures over the period 1958 to 1972 (exclusive of 1971) to be 1,997,484 kg, with the peak year being 1967. The export data from Colombia is probably more accurate, but the figure of 11,649,000 caiman exports from 1951 to 1980 still may be a considerable underestimate (Medem 1981). Pachon Rivera (1982) reported that official Colombian exports of tanned caiman skins from 1970 to 1978 totaled 5,060,972, with a peak of 1,495,401 in 1973. The export revenue for these skins was calculated to be U.S.$ 31,035,759. Total caiman exports including crude hides, tanned parts, or manufactured products was U.S. $33,327,460, or an average of U.S. $3,703,051 per year.

Venezuela instituted a countrywide ban on commercial hunting in 1972. Although illicit trade continued in some areas (especially bordering Colombia), much of the commercial hunting was brought to a halt. The ban on commercial hunting extended until 1982, when the Venezuelan government initiated an experimental caiman harvest.

Chronological Development of the Venezuelan Caiman Harvest Program

The experimental caiman harvest in Venezuela was authorized in 1982 (Ministerio del Ambiente y Recursos Naturales Renovables [MARNR] Resolución No.445). The original regulations established a harvest season from 1 January to 30 April (during the dry season) and a harvestable quota of 7% to 12% of the total population. Only caiman longer than 1.8 m could be taken, although an error factor allowed 10% of the quota to be between 1.2 to 1.8 m long. The regulations placed a 2 bolívares (Bs) tax on each caiman authorized for harvest and prohibited the export of crude or "semitanned" skins. Harvest quotas were to be assigned based on the size of the ranch applying for hunting permits and ranged from 8% (ranches over 40,000 ha) to 15% (ranches between 1,400 ha and 4,999 ha) of the censused population. Small ranches under 1,400 ha were to be assigned a quota of 50 caiman each (MARNR, unpubl. ms.)

During the first harvest in 1983, only eleven out of fifty ranches authorized to harvest caiman did so. This resulted in only 15.8% of the authorized quota being filled (table 16.1). In addition, meat (termed *salónes*) was taken and sold from an even smaller fraction of the caiman (13.3%). The following year a total of fifty-five licenses (out of 115 requests) were granted for a total authorized quota of 85,233 caiman. The ranchers' response improved greatly and resulted in a total harvest of 72,612 skins (85.2% of the total quota) and 28,780 salones (MARNR, unpubl. ms.).

The government modified regulations controlling the caiman harvest in 1985 (MARNR Resolución 33). The government tax was raised to Bs 20 (= U.S. $1 at exchange rate at the time) per caiman. Although permits had never been issued to hunt in the state of Bolívar, this state was removed from the list of areas where hunting would be considered. In the remaining states, hunting was no longer permitted in April, and a minimum exploitable population limit (on private land holdings) was established at 2,000 caiman. The harvest rate was reduced to a maximum of 7% of the estimated population size, and hunting

TABLE 16.1.
Permit Requests, Number of Authorized Licenses, and Harvest Totals for
the Experimental Harvest of *Caiman* in Venezuela, 1983–87

	Year				
	1983	1984	1985	1986[a]	1987
No. permit requests	56	115	339	—	358
No. licenses authorized	50	55	178	—	197
No. caiman authorized	13,975	85,233	235,964	—	104,260
Total skins obtained	2,214	72,612	232,063	—	99,453
Caiman meat harvested	1,865	28,780	110,357	—	64,846

Note: Meat harvest figures are in salones.
[a]The caiman harvest was banned in 1986 for 1 year.

with firearms, or at a distance of less than 150 m from a public road, was prohibited. The transport of meat was restricted by requiring government inspection before removal from the ranch. The new regulations also permitted the collection of caiman eggs for establishing commercially oriented captive rearing centers.

For the 1985 harvest, the number of permit requests almost tripled, and the authorized quota was raised to 253,575 caiman. A record number of caiman— 232,063 (91.5% of the quota)—were taken. Additionally, 110,357 salones of caiman meat were sold (MARNR, unpubl. ms.; table 16.1).

In 1986 the commercial harvest of caiman was banned for 1 year in order to evaluate the management program (MARNR Resolución 61 of 1985). However, censusing was done on sixty-five ranches to assess caiman population levels (MARNR, unpubl. ms). The caiman harvest was resumed in 1987 with an authorized quota of 104,260, of which 99,453 were taken (MARNR, unpubl. ms.).

Census and Harvest Procedure

During the first year of the experimental harvest population estimates were to be based on direct counting of caiman on ranches to be hunted using the censusing techniques developed by Seijas (1984). However, limitations on time and manpower prevented this being done for all ranches, and a mean density value of 0.241 caiman/hectare was used in these cases (MARNR, unpubl. ms.). The following year the number of permit applications increased greatly, which placed a great strain on MARNR to provide accurate census figures. Population estimates were derived by calculating an average density for several bodies of water on each ranch and using topographic maps to estimate the total amount of aquatic habitat on each ranch. The average density values were then applied to the ranch as a whole to arrive at a total population figure. Most censusing was done during the day; to correct for reduced diurnal caiman sightability a correction factor of 3.29 was used (Seijas 1984).

For the 1985 season, a new census methodology was employed. One-quarter hectare sections of each body of water were selected for census. Each section was counted several times, and the maximum number counted was used as the best estimate of caiman present. As in previous years, much of the censusing was done during the day and a correction factor of 3.29 was employed. In this manner, population densities were calculated for individual bodies of water and used to estimate total population for each ranch.

The legal harvest of caiman in Venezuela is restricted to privately owned lands in the Llanos. After the governmental regulatory agency (MARNR) establishes the quota and issues the permits, the landowners may begin to harvest. Although the official hunting season is from January through March, in practice, permits have generally been issued late and most harvesting has been done hurriedly in the late dry season (March to April). Caiman are taken from caños, natural ponds, or borrow pits where they concentrate during the dry season. In most areas, the caiman are captured with a harpoon, lassoed, and pulled out of the water, where they are killed, usually by clubbing (Rivero-Blanco 1985). Caiman are then transported to a *matadero*, where they are skinned and the meat removed. Skinning is done by first making four cuts, two dorsal and two ventral. In most areas these initial incisions are made with machetes or knives, but on some ranches chain saws are used (Rivero-Blanco 1985). During the skinning process virtually the entire skin is removed from the caiman, but only the lateral scales or flanks, leg, and lateral tail sections are used. The rest of the skin is discarded. The skin is preserved by salting.

The meat is taken off the carcass in one piece, called a *salon*. After it is washed the meat is also preserved by salting (Rivero-Blanco 1985).

Before being transported off the ranch, caiman hides are marked with plastic tags that remain attached through the tanning process until the skins are exported. To prevent the sale or use of illegal caiman skins, the hides are checked by representatives of MARNR and the National Guard on the ranch, in the tannery, and again before shipping. Meat is also checked and sealed by MARNR before leaving the ranch.

Economic Value of the Caiman Harvest

The economic value of the caiman resource may be quantified on a variety of levels. First, it provides a source of revenue for landowners whose property contains caiman habitat. The harvest itself and related support services (e.g., cooks, drivers) also provides employment and income for local campesinos who work on the ranch full-time or on a seasonal basis. The sale of the meat is important seasonally in the Llanos and in some of the larger cities in the northern part of the country. Lastly, the tanning of the caiman skins is a lucrative industry and provides an important source of foreign exchange for the country. This section examines some of the economic aspects of the harvest (based largely on data from Rivero-Blanco 1985) and provides quantitative estimates of the value of the caiman resource. Because of the continually changing value of the Venezuelan currency (the bolívar, or Bs), and the international price paid for caiman skins, this analysis deals principally with the 1985 harvest. Conversion of 1985 bolívares into U.S. dollars was made using a conversion figure of 20. A conversion factor of 30 was used for 1987 bolívares.

Value of Caiman to Landowners and the Local Community

For the 1985 season, the average value of each harvested caiman to the landowner has been estimated at Bs 220 for the hide (Bs 150) and meat (Bs 70) combined (MARNR). Rivero-Blanco (1985) estimated that 53% of the gross value of the caiman goes to the landowner; however, Rivero-Blanco used a mean gross value of only Bs 159/caiman in his analyses. If we use the MARNR value of Bs 220/caiman, the expenses fall to 34% of the gross value of each caiman, and the estimated net worth of each caiman to the landowner is Bs 144 ($7.20). Seijas (1984) estimated the mean caiman density on sixteen Llanos ranches (covering an area of 233,769 ha) to be 0.24/ha. If we assume an average of 75% of the surface area of an average ranch is covered by wetlands habitat suitable for caiman in the wet season (Woodward and David 1985), the mean ecological density of caiman is increased to 0.32/ha. At a harvest rate of 7% of the total population, the gross value of caiman per hectare is: (0.32 caiman/ha) $\times$ (0.07/yr) $\times$ (Bs 220/caiman) = Bs 5.28/ha yr. The net value to the landowner would be (0.32 caiman/ha) $\times$ (0.07/yr) $\times$ (Bs 144/caiman) = Bs 3.22/ha yr.

During the 1987 harvest, landowners were paid in the vicinity of Bs 600/caiman (J. Rabinovich, pers. comm., 1989). At these prices the revenue would increase substantially to a gross value of Bs 13.44/ha yr and be comparable to proceeds from cattle ranching (Bs 15/ha yr; calculated from data for a Paraguayan cattle ranch in Simpson and Farris 1982).

Per caiman expenses for the 1985 harvest were estimated to be Bs 76 (Rivero-Blanco 1985). A breakdown of costs reveals that 27% (Bs 20) went to the government to obtain the license, 6% (Bs 5) for transportation, 13% (Bs 10) for salt, and 54% (Bs 41) for contractual and other expenses. A further breakdown of the last category shows that for each caiman, Bs 24 was to pay skinners, Bs 1 for purchasing chain saws for skinning, Bs 1 for cooks, Bs 5 for hide salters, Bs 3 for hunters, and Bs 6 for other expenses (calculated from Rivero-Blanco 1985). According to this analysis, at least Bs 33 from each caiman taken during the 1985 harvest (Bs 7,658,079, or $382,904) went directly to ranch employees. Net returns to the ranch owners were Bs 33,417,072 ($1,670,845) (table 16.2).

According to MARNR estimates, the 1985 caiman harvest involved an investment of some Bs 50,600,000 ($2,530,000) in the llanos states of Apure, Barinas, Cojedes, and Portuguesa and employed directly no fewer than 5,000 people.

Value of Caiman to the Tanning Industry

According to MARNR, five legal tanneries are operating in Venezuela and employ approximately 250 people. In Venezuela, caiman skins are tanned to obtain what is referred to as a "crust." These crusts are then sold to buyers overseas (in the United States, Europe, or Japan), who dye and polish the skins to produce a finished hide. According to MARNR, the average price for raw untanned hides paid by the tanners was Bs 150 for the 1985 harvest. Rivero-Blanco (1985) places the value of a crusted hide at Bs 468, representing a threefold increase in value during tanning. A breakdown of expenses indicates that 32% (Bs 150/caiman) was spent to purchase the salted hide, 5% (Bs 23/caiman) was invested in machinery, 8% (Bs 37) in transportation costs, 10% (Bs 47) for administration, 20% (Bs 94) for manual labor, and 25% (Bs 117) in chemicals (Rivero-Blanco 1985). Based on these figures, total personal income for manual laborers in the tanneries totaled Bs 21,813,922 ($1,090,696). The corresponding figure for tannery administrative personnel would be Bs 10,906,961 ($545,348) (table 16.2).

For the 1985 harvest, MARNR estimates that 700,000 ft^2 of skins were exported. At an average price of $8/ft^2 this represented foreign exchange earnings of $5,600,000 for Venezuela. However, according to a buyer of Venezuelan caiman skins, the value of a crusted hide was underestimated in the reports by Rivero-Blanco (1985) and MARNR, and the actual price paid was $12 to 15/ft^2 (J. Wilson, pers. comm., 1986). Using a conservative figure of $12/ft^2 for 1985 hides, export earnings would have been $8,400,000.

Prices paid for caiman crusts rose significantly for the 1987 harvest. The

TABLE 16.2.
**Estimated Incomes of Skin Producers and Tanners Generated by the
1985 Caiman Harvest in Venezuela (Bs 20 = U.S.$)**

Category	Income per Caiman		Total Income	
	Bs	$	Bs	$
Ranch				
Employees	33	1.65	7,658,079	382,904
Owners	144	7.20	33,417,072	1,670,854
Tannery				
Employees	94	4.70	21,813,922	1,090,696
Administration	47	2.35	10,906,961	545,348
Total	318	15.90	73,796,034	3,689,801

Note: Based on data in Rivero-Blanco 1985.

mean value per square foot was conservatively estimated at $28 (J. Wilson, pers. comm., 1986) and reached $ 33.50 by the end of the year. Based on an average 3 ft^2/caiman this would suggest the sale of crusts totaled $8,354,052. Caiman harvest levels for the short-term future are expected to remain near 150,000. Based on a value of $28/ft^2 this would yield an annual revenue of $12,600,000.

Value of Caiman Meat

The demand for caiman meat is highly seasonal in Venezuela. The majority of this meat is consumed in the state of origin (J. Wilson, pers. comm., 1986), but some meat is sold in the northern urban centers as well. Venezuela is a predominantly Roman Catholic nation, and religious taboos forbid the consumption of meat during Lent. The Roman Catholic Church, however, has classified caiman as a fish and permits its consumption during this time. This results in higher prices being paid for caiman meat before Easter. MARNR reports a total of 110,357 salones of caiman meat were obtained during the 1985 harvest. According to Rivero-Blanco (1985) the mean weight of salones from two ranches was 17 kg, and the mean price paid for caiman meat was Bs 10 before Easter and Bs 5 afterward. However, during salting, the meat loses weight. If we assume a mean weight of 10 kg/salon, and an average price of Bs 7.5/kg, the total retail value of the caiman meat was (110,357 salones) × (10 kg/salon) × (Bs 7.5/kg) = Bs 8,276,775 ($413,839).

The local sale of caiman meat has resulted in only modest monetary profits for the ranchers; nevertheless, caiman meat has great potential as an export product, especially to the Asian market. A Korean company has expressed interest in buying frozen Venezuelan caiman meat at $4/kg (J. Wilson, pers. comm., 1986), increasing its present value some eightfold. However, use of the meat as an export product would require improved slaughter techniques and facilities. The lack of refrigeration facilities on most ranches would be a problem in this respect.

Other Products Derived from Caiman

Presently, hide and meat are the only commercial products derived from the caiman. However, caiman could potentially supply at least two other sources of revenue. Following skinning and fleshing out, the caiman skeleton is usually discarded (Rivero-Blanco 1985), but the skeleton could have economic value as a source of bone meal. The marketing of caiman skeletons for bone meal would require improved slaughter facilities on most ranches, and the use of the skeleton may only be feasible in conjunction with the sale of frozen meat.

Another product that could be used is the secretion of the cloacal musk glands. Medem (1983) reported that during the commercial hunting of Orinoco crocodiles, musk was sold as a base for making perfume. If a market could be developed for caiman musk, these glands could be easily collected and stored during skinning and may provide an important additional source of revenue.

Value to Venezuelan Government

For the 1985 caiman harvest, a tax of Bs 20 was required for each caiman authorized in hunting quotas. Although the total harvest quota was 253,575 caiman, MARNR estimates for total government income were based on the total number of caiman harvested, yielding a total estimated income of Bs 4,600,000 ($230,000). For the 1987 harvest, the tax would have yielded an estimated Bs 1,989,060 ($66,302).

Overall Economic Value of the Caiman Harvest

The net value of each caiman harvested was estimated for the 1985 harvest by adding the amount received per caiman by the landowners (Bs 220) to the value of the crust hide (Bs 468, Rivero-Blanco 1985; or Bs 720, J. Wilson pers. comm., 1986) minus the amount paid for the raw salted hide (Bs 150). Because the two estimates for the value of the crusts differed, high (Bs 790) and low (Bs 538) estimates were obtained.

Based on these estimates of net value per caiman, the total value of the 1985 harvest was Bs 124,849,890 to Bs 183,329,770 ($6,242,495 to 9,166,489), or a mean value of Bs 154,089,830 ($7,704,492). Using the estimated net values per caiman we can also calculate the total value of caiman habitat in economic terms, Low estimate: (0.32 caiman/ha) × (0.07 harvest rate/yr) × (Bs 538/caiman) = Bs 12.1/ha yr; High estimate: (0.32 caiman/ha yr) × (0.07) × (Bs 720/ha) = Bs 17.7/ha; or a mean value of Bs 14.9/ha/yr.

Similar calculations can be made for the 1987 harvest: per caiman gross value to land owners, Bs 600; value of crust, Bs 2,520; amount paid for crude skin, Bs 400; total net worth per caiman, Bs 2,720. The estimated total value of the 1987 harvest was Bs 270,512,160 ($9,017,072), roughly equivalent to the value of the 1985 harvest even though it was based on less than half the number of caiman (table 16.1). However, because of the increased net value per caiman the commercial value of habitat in terms of the caiman harvest is raised significantly to Bs 61/ha/yr.

Sustainability of Caiman Harvest

The Venezuelan management program targets adult males for harvest. The basis of the male only harvest is twofold: (1) a reproductive surplus of males due to a presumed polygynous mating system and (2) larger males size and consequently a larger and more valuable flank hide. Surveys of caiman populations in the Llanos reveal that large adult caiman (over 90 cm SVL) normally comprise 10% to 30% of the total nonhatchling population (average value of 17.4%; Seijas 1984). Caiman populations annually pass through a dry season bottleneck, during which time mortality rates peak and somatic growth slows or even stops (Staton and Dixon 1975; pers. obs.). Large caiman assume dominant social positions in the dry season habitats and presumably act as a density-dependent check on population growth. This would occur through competition for limited resources (food, space), increased susceptibility to disease caused by high densities and stressful conditions, or cannibalism of juvenile or subadult animals (Staton and Dixon 1975; pers. obs.).

The removal of a certain percentage of the large adult males would be expected to drop populations below carrying capacity, or perhaps even raise the carrying capacity of the dry season habitats and increase rates of population and somatic growth. This could take place through a variety of mechanisms: higher per capita resource availability, increased juvenile or subadult survivorship, and increased fecundity.

Current management procedures allow a maximum harvest of 7% of the censused population, which represents an average of 40% of the adult males over 90 cm SVL. Estimates from Hato Masaguaral predict a current annual recruitment rate of 2% to 3% of the total nonhatchling population into this size class (Thorbjarnarson, unpubl. data). No quantitative data exist on how this recruitment would be affected by a reduction in density of large adult males, so it is difficult to assess the long-term effects of the harvest on population size-class structure and reproduction. One potential problem would be reducing the sex ratio below a threshold value where it would negatively effect fecundity (Caughley 1977). However, male *Caiman crocodilus* reach sexually maturity at sizes less than 90 cm SVL (Blohm 1973; Ayarzaguena 1983). A recent computer simulation of caiman population dynamics predicted that fecundity would not be affected even if all the males over 90 cm SVL were harvested (Rabinovich, pers. comm., 1989).

Intensive, unmanaged harvesting of caiman is known to severely deplete population densities (Medem 1981, 1983); however, current illegal hunting in Brazil is selective for larger animals (Rebelo and Magnusson 1983). In this respect the small reproductive size of female caiman is a decided advantage. Rebelo and Magnusson (1983) estimate that 60% and 46% of the female caiman from two populations would have been large enough to breed before being large enough to be cropped. The Venezuelan harvest is very conservative in that it should not at all affect the number of breeding females. A similar harvest quota of 7% to 8% of the total population has been used for American alligators in Louisiana (Palmisano et al. 1973) and Florida (D. David, pers. comm., 1987). In Louisiana, the managed alligator harvest began in 1972 and has been restricted to private lands. Hunting procedures were designed to take a greater percentage of males, and during 1972 to 1977 the harvest ranged from 66.3% to 82.7% male. Nesting surveys in Louisiana from 1970 to 1983 reveal a 9.7% increase in nests on nonhunted refuges and wildlife management areas. However, over the same period of time nesting on privately owned lands that were hunted increased 11.0% (Joanen and McNease 1987). Similar results have been found in Florida, where commercial cropping began in 1981. In one study population, nesting rates increased (71.3 to 88.7 nests/year) after the harvest began, even though a total of ninety-three adult females were taken during the first 3 years of cropping (Hines and Abercrombie 1987). These data on the American alligator indicate that a 7% to 8% harvest level has no negative impact on the wild populations and suggest that reproduction levels increase, even with (or possibly because of) the removal of a certain fraction of the female population.

Unfortunately, no good follow-up studies have been done on harvested caiman populations in Venezuela. The few available data deal with estimates of population density and indicate that in three states no significant changes in population density have taken place over the period 1984 to 1987, during which time 304,675 caiman were harvested. In summary, these data do not allow direct assessment of the effects of the current harvest program on caiman populations in Venezuela. However, based on known aspects of caiman life history (fast maturing, high reproductive potential), the conservative nature of the harvest (7% quota, males only) and the fact that males become sexually mature below the minimum legal harvest size, if the program is administered correctly, the harvest program should not negatively impact wild populations and could be sustained indefinitely.

Additional Management Considerations

Increasing Caiman Density

One obvious means of increasing revenue from the caiman harvest is to increase caiman density in llanos habitats. The Venezuelan government and private landowners have recently expressed interest in increasing wild stocks of caiman by collecting eggs, rearing the young to a certain size, then releasing them into the wild. Such a method is seen as a means of avoiding the high mortality rates of eggs and neonates. A restocking program of this type, however, may be counterproductive, as many llanos caiman populations are already at or near carrying capacity. The principal objective of harvesting management is to reduce population densities below carrying capacity and thereby increasing fecundity and survivorship. This would increase the rate of population growth and provide the basis for sustained yield cropping. Restocking caiman into the habitat would lead to greater density-dependent controls on population growth. This would be manifested in reduced growth rates, reduced fecundity, and increased mortality. Higher densities and increased levels of stress would also increase the probability of massive die-offs due to disease.

The only practical method for increasing caiman density would be to create more dry season habitat, which could easily be accomplished by digging canals or borrow pits or by damming caños so that they retain water over the dry season. Over the long term this would almost certainly cost less than the annual collecting and rearing of hatchling caiman for release. Caiman populations would then increase naturally to a new, higher density levels. Habitat modification is commonly practiced in relation to cattle ranching. With a little planning this can also be used to benefit the caiman populations.

Population Monitoring and the Establishment of Study Populations

Population monitoring is a critical part of any sustained yield management program. The annual monitoring of population density is an inherent part of the current harvest program in Venezuela. However, to better understand the effects of the harvest it would be beneficial to establish several study populations where more detailed information on population density, size-class composition, and reproduction could be gathered. Although considerable information exists on the population ecology of caiman, virtually nothing is known about density-dependent compensatory mechanisms. Because these mechanisms form the basis for harvesting on a sustained yield basis, investigations of this sort would provide valuable information pertaining to cropping schemes.

In the Venezuelan llanos, compensatory mechanisms may be studied in two situations: (1) dense populations at or near carrying capacity that are harvested or (2) populations that have not been well protected in the recent past and that have reduced densities due to unmanaged human exploitation. These studies should be coordinated by the Venezuelan wildlife research department (Servicio Nacional de Fauna) and funded by the government or a private group (see following discussion).

Value Added Conservation

Using a portion of a species' commercial value for its conservation is critical to the success of a management program such as the one in Venezuela (Hines and Abercrombie 1987). Inherent to the utilization program concept is the fact that the species' value provides a commercial incentive to protect the wild populations and their habitat. However, to develop a really effective management program, a certain fraction of the proceeds obtained from the harvest should be invested in a research and management program. The state of Florida, for instance, uses 30% of the proceeds from the sale of alligator skins for alligator research and management (Hines and Abercrombie 1987).

In Venezuela, the government has placed a Bs 20 tax on all caiman authorized in the hunting permits; however, this tax money returns to the general treasury and is not earmarked specifically for caiman programs. A change in revenue legislation would be required to make this money available specifically for wildlife management.

Another alternative for generating funds for caiman programs would be through a private group of ranchers and tanners that benefit from caiman harvests. The organization of such a group is now in progress in Venezuela (J. Caraguel, pers. comm., 1988). The members understand that the development of a sound management program is in their own best interests and have agreed to tax themselves in order to make money available for research and management. The establishment of this association will be a major step forward for the caiman management program. To be most effective, the association should be encouraged to establish strong ties with the Servicio Nacional de Fauna to support caiman-related work.

Sustained-Yield Conservation Programs in Latin America

The caiman harvest, if managed properly, can produce both economic and conservation benefits. Caiman provide a significant source of income to ranchers whose land contains caiman habitat and to the ranch employees who are employed for the harvest. Proceeds come from selling the meat for local consumption and the caiman skins for tanning. The sale of tanned, crusted hides represents a considerable source of revenue for Venezuelan tanners and can produce an export product valued in excess of $10 million annually. The government generates revenue directly through the taxation of hunting permits.

From a conservation perspective, the harvest generates an economic incentive for protecting wild stocks of caiman and their wetland habitats. Caiman harvesting, especially if done in conjunction with controlled harvests of other species of wildlife (e.g., capybara), could represent the most efficient economic use of wetland habitats. In savanna regions such as the llanos, these wildlife management programs could be carried out harmoniously in conjunction with cattle ranching, as has been done on several Venezuelan ranches (El Frio, El Piñero). Preserving wetlands to support populations of these economically valuable species would also benefit other wetland species for which no economic basis for conservation can be applied.

The development of a management program for caiman in the Venezuelan llanos has been facilitated by a number of institutional and biological factors. The institutional factors that have contributed to the programs' success are (1) the relatively advanced stage of wildlife management programs in Venezuela, (2) the presence of a large group of biologists who have carried out ecological studies on caiman, (3) a strong group of nongovernmental conservation organizations, (4) an in-place cattle-ranching infrastructure in the llanos, and (5) relatively good enforcement capabilities through the National Guard. In biological terms, management has been facilitated by (1) the high reproductive potential of caiman, (2) many populations being at or near carrying capacity, (3) the dense seasonal concentrations that make censusing and harvesting quick and easy to accomplish, and (4) the relatively large size of llanos caiman and their resulting higher commercial value. Nevertheless, program implementation has been fraught with administrative problems and is still evolving.

Applying a similar harvest programs in other parts of the country would necessitate certain changes. For instance, in Bolívar state, caiman do not attain the minimum legal size of 1.8 m mandated for llanos populations. A planned harvest for Bolívar caiman would require a smaller minimum size limit, which in turn, would require a system for identifying caiman that originate from Bolívar to prevent the illegal harvest of undersized animals from llanos populations (S. Gorzula, pers. comm., 1988).

The Venezuelan caiman management program is a pioneering effort among South American nations. It represents the first effort by a Latin American government to replace the old unregulated and, in many cases, illegal harvests managed by the reptile leather industry with one based on sustained yield management. Venezuela, with its superior institutional capacity, will serve as a proving ground for this type of applied management, the success of which will be critical for the future of crocodilian conservation in South America. If the program is successful in the long term, it could serve as a model for similar programs in other Latin American countries.

In other parts of South America, the regions with the greatest biological potential to successfully implement similar harvest programs would be other seasonal savannas such as the Brazilian pantanal, the Bolivian Beni region, and the Colombian llanos. However, the political and administrative realities of these regions would play an overriding role in the success of such programs. Strong commitments must be obtained from governments to establish the necessary regulations and enforce them, but in many remote areas where caiman harvest would be contemplated, the functional role of the government is minimal. In these areas the active cooperation of landowners will be the key ingredient to success. In this respect the success of the Venezuelan program in providing a secure source of income for landowners may play a critical role for program implementation.

17

Human Exploitation of Capybara

JUHANI OJASTI

The endemic hystricognath rodents of Latin America occupy ecological niches of large- and medium-sized herbivores and frugivores in many neotropical ecosystems and comprise an important fraction of their mammalian biomass (Dubost 1968; Eisenberg 1980; Hershkovitz 1969;). Hystricognath rodents that are widely hunted for food and other animal products include agoutis (*Dasyprocta* spp.); pacas (*Agouti paca*) of the tropical forest (Collett 1981; Gaviría 1980; Mondolfi 1972; Redford and Robinson 1987; Smith 1976b); mocó (*Kerodon rupestris*) of the dry Brazilian Northeast (Avila-Pires 1977; Lacher 1979); cavies (*cavia* spp.) of the Andean highlands (Dourojeanni et al. 1968; Nogueira Neto 1973); hutias (*Capromys*) of Cuba; nutria (*Myocastor coypus*) of the wetlands and vizscacha (*Lagostomus maximus*) of the Pampa of southern South America (Fauna Argentina No. 20, 1983; Fauna Argentina No. 30, 1984; Mares y Ojeda 1984, Torres 1980), and the capybara. All these species are important sources of wildlife protein in the areas in which they occur.

The capybara of the lowlands of South America (*Hydrochaeris hydrochaeris*) (fig. 17.1) and its smaller counterpart from eastern Panama and northern coastal areas of Colombia and Venezuela (*H. isthmius*) have biological features that make them especially suitable for exploitation as a resource using appropriate management. Little is known about *H. isthmius*, so the information reported here concerns *H. hydrochaeris*.

The capybara is the largest living rodent and one of the heaviest mammals of South America. The average body mass of fully adult capybaras in the Venezuelan llanos is 59 kg. The average individual mass, a statistic that incorporates the prevalent age structure in the natural herds, is about 30 kg. The maximum recorded mass in Venezuela is 65 kg (Ojasti 1973). Even higher values have been recorded from Uruguay and southern Brazil, where Mones (1973) reports a figure of 91 kg. The head and body length of adults varies from 120 to 135 cm, and the height at withers varies between 55 and 62 cm. Large size means more edible meat, with an adult animal producing 20 kg or more.

The capybara is restricted to the proximity of water and rarely is found more than 500 m from water. The species occupies a wide array of habitats, from forested riversides to open savannas and brackish mangrove swamps (Mones and Ojasti 1986). Capybara require grazing areas, water for drinking, wallowing, and protection, and dry ground to rest. They apparently prefer some bush or tree cover, but this is not an absolute requirement. In seasonal environments the availability of water during the dry season limits the extent of habitat suitable for capybara. The proportion of suitable habitat for capybara in the dry season in the low llanos of Venezuela has been estimated at between 5% and 30% of the total area, depending on the distribution of water. In the wet season the amount of suitable habitat is much greater due to the presence of temporary pools (Ojasti 1973).

The capybaras are widely distributed in South America. West of the Andes they extend westward up to eastern Panama and eastward into northern Colombia. East of the Andes, they occur northward into Venezuela and southward to central Argentina (fig. 17.2). Large populations exist in Brazil, Colombia, the Guianas, Paraguay, Uruguay, in the Amazonian parts of Bolivia, Ecuador, and Peru, and in northeastern Argentina. All South American countries except Chile therefore contain populations of capybara.

Surprisingly enough, the ecology of capybara remained almost unknown until 1966, when the Venezuelan Ministry of Agriculture initiated a research program in the llanos region (Ojasti 1973), where the exploitation of capybara is traditionally important. Several other studies have since been conducted in Bra-

Figure 17.1. Capybara (*Hydrochaeris hydrochaeris*) foraging at the water's edge in the llanos of Venezuela. (Photo, John Robinson.)

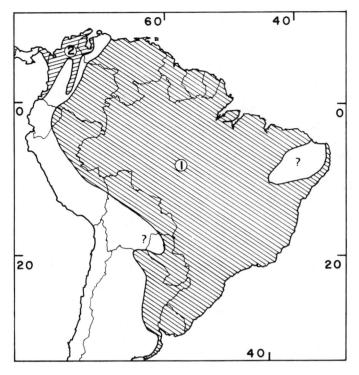

Figure 17.2. The geographical distribution of capybara. 1, *Hydrochaeris hydrochaeris*. 2, *H. isthmius*. The inclusion of all populations in western Colombia into *H. isthmius* is tentative and requires further study. Redrawn from Mones and Ojasti (1986).

zil, Colombia, and Venezuela, and the capybara is now one of the best-known native mammals of South America.

This paper reviews the human exploitation of capybara and discusses the background and prospects of sustained harvesting of this rodent in Venezuela and elsewhere in South America.

Exploitation of Capybara

Subsistence Hunting

To varying degrees, capybara are hunted throughout their range for direct consumption of their meat. This subsistence hunting is practiced by millions of peasants and many Indian communities.

The method of hunting capybaras depends on the abundance and behavior of the animals, the protection provided by the habitat, and the available weapons.

Most subsistence hunters chase down animals in areas where capybara are dispersed in difficult terrain, dense cover, and abundant water. In coastal areas, dogs are often used to drive the animals from the thickets to the shore or into water, where they are shot, struck down with a heavy stick, or taken with a harpoon. Harpooning is preferred by experienced hunters because it causes less damage to the skins, facilitates the recovery of animals from water, and saves expensive shotgun shells. In wetlands the hunters may pursue the capybara on horseback or in a canoe. Capybaras, along with other large mammals, are also hunted at night by searching the shoreline from a boat with electric lights. Iron traps, gun traps, and pitfalls along the pathways of the animals are used in some regions. The animals shot on the shore often jump in the water and sink, but with 20 to 30 minutes they will float because fermentation gases are produced in the digestive tract (Barlow 1965; Becker 1981; Hvindberg-Hansen 1970d; Krieg 1929; Ojasti 1973). Many animals are taken for food in accidental encounters between an unwary capybara and an armed peasant.

The meat of capybara, fresh or salted, is highly esteemed in some regions. Capybara meat is consumed less frequently by rural people than are other large mammals such as peccaries, deer, and tapir (Ojasti 1986; Redford and Robinson 1987). The highest figure recorded in peasant communities is 11.6 kg of capybara meat per person per year (Pierret and Dourojeanni 1966). In Indian communities, capybara comprises about 1% of the total consumption of meat (Hames 1979; Lizot 1979; Vickers 1980); however, most of the available data are from forested areas. The consumption rates of capybara meat in savanna and floodplain habitats are probably much higher.

The chemical composition of capybara meat is similar to that of domestic mammals, but it has a lower fat content (Assaf and Cruz Marcano 1976; Torres Caona 1974). The taste of the meat varies with the age of the animal, the processing of the product, and the region of origin, and probably depends on the animal's diet. The more tender meat of subadults is preferred to that of adults, and the meat of animals from grassland habitats seems to be of higher quality than that from forested areas. In some regions the consumption of capybara meat is believed to produce skin diseases. In many cases the hides of capybara hunted for meat are sold for cash income.

Commercial Hunting

Hunting is the principal occupation and source of income for many peasants in remote areas of tropical America. These hunters generally hunt on public lands for meat to be sold for local consumption and for skins to be sold to the tanning industry or exported. Capybara are hunted mainly for their hides in Argentina (Fauna Argentina No. 2, 1983; Godoy 1963; Lombardero 1955), Brazil (Carvalho 1967; Smith 1980), Paraguay (Krieg 1929), Peru (Hvindberg-Hansen 1970d; Ponce 1973), Colombia (Borrero 1967; Lemke 1981) and Uruguay (Mones 1980). Limited quantities of salted capybara meat is frequently sold in villages and towns along with other bush meat (Aquino and Ayala 1979; Mones 1980; Smith 1980; Ojasti, pers. obs.).

The only large-scale exploitation of capybara meat for city markets occurs in the Venezuelan and Colombian llanos. This activity has developed to meet the demand for dry salted capybara meat, traditionally a dish of Lent in some Venezuelan cities (Codazzi 1841; Ojasti and Medina 1972; Marta 1986).

The small-scale commercial hunters of capybara employ the same methods as the subsistence hunters but probably select for large animals, which produce bigger hides and more meat. In contrast, the large-scale commercial exploitation for meat in the Venezuelan llanos is carried out during the dry season on rather open terrain occupied by moderate- to high-density capybara populations. Under these conditions, the most efficient method of hunting involves teams of men on horseback who locate, round up, and drive herds of capybara to an open place, where workers on foot surround the herd and kill the adult animals with wooden clubs (fig. 17.3). Young and subadult animals and sometimes the visibly pregnant females are saved. Most of the actual killing depends on one or two expert hunters. The other workers keep the herd together and kill only those that run out. The procedure is quick, efficient, inexpensive, and allows selective harvest of the different age and sex classes. This method also presents fewer risks to the personnel than hunting with firearms. The capybara

Figure 17.3. Commercial harvesting of capybara in open habitat in the llanos of Apure state, Venezuela. The expert hunter (in the center) strikes down adult capybara while other workers keep the herd together. (Photo, Juhani Ojasti.)

viscera are then removed and the carcasses transported by vehicle to a camp or slaughterhouse for processing. The average daily harvest is between 200 and 300 capybara by a team of about twenty men. In some cases the capybaras are harvested at night by shooting them from a vehicle with .22 rifle (Ojasti 1973; Ojasti and Medina 1972; Sunquist 1984).

The traditional processing of capybara meat is by salting and drying. The carcass is first skinned, all meat is separated from the skeleton in one piece, washed thoroughly to eliminate the blood, and then covered with coarse salt. The next day the meat is salted again and then dried by hanging in the sun for a week or more. All subcutaneous fat is removed to avoid rancidity. The dressed carcass comprises about 52% of the total body mass of adult capybara—the fresh boneless meat 39%, and the dry salted meat 17%. An adult capybara produces an average of 7.5 kg of salted meat (Ojasti 1973). The market price per kilogram of this product during the 1987 season in Venezuela equaled 80 bolivares (about U.S. $3.50), or roughly the daily wage of a ranch hand.

The hides are the most valuable capybara product in most South American countries. After skinning, the subcutaneous fat is removed and the skin salted or stretched to dry in the shade. The quality of the hide depends mainly on size: first-quality raw hides measure 100 cm or more in length from the eyeholes to the rump and 80 cm or more in width. However, many holes, due to shots or careless skinning, may decrease the value. The price paid in May 1987 by tanning factories in Argentina for first-quality, legally hunted raw hides was 8 australes (about U.S. $4). The product of the 30-day tanning process is a soft, pale yellowish brown chamois leather, which sells in Argentina for about U.S. $20 m². This leather is mainly used for making fine gloves but is also suitable for handbags, belts, jackets, and leather furniture. Most of the leather, known in international markets as *carpincho*, is exported.

The third commercial product of capybara is the oil, which is extracted from the subcutaneous fat and yields up to 4 liters per adult animal (Avalos, pers. comm.). The capybara oil is highly esteemed as a popular medicine (e.g., for asthma) in southern South America. It may also be economically feasible to extract hormonal products from some organs of capybara for medicinal uses (Lopez Barbella, pers. comm., 1984).

Management Policies

Capybara cannot be legally harvested at present time throughout most of its range: national or provincial laws proscribe hunting in Brazil, Panama, Colombia, Paraguay, Uruguay, and in several Argentinean provinces including Córdoba, Entre Ríos, Jujuy, Misiones, and Salta. In some Argentinean provinces there is regulated hunting. In Formosa province the hunting season is from April to July, with a bag limit of five per season. The wildlife service of Corrientes province allows controlled hunting on ranches where capybara have damaged the pastures or crops. In Peru, subsistence hunting is allowed in the forest districts of Ceja de Selva and Selva from April to November. Suriname has an open season without bag limit for the entire year.

Venezuela has carried out controlled exploitation of capybara in the llanos since 1968, which at present is guided by a decree issued in 1984. The management system is based on sustained harvest of natural populations of capybara on ranches located in the states of Apure, Barinas, Cojedes, and Portuguesa. On each ranch where the owner requests a license, wildlife officers estimate the population size of capybara. Where populations are abundant, the authorized harvest is 30% of the population size. This harvest rate is based on an estimate of the annual net production (see Productivity and Sustained Harvest). If the populations are low or decreasing in comparison with earlier estimates, the licence is denied. In addition to the hunting licence, a permit is required to transport every load of meat from the ranch to the markets. This arrangement allows law enforcement officers to detect illegally hunted capybaras. There is also an open season for sport hunting of capybara in February and March, with a bag limit of two per season. The widespread subsistence and small-scale commercial hunting of capybara is illegal in Venezuela as well as in most other South American countries.

Impact of Harvest on Populations

Assessing the impact of exploitation upon the populations of capybara is difficult, because of the paucity of information concerning the past and present status of capybara populations and the intensity of their exploitation. However, a preliminary assessment is critical if we are to develop management strategies for this resource.

There is no evidence that the geographical range of capybara has decreased in recent years. Local extinctions have undoubtedly occurred, especially in open areas with few permanent bodies of water and high hunting pressure. Capybaras are still common in many regions, although in most cases the population densities are much lower than the habitats could support (Barlow 1965; González-Jiménez and Ojasti 1987; Mondolfi 1957; Ojasti 1973; Ximénez 1978).

The status of capybara in a region depends on its management: The Argentinean province of Corrientes allows a controlled harvest of dense capybara populations, all the products are used and sold legally, many landowners see capybara as a resource, and abundant populations exist in many areas. In the nearby Entre Ríos province, hunting is prohibited; however, animals are commonly taken for local meat consumption and the hides are wasted. Landowners do not protect capybara populations, which are generally low (González-Jiménez and Ojasti 1987).

The 30-year record on the legal harvest of capybara in the Venezuelan llanos gives insight to the impact of exploitation on overall population of the region (fig. 17.4). The data cover three periods: Exploitation in the absence of population estimates (1958–62), 5 years of closed hunting, and exploitation based on sustained harvest since 1968.

During the first period, the Ministry of Agriculture (MAC) provided commercial hunting licenses to anyone who requested and paid a given tax. Licensees could hunt wherever and whenever convenient, regardless of the population size and land ownership. This policy discouraged landowners from protecting capybara and resulted in diminishing harvests (fig. 17.4), probably due to overexploitation of the resource. As a result, in 1962 hunting was banned for 5 years, and the Venezuelan market for capybara meat was supplied by Colombia.

In 1968, the commercial exploitation was again permitted, but restricted to owners of ranches with exploitable capybara populations (see Section on Management Policies). The legal harvest increased slowly from 17,700 in 1968 to 46,200 in 1973, mainly because the number of ranches associated with the program increased (fig. 17.4). The harvest decreased starting in 1974 and was associated with severe drought. Thereafter, the number of licenses and total

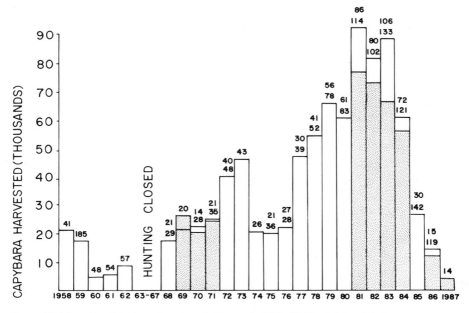

Figure 17.4. Legal exploitation of capybara in Venezuela 1958–87. The height of the bars denotes the total authorized harvest (in thousands of capybara) and the hatched portion the total actually harvested as indicated by transportation permits. The upper number above the bars denotes the number of licenses granted, the lower the number of applications for licenses. When only one figure is given, it is the first number.

harvest increased; by 1981, eighty-one licenses were granted, allowing the maximum harvest of 92,734 capybaras. The sharp increase from 1976 to 1977 coincided with the transfer of the management program from MAC to the new Ministry of Environment (MARNR). This administrative move involved personnel and program changes. Large harvests were authorized from 1981 to 1983, but these were not achieved. Beginning in 1985 the legal harvest decreased sharply. I believe that this decrease was caused mainly by overly optimistic population estimates and concomitant overexploitation between 1981 and 1984. When a decrease in the population was detected, tighter policies were applied to allow population recovery. In 1988, the formula for calculating the harvest quota changed. The quota now is based on the number of capybara actually counted in a ranch, instead of the total estimated population, and on a harvest rate of 20%. In accord with these restrictions, only 7.5% of the 41,810 capybara counted on twenty-two ranches was assigned to be harvested in the 1988 season. Increased subsistence hunting in recent years has also diminished populations according to Medina Padilla (pers. comm., 1986).

Exploitation selectively acts on the population structure. Because large animals are preferred in commercial hunting for meat and hides, the age distribution is skewed toward the younger age classes. This trend was verified by Cordero and Ojasti (1981), who found a lower average age for capybaras in heavily harvested habitats (savannas) in comparison with forests. Herrera (1986) monitored capybara herds for 3 years and reports higher average weight and age in unharvested areas. In addition, Ojasti (1973) detected a statistically significant correlation between the age of female and the litter size, and a higher incidence of pregnancy in large females (size class 50 to 60 kg). Accordingly, the higher proportion of younger females in exploited populations would imply a lower average fecundity.

Given the haremlike social organization of the capybara herds (Azcárate 1980; Herrera 1986), a heavier harvesting of adult males should result in a more productive population. Bone (1977) demonstrated with a simulation model that when a higher proportion of males (60% to 70% of animals harvested) is taken, production increases. However, according to the model, fully adult males are infrequently seen and difficult to find after 2 years and disappeared in a few years.

The hunting pressure also alters habitat use. In heavily hunted areas, capybara survive only in the least accessible habitats with thick cover and abundant water. Grassland habitats offer more forage but require a careful hunting management. Huge areas of neotropical savannas may sustain very sparse capybara populations due to overhunting. Habitat selection as a response to high hunting pressure is linked with changes in behavior. Capybara are quite diurnal and fearless when unmolested but turn shy and strictly nocturnal if pursued frequently. An increase in alertness and in the flight distance is often observed after the seasonal harvest (Azcárate 1980; Ojasti 1973). Heavy hunting undoubtedly breaks down the social structure of capybara herds, but no data are available on this or on the reorganization of the herds after a perturbation.

Sustainability of Harvest

Many wildlife species are exploited in rural Latin America for food and other animal products (Becker 1981; Carvalho 1967; Ojasti 1984; Ponce 1973; Redford and Robinson 1987; Smith 1976b). It is not clear, however, if the present levels of extraction can be sustained in the long run. The sustainability of the wildlife resource is also linked with conversion of habitats, land use, and demand for wildlife products and thus depends on both biological and economic factors.

Biological Aspects

Habitat

While the advancing conversion of tropical forests reduces the habitat available for most large neotropical mammals, the capybara lives perfectly well in open country. In fact, probably most of the best capybara habitat is located on large ranches dedicated to extensive livestock production. Grazing by cattle, which keeps the grass short and palatable, and managing rangeland for livestock, such as the provision of water during the dry season and predator control, generally improves the habitat for capybara. The carrying capacity of many areas for capybara could be improved further by properly distributing artificial pools (Herrera 1986; Ojasti 1982). Open habitats also facilitate assessment of population size and harvest. Accordingly, the adaptability of capybara to open habitats and areas modified by human activities provides a significant advantage for its management.

Nutrition

The use of habitats by capybara is closely linked with their role as grazing herbivores. Capybara are the most abundant large primary grazers among extant native mammals of South America. They feed mostly on grasses growing in low, seasonally inundated savannas and wetlands—areas less used by domestic herbivores (Escobar and González-Jiménez 1976). Capybara digest an average 52% of the total intake of their native forage (Ojasti 1978). This digestive efficiency is similar to that of ruminants and results from the efficient grinding and hindgut fermentation of the forage ingested (González-Jiménez 1978; Ojasti 1973; Parra, Escobar, and González-Jimenez 1978). The use of the most abundant resource in savannas enable capybara to attain high population densities.

Abundance

The direct counting of capybaras present in a given area seems to be the most practical method for estimating the abundance of capybara in open country (Alho, Campos, and Concalves 1978a; Cordero and Ojasti 1981; Jorgenson 1986; Ojasti 1973; Schaller and Crawshaw 1981). This method works best in the dry season, when the animals are concentrated around the remaining bodies of water and the cover is less dense than in the rainy season.

The reported crude population densities in the Pantanal of southern Brazil vary between 1.6 and 7 individuals/km^2 (Alho, Campos and Concalves 1987a; Schaller 1983) and from 0.3 to 36 individuals/km^2 in the Venezuelan llanos (Eisenberg, O'Connell, and August 1979; Ojasti 1973). The ecological densities (the average number of animals per unit area actually used by capybara) attain values between 10 and 200 individuals/km^2 in the llanos (Eisenberg, O'Connell, and August 1979; Ojasti 1973; Ojasti and Medina 1972), but even higher figures are reported in the temporary concentrations in the dry season (Cordero and Ojasti 1981). According to present evidence (Ojasti 1973, 1978; Herrera 1986), the optimum ecological density for capybara production in the floodplain savannas of the Venezuelan llanos is somewhere between 100 and 200 individuals/km^2. The upper density limit is set probably by the territoriality of the herds and dispersion of surplus subadults (Azcárate 1980; Herrera 1986).

Growth and Reproduction

The average growth rate of capybara on natural pastures in their first year and half is between 62 and 67 g/day (Ojasti 1973, 1978), and a twofold increase of this growth rate can be achieved with protein-rich concentrates in captivity (Parra et al. 1978). They attain sexual maturity at a body mass of 30 to 40 kg or between 1 and 2 years of age, depending on the quality of habitat and diet. One litter per year is the rule in most habitats, but two litters can be achieved in confinement and in favorable natural habitats (Ojasti 1973; Parra, Escobar, and González-Jimenez 1978). The litter size is normally between three and five (Bone 1977; Jorgenson 1986; Ojasti 1973). The average number of young produced by a female per year in the llanos is six. The maximum number that has been achieved in captivity is sixteen per year (Parra, Escobar, and González-Jimenez 1978). However, the reproductive performance of capybara is probably less important than newborn mortality as the factor limiting population growth and thus production (Bone 1977; Jorgenson 1986; Ojasti 1973; Schaller and Crawshaw 1981).

Productivity and Sustained Harvest

Sustained harvesting of any population require data on its rate of increase (Caughley 1977). The harvest rate of 30% of the population size in Venezuela was based originally on estimates of population increase derived from the fraction of animals younger than 1 year in capybara populations at the beginning of the dry season (Ojasti 1973). This estimate accords with observed rates of population increase computed from the 20-year census and harvest data of El Frío ranch in the state of Apure, Venezuela (source: statistics of MARNR).

During the period 1967–71, when the population was estimated by the same person, the observed rate of increase r varied between 0.35 and 0.46 per year. The isolated rate of sustained harvest h, which applies to a single annual harvest (Caughley 1977) varied from 0.30 to 0.37. The population assessments were less uniform in later years, and some major changes of the reported population size are likely biased by uneven counting effort or differences in methods. The average r, based on 12 years of data from El Frío that I consider reliable, was 0.42 (range 0.24 to 0.59). The respective mean value for h was 0.34, varying from 0.24 to 0.55. These harvest rates computed from field data are in close agreement with the officially sanctioned rate of 30%.

Another population studied by Ojasti (1973) in Apure state during 2 years increased during this period from 124 to 190, and 36 animals were harvested, resulting in an r of 0.30/year ($h = 0.26$). The populations studied by Jorgensen (1986) in llanos of Arauca, Colombia, and by Schaller and Crawshaw (1981) in Mato Grosso, Brazil, did not increase, however. Accordingly, the net production and sustained harvest of capybara will vary widely in time and from one area to another. Assuming an optimum density of 100 individuals/km², a harvest rate of 0.30, and an average mass of exploited capybara of 40 kg, the maximum sustained harvest of capybara in favorable habitats also grazed by cattle would be 30 individuals/km² or 1,200 kg/km²/year. Populations with a lower rate of population increase would have a concomitantly lower sustainable harvest.

Economic Aspects

The exploitation of capybara provides goods and income for rural peasants, landowners, commerce, and industry. I believe that capybara is less important as a commercial resource and more important as a source of the animal protein for the huge marginal population of rural South America through subsistence hunting. The prices obtained by the full-time commercial hunters for hides and meat are low, because much of this hunting is illegal and because the hunter is exploited by a chain of up to five middlemen, with profits increasing toward the upper end of the chain (Hvidberg-Hansen 1970d; Krieg 1929; Geronimi, pers. comm., 1987). The commercial hunting for meat offers temporary jobs for local peasants, but otherwise the economic value of capybara for common country folk is limited.

The commercial exploitation of capybara on private ranches in the Venezuelan llanos has produced an annual average of 400,000 kg of dry salted meat and a gross income of 16.5 million bolivars (about 0.7 million U.S. dollars at the January 1987 exchange rate) during the period 1975–85 (Marta 1986). Although this harvest of capybara represented only 1.63% of the total value of animal production in the state of Apure, capybaras were harvested only on an average of fifty-three ranches, which comprise a small fraction of the entire state. On these ranches, the exploitation of capybaras provided an important additional income. The profits from exploitation of capybara were probably similar in the Colombian llanos in the 1960s, when Venezuela imported between 162,000 and 409,000 kg of capybara meat per year from Colombia (Ojasti 1973).

The predominant economic activity in many prime habitats of capybara is extensive cattle raising. When these rodents are abundant, they significantly affect the pastures. The landowner must therefore decide what to do with the capybara: harvest them as a resource or eradicate them as a pest.

Capybara have important advantages compared to cattle. As a native species it is better adapted to its environment. Because of the sedentary habits of the rodent, no fencing is necessary. The reproduction efficiency of capybara is six-fold that of cattle and the meat-producing efficiency 2.6-fold (table 17.1), which means higher population turnover and harvest rates: capybara 30%, cattle 10% in Apure state, Venezuela (Estrada 1966). In a preliminary economic comparison, Escobar (1973) demonstrated that the net profit from cattle in Apure State was 4.1% of the selling price, while it was 60% from capybara.

TABLE 17.1.
The Reproductive and Meat-producing Efficiencies of Capybara and Cattle under Natural Conditions (Apure State, Venezuela)

	Capybara	Cattle
Reproductive efficiency		
A. Gestation period (days)	150	275
B. Litter size	4	1
C. Parturitions per year	1.5	0.5
D. Weight of dams (kg)	40	350
E. Weight of newborn (kg)	1.5	28
Reproductive efficiency	0.23	0.04
Meat-producing efficiency		
A. Individual growth rate (g/day)	62	203
B. Body weight at slaughter (kg)	40	363
C. Daily growth/slaughter weight (%)	0.16	0.056
D. Carcass yield	0.52	0.45
E. Time to slaughter weight (yr)	2.0	4.5
F. Meat-producing efficiency per individual[b]	10.4	36.3
Meat-producing efficiency per kg[c]	0.26	0.10

Source: Gonzalez-Jimenez 1977 (updated for capybara).

[a]Kg young/kg mother $= \dfrac{B \times C \times E}{D}$.

[b]Kg carcass/animal/year $= \dfrac{B \times D}{E}$.

[c]Based on body weight at slaughter.

This huge difference is attributed to the high investment of capital and labor required for livestock raising. In the case of capybara, the bulk of the costs are the direct expenses of the harvest and processing. However, the limited market for capybara meat, in comparison with beef, diminishes the value of capybara throughout most of its range. Accordingly, the economic feasibility of the management of natural populations of capybara on rangelands beyond Venezuela depends on the development of markets for capybara meat and integrated utilization of the hides and other derived products.

Capybara hides, compared with other large herbivores, are infrequently exported in spite of the high quality and unlimited potential market of the capybara leather. An annual average of 11,200 hides was exported from Argentina between 1972 and 1978, 150,000 from Brazil (1960–69), 7,680 from the Peruvian Amazon (1962–72), and 25,900 from Colombia (1970) (Mares and Ojeda 1984; Lemke 1981; Ponce 1973; Smith 1981). The tanning industry and manufacturing of products of capybara leather for local markets and exportation is more developed in Argentina. At present exportation is restricted by harvest and trade restrictions taken by several South American countries.

Capybara Farming

Capybara farming is very feasible. The capybara is large, has a high reproduction potential, grows fast, eats grass, has no major sanitary problems, lives in groups, and is easy to handle. Farming would provide employment, food, and income for small farms and peasant communities. Farming would produce the continuous supply of meat required by the meat processing industry. Capybara meat is suitable for sausages, smoked and canned meat, and other industrial applications (Assaf and Cruz Marcano 1976; Fauna Argentina No. 2, 1983; González-Jimenez 1977). Production systems for capybara have been developed and tested in Brazil (Alho 1986; Nogueira Neto 1973; Lavorenti, pers. commun. 1987), Colombia (Fuerbringer 1974), and Venezuela (Parra, Escobar, and González-Jimenez 1978; Sosa-Burgos 1981), and the feasibility of raising capybara in captivity has been demonstrated beyond any doubt. The wildlife laws and policy of many countries also encourage the breeding of native species in captivity. Two main types of production systems have been developed.

Semi-intensive System

In the semi-intensive system, capybaras live in large fenced areas of natural habitat with access to a permanent source of water. The fence restricts the movements of the animals, excludes terrestrial predators, large herbivores, and poachers, and facilitates the capture of animals for sanitary control, transfer, or slaughter. This system can be operated in properties as small as 5 ha. The animals normally graze on natural pastures, but supplementary feeding is feasible during periods of seasonal food shortage (Alho 1986; Cruz 1974). The appropriate stocking rate of this system is not well established. In a 3-year experiment on seasonally inundated savannas in Venezuela, population densities above three individuals/ha resulted in depletion of pastures through trampling (Ojasti 1978). Alho, Campos, and Concalves (1987b) report a value of 4.3 individuals/ha in a similar experiment in Pantanal of Mato Grosso, Brazil.

The semi-intensive system may be suitable under some conditions and deserves further study. Its economic feasibility is uncertain, however. Capybara-proof fences are expensive, and the confined animals seem to be unable to attain much higher population densities than in the wild, even in the absence of cattle. This may be related with their territoriality. Large enclosures of natural pasture would be most convenient as feeding areas of groups of weaned young.

Intensive System

In the intensive production system, animals are closely confined in corrals similar to pig breeding plants and are provided with forage, a pool, and some shade. In the system developed by the research team of Facultad de Agronomvía, Universidad Central de Venezuela in Maracay, the animals are divided in (1) permanent breeding groups of one adult male and four females, (2) larger production groups for weaned young, and (3) small maternity pens for each female and her newborn offsprings until they are weaned at the age of 5 weeks. The staple diet is green forage (*Pennisetum purpureum,* 70% of the dry matter intake) and a protein-rich concentrate, 30%. With this husbandry, most females can produce two litters per year, and growing animals can attain the market weight of 35 kg in 10 months (Parra, Escobar, and González-Jimenez 1978).

Capybara adjust quickly to confinement and reduced living space; however, precautions are needed to control the agonistic behavior associated with the social organization. The composition of groups should not be changed, and new individuals should never be added to an established group. Sosa-Burgos (1981) detected an increase in the agonistic behavior and a decrease of the reproductive output per individual when the breeding group increased from five to fifteen. According to this study, the recommended group size is one male with four to six females in a corral of 30 m².

The economic feasibility of this production system has not been tested, and no commercial capybara farms are known to exist. However, when cheap agricultural residues such as the leaves of sugar cane or bananas are available, it should be possible. The workshop on the management of capybara, caiman, and river turtles, held in Piracicaba, Sao Paulo, December 1987, recommended economic research on captive breeding as a top priority.

Discussion and Conclusions

The heavy exploitation of wildlife in tropical America by increasing human populations is gradually depleting the most valuable species. The overall status of capybara populations is probably better than that of other native mammals of similar size, because these rodents are less affected by deforestation, have lower commercial value over most of their range, and much higher natality rates than the ungulates.

The Venezuelan experience proves that sustained harvesting of capybara in open habitats is possible and profitable. Several reasons contribute to the success of the Venezuelan management policy: (1) It is based on old traditions and a well-established market for meat; (2) it produces income to ranch owners, and at least some ranches protect the herds against outsiders; (3) the harvest quota is based on assessment of the population size and realistic estimates of annual net production; and (4) the Venezuelan wildlife service regards the capybara as a manageable natural resource and has the technical capacity to conduct the program. The continuity of the management, in spite of political changes during the last 20 years, is equally important. However, as indicated by the diminishing populations in the last years, the management system is very sensitive to errors in the assignment of the exploitation quota. This kind of fault can be avoided by more careful population estimates. It is also possible to use floating harvest rates computed from the actual rates of population increase in each ranch.

The current Venezuelan system manages the commercial harvest from large- and medium-sized ranches but does not benefit the small farmers and landless peasants, whose access to the resource is through poaching. This problem is very important, especially because most prime habitats of capybara are privately owned. This is part of the general issue of subsistence hunting, which is closely linked with the fundamental problems of rural tropical America: poverty, inadequate land ownership, isolation, limited basic services in education and health, and lack of adequate development planning. The design of wildlife management strategies that would benefit the common country people is a top priority in Latin America and a potential tool for rural development in general (Dourojeanni 1974; Lopez Pizarro 1986; Ponce 1987).

To address this problem in the case of capybara, Alho (1986) recommends small-scale breeding in captivity. The economic feasibility of this approach is doubtful and should be tested. Official policies encouraging landowners to share more widely the benefits from wildlife with the workers living on the ranch would be another possibility to increase the social value of capybara. It could also be feasible to organize cooperative management plans and harvest quota for peasant hunters on public lands.

The Venezuelan system of controlled commercial exploitation in open country could be operated with some adjustments in other savanna regions, especially in the Colombian llanos. On the other hand, most of the subsistence and small-scale commercial hunting in South America takes place on riverine habitats in forested areas. We can assume that these habitats provide more protection and less food than savannas, but nothing is actually known about the population density and productivity of capybara in forested regions. An ecological survey of the riverine capybara populations is therefore the first step required for the management of capybara for subsistence hunting.

Most Latin American governments have attempted to resolve the management of capybara by banning all hunting. If the protection is effective, the populations will increase in a few years, demanding some kind of harvesting. This seems to be the case in some ranches in the Colombian llanos (Hernández-Camacho, pers. comm., 1988). If protection is not effective and only makes the hunting illegal, the populations are controlled by furtive hunting for subsistence needs or for vermin control. This policy may actually work against the original purposes by undermining the resource value of these animals. In some cases the reason behind the protective policies may be the inability of official wildlife agencies to develop and supervise controlled harvesting programs.

The prospects for capybara management depend on the development of enlightened policies and efficient wildlife services in South America. The developing countries of the areas must learn to properly utilize their natural resources to sustain their expanding populations. They cannot afford to lose valuable wildlife species like capybara.

The value of this rodent can be increased by industrialization of its meat, processing the hides to first-class final products, appropriate use of the byproducts, and simplifying the commercial networks. The domestication and further genetic improvement of capybara is another promising approach. Capybara contribute to the scenic values of some tropical American landscapes, a feature that can be exploited by nature-oriented tourism.

The data base on the biology of capybara is extensive and should be more widely applied to its management. Additional research is necessary, especially to develop techniques for the estimation of abundance in forested habitats, elucidate the distribution, abundance, productivity, and habitat use of capybara in different regions, and in the socioeconomic aspects.

Acknowledgments

I am grateful to Peter Crawshaw, Daniel Navarro, and Jody Stallings, graduate students of the Program for Studies in Tropical Conservation, for their critical review of the first draft and many editorial suggestions, which greatly improved the final manuscript. I am also indebted to Mirna Quero de Peña of Division de Fauna, Ministerio del Ambiente, Caracas, for access to unpublished data on the capybara program.

Part 5
Sport Hunting

18

The Eastern White-Winged Dove: Factors Influencing Use and Continuity of the Resource

PAUL C. PURDY AND ROY E. TOMLINSON

The white-winged dove (*Zenaida asiatica*) is an important sustainable natural resource throughout its range in the western hemisphere. Two major subspecies nest in the southwestern part of the United States and northern Mexico (fig. 18.1). The western subspecies (*Z. a. mearnsi*) nests mainly in the southern parts of Arizona and California and the Mexican states of Sonora and Sinaloa. Although some whitewings of this race nest in colonies, most nest in solitary locations throughout the dry, desert areas. These populations migrate along the Pacific Coast and winter primarily in the southwestern Mexican states of Jalisco, Colima, Michoacán, and Guerrero (Brown 1982).

The eastern subspecies (*Z. a. asiatica*) nests in southern Texas and northeastern Mexico (Tamaulipas and Nuevo León). This population is separated into a series of large and densely populated colonies but interchange of individual birds among colonies occurs from year to year. Doves from all of the colonies have identical migration patterns. They move south along the east coast of Mexico and cross the Isthmus of Tehuantepec into southern Mexico and Central America. Wintering areas are concentrated along the Pacific Coast of Central America as far south as northwestern Costa Rica. Thus, the eastern and western white-wing races are mutually exclusive in nesting and migration behavior and seldom meet on common ground.

In the nesting range of the eastern subspecies, the clearing of native brush for agricultural development has directly affected populations. For years, a major concern has been that the loss of nesting habitat combined with increasing hunting pressure will eventually spell the end for white-wings. The purpose of this paper is to provide information on the status of the eastern race; to document changes in habitat resulting from agricultural development in Texas and Mexico; to illustrate the continuing impact of these changes on white-wing populations; to indicate the need for protection of existing habitat; to indicate the impact of hunting on the species; and to provide some insight into management needs for the species.

Figure 18.1. Distribution of the two major subspecies of white-winged doves. Arrows indicate migratory routes of each population.

Agricultural Development and Habitat Destruction

The breeding range of the eastern white-winged dove extends from upper south Texas to southern Tamaulipas. The most productive nesting areas fall within the Tamaulipan biotic province on the Gulf of Mexico coastal plain.

White-wings nest in a vegetative complex referred to as Tamaulipan thorn scrub or native brush. The vegetation may reach 2 to 5 meters in height and is composed of shrubs and small trees such as ebony, huisache, mesquite, brasil, coma, barreta, guajillo, anacahuite, manzanita, and several species of cactus. The best nesting areas are in associations of these and other plant species that form dense entangled expanses, largely impenetrable to humans without machetes or other cutting instruments.

Many soils of the Tamaulipan biotic province are fertile and well suited for agricultural use after the thorn scrub vegetation has been cleared. Since the middle 1920s, the native brush of the Lower Rio Grande Valley of Texas has been systematically cleared for agricultural development (Uzzell 1950). Over 200,000 ha of potential nesting cover had been destroyed by 1942 (Marsh and Saunders 1942), and an additional 30,000 ha of thorn scrub were removed between 1939 and 1971 (Marion 1974).

Grain sorghums, corn, and cotton have become increasingly important to agricultural production in the Lower Rio Grande Valley since the early 1920s. In addition, citrus production has increased from nil in 1920 to 15.4 million boxes of fruit in 1979 (U.S. Department of Agriculture, 1936, 1980). In 1981, 436,000 ha (40%) of the total of 1,093,000 ha of the Lower Rio Grande Valley were in cultivation (G. L. Waggerman, pers. comm., 1984). Of these, nearly 250,000 ha were in grains, 107,000 ha in cotton, 28,000 ha in citrus, 34,000 ha in vegetables, 15,000 ha in sugar cane, and 2,500 ha in other crops such as aloe vera and sunflowers.

Agricultural development has been slower in Tamaulipas and did not intensify until the middle 1970s, when the Mexican government initiated a program called the Green Revolution. This program introduced new production techniques into the traditional system, including fertilization, changed agricultural practices, pest control methods, and new genetic varieties. A contributing factor that increased crop production was the Sistéma Alimentario Mexicano (SAM), which was implemented in 1980 as a central agricultural and nutritional plan for Mexico. Its primary goals were to improve the diets of some thirty-five million Mexican citizens judged by the government as being undernourished and to attain self-sufficiency in the production of rice, wheat, safflower, soybeans, sesame, and sorghum (SAM 1980; Fernandez Gonzalez 1980). This program was phased out in the middle 1980s.

Cultivated cropland has increased significantly in Tamaulipas during the last 30 years. The cultivated area of about 1.3 million ha in 1980–81 was five times the cultivated area in 1953–54 and three times that in 1977–78 (Secretaria de Agricultura y Recursos Hidráulicos [SARH], 1977, 1978, 1979a). Cultivated areas represented only 3% of the total land area in 1953–54, but over 16% in 1980–81. Since most of the new cropland was converted from native thorn scrub, it can be deduced that nearly 1.1 million ha of actual or potential white-winged dove habitat was destroyed in the period of 1953–81 (Purdy 1983). Data on habitat loss during the last 2 to 5 years has not been obtained. The total amount of existing natural (and useable) habitat has not been determined.

White-winged Dove Populations

Because of the alarming loss of nesting habitat in Texas, studies began in the 1940s and 1950s to monitor the status of white-wings there (Saunders 1940; Cottam and Trefethen 1968). Similar studies began in Tamaulipas in the middle

1960s (La Paloma 1968; Blankinship 1970; Blankinship, Teer, and Kiel 1972). These studies have been continued in the respective states by the Texas Parks and Wildlife Department and the Dirección General de la Fauna Silvestre and more recently, on a cooperative basis, under the aegis of the U.S.–Mexico Joint Agreement on Wildlife Conservation.

White-winged doves were abundant before 1924 in the Lower Rio Grande Valley of Texas. Population estimates varied from four million to twelve million birds in flights during the fall of 1923 (Saunders 1940; Marsh and Saunders 1942). Beginning in 1924, a continuing reduction in white-wing numbers coincided with the destruction of large tracts of nesting habitat during the "land boom" in south Texas (Saunders 1940). By 1939, Saunders estimated the fall white-wing population to be only 500,000 to 600,000 birds. Although the 1923 estimate was based on the recollection by long-time State Game Warden, C. G. Jones (Jones 1945) and was therefore not precise, white-wing populations obviously declined drastically during the 16-year period of 1924–39, perhaps by as much as 85% to 95% (Saunders 1940; Marsh 1941). By 1965, biologists estimated that more than 95% of the native nesting habitat had been destroyed (Cottam and Trefethen 1968). We have concluded that the conversion of white-wing habitat into agricultural land was the major factor contributing to the decline of white-wing populations; however, excessive hunting pressure probably also contributed (Jones 1945). Dr. G. B. Saunders, a U.S. Fish and Wildlife Service biologist stationed in the Lower Rio Grande Valley, and E. G. Marsh, Jr., a biologist for the Texas Game, Fish and Oyster Commission, both recommended several measures to alleviate the problem in a series of letters to officials in 1939 and 1940 (letters on file, U.S. Fish and Wildlife Service, Albuquerque, N.M.). Among the recommendations were purchase or lease of remaining nesting habitat and reductions in hunting season and bag limits.

During the more than 40 years since Saunders' and Marsh's pleas, much progress has been made in fulfilling the early Texas recommendations. Through cooperative projects, state and federal agencies have purchased about 4,000 ha of prime white-wing nesting habitat as refuges, and more land has been earmarked for purchase. The total extent of native brush habitat used by white-wings for nesting in Texas in the early 1980s was about 8,500 ha (Waggerman and George 1982; G. L. Waggerman, pers. comm.). In addition, the establishment of extensive citrus groves (about 28,000 ha) since the 1930s has provided an unexpected source of white-wing nesting habitat. During the last 20 years, about 50% of the Lower Rio Grande Valley white-wings have nested in this citrus (Waggerman and George 1982; G. L. Waggerman, pers. comm., 1984). A severe freeze in the Lower Rio Grande Valley citrus in 1983 resulted in loss of habitat and reduced use of citrus by white-wings. Populations were reduced to the point where closing of the hunting season was necessary in 1985. Citrus has recovered in the last 5 years and white-wing populations are slowly responding to the increased nesting habitat (G. L. Waggerman, pers. comm.,

1984). Since 1941, the white-wing season has been restricted to 4 or 5 half-day hunts in early September with bag and possession limits of ten and twenty birds, respectively.

Habitat acquisition and strict hunting seasons have caused Texas white-wing populations to stabilize at about 530,000 nesting birds and a post-breeding population of about 1 million birds during the period 1967–81. During this same period, the Texas population sustained a harvest of about 416,000 birds annually (R. Tomlinson, unpubl. compilation from Texas Parks and Wildlife Fed. Air Perform. Reps.). The present management program in Texas has been designed to increase the population to the 1981–82 levels.

Little was known about white-winged dove populations in Mexico until the middle to late 1960s, when D. R. Blankinship conducted an intensive study of nesting colonies in Tamaulipas (Blankinship 1970). From the eight major colonies identified, he estimated postbreeding season populations ranging from 5.3 to 6.2 million white-wings during 1966–68 (table 18.1). The total breeding population remained relatively constant at between 3.1 and 3.4 million birds, although numbers of birds in individual colonies varied during the 3 years, which indicated some interchange among colonies. Analysis of banding records (Blankinship, Teu, and Kiel 1972) confirmed that considerable interchange occurred among the colonies as well as with the Texas population, at least among years. During Blankinship's studies, clearing of land for agricultural development was already underway, and he noted that habitat in two colonies had been affected by brush removal between 1966 and 1968.

From 1968 to 1976, white-wing colonies changed drastically, for a variety

TABLE 18.1
**Post-breeding Season White-winged Dove Populations in
Tamaulipas, Mexico, for Selected Years**

Year	Number of Colonies				Number of Doves			
	North Zone	Central Zone	South Zone	State Total	North Zone	Central Zone	South Zone	State Total
1966[a]	2	4	2	8	641,400	2,818,800	1,864,000	5,324,200
1967[a]	2	4	2	8	598,800	2,954,000	2,178,500	5,731,300
1968[a]	2	4	2	8	631,200	1,348,500	4,259,500	6,239,200
1978[b]	5	9	8	22	6,903,859	330,001	1,721,600	8,955,460[c]
1982[d]	4	6	6	16	4,740,000 to 6,320,000	6,204,000 to 8,272,000	1,056,000 to 1,408,000	12,000,000 to 16,000,000

Source: Purdy and Tomlinson, in press.

[a] Blankinship 1970.

[b] Ortega M. 1979.

[c] Incomplete count of all colonies.

[d] Populations estimated without supporting transect data.

260

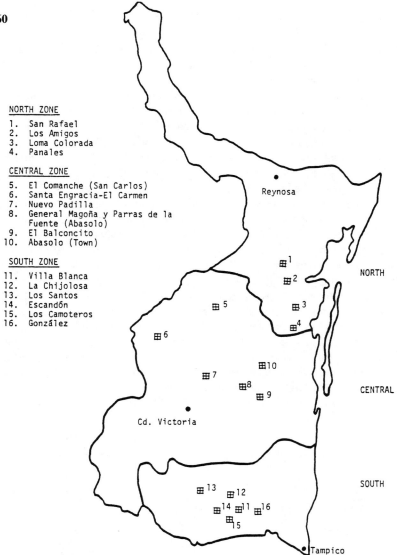

Figure 18.2. The distribution in 1982 of white-winged dove colonies in Tamaulipas, Mexico (H. Ortega, pers. comm., 1983; Purdy 1983)

of reasons, both human and natural. Under the auspices of the Green Revolution, hundreds of thousands of hectares of brush habitat were cleared for agricultural development. Habitats of several colonies were cleared or flooded by dam and irrigation systems. By 1976, five of the original eight colonies no longer existed, and two had been severely altered. In 1978, however, the number of known colonies in Tamaulipas had increased to twenty-two, with a combined population estimated at over nine million post-breeding season white-wings (Ortega M. et al. 1979) (table 18.1). Because a considerable amount of thorn scrub nesting habitat was still available, dove populations had been able to move to other areas when their original nesting habitat was destroyed. This factor, plus the availability of increased food (sorghum) and water, allowed white-wings to increase dramatically in numbers.

By 1982, the number of colonies had decreased again, and there were sixteen known colonies (fig. 18.2) in Tamaulipas (H. Ortega M., pers. comm.), with an estimated post-breeding season population of between twelve and sixteen million whitewings. Several of the 1978 colonies had been destroyed by brush removal, but new colonies were subsequently discovered. The reason for the relocation of some colonies is unknown, but probably it was a response to the creation of more favorable food and water conditions in other areas. Whitewings readily adapt to a diet of cultivated grains, particularly sorghum. The doves will eat grain that has fallen to the ground but prefer to alight on the grain heads and feed from the standing plant. Many Mexican farmers consider whitewings to be nothing more than a plague and expend much time and effort in frightening birds from their fields.

Because of the rapid agricultural development in Tamaulipas, most whitewing colonies are threatened. It is necessary to plan now to preserve existing colonies to prevent the situation destruction of the 1930–70 period in Texas

TABLE 18.2
Ranking in 1987 of thirteen White-winged Dove Colonies in Tamaulipas, Mexico, According to Importance (60%) and Threat of Loss (40%)

	Importance Priority[a]	Threat Priority[a]	Composite Priority[b]	Rank
North Zone				
San Rafael	2	9	4.8	8
Loma Colorada	4	6	4.8	9
Laguna Madre	4	5	4.4	10
Central Zone				
Panales	7	10	8.2	2
Arroyo	2	2	2.0	13
El Comanche	10	2	6.8	5
Parras de la Fuente	10	8	9.2	1
El Balconcito	5	6	5.4	7
South Zone				
Los Santos	8	7	7.6	3
Presa San Lorenzo	4	4	4.0	11
El Rosillo	9	2	6.2	6
Escandon	7	7	7.0	4
Aragon	3	4	3.4	12

Source: Tomlinson 1987b.

[a] Priority rating on basis of 1 to 10, where 10 is highest rating.

[b] Composite rating based on 60% for importance and 40% for threat to existence of colony (deforestation).

from recurring. The thirteen most important colonies have been rated according to their "perceived status" in 1987 (table 18.2). The top-ranked colony is Parras de la Fuente, followed closely by Panales, Los Santos, Escandon, and El Comanche. These five colonies should be investigated thoroughly to determine land ownership; the ultimate goal would be to establish nesting sanctuaries. The protection of these important areas would safeguard about 70% of the nesting white-wings in Tamaulipas. Action should be initiated promptly to prevent further habitat destruction (Tomlinson 1987b).

Hunting

Hunting activity by Mexican citizens is minimal (Cottam and Trefethen 1968; Mazzaccaro 1980; F. Trevino, pers. comm., 1982). Throughout Mexico, shotguns, rifles, and ammunition are scarce and expensive. In northeastern Mexico, white-winged doves are hunted mainly by hunters from the United States. Mexican hunting regulations are set by the Dirección General de la Conservación Ecológica de los Recursos Naturales (formerly Dirección General de Flora y Fauna Silvestre) and published annually in their Diario Oficial (equivalent to the U.S. Federal Register). Since 1975, daily bag and possession limits have been set. Possession limits are two or three times the daily bag limit and U.S. regulations permit the importation of one possession limit per licensed hunter. It is customary for many U.S. hunters to remain in Mexico long enough to attain the possession limit before returning. Before 1981, U.S. citizens could hunt throughout Mexico with a valid Mexican federal hunting permit. Since that time, Mexican regulations have been established by the states and a combined federal-state permit is necessary for each state in which hunting is to occur. Since bag and possession limits may vary by state for any species, presentation of the state permit at the border is necessary to validate declarations. In addition, each hunter must provide proof that he has been in Mexico for the required period of time. This may be satisfied by obtaining a date-stamped entry card from Mexican Customs or a signed voucher from any hotel or resort. During 1986, white-winged dove seasons began on 15 August in Tamaulipas, Nuevo León, and Coahuila and concluded in October and November (table 18.3). The major hunting state, Tamaulipas, established three hunting zones from north to south. The season dates were the same for all zones (15 August to 26 October), but bag and possession limits varied. In the north zone,the limits were 20/60, central zone 25/75, and in the south zone 30/90. This was done to draw hunters to the less heavily hunted southern areas of the state (Tomlinson 1987a).

Only in recent years has the white-wing harvest reached large proportions. Examination of game bird importation declarations (Customs Form 3315) revealed that U.S. citizens declared approximately 17,000 white-wings at Texas border ports during the 1963 hunting season. This number has increased substantially over the past 23 years (Tomlinson 1987a) (table 18.4).

TABLE 18.3
**The 1986–87 Mexican Hunting Season Dates and Bag/Possession
Limits for White-winged Doves in the Major Harvest States**

State	Dates	Bag/Possession
Tamaulipas		
Zone 1	15 Aug.–26 Oct.	20/60
Zone 2	Same	25/75
Zone 3	Same	30/90
Nuevo Leon	15 Aug.–16 Nov.	20/60
Coahuila		
Zone 1 & 2	15 Aug.–16 Nov.	5/15
Zone 3 & 4	Closed	
Sinaloa		
All Zones	10 Oct.–8 Feb.	20/60
Sonora		
Zone 1	12 Sep.–11 Jan.	20/60
Zone 2	Special Permit Only	
Zone 3	10 Oct.–8 Feb.	20/60

Source: Tomlinson 1987a.

TABLE 18.4
**The Number of White-winged Doves Harvested in
Mexico and Declared at Texas Ports, 1963–86**

Year[a]	Number harvested
1963	17,004
1965	24,922
1966	54,256
1968	139,956
1969	183,379
1970	178,591
1974	168,112
1976	165,036
1977	232,692
1978	260,977
1979	419,251
1980	636,478
1981	507,694
1982	548,273
1983	566,542
1984	777,815
1985	888,686[b]
1986	796,844

Source: Tomlinson 1987a.

[a] Data incomplete for the years 1964, 1967, 1971, 1972, 1973, and 1975.

[b] 1985 total revised to include late receipts.

The numbers of doves declared at border ports provide a general index to harvest success of American hunters in Mexico. However, an estimate of the total kill is important to assess the impact on white-wing population in northeastern Mexico. Perhaps in the future, a mail survey of license purchasers will provide a more accurate estimate of total harvest. In the meantime, because most U.S. citizens eat or otherwise leave many doves in Mexico, it is believed that the actual kill is about three to four times the number of birds declared at the border. If this estimate is correct, U.S. hunters probably harvested between 2.4 and 3.2 million white-wings in northeastern Mexico during 1986. This represents a kill of about 13% to 17% of an estimated nineteen million white-wings in the fall population (Tomlinson 1987a). As long as the white-wing populations remain stable, they will be able to sustain a harvest of this magnitude. Whether the populations remain at this high level depends on the ability of resource managers to assure continued maintenance of nesting habitat.

Conclusions and Management Considerations

Agriculture in South Texas and Tamaulipas has greatly influenced the development of both areas. In the Lower Rio Grande Valley, production of citrus, vegetables, sorghum, and cotton accounts for a large share of the economic income. In Tamaulipas, it can be said that sorghum and corn production is now the major agricultural influence.

White-winged dove populations have fluctuated as agricultural practices have changed. In Texas, white-wings were depleted because of the loss of significant portions of their nesting habitat. It is our opinion that so much of the native habitat was destroyed in Texas that some white-wings were forced to remain in Mexico to find suitable nesting areas. The lack of nesting habitat and heavy hunting pressure resulted in the depressed populations of the 1940s and 1950s. After the introduction of citrus to the Lower Rio Grande Valley, more nesting habitat became available and the population of white-wings responded by increasing to the 1981–82 level. The acquisition and protection of native brush habitat has been a big step in assuring that white-wings will continue to have nesting areas; however, an increasing human population in Texas and changing agricultural practices will undoubtedly affect white-wings adversely in the future. New management procedures must be developed to provide the birds with food and water sources if their populations are to be maintained.

In Tamaulipas, white-wings have responded to increased food and water by nearly quadrupling their numbers since the late 1960s. Thousands of hectares of native brush remain that appear suitable as nesting habitat. Some nesting populations have simply changed locations when former colonies were altered or destroyed. However, it is predicted that white-wing populations in Tamaulipas are nearing peak levels consistent with food supply and availability of nesting habitat. As brush removal continues, essential nesting habitat will eventually be destroyed and dove populations will decline. If the population does begin to decline as a result of nesting habitat loss, harvest pressure may become a negative factor. Careful considerations should be given to setting regulations that guard against overharvest. A hunting season opening no earlier than 20 August and a daily bag limit of no more than twenty-five birds may be necessary at present population levels. If evidence indicates that populations are continuing to decline in the next few years, more restrictive hunting regulations should be considered. Institution of an immediate program to protect important expanses of remaining native brush as sanctuaries would safeguard about 70% of nesting white-wings in Tamaulipas.

Future management considerations should encourage cooperation among state, national, international, and private organizations. Many areas need to be considered in the development of appropriate management options for this important international resource.

An effort should be made to identify those individuals and organizations directly and indirectly involved in the management or use of the resource. We must determine their level of involvement and how they could or should participate in the management of the resource. In this situation, the process is more complex because the species occurs internationally.

Comprehensive nesting habitat and population studies should be conducted in Tamaulipas and Nuevo León to document location of all major white-wing nesting colonies. Research personnel should continue development of standardized nesting population survey techniques.

Methods must be developed to analyze the magnitude of the dove harvest in northeastern Mexico through the use of questionnaires, surveys, customs declarations, and field data collection.

A standard format should be developed to evaluate the economics of dove hunting: license and permit sales and associated costs such as ammunition, hotels, food, and gasoline. How much money is spent and where does it go? Research personnel must determine the extent of depredations on agricultural crops by white-wings, develop ways to alleviate depredations, and if alleviation is impractical, explore means of compensating farmers for losses.

Immediate preservation of critical habitat is necessary. Agreements must be established with those agencies involved with the resource to acquire the approximately 12,000 ha containing the more than twenty major colonies nesting in Tamaulipas. The possibility of purchasing privately owned land or the development of long-term lease agreements should be explored.

Research personnel should be assigned to projects in a manner that provides continuity in research effort and results obtained. Additional personnel should be assigned for training as techniques are developed and improved during ongoing projects. Carryover value and application of results to other research projects should be encouraged. Results of research and management decisions should be provided to all key individuals and agencies (private and governmental) involved in management of the resource.

19

Whistling-Ducks as a Manageable and Sustainable Resource in Venezuela: Balancing Economic Costs and Benefits

FRANCISCO DALLMEIER

For more than 20 years damage to rice crops by whistling-ducks (*Dendrocygna spp.*) has been reported in Venezuela. Whistling-ducks are known to feed regularly on planted fields of rice (Bourne and Osborne 1978; Bruzual and Bruzual 1983; Casler, Rivero, and Liva 1981; Ffrench 1973; Gómez 1979c; McCartney 1983; Meanley and Meanley 1959; Rios Soto, Gutierrez, and Casler 1981). In the central and western Venezuelan llanos there are important rice production regions that provide critical habitats for ducks during reproduction. During the 1960s, farmers began trying to control crop damage by scaring ducks off fields. In 1967, a special hunting season was created to control the damage caused by ducks in the rice fields.

For several reasons, it is difficult to accurately measure the net damage caused by ducks. First, certain farms are more susceptible to depredation than others. Some farmers claim losses as high as 100% of the crop, while other fields in the same area remain untouched. Second, ducks are not the only predator of rice. Predation in the rice fields is caused primarily by rodents. The second most important predators are the three species of whistling-ducks (*Dendrocygna spp.*) in the central llanos or the white-faced whistling-duck (*Dendrocygna viduata*) and the fulvous whistling-duck (*Dendrocygna bicolor*) in western llanos. Third, ducks provide benefits as a source of protein to the rural human population. Duck meat and eggs in rural areas are a basic element of the diet (Gómez and Cringan, in press; Gómez unpubl. data). During the breeding season, eggs are harvested constantly. During the molting season, ducks are vulnerable because they are gregarious and use easily accessible bodies of water. At this time they provide food for the local human residents for 2 to 4 weeks. Fourth, duck hunters generate income to local residents. Waterfowl hunters in Venezuela purchase firearms, ammunition, clothing, equipment, transportation, meals, and accommodations. They also buy optical equipment, books, art, and other items related to waterfowl appreciation.

Whistling-ducks are a pest that needs to be controlled to minimize crop damage. They are also an important resource for sport hunting and subsistence that should be managed and exploited in a sustainable manner. In this paper I discuss the problems with achieving both objectives: the goal of reducing the whistling-duck population to minimize impact on rice farms while maximizing hunters' involvement.

Whistling-ducks in the Llanos of Venezuela

Whistling-duck is the common name for nine species in the family Anatidae and tribe Dendrocygnini (Bolen and Rylander 1983). Eight of these species are placed in a single genus (*Dendrocygna*), three species of which are found in Venezuela: fulvous whistling-duck (*D. bicolor*), black-bellied whistling-duck (*D. autumnalis*), and white-faced whistling-duck (*D. viduata*).

The reproductive period of whistling-ducks in Venezuela starts at the beginning of the rainy season at the end of April and reaches a peak in July. Whistling-ducks are considered mature when they are 1 year old, and both sexes participate in the rearing of the young. Whistling-ducks feed in shallow water by walking or standing rather than swimming or diving and feed on plant seeds and vegetable parts.

Fulvous whistling-ducks inhabit the New World from the southern United States to central Argentina and Chile. In East Africa and Asia, they are found from Ethiopia to Madagascar, India, Ceylon, and Burma. In Venezuela, fulvous whistling-ducks regularly inhabit freshwater marshes and ponds and are occasionally found in lowlands in the savannas. Resident populations nest in the rice fields of the llanos and are the least abundant of the three species of whistling-ducks. These ducks build their nests on dense, emergent vegetation over the water. Single hen clutches average nine to twelve eggs. These ducks are highly adaptable to changing environmental conditions, and late nests (July to early September) occur frequently as the rice becomes high enough to provide suitable nesting material and cover.

White-faced whistling-ducks occur from Costa Rica to northern Argentina, Paraguay, and Uruguay. The species occurs commonly in Africa, south of the Sahara to southern Angola and the Transvaal. They are common residents in Madagascar and on the Comoro Islands. In Venezuela, white-faced whistling-ducks are the most abundant resident species, and major concentrations occur in the savannas of the central and western llanos. These ducks breed in Venezuela in dry areas with abundant long grassy vegetation and within 50 m of water. Clutch size varies from seven to twelve eggs.

The black-bellied whistling-duck is exclusively a neotropical species ranging from the southern United States to northern Argentina. In Venezuela it is the second most abundant waterfowl species found and is widely distributed throughout the country. Large concentrations are common in the central llanos. In contrast to the preceding two species, black-bellied whistling-ducks are adapted to arboreal environments. They frequently perch in trees, on wire fences, and electric poles. This tendency is more frequently observed during the nesting season, when they search for natural cavities in which to nest. Black-bellied whistling-ducks generally lay compound clutches of unusually large size (sixteen to twenty-three).

The Llanos Region

The Venezuelan llanos, or savannas, are flat grassy landscapes including isolated shrubs or trees that seasonally are submerged by floods. The llanos also include transitional areas with dry forest, deserts, or both and patches of herbaceous vegetation dispersed throughout the tropical forest (Ojasti 1984). This region constitutes 30% of the country surrounding the Orinoco and Apure rivers. Considered together, the Colombian and Venezuelan llanos are the largest uninterrupted area of neotropical savanna north of the equator and include an area of 500,000 km² (Sarmiento 1984).

The annual distribution of rain has important effects on plants in the llanos, and consequently, on animals. During the rainy season there is an excess of surface water, while during the dry season the soil is dry and often hard. Some years are extremely dry. Thus, there is a period of intense and diverse vegetation growth and one of semidormancy. The savanna frequently burns toward the end of the dry season. While the fire consumes most of the standing vegetation, a buried seed bank is relatively protected.

Field studies were conducted at Hato El Frío and Módulos de Mantecal (cattle ranches), Apure State (1976–89) in the southern llanos, in the rice fields of the central llanos in Calabozo, Guárico State, and in the rice fields of the western llanos in the states of Portuguesa and Cojedes (1976–86) (fig. 19.1). Ramia (1972, 1974a, 1974b) and Sarmiento (1984) summarize the soil, climate, vegetation, and geomorphology of the region.

The study areas differed somewhat in their vegetation characteristics, total annual precipitation, and farming practices. Hato El Frío and Módulos de Mantecal generally receive greater rainfall during the rainy season than the central and western llanos. Histograms of the seasonal patterns of rainfall for the reporting stations located closest to the study areas are shown in figure 19.1. The southern llanos are predominantly used for grazing cattle. In contrast, the central and western sites are used primarily for agriculture, principally rice production. In this region the typical rice farm ranges in size from 200 to 600 ha, with some farms having more than 1,000 ha. Two species of rice, *Oriza sativa* L. (Asian origin) and *Oriza gluberrina* Steud (African origin), are cultivated commercially. The growing cycle of rice has three distinct stages: vegetative (seedling and tilling); reproductive (panicle initiation, booting, and flowering); and ripening. Rice is susceptible to waterfowl damage during each stage. The cash value per year of rice in the western region is $42.2 million (Ministerio de Agricultura y Cría 1984; Páez et al. 1981).

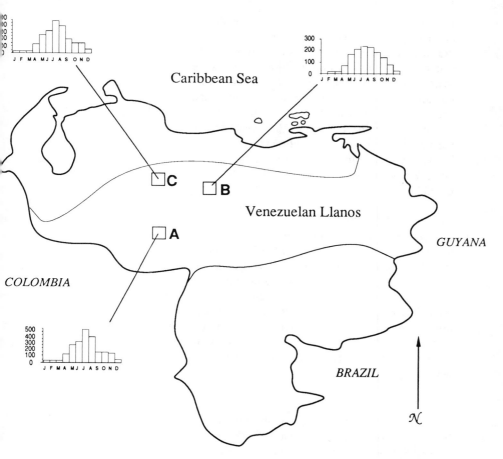

Figure 19.1. Location of the study areas and average seasonal rainfall patterns (mm) in Venezuela. A, Hato El Frio and Módulos de Mantecal. B, Central llanos. C, Western llanos.

Hato El Frío and Módulos de Mantecal Study Areas

Hato El Frío is a private cattle ranch where hunting has been controlled for many years and where wildlife abounds. This 150,000-ha ranch is located between the towns of El Samán de Apure and Mantecal, Apure State. On this site, most of the waterfowl collected came from the northern part of the ranch, where extensive wetlands formed by small dikes retain water during the dry season.

Módulos de Mantecal includes both public and private lands on which a series of dikes were constructed to control excess water during the rainy season. Throughout the 500,000-ha area, the dikes retain excess water until the beginning of the dry season in order to provide pasture for cattle.

These two sites in the southern llanos of Venezuela are characterized by large open savannas where grasses are the dominant vegetation. Gallery forests are usually present along the main water courses. Isolated forest islands within the savanna, or *matas,* are also common. Hunting is prohibited in both areas and strongly enforced in Hato El Frío. Intense grazing by cattle at Hato El Frío maintains open wetlands favorable to water birds. Most of the dikes are periodically checked for water level to ensure adequate amounts of water and to control excessive plant growth. At the Módulos de Mantecal waterfowl abundance was high the second and third years following construction. At that time, the vegetational succession attracted large populations of waterfowl, wading birds, and many other species of wildlife. After about 5 years, however, vegetational changes reduced waterfowl and wading bird habitats by 60% (Gómez, unpubl. data).

Central Llanos Study Area

The central llanos study area is located in the Guárico River Irrigation System near the city of Calabozo at the Guárico River Dam northeast of Calabozo. Rice here is irrigated and cultivated year-round on 20,400 ha of land, which accounts for 12.4% of the total rice production in Venezuela.

The biogeography of the central llanos is highly diverse, containing five ecological regions: mountains, hills, alluvial plains, floodplains, and sandy marshlands (Sarmiento and Monasterio 1971). Irrigated fields occupy much of the alluvial plain. The land is also intensively used to cultivate corn, papaya, bananas, and other crops. Year-round irrigation of the fields attracts thousands of waterfowl and wading birds.

Western Llanos Study Area

The western llanos study area is south of the city of Acarigua, Portuguesa State. This area contains about 150,000 ha cultivated for rice and represents 80% of the total rice production in the western llanos. Most of the rice planting here occurs during the rainy season. Only 11% of the total annual rice production is grown during the dry season with irrigation. This diverse region is intensively cultivated not only for rice but also for tobacco, sugar cane, sesame, and sorghum. In addition, cattle raising plays an important role in the local economy.

Whistling-duck Populations in Venezuela

Methods

To estimate the population levels of ducks, waterfowl censuses in the study areas were conducted during the rainy season on foot and from motor vehicles and aircraft between 1975 and 1985 (May to October) and during the dry season (November to April). Additional waterfowl counts were provided by the Servicio Nacional de Fauna of MARNR (Ministerio del Ambiente y de los Recursos Naturales Renovables). During the rainy season, transects from 2 to 5 km in length and 400 m in width were selected along the main dikes and roads of the Módulos de Mantecal and Hato el Frío and along the rice fields of the central and western llanos (Gómez 1979a; Madriz et al. 1981; Gómez and Cringan, in press). The counts for all visible birds were conducted between 0700 and 1000 and between 1500 and 1800. An area of 6,000 ha was censused at Hato El Frío and Módulos de Mantecal and of 14,000 at the central and western llanos areas. During the dry season waterfowl were counted in areas that still retained bodies of water, reservoirs, and irrigated cultivated areas. Additional censuses of waterfowl were done by aircraft.

To determine the number of fulvous whistling-duck nests intensive surveys of 43 ha of wetland habitats were conducted in 1977, 1980, and 1982. Of these 43 ha, 32 ha were in rice farms of the western llanos and 11 ha in Hato el Frío and Módulos de Mantecal. To determine the number of nests of white-faced whistling-ducks, intensive surveys of the dry savanna area surrounding wetland habitats were made at Hato El Frío and Módulos de Mantecal: 24 ha in 1977 and 19 ha in 1984. To determine the number of eggs in the black-bellied whistling-duck nests, seven tree cavities were examined in the central llanos in 1979, six in Hato El Frío in 1977 and 1982, and five Módulos de Mantecal in 1979 and 1983.

Seasonal Distribution of Ducks

During the dry season, ducks are observed in mixed flocks in the remaining bodies of water. With the advent of the rainy season in mid-April, ducks begin to move to the new marshes and rice fields. Whistling-ducks disperse toward less flooded and more suitable habitats as water levels rise in the savanna wetlands of southern Venezuela. Black-bellied whistling-ducks tend to feed in areas near tree cavities, where nesting may take place close to feeding areas. In comparison with other areas, the central llanos provide a particularly suitable breeding habitat for this species because natural cavities are common and the species is most abundant in this area during the rainy season. White-faced and fulvous whistling-ducks are common in all areas, especially in rice fields, where the food and nesting habitats are abundant.

Ducks in the Venezuelan llanos move considerable distances during the year. Chang, Seijas, and Figueroa (1985) reported preliminary results of banding black-bellied whistling-ducks on the molting grounds of the southern llanos of Venezuela. Of 15,786 ducks that were banded during 4 years at Hatos El Frío and La Palmera, Apure State, 54 have been recovered and returned by hunters and 64 have been recovered on the molting grounds. The bands recovered indicate that black-bellied whistling-ducks can move to the central and western llanos, to the eastern part of Venezuela, and south to the llanos of Colombia with a maximum recorded distance of 416 km. This suggests that the waterfowl populations of Venezuelan and Colombian llanos migrate throughout the year to follow suitable habitats. In addition, during the dry season most waterfowl probably concentrate in the southern llanos of Venezuela and Colombia, where large extensions of wetlands still occur. While little is known about the waterfowl populations of the Colombian llanos, they are subjected to the same climatic and physiographic conditions that regulate the Venezuelan llanos. Any drastic impact on the waterfowl population and habitat change in either of the two countries will affect the regional waterfowl population.

Ducks prefer wetlands and rice fields with low water levels for foraging on pregerminated rice and other species. Wetlands with depths between 30 and 120 mm, located in open areas with 360° visibility, and in some cases with earth clods, provide a very suitable feeding habitat for ducks and many other species of waterfowl and wading birds. These conditions characterize those of sprouting rice.

Ducks in the undisturbed areas of Hato El Frío and Módulos de Mantecal feed mostly early in the morning between 0600 and 0800 and at 1730 to 1830. They also are very active during the night, roosting and feeding in large mixed flocks. In the rice areas, feeding occurs mostly at night during the hunting season. Small flocks leave the roosting areas at dusk to feed in the rice fields until sunrise, when they return to the roosting areas. At other times of the year mixed flocks of from 20 to 150 ducks were observed feeding at various times throughout the day.

From surveys conducted to determine the number of nests of ducks in the study areas, a density of two nests per hectare, with a range from none to five, was observed for white-faced whistling-ducks in the southern llanos. Nest predation by animals is very high in these areas for white-faced whistling-ducks (Gómez 1979a). For fulvous whistling-ducks in the western llanos, an average of four nests per hectare, with a range from zero to nine, was observed. Fulvous whistling-duck nests are often disturbed by hunters and local human residents. Deforestation has reduced the occurrence of tree cavities, which limits breeding by the black-bellied whistling-duck in the western llanos.

Historical Population Levels

Two factors are mainly responsible for the increased duck population in the central and western llanos of Venezuela in recent years: (1) an increase in the area under rice cultivation in the region (fig. 19.2) that provide newly flooded habitat suitable for waterfowl and (2) a constant conversion of natural wetlands into agricultural land in the central and western llanos. The central llanos historically had a resident population of ducks that increased considerably following the completion of the Calabozo dam and irrigation system. The western llanos supported a small population of waterfowl that also increased considerably when more than 150,000 ha of rice fields were established. Waterfowl traditionally migrated from these cultivated areas to the wetlands of the south-

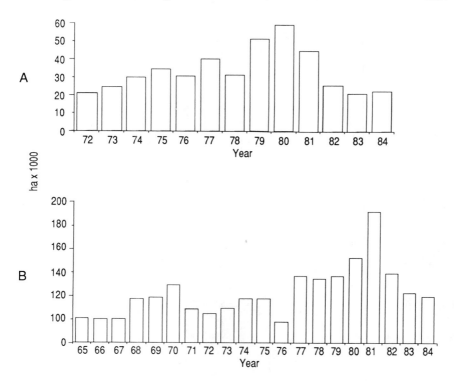

Figure 19.2. Area cultivated for rice in Venezuela. A, Central llanos. B, Western llanos.

ern llanos during the dry season. Within the last 10 years, however, a resident population has become established in the western llanos, where wetlands from the Majáguas Reservoir and the rice-cultivated areas provide habitats for ducks year-round. The three species of whistling-ducks are equally abundant in the central llanos; however, in the western llanos, 83% of the whistling-ducks are fulvous, 16% white-faced, and only 1% are black-bellied.

The population of ducks varies annually on the three study areas (fig. 19.3A, B, C). In 1970, the central llanos population of ducks was estimated at 180,000 ducks (Madriz 1984). The closing of the hunting season in 1973 (following heavy hunting from 1967 to 1970) and the increase of rice cultivation in the area allowed the duck population in the central llanos to approach 120,000 in 1987.

In the western llanos, the duck population increased rapidly to over 200,000 in 1980. Between 1978 to 1981, rice was at its peak of production in Venezuela with more than 280,000 ha cultivated in the country. In 1981 the duck population of the western llanos decreased by 100,000 because local farmers began using pesticides, collecting duck eggs, and destroying nests in an attempt to

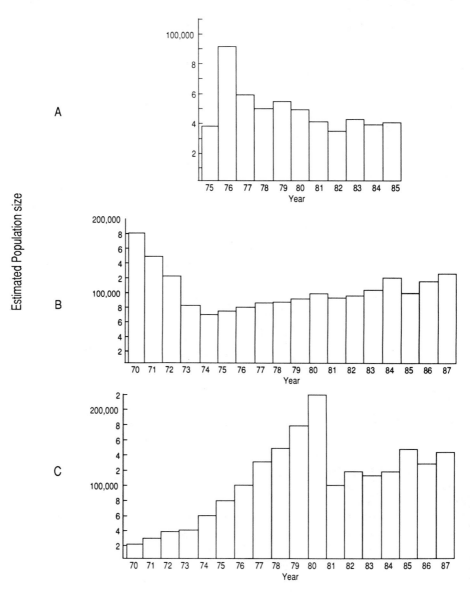

Figure 19.3. Size of the whistling-duck population during the rainy season in the Hato El Frio and Mantecal (A), central llanos (B), and western llanos (C).

reduce crop damage. Since then, the waterfowl population has increased slowly to around 150,000.

The duck population in the southern llanos was highest in 1976 as a conse-quence of the dikes constructed 2 to 3 years earlier. After 1976, vegetation succession reduced the waterfowl habitat, and most of the duck population was concentrated in the Hato El Frío, where overgrazing by cattle controls the vegetation.

Impact of Whistling-ducks on Rice Harvest

Methods

To document the importance of rice in the diet, ducks were shot early in the morning and late in the afternoon in feeding and the resting grounds and during their daily flights between the two areas. Every month we tried, in some months unsuccessfully, to collect five to ten individuals of each whistling-duck species per study area. During the hunting season, birds taken by hunters in the central and western llanos study areas were examined, and in some cases their crops were removed and studied. I collected and examined 310 ducks (table 19.1) and hunters collected an additional 63. Thirty-nine specimens were excluded from most of the following analysis because we were unable to determine sex, age, and other biological information.

A detailed necropsy documented the ducks' food preferences and general biological information. Specimens were examined within the first 3 to 4 hours after collection. Standard ornithological measurements were taken using a steel tape. Photographs of important characteristics were taken when considered necessary. Crop contents (131) were separated and placed in 5% formalin solution immediately after collection, and food items from the crops were removed, segregated, and identified under a stereomicroscope. The percentage in dry weight of each food item for the three species of whistling-ducks was recorded (Gómez 1979b; Gómez and Rylander 1982; Gómez and Cringan, in press).

To document the effect of ducks on rice fields between 1977 and 1984, more than 100 3- to 10-day visits were made to rice farms of the central and western llanos region and other study areas. Visits to forty-two farms and ranches produced information from farmers, ranchers, and local people about the numbers of active rice farms, inactive rice farms, areas cultivated under irrigation, and

TABLE 19.1
**Number of Whistling-ducks Collected in Venezuela
from Each Study Area (1976–84)**

Study Area	White-faced Whistling-duck	Fulvous Whistling-duck	Black-bellied Whistling-duck
Hato El Frío and Módulos de Mantecal	48	29	37
Central Llanos	36	43	39
Western Llanos	41	37	0
Totals	125	109	76

cattle ranches with large extensions of wetlands. Farmers and managers provided information about crop damage, farming practices, and damage prevention methods. To document the damage caused by ducks on four rice farms, we placed six cages per farm to exclude ducks (10 m long × 8 m wide × 2 m high and 3 cm mesh diameter).

Food Preferences and Feeding Behavior

Whistling-ducks feed almost exclusively on plant seeds and vegetable parts. Invertebrates, principally insects (Coleoptera and Hemiptera), probably are consumed accidentally by waterfowl when searching for seeds, but do not form an important part of the diet (Gómez 1979a, 1979b; Gómez and Rylander 1982). Ducklings, on the other hand, feed actively on invertebrates during the first few weeks of life.

Grass and other seeds are the most common component in the diet of ducks and were found in all the crops analyzed. In the rice fields of the central and western llanos, *Oriza sativa, O. perennis,* and *Echinochloa colonum* are important sources of food during the rice season. Rios Soto, Gutierrez, and Casler (1981) reported that fulvous whistling-ducks consumed less rice in the western llanos than in the central llanos, but the opposite situation applied to the white-faced whistling-ducks. In four specimens of fulvous whistling-ducks collected after a few hours of feeding in harvested fields, the crop contained on average 34% rice. In the western llanos, *Echinochloa* was an important source of food during the rainy season for white-faced and fulvous whistling-ducks. In the Hato El Frío and Módulos de Mantecal study areas, where rice is not available, the most common species present in the ducks' diet were *Bracharia plantaginea* and *Panicum* sp.; *Heliotropium indicum* vegetative parts (leaves, roots, and stems) are also consumed in considerable amounts. Rice (*O. sativa*) is an important source of food for ducks and other species in Venezuela (fig. 19.4).

The amount of rice consumed by the three species of whistling-ducks varies and is consistent with the pattern reported by Bruzual and Bruzual (1983). These authors found that in the central llanos, rice consumption was significantly lower ($p < 0.05$) in white-faced whistling-ducks than for the other two species. They did not find differences in rice consumption between fulvous and black-bellied whistling-ducks. Twenty-nine species of plants were identified as being eaten by whistling-ducks in Venezuela (Bruzual and Bruzual 1983; Gómez 1979a, b; Gómez and Cringan, in press; Gómez and Rylander 1982; Madriz et al. 1982; Rios Soto et al. 1981).

Based on thirty-five visits and twenty-seven interviews with representatives of rice farms of the central and western llanos study areas between 1978 and 1982, farmers estimated an average 32% loss of rice during the rainy season and 45% during the dry season. These results are subjective and are based on estimates of total annual rice production, on the farmer's direct observation, and on the assumption that 50% of the rice loss was caused by ducks and 50% by rodents, dickcissel, wattled jacana, and gallinules. Ducks are more often

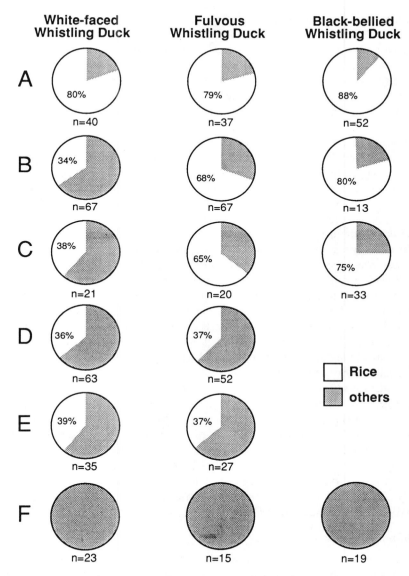

Figure 19.4. Percent of rice (g) (*Oriza sativa*) consumed by whistling-ducks in Venezuela. A, Central llanos (Madriz 1982). B, Central llanos (Bruzual and Bruzual 1983). C, Central llanos (present study). D, Western llanos (Rios Soto et al. 1981). E, Western llanos (present study). F, Hato El Frio and Mantecal (present study).

blamed for the damage simply because they are the most easily observed predators. The reliability of farmers' responses is questionable. Farmers generally tend to overestimate the damage, and their opinions changed from 1 year to another. From interviews conducted by Casler, Rivero, and Lira (1981) in the western llanos between 1970 and 1977, the damage estimated by farmers ranged from 26% (1970) to 53% (1977) during the dry season. In 1977, however, they reported a decrease to 16% after the hunting season was opened.

Casler, Rivero, and Lira (1981) estimated the damage caused by ducks in the rice fields of the western llanos. They reported 1.2% to 1.6% of damage during the rainy season (May to October) and 6.2% to 9.0% during the dry season (November to April), with an annual average of 1.8% to 2%. This percentage represents 11,400,000 to 16,000,000 kg of rice consumed or trampled by ducks. These estimates were based on the assumptions that (1) the size of the waterfowl population is the product of nest density (breeding pairs) and the total area cultivated, (2) each pair of adults produces at least two ducklings that become adults, (3) the population size during the dry season decreased by 60%, (4) the daily consumption of rice per duck is 65 g, (5) the percent of rice in the diet during the dry season varies between 48% and 70% and, during the rainy season, between 30% and 41%, (6) average rice production is 3,700 kg/ha, and (7) waterfowl trample the same amount of rice as they consume.

Our observations in the western llanos study sites suggest ducks are more likely to be attracted to already harvested fields. Newly harvested fields are characterized by good visibility and plenty of food. During observations of twenty-two harvested fields, about 220 ha, very little duck activity was observed in nearby unharvested rice fields. On two farms with harvested fields, ducks were hunted and three other flocks being observed flew and landed in adjacent unharvested rice fields.

Predation by ducks would therefore not represent a major problem if the damage were uniformly distributed among all farms. However, certain farms are depredated more heavily. Using cages to exclude waterfowl, Casler, Rivero, and Lira (1981) reported 10% and 12% of the rice crop was damaged by waterfowl on two rice farms of the western llanos. I found 3%, 6%, 15%, and 16% damage on four rice fields of the central llanos using the same method. Variation is greater during the dry season, when rice is cultivated by irrigation in 15% of western llanos. Waterfowl concentrate on these irrigated farms, where total damage can increase to 45% to 50%.

Minimizing Rice Loss

Damage to rice crops by ducks can be averted by preventing waterfowl from landing in the fields. If ducks are allowed to feed on harvested fields, waterfowl can be attracted away from nearby unharvested rice fields. When a sufficient number of fields have been harvested and protected from hunting, they will provide ducks with a place to feed where they can do no harm, since they would be eating waste grain. Hunters should be encouraged to hunt unharvested rice fields to encourage ducks to feed at the desired locations. The problem with this management technique is that hunters prefer harvested fields, where they can easily spot the ducks.

At three farms in the western llanos, the farmers agreed to provide rice at two places where ducks concentrated due to their established flight line. In the two places of duck concentration, 300 kg of rice were provided during 3 weeks, and the population of ducks increased from 670 and 920 to 2,140 and 3,630, respectively. In one of the sites, rodents, purple gallinules, dickcissels, and wattle jacanas were also attracted to the rice. In another experiment 100 kg of rice was spread on 400 m of an established flight line, and twenty-five decoys were placed in the area. Three days later, 1,200 ducks were observed feeding in the area. This type of practice reduces waterfowl movements and is effective in diminishing waterfowl depredation if used in conjunction with scaring programs in nearby, unharvested rice fields.

Impact of Sport Hunting on Whistling-ducks

Methods

To estimate hunter pressure on the duck population, we established five check stations to interview the hunters and check game in possession. Four of the stations were located in the western llanos and one in the central llanos. The station in the central llanos at Puente Aldao provided the best location because hunters coming from the rice fields of the central llanos had to pass right by it. The western llanos is an extensive area with many local roads, which makes it difficult to control hunters. During the seven weekends of the hunting season of 1980 and 1981, we interviewed hunters to determine the number of ducks (1) hunted, (2) in possession, and (3) shot but not reported (these included ducks given to the local people, not recovered, or consumed locally). The results were analyzed using the student's t-test for proportions. Unidentified ducks were not included in the data set. Hunting pressure out of season in the central and western llanos is more difficult to quantify. Human residents of local farms and ranches regularly hunt ducks for food, and hunting is certainly the principal cause of death for waterfowl in the area near human settlements.

In the southern llanos, harvest information is not known. However, discussions with poachers, local residents, and government officials in El Frío and Mantecal study areas suggested that between 800 and 1,300 ducks per year are taken from the southern part of El Frío and from the northern part of Mantecal.

Whistling-ducks Harvested per Year

Because of the expanse of the western llanos, many hunters stay overnight on private farms, and many of the harvested waterfowl are consumed locally by the hunters or given away to the locals. Only about 60% of ducks were in the hunters' possession in the western llanos area, whereas approximately 85% of the ducks taken in 1982 in the central llanos area were in the hunters' possession.

The number of registered waterfowl hunters averaged about 3,000 (fig. 19.5), and the average number of ducks harvested per hunter was about twenty

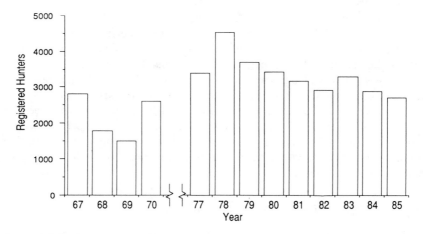

Figure 19.5. Registered waterfowl hunters in Venezuela.

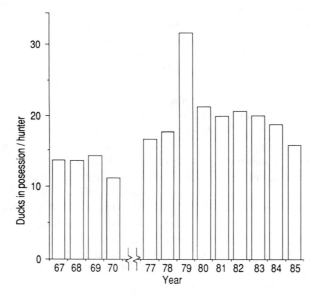

Figure 19.6. Average of whistling-ducks in possession per hunter in the central and western llanos of Venezuela.

(fig. 19.6). The harvested waterfowl reached the maximum amount of 30,000 in the central llanos and around 70,000 in the western llanos in 1979–80 (fig. 19.7).

In the central llanos, 37% of the duck population was harvested during the hunting season of 1982 (tables 19.2, 19.3; fig. 19.7). About 36,000 ducks

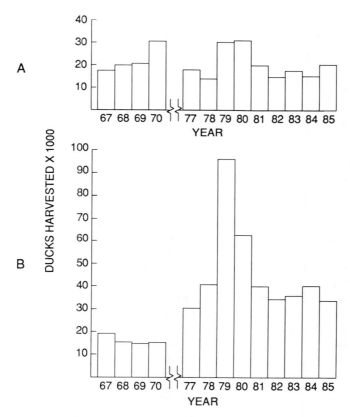

Figure 19.7. Number of whistling-ducks harvested in the rice fields of Venezuela from 1967 to 1985. A, Central llanos. B, Western llanos. (No data available from 1971–76.)

TABLE 19.2
**Population Estimations from the Central and
Western Llanos of Venezuela (1982)**

	Central Llanos		Western Llanos	
	N	%	N	%
Population size				
before hunting season	95,120		121,900	
Total harvested ducks	35,100	(36.9)	96,400	(79.1)
Migration and/or				
dispersion	35,800	(37.6)	300	(0.2)
Population size				
after hunting season	24,200	(25.5)	25,200	(20.7)

TABLE 19.3
Harvested Ducks from the Central and Western Llanos
of Venezuela (1982)

Harvested Ducks	Central Llanos		Western Llanos	
	N	%	*N*	%
Harvested ducks registered	20,300	(84.4)	35,800	(58.2)
Estimated number harvested ducks not registered	14,800	(15.6)	60,600	(49.7)

(38% of total) dispersed or migrated to other areas, and around 24,000 (25% of total) remained to form the post-hunting season population, most of which were probably yearlings. In the western llanos study area, about 79% of the population was harvested by the end of the hunting season of 1980. This is probably an overestimate because of the difficulty of calculating the size of the immigrant population arriving during the hunting season. Census of the waterfowl population in the central and western llanos prehunting season 1981, indicated a population size 55% lower than the previous year's. The population estimates after the hunting season in 1980 indicated that 25,000 ducks were present in the study areas, which was only 20% of the initial population size. Few ducks, about 300, dispersed or migrated from the area.

Commercial Value of Whistling-ducks

The commercial value and extent of exploitation can be measured as the income derived from selling, trading, or consuming waterfowl species or their parts. Total value includes the value of meat, eggs, and taxidermy charges. In 1984 Venezuelan waterfowl harvesters took 60,000 ducks, more than $24,000 worth of meat, from Venezuelan rice fields. The income received by residents of the Venezuelan town of Calabozo during the 1982 waterfowl hunting season was about $350,000 during three weekends (Gómez, unpubl. data). An estimate of the total income for the entire season in Calabozo would exceed $2 million. The commercial value of waterfowl in that town also includes a portion of the income received by the local businesses. The money generated by waterfowl hunters in the local economy also generates a secondary, or multiplier, effect because business people invest some of the money received from hunters locally, improving the business condition of the area.

The Management of Whistling-ducks by Hunting

The number of birds that exceed a specified number of breeders required to maintain a certain population size can be termed the annual surplus (fig.

19.8A). This is determined by surveys of broods and breeding birds during the spring. In addition, harvest data from the previous hunting season may produce a more precise estimate of the annual surplus that consists of the percentage of total mortality that can be allocated to harvest. Ideally, waterfowl can be manipulated to maximize the annual harvestable surplus. Harvest of the annual increase will return the population to the same size (fig. 19.8B). Natural and harvest mortalities are partly compensatory and partly additive and noncompensatory (fig. 19.9). Compensatory harvest mortality is harvest-caused mortality that directly reduces mortality due to other factors and does not increase total mortality. Noncompensatory harvest mortality is harvest-caused mortality that directly increases total mortality.

Waterfowl differ in their productivity, biological characteristics, and harvestable surplus. The number of surplus individuals that can be harvested differs for each waterfowl species. The harvestable surplus for species that matures when

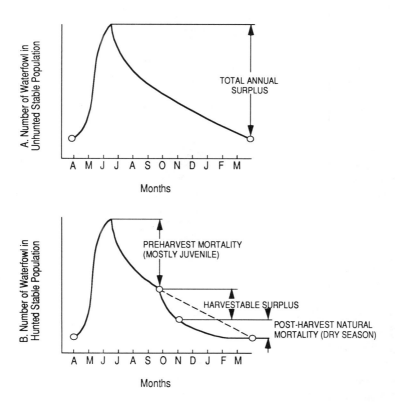

Figure 19.8. Theoretical annual abundance of waterfowl. A, Unhunted waterfowl population. A large number of ducks is added to the population each breeding season, and a large annual surplus suffers natural mortality before the next breeding season. B, Hunted waterfowl population. Some of the annual surplus can be harvested to replace natural mortality.

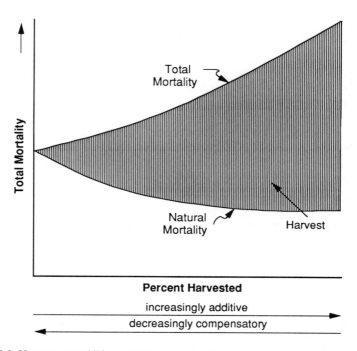

Figure 19.9. Harvest as an additive or compensatory mortality factor. Low levels of harvest tend to be compensatory; as the harvest rate increases, harvest becomes additive rather than compensatory.

a year old and has large clutches is greater than that of a species maturing at 2 years of age and having a small clutch. Brood production varies among different years, species, and individuals. Species with large clutches tend to have higher mortality and lower survival rates than species with small clutches. Experienced hens seem to be more successful in rearing broods than yearling hens. Waterfowl behavior also changes with experience, and yearlings are more susceptible to predation and hunting. Ideally, therefore, waterfowl hunting regulations should be species specific.

Venezuelan Hunting Regulations

Venezuelan hunting regulations are established in the Law of Wildlife Protection (Ley de Protección de la Fauna Silvestre Gaceta Oficial No. 29,289 del 11 de Agosto de 1970), which permits four categories of hunting: sport, commercial, scientific collecting, and predator control. This law lists game animals (Resolución MAC-RNR 5-276) that are the only species allowed to be hunted under special regulations. All three species of ducks are included on this list.

There are three kinds of bag limits. The daily limit specifies the maximum number of individuals per species that can be harvested in 1 day. The possession limit establishes the maximum number of waterfowl of a species that a person may have in his possession. The season limit is the maximum number of ducks of all species combined that can be harvested during the whole season. To obtain a hunting license, a person must be 18 years old or older and be registered as a hunter by the MARNR (Resolución MARNR No. 167 del 23-7-80) if the individual has purchased a license in the past. The hunter is also required to return the hunting questionnaire from the previous hunting season and must not have had his license suspended. There are three classes of hunting licenses. Class A licenses are for members of hunting organizations registered by the MARNR and cost $1.07 (Bs 50) in 1987–88. Class B licenses are for unaffiliated individuals and cost $6.70 (Bs 200) in 1987–88. Class C licenses are for people registered under a former league (sindicatos, ligas campesinas, uniones de prestatarios), and cost $0.33 (Bs 10).

Venezuelan hunting regulations do not allow the use of motor vehicles while hunting. The burning of vegetation and use of poisons and explosives for killing game is prohibited. Hunting must be done between 0500 and 1900 and is not allowed with the aid of artificial light. Collection or destruction of nests, eggs, and ducklings is prohibited. Hunters transporting waterfowl from the hunting area must possess a hunting license. Duck carcasses must still have the head and legs attached to allow for identification at the check stations, where the harvested ducks must be presented. Violators are subject to license suspension or revocation, fines, and confiscation of property, according to the severity of any violation.

The Venezuelan Law of Arms and Explosives and associated regulations (Decreto Presidencial No. 2371 del 13-09-77) establish which firearms are legal. Shotguns with a capacity of two or fewer shells and ranging in gauges from 12 to .410 are allowed for hunting purposes. Shotguns must be registered in the county (Prefectura).

Venezuelan waterfowl hunting regulations provide for recreation, limitation of the harvest size, and distribution of the harvest among the human population. Duck hunting starts during the dry season in some areas, and at the beginning of the rainy season in others (table 19.4). Because ducks are the most abundant species and are frequently associated with depredation problems in the rice fields, there is a special hunting season for them in the central and western llanos of Venezuela between April and June, from Friday to Sunday.

The 1987–88 duck hunting calendar allows hunting from 4 April until 29 June. By the end of May and the beginning of June most of the waterfowl breeding pairs had already formed, and by the middle of June most of the females had started to lay their eggs. I frequently received complaints by the hunters that they were shooting females with eggs. To maximize hunting opportunities and minimize rice depredation, I propose the following changes in the duck hunting calendar (table 19.5): (1) extend the hunting season from 15 January to 22 April, which would provide hunting opportunities for a longer

TABLE 19.4
Venezuelan Whistling-ducks Hunting Information (1986–87)

	Area and Observations	
	Central and Western Llanos[a]	Rest of Country
Hunting dates	4 April–29 June	1 December–28 February
Ducks/hunter		
Per day	12	4
Total in possession	24	8

[a] Barinas, Cojedes, Guárico and Portuguesa states. Only Fridays, Saturdays, and Sundays.

TABLE 19.5
Venezuelan Whistling-ducks Hunting Information Proposed (15 January–22 April)

	Area and Observations							
	Central Llanos Guárico State			Western Llanos Barinas, Cojedes and Portuguesa States		Entire country except Central and Western Llanos		
	FWD	WWD	BBWD	FWD	WWD	FWD	WWD	BBWD
Ducks per hunter								
Per day	3	3	3	6	3	2	2	2
Total in possession	6	6	6	12	6	4	4	4

Note: Hunting allowed only on Fridays, Saturdays, and Sundays. Hunter must be able to differentiate between the three species of whistling ducks. FWD = fulvous whistling-duck; WWD = white-faced whistling-duck; BBWD = black-bellied whistling-duck.

period of time and would harvest the desired amount; (2) permit hunting every-day and not only on weekends if necessary to reduce the population size; and (3) establish different bag limits for different species and different areas. This is important because they occur in different proportions in the central and western llanos. The present bag limits allow hunters to shoot twelve ducks daily, of species combination, or to have twenty-four in possession by the end of the three days hunting weekend. In the central llanos the three species are present in about the same proportion. There, harvesting can be allowed in the same proportion—three of each species daily or six of each species in possession. For the western llanos, fulvous whistling-ducks are the most abundant species (93%), so they can be harvested in greater numbers—six per day and twelve in possession. In other areas where hunting is permitted that are not rice fields, I propose an equal proportion of ducks per day (2) and in possession (4) until the abundance of the three species is recorded. This hunting season proposal provides an alternative to reduce the duck population to the level desired, to reduce crop depredation, and provide hunter opportunities. One problem is that hunters must be able to differentiate the three species of whistling-ducks. This could be easily solved by a mandatory hunters' education program.

Conclusion

Hunting is an important management tool to control the waterfowl population. Harvest can be increased or reduced annually to maintain an optimal population size, which in turn will determine the amount of damage in the rice fields. The goal is to maintain the population at a level that minimizes damage to the rice crop without adversely affecting local economics, which depend on the waterfowl hunting. Censuses during the hunting season will provide a better estimate of the waterfowl population that migrate to the area than the data available. A better control of bag limits, pesticide use, and poaching is also necessary.

20

White-Tailed Deer Management in Costa Rica

CHRISTOPHER VAUGHAN AND MIGUEL RODRIGUEZ

The white-tailed deer (*Odocoileus virginianus*) is the most widely distributed and important big game animal in North America (Hesselton and Hesselton 1982). In 1982, twelve million hunters harvested nearly three million deer in the United States and Canada (Stransky 1984). It is also one of the principal game species in Central America (Mendéz 1984). The white-tailed deer also has cultural, ecological, psychological, and social importance to humans (Langenau, Kellert, and Applegate 1984).

Until recently, there have been few studies on deer natural history in the neotropics (but see Brokx 1984; DiMare 1986; Janzen 1983b; Mendez 1984; Solís 1986a; Solís, Rodriguez, and Vaughan 1987). No studies have considered deer management in Latin America. Such work is badly needed, as white-tailed deer have been overharvested in many areas (Brokx 1984; Méndez 1984; Solís and Rodriguez 1987), and optimum habitat has been converted to intensive agriculture land (Janzen 1987). The only population or habitat management practiced in the neotropics has been poorly enforced hunting seasons.

This paper documents the importance of white-tailed deer as a game species in the neotropics, the impact of hunting and harvesting on deer populations in Costa Rica, deer management in Costa Rica, and the feasibility of harvesting white-tailed deer on a sustainable basis in Costa Rica.

Deer as a Natural Resource in the Tropics

The white-tailed deer is distributed from Canada through Central America to northern Brazil and southern Peru. Thirty or more subspecies have been named from North and Central America and eight in South America (Halls 1984). Although Mendéz (1984) reports limited information on populations and distribution of white-tailed deer in Mexico and Central America, he includes a distribution map of sixteen subspecies for the area. Brokx (1984) found that the seven South American subspecies of white-tailed deer occur from sea level to at least 4,000 m in the Andes from Bolivia north to Venezuela and Colombia. A major part of white-tailed deer habitat in South America is covered by broad-leafed evergreen and semideciduous forests. In Mexico and Central America *Odocoileus* prefer well-watered pasture lands with interdispersed wooded areas, although they occur in a wide variety of habitats from dense tropical rain forests to upland desert (Mendéz 1984). White-tails were absent or uncommon in tropical rainforests, humid montane forests, open steppe, and xerophytic steep slope habitats. Of an approximate 5.5 million km^2 distribution in South America, the effective range of white-tailed deer is about 1.7 million km^2, which supports habitats with shrubs and low trees that animals use for browse and cover. While habitat disturbance has favored expansion of white-tailed deer range by increasing the extent of regenerating edge and woody vegetation (Harlow 1984), deer populations in Latin America have declined since the 1950s through intensive agriculture, cattle ranching, lowland drainage, destruction of forests, pollution of water, indiscriminate hunting, and excessive use of insecticides and herbicides (Mendéz 1984). Brokx (1984) notes population declines in overgrazed areas and areas where a burgeoning human population inhabits prime white-tailed deer habitat.

Within its historical distribution, the white-tailed deer has provided people with recreation, food, clothing, footwear, decorations, and even utensils (Baker 1984). In pre-Columbian times, white-tailed deer were one of the most desired terrestrial game species in the Central American lowlands (Bennett 1968; Kerbis 1980). In the 1800s, authors such as Solano (1857) documented its use for meat, skins, and trophies by indigenous groups in Nicaragua.

The white-tailed deer is still hunted for sport and subsistence. This species has been the most important big game species in Mexico (Leopold 1959), Central American countries (Handley 1950; Mendéz 1984), and parts of South American countries such as Venezuela, Peru, and Ecuador (Brokx 1984). This importance is due to its large size and its ability to adapt to altered environments and savannas. It is more widely distributed and abundant than other ungulates such as peccaries and tapirs, and it persists near human population centers (Brokx 1984).

Deer as a Natural Resource in Costa Rica

In Costa Rica, Goodwin (1946) distinguished two subspecies of white-tailed deer: *O. v. truei* (Merriam) is found on mountain slopes and lowlands of the northern and Caribbean part of the country, while *O. v. chiriquensis* (J. A. Allen) is found in the lowland pastures and secondary vegetation up the mountains on the Pacific slope. We will treat the second subspecies in this chapter. It is found in the mosaic of pasture-shrub-forest in the tropical–dry forest vegetation covering about 8,000 km^2 in northwestern Costa Rica. This area corresponds politically to the Guanacaste Province and forms part of the tropical–

dry forest corridor extending from southwestern Mexico to northwestern Costa Rica, which historically included over 550,000 km² (Janzen 1986).

Before human settlement of Central America at least 10,000 years ago, some of the large herbivores such as the mastodon, giant sloth, and horses may have opened clearings in the dry forest, producing adequate habitat for white-tailed deer (Janzen 1987). When humans arrived and eliminated these large herbivores, deer habitat was reduced (Janzen 1987). Later, deer concentrated near indigenous clearings, which provided excellent deer habitat and food in the form of corn, beans, and pasture (Caufield 1984).

Extensive forest clearing in Guanacaste Province in the mid 1600s associated with the livestock industry (Sequeira 1985) created excellent deer habitat (Solís and Rodriguez 1987). Deer density was probably at its highest between the middle 1600s and early 1900s. Since then, especially in the 1950s, the creation of monocultures of sorghum, rice, cotton, sugar cane, and pasture has eliminated quality deer habitat (Janzen 1987). Hunting pressure and habitat alteration caused deer to become rare in Costa Rica by the late 1960s (Janzen 1983, 1987). The opening of the Pan American highway in 1947 permitted easier hunter access from Costa Rica's Central Valley to Guanacaste Province, and a period of intensive exploitation began.

By 1983, forest cover in Costa Rica had been reduced from an estimated 99.8% of the national territory (50,000 km²) to about 24% (Vaughan 1983). High deforestation rates in Costa Rica and the resulting increase in secondary forest growth and forest edges increased white-tailed deer habitat, especially in the dry forest zone (Vaughan 1983). White-tailed deer never were as abundant in other regions (Alfaro and Allen 1987).

In Costa Rica, early Spanish explorers mentioned that the species formed part of the diet of indigenous tribes in Guanacaste Province (Fernández de Oviedo 1851–1855). Between 1800 and 1940, the estimated annual harvest in Guanacaste Province was between 10,000 and 40,000 animals, and deer meat was less expensive than beef (DiMare 1986). Between 1900 and 1950, an estimated 832,000 white-tailed deer skins were exported from Costa Rica; an average of 16,640 skins a year (Solís and Rodriguez 1987). In decreasing order of importance the importing countries were the United States of America, Germany, Panama, England, Spain, Colombia, and Japan (Solís and Rodriguez 1987). Trade with the United States was particularly heavy between 1901 and 1906 because in the U.S. deer were rare and interstate trade in wildlife had been prohibited. During this period, the golden age of deer exploitation, Costa Rica exported about 34,000 deer pelts per year (Solís and Rodriguez 1987).

Hunting in Costa Rica

The white-tailed deer is still one of the most important game species in Costa Rica. It was hunted by 75 (48%) of 157 rural hunters interviewed in 1980–81, making it the second most important game species by numbers taken (after *Agouti paca*) and the most important by meat biomass (Vaughan, Carrillo, and Wong, unpubl. data). National hunting associations have always focused on deer hunting and hold annual tournaments for the largest antlered buck taken (Fernández 1987).

Three types of hunting permits are issued by the Costa Rican Wildlife Service, the agency responsible for the management of wildlife outside the national parks and equivalent areas. Permits are issued for sport hunting, scientific hunting for research or teaching purposes, and subsistence hunting. In 1987, there were 529 licensed white-tailed deer hunters, mostly seeking trophy antlers, and probably 3,000 to 4,000 illegal hunters in Costa Rica. The country had a 1986 population of three million. According to the Wildlife Conservation Law and its bylaws, white-tailed deer hunting in the Guanacaste Province is limited to one male per year during the 4-month period (August to November), when males have antlers. Hunting with dogs is legal and practiced by most hunters. Many illegal hunters and an unknown number of legal hunters jack-

Figure 20.1. Map of Guancaste Province, Costa Rica, showing white-tailed deer distribution (hatched) in 1987. Scale 1 : 1,000,000.

light at night, sometimes with dogs. This is most common during the dry season around waterholes. Unfortunately, no records exist on most deer killed by most hunters (Fernández 1987).

Rodriguez (1987) determined white-tailed deer distribution and relative abundance in Guanacaste Providence during the dry season (January to March) of 1987 (fig. 20.1). The highest deer densities were on San Lucas Island in the Nicoyan Gulf. On this 500-ha penal colony island, density was calculated at about 0.8 deer/ha. The island contains a mosaic of pasture and altered natural forest environments vegetatively similar to the nearby mainland and is grazed by approximately 200 head of cattle. The deer herd derives from two females and a male placed on the island about 16 years ago. Similar dense deer populations are found in protected wildlands, especially in Santa Rosa National Park and the Santa Elena Peninsula and the complex formed by Palo Verde National Park and Palo Verde National Wildlife Refuge near the mouth of the Tempisque River. In all areas, it is possible to see eight to ten white-tailed deer in an hour's walk. In other areas, densities are generally lower (Rodriguez 1987). Deer tracks and feces are very uncommon in sorghum, rice, sugarcane, and cotton fields, the forested savannas at the foot of the Guanacaste volcanic mountain chain, and the coastal mountain chain. In these areas, deer are more cautions and can usually only be seen at night with spotlights. Throughout most of the Nicoyan Peninsula, white-tailed deer have been eliminated and only survive in low numbers in protected wildlands, protected farms, and the more inaccessible regions.

Deer Management in Costa Rica

No effective management is presently practiced in Costa Rica, except for limited law enforcement. If a drastic measure such as the 5-year hunting ban proposed by the former head of the Costa Rican Wildlife Service were enforced (López 1987), this would no doubt promote recovery of white-tailed deer populations in adequate habitats where they still occur or can easily invade. However, deer management practices common in temperate regions, such as restocking, habitat management, population management, predator control, and effective law enforcement, could produce equal or better recovery without depriving residents of deer use.

Demographic studies of unhunted and hunted white-tailed deer populations in Costa Rica are necessary to determine the density dependence of fecundity and survivorship. The only population for which we have sufficient information occurs on San Lucas Island.

The white-tailed deer herd at San Lucas Island is unhunted. Using transect counts in May 1987 and information from a social organization study (Rodriguez and Vaughan, unpubl. data), Rodriguez and Vaughan (1987) estimated a total population of 400 animals at a density of 0.8 animals/ha, higher than the highest deer densities in the United States (Teer 1984). The tropical year-round growing season, the insular nature of the site, appropriate food, water, refuge, and lack of predation presumably all contribute to make San Lucas Island an excellent deer range.

To estimate deer survivorship, ninety-four crania were collected in the field from 1984 to 1985. Aging relied on tooth wear and eruption structure following Severinghaus (1949). Thirty-six percent of the animals died before 2 years of age; 18% were less than 9 months old. Thirty-nine percent died between 2 and 4 years of age, 20% died between 4 and 5 years, and 4% lived over 5 years. San Lucas Island deer survival cohorts are similar to those in the United States (Hayne 1984). Documented causes of mortality included heavy tick infestations and vampire bat (*Desmodus rotundus*) bites, followed in some cases by ectoparasite larvae. The high mortality rate in young animals suggests that the population may have reached or exceeded carrying capacity.

Social and reproductive cycles were studied on San Lucas Island between 1984 and 1985. The deer occurred as family units and usually included a doe, one or two yearlings, and the fawns produced that year. Family groups formed from March to April, 3 or 4 weeks after the birth of fawns, and were stable throughout the wet season. As in North America (Marchinton and Hirth 1984), groups rarely included more than one adult female.

Births occurred from January to June, although 94% were concentrated in a period of 60 days. Of sixty-seven fawns captured between 7 February and 27 April, 1985, two were born the end of January, thirty-four during February, twenty-six in March, and two in the beginning of April. Only two newly born fawns were observed in May and one in June. If white-tailed deer in the tropical dry forest follow a similar reproductive pattern, newly weaned fawns feed on abundant forbs produced by the wet season rains (Rodriguez and Solís 1987). Observations at Santa Rosa National Park and Palo Verde National Wildlife Refuge indicate that births occur in January and July, well into the wet season. Thus fawning seasons are spread over a much greater period than in the United States (Marchinton and Hirth 1984). In Guanacaste Province, the corresponding period of conceptions, calculated by back aging from the date birth, extended from June to September, with a peak between the second week of August and the second week of September.

Bucks form all-male groups except during June, when they lose the velvet from their antlers and commence the rut. At this time they are frequently observed singly. Groups composed of a doe and buck were more frequent in August and September during the height of courtship. The antler cycle lasted 12 months, while the molt peaking in January and February. Older males were the first to lose their antlers, with growth beginning immediately on the new ones.

During the dry season (December to early May), average group size increased significantly. Between March and May, large temporary groups of all sexes and age classes formed; apparently the result of the concentration of deer in the limited habitats that provide fallen fruits, water, and thermal cover (Rodriguez and Vaughan 1987).

When interpreted by studies from northern latitudes, this information indicates that intensively managed white-tailed deer populations can withstand harvest of up to 30% of the total population. Creed et al. (1984) provide us with guidelines that we can use for experimental management of the San Lucas deer herd. We propose an annual maximum removal of 20% that continues for 3 years. Take should be adjusted each year according to yearly census and productivity estimates (Rodriguez, Solís, and Vaughan 1987). We suggest that to maintain current sex ratios, forty does and forty bucks be removed in September, October, and November, following the breeding season and weaning of young-of-year in August. Of the eighty animals removed, thirty spike bucks should be killed to provide biological data and meat for the prisoners in the penal colony. Ten bucks with suitable antlers and forty females should be restocked on favorable sites on the mainland. This program will serve in population management on San Lucas Island and white-tailed deer restoration on the mainland. Also, twenty fawns should be removed yearly for rearing at agricultural high schools. The removal of fawns should have minimum impact on recruitment because most fawns at San Lucas Island die before the age of 6 months.

Habitat Management

The principal components of white-tailed deer habitat are water, shelter, escape cover, and food (Dasmann 1964). The goal of habitat managers is to assure that these components will be available at the right time and place. Manipulation of habitat may involve a number of approaches, including controlled burning, plantings, farming and maintaining openings, forestry practices, grazing modification, and land use planning (Crawford 1984).

Based on deer numbers, San Lucas Island offers an excellent example of quality deer habitat. Habitat management for other dry forested areas in Costa Rica should attempt to create similar habitat characteristics. Seventeen percent of the 500-ha island is covered with secondary forest, most of which is used for firewood by the prisoners. Over 200 head of Cebu cattle graze the pastures (with tree densities up to ten per hectare), which cover most of the rest of the island. Major forage classes at San Lucas Island were browse and forbs (DiMare 1986). Forbs were dominant in the wet season, whereas browse was dominant in the dry season. Grasses and sedges usually represented only a very small proportion of the total diet and were most abundant during the wet season. Wet and dry season diets were not significantly correlated, although some species were important in both seasons (DiMare 1986). Ten watering tanks for cattle in the dry season are used by the white-tailed deer. There are no predators on the island, and hunting is totally controlled. Under these conditions, the deer population apparently has no problem in meeting its food, shelter, and water requirements (Rodriguez, Solís, and Vaughan 1987).

In Costa Rica burning is commonly practiced during the dry season to clear land for planting. Fires often become uncontrolled and damage large areas. In Santa Rosa National Park, fires are used to maintain certain vegetational successional stages and to create fire lanes (Janzen, pers. comm., 1986). Thus land managers inadvertently maintain and or create white-tailed deer habitat. Burning is recommended in some areas of San Lucas.

Although nutritious, palatable, and digestible foods are not presently planted specifically for white-tailed deer in Costa Rica, food habit studies in Costa Rica (DiMare 1986; McCoy and Vaughan 1981) indicate that several species would be appropriate for forage improvement. Trees that produce desirable fruits or seeds include *Anacardium excelsum, Mangifera indica, Enterolobium cyclocarpum, Pithecellobium saman, Brosimum alicastrum, Eugenia salamensis, Manilkara zapota, Agonandra macrocarpa, Mastichodendron capiri,* and *Guazuma ulmifolia*. Preferred forbs include *Ipomoea* sp., *Sida* sp., and *Archyranthes* sp.

Deer depredation on annual or perennial crops and tree seedlings would be expected where there are high deer densities. If restoration programs are successful, control of deer movements may be necessary. For instance, in San Lucas Island, the prison authorities found that they were unable to plant gardens or many fruit trees due to deer damage. To ensure that deer would not be shot for destroying crops, our white-tailed deer project had to purchase 400 m of 2.5-m-high cyclone fencing and enclose a 1-ha plot on good soils for planting crops.

Restocking

Restocking of white-tailed deer in the United States is one of the major success stories in wildlife management (Dasmann 1964). At the turn of the century, private, state, and federal agencies cooperated to reintroduce deer into ranges from which they were eliminated (Barick 1951). Between 1890 and 1971, over 32,330 deer were restocked into eleven states in the southeastern United States (Blackard 1971). In Alabama alone, deer populations increased from several thousand in 1925 to 207,000 in 1965 (Allen 1965). In restocking, deer must be moved to habits with appropriate food, water, and refuge at the proper time of the year to avoid upsetting population dynamics.

Although many problems are associated with deer capture and transport (Rongstad and McCabe 1984) and subsequent release (O'Bryan and Mc-Cullough 1985; Evans 1980), restocking will form part of our program in Costa Rica because (1) several good restocking sources exist, (2) restocking has proven important in recovery of United States white-tailed deer populations (Barick 1951; Allen 1965; Blackard 1971; Hillestad 1984), and (3) restocking makes for better public relations and allows the active participation of local communities, both important ingredients in a successful program.

We plan to use animals from San Lucas Island, where forty does and ten bucks could be captured yearly for restocking; Palo Verde National Wildlife

Refuge, where twenty does and five bucks from a population estimated at 500 deer could be captured yearly for restocking; and captive animals. Before restocking, Teer (pers. comm., 1987) recommends inspecting the release site to verify appropriate habitat. Texas Parks and Wildlife Department usually requires a minimum of 9,000 ha, although a smaller area of high-quality habitat is sometimes acceptable. If deer are to be released onto private land, there should be an agreement with the landowner to protect the transplant for not less than 5 years. There should be a minimum release of about twenty deer and a sex ratio of one buck to three or four does.

In October 1987, the first white-tailed deer restocking attempt in Latin America began. We used five fawns born on San Lucas Island and raised on the mainland in a 0.5-ha enclosure and adults captured at Palo Verde. Animals were released in a 5,100-ha farm, which produces livestock, sugarcane, rice, and sorghum. Patches of semideciduous and evergreen forest, swamp forest, and swamp combined with the pastures provided the necessary habitat mosaic. The interest of the owners in reestablishing white-tailed deer populations and their promise to actively protect the wildlife were major factors in choosing this ranch as the first reintroduction site.

The movement site of each transplanted animal is presently being monitored over a 24-hour period at least once a week. Location data are taken at 30-minute intervals. This will continue for 1 year to determine daily movements, activity patterns, habitat utilization, and survival. Results will be compared between deer from San Lucas Island and Palo Verde (Saenz 1987). In 1988, a similar restocking study involving thirty radiotagged pregnant female deer, fifteen from San Lucas Island and fifteen from Palo Verde, was carried out on another large ranch. We will monitor the survival and breeding success of the two populations.

Law Enforcement and Environmental Education

In 1986, the drastic decline in white-tailed deer populations in the Guanacaste Province prompted the Costa Rican Wildlife Service to propose a 5-year hunting ban in Guanacaste Province to allow deer and other wildlife to recover to former population levels (López 1987). Unfortunately, the proposal met with opposition from hunting groups and was never initiated.

Hunting seasons presently permit harvest of one deer during the hunting season between August and November. However, illegal hunting occurs throughout the year, and bag limits are frequently exceeded. If illegal hunting cannot be controlled, no large-scale restocking, habitat, or population management programs will be successful. In many regions, Costa Rican subsistence and weekend hunters have depleted deer populations to levels from which they will take years to recover. Law enforcement is very difficult. There are only four wildlife inspectors for all 50,000 km² of national territory. Under these conditions, it is impossible to curtail illegal hunting.

An alternative approach for curtailing illegal hunting emphasizes environmental educational campaigns at all levels. Public pressure in local communities where everyone knows who hunts may be more effective than additional wildlife agents (López 1987). It is important to train local community leaders, teachers, students, and other interested individuals who will initiate programs stressing the protection and rational use of wildlife species and the need for a harmonious relationship between humans and their environment (Solís 1986b).

Environmental education is being carried out in two communities that were very different in land tenure, human population density, and direct involvement in the project. At one site, the agricultural high school and some interested landowners have established deer enclosures for future releases. The other site is a large, privately owned ranch, whose environmental education has concentrated on schools inside or surrounding the farm.

Predator Control

Our opinion is that wild animals do not significantly affect white-tailed deer populations in Costa Rica and that humans are the major predators to be controlled. The mountain lion (*Felis concolor*), an important predator of white-tailed deer in the United States, and the jaguar (*Felis onca*), are rare in Northwestern Costa Rica and thus of no significance in regulating deer populations (Vaughan 1983). Even the coyote (*Canis latrans*), a major predator on white-tailed deer fawns in the United States, where it caused up to 80% fawn mortality (Cook et al, 1971), may not be an important predator in Costa Rica (Vaughan and Rodriguez 1986). A yearling released for restocking, however, was taken by coyotes. We have also seen boa constrictors (*Boa constrictor*) eat deer fawns.

Sustainability of Deer Harvest

No sustained wildlife harvesting will be achieved without the understanding, cooperation, and good will of the local human inhabitants. Even on large haciendas with hired guards, poaching can quickly eliminate wildlife populations. Environmental education programs and community involvement must begin at least 1 year before population management and restoration are attempted. Wildlife biologists must understand the cultural context and needs of a region as well as the biology of deer. Based on 2 years of analysis and extension work in two rural communities in Costa Rica, successful extension programs must include the continuous presence of extension specialists and researchers, the distribution of didactic material and handouts relevant to the inhabitants, and the involvement of community leaders, who will eventually manage the educational projects such as the model management projects. A model management project should be developed in each region as a showcase to encourage widespread imitation. Examples of model projects might be a population and habitat management program on one or several adjoining farms, a community plan to protect wildlife resources, or a deer-rearing enclosure at an agricultural high school. Activities in extension projects must be communicated at a regional and national level so that the country is aware of the efforts.

As mentioned earlier, current laws are adequate, but enforcement is poor. Because funds for strict enforcement are likely to be inadequate in the future, environmental education at all levels and community action in controlling violators should be employed. If wildlife resources are considered community property and if a large landowner places an economic value on his deer, violators will be prosecuted and think twice about poaching. This will require cooperation among local communities, hacienda owners, wildlife inspectors, and law enforcement. As an example of this, a Costa Rican community recently complained about excessive hunting and insisted on governmental action to control poaching.

If an adequate initial population of deer reproduces in good habitat, it will overpopulate the area in a few years time, a fact well documented in temperate areas (Creed et al. 1984; McCullough 1984; Teer 1984) and tropical areas such as San Lucas island (Rodriguez, Solís, and Vaughan 1987). To maintain harvestable populations in northwest Costa Rica, a focus on habitat and population management is essential. Yearly burning can be important to ensure uneven-aged stands of vegetation and tender and highly nutritious shoots at the beginning of the dry season. We also recommend that secondary forests be interspersed with charral and pasture to provide more edge and refuge for deer.

We recommend that yearly censuses be conducted on farms and other possible hunting areas throughout the Guanacaste Province and quotas on deer hunting be established based on these censuses. Hunters should be required to give data about animals harvested and turn in mandibles for aging at check stations along the Pan American highway. If reproductive tracts are also taken at these stations, the reproductive condition of the population can be closely monitored. These data will be used for studying population dynamics and to refine regional harvesting programs.

It is possible to harvest white-tailed deer on a sustained yield basis in the tropical dry forest region in Costa Rica. However, it will required a tremendous amount of cooperation between land owners, law enforcement agencies, aware citizens, and enlightened hunters. What we know of the biology of the white-tailed deer in tropical environments tells us that it has a similar natural history to deer in temperate environments and can exist in Guanacaste Province in high densities, which can be harvested on a sustained-yield basis. More biological studies must be made, but we must also understand the deer users. Only then can deer in Costa Rica recover and be sustainably harvested in the future.

Acknowledgments

We wish to thank Vivienne Solís and Maria Isabel DiMare for contributing information to this study; to Drs. Lynne Irby and James Teer for revising the manuscript; and the World Wildlife Fund-US, Organization of American States, and our institutions, the Universidad Nacional and the Ministry of Natural Resources, Mines and Energy, for supporting this project.

Part 6

Commercial Uses

21

Tupinambis Lizards in Argentina: Implementing Management of a Traditionally Exploited Resource

LEE A. FITZGERALD, JOSÉ MARIA CHANI, AND OSCAR E. DONADÍO

Two species of tegu lizards of the genera *Tupinambis, T. teguixin,* and *T. rufescens* (fig. 21.1), are heavily exploited for their skins in Argentina. Each year, more than 1,250,000 skins are exported from Argentina to the United States, Canada, Mexico, Hong Kong, Japan, and several European countries. Some skins are reexported or made into exotic leather accessories, but the majority of the tegus are destined to become cowboy boots in Texas (Hemley 1984a). Surprisingly, the trade has continued at this level for at least 10 years (Hemley 1984a: Norman 1987). An internal Argentine market also exists for tegu skins, but it has not been quantified.

The large trade in *Tupinambis* has caused concern among some government and nongovernment organizations because the biology of the lizards is essentially undescribed, and the effects on the tegu populations and associated biotic communities of removing more than one million individuals annually are unknown. Although population declines have not been documented, it seems prudent to study *Tupinambis* biology and formulate long-term management and conservation plans if the ecological, economic, and cultural values of the resource are to be guaranteed.

The *Tupinambis* trade is important to the Argentine economy. The export value of the resource is worth millions of dollars annually, and for rural peoples in northern Argentina with low wages or intermittent employment, tegu hunting is a significant source of income. In the vicinity of Joaquin V. Gonzalez, Salta, where we concentrated field work in 1987–88, hundreds of people hunt tegus, and the sale of each skin (about U.S. $4) is equivalent to a day's wages for a farm hand. Additionally, about half the families eat the meat, and tegu fat is highly valued for medicinal purposes (Donadío and Gallardo 1984).

This project was funded by the World Wildlife Fund-US (WWF-US), the Convention on International Trade of Endangered Species of Flora and Fauna (CITES), and the Camara de Industriales de Curtidores de Reptiles de Argentina (CICuR) with the aim of describing the population biology and ecology of

Figure 21.1. A juvenile (approximately 280 mm SVL) *Tupinambis teguixin,* the common tegu top) and an adult male (approximately 430 mm) *Tupinambis rufescens,* the red tegu (below). (Photo, Larry E. Naylor)

Tupinambis in Argentina. The project is unusual in that the reptile skin traders, who benefit the most from exploiting the lizards, finance the majority of the project. Hopefully, the *Tupinambis* project will serve as a model for funding other studies of natural resources in Latin America.

The long-term goals of the project are to determine the factors necessary to ensure the conservation and rational use of Argentine *Tupinambis* populations and develop a workable management scheme. To achieve this goal, we have begun studies of *Tupinambis* reproductive biology, behavior, demography, habitat use, activity patterns, growth rates, diet, morphology, and hunting methods. In this chapter we elucidate the relationships between *Tupinambis* natural history and the present exploitation system and explore the implications of these relationships for *Tupinambis* management and conservation. We present results from the first 6 months of field work and finally we outline future research and potential management approaches.

Distribution and Natural History of *Tupinambis* in Argentina

Tupinambis systematics are unresolved, but at least three, and possibly other *Tupinambis* species occur throughout South America east of the Andes (Presch 1973; Gudynas 1985).

In Argentina, *T. teguixin,* the common tegu, occurs in the provinces of Misiones, Corrientes, eastern Formosa, Entre Rios, eastern Chaco, Santa Fe, southeastern Córdoba, eastern La Pampa, and Buenos Aires (Presch 1973; Donadío 1984) (fig. 21.2). *T. rufescens,* the red tegu, occurs in the northwestern part of the country, in the provinces of Salta, Jujuy, western Chaco, western Formosa, Santiago del Estero, eastern Tucuman, San Juan, Mendoza, and as far south as northeastern Patagonia (Cei and Scolaro 1982) (fig. 21.2).The distribution of *T. rufescens* extends into the Paraguayan and Bolivian Chaco, some arid parts of eastern Paraguay, and southern and southeastern Brazil (Presch 1973; Norman 1986). Both species may occur sympatrically in eastern Paraguay (Presch 1973; Norman 1986) and in the provinces of Chaco, Formosa, and Santiago del Estero, Argentina.

Tupinambis rufescens is a more arid land species than *T. teguixin,* but within their ranges both species use a variety of habitats, including primary forest, disturbed and regenerating forest, fence rows, and shelter belts between plowed fields. They are capable of excavating their own burrows, but commonly take refuge in burrows made by other animals or in natural cavities. Tegus are omnivorous, including carrion and fruit in their diets as well as snails, insects, and small vertebrates (Gudynas 1981; Dessem 1985).

Tupinambis are the largest members of the Teiidae; males of both species can exceed 500 mm snout-vent length (SVL) (1300 mm total length) and weigh up to 4.7 kg (unpubl. data). *Tupinambis* exhibit sexual dimorphism in that adult males are longer and heavier than females on average, with wider heads and enlarged jaw musculature. Male tegus also possess two "buttons" of enlarged scales in the postanal region.

With preliminary data from wild and captive populations, we have assembled a fairly clear picture of tegu breeding chronology in Argentina. Both species overwinter in burrows and emerge during the first hot days in September and October. *Tupinambis teguixin* mates from September through early Jan-

Figure 21.2. Estimated distributions of *Tupinambis teguixin* and *T. rufescens* in Argentina. The provinces where commercial tegu harvests were authorized at the time of writing are numbered: 1 = Salta; 2 = Formosa; 3 = Chaco; 4 = Santiago del Estero.

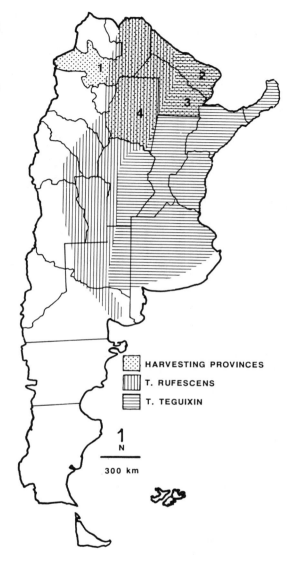

HARVESTING PROVINCES

T. RUFESCENS

T. TEGUIXIN

1
N

300 km

uary, and in the dry chaco *T. rufescens* starts breeding a few weeks later, probably depending on the start of the rainy season (fig. 21.3). In captivity at Guaycolec Reserve, Formosa, of thirty male and thirty female *T. teguixin* that had opportunities to mate, only large individuals did so. Small males were rejected by breeding females, and small females would not copulate. Five successfully breeding males averaged 438 mm SVL, with an average weight of

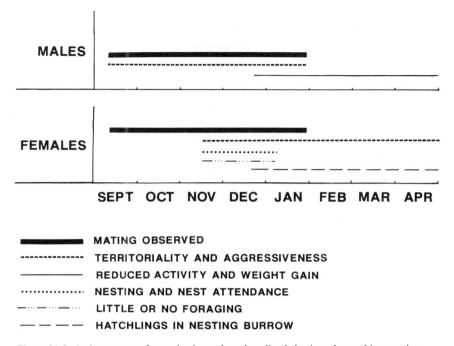

MALES

FEMALES

SEPT OCT NOV DEC JAN FEB MAR APR

▬▬▬▬▬ MATING OBSERVED

------------- TERRITORIALITY AND AGGRESSIVENESS

——————— REDUCED ACTIVITY AND WEIGHT GAIN

················ NESTING AND NEST ATTENDANCE

—···—···—··· LITTLE OR NO FORAGING

— — — — HATCHLINGS IN NESTING BURROW

Figure 21.3. A chronogram of reproductive and postbreeding behaviors observed in a captive population of *Tupinambis teguixin* at Guaycolec Reserve, Formosa. The same trends were observed in the wild at National Park El Palmar, Entre Rios.

3,759 g, whereas the five breeding females averaged 382 mm SVL and weighed 2,263 g.

Nesting begins in mid-November and peaks in December, but occasionally gravid females can be found as late as February. Females of both species construct nests out of moist grass, small sticks, and miscellaneous litter in burrows. *Tupinambis teguixin* laid twenty-nine to thirty-nine ($n = 5$; $\bar{x} = 33.75$) eggs at Guaycolec, and clutch sizes of twenty to fifty-four were reported by Donadío and Gallardo (1984). Two nests of *T. rufescens* from the wild contained twenty-five and twenty-four eggs, but clutch sizes greater than thirty are known (pers. obs.). After the incubation period of 45 to 75 days, young hatch from late December through March (fig. 21.3).

Interestingly, females remain with their nests throughout the incubation period, possibly to provide protection. Hunters claim that females attend nests, and this has been the case with nests we have excavated. At the Guaycolec facility, females remained near their nesting burrows once nests were constructed, and nesting females were noticeably aggressive towards intruders. Hatchlings remain for at least a few weeks in the nesting burrow with the female. Whether parental care is involved in this relationship, whether the mother and young overwinter together, and the effects of maternal presence on offspring survival are topics of current and future research.

Observations at El Palmar National Park indicate that during the courting period, tegus roam over relatively large home ranges, and much fighting ensues between males. Males frequently mark along trails and around the burrows they visit by rubbing their thighs, tails, and cloacas along the ground, presumably leaving behind secretions from the femoral pores and cloaca. Females also leave marks but much less frequently than males. We observed such marking behaviors both in captivity and in the wild at El Palmar National Park. After the mating season, both sexes apparently mark less frequently, and their home range size decreases.

Dominance in *Tupinambis* clearly depends on size (Chani and Fitzgerald, pers. obs.). Displacement aggression can occur between individuals of all sizes and either sex and usually results in the largest individual displacing the smallest. In captivity during the breeding season, these aggressions result in dominance hierarchies between males and the formation of temporary pseudoterritories.

Captive Rearing Projects

At least five captive rearing efforts of both species of *Tupinambis* are ongoing in Argentina; we have information on three of the facilities. The captive breeding program at Guaycolec Reserve, Formosa, is supported by the Province of Formosa, WWF-US, and the Curtiembre Formosa tannery. The main objective of this program is to contribute to *T. teguixin* conservation by transferring captive rearing technology to indigenous communities and colonists in northeastern Argentina. The hope is that small-scale captive operations may be operated by families as a source of meat and skins. At Guaycolec, *T. teguixin* has successfully reproduced, and approximately 160 young hatched in 1987–88. Another facility in the city of Presidente Roque Saenz Peña, Chaco, supported by the province of Chaco and financed by the Curtiembre Chaco tannery, shares objectives and information with Guaycolec. Saenz Peña is located in a zone where both *T. teguixin* and *T. rufescens* occur, and both species are used there. A large facility in Rosario de la Frontera, Salta, forms part of the "Programa Iguana Colorado," which is operated and financed by S. y F. Trachter e Hijos S. R. L. and Cueros Salta S. R. L. This facility is commercially oriented, operating on the idea that it might be economical to raise *T. rufescens* in large quantities as a skin source. More than 600 animals are in captivity there, and capacity exists to incubate more than 3,000 eggs. Reproduction in captivity was achieved in 1987–88. All three facilities have allowed us to use their captive animals for our research and are valuable resources for a variety of research questions.

The Traditional System of Exploitation

The tegu harvest system could be described as "a million hunters for a million skins." Of course, fewer people really hunt, but in the areas of regular exploitation, almost anyone will catch a tegu if the opportunity arises. The hunting season corresponds with the activity of the lizards, beginning in September and lasting through March. Most hunters in Argentina use one to three trained dogs to track the lizards to their burrows, where they are dug out and captured alive. Occasionally the dogs jump an active lizard and chase it to a temporary refuge such as a hollow log, underneath a thicket, into a hole, or up a tree. Along rivers in eastern Argentina, baited hooks left near burrows are a common capture method.

Hunters can be classified as professional or occasional. There are many, many occasional hunters, and they typically hunt on weekends or during time off from their jobs. Professional hunters use superior dogs and spend much more time hunting than occasional hunters. A professional can bag fifteen tegus on a good day. In ten outings near Joaquin V. Gonzalez, Salta, hunters covered an average of 16.23 (SD = 7.89) ha/day and averaged 3.6 (SD = 3.07) captures.

Once killed, the lizards are skinned from the dorsal side, leaving the ventral plates intact. Skins can be sold directly to the tanneries, but more often the skins pass through middlemen. Hunters in remote areas sell skins or trade for goods to mobile *acopiadores,* who resell the skins to tanners or to another level of middlemen, *barraqueros* (Donadío and Gallardo 1984) (fig. 21.4).The skins' market value depends on their width when dry, so a strong incentive exists to stretch them as much as possible. Acopiadores and barraqueros even restretch skins in order to sell them as a larger size. Skins are traded according to three size classes: in the vicinity of Joaquín V. González during 1987–88, class I skins (more than 300 mm wide) fetched about US$4; class II skins (250 to 299 mm wide) brought US$2, and class III skins (less than 250 mm wide) were worth less than US$1. Skins may be devalued if they are scarred or poorly prepared. The tanneries need class I and II skins and actually prefer not to buy smaller skins. Paying low prices for class III is a way the tanneries put economic pressure on hunters not to collect small skins, and over time, this pressure may have resulted in fewer small skins circulating. The tanneries deal with many middlemen who will sell class I only on the condition their entire stock is purchased, so some class II and III skins always enter the trade (Casado Sastre, pers. comm.).

Four provinces in northern Argentina traditionally authorized *Tupinambis* harvests: Santiago del Estero, Formosa, Chaco, and Salta (fig. 21.2). Each year, these provinces formulated legal decrees that set harvest quotas for tegus based on the needs of the industry and the province.

Harvest quotes have had little or no biological basis in that tegu population

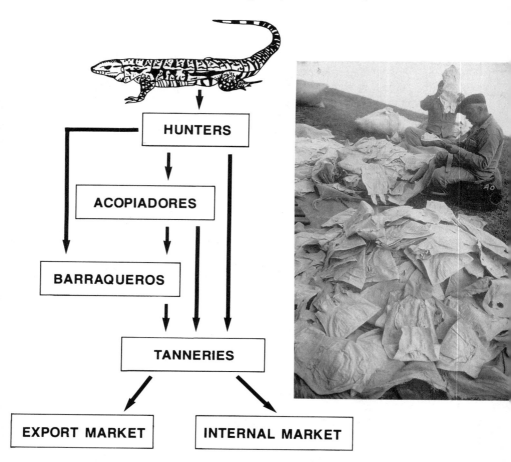

Figure 21.4. (above) The flow of tegu skins in Argentina. Hunters sell skins directly to tanneries or to either level of middlemen, who then resell to the tanneries. The internal market in Argentina has not been quantified.

Figure 21.5. (above, right) Semitanned tegu skins, or "crusts," being sorted at a tannery. Skins in this stage of the tanning process may be legally exported from Argentina or may be further processed into finished leather. (Photo, Ginette Hemley/WWF-US)

size and structure have never been estimated. Not all tegu skins derive from the four provinces where hunting is legal, but we have no estimates of what proportion of the total annual harvest originates in other provinces. Skins collected in other areas may pass into one of the four harvesting provinces and figure as part of that province's quota. Additionally, skins cross the borders from Paraguay and Bolivia into Argentina and enter the Argentine trade (Norman 1987). Thus it is likely that the quotas of the harvesting provinces do not reflect well the level of exploitation there.

But the provinces' approach to tegu commercialization is rapidly changing, and a new system controlling tegu commerce is already being implemented. A group called the Comisión *Tupinambis* was formed in 1988 and consists of directors of provincial wildlife agencies, skin traders, and others interested in tegu management and exploitation. Ten provinces participate in the Comisión *Tupinambis:* Salta, Formosa, Chaco, Santiago del Estero, Jujuy, La Rioja, Santa Fe, Corrientes, Entre Rios, and Catarmarca. All of these provinces except Corrientes, Catamarca, and Entre Rios had legalized tegu harvests for the 1988–89 season at the time of this writing. The main thrust of the Comisión *Tupinambis* is to stabilize tegu commerce within the provinces through tax incentives. Fewer taxes are levied on tanned and semitanned skins leaving the province of origin than for raw skins. Taxes on transport permits for raw skins in 1989 were $1 per skin, $0.16 per semitanned skin, and only $0.08 per finished skin. Because of the tax breaks, it is hoped that skins originating in a province remain there throughout the tanning process. In this way, the provinces hope that the tanning industry will build more tanneries in the provinces where tegus are harvested, resulting in industrial development and creating jobs.

The Comisión *Tupinambis* plan has important implications for management. Once a legal harvest and control system is in place, wildlife managers will know the number of skins harvested in each province and will be able to monitor the effects of management practices.

Argentina is signatory to CITES, and *Tupinambis* skins leave the country with CITES export permits according to appendix II rules. Skins must be tanned or semitanned before export, which facilitates monitoring the trade and also means that more of the industry is a national endeavor than if raw skins were exported (fig. 21.5).

Impacts of Hunting on Tegu Populations

Seasonal differences in activity among males, females, and juveniles may play an important role in which sizes and sexes of tegus are most vulnerable to hunters at a given time. Hunters' dogs track tegus by their scent, and if males are indeed more active and leave marks over larger areas than females, a logical prediction is that males should be especially vulnerable to hunters during the breeding season. Conversely, fewer females should be hunted if they occupy smaller home ranges and remain near their nesting burrows. If territoriality in tegus is strictly related to the mating process, then one would not expect juveniles of either sex to be heavily hunted. If males reduce their activity after the mating season, then at this time, they may be no more vulnerable than females.

These predictions were supported with data from 118 adult *Tupinambis rufescens* purchased from hunters in 1987–88. Seventy-eight percent of adults collected in the breeding season month of November were males (chi-

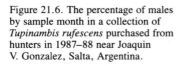

Figure 21.6. The percentage of males by sample month in a collection of *Tupinambis rufescens* purchased from hunters in 1987–88 near Joaquin V. Gonzalez, Salta, Argentina.

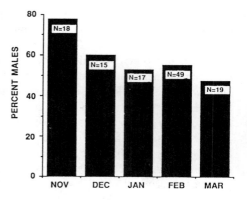

square $= 4.500$; $p < 0.05$), compared to 47% to 60% males in other months (fig. 21.6).The association between the number of each sex collected and month was not significant (chi-square $= 4.128$; $p > 0.25$), but the trend suggests that males were more active during the breeding season and that there was little difference in activity levels between the sexes at other times of the year.

Not only were more males hunted in November, but interestingly, they were significantly longer than males taken in other months (d.f. $= 4,92$ F-ratio $= 3.217$; $p < 0.02$). Female SVL did not differ among sample months (d.f. $= 4,79$ F-ratio $= 0.540$; $p > 0.50$).

We also searched for evidence of differential vulnerability of male and female tegus to hunters by examining trends in harvested skins. We measured and sexed thousands of skins in Curtiembre Formosa tannery in December, January, March, and April and tested for deviations from equal sex ratios among the three skin size classes (table 21.1).We predicted that more male than female class I skins should appear early in the season because those skins belonged to large adult lizards. Most of the skins in classes II and III probably came from immature individuals, thus sexes in those size classes should have been equally represented.

Male and female *T. teguixin* sampled in December were represented equally in classes I and II, and significantly more females were tallied in class III (table 21.1). In the January sample, however, significantly more males of both species occurred in class I, and there was no difference in class II for either species. Significantly more females occurred in class III *T. rufescens,* but there was no difference in class III *T. teguixin.* Significantly more males occurred in the March sample of class I *T. teguixin,* but there was no difference in class I *T. rufescens.* Sexes were equally represented in classes II and III *T. teguixin* in March, but significantly more females occurred in class II and III *T. rufescens.* Class I males of both species were equally represented in the April sample, but again, significantly more females were tallied in the smaller size classes. It is curious that more females often occurred in classes II and III (table 21.1). We

TABLE 21.1
Percent Male Tegus (total *n*) in Samples of Each Skin Size Class
Measured in Curtiembre Formosa Tannery

	Skin Size Class		
	I	II	III
	Tupinambis teguixin		
December	53.9 (306)	40.9 (110)	40.5 (190)
	$p > 0.1$	$p < 0.1$	$p < 0.01$
January	66.3 (725)	51.7 (594)	51.5 (301)
	$p < 0.001$	$p > 0.50$	$p > 0.50$
March	58.6 (1421)	50.9 (678)	45.2 (416)
	$p < 0.001$	$p > 0.75$	$p = 0.05$
April	59.3 (86)	67.3 (150)	46.0 (150)
	$p > 0.25$	$p < 0.001$	$p > 0.25$
	Tupinambis rufescens		
January	57.4 (584)	44.2 (163)	32.7 (202)
	$p < 0.001$	$p > 0.1$	$p < 0.001$
March	51.2 (704)	33.4 (411)	29.6 (584)
	$p > 0.75$	$p < 0.001$	$p < 0.001$
April	50.9 (214)	27.3 (150)	28.0 (150)
	$p > 0.75$	$p < 0.001$	$p < 0.001$

Note: values were calculated from goodness-of-fit tests to show deviations from equal sex ratios.

could have made sexing errors, or the secondary sexual characteristics of males may not be readily evident in classes II and III.

To summarize, the results indicated differential harvests of male and female tegus, but the pattern differed from that obtained in the analyses of collections. Adults (class I skins) were equally represented in December and April, but significantly more males appeared in January and March. Perhaps males were more vulnerable than females throughout the season, or geographical variation in tegu activity was responsible for the observed pattern. It is also likely that middlemen held large skins while waiting for better prices late in the season, thus influencing the data.

Implications for Management and Research Priorities

Understanding the biological and socioeconomic factors that have allowed tegu populations to endure harvests greater than 1,250,000 every year for at least 10 years might enable us to design management practices that operate within the traditional exploitation system, as well as assess the security of *Tupinambis* in Argentina. Tegu populations may have endured high harvest rates because there simply were a lot of tegus and habitat available. New areas may be hunted as populations decline in other areas, or alternatively, populations may persist in spite of hunting pressure. As wildlands are developed and roads built, previously unexploited regions become hunting grounds, but it is also certain that the same areas where tegus have been hunted for years, such as the province of Santiago del Estero, continue to produce skins. Other than plowed fields and urban centers, we know of no historical locality where tegus cannot still be found today. Thus it seems promising that *Tupinambis* populations in traditionally harvested areas tolerate hunting without obvious extirpations. Still, it is dangerous to assume that a sustainable harvest level has been reached merely because large numbers of skins can be gathered year after year. An alternative hypothesis is that traditionally exploited populations might not produce many large skins even though they still tolerate hunting. The international market for tegus requires large skins, so in this case new hunting areas would continually be required. Development and wildlife exploitation in northern Argentina are both increasing (Bucher 1986; Ojeda and Mares 1984), and the extent of new hunting grounds for tegus is finite. Clearly, the relative contributions of traditional and new hunting grounds to the annual tegu harvest has far reaching ramifications for the long-term stability of *Tupinambis* populations and the tanning industry that depends on them.

In many areas that have historically been hunted, tegu populations might have been maintained due to the difficulty of hunting tegus in certain habitats and the proximity of refugia. If an exploited area adjoins an adequate refugium, such as a dense forest inaccessible to hunters, then the lizards that are removed could be replenished by recruitment and immigration. Many areas are not frequented by hunters because they are either remote or terrain makes hunting difficult. In the dry chaco, expanses of dense thorn forest are ignored, whereas roadsides, fence rows, and shelter belts are favored hunting sites. Hunters rarely venture more than 25 km from their homes and usually return the same day. Roadsides constitute potential hunting areas, as does any primary or secondary forest surrounding pastures, plowed fields, and ranchers' line camps.

Hunters are also limited by the number of hours they can hunt per day, by weather that inhibits tegu activity, and the entire hunting season lasting about 7 months. We observed that tegus sometimes escape into inaccessible holes and burrows, notably viscacha (*Lagostomus maximus*) warrens or abandoned leaf-cutter ant (*Atta*) mounds, but need to quantify hunter efficiency before we can evaluate if a meaningful number escape. Additionally, it is likely that hunting pressure drops in localities where fewer and smaller tegus are hunted per unit time, and such a respite could reduce impacts on populations, especially if reproductive individuals are left. To test the hypothesis that it is difficult to reduce populations to nonrecoverable levels, we need to work with hunters who will repeatedly visit established hunting plots until, after repeated attempts, they cannot find any tegus.

Growth rates and the reproductive output of females of different sizes are undescribed *Tupinambis* life history parameters that influence population growth rates and, hence, their recoverability. Newborn *T. rufescens* from the "Programa Iguana Colorada" captive rearing facility near Rosario de La Frontera, Salta, measured 82 mm SVL on average ($n = 20$; SD $= 4.90$) and captive yearlings 274 mm SVL ($n = 20$; SD $= 35.58$). Assuming slower growth rates in the wild of about 100 mm/yr during the first 3 years, a tegu in its third year would measure more than 350 mm SVL and be within the size range of known breeding females. We are determining size at first reproduction by analyses of reproductive tracts and quantifying growth rates from skeletal characteristics and by mark and recapture of *Tupinambis teguixin* in El Palmar National Park. Establishing size-specific growth rates and fecundity (clutch size) will allow estimation of the reproductive output of females that are harvested as different size classes.

Our preliminary results indicated male and female tegus were not equally vulnerable to hunters at all times; more and larger males were hunted during the breeding season. The effects of removing a disproportionate number of large breeding males from a *Tupinambis* population have not been determined. Tegus are polygynous, so some males could be removed without reducing female reproduction. On the other hand, if hunting pressure is strong and tegu population densities are low, then breeding males could become a limiting resource to females. Additionally, there is no evidence that females are hunted less during the period when males are apparently more vulnerable; it is possible that an increase in male vulnerability merely results in a higher total of tegus hunted. Future research should be aimed at understanding tegu activity and patterns, and armed with this knowledge, we can then work to modify hunting patterns to theoretically maximize female survivorship and reproduction.

Our experiences and those of Norman (1986) in Paraguay indicate that when there is no immediate outlet to whom hunters can sell skins, they hunt less. Assuming differences exist in activity patterns among sexes and sizes, buying skins early would cause hunters to take more large males. Similarly, halting skin purchases in December, for example, could enhance survivorship of nesting females. Perhaps it is feasible, if industry and government were in agreement, the economic pressures already in action could be extended to further reduce the number of small skins entering the trade. The purchase of class III skins could be banned, but the plan would collapse if some buyers did not participate. Middlemen could continue to manipulate buyers into purchasing mixed lots of skins.

It is essential to monitor management practices that are supposed to result in the harvest of specific *Tupinambis* population segments. But *Tupinambis* are difficult to census by trapping or by sight due to the effects of weather on daily activity complicated by variable observability according to habitat. In over 400 trap-days with lines of 20 to 35 live traps, we captured two tegus, and in 3 months of continuous trapping with a system of drift fences and 103 pitfall traps we caught only four. Censuses conducted while walking or driving were equally problematic. We saw fewer than one individual per 40 km of road while driving in localities where large numbers of tegus were hunted. Based on these experiences, it is doubtful that biologists would be able to meaningfully estimate *Tupinambis* population sizes on a regional basis by sampling populations in the field using these methods. Instead of a system where population information originates from estimating the number of living individuals, we envision a system that depends on monitoring demographic changes in the yearly harvest in the tanneries. Species, sex, SVL, and total number of skins of each size class are data potentially available in tanneries, thus a fairly complete demographic picture of the harvested population could be obtained on a regional basis. Operationally, large-scale data collection for management purposes could be rapid and inexpensive. Authorized observers or agency personnel could sample skins of each size class several times yearly to quantify sex ratios and size distributions and confirm the total number of skins of each size class and species. With this information, national or provincial wildlife agencies could then compare the characteristics of harvested populations over time.

The preliminary skin harvest analyses did not include data from most of the breeding season; thus it is difficult to conclude whether the results indicated real differences in tegu activity patterns and vulnerability. We hope to add rigor to the monitoring experiments by measuring skins throughout the entire season and by taking into account the zone of origin and approximate collecting dates of the harvested tegus. Future research should identify the sources of variation in these sorts of analyses in order to determine how accurately *Tupinambis* population trends are represented.

Acknowledgments

We especially thank Felix Cruz, Marcelo Del Hoyo, Cinthia Karlsson, and Gabriela Perotti for their unflagging assistance and good humor throughout the entire season. Patricia Silva and Silvina Chauvin also assisted in National Park El Palmar and in the Guaycolec Reserve breeding facility. Ing. Carlos Saravia Toledo of Campos del Norte S. A. opened the doors of Campos del Norte to our research in the Chaco and housed our entire crew. Sebastian Casado Castre, president of the Curtiembre Chaco and Curtiembre Formosa tanneries, enthusiastically supported the harvest monitoring experiments. We also thank Sergio Trachter, President of CICuR, for solving many of our logistical needs and providing access to the captive breeding facility of the "Programa Iguana Colorada," Cueros Salta, S. R. L. We gratefully acknowledge the support of the provincial wildlife agencies of Buenos Aires, Chaco, Corrientes, Entre Rios, Formosa, Salta, and Santiago del Estero as well as the Dirección Nacional de Fauna Silvestre, the Administración de Parques Nacionales, and Salta Forestal S. A. Thomas H. Fritts, Ginette Hemley, Norman J. Scott, and Dagmar Werner kindly reviewed the manuscript.

22

Sustained Harvesting of the Patagonia Guanaco: Is It Possible or Too Late?

WILLIAM L. FRANKLIN AND MICHAEL A. FRITZ

The more we can demonstrate the economic value of wild species, the more we shall add a much-needed weapon to our arsenal of conservation arguments. There is hardly another argument in support of threatened species that carries so much weight as the economic argument.[Myers 1983]

As elsewhere in the world, increasing human pressure and use of marginal and arable lands in South American has threatened wildlife and their habitats. Overhunting and habitat destruction are consistently the most severe and widespread causes of wildlife decline. However, rigid protection of wildlife is clearly not a panacea. We are now entering an era of wildlife conservation and management in Latin American countries that dictates a "use it or lose it" philosophy. The world conservation strategy set the stage for this approach, proposing the managed harvesting of wild animals in those situations where economic incentives are likely to be the most effective motivator for species conservation (IUCN 1981). This might apply even to rare and endangered species. A classic example of the use it or lose it philosophy in Latin America is the South American vicuña (*Vicugna vicugna*), whose valuable wool and high economic potential to the indigenous Andean people was the primary rationale used to preserve this species from extinction in the 1970s (Franklin 1982a; Hofmann et al. 1983; Cueto and Ponce 1985). The South American guanaco (*Lama guanicoe*), whose numbers have dramatically declined over the past century, is another species for which a rational and scientifically managed harvest could contribute to its conservation and perpetuation.

Despite their dramatically reduced numbers throughout their former range, guanacos continue to be an important and viable asset to local and regional economies in South America. In Argentina, legal harvest of newborn guanacos (chulengos) is a multi-million dollar industry. During the years 1972 through 1979, 443,655 guanaco skins were exported from Argentina. In 1979 alone over 86,000 chulengo skins were legally exported at a total worth of $3.6 mil-

317

lion dollars (Ojeda and Mares 1982). From 1976 to 1979, 223,610 chulengo pelts valued at $5.6 million were exported (Mares and Ojeda 1984).

With reduced numbers, fewer populations, and uncontrolled harvesting of guanacos, it is critical to acquire basic biological information and to develop effective field methods for harvesting guanaco on a sustained yield basis. Sustained yield management of guanacos is not a new idea. It has been proposed by a variety of workers, including Miller, Rottman, and Taber 1973; Miller et al. 1983; Franklin 1978, 1982b, and Cunazza 1980. Miller et al. (1983) rightfully warned that implementation of management for economic return requires "substantial augmentation of the biological data bases upon which effective conservation plans must be based." Thus, the economic argument for wildlife conservation must be based upon sound biological principles and data.

Our ultimate objective as wildlife ecologists and managers is to preserve the guanaco and the ecological system in which it lives. Toward this goal, a series of field studies on the natural history, population biology, ecology, social behavior, and social systems of the guanaco have been underway in southern Chile for the past 15 years (see Raedeke 1979; Franklin 1982a). With these studies, we can begin to apply our knowledge to management.

The guanaco is a wildlife resource that could have immense value for regional economies. Yet, management of populations of these large grazers could significantly affect other land use practices. The critical questions we now face are: How can we harvest guanacos on an optimal yield basis without interfering with normal reproduction and social organization? Is it too late to apply such a progressive, although traditional, approach?

The Animal: Its Biology and Distribution

The guanaco is one of four members of the South American camelid family, which also contains the llama (*Lama glama*), a domestic beast of burden; the alpaca (*Lama pacos*), a domestic wool producer; and the vicuña, a nondomestic animal with silky fine wool. The guanaco is the wild progenitor of the domestic llama, whereas the alpaca appears to be a product of selective breeding of guanaco with vicuña and/or llama with vicuña. Of the four, guanacos are the most widely distributed in South America. Their flexible social and feeding behaviors enable them to occupy a variety of arid land habitats and a wider range of altitudes (Franklin 1975, 1982b, 1983).

Guanacos are uniformly cinnamon brown with a white underside and gray to black heads. They weigh 100 to 150 kg with little difference between males and females. Their wool is second only to the vicuña in fineness, averaging 16 to 18 μm in diameter. Depending upon the dryness of the environment, cover, or the amount of snow, populations may be sedentary or migratory (Franklin 1975; Raedeke 1979). Individuals in a population are socially and spatially divided into family groups (one territorial adult male, several females, and their offspring less than 15 months old), male groups (immature, nonterritorial males), and solo males (single, territorial males without females). Winter aggregations of all ages and both sexes form in the migratory populations, and female groups may form in any population, especially in the nonterritorial season.

The guanaco was historically the dominant, large mammalian herbivore on the southern grasslands, scrublands, and steppes of South American (Franklin 1982b). The heartland of the guanaco's distribution was Patagonia, the high cold plateau desert that is the ecological counterpart to the North American Great Basin desert. When Charles Darwin visited South America in the early 1830s, he noted that "The guanaco . . . an elegant animal . . . is the characteristic quadruped of the plains of Patagonia . . . it is common over the whole of the temperate parts of the continent . . ." (Darwin 1845). Other great naturalists who first explored South American continued to marvel at the large numbers of guanacos. Prichard (1902, 1911), in his extensive travels throughout the Patagonia at the turn of the century, observed that "during the whole course of our travels in Patagonia (save when in the forests) a day rarely passed without our seeing guanacos. . . . The range of the guanaco extends over the plain of Patagonia. . . . Enormous herds from three to five hundred live upon the pampas. . . . Literally thousands of guanacos appeared on the summits of the surrounding barren ridges. . . ." During his visit to the Patagonia, Musters (1871) also saw guanaco herds with thousands of animals.

Today, such spectacular sights of enormous herds of guanacos on the Patagonia are no more. There were millions of guanacos on the Patagonia when the Europeans first arrived in the 1500s. Based upon post-European maximum stocking rates, Raedeke (1979) estimated the potential pre-European numbers of guanacos on the pampas to have been 30 to 35 million. During the last century almost 7 million guanacos still remained (Torres 1985) in Argentina, Bolivia, and Peru (Cabrera and Yepes 1940). Their numbers continued to drastically decline because of overhunting for their valuable pelts and wool, persecution because of suspected competition with livestock (especially sheep), and the interference by fences with routes of movement. By the mid-1900s, most guanacos had been all but eliminated from the large Patagonia pampa (Dennler de la Tour 1954; Howard 1970). The currently accepted number of guanacos remaining in South American is approximately 600,000, of which about 95% are in Argentina (Franklin 1982b; Torres 1985). Recent aerial surveys by Garrido, Mazzanti, and Garrido (1988) are more optimistic and estimate the number of guanacos on the Argentine Patagonia to be 1.5 million ($\pm$ 20%).

Guanacos have long been an important life-sustaining and economic resource for residents of the Patagonia. The Tehuelche Indians of southern Patagonia and the Ona Indians of the highlands of Tierra del Fuego were both guanaco-dependent cultures (Gilmore 1950b). They made full use of the animal by using its meat for food, hides for shelter, wool for cloth, pelts for clothing and robes, bones for tools, and internal organs and glands as medicines. Bridges (1950) described numerous uses and applications of guanaco products that helped the Ona Indians survive on the harsh pampas and forest of Tierra del Fuego.

Harvesting Guanacos

Previous Studies

Because of their declining numbers in Chile, guanacos became a protected species in 1929 (Miller, Rottman, and Taber 1973; Iriarte and Jaksic 1986). In the mid-1970s, a conservation and protection program was established in southern Chile, where guanacos were most abundant on the mainland and Tierra del Fuego Patagonia (Cunazza 1980). This concern with protection did not preclude studies of the potential for harvesting guanacos (Sielfeld and Venegas 1985). Miller, Rottman, and Taber (1973) observed that guanaco meat could be sold for as much as three times the price of beef in Chile. Verscheure (1979) investigated the marketability of guanaco meat, wool, and skin products and believed meat to be the best potential product for Chile.

Guanacos were harvested experimentally on Tierra del Fuego in 1980 and 1981 by the Chilean Forestry and Wildlife Service (CONAF). Costs and potential returns were carefully analyzed to determine the economics of the 1981 harvest of 98 guanacos (Cunazza 1985). The total cost of the harvest was $8,100 (U.S. dollar equivalent at that time), with personnel representing 35%, transportation 26%, tanning of skins 26%, and materials and miscellaneous 13%. The projected total income $9,800 was from meat ($58% at $1.40/kg) and tanned skins (42% at $52/skin). Potential wool sales were not included.

This guanaco harvesting program was terminated when it was determined that the population under study had a high incidence (76% of the animals harvested) of sarcocystosis caused by the parasitic protozoan *Sarcocystis*. Guanacos were the intermediate hosts for a parasite with an undefined carnivore-definitive host. Sarcoystosis produced lesions in meat, which although not harmful for human consumption, were disagreeable to the consumer. The high costs of tanning skins ($26 each) and the lack of a ready market for the end products were also problems. The alternative of marketing the sheared wool ($35 to 45/kg) from the skins instead of selling them as tanned pelts might have increased income (fig. 22.1). Although this was only a pilot study, a number of important lessons were learned and conclusions made: late summer and early fall (February to March) was the best time of year to harvest because guanacos were in peak physical condition and it was a good time to minimize the accidental shooting of females that were still in family groups; techniques and methods to allow efficient use of horses and vehicles were developed; and hunting tech-

Figure 22.1. Shearing wool by hand from a guanaco. (Photo, William Franklin).

niques, procedures for dressing carcasses, and refrigerating the meat were refined (see Cunazza 1985). This valuable work also clearly illustrated the numerous variables that had yet to be considered when harvesting guanacos.

Current Studies

The overall goal of this phase of our studies was to expand the biological base of knowledge of guanacos as it applied to their potential harvest. Our study area was Torres del Paine National Park in southern Chile. As a protected area, it offered the opportunity to assess social organization, distribution, movements, and population parameters of an undisturbed population. Earlier studies had established that the guanaco population was migratory, that males and females formed large (150+) mixed nomadic aggregations in winter and that females became members of family groups (14–20 animals) in summer, on single male-defended territories, and bachelor males formed male groups (Franklin 1982a; Wilson and Franklin 1985; Ortega 1985).

Our specific objectives were to (1) study guanaco population biology and dynamics, including natality, survival, and mortality rates; (2) explore the harvestability of the population using a modified Leslie matrix simulation model (Leslie 1945; Clark 1985); and (3) to incorporate into the harvest model features of the guanaco's social system.

This information was collected at Torres del Paine National Park (72°55'W, 51°3'S) on the western edge of the southern Patagonia and on the east slope of the Andes. The park was established in 1969 and expanded in 1975 to include the eastern half of the study area. Before 1975 much of rangelands of the park, including the study area, was overstocked with sheep and cattle. Invader shrubs still dominate the landscape, although it is in the process of recovery (IUCN 1982).

The study area itself is a "peninsula" surrounded by Lake Nordenskjold and Paine River on the north and northwest, Lake Pehoe on the west, Lake Sarmiento on the south, and the Goic sheep and cattle ranch on the east. Rugged shale and conglomerate foothills, 100 to 250 m above sea level, transect the study area north to south in a series of four almost equally spaced ridges. Some thirty medium-sized permanent freshwater lakes and lagoons and numerous intermittent ponds are present.

Despite there being numerous large and small bodies of water in the region, this is part of the treeless Patagonian steppe (grass/shrub land). The area is in the rainshadow of the 2,346 m Paine Mountain massif, and although the approximate 400 mm annual precipitation has a fairly uniform seasonal distribution, this is basically a desert environment induced by high wind evaporation. Temperatures average 15°C in summer and 1°C in winter, with only 1 or 2 frostfree months in summer (Pisano 1974). Seasonal and daily oscillations of temperature are great. High winds occur all year but are less frequent in winter. This desertlike shrubland is dominated by the shrub *Mulinum spinosum* and is classified as a *matorral xerófito Pre-Andino* association (Pisano 1974).

Methods

To examine what number, sex, and age of guanacos could be harvested without damaging the population, we used a modification (Clark 1985) of Leslie's (1945) projection matrix population model, called NOLES. Modifications of Leslie's (1945) projection matrix population model have been widely used in modeling the harvesting of populations (e.g., Fowler 1980).

Population Size and Growth

Census results from 1975 to 1980 were generously provided by the CONAF (unpublished reports, Torres del Paine National Park, Puerto Natales, Chile). Sixteen censuses (complete counts) were conducted during our study from July

1981 to February 1984 by following fixed routes on foot and using binoculars and spotting scope to count and identify the sex and age of all guanacos encountered. To compare the growth rate calculated from census results with computer-simulated population growth (using the initial age-specific survival and natality rates without harvest), the program was run to simulate twenty annual cycles of births and deaths.

Sex and Age Structures

Live Guanacos. All guanacos counted during our censuses at Torres del Paine National Park were sexed and aged based on field criteria and techniques developed during preceding field studies (Franklin 1983). Adults were animals >2 years old, yearlings 1 year old, and chulengos (juveniles) <1 year old.

Dead Guanacos. All skulls and mandibles found during the study were sexed and ages using criteria developed by Raedeke (1979) for another guanaco population (Tierra del Fuego). An age-specific sex ratio of guanacos 3 years old and older was obtained from the censuses following the November to December birth season. We assumed 50% of the chulengos (see Raedeke 1979) and 55% of the yearlings were females.

Survival and Mortality Rates

Sex- and age-specific survival rates were calculated from life table analysis of 243 guanaco skulls collected in the study area; inputs for males and females were regarded as the same. The initial age distribution input was the Lx series, calculated from the life table using $L_x = C_x N_t$, where $C_x = 1_x/\Sigma l_x$ (Pielou 1969), and $N_t = 800$ to approximate the population size at the time.

Time-specific life table analysis assumes (1) zero growth, (2) stable age distribution, and (3) accurate aging (Caughley 1966; Seber 1973). Since the Paine population had been increasing, the frequencies of ages at death were adjusted by the e^{rx} factor to approximate zero growth (Caughley 1966). The skull sample had been collected over a 25-year period since the beginning of the park's protection. The large sample size (>150) was assumed to balance out the effects of fluctuations in growth rate on the age distribution and to approximate a stable age distribution (Caughley 1977). For additional details of these assumptions and the results of the life table analysis, see Fritz (1985) or Fritz et al. (unpubl. ms.)

Natality Rates

Age-specific natality rate for all adult females 3 years and older was the mean rate calculated from our 1981–84 censuses (January or February). Exact age-specific natality was unattainable in this study because free-ranging females could not be aged as 2 year olds and beyond in the field. For the natality rate of 2-year-old females we used Raedeke's (1979) estimate of 2-year-old fecundity (37%) based upon analysis of reproductive tracts.

Degree of Polygyny and Territoriality

The initial degree of polygyny (the maximum number of females one male of each age class can breed with per season) was the mean number of females in family groups counted in the postreproductive censuses. Thirty-two male guanacos were live captured by immobilization, aged, and ear-tagged in order to document their territorial histories. Free-roaming animals were approached on foot and immobilized with projectile syringes shot from Long Range Projectors (modified rifles). Others were captured in a walk-in corral located in a *vega* meadow within the male group zone, and then immobilized (Franklin and Fritz, unpubl. ms.)

Harvest Rates

Computer simulations of age- and sex-specific harvest rates were calculated, harvested animals were removed from the population after reproduction, and natural mortality had been calculated for each annual cycle. Thus, simulated harvest mortality was in addition to natural mortality. For simulation of harvesting males, the NOLES program indicated the cycle in which there would be too few males to breed all the adult females according to the degree of polygyny input in order to maintain population size.

Results and Discussion

Population Size and Growth

Population counts from 1981–84 were done by experienced observers following similar census routes each year. Censuses from 1975–80 were in the early years of the park's administration, and varying methods and inexperienced workers resulted in erratic and inconsistent results (table 22.1). Just the same, the 1975–80 counts indicated growth of the guanaco population after the exclusion of livestock and the institution of park protection. The mean observed exponential rate (r) of increase as calculated from 1981–84 data, was $\bar{r}_s = 0.12$ ($r^2 = 0.92$, $p < 0.05$). Computer simulations of population growth based upon the separate manipulation of 2-year-old natality, 3-year-old natality, and chulengo survival (Fritz et al., unpubl. ms.) were all lower than the $\bar{r} = 0.12$ observed population growth rate. Accordingly, both natality and chulengo survival must have been underestimated, and some combination of increases in these inputs would increase r_s to 0.12.

Sex and Age Structures

Averaging the 1982, 1983, and 1984 censuses (excluding the animals classified as unknown), adults (2 years old and older) comprised 63% of the population, yearlings 13%, and chulengos 25%. In the weeks following the birth

TABLE 22.1
Postreproductive Censuses of the 40-km² Study Area

Date	Total Count	Adult Males	Adult Females	Yearling Males	Yearling Females	Chulengos	Unk
Feb 75	97[a]	—	—	—	—	36	—
April 76	218	69	60	—	—(29)[b]	60	—
Jan 77	262	56	56	—	—(80)	56	14
Jan 78	143	58	27	—	—(34)	13	11
Apr 79	700	76	203	—	—(307)	114	—
Jan 80	392	15	126	—	—(167)	84	—
Apr 81	560	210[c]	244	—	—	106	—
Jan 82[d]	616	162	200	48	36	128	42
Jan 83[d]	770	174	296	26	36	200	38
Jan 84[d]	787	196	275	71	51	188	6

[a] In 1975, adults were not sexed and yearlings were counted as adults.

[b] In 1975–80 censuses, all males in male groups were counted as yearlings.

[c] In 1981, all yearlings were counted as males.

[d] This study (see text for sources of other data).

season during the postreproductive censuses, 67% of the adult females had chulengos at their sides (table 22.1).

The proportion of females (P_f) in the adult population was the number of adult females divided by the total number of adults in the postreproductive censuses (Downing 1980). Because observers were less experienced at sexing adults in the 1982 census, only the 1983 and 1984 counts were used. Using a large-sample approximation of a binomial test statistic (B*) (see Hollander and Wolfe 1973; 16), the observed proportion of females was significantly ($p < 0.05$) greater than 0.50 for both years. The mean P_f for 1983 and 1984 was 0.61, with a 95% confidence interval of 0.58 to 0.64. Thus, adult females outnumbered adult males almost 3 to 2. Observations of marked animals and conversations with CONAF park guards and neighboring ranchers did not indicate a significant movement of animals in and out of the study area sufficient to affect the male-to-female ratio.

The observed skewed sex ratio was attributed to differential sex mortality. Males presumably suffer higher mortality rates than females due to the accidents and injuries incurred in play fighting (see Wilson and Franklin 1984) in male groups and sometimes in violent fights between adult males over territorial ownership. On several occasions we have seen adult males with severe neck and body wounds. Because of fighting, territorial males can be debilitated and even suffer broken leg bones.

Survival and Mortality Rates

To check the accuracy of tooth wear and replacement aging technique, we had incisors form 42 adults aged by the cementum annuli method. The age distributions generated by the two methods were significantly different ($p < 0.001$) with no justifiable correction factor. Until a more accurate aging criteria is accomplished, based upon a large collection of *known aged* guanaco skulls from this population, the assumption of accurate aging can only be approximated.

Dead chulengos were very difficult to find in the field, especially during the first few weeks after their birth. If puma (*Felis concolor*) predation on chulengos was important, as suspected, their ability to eat nearly the entire chulengo and the behavior of burying their prey could explain chulengo absence. As a consequence, we believe that we underestimated chulengo mortality, which would also have caused us to underestimate the number of live chulengos born each year to adult females (natality).

When the curves for guanaco survivorship (l_x = the proportion of individuals surviving from birth to age x) and mortality rates (q_x = the probability at age x of dying in the interval between x to $x + 1$) are compared for populations at Torres del Paine National Park (this study) and Tierra del Fuego (Raedeke 1979), they are remarkably similar (fig. 22.2). The mortality rate curve (fig.

Figure 22.2. Guanaco survivorship curves based upon life table analysis of skulls (N) collected from guanacos that died from natural causes at Torres del Paine National Park (this study) and Tierra del Fuego (Raedeke 1979).

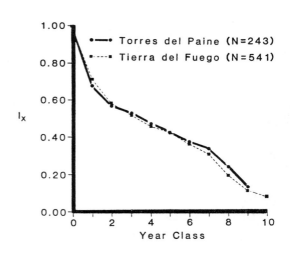

22.3) is the most suited for comparing results between studies (Caughley 1966). Guanacos are clearly the most vulnerable during their first 2 years of life. Three factors that occurred in both populations were suspected contributors to subadult mortality: (1) predation by pumas (Torres del Paine) or humans (Tierra del Fuego); (2) starvation during winters, especially in severe years with heavy snow cover (see Raedeke 1978 and 1979); and (3) the often violent expulsion of young from their natal family groups at about 1 year of age and their subsequent wandering.

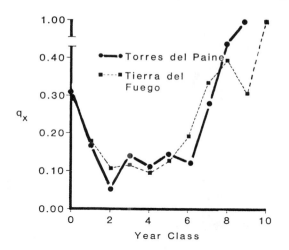

Figure 22.3. Guanaco mortality rate curves based upon life table analysis of skulls collected from guanacos that died from natural causes at Torres del Paine National Park (this study) and Tierra del Fuego (Raedeke 1979).

Natality Rates

Most female guanacos do not breed until 2 years of age. After an 11.5-month gestation they give birth to one offspring and usually breed within a few weeks of giving birth (Franklin 1982b). Young-primarous (2 years old) females are often less fecund than fully mature females (3 years and older). Raedeke (1979) reported a fecundity of 0.37 for 2-year-old female guanacos necropsied on Tierra del Fuego. Unfortunately, we could not visually distinguish 2-year-old from 3-year-old females during field censuses.

To estimate natality for females 3 years and older, the number of 2-year-old females was estimated and subtracted from the adult female counts, as was the estimated number of chulengos born to those females. Life table survival rates of yearlings (0.83) multiplied by census counts of female yearlings 1 year old (1982 = 36, 1983 = 36) estimated the number of 2-year-old females the next year (1983 = 30, 1984 = 30). Assuming the 0.37 fecundity rate, they produced eleven chulengos each year. Subtracting these eleven chulengos from the estimated total numbers of chulengos born and all 2-year-old females from the original adult female counts, natality was 1983 = 0.733 (195/266) and 1984 = 0.747 (183/245), resulting in an average of seventy-four chulengos per 100 adult females 3 years old and older. There was no adjusted natality rate for 1982 since a reliable yearling count was not done in 1981.

Degree of Polygyny and Territoriality

With the entire population, male guanacos were in family groups as chulengos (27% of all males), in male groups (45%), or were territorial males (27%). Of the males not in family groups (1 year and older), 63% were in male groups and 37% were territorial. Out of all adult males that were territorial, 45% were

TABLE 22.2.
Social Distribution of Males from 3 Postreproductive Censuses (percent)

| | | Territory | | | |
| | | Family | | Male | |
Year	N	Groups	Solitary	Groups	Chulengos[a]
1982	275	11	20	46	23
1983	300	14	12	40	33
1984	361	11	13	50	26
Mean		12	15	45	27
SD		1.7	4.4	5.0	5.1

Note: [a]Assumes a 50:50 sex ratio for chulengos.

Figure 22.4. Guanaco male group in the Torres del Paine National Park, Chile. (Photo, William Franklin).

"operative" with family groups and 55% were nonoperative without females (table 22.2).Thus, of all males 1 year and older, only 17% were breeding territorial males.

The social dynamics of guanaco male groups (fig. 22.4) has been described by Franklin (1978, 1982b, 1983) and Wilson and Franklin (1985). Males join male groups as 1 year olds when they are expelled from their family groups by the resident territorial male. It has not been determined, however, when males become territorial. Franklin (1978) estimated that "large-prime individuals" in male groups are 4 to 6 years old. The mean age of six family group territorial males collected (shot) by Raedeke (1979) was 8 years old (range = 6 to 8).

If animals in male groups are to be harvested, knowledge of when males become territorial is important to understand and model population dynamics and harvestability. Enough males should be left in male groups in the adult (see Wilson and Franklin 1985) or senior age class graduating to territoriality, so as not to undermine the annual supply of physically and socially mature males.

Of the thirty-two males ear tagged, there were seven yearlings, six 2 year olds, six 2 to 3 year olds (i.e., not clearly one or the other), three 3 to 5 year olds, and ten fully adult males (Fritz 1985). We observed that male guanacos spent their first year in a family group and the next three summers in male groups (i.e, from 1 to 3 years old). At 4 years of age, most males became territorial at least part time. Some animals left male groups to become territorial before 4 years of age, and some older territorial males visited male groups sporadically. Thus, male groups in summer were composed principally of males 1, 2, and 3 years old but also contained some older visitors.

Harvest Alternatives

What Age-sex Classes Should be Harvested?

Although in some areas rough terrain or tall shrubs are a problem, harvesting guanacos is made easier because the size of many populations can be accurately assessed. Guanacos typically occupy open habitat and are highly social, which facilitates censuses of populations.

There are three alternatives as to which animals should be harvested: (1) harvesting guanacos unselectively, (2) chulengos from family groups, or (3) males from male groups. Unselective hunting (taking whatever animals are encountered) is unacceptable because of the lack of control over the sex and age structure of harvested individuals. Adult breeding females and territorial males would be indiscriminately removed, with the potential to damage the social structure and reproductive success of those not taken.

Hunting chulengos for their soft pelts, especially within the first few days after birth, has long been the most common type of guanaco hunting. Chulengos are easy to catch compared to adults (the technique being to grab them by

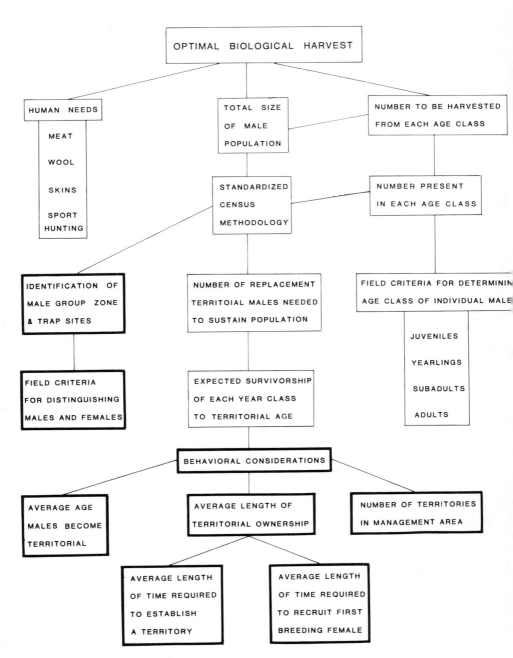

Figure 22.5. Variables and types of information that must be considered to assess the optimal biological harvest of male guanacos. Bold rectangles indicate territorial and behavioral parameters.

hand or run them down on horseback); the meat is tender; and the silky pelts are valuable ($20 to $40 untanned). Tanners report they prefer guanaco-chulengo pelts over the thin-skinned pelts of juvenile vicuña (crias) because chulengo skins do not tear during the vigorous tanning process, as they possess thicker hide with nearly equal softness. Chulengo pelts are made into throw rugs and bedspreads that can be worth several thousand dollars. Without knowing the impact of removing chulengos on population size, however, chulengo hunting must be approached with great caution.

Removing individuals from male groups for their meat and wool is the third alternative. In a polygynous breeding mammal, guanaco male groups could well contain a "surplus" of males. Caution must be exercised, however, until a number of biological and behavioral variables are known, for example, (1) the number of males in the population (which is dependent upon a standardized census technique and identification of where male groups are found, conducted by personnel familiar with field criteria for distinguishing social groups and males from females); (2) the recruitment rate of additional males into the population (natality rate of adult females); (3) the number of females a male can recruit and mate, that is, the degree of polygyny; (4) whether hunting within male groups is unselective or selective (if the latter, the number present and number to be harvested from each male age class must be determined); (5) how rapidly males recruit from male groups into territories of their own, that is, into the breeding population; and (6) a series of factors dealing with territoriality and the number of adult males required to sustain the guanaco's territorial breeding system (fig. 22.5)

How Many to Harvest?

Until the accuracy of aging and estimates of survival and natality rates is improved and their density-dependent and stochastic natures are included in the model, these simulations with NOLES provide tentative estimates of guanaco harvestability. The simulations explore the effects of harvesting on the long-term (20-year mean) exponential growth rate (r_s) of the population. Our goal is to assess whether we can harvest guanacos on an optimal yield basis without reducing population size or without interfering in normal reproduction and social organization.

Simulations

Harvesting Chulengos From Family Groups

Several NOLES simulations were run using the natality rates calculated from census and life table survival rates to explore the effects of harvesting chulengos on population growth. Population growth rate sharply declines as the fraction of chulengos harvested increased (fig. 22.6). When more than 20% of the chu-

Figure 22.6. The effects of harvesting chulengos on the 20-year
mean exponential population
growth rate (r_s) using the
NOLES model.

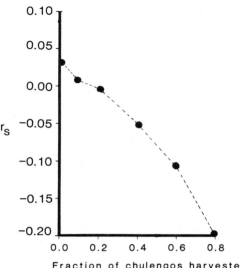

Fraction of chulengos harvested

lengos were harvest for 20 years, population growth rate (r_s) became negative. We urge a note of caution, however, as such a fixed annual chulengo harvest rate discounts the important effects of potentially large year-to-year variations in natality and natural chulengo mortality due to the stochastic nature or variability of the guanaco's environment. Because of the negative impact and the population's sensitivity of harvesting chulengos, any such program should be closely supported by continuous and accurate monitoring of population size and natality.

Harvesting Males From Male Groups

Male-only harvest programs are based on the idea that most polygynous mammal populations have more males than needed to mate with reproducing females. The feasibility of this assumption is supported by the observation that only 17% of the guanaco males 1 year old and older possess territories with females during the summer breeding season. Although tenure of territorial ownership has yet to be determined, one out of five postjuvenile males participating in reproduction at any one time suggests the probability of such a biological surplus.

Harvesting males is logistically feasible because male groups are often found within male group zones that are socially and geographically separate from family group zones. For more information on male group zones see Franklin (1978 and 1983), Fritz (1985), and Franklin et al. (unpubl. ms.)

Although older marked males are found intermittently in male groups, simulated harvesting was applied only to year classes 1, 2, and 3, the age classes primarily making up male groups. The allowable harvest rate of males 1 to 3 years old depended upon the maximum number of females one breeding territorial male 4 years and older could breed each year. The mean number of females in family groups was seven during the postreproductive censuses. Assuming seven females to be the maximum number that each breeding male could mate, and that all males 4 years and older were fertile and available, approximately 30% of the male group males could be harvested before reproduction was affected (fig. 22.7). On the other hand, if twenty females could be bred by each territorial male, then about 50% of the male group males could be harvested. Seven females per territorial male seems low, and few territorial males consistently had as many as twenty. Although the actual breeding potential of adult male guanacos is unknown, a first approximation is that 30% to 40% of the males 1 to 3 years old could be sustainably harvested from male groups.

Density-dependent responses to harvesting were not included in this model, although most large mammals respond to changes in density with changes in their natality and survival rates (Eberhardt 1977; Hanks 1981). Harvesting "surplus males" from male groups would most likely decrease intraspecific competition for food, territorial space, and mates, as well as reduce any interference of nonterritorial males with territorial stability and the rearing of chulengos. Also with the reduction of guanaco density, it could be expected that chulengo survival, 2-year-old natality, adult natality, and adult survival would increase. When a sustained-yield guanaco harvest program is implemented, this simulation model could be improved as empirical data on the response of the population to harvesting became available.

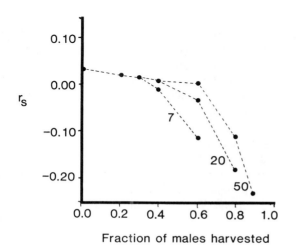

Figure 22.7. The effects of harvesting males from male groups on the 20-year mean exponential population growth rate (r_s) using the NOLES model. Simulations were done for three levels of polygyny. Males are 4 years old or older and breeding with seven, twenty, or fifty females per year.

Considerations for Harvest Management

Improved data on adult female natality, chulengo mortality, and age should be obtained. To obtain these, it will be necessary to annually mark a high percentage of the newborn chulengos. Accurate assessment of chulengo mortality/survival will give information on natality, and known aged skulls will provide reference animals for improving age determination.

Further modeling efforts should include the stochastic nature of survival and natality rates, as well as the density-dependent responses. Again, needed information can be provided by long-term monitoring of the survival and natality of marked animals and the concurrent changes in population density and habitat conditions. Studies should also be initiated to document the impact of conservative harvest rates on populations being concurrently managed with and without sheep, the impact upon reproduction, social structure, and economic return.

Marketing of guanaco products within and among producing countries is currently not an organized effort. Major efforts will need to be made to develop the products and markets for guanaco wool, pelts, cloth, and fresh and dried meat. Further development of capture and harvest techniques of wild populations will increase the attractiveness of managing free-ranging populations. Intensive ranching of captive and tractable herds of guanacos, while feasible, has not yet been successful.

Conclusions

Harvesting the Patagonia guanaco for meat, skins, and wool has been a long-time tradition that has provided life-sustaining resources and economic return. We are now ready on a biological and scientific basis to replace uncontrolled hunting with sustained-yield harvesting.

Sustained-yield harvesting is a proven and successful approach to using and managing wildlife species around the world. However, as illustrated here with empirical field data, it is not a simple process to determine the level of harvesting; the process depends upon a variety of variables that are difficult and time consuming to measure accurately in wild, free-roaming populations such as the South American guanaco. Resource managers are hoping to move forward with this important potential (Cunazza 1988) but only while armed with the necessary biological information.

The tolerable harvest rates estimated by the simulations in this study depended upon natality and survival rate inputs, but despite our best efforts, it appears we underestimated chulengo mortality and adult natality. The harvestability estimates presented here are preliminary and are not intended per se to be used as management recommendations. We feel the simulated harvest rates are important beginning points from which we can further perfect our understanding of an important biological and management process. However, these potential guanaco harvest rates, based upon field data, are the best estimates we have to date.

Several factors contribute to the biological and logistic feasibility of age- and sex-selective harvestability of guanacos for a sustained yield. The most significant is the polygynous mating system that creates a surplus of prereproductive males living in large groups in a zone apart from the breeding area. Depending upon the number of females one adult male can successfully mate during the summer breeding season, 30% to 40% of males in male groups could be cropped without disrupting or diminishing reproduction and population size.

Although chulengo pelts are traditionally the most desired guanaco product, great caution must be exercised in hunting this age class. Our simulations tentatively suggested that only a maximum of 20% of the chulengos could be annually harvested before causing the population to decline.

What about harvesting guanacos unselectively, that is, randomly taking any animal that is encountered? This would be impractical for a sustained-yield program because of the rigid separation of males in male groups and females in family groups. Under this approach, family groups would disband by removing territorial males, orphaned chulengos would be created, and unweaned chulengos would be separated from their mothers.

In response to the original questions posed in the title of this work, we feel that, yes, based upon the data herein, it is possible to harvest guanacos on a sustained biological basis without adversely interfering with reproduction or reducing population size. Nor is it too late to implement such a program. To the contrary, after a continuous decline for the past century, guanacos are recovering in some areas. A number of guanaco populations currently exist whose high densities warrant experimental harvesting based upon biological information.

There are ultimately two choices before us at this stage in the guanaco's tumultuous history with humans. First, as resource and wildlife managers, we have the opportunity to demonstrate to landowners and ranchers of the Patagonia that free-roaming guanacos can be harvested on a sustained-yield basis and provide an important source of income. It is our responsibility to illustrate the economics of managing and harvesting guanacos, as well as provide the technical advice that is needed and appropriate. Our second choice is to not act on the opportunity. Guanacos will continue to be considered pests and competitors by ranchers and be illegally hunted, resulting in local, if not regional, extirpation.

Let us opt for the sustained harvesting of guanacos based upon sound scientific information and management. The guanaco has been demonstrated to be a valuable wildlife resource. We can now wisely use it or irresponsibly lose it.

Acknowledgments

We are grateful to Oscar Guineo, Rene Sifuentes, Daniel Pedreros, Guillermo Santana, Jovito Gonzalez, and many other CONAF staff members at Torres del Paine National Park for their cooperation and assistance that made this work possible. Gladys Garay was especially helpful with the guanaco censuses and monitoring marked animals. Herardo Gunkel and Sergio Gallardo of CONAF in Puerto Natales provided essential logistical support. We appreciate the cooperation and administrative assistance given by Mauricio Rosenfeld and Claudio Cunazza of CONAF and Mateo Martinic and Claudio Venegas of the Institute of Patagonia in Punta Arenas. Thanks to graduate research assistants from Iowa State University (ISU): Issac M. Ortega and Paul Wilson, who preceded us in this work and provided preliminary data and logistic groundwork; and to Tom and Kathy Jurgensen for their valuable help in the field. Scott Watson, Betsy Martin, Boy Scouts of Puerto Natales, and members of the 1982 Earthwatch Expedition and the 1983 ISU Patagonia Guanaco Expedition were important contributors to the field work. Sincere appreciation to the many Chileans who brightened our time in their beautiful country with their unmatched hospitality.

William R. Clark and David Glenn-Lewin of ISU and Thia Hunter and Phil Hall of the University of Florida generously provided valuable input and suggestions on the writeup.

This research was supported by funds from the National Science Foundation Latin American Cooperative Science Program (Award No. INT8105084 to W. Franklin); a Fulbright Grant for International Educational Exchange (M. Fritz); EARTHWATCH; and the 1983 ISU Patagonia Research Expedition. This is Journal Paper No. J-13334 of the Iowa Agricultural and Home Economics Experiment Station, Ames, Iowa. Project No. 2171.

23

Vicuña Use and the Bioeconomics of an Andean Peasant Community in Catamarca, Argentina

Jorge E. Rabinovich, Angel F. Capurro, and Leonor L. Pessina

The vicuña (*Vicugna vicugna*) is a member of the camelid family (Camelidae) (fig. 23.1). Koford (1957) estimated their historical geographical range (confirmed by Franklin 1982b to be also its present, although discontinuous, geographical range) to be a stretch of about 2,000 km in the puna, a treeless pastoral zone in the central Andes of western South America between 10° and 29° south latitude. These limits are apparently determined by food availability. The altitudinal distribution of the vicuña is confined from about 3,700 to 4,800 m. In the 1950s, two-thirds of the population lived above 4,250 m. As strict grazers on forbs and grasses, the vicuña is ecologically confined to the high puna grassland, because lower elevations quickly turn to scrubland valleys and slopes under intense agricultural use or to barren foothills of the coastal desert (Franklin 1982b).

Because of their fine wool and delicious meat, vicuña have been hunted for centuries. Although millions of animals have probably been killed since they were recognized as a resource to humans, the system of the Inca seemed to be a sound game management practice (Koford 1957). It consisted of periodic hunts, or *chacos,* that were held every 3 to 5 years. On royal order, 20,000 to 30,000 people assembled to encircle an area of 4,000 to 5,000 km². Special corrals of stone and ropes with colorful fluttering cloth occasionally were used to assist the larger "human corral" in capturing, sorting, and killing vicuñas (Gilmore 1950b). Regulation of hunting, coupled with the harvest system rotating between provinces, was an enlightened management plan for maintaining the vicuña population. However, after the arrival of the Spaniards in America, hunting with guns and dogs, and excessive market hunting for the vicuña's valuable wool caused a population decline from millions in the 1500s to 400,000 in the early 1950s (Franklin 1973). In the late 1960s, there were fewer than 2,000 vicuñas in Bolivia, Chile, and Argentina combined and 5,000 to 10,000 in Peru (Jungius 1971, cited in Franklin 1982b).

An agreement for the conservation of the vicuña was signed by Peru and Bolivia in 1969; Argentina adopted it in 1971, and Chile in 1972 (Cajal 1983). Peru pioneered the conservation of the vicuña by establishing the Reserva Nacional Pampa Galeras in 1965 to protect the species and to manage the local population on behalf of the Andean peasants. This protection occurred simultaneously with the inclusion of the vicuña and its products in Annex I of CITES (Convention for the International Trade of Endangered Species). The results were spectacular; in the Reserva Nacional Pampa Galeras, Peru, with an initial population of about 800 individuals in 1967, numbers reached almost 5,000 by 1978 (Norton and Torres 1980) before starting to decline. This positive response of vicuña populations to protection opens the possibility of allowing their harvest with appropriate scientific and administrative controls. A vociferous debate started when Peruvian government scientists suggested a selective culling of the vicuña population, which conservation groups opposed. Technical studies against (Eltringham and Jordan 1981) and in favor of (Norton and Torres 1980) culling, harvesting, or both appeared.

There have been few attempts to evaluate the potential production of vicuñas based on their population dynamics. The first efforts to estimate a sustained yield were those of Norton and Torres (1980) and Rodriguez, Glade and Nuñez (1983), both of whom used the logistic model of population growth in their models. Later, Rabinovich, Hernandez and Cajal (1985) developed a computer simulation model to predict the size of unexploited and exploited vicuña populations; in addition to population modeling, they considered the economics of harvesting and shearing. More recently, Sandi, Sánchez, and Yarigaño (1987) analyzed the potential yield of vicuña populations for Peru, including the price of wool, leather, and meat and operating costs. They also used the logistic model and assumed a maximum sustained yield based at K/2 (where K is the carrying capacity of the environment).

The model developed by Rabinovich, Hernandez, and Cajal (1985) is limited to situations with certain technological capabilities: each operational unit, or *manga* (a funnel-type net with a corral at its end), represents an investment of about U.S. $18,000 and involves fifteen people, two vehicles, and twelve horses. Furthermore, the optimization analysis done by Rabinovich, Hernandez, and Cajal (1985) is based on a free offer and demand market, where the discount rates play an important role (Clark 1976). This framework may be applicable to other wild camelids, such as guanaco (*Lama guanicoe* Muller) populations, that live in open areas in Patagonia, where the sheep ranching landowner system allows for capital investment. However, it is not applicable to a typical Andean rural community with a barter system and little monetary exchange with other sectors of the country's economic system, unless the provincial government manages the effort as an economic enterprise.

This work discusses the importance of vicuñas as a renewable resource for an Andean peasant community, addressing questions such as the monetary impact to the peasant's economy produced by the use of vicuñas, the level of herbivore density that should be maintained, and the potential effect of vicuña use on vicuña conservation. To this end a simple computer model was developed to simulate the use that the peasant community could make of profits from the harvest of vicuñas and its impact on herbivore composition and on the community's economy.

The Study Area

The provincial reserve of Laguna Blanca (Province of Catamarca, Argentina) (fig. 23.2) was selected for this study. It has a growing population of vicuñas that was studied by Hofmann and Otte (1983) and Cajal (1985). There is a 6-year data base on the socioeconomic aspects of the local peasant population (Forni 1981; Forni, Tort, and Pessina 1987).

The Laguna Blanca Reserve is located in the southern Catamarca puna (Belén Department), with an area of approximately 973,000 ha. In 1982, the reserve was declared part of the International Network of Biosphere Reserves by the Man and the Biosphere (MAB) program of UNESCO.

The pampa is situated at an altitude of 3,500 m above sea level and is surrounded by high mountain peaks. It is a rather arid area, with insufficient rainfall for most crops, frequent frosts even in summer, strong winds, and an extreme temperature range. Groundwater from melting ice does, however, create locally moist edaphic conditions (*vegas*), where hardy grass grows abundantly.

There are two different areas, which are distinguished by their plant cover. The first has a sparse scrub and grass cover of about 20%; the other, the vega, has a grass and herb cover of almost 100% (Novaro and Teixido, pers. comm., 1985). The dominant species are members of the genera *Festuca, Stipa, Bouteloua, Panicum, Sporobolus, Eragrostis, Cortaderia, Hordeum, Distichlis, Tridens,* and *Pappophorum* (Nuevo Freire 1982).

The presence of vegas, combined with other high-altitude grasslands, has allowed human settlements. This is indicated by the presence of old Indian ruins and also by human populations that subsist on livestock ranching. The presence of an old mid-nineteenth century church shows the previous importance of Laguna Blanca, possibly as a point for livestock herding and mule production for Chile and Bolivia (Forni, Tort, and Pessina 1987).

The present human population is approximately 400 to 500 people, distributed in about ninety-five households, relatively dispersed but organized in three main areas: Laguna Blanca, Corral Blanco, and Aguas Calientes (fig. 23.2).

In the 1950s, vicuña fur traffic from Chile to Belén (Argentina) and the hunting of local vicuña were the most important activities in the Laguna Blanca area (Pais 1955).

When the Belén-Antofagasta de la Sierra road was built in 1980, it ended the extreme isolation of this community. The area was declared a reserve, and

Figure 23.1. Vicuña male group at the Pampa Galeras Reserve, Peru. (Photo, William Franklin).

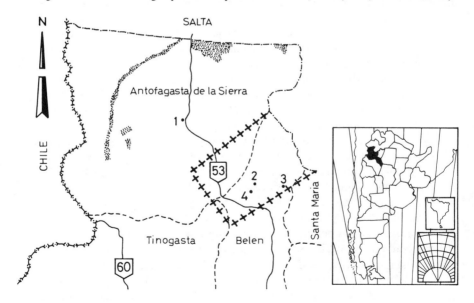

Figure 23.2. Location of the Laguna Blanca reserve in the Province of Catamarca, Argentina (from Forni, Tort, and Pessina 1987). Line drawn with crosses: reserve's boundary; numbers represent the four main peasant villages: 1 = Antofagasta, 2 = Corral Blanco, 3 = Aguas Calientes, and 4 = Laguna Blanca.

an experimental station was established. At the same time, the resulting ban on hunting the vicuña had a serious negative effect on the economy of some of the people in the region (Forni, Tort, and Pessina 1987). This negative effect was partially ameliorated by hiring twenty wildlife rangers recruited from the male Laguna Blanca population. This economically compensated those near the station for the hunting prohibition, but not persons living farther away.

The economics of the region is based on herding and the sale of sheep or llama wool. Many households have a predominantly self-subsistence economy that cannot absorb demographic growth; for decades this has forced the emigration of young adults (Forni, Tort, and Pessina 1987). This situation worsened with the ban on vicuña hunting and the resulting competition between vicuña and domestic animals. As a consequence, a strong shift toward wool spinning by most members of the households developed. More recently, peasants have bartered, assigning an economic value to the commodities that depends on the value of the fabric. The smaller herders spin wool for their neighbors who are owners of bigger herds. For the many families, with small-sized herds, spinning (and to a lesser degree knitting) is the main source of income. This activity is highly compatible with the labor necessary for herding and is performed by either sex and at any age (even very young children knit).

The trading tendencies generated by spinning and knitting forced the people to abandon other incompatible activities such as crop farming and other self-subsistence labors; both factors contributed to a breakdown of the Laguna Blanca isolation.

The recruitment of the wildlife rangers and their assistants increased the tendency toward a money-based economy of salaries and a diversification of consumption (food, clothes, and other commodities) and even different working schedules.

These changes in activities generated a social stratification that is presently measured by herd size. There are a few major herders (several hundred llamas and more than 1,000 sheep), a few dozen "economic units" (about 100 llamas or the equivalent in sheep), and the rest own just a few animals (Forni and Benencia 1985). This is now changing because of the possibility of working for a salary.

Methods

We estimated the following herbivore population parameters relevant to any land use and productivity study: population densities, the carrying capacity of the environment, the intrinsic rate of natural increase, and the actual population rate of growth. In addition, it was necessary to quantify the economics of resource use by the peasant community. A description of the estimation methods follows.

Herbivore Population Density

We obtained the vicuña population density from bibliographic information and wildlife rangers' personal communications. Livestock density was calculated using field information on livestock property by peasant families. The latter were classified in three size classes by the size of their domestic herds: small (0 to 30 llamas, 25 to 100 sheep, 2 cows, 50 goats, 1 horse), medium (80 to 100 llamas, 100 to 300 sheep, 5 to 10 cows, 80 to 100 goats, 4 horses), and large (200 to 1,000 llamas, 400 to 500 sheep, 25 cows, 100 to 300 goats, 10 horses, 50 donkeys). Livestock densities were converted to vicuña equivalents to simplify future calculations. The conversion was performed by multiplying the livestock number by an equivalence factor. These factors, which represent the ratio between consumption rates of each herbivore species and that of the vicuñas, were obtained from the literature: 1.63 for llamas (Rodriguez, Glade, and Nuñez 1983), 1.4 for sheep (Rodriguez, Glade, and Nuñez 1983), and 5.55 for cows, horses, and donkeys (Brack, Hoces, and Sotelo 1981). For goats the factor is 1.5 and was estimated by assigning consumption rates of 1.5 kg of dry matter per day for goats (N. J. Barassi, pers. comm., 1985) and of 1 kg of dry matter per day for vicuñas (Rodríguez et al. 1983).

Herbivore Carrying Capacity (K)

Although carrying capacity values depend upon many factors related to soil type, topography, temperature, wind, intensity and distribution of rains, and vegetation composition, we derived a first approximation of herbivore carrying capacity by using two methods: (1) looking at relationships between annual precipitation and herbivore biomass and (2) using data of herbivore consumption rates and net primary productivity. The former was used by Delaney and Happold (1979) to estimate the carrying capacity of savanna ungulates in Africa, while the latter are commonly used estimators.

The Precipitation-biomass Regression Method

We used Coe et al.'s (1976) linear regression:

$$Y = -1.2202 + 1.75596\,X \qquad (r = 0.894; n = 24) \tag{1}$$

where Y is the decimal logarithm of herbivore biomass (kg/km^2) and X is the decimal logarithm of rain (mm/yr). The division of herbivore biomass by the average adult weight provides the estimate of carrying capacity. Although equation (1) is based on data from African savannas and reflects different conditions from those of the Andean Puna, we used this equation to compare with results from the second method.

The Primary Productivity Method

This method estimates the potential densities by the following equation:

$$K = CF \times (NAPP \times 100)/(DR \times 365) \tag{2}$$

where K is the carrying capacity of the environment (ind/km^2), CF is the consumption correcting factor, NAPP is the net aerial primary productivity (in kg/ha/yr), DR is the daily requirement of a herbivore species, expressed as consumption rates (kg/ind/day) and the coefficients 100 and 365 are conversion factors from hectares to square kilometers and from days to years, respectively.

The value of NAPP was estimated from two independent sources: (1) an approximate field value (Dias 1982, cited in Puig 1986), and (2) a rain–primary production regression. The latter was adjusted by us based on fifty-seven data points: fifty-two values of grassland measurements from different parts of the World (Lauenroth 1979) plus five additional estimates from Argentine and Peruvian dry grasslands; R [rain in mm/year] = 150 (Cajal 1985) and NAPP = 330 (Cajal, Pujalte, and Reca 1981) for San Guillermo, San Juan, Argentina; R = 320 and NAPP = 294 (Norton and Torres 1980) for Pampa Galeras, Peru; R = 185 and NAPP = 246 (Puig 1986) for La Payunia, Mendoza, Argentina; R = 280 (Bertoni 1985) and NAPP = 1,170 (Bertoni, Sánchez Llena, and Vorano 1980) for Abra Pampa, Jujuy, Argentina; and R = 400 and NAPP = 870 (Defossé and Merino, in press) for northwestern Patagonia, Argentina). The resulting regression equation ($n = 57, r = 0.73$) was:

$$NAPP = 5.313 \, (\pm \, 0.67) \, (R - 66.89) \tag{3}$$

Intrinsic Rate of Natural Increase (r_o)

To estimate this parameter we used two methods: (1) a power regression between weight (W, in kg) and intrinsic rate of population increase (Caughley and Krebs 1983) and (2) Cole's (1954) formula relating the intrinsic rate of population increase with first age of reproduction (a), litter size (b), and last age of reproduction (c). The equation from Caughley and Krebs (1983) has the following form:

$$r_o = 1.5 \, W^{-0.36} \tag{4}$$

while Cole's formula is given as:

$$1 = \exp(-r_o) + b \exp(-r_o{}^*a) - b \exp(-r_o{}^*(c+1)) \tag{5}$$

where the symbol "*" stands for multiplication, and "exp" means the exponential operation. Most of the information necessary to apply these formulas was obtained from the literature. The average weight of an adult vicuña (40 kg) was the one given by Rodríguez, Glade, and Nuñez (1983). For Cole's formula, the value of 3 years for a as suggested by Koford (1957) was found to be too large; Raedeke (1979) found for the guanaco that 25% of juvenile females (12 to 24 months old) and 50% of subadult females (24 to 36 months old) were pregnant, giving an average of first reproduction of 1.6 years; as the guanaco is a much larger animal than the vicuña, it was considered that 3 years was an overestimation of the age at first reproduction. We resorted to a regression between body weight (W, in g) and age of first reproduction (a, in days) for artiodactyla (Western 1979), given as log a = log (35.48) + 0.27 (± 0.03) W (n = 11, r = 0.95) and obtained the value of 1.7 years as an estimate of a for the vicuña for Cole's formula.

For the parameters b and c we used the values given by Eltringham and Jordan (1981): 0.5 and 17 years, respectively. Actually, Eltringham and Jordan (1981) give 13 years as maximum life span; however, as in guanacoes it was observed that the maximum life span was still a reproductive age (Raedeke 1979), we assumed that for the vicuñas the maximum life span represented also the maximum reproductive age and preserved 13 years as an estimate of parameter c. This value is very close to 12.9 years, obtained for the vicuña from the regression of weight (W, in g) on maximum life span (MLS, in days) as estimated by Western (1979) for artiodactyla: log MLS = log 457.1 + 0.22 (± 0.027) W. n = 14, r = 0.92.

Actual Population Growth Rate (r)

We calculated the actual or present growth rate (r) assuming that all herbivore populations in Laguna Blanca grow following a logistic process. Thus, knowing r_o, K, and present animal densities (D), r is determined by

$$r = r_o (1 - (D_i/K_i)) \tag{6}$$

The specific carrying capacities (K_i) were calculated as

$$K_i = K_t - (D_t - D_i) \tag{7}$$

where K_t is the total carrying capacity, D_t is the present density of all herbivores, and where the subindex i refers to different herbivore species. All densities and carrying capacities are expressed in vicuña equivalents per square kilometer (VE/km²). We assume here that $K_i > 0$, that is, that some of the resources are presently unexploited, which implies some degree of undergrazing.

Socioeconomics of the Peasant Community

The data used here are the preliminary results of several years of surveys in the Laguna Blanca Reserve, carried out by one of the authors (L.P.) and her colleagues. Statistical analyses have not yet been completed, but we present here approximate results. Livestock property information was obtained from sixty-five of the ninety-five families living in the reserve. Goods consumed and their cost, as well as products and their prices, were obtained from a sample of thirty-nine people in a 2-year period, representing about 10% of the population; the same sample provided cultural information. All monetary values (Australes of February 1986) were converted to U.S. currency.

The Model

We evaluated the socioeconomic consequences of the use of vicuñas by the peasants by developing a simple computer model. Table 23.1 shows the explicit and implicit assumptions used in its construction. Two of them, the percentage of annual net profits that is invested in new livestock (see assumption E.9), and the minimum vicuña density that should be maintained (see assumption E.3),

TABLE 23.1
Implicit and Explicit Assumptions Used in the Development of the
Simulation Model to Evaluate the Economic Consequences of Vicuña Utilization to the
Laguna Blanca Reserve Peasant Community

Implicit	Explicit
Herbivore-plant assumptions	
I.1. Primary productivity is a constant and, as a consequence, herbivore carrying capacity does not vary with time	E.1. Ten percent of aerial primary productivity is consumed by all herbivores
I.2. Primary productivity is an average for the reserve as a whole (areas of higher and lower productivity are not considered separately)	E.2. The total herbivore density is limited by the global carrying capacity of the reserve (7.9 vicuña equivalents/km²), but is presently below that value (6.77 vicuña equivalents/km²); this means that the Laguna Blanca Reserve is not overgrazed
I.3. Herbivore species differ only in their plant consumption rates (that is there is no interference competition, only exploitation competition, by complete dietary overlap) (see assumption I.6)	
I.4. Plant consumption rates by each herbivore species are the same for all ages and sexes	
Herbivore population dynamics assumptions	
I.5. Livestock (the original population plus the one incorporated with the profits from vicuña utilization; see assumption E.5) remains constant with time; that is, the *net* population growth of livestock is zero (all excess is sold and/or consumed)	E.3. As new livestock is added, the vicuña density diminishes to a minimum arbitrarily set value; the values assigned vary between present density (0.5 vic/km²; see assumption I.7) and about 60% of its carrying capacity (1 vic/km²)
I.6 Vicuñas and livestock graze in the same places at the same time; they do not interfere with each other (see assumption I.3)	E.4. Vicuña's population growth is of a logistic type with $r_0 = 0.37$ and $K_v = 1.64$ vic/km² (the latter with present livestock load; see assumption E.2)
I.7. Present vicuña density (0.5 ind/km²) was considered compatible with its conservation: it is about 60% of the population density that has the maximum rate of growth assuming a logistic model ($K_v/2 = 0.82$ indiv/km²)	
I.8. Parasites and predators were not considered	

(*continued*)

TABLE 23.1 (*continued*)

Implicit	Explicit
Socioeconomic assumptions	
I.9. As wool sales represent about 90% of total income (see table 23.6) this is the only source of income considered	E.5. All additional *net* profits from vicuña utilization are converted into more livestock, within the reserve's carrying capacity limit (see assumptions I.10 and E.2), except the fraction used for other purposes (see assumption E.9)
I.10. The present tradition of the peasant community investing in more livestock any additional monetary income, is preserved (see assumption E.5)	
I.11. Vicuña harvest and associated labor do not affect other productive activities; potential profits from vicuña utilization will reduce emigration and even make previous emigrants return.	E.6. New livestock is purchased maintaining present proportions between llamas (30%), sheep (46%), and goats (24%) (see table 23.4)
I.12. Harvest methods remain traditional (horse herding and rifle shooting); this also means that zero cost is assumed	E.7. As determined by the logistic model of population growth, vicuñas, are harvested at a rate of $r_0 K_v/4$, where r_0 is the intrinsic rate of natural increase and K_v is the carrying capacity of vicuñas, a diminishing value as new livestock is incorporated (see assumption E.3)
	E.8. Only 50% of the *net* profits from vicuña utilization is available to the peasant community (the other 50% goes to the only large landowner and/or the provincial government)
	E.9. A **variable** fraction of E.8 (between 60% and 80%) is used to purchase new livestock; the remaining is used with other purposes (e.g., children's education, trips to Belén)

were applied at six levels each: 10%, 20%, 30%, 40%, 50%, and 60% for the former and 0.5, 0.6, 0.7, 0.8, 0.9, and 1.0 individuals/km² for the latter. The values of these two variables were changed simultaneously, generating a total of thirty-six combinations; for each of them the model was run for 20 years. The simulation was stopped whenever any of two assumptions were violated: (1) that the minimum vicuña density was reached (see assumption E.3 of table 23.1) or (2) the total carrying capacity of the reserve was surpassed (see assumption E.2 of table 23.1).

For each run of the model (1) the vicuñas were harvested, (2) the new livestock purchased with vicuña profits was calculated and added to the total herbivore density, (3) the vicuñas' carrying capacity was reduced accordingly, and (4) the vicuña population was allowed to grow. All these changes were converted, for each simulated year, in net profits from vicuña and livestock separately. The variables used to analyze the results were (1) the net total annual profits, (2) the number of years of incorporation of new livestock, and (3) the proportion of total profits originating in the additional livestock accumulated as the result of vicuña utilization. The model was programmed in FORTRAN77.

Results

Herbivore Population Parameters

Vicuña Population Density

There are two field estimates of the vicuña population for the Laguna Blanca Reserve. Cajal (1985), working on the relatively productive vega environment, found 679 vicuñas in 400 km², and Hofmann and Otte (1983) counted 1,345 vicuñas in the of Laguna Blanca sector (area of 670 km²). This gives a range of densities between 1.7 and 2.0 vic/km²; however, the variability of population densities is larger depending upon the type of environment. Hofmann and Otte (1983) also estimated numbers in two other sectors of the same area (Antofagasta and Cazadero Grande) and found 0.14 and 0.23 vic/km², respectively. The local wildlife rangers estimated the total vicuña population in the reserve as 5,000 individuals; with a total surface area of 9,730 km² the *average density* of the Laguna Blanca Reserve as a whole is 0.5 vic/km², intermediate between the highly productive areas and the almost uninhabited drier regions. We used 0.5 vic/km² as an estimation of present vicuña densities, that is, a *crude* density measure, because our primary productivity values (see Herbivore Carrying Capacity) represent a global estimate for the reserve, combining higher and lower productive areas.

Herbivore Carrying Capacity

As there is no rain gauge in the reserve itself, we had to resort to indirect information from nearby locations. Table 23.2 shows the average annual pre-

TABLE 23.2
Rain Values of Laguna Blanca Reserve and Nearby Localities

Locality	Geographical Coordinates	Rain (mm/yr)	Source
Antofagasta de la Sierra	67°20'W 26°02'S	105	De Fina (1976) cited in Fujalta and Reca (1985)
Laguna Blanca Reserve	66°40'W 26°30'S	ca. 100 ca. 200	Dias (1982 cited in Purg 1986) Forni, Tort and Pessina (1987)
Tinogasta	67°34'W 28°04'S	159	Irurzun (1978)
Andalgalá	66°20'W 27°36'S	305	Irurzun (1978)

cipitation for three different places (see also fig. 23.2), plus a general estimate found in two publications. Antofagasta de la Sierra is the station closest to the reserve and the most similar to it in general physiographical conditions; Tinogasta is also relatively close, although it is toward the south, thus more humid. Both are typical localities of the Andean Puna. Due to the lack of precise information we arbitrarily decided to use an intermediate value between Antofagasta de la Sierra and Tinogasta: 130 mm/year. This value is also intermediate between the two extremes given as general estimates for the Laguna Blanca Reserve.

The use of 130 mm of rain per year in equation (1) results in an herbivore biomass of 310.3 kg/km^2, equivalent to 7.76 vic/km^2, assuming 40 kg for an average vicuña adult.

With the same amount of rain, net aerial primary productivity (NAPP) estimated from equation (3) yields 335.3 kg/ha/year; using the standard error of the slope of equation (3) we have 247.8 and 422.0 kg/ha/year as lower and higher limits of NAPP, respectively. Murphy (1975) shows that most cases of low precipitation have actual NAPP values below predicted ones; this is particularly true for the five pieces of data from the dry grasslands added by us to the regression of equation (3); thus we preferred to use some lower value than 335.3 kg/ha/year and decided to take the mean between the NAPP value predicted using the estimated slope of the regression and the one predicted with the slope minus one standard error. This gives 291.5 kg/ha/year, very close to Dias' (1982 cited in Puig 1986) field estimate of 280 kg/ha/year. The latter was used for all calculations based in equation (2). We also needed an estimate of the consumption correcting factor (CF) in order to use equation (2). Processes such as effects of grazing on the plant itself, plant density-dependent growth, trampling by the herbivores, deficient nutritional values of plants in certain seasons are, among others, responsible for the fact that only a relatively small fraction of the net primary productivity is really transferred to herbivores. Seligman (1987, pers. comm.) considers that in many cases not more than 10% to 30% of the primary productivity is effectively utilized by herbivores. Additionally, several authors have found similar low consumption values by large herbivores: Delaney and Happold (1979) estimated 19% for ungulates; Crawley (1983) less than 10%; Lamotte (1983) between 8% and 20%; Rice (1986) approximately 26%, and Phillipson (1975) 8% for elephants. Based on energetic relationships between grazed and ungrazed grasslands, Sims and Coupland (1973) give data that yield 12.5% as total available plant energy actually used by herbivores. Application of equation (2) with NAPP = 291.5 and CF = 10% yields a carrying capacity of 7.99 vic/km^2, quite close to the value of 7.76 vic/km^2 derived from the regression between rains and herbivores biomass by equation (1). For future calculations we used the average between these two estimates, that is, 7.9 vic/km^2.

TABLE 23.3
Intrinsic Rate of Natural Increase (r_o) for Vicuñas, Sheep, and Goats, as calculated by
Caughley and Krebs' (1983) and Cole's (1954) formulas

Species	Cole				Caughley and Krebs	
	a	b	c	r_o	W	r_o
Vicuñas	1.7	0.5	13	0.329	40	0.397
Sheep	1.6	0.5	12.5	0.337	35	0.417
Goats	1.8	0.5	13.5	0.322	50	0.362

Note: a = age of first reproduction in years; b = litter size; c = reproductive life span in years; W = live weight of an average adult in kg).

Intrinsic Rate of Natural Increase

Table 23.3 shows the results of the intrinsic rate of natural increase using formulae (4) and (5) for vicuñas, sheep, and goats. Norton and Torres (1980) made four evaluations of r_o for different sectors of the Pampa Galeras National Reserve in Peru (0.43, 0.48, 0.38, and 0.34); Rodríguez, Glade, and Nuñez (1983) made an estimate of r_o for the National Park of Lauca in Chile of 0.29; Sandi, Sánchez, and Yarigaño (1987) uses 0.37 for r_o for Peruvian vicuña populations. The average of these six estimates is 0.38, intermediate between our lower (Cole's) and higher (Caughley and Krebs') values of 0.33 and 0.4, respectively. Cole's formula probably underestimates r_o (Hayssen 1984), so we calculated an average between the field mean (0.38), the Caughley and Krebs' estimate (0.4), and Cole's estimate (0.33); its value is 0.37, and this is the estimate of the vicuña's intrinsic rate of natural increase used for future calculations. The value of r_o for the vicuñas was used in the calculation of harvest rates, and the ones obtained for sheep and goats were used to estimate r with equation (6) to determine their economic profitability for the peasants.

Actual Population Growth Rate

Table 23.5 provides the values of present densities of all herbivores. These values of sheep and goats plugged in equation (7), with D_t = 6.77 and K_t = 7.9, resulted in carrying capacities of 3.42 and 2.39 animals/km², respectively. The carrying capacity for vicuña was calculated as 1.64 vic/km². To estimate the actual population growth rate of those three species applying equation (6), the r_o values are needed. For the vicuñas, 0.37 was used; for sheep and goats we used the average between Cole's and Caughley and Krebs' methods (table 23.2), that is, 0.38 and 0.34, respectively. The results of the actual annual population growth rates (r) are 0.257 for vicuñas, 0.125 for sheep, and 0.161 for goats. Expressed as finite annual rates of population growth (λ) they correspond to 29%, 13%, and 17%, respectively. We are interested in the actual population growth rates of sheep and goats and not of other domestic herbivores, because these are the only two species that contribute to the peasants monetary budget (selling or bartering to visiting merchants the population surplus); livestock is assumed to remain constant (see assumption I.5, table 23.1).

TABLE 23.4
Average Number of Domestic Animals of Laguna Blanca Reserve, by Peasant Classes and the Distribution of Families Per Class

Species	Peasant Class			Average Number of Animals per Family	Total Number of Animals
	Small	Medium	Large		
Llamas	15	90	600	112	10,631
Sheep	62	200	450	168	15,921
Goats	50	90	200	86	8,192
Cows	2	8	25	7	680
Horses	1	4	10	3	314
Donkeys	0	0	50	7	639
Total					36,377

	Number of families by class		
	Small	Medium	Large
Lessees	27	23	5
Landowners	2	6	2
Total	29	29	7

Note: Number of families in the reserve is ninety-five.

TABLE 23.5
Total Herbivore Numbers in Vicuña Equivalents in Laguna Blanca Reserve

Species	Total Number of Animals	Equivalence Factor (to Convert to Vicuña Units)	Total Number in Vicuña Equivalents	Density in VE/km^2
Llamas	10,631	1.63[a]	17,329	1.78
Sheep	15,921	1.40[a]	22,289	2.29
Goats	8,192	1.50[b]	12,288	1.26
Cows	680	5.55[c]	3,774	0.39
Horses	314	5.55[c]	1,743	0.18
Donkeys	639	5.55[c]	3,546	0.36
Total domestic herbivores			60,969	6.26
Vicuñas	5,000		5,000	0.51
Total herbivores	41,377		65,969	6.77

[a] Rodríguez, Glade, and Nuñez. (1983).

[b] Authors' estimate from the ratio between annual forage consumption between goats (545.7 kg) and vicuñas (365 kg).

[c] Brack, Hoces, and Sotelo. 1981.

Socioeconomics of the Peasant Community

Domestic Animals

Table 23.4 gives the herd size for each class of leaser and landowner and the resulting average number of animals per family and the total number of animals of each kind in the reserve. We converted all animal numbers to "vicuña equivalents" (VE) under the assumption of complete dietary overlap between herbivore species. Total animal numbers in the reserve are equal to a density of 6.77 vicuña equivalents/km^2 (VE/km^2) (table 23.5).

Annual Economic Budget

As mentioned before, the economy of the peasant community is mainly a subsistence one, with some degree of barter and a growing involvement in the market economy. The latter is represented by purchases that families make from visiting merchants. We calculated from the prices paid for essential commodities bought from the merchants the total expenses of an average family as U.S. $93.50/month. Adding the land leasing expenses (U.S. $26.50/month), each family spends a total of U.S. $120/month, that is, U.S. $1,440/yr. The two main sources of income are sheep and llama spun wool; Table 23.6 shows a

TABLE 23.6
Annual Incomes per Family for the Peasant Community of the Laguna Blanca Reserve Resulting from Selling Different Commodities and Net Profits

Commodity	Quantity Sold	Unit	Price (U$S) per Unit	Annual Income (U.S.$)
Spun llama wool	120.7	kg	10	1,207.00
Spun sheep wool	83.3	kg	7	583.00
"Puyos"	5.0	Piece	20	100.00
"Ponchos"	1.0	Piece	50	50.00
Livestock sales	8.0	Individuals	10	80.00
Total income				2,020.00
Total expenses				− 1,440.00
Net profit (U.S.$/yr)				580.00

total income per family of U.S. $2,020/year, which was used to evaluate the balance of the peasant's budget. The difference between annual income and expenses is U.S. $580, that is, a net profit of about U.S. $48.30/month. Most of this small excess goes into other unexpected expenses such as a trip to Belén, illness, or some nonquantifiable components such as coca and alcoholic drinks.

Vicuña Harvest

The potential harvest of the vicuña population can be estimated using some theoretical considerations. Under the assumption of a logistic population growth process to obtain the maximum sustained yield (MSY), we should let the population grow to a density of $K_v/2$, where K_v is the carrying capacity for vicuñas with all other domestic herbivores present, assuming the latter will remain constant at their present values. At this density the harvest rate (H) would be given by (Caughley 1977):

$$H = \frac{r_o K_v}{4} = 0.152 \tag{8}$$

where $r_o = 0.37$ and $K_v = 1.64$.

Thus, if we let the vicuña population grow from its present value of 5,000 individuals to 7,979 individuals, we can make a sustained harvest of 15.2% of that number, that is, a total harvest of 1,476 vicuñas per year. This is a conservative estimate, for this number could be increased if only males are harvested, a possible harvest strategy given the family organization of vicuñas. The monetary value of each vicuña is estimated at U.S. \$64 (Sandi et al. 1987): U.S. \$19 for the wool (at U.S. \$75/kg, with vicuñas producing about 0.25 kg of wool per animal), U.S. \$10 for the meat (20 kg/animal, at U.S. \$0.50/kg), and U.S. \$35 for the hide. So the total potential income for the peasant community of the Laguna Blanca Reserve, derived from the utilization of the vicuñas, is U.S. \$64 × 1,476 = U.S. \$94,464/yr. Assuming an equal distribution among the reserve's ninety-five families, it yields U.S. \$994.40 per family per year.

This figure is probably an overestimate, for most of the reserve belongs to one owner, who will claim a certain (probably high) share of the profits derived from vicuñas grazing on his property. Assuming a claim of about half of this profit, the peasants would be left with an additional net income of about U.S. \$500/yr; that is, vicuña utilization would double the average peasant's net income.

Also under the assumption of a logistic model of population growth, we can estimate the time (t) that should elapse before the vicuña's population size allowing MSY will be reached. This is explicitly calculated from

$$t = (1/r_o) \ln [((K_v/D_o) - 1)/((K_v/D) - 1)] \tag{9}$$

where K_v is the carrying capacity of the vicuñas for the Laguna Blanca Reserve with present-day domestic animal stocking ($K_v = 1.64$ vic/km²), D_o is the present vicuña density (0.51 vic/km²), D is the density to be maintained for sustained yield (in our case, using MSY, $D = K_v/2 = 0.82$), and r_o is the intrinsic rate natural increase (0.37). Thus, the necessary time that the peasant community should wait before starting to annually harvest vicuñas at a maximum sustainable yield (MSY) level is 2.2 years.

We also analyzed how sensitive these two results (increase in net income per family and waiting time to reach a harvestable vicuña population) are to some of the parameters estimated for the reserve. The carrying capacity, for example, using equation (1) with the standard values of the regression coefficient has a range between 4.3 and 14.2 vic/km²; the former is obviously incorrect, for even present numbers are above this value. The intrinsic rate of increase (r_o) is very sensitive to the parameters of Cole's (1954) equation (5), and also it was found to have a high variation from field estimates (between 0.29 and 0.48). We re-calculated the total annual profits per family and the waiting times for the combination of five values of r_o (0.2, 0.25, 0.3, 0.35, and 0.4) and eight values of the carrying capacity (8, 9, 10, 11, 12, 13, 14, and 15). The results (figs. 23.3 and 23.4) show a very strong interaction between these two parameters. The absolute effects are quite large: a doubling of the carrying capacity produces about a fivefold increase in the profits and about a fourfold increase in the waiting time. The effect of different r_o values is less dramatic on both variables (even at high carrying capacity values).

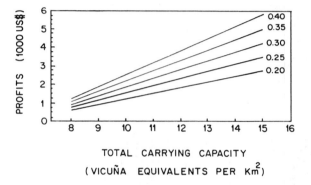

Figure 23.3. Sensitivity of total profits per family per year to changes in two model parameters: the intrinsic rate of natural increase of the vicuña population and the total herbivore carrying capacity of the environment. Numbers within the graph correspond to the intrinsic rate of natural increase.

The Simulation Results

As simulations using the computer model varied two parameters simultaneously in all combinations (see table 23.1, assumptions E.3 and E.9), the results can be best expressed as nomograms (Peterman 1977), a graphical method that compresses three-dimensional information on the plane (it simply interpolates valves of a simulation output variable on the x-y plane, linking the points of equal value).

The total net annual profits derived from vicuña utilization plus the new livestock accumulated on successive years with those profits is plotted in figure 23.5. Recall that all net profits derived from vicuña harvest are, in the model, invested in new domestic livestock (E.5, table 23.1). Figure 23.5 shows almost vertical lines, with increasing profits as the percentage of net profits invested in

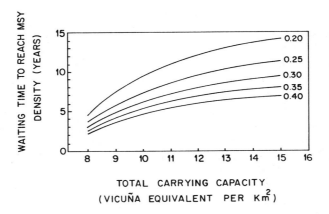

Figure 23.4. Sensitivity of the number of years to reach a harvestable vicuña population size (that would allow a maximum sustained yield) to changes in two model parameters: the intrinsic rate of natural increase of the vicuña population and the total herbivore carrying capacity of the environment. Numbers within the graph correspond to the intrinsic rate of natural increase.

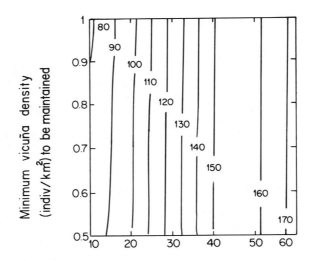

Percentage of annual net profits
from vicuña utilization that is
invested in new livestock.

Figure 23.5. Total annual net profits to the peasant community of Laguna Blanca from accumulated new livestock and vicuñas (lines in the graph represent net profits of simulated year 20, in thousands of U.S. dollars), as resulting from two possible scenarios of the simulation model: percentage of annual net profits from vicuña utilization that is invested in new livestock and minimum vicuña density to be maintained.

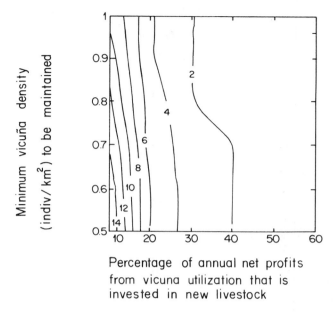

Percentage of annual net profits
from vicuna utilization that is
invested in new livestock

Figure 23.6. Number of years during which new livestock is incorporated to the peasants' economy as the result of investing a fraction of the vicuña utilization profits (lines in the graph are number of years), as resulting from two possible scenarios of the simulation model: percentage of annual net profits from vicuña utilization that is invested in new livestock and minimum vicuña density to be maintained.

livestock increases. This indicates that there is little effect of minimum vicuña density on net profit. The profits shown in figure 23.5 correspond to the last year of the computer simulation; however, under all the different x-y combinations, the number of simulated years varied depending upon certain restrictive conditions inserted into the model. Figure 23.6 shows that the number of years during which new livestock are added to herds diminishes as the percentage of vicuña profits invested in new livestock increases. This response results from the fact that the faster new livestock are added, either the earlier the reserve's total carrying capacity is reached or the earlier the vicuñas' minimum density is violated.

An interesting fact is that the nomogram of the annual profits from the accumulated new livestock, expressed as a percentage of the total profits (livestock plus vicuñas), also shows almost vertical lines (indicating a dominating effect of the x-axis), but *decreasing* with increasing values of percentage of vicuña profits invested in new livestock (fig. 23.7). This result reflects the fact that during the first years the vicuña harvest is much larger and diminishes as the animals are progressively replaced by the new livestock. As the *per capita* commercial value of vicuñas is much higher than that of livestock, the relative profits from new livestock decrease, essentially reflecting the smaller number of years of the process of vicuña replacement by livestock.

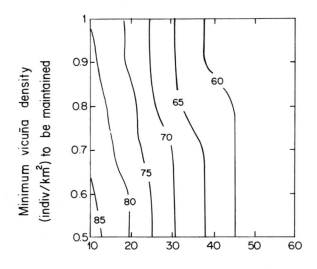

Percentage of annual net profits from vicuña utilization that is invested in new livestock.

Figure 23.7. Profits from accumulated new livestock (expressed as percentage of total net annual profits) in the last year of investment, as resulting from two possible scenarios of the simulation model: percentage of annual net profits from vicuña utilization that is invested in new livestock and minimum vicuña density to be maintained.

Discussion

With some minimum data on the biology and ecology of vicuñas, and with basic social and economic quantitative information, we have evaluated the potential consequences that vicuña harvesting would have on a typical Andean rural community. In so doing we have resorted to many implicit and explicit assumptions and simplifications. From the ecological point of view, the high variability of the Andean environmental conditions (mainly rain) is not reflected in our analysis. Nevertheless we have shown that for the economy of the peasant community, the consequences of vicuña harvesting are more sensitive to the environment's herbivore carrying capacity than to vicuña population parameters.

We have assumed that future profits from vicuña utilization will be destined mainly for the purchase of additional livestock, even to the expense of the vicuña population, despite the fact that vicuñas are commercially more valuable than livestock. This is so because the peasants consider llamas and sheep as the most stable and reliable source of subsistence. Not only is the future market of vicuñas more unpredictable, but recent experience has shown the peasants that government decisions are subjected to many factors (such as political changes, conservation pressures, individual decisions). This unpredictability makes such decisions unsuitable for use in making basic subsistence decisions.

Throughout this study we have assumed not only a logistic type of population growth for all herbivore species but also a vicuña population management based upon a *predetermined fixed rule* harvest system: the maximum sustained yield, obtained as harvesting $(r_o K)/4$ animals. This is not the best policy; a management system based on a vicuña population size estimation before each harvest (such as the bang-bang or fixed escapement rule) is preferable, for it takes into account several sources of variability, such as rains and vicuña reproduction) (Rabinovich et al. 1985). However, as our purpose was not an optimization analysis of vicuña management but the analysis of the potential consequences of vicuña utilization to the Andean peasants, a fixed rule management system was considered adequate.

We did not perform an analysis of the remaining cash left from the annual profits from vicuña utilization. Social and anthropological knowledge of this peasant community indicates that any money available, after livestock investments, would be oriented toward community action to improve children's education; this would be performed by school building improvements or restorations and an increase in teachers' salaries. The latter is essential because, due to the low provincial salaries and harsh living conditions, teacher turnover is very high, causing relatively long periods with no teachers. The other alternative to improving the children's education, also costly, is to send them to the nearby city of Belén, where better and more stable school systems exist.

The consequences of vicuña utilization here analyzed have a profound effect on the socioeconomics of this peasant community. However, more important consequences, related to the culture of these people, are more complex and have not been analyzed here. The possibility of a higher cash income due to vicuña utilization reverted to more livestock and children's education will inevitably break the present degree of isolation, with drastic changes in their culture, ways of life, and accumulated generational handicraft knowledge.

Our simulation results show that the fraction of vicuña profit that is invested in purchasing more livestock has a much larger effect on total profits than the minimum level of vicuña to be maintained. Thus, the predictions of our analysis suggest that conservation of the vicuña population may not be at stake if the assumptions used here are confirmed in the field. However, our results are very specific to the Laguna Blanca Reserve. Andean valleys of Peru, Bolivia, and Chile not only have different ecological conditions but also peasant communities with different cultural traits, and thus our results should not be extrapolated to other situations.

The sensitivity analysis carried out indicates that no reliable prediction of the socioeconomic consequences of the vicuña utilization can be made unless the following basic ecological, anthropological, and political information is collected: (1) a field estimation of the environment's herbivore carrying capacity, (2) a more accurate estimation of the vicuñas rate of natural increase, (3) the fraction of profits that might be retained by the local big landowner or the government, (4) the nature of the government's political decision regarding vicuña utilization in the near future, and (5) the degree of preference of the Laguna Blanca peasant community for livestock and not for vicuñas in light of (4).

Acknowledgments

The socioeconomic information used in this paper resulted from a research project in which one of the author's (L. P.) participated. We want to thank Dr. Floreal Forni, director of CEIL and head of the research project of Laguna Blanca of CONICET (National Council for Scientific and Technical Research) and two of the project's team members: Lic. María Isabel Tort and Lic. Dora Ginenez. Their collaboration and permission to use the preliminary results of the research project are greatly appreciated. We thank Dr. No'am Seligman of the Agricultural Resources Organization Volcani Center, Israel, for his many comments on this paper.

24

Sustainable Use of Neotropical Parrots

JORGEN BENT THOMSEN AND AMIE BRAUTIGAM

Among the diverse avifauna of the neotropics, parrots (Psittacidae) represent some of the most spectacular and unique species. The 141 neotropical parrot species discovered to date (Jorgenson and Thomsen 1987) are distributed almost throughout the neotropical realm, from the pine forests of northern Mexico to the islands of the Caribbean to the higher puna grasslands of the Andes and the cold temperate forests of the Fuegian region. Only the absolute deserts of coastal Peru and Chile appear devoid of parrots, and even these are known to be visited occasionally by one species (*Bolborhynchus aurifrons*) (Ridgely 1982).

Neotropical parrots are characterized by an equally broad range in size, from 1.5 kg—that of the largest parrot in the world, the hyacinth macaw (*Anodorhynchus hyacinthinus*)—to 0.025 kg, that of the smallest of the genus *Forpus*. Size is usually linked to population density, the largest species typically occurring in smaller numbers than the smaller species.

Because of their color, ease of feeding, size, ability to learn to talk, and variety, neotropical parrots are ideal target species for the cage-bird industry and some of them are the world's most popular avian companions. The vast differences among species can accommodate the individual tastes of almost any keen aviculturist or bird keeper, and as a result, these species have long been among the most popular in the cage-bird trade. Recent studies have documented the popularity of parrots as pets in urban areas in some South American countries. They have also figured prominently in the international cage-bird trade that has developed over the past 30 years: over the 5-year period of 1981–85, the United States alone imported a minimum of 703,000 neotropical parrots, representing at least 96 species (Jorgenson and Thomsen 1987).

While the high-volume national and international trade in neotropical parrots is a relatively recent development, parrots have been sought after as pets and for subsistence purposes by indigenous peoples in the neotropics for centuries. The larger species, such as amazons (*Amazona* spp.) and macaws (*Ara* spp.), are still important sources of protein in certain areas of South and Central America (e.g., Mittermeier 1977; Forshaw 1981; Ridgely 1982; Yost and Kelley 1983; Oren and Novaes 1986; Redford and Robinson 1987; Munn, Thomsen, and Yamashita 1987). Parrots are often hunted with traditional weapons such as blowguns (Yost and Kelley 1983) and with firearms in some of the more developed rural areas, for example, in the Brazilian states of Bahía, Minas Gerais, and Piauí (Munn, Thomsen, and Yamashita 1987; Thomsen, unpubl. data). Probably more important in actual numbers, and more widespread, is the traditional use of parrot feathers for ornamental and ceremonial purposes. A great variety of species have been and are still being used for these purposes. One of the most spectacular examples of ritualistic use is the fabrication of headdresses: a traditional headdress of the Brazilian Kayapó Indians may include the tail feathers from as many as ten hyacinth macaws (Munn, Thomsen, and Yamashita 1987).

Despite the long-standing socioeconomic importance of neotropical parrots to native and foreign peoples, our knowledge of them is generally no better than that of any other avian family. Other than Ridgely's (1982) analysis of status and distribution of mainland neotropical parrots, no systematic attempt has been made to assess the impact of exploitation on parrot populations nor has any investigation been carried out of the feasibility of using them as a renewable resource. Recent initiatives aimed at answering these questions are hindered by shortcomings in our current understanding of the reproductive biology and ecology of these species, and so we can only guess. This paper is about guessing and the conflict that inevitably arises when we have insufficient data to either advocate wildlife use or take measures to curtail it. As the subject of parrot use is a complex one, this paper is intended merely as an overview of some of the factors involved in sustainable use of neotropical parrot populations. It is hoped that a more thorough investigation of this problem will be made in the near future, for it seems increasingly evident that if we are to conserve parrots, we must learn to exploit them wisely.

Traditional Use of Neotropical Parrots

Parrots have traditionally been used for a variety of subsistence and ritualistic purposes by indigenous peoples throughout the neotropics. Recent excavations of the Sipan tombs of the Moche culture in Peru (A.D. 290) indicate widespread use of parrot feathers for ceremonial use (Alva 1988); parrots may well have been traded along with other commodities. As we do not know what the original ranges and population sizes of the mainland species were before the advent of human habitation in South America roughly 11,000 years ago or of Europeans in the 1500s, we cannot determine what effect this or other types of use has had on parrot populations. Certainly, however, any negative impact would likely have eased significantly when introduced diseases killed most of the natives long before Europeans and their African slaves began to penetrate and exploit the resources of the continent's interior.

Insofar as the Caribbean is concerned, we know that two endemic macaw species (*Ara autocthones* and *A. tricolor*) used for food and as pets are now extinct (Forshaw 1981). We do not know, however, if this use is the reason for their disappearance. Judging from reports from the expeditions of Columbus on the abundance of parrots coexisting with the Indians on the various islands of the Caribbean, Snyder, Wiley and Kepler (1987) conclude that although harvesting of parrots by Indians was a common practice throughout the Caribbean, it probably had relatively little effect on parrot populations. They state that the true decline of the endangered Puerto Rican amazon (*Amazona vittata*), for example, started with the arrival of the Spaniards in the 1500s and was not a result of the harvesting by the Taino Indians.

Mainland neotropical parrots continue to be harvested for subsistence use by many native peoples. Although not documented in great detail, there is little doubt that such hunting can significantly affect parrot population densities. Mittermeier (this volume and unpubl. data), reported that as a result of subsistence hunting, most larger animals, including parrots, were extirpated within a radius of 5 to 10 km around the Carib and Bushnegro villages he visited in Suriname. In all instances, *Ara* spp. were part of the diet, ranging from 0.1% to 1.6% of the total game biomass (Mittermeier 1977). Yost and Kelly (1983) reported that three species of parrots—*Ara macao, Amazona farinosa,* and *Pionus menstruus*—made up 2.2% of the total annual biomass consumed by the Waorani in Ecuador. Of all species consumed with a total annual biomass exceeding 10 kg, birds made up 43.2%. Among these, the relative biomass of parrots was 5.3%. The mealy amazon (*A. farinosa*) was the seventeenth most frequently killed animal by the Waorani. Similar observations, though not as detailed, have been reported by Hill and Hawkes (1983) regarding the Aché in Paraguay, by Posey (pers. comm.) with respect to the Kayapó Indians in Brazil, and by Plotkin (pers. comm.) regarding the Tirio Indians in Suriname and Brazil. In addition, Redford and Robinson (1987) provide a very detailed overview on the range of game species taken by hunters in the neotropics. Generally speaking, birds are the second most important group of game species (mammals come first) to Indian communities. Their analysis showed that between published studies on Indian nutrition, harvest of avian families was quite similar (W = 0.46; $p < .001$; $n = 12$). Psittacidae, primarily *Ara* spp. and *Amazon* spp., had the third highest ranking after Cracidae and Ramphastidae in terms of individuals killed per consumer-year. Sick (unpubl. ms.) observed quantities of dead orange-winged amazons (*Amazona amazonica*) for sale in local markets and noted that even smaller species such as *Touit* spp. are hunted for food in Brazil.

In addition to its importance as a source of protein, parrot meat is believed to have certain powers associated with it. The Kayapó, for whom parrot meat plays a significant dietary role, consider it to be very "powerful" or "strong" but caution that the more powerful it is, the easier it is to be "seduced" by it if one eats too much (Posey, pers. comm.). Such a superstition, like other tribal traditions and taboos, may have served the practical purpose of preventing overharvest of this resource.

Subsistence use of parrots has been documented among colonists as well as Indians and Bushnegroes (Redford and Robinson 1987). It has been reported as a delicacy in some parts of the neotropics (Mittermeier, pers. comm., Plotkin, pers. comm.; Posey, pers. comm.; Huyghe 1987).

Aboriginal plumeary art is known from many parts of the neotropical region; examples are the feather works of the Wayana Indians from Suriname and French Guiana, the Yanomamo from Venezuela, and the famous work of the Kayapó. The Kayapó use parrot feathers—mainly from blue and yellow macaw (*Ara ararauna*), scarlet macaw (*A.macao*), hyacinth macaw, conures (*Aratinga* spp.), and amazons—almost exclusively for their ceremonial headdresses; many other avian species are used for body dresses (Posey, pers. comm.). (See also photo documentation in Posey et al. 1987.) Posey (pers. comm.) reports that some headdresses may include the tail feathers from as many as fifty individuals of the same species. The tail feathers of certain captive-reared individuals are pulled year after year and are used this way without harming the parrot; others still are killed in the wild, the meat eaten, and the feathers used for ornamental purposes.

It is worth noting that Kayapó production of plumeary art has increased dramatically in recent years due to the steady commercialization of their craft. While they still fabricate headdresses and other ornamentation from feathers for ceremonial purposes, they also create them for sale on the tourist market. One large feather headdress may sell for as much as U.S. $200 (Munn, Thomsen, and Yamashita 1987). This commercialization has obvious implications for the sustainability of parrot populations thus used.

Parrots have long been kept as pets by indigenous peoples. Verbal and pictorial records from the sixteenth-century Drake Manuscript illustrate Nicaraguan Indians trapping live parrots with arrows blunted with cotton. Jeffreys (1760) verified another trapping technique mentioned in the Drake Manuscript (fig. 24.1) whereby Hispaniolan Indians used a tame parrot to attract other parrots, thereby trapping considerable numbers. More recent examples of keeping of parrots by indigenous peoples in the neotropics include the Panare and the Hoti in Venezuela, the Ayoreo in Bolivia, the Waorani in Ecuador, and the Kayapó (Plotkin, pers. comm.; Thomsen, unpubl. data.; Posey, pers. comm.; Oren and Novaes 1986; Yost and Kelley 1983; and Sick, unpubl. ms.). Many species are apparently popular, ranging from the smaller *Forpus, Brotogeris,* and *Aratinga* spp. to the largest of the macaws, including *Anodorhynchus hyacinthinus.*

While these parrots may be kept purely as pets, they may, as mentioned previously, have other uses, such as providing feathers, serving as lures for

Figure 24.1. The sixteenth-century Drake Manuscript documents highly developed techniques for capturing parrots in the wild. The use of lures to attract other parrots is a technique still widely used in the neotropics. (Courtesy of the J. P. Morgan Library, New York).

trapping other birds, or acting as a means for hunters to learn behavioral characteristics, thus making the species easier prey. Domestication of parrots and other animals for this last purpose is a well-developed practice according to Yost and Kelley (1983).

Commercial Trade in Neotropical Parrots

When Columbus first arrived in the New World, he and his crew were met by natives offering them skeins of spun cotton, wooden spears tipped with stingray tails, and live parrots. Since that first contact, parrots and macaws have featured in domestic and international trade in live birds.

No detailed studies have been carried out on the magnitude of the domestic cage-bird trade in the neotropics. Colonists have a strong tradition of keeping parrots in captivity, however, and ornithologists estimate that tens of thousands of these species may be taken every year for domestic markets. They are sold in local markets and pet shops and are offered for sale by peasant farmers along roadsides.

A recent study of the notorious Duque de Caxias live-animal market on the outskirts of Rio de Janeiro revealed that several thousand live animals from 246 species were offered for sale during the years 1980–83 (Carvalho 1986); 209 species were birds, among them 33 species of parrots. Carvalho (1986) further reported that this market is only one out of many, and that nearly all large Brazilian cities have bird markets. This is also the case in other Latin American countries, although the trade may not be of the same magnitude. Plowden (1987a) reported that Peruvian parrot trappers earn extra money during the closed export season by selling parrots at the Lima central market. He recorded conures and grey-cheeked parakeets (*Brotogeris pyrrhopterus*) for sale at U.S. $10 to $12/bird and Pacific parrotlets (*Forpus coelestis*) at U.S. $5/bird, as well as the following species: canary-winged parakeets (*Brotogeris versicolurus*) and red-lored amazon (*Amazona autumnalis*) (U.S. $150/bird), yellow-crowned amazon (*Amazona ochrocephala*) (U.S. $170/bird), and mealy amazon (U.S. $150/bird). The fact that *Amazona autumnalis* is not known to occur in Peru illustrates that domestic markets are not necessarily restricted to trading in domestic species. In addition, the fact that the prices set by the trappers for these birds were slightly higher than the prices paid to them by exporters during the open season may indicate that there is a competitive domestic market for these birds.

Sick (1985) concluded that the reason for the decline in the number of birds sold in some markets in Brazil was the decline in their numbers in the wild. He believed these declines to be the result of excessive trapping for the domestic market. Recent information on some threatened parrot species seems to support the contention that domestic bird markets may negatively impact species' populations. The endangered golden conure (*Aratinga guarouba*), for example, is illegally sold "in hundreds" every year for U.S. $100 to $300/bird in Brazilian urban markets, such as Belém (Oren and Novaes 1986). In addition, 50% of the threatened hyacinth macaws trapped annually are reportedly acquired by Brazilian parrot keepers (Munn, Thomsen, and Yamashita 1987, 1989.). The exact number of hyacinths taken every year from the wild is difficult to determine, but based on information from Brazilian parrot trappers and dealers, at least 300 individuals were probably captured in 1986 (Thomsen, unpubl. data); only about 50 individuals were reported in international trade in that year, although a certain additional number may have passed into international trade undetected. Last, although the wild population of the endangered Brazilian endemic Spix's macaw (*Cyanopsitta spixii*) numbers only three individuals in the wild (Roth, unpubl. ms.; Thomsen and Munn 1988), of the thirty-odd individuals located so far in the hands of aviculturists throughout the world, half have been located within Brazil (Thomsen, unpubl. data; Thomsen and Munn 1988).

It is only in somewhat recent times that the large-scale keeping of parrots as pets outside of their natural ranges has become common. Although neotropical parrots have been known as pets in Europe for 500 years, most species remained relative novelties in the United States, Europe, and Japan—the main importing regions—up until the 1940s, when air transport began to allow for their rapid movement from the tropics to the consumer countries. Parrots were in particular disfavor early in this century because of their presumed association with psittacosis, a disease carried by birds and to which humans are susceptible, now called *ornithosis*. The importation of parrots into the United States, for example, was prohibited by the Public Health Service in the 1930s after several psittacosis outbreaks led to a number of human fatalities, and was not lifted until 1967 (Banks 1976). Since then, except for a brief period during 1972–74, when exotic bird imports were banned as a result of an outbreak of exotic Newcastle disease in domestic poultry flocks (Clapp 1975), parrot imports into the United States have increased steadily.

The trends apparent in the international parrot trade have been documented by a number of authors (e.g., Roet, Mack, and Duplaix 1981; Gilbert 1983; Jorgenson and Thomsen 1987) based largely on statistics gathered by customs or agriculture agencies or by wildlife agencies operating under the auspices of the Convention on International Trade in Endangered Species of Wild Fauna and Flora (CITES). Shifts in the trade are often a reflection of changes in the regulation of harvest and export at the national level or under CITES, whereas improvements in reporting on parrot trade or, conversely, the illegality of trade may account for others.

Statistics nevertheless afford a basis for assessing the role of international trade on the conservation of neotropical parrot species. During the period 1982–86, a minimum of nearly 1.4 million neotropical parrots were exported by mainland neotropical countries (table 24.1). (The figure excludes exports from the Caribbean because they were largely insignificant or of nonindigenous

TABLE 24.1
Minimum Exports of Psittacine Species from Mainland Neotropical Countries, 1982–86

	1982	1983	1984	1985	1986
Argentina	88,851	114,019	109,206	179,473	177,992
Bolivia	56,340	48,774	11,584	115	17
Brazil	27	30	47	16	75
Chile	16	56	138	952	1,137
Colombia	260	220	188	31	30
Ecuador	3,648	398	3,989	278	62
Guiana	0	0	1	0	0
Guyana	26,693	25,300	38,177	27,386	30,324
Peru	39,303	19,463	51,671	33,921	16,977
Paraguay	10	7	25	5	42
Suriname	1,984	1,924	1,764	7,322	8,737
Uruguay	19,544	33,516	39,211	18,455	20,667
Venezuela	67	81	21	53	9
Sub-Total	236,743	243,788	256,022	268,007	256,069
Belize	13	29	7	15	41
Costa Rica	47	46	5	313	4
Guatemala	87	69	3,142	10,043	3,628
Honduras	6,501	9,253	14,483	17,164	14,769
Mexico	7,042	135	28	9	227
Nicaragua	100	121	96	282	1,827
Panama	184	101	55	50	54
El Salvador	877	552	1,388	2,065	16
Sub-Total	14,851	10,306	19,204	29,941	20,566
Total	251,594	254,094	275,226	297,948	276,635

Source: CITES annual reports.

species (Brautigam and Thomsen 1988). Because, as indicated previously, not all exporting and importing countries reported on their trade in parrots during that period, this is a minimum export figure. Smuggled birds, having crossed international borders undetected, would further add to the figure; it is estimated that 150,000 parrots are smuggled across the Mexican border into the United States alone every year (Thomsen and Hemley 1987). Preexport mortality would also have to be considered in assessing a true export figure. If one were to apply the estimate determined by Iñigo and Ramos (this volume) for preexport mortality of Mexican parrots (60%) to the entire neotropical realm, the total harvest for export for this period would have been at least two million individuals.

The monetary value of these parrot exports is significant. The estimated total retail value of the 1.4 million parrots reported exported by mainland neotropical countries during 1982–86 is U.S. $1.6 billion (table 24.2). The estimated total revenues collected by middlemen and trappers in local currency, the net profit

TABLE 24.2
Estimated Income Earned from Psittacine Species Exported from Mainland Neotropical Countries, 1982–86

	Total number of birds reported in trade	Estimated minimum gross income at different levels of trade (U.S.$)		
		Trapper[a]	Middleman[b]	Retailer[c]
South America				
1982	236,743	5,894,900	19,924,291	284,965,181
1983	243,788	6,070,321	20,517,198	293,445,178
1984	256,022	6,374,948	21,546,812	303,171,121
1985	268,007	6,673,374	22,555,469	322,597,345
1986	256,079	6,376,118	21,550,767	308,227,694
Central America and Mexico				
1982	14,851	369,790	1,249,860	17,876,000
1983	10,306	256,619	867,353	12,405,229
1984	19,204	478,180	1,616,209	23,115,663
1985	29,941	745,531	2,519,835	36,039,682
1986	20,566	512,093	1,730,835	24,816,787

[a] $N = 7$; $ × = 24.9; $ range = 2.5–65.0.
[b] $N = 25$; $ × = 84.16; $ range = 5.0–650.0.
[c] $N = 61$; $ × = 1203.7; $ range = 37.5–9,000.0
$N = 61$ species represents a total sample of 310 prices for 61 species; when more than one price was found for a species, an average was used.

made by the middlemen on these birds, is probably even larger than estimated in table 24.2.

The single most important exporter of neotropical parrots in recent years has been Argentina (table 24.1). This country has exported more than 660,000 parrots during the period 1982–86. The total retail value of Argentina's parrot exports is an estimated U.S. $800 million. Other important exporters were Peru, Guyana, Uruguay, Bolivia, Honduras, and Suriname, in that order.

The United States is the single largest importer of neotropical parrots. For example, of the 275,266 neotropical parrots reported exported in 1984, the United States reported importing 149,164, or 54%. The majority of these birds came from only five countries. Seven of the sixty-two species were imported in numbers exceeding 10,000 individuals and comprised more than 60% of the total trade. They were *Amazona aestiva* (10,406); *Amazona amazonica* (12,270): *Aratinga acuticaudata* (11,422); *Aratinga erythrogenys* (13,489); *Brotogeris pyrrhopterus* (12,931); *Myiopsitta monachus* (15,446); and *Nandayus nenday* (15,152). Only *Brotogeris pyrrhopterus* had at that time been identified as being "presently or potentially at risk" (Ridgely 1982). All U.S. imports of neotropical parrots for the years 1981 to 1985 are listed in table 24.3. The fifteen species imported in the greatest quantities to the United States are listed in table 24.4. Eight of these species have been identified by Inskipp, Broad, and Luxmoore (1988) as being insufficiently known to determine

TABLE 24.3
United States' Imports of Psittacine Species from the Neotropics, 1981–85

	1981	1982	1983	1984	1985
Amazona spp.	22,008	34,767	41,034	44,698	55,295
Anodorhynchus	98	316	267	37	16
Ara spp.	7,941	13,357	17,944	7,087	3,655
Aratinga spp.	24,227	45,118	43,686	44,289	53,251
Bolborhynchus spp.	0	105	352	68	0
Brotogeris spp.	14,756	30,778	6,956	13,917	6,464
Cyanoliseus	1,347	3,501	3,295	2,072	0
Deroptyus	51	197	268	139	39
Enicognathus spp.	0	1	0	2	0
Forpus spp.	1,293	634	1,706	1,763	0
Graydidascalus	0	0	1	0	0
Hapalopsittaca spp.	0	1	4	0	0
Myiopsitta	9,740	8,447	9,308	15,446	9,716
Nandayus	11,984	17,579	24,361	15,152	5,122
Pionites spp.	217	520	217	302	126
Pionopsitta spp.	376	7	16	2	1
Pionus spp.	1,805	2,077	3,086	2,316	1,883
Pyrrhura spp.	2,989	2,169	5,872	1,884	856
Psittacidae spp.	0	2	0	0	0
Total	98,832	159,590	158,373	149,164	136,454
Number of species	60	79	79	62	56

Note: Data obtained from U.S. CITES annual reports. Data for 1985 are incomplete.

TABLE 24.4
The Fifteen Neotropical Psittacine Species Most Frequently Imported
by the United States, 1981–85

	1981	1982	1983	1984	1985	Total
Nandayus nenday	11,984	17,579	24,361	15,152	5,122	74,198
Amazona aestiva	2,559	9,652	16,946	10,406	25,554	65,117
Aratinga acuticaudata	6,258	9,695	13,532	11,422	13,959	54,866
Myiopsitta monachus	9,740	8,447	9,308	15,446	9,716	52,657
Brotogeris pyrrhopterus	12,261	21,833	529	12,931	2,632	50,186
Amazona amazonica	9,443	9,765	11,893	12,270	5,912	49,283
Aratinga mitrata	6,080	9,892	11,907	3,154	10,516	41,549
Amazona ochrocephala	2,681	5,275	5,169	8,144	11,078	32,347
Aratinga wagleri	2,802	11,102	5,756	9,379	1,661	30,700
Aratinga erythrogenys	0	0	2,307	13,489	10,579	26,375
Ara ararauna	4,088	4,701	7,842	2,853	2,052	21,536
Brotogeris versicolurus	2,485	7,935	6,009	948	3,807	21,184
Amazona autumnalis	750	1,608	3,232	7,232	5,995	18,817
Aratinga weddellii	2,885	5,592	4,559	860	56	13,952
Aratinga leucophthalmus	1,425	2,172	2,773	2,127	4,859	13,356

Note: Data obtained from U.S. CITES annual reports.

whether their populations are being detrimentally affected by international
trade.

Major changes have taken place since the first data were published on imports of neotropical parrots into the United States (Banks and Clapp 1973b). Both the species composition and the exporting countries involved in the trade have changed dramatically, not because of changing taste in the United States but because of changes in the export policies of the countries involved (fig. 24.2). In the early 1970s the major exporters to the United States were Peru, Colombia, Paraguay, and Mexico. Legal imports of parrots from the latter three countries virtually ceased because of export bans, although illegal trade appears to have continued. Due to these bans, other countries, particularly Argentina and Bolivia, assumed major exporting roles. When Bolivia banned live wildlife exports in mid-1984 in response to allegations that it had become a major "launderer" of wildlife illegally taken in neighboring countries, Argentina became the major exporter of neotropical parrots. It accounted for more than 50% of all neotropical parrot imports into the United States in 1985 (Jorgenson and Thomsen 1987) and 64% of all reported parrot exports from the mainland neotropics in that year. Other countries have also increased their parrot exports since Bolivia instituted its export ban. Guyana, for example, was reported as the country of origin for some 90% of the 3,400 macaws imported into the United States in 1985 (Jorgenson and Thomsen 1987), while Bolivia had provided almost 90% of the macaws imported into the United States in 1980–82, before the export ban (Gilbert 1983). Total U.S. imports of macaws have, nevertheless, declined by approximately 80% since the Bolivian export ban was instituted (Jorgenson and Thomsen 1987).

Unlike its trade in macaws, U.S. trade in amazons has more than doubled from 1981 to 1985. The most dramatic increase has been in imports of the blue-fronted amazon (*Amazona aestiva*), from about 2,500 in 1981 to more than 25,000 in 1985 (table 24.4; Jorgenson and Thomsen 1987). Argentina exported more than 95% of all the specimens of this species imported into the United States in 1985 under special legal provisions for "pest" animals. While recent reports from Argentina refute the claim that the blue-fronted amazon is a pest and, moreover, indicate that in certain Argentinian provinces the species is declining (Bucher and Martella 1988), it is evident that such a designation has served other economic interests. Argentinian exporters received approximately U.S. $45/bird (see Plowden 1987b) or a total of U.S. $1,080,000. Before export, the trappers had received an average of only U.S. $4.50/bird (Bucher and Martella 1988) or a total of U.S. $108,000. The total retail value of these birds in the United States exceeded U.S. $5 million.

Impact of Trade on Parrot Populations

Until quite recently, the only systematic effort to place international trade in neotropical parrots into its biological context has been Ridgely (1982). Ridgely argued that habitat destruction is the major threat to the continued survival of neotropical parrot species. He concluded on the basis of his research that the

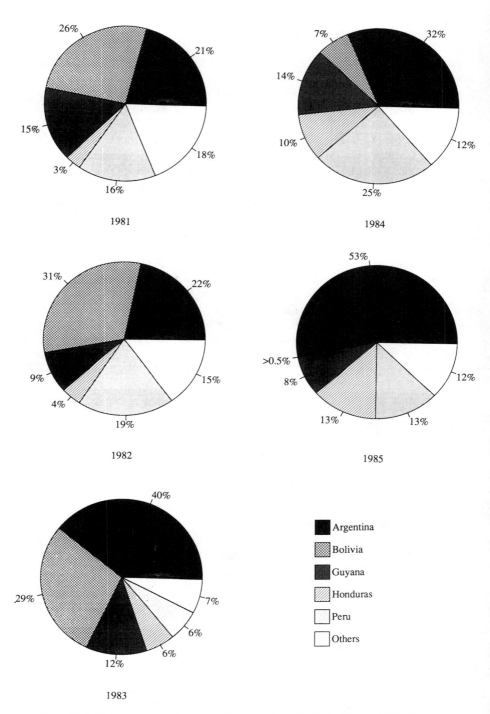

Figure 24.2. Major exporters of parrots in the neotropics to the United States, 1981–85.

impact of international trade on populations of many neotropical parrot species was not great and appeared convinced that many of the more numerous species could maintain their numbers even if subject to a considerably greater harvest than that taking place at the time.

The conclusions of a recent investigation carried out under the auspices of CITES (see Inskipp, Broad, and Luxmoore 1988) attest to the increasing threat posed to many parrot species by trade. In our opinion, this threat is second only to habitat destruction and considerably outweighs the impact of subsistence hunting by indigenous peoples. For some species, trade may be the primary factor threatening their survival. The lack of baseline data for most parrot species prevents us from assessing the effects of different threats on specific parrot populations. The limits of our understanding are highlighted by Munn's findings that only one-third of the breeding population of any of three macaw species attempts to breed in a given year (Munn 1988a; 1988b; Munn, Thomsen, and Yamashita 1987). The implications of these findings for the ability of these populations to sustain trade or other pressures are very serious indeed.

Central America is also an important supplier of parrots to international markets (table 24.1). In Honduras (Jorgenson and Thomsen 1987) exports are largely confined to four species of amazon parrots. Despite the export ban in effect in Mexico over the past several years, an estimated 150,000 parrots are thought to be exported from that country every year. Ramos and Iñigo (1985) and Iñigo and Ramos (this volume), report that trapping has significantly affected the country's parrot populations, a conclusion that accords with Ridgely (1982). A recent study by Perez and Equiarte (unpubl. ms.) further documents this problem. They concluded that populations of three amazon parrots (*Amazona ochrocephala, A. viridigenalis,* and *A. autumnalis*) in Tamaulipas state remained small primarily because of intense trapping pressure: In their study area, more than 30% of the nests were emptied by trappers.

The situation of the hyacinth macaw (fig. 24.3) exemplifies the negative impact trade can have on parrot species and the difficulties experienced in assessing sustainable levels of trade. Although the species is now thought to number fewer than 5,000 individuals in the wild (Munn, Thomsen, and Yamashita 1987), its original range and population size are unknown. We know that in the early part of this century, explorers reported flocks of hundreds of hyacinth macaws at localities in Piauí in northeastern Brazil, where now it is totally extirpated (Munn, Thomsen, and Yamashita 1987; Roth pers. comm.). Based on reports of numerous collecting expeditions dating from 1930 to the 1960s and from personal observations, Yamashita (unpubl. data) has indicated that the species formerly existed in many parts of Goiás, Maranhão, and Mato Grosso, where there are few or none today. In all likelihood, the species originally ranged from just south of the Amazon in Pará to the drainage of the Paraná and Paraguay rivers in Paraguay and southern Brazil.

A combination of habitat destruction for agriculture, capture for the bird

Figure 24.3. The hyacinth
macaw (*Anodorhynchus
hyacinthinus*) is one of the most
highly prized parrots from the
neotropics. (Photo, C. Munn.)

trade, and hunting for meat and feathers have decimated populations of hyacinth macaws (Munn, Thomsen, and Yamashita 1987). Until the 1960s and
early 1970s, it seems likely that habitat destruction (palms and nest trees) and
hunting for meat and feathers were the predominant causes of the species' decline. Now it appears the international trade in live hyacinth macaws takes a
greater toll on the species than either destruction of its habitat or hunting. Field
surveys and interviews in former strongholds of the species (Munn, Thomsen,
and Yamashita 1987), analyses of international trade records for the species
(Nilsson and Mack 1980; Nilsson 1985a; Inskipp, Broad, and Luxmoore 1988;
Thomsen, unpubl. data), and ground and air surveys and detailed interviews in
many parts of the Pantanal of Brazil, northeastern Brazil, Bolivia, and Paraguay over the last 15 years indicate that bird trappers systematically harvested
entire large populations of hyacinth macaws to sell to national and international
bird dealers (Munn, Thomsen, and Yamashita 1987; Roth, pers. comm.; Yamashita, unpubl. data).

Records of international trade in hyacinth macaws during the past several
years indicate that the reported trade may represent only a minor portion of the
trade actually occurring. For example, data from quarantine stations in the
United States indicate that 1,382 hyacinth macaws entered the United States
from 1981 through 1984, while CITES data for the same period indicate that
only 702 entered the country (Inskipp, Broad, and Luxmoore 1988). If CITES
data for other countries are less accurate than those of the United States, then
easily two or three times more hyacinth macaws may have been traded during
this period than CITES data suggest.

Although the hyacinth macaw was accorded complete protection from international trade under CITES in late 1987, large-scale international trade in the
species continues; indeed, it may have increased. It is estimated that during the

first half of 1988, more than 500 hyacinth macaws were trapped in the Pantanal and northeastern Brazil and moved through countries such as Argentina and Paraguay (Thomsen, unpubl. data; Villalba-Macías, unpubl. data; Roth, unpubl. ms.) to international markets.

The impact of this trade is cause for concern, particularly in light of recent information on the species' reproductive biology. Findings similar to those of Munn in Manú suggest that only 15% to 30% of the adult population in the Pantanal attempts to breed in a given year (Yamashita, unpubl. data; Hart, unpubl. data; see also Munn, Thomsen, and Yamashita 1987); this percentage may be as small or even smaller in the eastern Amazonian and northeastern Brazilian populations (Yamashita, unpubl. data). In addition, according to Munn, Thomsen, and Yamashita (1987), not all breeding pairs of hyacinth macaws fledge young, and those that do almost never fledge more than one bird. Thus, 100 mated pairs of breeding age macaws may produce between seven and twenty-five young per year, a very low reproductive rate. It would appear, then, that given its current population, the species does not have a high enough reproductive rate to withstand any substantial, long-term harvesting for either trade or subsistence use.

As early as 1984, members of the CITES community raised the issue of high-volume trade in species for which limited biological data were available (Hemley 1984b). Recognizing that such trade was undermining the effectiveness of CITES as a conservation mechanism and that baseline biological data are essential for determining the availability of species for harvest for trade and other purposes, the CITES parties agreed to review species deemed subject to high-volume trade. Among the species identified as of particular concern were neotropical parrots.

In 1985, the IUCN Conservation Monitoring Center (CMC) in Cambridge was contracted by the CITES Secretariat to assess the biological and trade status of certain animal species traded in high volumes. The trade data were compiled largely on the basis of annual reports submitted by the CITES parties and were analyzed by the CMC's Wildlife Trade Monitoring Unit in conjunction with the TRAFFIC (Trade Records Analysis of Flora and Fauna in Commerce) network. The preliminary findings of the CITES Significant Trade Study were released in 1986. Of the forty-five neotropical parrot species traded in high volume, one, the hyacinth macaw, was identified as probably being overexploited. Information on twenty-eight species was too incomplete for an assessment of the impact of the trade.

Since the study was published, two of these high-volume trade species have been completely protected from international trade under CITES. The data needed to change the status of the other species under CITES are lacking. Not until additional field research is carried out will such a policy move be made. In the meantime, most species continue to be traded at high levels; together they were traded at an average of 77,491 individuals per year from 1981 to 1984.

Sustainable Use of Parrots Through International Trade

While trade has been identified as a major factor threatening the survival of some parrot species, its impact on others has yet to be conclusively determined. Data on reproductive biology, essential for determining sustainable use ratios, are largely lacking. Despite an almost universal lack of such data and based on educated guesswork, policy measures restricting different types of use have already been adopted at both national and international levels. As with so many initiatives aimed at restricting or abolishing socially and economically entrenched practices, their success has been limited. New approaches that allow limited harvest and export and involve those engaged in harvesting and exporting parrots seem much more likely to succeed. Such measures will require a regulatory framework that is much more sophisticated than that currently in place.

Unlike most other countries, the United States began monitoring imports of exotic birds as far back as the late 1960s (see Banks 1970; Banks and Clapp 1972; 1973a; 1973b; Clapp 1975). This policy was institutionalized by CITES in 1975. In addition to establishing a regulatory framework for controlling trade in species listed on its appendices—prohibiting trade in species included in appendix I and allowing trade in appendix II species only on the basis of export permits certifying that the trade will not be harmful to the species' wild populations—the treaty requires monitoring trade levels by annual reports that document all CITES trade submitted by its member states. Thirteen neotropical parrot species were included in the original CITES appendices, and all parrot species not listed in appendix I were listed in appendix II in 1981 (except for *Melopsittacus undulatus, Nymphicus hollandicus,* and *Psittacula krameri*). Currently twenty-two neotropical species are listed in appendix I. CITES now counts 106 countries as parties, including all but Mexico in the mainland neotropics and the Bahamas, Dominican Republic, Saint Lucia, St. Vincent, and Trinidad, and Tobago in the Caribbean.

CITES specifically permits individual countries to adopt stricter domestic legislation to control wildlife imports and exports. Several Latin American countries have taken domestic measures to prohibit the harvest or trade in neotropical parrots or restrict it to specific user groups. Brazil banned all commercial wildlife exports in 1967; Paraguay followed suit in 1975, Ecuador in 1981, Mexico in 1982 and, most recently, Bolivia in 1984. Other countries, among them Colombia, Uruguay, and Venezuela, also severely restrict wildlife trade. While these efforts to protect species are laudable, they have not successfully limited the international parrot trade. Exports have continued, clandestinely or openly, with few or no repercussions.

In addition to their being a practical failure, export bans do little to promote sustainable use of wildlife. The result of political decision making, they ignore the possibilities that wildlife might be managed as a renewable resource. So long as export bans are in effect, there often is no government oversight of harvest for export, monitoring of trade levels, research, or cooperation with those involved in trapping and trading wildlife in determining the effects of harvesting.

The current CITES appendices is an example of one possibility for promoting sustainable use of parrots through appropriate regulation of the trade. All of the 141 neotropical parrot species are included in these appendices. While a number of these species have satisfied the strict biological criteria allowing for an international prohibition on trade through an appendix I listing, the remaining species are available for regulated international trade through their inclusion in appendix II. While the harvest of many of the appendix II species may be unsustainable, there is little scientific evidence available to indicate that any they should be completely removed from international trade through transfer to Appendix I.

The Case of Suriname

Although Suriname's fauna and flora do not compare with those of much larger neotropical countries, Suriname is nevertheless rich in wildlife, with 674 species of birds, 200 species of mammals, 130 species of reptiles, and 99 species of amphibians (Mittermeier and Plotkin 1986). Despite its relatively small size, it retains large tracts of forested area and has one of the lowest rates of forest destruction in the world; in the interior this rate is probably under 0.1% per annum (Mittermeier and Plotkin 1986).

The Nature Protection Division of the Suriname Forest Service (LBB) is responsible for developing natural resource conservation policies, enforcing wildlife protection laws, and implementing and enforcing CITES in Suriname. Scientific research and tourism are under the jurisdiction of STINASU, the Foundation for Nature Conservation in Suriname, which has placed special emphasis on developing tourism as a revenue-generating activity to make nature conservation self-supporting. Together, LBB and STINASU have developed a strategy for the sustainable use of some of Suriname's more abundant wildlife species, including twenty-one species of parrots. Most parrot species are still in great abundance in the forested areas, and in coastal agricultural zones some species are destroying crops. Instead of allowing these problem animals to be hunted, the government has established an export scheme that generates foreign exchange. The formula they have developed encompasses such contingencies as incomplete biological data for most species and the existence of subsistence hunting.

To set export quota for the targeted species, LBB and STINASU reviewed available data on their status and distribution in Suriname in consultation with the international scientific community. They also used information from surveys conducted by STINASU and analyzed the wildlife exports of neighboring countries, particularly those of Guyana. On this basis, they set what appear to be conservative export quotas for twenty-one of the thirty indigenous parrot species (table 24.5). Based on the assumption that larger species produce fewer young and have slower reproductive rates, they set larger quotas for the smaller species.

With the World Wildlife Fund, LBB will initiate a long-term investigation of the effects of trapping on species subject to export quotas. Quotas will be adjusted yearly to incorporate new information. So far, new information on species abundance has indicated quotas might be increased rather than decreased. To ensure compliance with the quota system, LBB has established an authorization system for all export shipments. To apply for an authorization, an exporter must be a member of the Association of Animal Exporters. The Secretariat of this association participates in the negotiation of quotas, which are then divided among the members. The members are required to report on their trapping activities and keep a logbook of all birds in their holding facilities. Underlying the authorization system is the philosophy of mutual responsibility, both for the wildlife resource and for the Association's activities. The fact that

TABLE 24.5
Fixed Values and Commercial and Noncommercial Quotas for
Psittacine Species Traded in 1987 under Suriname's Export Scheme Compared
With Commercial Export Quotas Established by Guyana

	Fixed Value (U.S. $)	Commercial Quota	Noncommercial Quota	Total	Guyana's Export Quotas
Amazona amazonica	22.50	1,207	217	1,424	17,500
Amazona dufresniana	125	50	0	50	240
Amazona farinosa	46	50	14	64	2,300
Amazona ochrocephala	46	50	2	52	2,300
Ara ararauna	140	216	22	238	2,400
Ara chloroptera	175	50	16	66	1,800
Ara macao	300	10	14	24	0
Ara manilata	35	500	0	500	1,500
Ara nobilis	24	150	35	185	1,000
Ara severa	65	30	8	38	0
Aratinga leucophthalmus	5	1,000	210	1,210	300
Aratinga pertinax	6	1,210	214	1,424	3,000
Aratinga solstitialis	20	50	0	50	600
Brotogeris chrysopterus	10	817	140	957	180
Deroptyus accipitrinus	200	176	0	176	480
Forpus passerinus	5	2,310	458	2,768	600
Pionites melanocephala	25	711	112	823	600
Pionopsitta caica	50	50	0	50	0
Pionus fuscus	30	750	91	841	300
Pionus menstruus	12.50	524	91	615	900
Pyrrhura picta	25	780	105	885	300
Total		10,671	1,749	12,420	

Note: Data from the Suriname Forest Service and the Guyana Ministry of Agriculture.

an authorization may be withdrawn further encourages each member to ensure the good conduct of his colleagues.

STINASU biologists are authorized to check the parrot trappers' holding facilities and trapping methods in order to limit preexport mortality. Exports are allowed only after an export permit and veterinary certificate are issued. The export permit is only valid with a special "security" stamp, the cost of which is determined by the number of birds being shipped. The money derived from these fees is allocated toward implementation and monitoring of the quota system.

LBB has established a minimum value in U.S. dollars for every quota species. The minimum value of one individual of *Ara ararauna* exported from Suriname, for example, is fixed at U.S. \$140 (see table 24.5). To comply with the foreign exchange regulations, an exporter must receive payment for the shipment in U.S. dollars and must receive at least the minimum value fixed for this particular species. The full amount in dollars is then paid to the Central Bank, which in turn pays the exporter back in local currency. Every export must be reported to the Central Bank before export, and the exporter must document the number of individuals in the shipment (which will be inspected by STINASU). Control of the foreign exchange rules is carried out by the Central Bank. In 1987, Suriname's export scheme for parrots earned a minimum U.S. \$240,000 in foreign currency (table 24.5). One year following implementation of the quota system it was evident that illegal trapping and trade had been reduced (Ball 1986).

It is worth comparing Suriname's export quotas with those established for species by Guyana. Suriname's 1987 export quotas total 12,420 parrots (table 24.5), just one-third the number exported by Guyana (Thomsen 1988). Suriname has recognized that the long-lived parrot species, in particular the larger species such as macaws, have low reproductive rates and that their populations probably cannot sustain large-scale harvest. This is not the case for Guyana. Guyana's export of 2,400 *Ara ararauna* per year, for example, is ten times greater than Suriname's for the same species.

Discussion

Much has been said to provide incentives for conserving wildlife species through exploiting their commercial value. Natural habitat can frequently be protected if it provides breeding or foraging opportunities for exploited species. Such an approach to parrot conservation and management seems worth investigating given the current high levels of trade and the fallibility of wildlife protection legislation in virtually every Latin American country.

Current levels of trade are such that a system for determining specific levels of exploitation of neotropical parrots must be devised. Otherwise we risk losing some of these species completely. Suriname's quota system seems a worthwhile model for other countries to follow and develop. Other management techniques might include ranching—taking a certain number of individuals or eggs from the wild and raising them for sale or export. The reproductive biology of some parrots might lend itself to such a method; the hyacinth macaw, for example, is known to always lay two eggs (Munn, Thomsen and Yamashita 1989) but never succeed in raising two young. One always dies in the first few weeks after hatching. One hyacinth egg or young might be taken from the nest and raised in a controlled environment without affecting recruitment in the wild population. However, with initiatives focused on intensive management, much capital investment would be needed. There would be high maintenance costs in raising young birds known to be susceptible to parasites and disease. There would also be a risk involved in allowing trade when wild-caught individuals might be passed off as having come from such a facility.

A system of sustainable use of parrots for international trade includes four major elements:

1. Quotas for capture and export must be established on the basis of the most complete and accurate scientific data, not arbitrarily as some countries have done (e.g., Honduras) or on the basis of average exports over a given period (e.g., Guyana). In the absence of a complete set of biological parameters such as population size, distribution, and reproductive potential, conservative quotas must be set. Appropriate attention must focus on the methods used in assessing population size; in Nicaragua, where population surveys using line transects resulted in inflated population estimates, the quotas that have been established are believed to be too high for the populations to withstand (Duffy, unpubl. ms.). Consultation with the international scientific community should be extensive.

2. The appropriate infrastructure must be put in place to monitor trapping and export activities. While the necessary mechanism for issuing permits and controlling the numbers of species traded already exists in CITES, additional emphasis needs to be placed on promoting compliance with export regulations and on cooperation between exporters and the regulating agency. There must be an incentive for exporters to comply with export restrictions. In Suriname, for example, requiring the organizing of exporters into an association with legal responsibility increases the chances that the industry will be self-policing and as a result eases enforcement by the government.

3. Wildlife exports must generate foreign exchange. When a country with increasing economic expectations must exploit its natural resources to generate foreign exchange, an incentive must be found to conserve wildlife and wildlife habitat. In such cases, species must pay their way. They can only pay their way when a country benefits from such harvest. Establishing a minimum fee for each exported bird ensures a predictable amount of foreign exchange per year through the sale of these birds.

4. Wildlife use and conservation must involve and profit local communities.

The current situation in many countries is that the campesino who actually traps a parrot receives a mere fraction of what the exporter, importer, and ultimately the retailer receive. The wildlife trade brings little benefit to the campesino and his family. Communities involved in parrot trapping should be involved in managing populations, through having sole rights to capture birds on certain areas of land, controlling the amount of trapping, and policing breeding sites. They can also be involved in captive breeding and ranching schemes on a cooperative basis, as has been suggested by Duffy (unpubl. ms.) for local communities in Costa Rica. Such conservation and management schemes can encourage the preservation of habitat and benefit both the community and the species involved.

There is little disagreement within the scientific and conservation communities that current levels of exploitation of neotropical parrot populations, when coupled with habitat alteration and conversion, will not ensure their long-term viability. Unilateral efforts to ban the trade have proved ineffective, and the data necessary for adopting multilateral measures under CITES are insufficient. A regulated export system based on levels of trade specific to the status of individual species seems most likely to succeed in rationalizing exploitation and holds promise for initiatives aimed at promoting use of parrots as a renewable natural resource.

25

The Psittacine Trade in Mexico

EDUARDO E. IÑIGO-ELIAS AND MARIO A. RAMOS

Large numbers of animals are traded from developing countries in Latin America, Asia, and Africa to the United States, Japan, and some countries of Europe (Nilsson, 1983; Ramos 1982). This wildlife trade involves both live animals, which are sold as pets and for zoos and research, and as animal products such as meat, eggs, oil, feathers, skins, and ivory (Harrison 1974; Nilsson 1981). The trade in animal products is immense: it is estimated that for each live animal traded, 100 to 1,000 animal products are sold (King 1978).

The total value of this world trade in wildlife is estimated at $2 to $5 billion U.S. dollars yearly (Toufexis 1983). Of all animal and plant species involved in this wildlife trade, birds are probably the most exploited. During the last 20 years the harvest of live birds from the wild has increased to sustain the national and international pet markets. The world trade in wild birds is estimated at between 3.5 million (Thomsen and Hemley 1987) and 7.5 million individuals per year (Inskipp 1975; Inskipp and Gamell 1979; Nilsson 1983).

Ornithology sometimes involves the collection of specimens, and it has been argued, particularly by wildlife dealers, that scientific collecting has caused the population decline of several species. The data do not confirm this. Scientific collecting began about 1800, and since that time a total of about 5,200,000 birds from 8,919 described species have been collected for scientific reasons from around the world (Banks and Barlow 1973). These numbers are small compared to the totals in the commercial bird trade. Between 1901 and 1986 for instance, 25,661,267 wild birds of 488 species were legally imported into the United States from around the world (Banks 1976; Nilsson 1981, 1985a; USDA 1987), with an average of 47,437 birds per species. Figure 25.1 shows the pet trade share of world imports of wild birds into the United States for this period, excluding the years 1943–67, when no records were available (Banks 1976; Nilsson 1981, 1985a; USDA 1987). Declines in the total birds imported into the United States coincide with wars and economic crises. During the 10

years between 1968 and 1982 for which records are available, 1,064,113 individuals of 104 psittacine species were imported into the United States from
around the world (TRAFFIC 1983).

The psittacine family, which includes parrots, macaws, cockatoos, conures,
and parakeets, has been the group of tropical birds most directly exploited by
humans for hundred of years (Iñigo 1986). The world trade in psittacines is
estimated at one million birds per year (Nilsson 1981; Roet, Mack and Duplaix
1981). Jackson (1985) estimated that in the United States, annual profits from
the sale of psittacines might be as high as $300 million each year. Between
1981 and 1985, the United States imported more than 250,000 psittacines
a year (Thomsen and Hemley 1987), a figure that comprised 25% of the
world import of psittacines. Approximately 47.1% of these came from Latin
America.

Mexico has been considered to be one of the ten major exporters of wild
birds in the world (Iñigo 1986; Nilsson 1981, 1983). In 1979, Mexico was the
most important Latin American supplier of wild birds to the United States
(Nilsson 1981). In 1980, it was the second most important Latin American
exporter to the United States (Roet, Mack and Duplaix 1981) Of the twenty-
one species of parrots known to occur in Mexico, 28.5% of the species and
79% of subspecies are endemic (AOU 1983; Forshaw 1977; Freidmann, Gris-

Figure 25.1. Wild birds imported by the United States from 1901 to 1986. (Data from Banks
1976; Nilsson 1981; Nilsson 1985a; USDA 1987.)

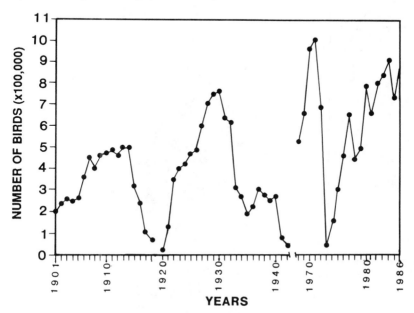

com, and More 1950). All of these species have been exploited for both national and international pet trade (Iñigo 1983; Nilsson 1981; Quiñones and Castro 1975; TRAFFIC 1983), even though Mexican laws allow the capture and trade of only a few species (SARH 1979; Diario Oficial 1987).

In this chapter we discuss the importance of psittacine birds as a tropical resource in Mexico and how this resource has been overexploited and mismanaged. In particular, we discuss the locations where parrots are captured, the ways in which they are trapped, the nature of the trade, and the protective legislation in Mexico. We discuss the illegal aspects of this trade, particularly the traffic, seizures, and reexport. Finally, we review the psittacine mortality during the legal trade process and the socioeconomic aspects for both the exporting and the importing countries.

Capture Areas of Psittacine Birds

Official permits in Mexico that allow the capture and trade of song and cage birds, including ten species of psittacines, record the state of origin. Our ex-

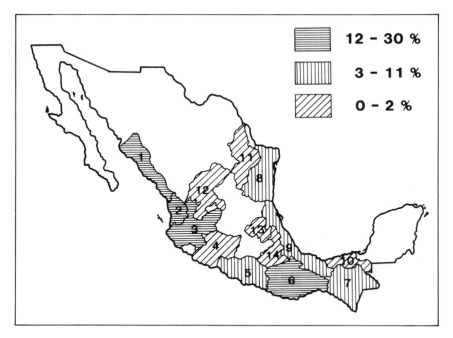

Figure 25.2. Capture zones of parrots in Mexico and percent of total capture per state. *Pacific zone:* (1) Sinaloa (five species); (2) Nayarit (nine species); (3) Jalisco (six species); (4) Michoacan (ten species); (5) Guerrero (seven species); (6) Oaxaca (seven species); (7) Chiapas (five species). *Gulf zone:* (8) Tamaulipas (six species); (9) Veracruz (eight species); (10) Tabasco (four species); *Central zone:* (11) Nuevo Leon (one species); (12) Zacatecas (one species); (13) Hidalgo (three species); (14) Puebla (one species). Data from DGFFS 1983.

amination of 1982 and 1983 records revealed three main capture zones in Mexico (DGFFS 1983) (fig. 25.2). Most birds are captured in the Pacific zone, which comprises seven states; 86.2% of all birds captured come from this region. All ten psittacine species are legally harvested here. The most frequently captured species was the white-crowned parrot (*Pionus senilis*) (40.9% of all birds captured in this zone) and the orange-fronted parakeet (*Aratinga canicularis*) (37.0% of all birds captured). The Gulf zone, comprising three states, accounts for 12.7% of all birds captured. Eight species of parrots are taken here. The most frequently captured species was the red-lored amazon (*Amazona autumnalis*) (25.6% of all birds captured in this zone). The central zone, which comprises four states, accounts for 1% of all birds captured. Four species were caught in these states. The green parakeet (*A. holochlora*) contributed the greatest proportion (41.8% of those captured) (table 25.1).

TABLE 25.1
Species Captured in Mexico for Commercial Purposes by Zone, 1982–83

Species	Pacific Zone		Gulf Zone		Central Zone		Total	%
	No. Birds	%	No. Birds	%	No. Birds	%		
Aratinga holochlora	1,330	1.4	2,250	18.4	490	41.8	3,870	3.8
Aratinga nana	20	0.02	1,400	11.4	—	—	1,420	1.3
Aratinga canicularis	30,060	37.0	2,230	18.2	390	33.3	32,680	31.2
Bolborhynchus lineola	3,580	4.4	—	—	—	—	3,580	3.5
Forpus cyanopygius	3,960	4.8	360	2.9	100	8.5	4,420	4.2
Brotogeris jugularis	740	0.9	—	—	—	—	740	0.7
Pionus senilis	33,220	40.9	530	4.3	—	—	33,750	32.2
Amazona albifrons	2,320	2.8	800	6.5	—	—	3,120	3.0
Amazona finschi	15,760	7.1	1,500	12.2	—	—	17,260	16.5
Amazona autumnalis	370	0.4	3,130	25.6	190	16.2	3,690	3.6
Totals	91,160		12,200		1,170		104,530	
		87.2		11.7		1.1		

Source: DGFFS 1983. Unpublished document.

Note: The percentage was calculated based on the total number of individuals (104,530)

It is important to note that this analysis is derived from data provided by only 320 tappers who were registered in fourteen states in the country, and that capture data include only the ten species of psittacines whose capture was permitted in the 1982–83 season (table 25.1). Capture and trade are not always restricted to those species whose exploitation is legally permitted. For example, the yellow-headed amazon (*A. oratrix*), the yellow-naped amazon (*A. auropalliata*), and the scarlet macaw (*Ara macao*) have always been captured in large quantities. Moreover, the number of trappers is larger than those recorded in the 1982–83 season, as is the number of states in which parrots are captured (e.g., San Luis Potosí [Eitniear 1980]; Quintana Roo [Chávez 1984]; Yucatán [Iñigo, pers. obs.]).

Methods of Capture

The major technique used in Mexico to capture psittacines consists of removing chicks from nests (Iñigo, pers. obs.; Rodriguez 1983). This method is prohibited by Mexican law (Diario Oficial 1987; SEDUE 1983). The bird trapper will either climb the tree, with or without the aid of pitons, or will cut down the tree that contains the nest (Estudillo, pers. com.; Iñigo, pers. obs.). A second method involves the use of nets, sometimes combined with a live parrot as a decoy. This technique is used more often for capturing small species such as parakeets (Iñigo, pers. obs.). A third method involves placing a live parrot on the branch of a fruit tree next to a slip knot, and trapping alighting birds by their legs (Iñigo, pers. obs.). Rodriguez (1983) also mentions that sticky gums are commonly used to catch parrots.

Legal Trade in Psittacines

Between 1970 and 1982, the minimum number of psittacine birds legally imported into the United States from Mexico totaled 133,299 birds (Nilsson 1981, 1985a; Roet, Mack, and Duplaix 1981; TRAFFIC 1983; USFWS 1981) (fig. 25.3). During this period, approximately 76,244 orange-fronted parakeets

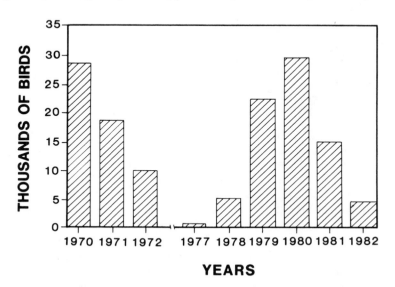

Figure 25.3. Psittacines exported from Mexico to the United States from 1970 to 1982 (no data available in 1973–76). (Data from Nilsson 1981; Nilsson 1985a; Roet, Mack, and Duplaix 1981; USFWS 1981.)

(accounting for 57.1% of the total imports from Mexico) and 16,490 endemic red-crowned amazons (*A. viridigenalis*) (12.3% of the total) were imported.

The species and number of individuals authorized for export by the Mexican government between 1981 and 1982 (DGFFS 1982), is compared with the list of birds imported into the United States during the same period (Nilsson 1981, 1985a; TRAFFIC 1983; USDA 1979, 1980, 1981, 1982b) in table 25.2. Of the

TABLE 25.2
**Psittacine Species Whose Capture was Legally Permitted in Mexico in 1981 and 1982,
Compared with Those Legally Imported by the United States from Mexico over
the Same Period**

Species	Birds Authorized for Export (21 Permit Holders) 1981–82[a]	Birds Imported by U.S. 1981–82[b,c]	% Received by U.S.
Aratinga holochlora	2,600	198	7.6
Aratinga canicularis	16,650	5,515	33.1
Ara militaris	—	110	—
Ara macao	—	2	—
Bolborhynchus lineola	6,500	—	—
Forpus cyanopygius	1,500	—	—
Brotogeris jugularis	2,000	—	—
Pianopsitta haematotis	1,300	200	15.3
Pionus senilis	6500	10	0.1
Amazona albifrons	—	1,924	—
Amazona viridigenalis	8,000	4,372	54.6
Amazona finschi	7,300	2,843	38.9
Amazona autumnalis	3,450	999	28.9
Amazona farinosa	—	321	—
Amazona ochrocephala	7,200	2,976	41.3
Totals	63,000	19,470	30.9

Sources: [a] DGFFS 1982; unpubl. records; [b] Nilsson 1985a; [c] USDA 1981, 1982. Quarantine report forms "17-13."

63,000 birds that the Mexican government authorized for export, only 31% were imported into the United States; the remaining 69% went to other countries. Table 25.2 also reveals that four species whose export was prohibited by the Mexican government were "legally" imported into the United States; these included the military macaw (*A. militaris*) (*n* = 110), the scarlet macaw (*A. macao*) (*n* = 2), the white-fronted amazon (*A. albifrons*) (*n* = 1,924), and the mealy amazon (*A. farinosa*) (*n* = 321).

Analyzing a sample of "17–13" forms used by the U.S. Department of Agriculture (USDA), we determined that 25,376 psittacine birds (eleven species) were imported into the United States from Mexico between 1979 and 1982. These birds were delivered in ninety-four shipments (median of 193 birds per shipment, ranging from 1 to 3,250 birds) (USDA 1979, 1980b, 1981, 1982). The majority of the Mexican shipments were received by cities in the United

States that were close to the U.S.–Mexican border. Los Angeles, California, alone received 32.2% of Mexican psittacine exports.

The Ley Federal de Caza (Federal Wildlife Law), passed in 1952, established the standard for all wildlife regulation in Mexico (Diario Oficial 1952; Fuller and Swift 1984; SEDUE 1983). In 1979, regulations for the capture and trade of song and cage birds were first established, covering the 1979–80 season. In 1979, the capture of four psittacines was banned (SARH 1979a). Since that date, banned species have been added and deleted from the list (table 25.3). In 1982, legal exportation of Mexican wildlife was banned (SFF 1982). This regulation affected the Mexican wildlife exports but not the local trade. The new Ley General del Equilibrio Ecológico y la Protección al Ambiente (Diario Oficial 1988) proposes new measures for conservation and exploitation of Mexican wildlife. Unfortunately, Mexico is one of the few countries that is not a

TABLE 25.3
Mexican Psittacines Legally Exploited in Each Season

Species	1979 1982[a]	1982 1983[b]	1983 1984[c]	1984 1985[d]	1985 1986[e]	1986 1987[f]	1987 1988[g]
Aratinga holochlora	x	x	x	x	x	x	x
Aratinga strenua[1]	x	x	x	—	—	x	x
Aratinga nana[2]	x	x	x	—	—	x	x
Aratinga canicularis	x	x	x	x	x	x	x
Ara militaris	—	—	—	—	—	—	—
Ara macao	—	—	—	—	—	—	—
Rhynchopsitta pachyrhyncha	—	—	—	—	—	—	—
Rhynchopsitta terrisi	—	—	—	—	—	—	—
Bolborhynchus lineola	x	x	x	x	x	x	x
Forpus cyanopygius	x	x	—	—	—	—	—
Brotogeris jugularis	x	x	x	x	x	x	x
Pionopsitta haematotis	x	—	—	—	—	—	—
Pionus senilis	x	x	x	—	—	—	—
Amazona albifrons	x	x	x	x	x	x	x
Amazona xantholora	x	—	—	—	—	—	x
Amazona viridigenalis	x	—	—	—	—	—	—
Amazona finschi	x	x	—	—	—	—	—
Amazona autumnalis	x	x	x	x	x	x	x
Amazona farinosa	x	—	—	—	—	—	—
Amazona oratrix[3]	x	—	—	—	—	—	—
Amazona auropalliata[4]	x	—	—	—	—	—	—

Sources: [a] SARH 1979; [b] Diario Oficial 1982; [c] Diario Oficial 1983; [d] Diario Oficial 1984; [e] Diario Oficial 1985; [f] Diario Oficial 1986; [g] Diario Oficial 1987.

Note: x = Species allowed to be captured; — = Prohibited Species

[1] Sometimes considered a race of *A. holochlora*

[2] Sometimes considered a race of *A. astec*

[3] Sometimes considered a race of *A. ochrocephala*

[4] Sometimes considered a race of *A. ochrocephala*

member of CITES (Convention on International Trade in Endangered Species of Wild Fauna and Flora) and does not strictly control wildlife exports and imports. As a result, smuggling of Mexican birds into the United States and Europe has increased (Parrot 1988; Polly 1988; CITES-Switzerland, unpubl. records; Gaski 1987; IUCN-Wildlife Trade Monitoring Unit, England, unpubl. records; Rohter 1987; Schouten, pers. comm; Villalba-Macías, pers. comm.; Weiser 1988).

Illegal Trade in Psittacines

Species that are either threatened or protected by law become more valuable in the illegal wildlife market (Harrison 1974: Nilsson 1983). This has occurred with the yellow-headed amazon (*A. oratrix*) and scarlet macaw (*A. macao*) in Mexico. Documents are falsified to legalize shipments of banned species within Mexico; legal permits that authorize the trade of a particular parrot shipment (which must specify species and number of birds) are used repeatedly for additional shipments, and illegal permits are used to reexport wild caught birds from countries in which they do not occur (Iñigo and Ramos, pers. obs.; Inskipp 1975; Nilsson 1981; Witt 1981). Common psittacine species are dyed to look like rare and valuable birds or to resemble birds that can be traded (Iñigo, per. obs.).

Mexico has been one of the big "laundry and springboard" countries in the illegal trade of psittacines. The Division of Law Enforcement of the U.S. Fish and Wildlife Service pointed out that in 1987 Mexico was the major source of smuggled wildlife entering the United States (Rohter 1987). This smuggling is considered a problem of great importance (Pasquier 1981; Rohter 1987) for both countries. Thomsen and Hemley (1987) estimated that each year approximately 150,000 birds, mostly psittacines, are smuggled across the border from Mexico into the United States. The Wildlife Section of the U. S. Department of Justice (USDJ) estimated that of 100 seizures between October 1979 to November 1980, the eight most important were along the border with Mexico (Witt 1981). A total of 1,246 birds were captured during these seizures, including one shipment of fifty macaws (Nilsson and Mack 1980). The recent Operation Psittacine of the U.S. Fish and Wildlife Service (Anon., 1988) seized a large number of endangered psittacines worth approximately $468,000, smuggled into the United States from Mexico, Latin America, and other countries. During 1987, approximately 200 palm cockatoos (*Probosciger aterrimus*), an endemic and endangered species from northern Australia, Papua New Guinea, and Indonesia, were smuggled into Mexico (Rice 1988). The Palm Cockatoo is protected by the laws in all three countries where it occurs, and is listed in Appendix I of CITES. These birds were presumably reexported to the United States, where they retail for $15,000 each and where large pet dealers and rich aviculturists can afford the price.

Frequently, parrots are exported at the nestling stage, 2 weeks old or less, making it difficult to distinguish commercial and endangered species. Nilsson (1981) reported that between 1975 and 1979, the U.S. Department of Agriculture confiscated a total of 7,219 Mexican parrots that were illegally imported into the United States; of these, 58% of the birds could not be identified as to the species because they were too young.

The reexport of native wildlife from one country or region to a second country is sometimes another form of illegal wildlife trade (AFA 1981; Inskipp and Thomas 1976; Nilsson 1981). The problem with monitoring this trade is distinguishing which species are truly reexports and which are merely misidentified by dealers. Table 25.4 shows the reexport of three endemic species from Mex-

TABLE 25.4
Exports and Reexports of Endemic Mexican Psittacine Species to the United States

Species (Region)	No. Birds Imported from Mexico	No. of Mexican Birds Exported to U.S. from Other Countries	Total Birds	%
Forpus cyanopygius (northeast Mexico)	500 in 1979[a,b,c]	280 from Bolivia, Surinam, and South Africa, 1980–81[b,c]	780	35.8
Amazona viridigenalis (northeast Mexico)	12,431 between 1971 and 1982[a,b,c]	3,106 from Colombia in 1970, and from unknown countries between 1968–82[a,b,c]	15,537	20.0
Amazona finschi (Sierra Madre Occidental)	5,666 between 1979 and 1982[a,b,c]	1,030 from Colombia in 1970 and 1971 and others from unknown countries in 1977[a,b,c]	6,696	15.3

Sources: [a] Nilsson 1981; [b] Nilsson 1985a; [c] TRAFFIC 1983.

ico. Apparently the red-crowned Amazon (*A. viridigenalis*), a species restricted to northeastern Mexico (Friedmann, Griscona, and More 1950; Ridgely 1981), has been imported by the United States from Colombia (Nilsson 1985a; TRAFFIC 1983). However, Colombia has a species, *A. autumnalis,* which is similar to *A. viridigenalis.* Similar circumstances exist for *F. cyanopygius* and *A. finschi* (see table 25.4).

Trade Mortality

Wild birds have a high mortality rate during different parts of the trading process. The causes and extent of mortality of psittacines at each stage during the legal trade process in Mexico is indicated in table 25.5. The mortality rate during nestling capture is at least 10%, depending on the species captured and the techniques used. The greatest mortality rate, approximately 30%, occurs

TABLE 25.5
Survivorship of Nestling Psittacines[1] at Various Stages of Legal Trade[a,b]

Stage	Survivorship[2] (l_x)	Mortality rate[3] (q_x)	Mortality[4] (d_x)
Capture	1.00	0.10	0.10
Confinement by trapper	0.90	0.30	0.27
Transportation within Mexico	0.63	0.20	0.13
Confinement by exporter	0.50	0.10	0.05
International transportation	0.45	0.04	0.02
Quarantine in importer country (U.S.)	0.43	0.06	0.03
Pet store	0.40	0.03	0.01
Pet owner	0.39	—	—

Sources: [a] USDA 1979, 1980b, 1981, 1982.

[b] Iñigo, unpubl. data.

[1]Data from 25,376 Mexican psittacine birds in ninety-four shipments from twelve species ($\bar{x}$ 1,372; birds per shipment)

[2]Proportion of birds still surviving at a given stage out of the original 25,376.

[3]Proportion of birds entering in a particular stage that die during it.

[4]Probability of dying during each stage.

during the confinement of birds by trappers waiting to ship to Mexico City. The high rate occurs mainly from poor nutrition, stress, and overcrowding (Brookland, Hora, and Carter 1985; Carter and Currey 1987; Fowler 1974; Iñigo, pers. obs.; Nilsson 1985b; Svedeen 1983).

These mortality rates vary enormously with the species. Moreover, the probability that an individual psittacine will die depends on the length of time each bird or shipment spends in any one stage of the trade process, as well the age and health conditions of each bird. The mortality rate of psittacines in the illegal trade is estimated as 40% to 50% greater than in the legal (Brookland, Hora, and Carter 1985; Inskipp and Gamell 1979; Nilsson 1981, 1985b). In 1981 one bird dealer mentioned to one author (EIE) that in one shipment of twenty-four wild amazon parrots and macaws (*A. macao*) from the state of Chiapas and shipped to the Mercado de Sonora in Mexico City (a distance of over 1,000 km), only fifteen birds survived to the final destination.

Socioeconomic Aspects of the Psittacine Trade

A juvenile parakeet (*Aratinga spp.*) can be bought in Mexico for less than U.S. $1 and a juvenile amazon parrot (*Amazona spp.*) for less than U.S. $10 and sold in the United States for over $400 (Iñigo, pers. obs.; Nilsson 1981; Olswang 1983; Smylie 1983). Permits to trap and sell birds issued by the Mexican government are very inexpensive. The revenues for these permits go to the government wildlife department (SEDUE), but the amounts are minimal. For example, during the 1987–88 season for the capture and trade of wild birds in

Mexico, the price for a permit to capture song birds and psittacines was 9,600 pesos ($4), and a commercial vendor permit to sell birds was 152,000 pesos ($66) (SEDUE 1987).

During 1988 a scarlet macaw (*A. macao*) could be sold in pet stores and illegal markets in Mexico City like the Mercado de Sonora (Iñigo, pers. obs.) for 300,000 pesos ($450). In 1983, for instance, a scarlet macaw was worth over $2,000 in a pet store in California (Aves International 1983); during 1988 the price for this macaw was as high as $4,000 in a pet store in Florida, depending on the age, feather conditions, and whether it was a captive or wild hatched bird (Iñigo, pers. obs.). Most of the value of a parrot is added by major exporter and importer commercial dealers. The same bird sold by an exporter in Mexico for between $400 and $3,000 brings only 50,000 to 200,000 pesos ($19) or less to the bird trapper in the Lacandona forest, Chiapas. The trapper thus receives 2.5% of the final value for the bird. The utility added by commercial dealers accounts for 97%.

These figures indicate that the trade in wildlife does not benefit the country as a whole, nor does it profit the trapper in the field. Profits accrue mostly to a few influential Mexican citizens (Garza 1987; Ortíz 1983) and pet dealers in the United States (Nilsson 1981). The profits are considerable; just between 1981 and 1982, the U.S. Department of Commerce recorded the legal importation of 15,461 Mexican birds with a registered value of over $77,000 (USDC 1981, 1982). The U.S. Fish and Wildlife Service estimates that animals, plants, and their products, worth approximately $100 million, are smuggled annually (Witt 1981). The U.S. Department of Justice and the U.S. Fish and Wildlife Service estimated that in 1979, 50,000 psittacines worth $10 million were smuggled across the border between Mexico and the United States (Exotic bird 1980; Roet, Mack, and Duplaix 1981). Recently the U.S. Fish and Wildlife Service and the U.S. Customs Service (USCS) arrested a pet shop owner from California who smuggled during the spring 1988, twenty yellow-headed amazon (*A. oratrix*) and three military macaws (*A. militaris*) from Mexico, worth over $25,000.

Another cost associated with the trade in live birds that is often neglected is the importation of diseases. Exotic diseases can be introduced and transmitted to poultry, wild populations of birds, or even to humans (AFA 1980, 1982; Baer 1981; Courtenay 1978; Jennings 1977; Morin 1977; Nilsson 1981). A compelling example of a damaging introduction was an outbreak of viscerotropic velogenic Newcastle disease (VVND) in 1971, apparently derived from some smuggled Mexican yellow-headed amazons (*A. oratrix*). The disease affected the poultry industry in California and part of Arizona. Approximately twelve million poultry birds were destroyed at a cost of $28 million. It is estimated that 113 million doses of vaccine were used to eradicate this disease over a 3-year period (Nilsson 1981; USDA 1980a).

Recommendations

While habitat destruction is the major cause of population decline in most species, the wildlife trade has a very significant impact on others (King 1978; Toufexis 1983). In the case of psittacines, the exploitation for the wildlife trade has been a most important cause of population decline and extinction of several species (Collar 1988; Hardie 1987; Munn 1988b; Snyder, Wiley, and Kepler 1987). The U.S. Fish and Wildlife Service estimates that over 85% of all birds imported into the United States are wild-caught (Nilsson 1981), and of all imports 98% are destined for the commercial pet trade. Only 2% are for zoological and research institutions (King 1978).

The long-term exploitation of psittacine birds is not feasible unless the resource is carefully managed. In general, psittacine birds have a low rate of reproduction with an average of only two young per year, an incubation period averaging 25 days, a nestling stage between 30 and 70 days, high chick mortality rate, a high competition for nest sites, and highly specialized diets (Alvarez del Toro 1980; Forshaw 1977; Iñigo and Ramos, unpubl. data; Munn 1988a, 1988b; Snyder, Wiley, and Kepler 1987).

Several legal and policy decisions are needed within the importing and the exporting countries in order to prevent the extinction of several psittacine species in Mexico:

1. Mexico needs to develop a workable internal control program for its wildlife trade and simultaneously become a party to the Convention on International Trade in Endangered Species of Fauna and Flora (CITES). This probably will help to control smuggling of endangered species and suppress the illegal trade.

2. The Mexican laws, Ley Federal de Caza and Ley General del Equilibrio Ecológico y la Protección al Ambiente, should be amended to include strong measures for the protection of endangered species, as well as species with commercial value.

3. In accord with the proposals by the Conservation Committee of the AOU (AOU 1973), the recommendations by the Conference on Conservation of Neotropical Parrots in St. Lucia 1980 and Brazil 1988, the recommendations of the International Council for Bird Preservation (ICBP) Mexican Section, we suggest (Iñigo 1983, 1986; Iñigo et al. 1988; Ramos 1982; Ramos and Iñigo 1985) that because of the continued exploitation of some Mexican psittacines species and the lack of information on the current status of the wild populations, the Mexican government should temporarily ban commercial exportation and reduce the local trade of psittacine populations that occur in Mexico until the population status of all species has been determined and, the recovery of the wild populations most affected by the trade has been established; they should then develop an appropriate sustainable exploitation system that allows the long-term survival of psittacine species.

4. It is necessary to create in Mexico an effective system of parks and reserves that will protect the long-term survival of endangered and endemic species, regardless of their commercial value.

5. Wildlife surveys of those species involved in the commercial trade should be implemented. Federal institutions, international organizations concerned with wildlife conservation, and national and international wildlife dealers must begin to support surveys to determine and monitor the status of wild populations that are traded, to establish optimal capture rates or quotas, and to banish the trade of those species in critical condition. The principal nations importing or exporting wildlife must ban the trade of wild endangered species, support research on ecology and conservation of those species implicated in the wildlife trade, and more strongly punish those people involved in the illegal wildlife trade.

Acknowledgments

To the memory of my father Ernesto Iñigo for his continuous support and belief in me. We thank Greta Nilsson from the Animal Welfare institute for providing valuable information and suggestions in the first manuscript and for her interest in the problem of the trade in Mexican wildlife. Húgo Rodriguez Uribe, from Dirección General de la Fauna y Flora Silvestres (now Consejo Nacional de Ecología-SEDUE) of Mexico, Sheryl Gilbert of TRAFFIC (U.S.A.), Dr. Kees C. Shouten, Scientific Consultant to the European Commission for CITES, and Juan S. Villalba-Macías, Director TRAFFIC (SUDAMERICA) provided information for this study. Dr. Jesus Estudillo Lopez, commented on the problem of wildlife trade in Mexico. Dr. Michael W. Collopy, Daniel Navarro, Damian Rumiz, and Rodrigo Medellin critically reviewed this manuscript. Dr. John A. Smallwood made suggestions in table analysis. Finally, we thank all the anonymous bird trappers and dealers (*Pajareros*) we interviewed in the field, streets, and markets of Mexico for their help and information. This is a contribution No. 38 of the Program for Studies in Tropical Conservation, University of Florida. This publication was partially supported by Consejo Nacional de Ciencia y Tecnologia (CONACYT) through a grant (#6366) to Eduardo Iñigo.

26

Tourism as a Sustained Use of Wildlife: A Case Study of Madre de Dios, Southeastern Peru

MARTHA J. GROOM,
ROBERT D. PODOLSKY,
AND CHARLES A. MUNN

Nature tourism is a means of using wildlife to benefit human populations that is nonconsumptive, which distinguishes it from many of the other uses discussed in this volume. Whereas the success of harvesting wild animals may depend on their population growth rates or behavior in captivity, tourism brings a different list of concerns, including the impact of tourists on natural communities, the effects of foreign culture and capital, and the challenge of educating the public about problems facing natural systems. Perhaps the largest distinction between nature tourism and other uses of wildlife, however, is the potential size of the industry created. Whereas most consumptive uses lead to smaller commercial or subsistence economies, a well-managed and promoted tourism program can easily rival other major forms of national income, particularly in developing countries.

Tourism is a major world industry, and international tourism is its largest and fastest growing segment (R. T. Devane, unpubl. data). Many argue that investment in international tourism is risky because it depends on the vagaries of worldwide economic patterns and is sensitive to unpredictable political acts such as terrorism. However, even in countries like Peru and Zimbabwe, where terrorist incidents have resulted in large setbacks, these have proved temporary, and tourism has remained a steadily growing industry (R. T. Devane, unpubl. data). International tourism currently generates more than $40 billion per year worldwide (excluding airfares), the fastest growing portion going to goods and services that support adventure tourism (R. T. Devane, unpubl. data; Alpine 1986). Thus, from a purely economic standpoint, investment in services supporting adventure tourism is likely to pay off increasingly for governments and private businesses willing and able to take the risks of investment.

Linking tourism to conservation, however, requires that economic gain by investors be coupled with at least three additional goals. First, a tourism/conservation program ideally should extend the economic benefits of development to a broad base of the local human population through employment, compensation fees, or the development of social services. Such an approach in Kenya's Amboseli National Park (Western 1982) has demonstrated that local people are more likely to protect lands and wildlife when they have an economic incentive to do so. Second, for tourism on reserve lands, the goals of park management must be furthered by economic gains and not counteracted by tourist activity. This involves not only supporting research on human impacts, but also creating a mechanism for visitors excited by their experience to contribute to the park following their visit, either through contributions or word-of-mouth advertising. Finally, the program ultimately should accommodate visitors of a wide range of economic status, so that access to wildlife is not restricted to the rich or foreign.

Problems in the Distribution of Income

The economic effects of tourism can be felt at four levels: the private investor, the national economy, the local economy, and, if on reserve lands, the reserve budget. Benefits are rarely well distributed, however, with revenues usually decreasing rapidly in the order listed. Creating a more equitable distribution of income among these levels is one of the main challenges to a tourism/conservation program.

Although tourism infrastructure often needs only modest capital input and can sometimes capitalize on government-supported development of transportation, entrepreneurs from developing countries usually lack the capital for initiating a tourist business. Often control of development rests in the hands of wealthy foreign investors who do not understand or appreciate local problems and who place profits above conservation and the support of local economies. Revenues from tourism are moved out of the host country to avoid devaluation associated with the high inflation rates characteristic of developing countries. Although the exportation of profits is common to many industries, tourism usually allows a greater fraction of revenues to remain in the host country.

Of foreign capital brought into the host country, most is normally spent in the larger cities for transportation, lodging, food, and supplies (De Kadt 1979). The share that actually goes into economies near the tourist site can be minimal (Weber 1987). As mentioned, local people rarely have resources or experience to invest, and most therefore end up with low-paying jobs (Jenkins and Henry 1982; Mishra 1982). On the other hand, because it is a labor-intensive industry, tourism can provide jobs for large numbers of nonskilled workers, which makes it especially important in areas with high unemployment (Beekhuis 1981; Cohen 1982). If properly practiced, the industry can also stimulate local economies through increased local demands for transportation, lodging, food, materials, and nature interpretation (e.g., Saglio 1979). Thus, even a relatively small share of tourism revenues can provide an extremely strong boost to the local economy.

What is the Potential of Tourism as a Conservation Strategy in Developing Countries?

Meeting conservationist goals has had mixed success in East Africa, where the economic potential of watching, rather than hunting, large and attractive mammal populations has been recognized for many years. For example, tourist interest in a single—albeit spectacular—species, the mountain gorilla, is estimated to bring in $4 million/yr to Rwanda, making gorilla tourism alone the country's second largest industry (A. W. Weber, pers. comm. 1988). The small portion of revenues received by local people has played a major role in reversing negative attitudes toward wildlife. Whereas poaching was a major problem for gorillas at the start of the project, no gorillas were known to have been killed by poachers for several years, and gorilla populations showed their first size increase in 1986 (Weber 1987). Newly habituated gorilla troops in Zaire have provided less expensive opportunities to see the gorilla, broadening access to new socioeconomic classes and enabling better management of the entire gorilla population in Rwanda and Zaire.

Tourism development in the neotropics has had a slower start. Since the explosion of nature tourism in Africa during the last decade, however, tourists have begun looking toward the Amazon as a destination with romantic appeal and smaller crowds. Informal interviews with tourists coming to see the cultural and natural sites of Peru indicate that, of those planning to visit the Amazon, about 70% are primarily interested in seeing animals and are less interested in indigenous cultures or Amazonian panoramas (C. Munn, unpubl. data). Unfortunately, the neotropical species that are exciting to see (e.g., giant river otter, woolly monkey, spectacled bear, macaw and parrot species) are less familiar to the average tourist than are the large mammals of East Africa. Many tourists therefore travel to areas like Iquitos, which are well advertised but, because of hunting and land conversion, are depauperate in animal species and primary forest. Interviews with the same tourists leaving Iquitos give the impression that many are happy with their experience, but probably not excited enough to spread the appeal of a visit by word of mouth (C. Munn, unpubl. data). This also means that most feel no commitment to contributing financially to the preservation of the area.

In this chapter we evaluate how tourism development in the Madre de Dios region of southeastern Peru is achieving a link between private enterprise and land and wildlife protection. We focus on the magnitude and distribution of revenues coming into the region, and emphasize the degree to which growth in the tourism industry can aid development and conservation in the area. Finally, we discuss current and future limitations to tourism development in southeastern Peru and potential problems with using Madre de Dios as a model for the development of nature tourism in other countries.

Case Study: Tourism in Madre de Dios, Peru

The Madre de Dios region contains some of the most diverse and spectacular cloud and lowland tropical rainforest in the world, which is largely unmolested by hunting or commercial activity. Forests of this region boast an astounding diversity of species (with >15,000 plants, 200 mammals, 1,000 birds). Some of the only large and easily observable populations of highly endangered species are found in this area, including those of the giant river otter, jaguar, woolly monkey, spider monkey, white-lipped peccary, tapir, black caiman, and several species of macaw, parrot, toucan, and curassow. These characteristics have made the region of prime importance to conservationists and other scientists, and suggest its potential attraction to tourists wishing to see and contribute to the protection of one of the most pristine areas in the entire Amazon basin.

History of Development and Use

One of the major departments in Peru, Madre de Dios is situated at the Brazilian and Bolivian borders, just east of the department of Cuzco (fig. 26.1). It is sparsely populated, with fewer than 0.40 people/km², 39% of whom live in the region's capitol, Puerto Maldonado (Statesman's Yearbook 1987). Development of the region has been slow. Aside from minor rubber, Brazil nut, and hardwood extraction during the early part of this century, little commercial use was made of the area before the 1940s, when gold extraction began near Puerto Maldonado (Ríos et al. 1986). Gold is now the major industry of Madre de Dios, followed by rubber, Brazil nuts, tourism, and lumber. A recent surge in the government-supported development of cattle ranching has accelerated forest conversion in Puerto Maldonado and the surrounding lands to the north of the city (Riós et al. 1986). Colonists along roads leading into the area have also cut some forest for small-scale agriculture.

In 1973, 1.5 million ha (18%) of Madre de Dios was set aside, along with some highlands of the department of Cuzco, as the Manu National Park. The park encompasses the entire drainage of the Manu River, and spans páramo at 3,650 m to lowland tropical rain forest at 300 m. In 1977, with the addition of a reserved zone and a cultural zone near native and colonist settlements, the park was designated a UNESCO Man and the Biosphere Reserve, and the total area now included in the Reserve is over 1.88 million ha (Ríos et al. 1986). Although rubber was extracted briefly at the turn of the century and mahogany trees were removed from along a portion of the Manu River in the 1960s, little hunting or other exploitation occurred within the park boundaries, leaving Manu Park in a near-pristine state. As in all areas of Madre de Dios where natural communities have not been disturbed, the diversity of species is high, and most species are tame and easily observable.

Four smaller reserves in Madre de Dios, the Tambopata Reserve Zone (5,500 ha), Lake Sandoval (<2,000 ha), Cuzco-Amazonico Reserve (10,000 ha), and

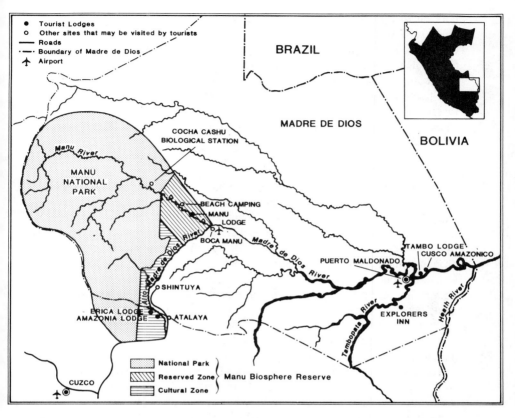

Figure 26.1. Map of Madre de Dios showing tourist destinations. Triangles mark locations of guard posts for Manu National Park.

the Pampas del Heath National Sanctuary (107,000 ha), are all located near Puerto Maldonado; the first three serve as the main destinations for tour groups. All reserves are in a semipristine state and include potential attractions not found elsewhere in Madre de Dios, such as the maned wolf in the Pampas del Heath and the grade 4 to 5 rapids on the Tambopata River. At present, only the Heath Sanctuary is officially protected, and none of the four is actually protected by guards. In February 1990, the Peruvian government established a much larger reserve (1.5 million ha) that encompasses most of the drainage of the Tambopata and Heath rivers above and between the four existing reserves.

Little organized tourism existed in any part of the Madre de Dios region before 1975 (Ruiz 1979). For many years the lack of transportation had restricted tourist flow into the region. Even now, of the two major roads from Cuzco, the nearest major city, one (to Puerto Maldonado) is too long to transport tourists. The other (to Shintuya (fig. 26.1), a small town on the Alto Madre de Dios River) is used frequently by tour companies operating in Manu. Large commercial jets began flights regularly into the Maldonado airport only after its dirt airstrip was paved in 1983. In addition, small twin-engine charter flights have come to Manu since 1983 by using a hard gravel airstrip at Boca Manu, a small settlement at the mouth of the Manu River. Air transportation thus has increased tourist access to the natural attractions around Puerto Maldonado and Manu, although ground transport for tourists through the area still depends chiefly on river transportation.

Tourism near Puerto Maldonado

Although more than 60,000 people now fly to Puerto Maldonado each year, little infrastructure exists to tap the potential nature-oriented tourism market. Only three lodges and relatively few independent guides regularly bring tourists to sites near Maldonado. One reason is that, at present, tourism is not perceived by the local and national governments or by most potential investors to be a profitable industry in the southern rainforest. Furthermore, most local people lack the expertise and resources to start such a business. As we will argue, figures on current revenue suggest that tourism is a viable industry for the region, but that it has not yet developed fully in size nor in the equitability of profit distribution.

The largest share of the tourism market in Puerto Maldonado is held by three tourist lodges, Explorer's Inn, Cuzco-Amazonico, and Tambo Lodge, each of which have about seventy beds. Explorer's Inn was established in 1975, originally as a hunting lodge for a largely European and North American clientele. When the government outlawed trophy hunting in 1975, the Inn converted to nature tourism. Cuzco-Amazonico, which started in 1977, has from the start emphasized low-intensity, jungle wildlife viewing with an antiquated but very widespread "dangers of the Amazon" approach. While both lodges offer a comfortable stay in intact forest, they do not offer an intact fauna. A history of hunting at the lodges, as well as continued subsistence hunting nearby, has depleted some of the more spectacular wildlife, such as large monkeys, cats, otters, caiman, and curassows (C. Munn, pers. obs.; K. Renton, former guide at Explorer's Inn, pers. comm. 1988). Both lodges, however, offer day trips to nearby oxbow lakes on the Madre de Dios and Tambopata Rivers, where more wildlife can be dependably seen. A two-night stay is about $150 at either lodge, and both are usually full during the tourist season (June to September). Both Cuzco-Amazonico and Explorer's Inn are owned by wealthy Peruvians of European extraction, and the clientele remains mostly North American and European. A third lodge, Tambo Lodge, recently was opened by a Peruvian from Cuzco formerly employed by Cuzco-Amazonico. It is similar in goals and services to Cuzco-Amazonico, but less fancy and less expensive.

Other than the three lodges, about five independent tour guides based in

Puerto Maldonado will bring people to oxbow lakes and other areas to see wildlife for relatively modest fees. Several guides are mentioned in the South American Handbook (South American Handbook 1989), and most advertise from the hotels in Puerto Maldonado and try to attract customers as they arrive at the airport. As with the lodges, some guides have moved from marketing consumptive (hunting) to nonconsumptive (photo or adventure) tours in the last few years. One guide, who now grosses $8,000/yr, led hunting safaris successfully for more than 5 years before learning he could make much greater profits by guiding people to see live animals. Most guides take people for 1- or 2-day trips to close attractions ($15 to $25/day), particularly to Lake Sandoval, only 45 minutes by boat from Puerto Maldonado. A few guides will run longer trips to particular sites ($20 to $30/day), while rafting outfitters specialize in trips down the Tambopata rapids or to what is perhaps the largest macaw mineral lick in the world, attracting hundreds of macaws daily.

Where does the money go? Negative perceptions of the profitability of tourism in Madre de Dios seem unwarranted given that over $1.27 million were paid for tourist services in Puerto Maldonado in 1987 (table 26.1). This amount does not include the increase in revenues to Peru as a whole from tourists who come to Peru principally to see wildlife in Madre de Dios (particularly naturalist/bird tours), but also visit the more traditional cultural attractions of Cuzco and Macchupicchu. The average tourist spends $1,050 per visit for lodging, food, transportation, and gifts in the major cities of Peru (Ministry of Industry, Tourism, and Integration (MITI)). Thus, the 6,520 tourists to Puerto Maldonado contributed about $6.8 million to the Peruvian economy above their payment to the tourist companies in Madre de Dios.

Explorer's Inn grosses over $350,000 per year in recent years, although prof-

TABLE 26.1
1987 Revenues of Tourist Companies and Independent Tour Guides in
Puerto Maldonado, Madre de Dios, and Cuzco, Peru

Company	No. Tourists	Average Length of Stay (Days)	Price/day (US$)	Total Gross Revenues (U.S.$)
Cuzco-Amazonico Lodge[a]	3,000	3	48	432,000
Explorer's Inn[a]	2,550	3	50	382,500
Tambo Lodge[a]	350	3	25	26,250
Independent Guides[a]	450	3	25	33,750
Ind. Guides (short trips)[b]	100	1	15	1,500
River Rafting[b]	70	14	90	88,200
Hotel/Food in Pto. Mdo.[b]	550	1	30	16,500
AeroPeru/Faucett round-trip Cusco-Pto. Mdo[b]	6,520	—	45	293,400
Total gross earnings				1,274,100

[a]Sources: Lodge owners, employees, South American Handbook 1989 and information supplied to ACSS.
[b]Figures estimated by average costs of services and estimates of numbers of participants supplied to ACSS.

its were temporarily affected by one severe but isolated terrorist incident in Cuzco in 1986 (M. Gunter, pers. comm. 1988). The larger Cuzco-Amazonico grosses more: $432,000 in 1987 and $770,000 in 1988. Independent guides earned about $35,000 in 1987, while special interest tours (e.g., river rafting) grossed $88,200. The combined gain of the airlines and local hotels and restaurants was at least $310,000. By gross revenue, nature tourism is thus the fourth largest industry in Madre de Dios, comparable to or above rubber and Brazil nuts (MITI).

Tourism has been profitable to business owners, but the benefits are not generally widespread. The tourist lodges and some independent operators enjoy profit margins as high as 30% to 45%. Discounting revenues to the airlines and specialized tours, and assuming a 35% profit margin for the lodges and a 25% profit margin for all other tour operators, Puerto Maldonado tourism in 1987 paid out approximately $575,550 in salaries and for the purchase of food and local materials. These estimates are conservative, as more people may be visiting the forest than are traveling with guides known to us, and tour companies may underrepresent tourist volume for tax purposes. In any case, nearly all of the $1.4 million or more generated by tourism in Madre de Dios went to Peruvians. Tours packaged through U.S. or European companies are marked up nearly 100% in cost (B. Gomez, pers. comm.), indicating that if Peruvian companies marketed directly at prices closer to those charged by foreign companies, revenue to Peru could increase.

Potential for growth. Now that transportation problems have eased with the addition of a major airport, tourism development in Maldonado is limited mostly by a lack of infrastructure. Maldonado receives less than one-tenth of the tourism volume of Iquitos (MITI), despite the fact that forest clearing and hunting have decimated wild populations of large birds and mammals in Iquitos. Iquitos has the lure of being located on the banks of the Amazon and still retains some reputation as a site where wildlife can be seen. We believe that the creation of new lodges, wider advertising, and better nature interpretation in the Madre de Dios area would help to improve and spread the area's reputation and ultimately lead to an increase in tourist revenues. This process appears to have already begun: Cuzco/Amazonico received 5,000 visitors in 1988, up 67% from 1987.

The new Tambopata/Candamo reserved zone established in February 1990 will likely foster the development of new tourist markets such as river rafting and giant otter or macaw watching. Interest in river rafting is evidenced by the popularity of day-trip rafting in the Urubamba River basin near Cuzco (3,500 tourists/yr: Association of Canoeing Companies of Cusco (ASEC)). Currently, the Tambopata rapids are not well advertised, and this sector of the market will almost certainly grow once the area gains a reputation. The large size of the proposed reserve makes it likely that several new lodges could be built and operated without adverse impacts on the forest and its wildlife.

Tourism in the Manu Biosphere Reserve

The value of Manu Park as an educational and recreational area has been repeatedly emphasized in statements of the park's goals and purposes (Ruiz 1979; Riós et al. 1986). Nevertheless, tourism has been introduced to the lowland forests of Manu with a great deal of caution. The first tourists to the lowlands were naturalists visiting the Cocha Cashu Biological Station (fig. 26.1) in the early 1980s. In 1985, more than 100 people visited the park in a single year for the first time. Current policy restricts the number of tourists to 500/yr, although that figure is likely to be raised pending a current reevaluation of human impacts (L. Yallico and G. Ruiz, pers. comm. 1988). All tourism is now restricted to the reserved zone of the park to avoid any adverse impacts on the original protected area. Tourism has been controlled tightly by the park to avoid compromising the other goals of park administration, including the conservation of flora and fauna and concern for the well-being and traditions of several groups of indigenous peoples.

Three organized tour companies (Expediciones Manu, Mayuc, and Manu Nature Tours) currently have permission to bring tour groups by canoe into the park. In 1987, the first tourist lodge in the reserved zone (Manu Lodge) was built near an oxbow lake to accommodate tourists brought in by Manu Nature Tours (fig. 26.2). Other groups are restricted to camping on sand beaches ex-

Figure 26.2. Manu Lodge, as seen from the oxbow lake (Cocha Juarez). A platform boat used by tourists for viewing wildlife on the lake is in the foreground. (Photo, K. Renton.)

posed along the Manu River from May through August. The park has designated two beaches adjacent to oxbow lakes as camping and recreation areas, and only allows camping on other beaches as long as tourists do not camp on beaches with colonies of nesting birds (see Groom 1986, 1990).

While only 315 tourists entered the park in 1987 (fig. 26.3), tourist companies and independent guides grossed about $172,225, or $547 per tourist from those few visitors (table 26.2). Company tours are fairly expensive ($75 to $90/ day) and bring in mostly European and North American clients, although much lower rates have been offered for Peruvian nationals and students. Independent guides are less expensive ($30/day) and therefore accommodate the majority of foreign backpackers and nationals.

Although visitation to the park's cultural zone is not restricted, the two tourist lodges located there (Erica and Amazonia Lodges) receive fewer than 200 tourists each year. Both are close to human settlements, and while wildlife is still plentiful when compared to the Iquitos region, it is generally less observable than along the Manu River. Both lodges appear to lack the advertising and infrastructure necessary to maintain a healthy business. Most clients, in fact, are Expediciones Manu and Manu Nature Tours groups stopping for one night en route to the reserved zone of the park.

Access to the park is still one of the main limitations to tourism in Manu. The cultural zone lies a day's journey by car from Cuzco on a dirt road that is closed by landslides for parts of the year and is too narrow to accommodate

Figure 26.3. Tourists watching macaws in Manu National Park. (Photo, D. O. Johnson.)

TABLE 26.2
**1987 Revenues of Tourist Companies and Independent Tour Guides in
Manu Biosphere Reserve, Madre de Dios, and Cuzco, Peru**

Company	No. Tourists	Average Length of Stay (Days)	Price/day (U.S.$)	Total Gross Revenues (U.S.$)
Manu Nature Tours[a]	38	7	90	23,940
Manu Lodge[a]	32	7	90	20,160
Expediciones Manu[a]	180	6	75	81,000
Mayuc	25	6	65	8,125
Independent Guides[a]	40	5	30	6,000
Amazonia Lodge[a]	150	2	30	9,000
Erica Lodge[a]	50	1	20	1,000
Hotel/Food in Pto. Mdo.[b]	100	1	30	3,000
AeroSur round-trip Cusco-Boca Manu[b]	100	—	200	20,000
Total gross earnings				172,225

[a]Source: Owner or guide of tour group and information from employees.
[b]Figures estimated from known costs and number of tourists.

more than one-way traffic (switched on alternate days). The reserved zone of the park lies an additional 6 to 12 hours by river. Tourists generally reach the reserved zone by boat from the river ports on the Alto Madre de Dios River. A more comfortable (but more expensive) option is to charter a small plane from Cuzco to the mouth of the Manu River, less than a day by boat from all points in the reserved zone. Only relatively wealthy groups with Manu Nature Tours and Expediciones Manu charter a plane directly to the area.

Where does the Money go? Manu Biosphere Reserve presently accommodates many fewer tourists than Puerto Maldonado and only grosses about one-seventh of the revenues (tables 26.1 and 26.2). Still, Manu's reputation for spectacular wildlife attracts wealthier clients, who stay longer and spend more per day. Thus, Manu earns about three times as much per tourist as Maldonado ($547 versus $195), demonstrating that the two areas cater to different economic classes.

Table 26.3 gives the estimated distribution of revenues to private companies. Due to an explicit emphasis on the quality of a tourist experience, Manu Nature Tours employs a greater number of people per tourist (currently about 1:1) and has a lower profit margin than any other tour company in Madre de Dios, choosing to reinvest profits to improvements in services. The other tour operations in Manu also have lower profit margins than those in Puerto Maldonado; in general, revenues are more evenly distributed among employees. Both Expediciones Manu and Manu Nature Tours use mostly Peruvian guides and employees. Nearly all food and gasoline must be brought directly from Cuzco, reducing somewhat the money going into local economies. Most employees,

TABLE 26.3
Estimated Distribution of Gross Revenues of Tour Companies in Madre de Dios (1987)

Company	Gross Revenues[a]	No. of Employees[b]	Profit Margin (%)[c]	Local Expenditures (U.S.$)[d,e]
Manu Biosphere Reserve				
Manu Nature Tours				
and Manu Lodge	44,100	15	5	11,910
Expediciones Manu	81,000	15	30	17,000
Mayuc	8,125	6	25	?
Independent Guides	6,000	6	15	4,000
Amazonia Lodge	9,000	6	15	9,000
Erica Lodge	1,000	3	15	1,000
Puerto Maldonado				
Cuzco Amazonico	432,000	20	35	84,240
Explorer's Inn	382,500	20	35	74,590
Tambo Lodge	26,250	12	25	7,875
Independent Guides	35,250	15	25	26,000

[a]Figures from tables 26.1 and 26.2.

[b]Source: Tour companies and ACSS.

[c]Percentage of gross revenues taken as profits; source, tour companies and ACSS.

[d]Estimated amount spent on salaries and local materials; based on estimates reported by Manu Nature Tours and Manu Lodge and on costs to Independent Guides.

[e]Information not available for Mayuc tours.

however, are from the area, and boats and construction materials for Manu Lodge are purchased locally.

The park itself receives tourism-generated revenue directly from two sources (park fees and concessions) and indirectly from postvisit donations to private conservation group (table 26.4). The only park fee is a minimal per visit charge ($\approx$ $10 per foreign tourist and $1 per national tourist) collected from all tourists for entering the reserved zone, which generates less than $3,000 per year. Manu Lodge pays a concession fee of 5% of its gross revenues (about $1,000) for its access to 10 ha of reserve land. Indirect tourism-generated support for the park is collected mainly by Conservation Association of the Southern Rainforest (ACSS), a Peruvian group formed in 1984. In their fourth year, ACSS collected more than $13,000 in donations just from tourists who had visited Manu (D. Ricalde, president of ACSS, pers. comm. 1988). This money has been fed directly into park projects, including purchases of equipment, food, and medical care and supplies for park guards, payment for environmental education programs in local schools, applied research on the status of native groups in Manu, and other programs not supported by the park budget. Postvisit contributions thus play an essential role in furthering conservation goals in the park.

Potential for growth. If the cap on visitor numbers is raised in the next year, only infrastructure development will limit tourism growth in Manu. Manu

TABLE 26.4
Current and Projected Revenues to Manu Biosphere Reserve from Tourism Receipts

Income Source	No. Tourists Foreign	National	Total Gross Profits (U.S.$)
1987 earnings			
Park Fees[a]	280	35	2,835
Concession Fee (ML)			1,000
Donations from ACSS[b]			13,000
CORDEMAD Budget[c]			20,000
Total 1987 earnings			36,835
Projected Earnings[d]			
Park Fees[a]	1280	320	13,120
Concession Fees[e]			43,260
Donations from ACSS[b]			50,000
Total projected earnings			106,380

[a]Assumes fee of $10/visit to foreign tourists and $1/visit to national tourists. Numbers of tourists projected from average proportions of foreign and national tourists visiting Manu in 1988.
[b]Source: D. Ricalde, President ACSS (Conservation Association of the Southern Rainforest).
[c]Source: A. Cuentas, Director of Parks, CORDEMAD.
[d]Source: Calculations based on projections made in table 26.5.
[e]Assumes 5% concession fee is assessed to gross revenues of all lodges and organized tours (including Amazonia and Erica Lodges).

Lodge is well under capacity due to ongoing construction and lack of publicity, but when running at full capacity the lodge should gross a minimum of $200,000 per year. The success of the lodge will indicate if enough of a market exists to develop lodges on other oxbow lakes in the reserved zone. Expediciones Manu currently runs near capacity and could increase their business with more boats and guides. Growth in beach camping could increase modestly without negative impacts to wildlife as long as park regulations and guidelines for avoiding disturbing beach-nesting birds are followed (Groom 1986). Adding two more such lodges and continuing beach camping at its current level, nature tourism could gross $992,250 per year in Manu alone (excluding revenues to airlines; table 26.5). If each lodge employed local people and used local supplies, perhaps as much as 60% of this sum could stay within the region. Currently only about 30% of these revenues go into communities immediately adjacent to the Manu Biosphere Reserve.

As with other public lands, the potential of using tourist revenue to offset management costs is an attractive and, we believe, reasonable option for Manu Biosphere Reserve. The current entry fee easily could be raised, but maintaining a two-tiered rate structure is necessary so as not to exclude lower-income Peruvian nationals. Currently only Manu Lodge is paying a concession fee to the government, but the park is now considering charging Expediciones Manu and independent guides a concession fee for their use of the park (A. Cuentas, pers. comm. 1988).

TABLE 26.5
Projected Revenues to Tourist Companies in Manu Biosphere Reserve

Company	No. Tourists	Average Length of Stay (days)	Price/day (U.S.$)	Total Gross Revenues (U.S.$)
Manu Nature Tours	200	7	90	126,000
Manu Lodge	350	7	90	220,500
2 Additional lodges = ML	700	7	90	441,000
Expediciones Manu	250	6	75	112,500
Mayuc	150	6	65	48,750
Independent Guides	150	5	30	22,500
Amazonia Lodge	250	2	30	15,000
Erica Lodge	250	1	20	5,000
Aerosur round-trip Cusco-Boca Manu[a]	900	—	200	180,000
Total gross earnings				1,172,250

[a]Assumes 70% of all visitors to MNT, ML, and lodges = ML and 50% of visitors with Expediciones Manu will fly into Boca Manu.

The success of postvisit donations to the park relies on the quality of the tourist experience in Manu, and tourist satisfaction seems to be substantially higher than in Iquitos or in other parts of Madre de Dios. Currently, only Manu Nature Tours groups regularly are informed of the possibility of making contributions to ACSS. It is likely that increasing the direct solicitation of donations, which is not currently done, will substantially raise this source of revenue.

Simple calculations show that tourism (as we project it) could pay for the operating budget of the park, currently set by the regional government (CORDEMAD) at $20,000. With only a modest increase in tourist volume, $50,000 per year could be raised through a combination of collection of use fees and assessing a 5% gross revenue charge on all lodges and organized tour operations (table 26.4). An additional $50,000 could easily be raised through postvisit contributions. This income would be enough to quintuple the current operating budget of the park without the need for inputs from CORDEMAD.

Concerns With Tourism Development in Madre de Dios

Economic Considerations

Although proving itself worth the risks of investment, nature tourism is not yet an economically important benefit to most of the people in Madre de Dios. A large share of the money brought into the region does not remain there. Most profits from Puerto Maldonado tourism currently return to the two lodge owners in Lima, while little is being reinvested in infrastructure or local employment. The average employee : tourist ratio (1 : 3), for example, is low relative to similar tour operations in Kenya (2 : 1; Western 1986). Explorer's Inn, and to a lesser extent, Cuzco/Amazonico Lodge use nonlocal or foreign managers and guides, while local opportunities are limited mostly to lower-paid positions as cooks, waiters, construction workers, boat drivers, and groundskeepers.

This situation results from a combination of inattention to local problems on the part of some tour companies and a shortage of local guides trained both in nature interpretation and in English. This is unfortunate, because nonlocal guides in Madre de Dios know much less about the forest. Tourists are given a minimum amount of information on only a few plants and animals, and leave with the impression that there is little to see. Local people know a tremendous amount about their surroundings, but have not been trained to deliver that knowledge in a systematic way. Some tourist companies are beginning to recognize that investment in service staff and in the education of local guides is linked with the health of their own business: local perception of the industry as an economic benefit is increased, and a high-quality experience greatly adds to word-of-mouth advertising among satisfied clients.

Tour operations in Madre de Dios do use local materials, and to some extent locally grown food, but local merchants still do not feel sufficiently patronized by tour companies. The supply of many local goods is erratic, and therefore greater awareness of the problem by tourist operators will not necessarily reduce the problem. It is difficult to envision how local suppliers can improve their dependability, since even basic supplies such as sugar and rice can be difficult to obtain in Cuzco. Patronage of local suppliers can also adversely affect availability of goods to local people. Unable to compete with the inflated prices paid by lodges, local people may suffer shortages for even basic goods (Myers 1975; Mishra 1982; Weber 1987). This type of inflation, driven not only by tourism but even more by the gold-mining industry, is already a concern of local people in Madre de Dios. Thus, the influence of a new industry can have many unexpected disruptive effects on the social structure of the local community (DeKadt 1979; Smith 1980; Jenkins and Henry 1982).

Economic benefits to the park at present come mainly through donations by independent conservation groups such as ACSS. This mechanism for indirect funding of the park through independent organizations is one great conservation success of tourism development in Manu Park. Such donations, originating mostly from satisfied customers in Manu, also support conservation projects throughout the region.

Effects on Wildlife and Indigenous People

Although nature tourism encourages the economic valuation of maintaining animal populations and intact forest, it clearly has negative side effects (Pigram 1980). In Manu, many animals (with the exceptions of giant river otters and beach-nesting birds) appear largely unaffected by people, although several species are sensitive to boat traffic and may experience some alterations in their ranging behavior or interruptions in foraging as a result (see Groom 1990). A large volume of otherwise innocuous tourists can disturb wildlife directly through noise and overuse of critical areas (e.g., nesting areas, watering holes), and indirectly through habitat degradation (e.g., pollution, alteration through trail cutting). Lodges outside the Manu Biosphere Reserve have suffered tourist-related reductions in wildlife and habitat degradation. In the past, the two large Maldonado lodges, for example, have sold arrows with macaw feathers, and one of them also sold necklaces with monkey hands to tourists. Vines and trees along trails at one of the lodges are heavily scarred or irreparably damaged by cutting to demonstrate their latex or water-holding properties.

In the Manu Biosphere Reserve, the currently small volume of tourists has not harmed the forest or wildlife at the most heavily used areas along the river or oxbow lakes. However, incidents have been reported of independent guides bow hunting, digging up turtle nests, disturbing beach-nesting birds, and chasing giant otters, swimming jaguars, and tapir so that all members of a tour group see them (see Groom 1990). Disturbance to nesting birds and turtles has been reduced by confining tourist activity to a few beaches, but problems with littering and hunting intensified in 1988 with an increase in independent tour groups, which are poorly organized and unregulated (Groom 1990). A proposal under consideration would have all tour guides entering Manu Park take a short course in park regulations and basic ecology, as is required of guides in the Galapagos (see De Groot 1983).

A particularly sensitive problem in Manu Park is how to handle interactions between tourists and native peoples. At present the park includes four contacted native groups, two of which (Machiguenga and Piro) are in settlements accessible by river. Several tours in the early 1980s visited a Machiguenga settlement, but such contact is now forbidden under park policy (G. Ruiz, pers. comm. 1988). People of that community and of a Piro/Machiguenga settlement in the cultural zone, however, have expressed interest in tourist visits and the potential income from selling ceramics and other handicrafts (H. Kaplan, pers. comm. 1988). The park is cautious about encouraging such interactions for fear of introducing outside diseases and of negatively affecting cultural traditions through participation in Western-style market activities. The introduction of indigenous peoples to diseases and cash economies has been a thorny issue throughout Latin America (Smith 1980; Halffter 1981).

It should be added that these concerns are not limited to indigenous peoples, but can create unforeseen stresses in any local community. In addition to the problems already mentioned, jealousies or power asymmetries from inequitable distribution of profits, greater movements between communities, and stresses from interacting with foreign tourists can cause a variety of social problems (DeKadt 1979; Smith 1980; Jenkins and Henry 1982). Finding ways to limit or mitigate social stresses that arise from tourism activity challenges not only national, regional, and local governments, but also tour companies. Here, the advice of sociologists and anthropologists must be sought and incorporated into tourism development (Smith 1980).

Nature Tourism in Developing Countries in Latin America

The economic success of nature tourism will depend on several factors: (1) the attractiveness of the natural area and its wildlife, and the degree to which the wildlife is easily seen, (2) the ease of access to the area and the comfort of the accommodations, and (3) the quality of nature interpretation and other guided services (Ferrario 1980). In addition, the success of nature tourism in fostering a sustainable industry and promoting habitat and wildlife conservation depends on the compatibility of tourism and wildlife conservation, and on whether tourism is perceived as a benefit at local and national levels.

Increasing the Attractiveness of Latin America Sites

One reason for the huge success of nature tourism in East Africa is that East African plains mammals are both extremely attractive to the public and easy to observe. Manu Biosphere Reserve offers a wide diversity of species that, while not as visible or spectacular as their East African counterparts, are nevertheless plentiful and diverse. Indeed, few tropical forest sites in Latin America will be able to equal Manu in its attractiveness to tourists. Other ecosystems in Latin America, such as the Brazilian pantanal, the Venezualan llanos, and similar open, wildlife-rich habitats have excellent visibility of attractive wildlife and are thus also likely to be successful nature tourism centers. In addition, unique sites, such as the Galapagos, are highly diverse and undisturbed.

Ultimately, it is possible that only a few sites across Latin America will be able to support large-scale nature tourism. Yet, skillful marketing could increase the attractiveness of many places. Individual Amazonian species, while not as well known as elephants and lions, could be publicized to increase their value. Thresher (1981) has estimated the worth of a single wild male lion to be $500,000 (which, given inflation and even greater interest in tourism in East Africa now, is a conservative value). We estimate that one jaguar, baited in order to be seen dependably by tourists, would increase revenues coming to Madre de Dios by at least a comparable value. Equally spectacular and rare sights such as spectacled bears, giant otters, harpy eagle nests, or salt licks that attract hundreds of macaws and parrots, could have nearly equal "worth" to the nature tourism industry of Latin America.

Infrastructure Improvements to Sustain Tourism to Natural Areas

A successful tour operation usually requires a lodge that is sufficiently comfortable to attract a wide variety of tourists. Good infrastructure support, consisting of (1) paved, reliable roads, (2) telephone or radio contact for logistics and emergencies, and (3) failsafe coordination of travel, housing, and meals is also crucial to the success of any tourist venture (Gray 1981). Many people would never consider going to Manu because it involves a relatively arduous trip, although they will go to Puerto Maldonado or Iquitos because they are accessible by air. The costs of infrastructure development, however, can be high, although they are often lower than for alternative industries (e.g., large-scale agriculture) that require machinery and other imported goods.

The capital necessary to begin a tourism project in the rainforest is $10,000 to $50,000, sums that are sufficiently large to pose an immediate barrier to local entrepreneurs (Gray 1981; Jenkins 1982a; Weber 1987). To overcome this barrier, economic support and guidance from governments and organizations cognizant of tourism's strengths and weaknesses is necessary (Jenkins and Henry 1982). Unfortunately, governmental subsidies are rarely targeted for tourism development (in Peru these are chiefly limited to tax incentives: International Tourism Reports 1988), although tourism is probably a more sound investment than some businesses that are currently heavily subsidized (e.g., cattle ranching, some agriculture). Thus, an important first step is for national governments to expand loans, grants, and other support for tourism development. Nongovernmental organizations (NGOs) can provide support to tourism projects, while stipulating that they be planned carefully to enhance local participation, conservation, and educational goals. Finally, foreign NGOs can contribute by playing a greater role in advising national projects or in training local entrepreneurs to avoid the financial, environmental, and sociological pitfalls of nature tourism (Jenkins and Henry 1982).

Environmental Protection

Creating the infrastructure to promote tourism can create problems for protected areas. Immigrants, attracted by employment opportunities or the opening of access roads, may abuse lands surrounding and within a park (Western 1986). At the present time, the majority of immigrants to southeastern Peru come not for tourism but for gold-mining and government supported projects such as cattle ranching and agriculture, which all promote land conversion. Madre de Dios is not an area with intense land pressures or severe conflicts between local needs and park preservation, as in Africa or Asia, where local people cut "protected" forest for firewood (Western and Henry 1979) or are resentful of the competition of large wild animals with their cattle at water holes (Western 1986). As such problems become more significant in Latin America, tourism may offer one of the most sustainable uses of land by requiring a minimal amount of forest conversion.

Littering, disturbance to wildlife, uncontrolled hunting, and species introductions can result from tourism programs that are underrregulated or oversubscribed (Nolan 1979; Beekhuis 1981). For example, the Galapagos—considered a model of nature tourism planning—is currently visited by more people than is legally permitted and is considered safe for the ecology of the islands (De Groot 1983). Tourists and guides in the Galapagos have not followed or enforced park rules designed to protect the wildlife and flora of the islands. One direct way of limiting environmental degradation due to tourism is by improving the training of guides. Guides knowledgeable of park regulations and of the impact of tourists on ecosystems can help to determine whether nature tourism projects are constructive or destructive. Training of guides should be supported by tour companies and by governmental and nongovernmental programs.

Improving Local Perceptions and Participation in Ecotourism

Exporting tourism revenues from a local area to the capital city or abroad eliminates the opportunity to build local support for land and wildlife preservation. It is vital that tour operators recognize the need to foster good relations and to promote economic and social cooperation with local communities to protect the park or other natural area upon which their success depends. It may be necessary for local or national governments to impose quotas for local hiring or to encourage some other means of profit sharing with local communities. Whenever possible, park policies should encourage and facilitate the participation or leadership of local and indigenous people in the tourism industry, particularly by subsidizing infrastructure development.

The degree to which local people can be assimilated into tour operations is often limited by their knowledge of tourist wants and needs, natural history, or foreign languages. Overcoming this problem may require novel approaches, such as using interpreters to communicate the knowledge of local or indigenous people to tourists. Many guides could learn English or other foreign languages under the support of government programs or grants from nongovernmental conservation organizations or by the tourist companies themselves. Tour companies should be willing to finance some education of their guides, and the use of protected areas should be limited to groups that are guided by registered people who meet certain standards of knowledge.

Local communities should be shown both how wildlife tourism benefits them economically and how tourism is dependent on good conservation practices. The indirect benefits of ecotourism must be highlighted, including the incidental expenditures by tourists in local towns, watershed protection, and other benefits of the conservation of animal and plant resources. Any indirect revenues that go to the local community must be shown to depend on intact forest and animal populations. At this time, slide shows about the benefits of conservation and appropriate development options for the southern rainforest are being given by members of ACSS in Puerto Maldonado, Cuzco, and elsewhere in southeastern Peru.

Initially, emphasis should be placed on pursuing nature tourism on a small scale in order to achieve the dual development and conservation goals described in this chapter. The successes of the Madre de Dios example come in part from the low number of tourists visiting the area and the slow development of the industry. Generally speaking, the more slowly and carefully tourist operations begin, the more equitably profits are distributed, and the greater the inputs of local food, labor, and materials, the more likely these projects are to succeed financially and foster conservation and community development (Smith 1980; Jenkins 1982b).

Conclusions

Nature tourism is a promising means of achieving sustainable development while preserving natural areas in Latin America. Examples of successful tourist operations that are managed by local people are increasing (e.g., Saglio 1979), and each provides particular lessons. In Madre de Dios these lessons come mostly from the successes and shortcomings of tourism in the Madre de Dios Biosphere Reserve and from the demonstration of how accessible areas (the lodges in Puerto Maldonado) can be highly profitable, even when not managed optimally. The slow introduction of tourism to Manu, the careful monitoring of tourism's effects on the habitat, wildlife, and people in and surrounding the reserve, and the provision of alternatives to large infrastructure investments (such as permitting beach camping and providing trails to oxbow lakes), have all contributed to a greater level of participation by local people than in most nature tourism projects. As tourism to Manu Biosphere Reserve continues to grow, we hope it can augment the benefits to local people as well as maintain its current low level of impact to the reserve and that it will serve as a model for the development of healthy nature tourism projects throughout Latin America. As with most sustainable development projects, nature tourism will require guidance and support from local people, governments, and nongovernmental agencies to achieve its goals.

Acknowledgments

We gratefully acknowledge the following individuals for their contributions: D. Ricalde, A. W. Weber, W. Henry, J. Laarman, G. Mellor, B. Gomez, G. Ruiz, L. Yallico, A. Cuentas, R. T. Devane, J. Koechlin von Stein, M. Gunther, H. Pepper, C. Bueno, S. Yabar, K. Renton, H. Kaplan, J. Serra, and spokespersons from the Association of Canoeing Companies of Cuzco (ASEC) and the Peruvian Ministry of Industry, Tourism and Integration (MITI). We also thank M. Romero, Director General of Forestry and Fauna of the Ministry of Agriculture, and A. Castillo and A. Cuentas of the Corporation for Development of Madre de Dios for permission to do research in Manu National Park. D. Harrison prepared the map of Madre de Dios.

This project was supported by National Science Foundation Graduate Fellowships (MJG, RDP), a Presidential Graduate Fellowship from the University of Florida (RDP), and Wildlife Conservation International (WCI), a division of New York Zoological Society (CAM). Any opinions, findings, conclusions, or recommendations expressed in this publication are those of the authors and do not necessarily reflect the views of the National Science Foundation, the University of Florida, or WCI.

Part 7

The Future

27

Sustainable Harvest of Neotropical Forest Mammals

JOHN G. ROBINSON AND KENT H. REDFORD

If humans are to continue to be able to use the products of neotropical forests, it is imperative that rates of harvest of these resources not exceed rates of production. If resources are overexploited, they will become depleted. One important resource in neotropical forests is game. In this chapter, we are concerned with identifying sustainable harvest rates of mammals living in neotropical forests. Both Indian and colonist groups living in neotropical forests rely extensively on wild game, especially mammalian game (see review in Redford and Robinson 1987). Yet as human populations increase, as settlements become larger and more permanent, as hunting technologies improve, as forest habitat is degraded, and as market participation increases, overexploitation of wildlife populations leads to resource depletion and the loss of an important source of animal protein. Cultural regulation of hunting can prevent or alleviate game overexploitation (e.g., Posey 1982; Smith 1983; Balee 1985; Vickers this volume), but these systems are not surviving in most regions. We need to develop alternate methods of game management in the neotropics, and the first step is to identify the sustainable levels of harvest from tropical forests.

The concept of the sustainable harvest of wildlife embodies two requirements. The first is that the maximum production from the population for human use is achieved. The second requirement is that the wildlife populations will not be reduced to levels at which the species is vulnerable to local extinction or the ecosystem functioning is affected. If either of these requirements is violated, a harvested population can be considered depleted. These definitions of sustainability and depletion are ambiguous and difficult to apply to real populations, but they were codifed in the Marine Mammal Protection Act and ratified by the U.S. Congress in 1969 (see Bean 1983), which defined an optimum sustainable population as follows:

Optimum sustainable population means, with respect to any population stock, the number of animals which will result in the maximum productivity of the population or the species, keeping in mind the carrying capacity of the habitat and the health of the ecosystem of which they form a constituent element.

A revision of this act in 1981 explicitly defined depletion as any population under the "optimum sustainable population" level. In effect, a sustainable harvest is one in which the resource is not depleted. Sustainable harvest requires both the maintenance of the resource so that it can be exploited for human welfare, and the conservation of the species being exploited and the biological community in which it lives.

These two requirements are not in conflict: human welfare in these forest ecosystems depends on the maintenance of the biological community. A harvest that is not ecologically sustainable cannot be economically sustainable or socially realistic. Neither is a concern for the conservation of the biological community antithetical to the harvest of wildlife species. It is becoming increasingly clear that, except for those in reserves, wildlife populations are and will be harvested. Even protected populations are vulnerable: Many mammal species will be unable to survive in the long term if isolated in the existing reserves and national parks in Latin America. Many parks, even the largest ones, will be too small to support viable poulations of large-bodied species, especially those at high tropic levels (Redford and Robinson in press). Many forest species will survive only in landscapes that include both protected areas and areas where wildlife populations are hunted. In many cases, the genetic and demographic viability of a species will be maintained only when populations in both types of areas are integrated.

We develop a simple model to provide a first estimate of harvest rates for different forest mammal species. We focus on fourteen mammalian species that traditionally have been important to subsistence hunters. We first calculated maximum production (in numbers of animals per square kilometer). This is the production that might be generated by a natural population under the best of all possible environmental conditions. This calculation required us to derive measures of population density and intrinsic rate of natural increase for each of these species. We then calculated potential harvest (in numbers of animals per square kilometer) for the different species. This is the optimum sustainable harvest expected if the production is at a maximum and harvesting has the minimum effect on the natural population.

Calculation of Production

For each species, the model required information on the population density at carrying capacity, the maximum rate of population increase, and the density that produces the maximum sustainable yield. The following variables were incorporated into the model.

The *actual density* (D_1) of a species is the number of animals (both adult and juvenile) recorded per square kilometer in appropriate habitat. Robinson and Redford (1986a) tabulated 480 density estimates of 103 neotropical forest mammal species from the literature. Average densities for each species were then calculated with the following restrictions: Most densities were estimated by different authors at different locations, but we also included estimates by different authors at the same location. Different estimates by the same author at the same location were averaged to produce a single estimate, and we took the midpoint if a range of values was presented. All included densities were from undisturbed, nonhunted, or lightly hunted sites so that they are the best approximation of the maximum density that could be carried in a given habitat.

The *predicted density* (D_2) was the species density (number animals/km²) predicted from a linear regression of $\log_{10}$ population density against $\log_{10}$ body mass for samples of neotropical forest mammals broken into dietary categories (see Robinson and Redford 1986a). Population densities declined with body mass within each of seven dietary categories: herbivore-browser, frugivore-herbivore, frugivore-granivore, frugivore-omnivore, insectivore-omnivore, myrmecophage, and carnivore. At a specified body mass, species in dietary categories at low trophic levels and with broad diets (categories at the beginning of this list) occurred at higher densities than species at high trophic levels and with restricted diets. Regression equations of $\log_{10}$ population density against $\log_{10}$ body mass accounted for between 31% and 84% of the variation within dietary categories.

The *intrinsic rate of natural increase* (r_{max}) of a population is the highest rate of increase that can be attained by a population not limited by food, space, resource competition, or predation. Robinson and Redford (1986b) estimated this value for thirty-nine neotropical forest mammal species using Cole's (1954) equation:

$$1 = e^{-r_{max}} + be^{-r_{max}(a)} - be^{-r_{max}w + 1}$$

where a is the age of first reproduction, w is the age of last reproduction, and b is the annual birth rate of female offspring. This formulation assumes no mortality in the population. The error introduced by this assumption is small if mortality is not significant before the age of first reproduction.

The *maximum finite rate of increase* (λ_{max}) is the exponential of the intrinsic rate of natural increase $(e_{r_{max}})$, and is the increase in the population size from time to time $t + 1$. Thus if time is measured in years, a population that is only replacing itself will have a finite rate of increase of 1.0, while a population that is doubling every year will have a rate of 2.0. The rate of population increase depends particularly on the number of adult females reproducing and their average birth rate (number offspring produced per adult female in a year).

Production (P) is defined as the addition to the population (through births and immigrations), whether these animals leave (through deaths and emigrations) or survive to the end of the specified time period (in this case one year).

Our simple model only considers the number of animals, not their size (see Banse and Mosher 1980). Production therefore can be calculated as

$$P = N_{t+1} - N_t \qquad (1)$$

where N_{t+1} is the population size at time $t+1$ assuming no natural mortality or harvest, and N_t is the population size at time t. P_{max}, the maximum possible production, will be achieved when

$$N_{t+1} = \lambda_{max} N_t \qquad (2)$$

As independent verification of this method of estimating production, we used two other empirically calculated formulae to estimate production. Both equations included the increase in size in their definition of production. In the first, Banse and Mosher's (1980) calculated an equation relating production, biomass, and body mass of a species. Based on a sample of seven mammalian species (four ungulates, two rodents, and the elephant), Banse and Mosher derived the following equation:

$$\log_{10}(P/B) = 1.11 + (-0.33)\log_{10}(M)$$

where P includes both the addition of more animals and also increases in their average size, M is the body mass (g) of the species averaging adults of both sexes, and B is the mean biomass calculated as population density (D_2 was used here) times body mass. In this equation, production is therefore determined solely by the body mass of the species and its population density. The effect of variation in the rate of increase of different species of comparable size (see Robinson and Redford 1986b) is not considered. In the second formula, Western (1983) developed an equation relating production to the body mass of a species:

$$P = 13.8 M^{0.67}$$

the derivation of this equation used a larger sample of mammal species (twenty-one, including herbivores, carnivores, and omnivores) but actual data on production was not available, and Western indirectly estimated production using finite birthrate (percentage of young born each year to the study population). Production values using this equation therefore are even more general than those from the Banse and Mosher equation.

To calculate P_{max} for the fourteen species, we made the following conservative assumptions and choices:

1. Predicted densities would be better approximations of the density of a species than the observed densities. Observed density estimates are notoriously unreliable. Because our sample sizes for many species are small, the mean observed densities we calculated were very sensitive to single outlier values. Predicted densities incorporate the estimates of the densities of other species

in a dietary category and thus minimize the deviations introduced by these single values. Predicted values tended to be less extreme and possibly more realistic. The assumption, of course, is that body mass and diet are excellent predictors of population density, and that variation around the regression line is the result of errors in the mean densities rather than departures by certain species from the group norm.

In two cases, however, we used observed mean densities rather than predicted densities. These two exceptions were *Dasypus novemcinctus* and *Myoprocta* spp. The armadillo *D. novemcinctus* commonly occurs at higher densities than predicted, and the average density was based on eight reliable estimates. Acouchis *Myoprocta* do not seem to attain the densities predicted from their body mass and diet.

2. Maximum production would be achieved when the population density (N_t) was at 60% of carrying capacity (0.6 K). In most studied populations, actual production varies with population density. Birth rate generally increases with a decreasing population density, presumably through a decrease in intraspecific competition. If birth rate does exhibit this density dependence, at some density below the habitat's carrying capacity ($< 1.0\ K$) the actual rate of increase of the population is maximized ($\lambda = \lambda_{max}$). If the population growth of a species approximates the logistic growth curve, this density will be close to 0.5 K. In species in which animals do not breed until relatively late in life, population growth will not approximate the logistic growth curve and this density will be closer to the carrying capacity (densities in the range of 0.65 K to 0.90 K have been suggested) (Eberhardt 1977; 1981; Fowler 1981; Smith 1984; but see Fredin 1984).

3. The predicted densities, which were derived from censuses of populations in lightly hunted or nonhunted areas, were close to or at the carrying capacity for each species in neotropical forest ($D_2 = K$).

4. We therefore calculated production assuming a population at 0.6K:

$$P_{max} = (0.6\ D_2 \times \lambda_{max}) - 0.6\ D_2 \tag{3}$$

Subtracting 0.6 D_2 maintains the population at the same density.

In all cases but two, our calculations were based on production values derived from this equation. In two cases, *Sciurus* spp. and *Myoprocta* spp., we did not have an estimate of λ, and therefore we used the production values from the Banse and Mosher equation, assuming a standing density of 0.6 D_2.

Calculation of Harvest

The *harvest* (H) is the number of animals of a species removed by humans per square kilometer in every year. In a table population, all production must go into either harvest or natural mortality. Figure 27.1 (adapted from Harris and Kochel 1981) illustrates a population subject to little harvesting. The standing

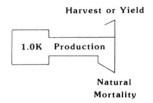

Figure 27.1. Interrelations among production, harvest, and natural mortality in a stable natural population at carrying capacity. A population at a given density (in this case 1.0 K) will have a specified production. Harvest and natural mortality together account for all of the production.

population, at a density equal to the carrying capacity of the habitat, produces "excess" animals, and almost all the production goes into natural mortality.

In a population subject to harvest, these relationships change. The standing population is reduced by the harvest. Some production is going into harvest, so the proportion going into natural mortality is reduced. Accordingly, the number of animals that can be harvested without *altering the size of the standing population* depends on the number of animals being produced and the proportion of those animals that die naturally and so cannot be harvested. In our model, the number of animals being produced is the production (P). In the extreme case,

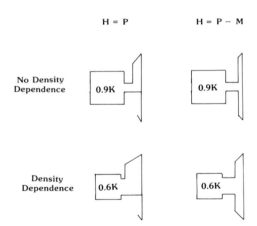

Figure 27.2. Four examples of the effect of density dependence (vertical axis) and whether harvest is compensatory or additive (horizontal axis) on production and harvest. Diagram as in figure 27.1, with the size of the box proportional to population density and the size of the output arrow proportional to production. The proportions of production which go into harvest and natural mortality are also reflected in the size of the arrows. If production does not vary with population density, maximum harvest will be achieved by keeping the population as close to carrying capacity as possible (in this illustration at 0.9 K). If production increases with a lowering of population density, harvest will be maximized at some lower density (in this illustration at 0.6 K). The proportion of production that can be channelled into harvest depends on whether harvest compensated for natural mortality, or is additive to it.

harvest (H) is maximized when it only takes the proportion of animals that would have died anyway and thus eliminates natural mortality (M). In this case, harvest takes all the production ($H = P$). In the more realistic case, harvest only takes a proportion of the production ($H = P - M$).

We illustrate four examples of how populations might respond to harvesting in figure 27.2. If populations exhibit no density dependence, then production would be maximized by keeping the harvested populations at densities as close to the carrying capacity as possible (in this illustration at a density of 0.9 K). If populations do exhibit density dependence, then production would be maximized at some lower density (in this illustration at 0.6 K). Harvests are high when natural mortality is low. Maximum harvest is therefore achieved with maximum production and little natural mortality (in this illustration when $H = P$ and density $= 0.6\ K$).

Unfortunately, little is known about the response of neotropical forest mammal species to harvesting. Accordingly we made the following assumptions:

1. A harvested population will have a lower density than that observed in un-hunted or lightly hunted habitats, and we assumed that this density would not fall below 60% of carrying capacity (0.6 K). As we assumed that maximum productivity is also achieved at 0.6 K, this assumes that harvested populations can be maintained at or above the density of maximum productivity.
2. The average lifespan of a species is a good index of the extent to which harvest takes animals that would have died anyway. We assumed that in short-lived species, natural annual mortality is high, and therefore harvest can take a higher proportion of the production without reducing the standing population. In long-lived species, this mortality is low, and harvest must take a lower proportion of production. To have a sustainable harvest, the rate of harvest must be such that the population will remain stable through time. We arbitrarily divided species into three categories: long-lived species whose age of last reproduction was 10 years or greater, short-lived species whose age of last reproduction was at least 5 years but less than 10, and very short-lived species whose age of last reproduction was less than 5 years. We assumed that harvest could take 60% of the production in very short-lived species, 40% in short-lived species, and 20% in long-lived species. These numbers fall within the range considered reasonable for other species. (For birds: Anderson and Burnham 1976; Roseberry 1979; Nichols and Haramis 1980; Gomez-Dallmeier, this volume. For mammals: Eltringham 1984; Taylor et al. 1987).

Results

Table 27.1 presents the values of body mass, density, and rate of increase

TABLE 27.1
Calculation of Potential Production

	Body Mass (g)	Average Density (no./km²)	Predicted Density (no./km²)	r_{max}	λ_{max}	Production (no./km²)	Production (no./km²)[a]	Production (no./km²)[b]
Primates								
Cebus apella	3,445	12.42	9.82	.14	1.15	.88	4.52	4.83
Alouatta spp.	6,466	34.22	19.32	.16	1.17	1.97	7.22	7.73
Ateles spp.	7,592	13.35	16.60	.08	1.08	.80	5.88	6.30
Lagothrix lagothricha	10,000	10.32	13.18	.14	1.15	1.19	4.26	4.57
Edentates								
Dasypus novemcinctus	3,544	21.85	4.92	.69	1.99	12.98	9.96	10.67
Rodents								
Sciurus spp.	338	98.90	75.50				74.72	80.04
Myoprocta spp.	552	8.60	56.53				7.24	7.75
Dasyprocta spp.	2,844	19.66	18.70	1.10	3.00	22.44	9.12	9.82
Agouti paca	8,227	27.51	11.49	.67	1.95	6.56	3.96	4.25
Ungulates								
Tapirus terrestris	148,950	1.61	1.22	.20	1.22	.16	.16	.17
Tayassu pecari	28,550	4.94	5.24	.84	2.32	4.16	1.20	1.28
Tayassu tajacu	17,520	11.83	8.05	1.25	3.49	12.03	2.17	2.32
Mazama americana	26,100	10.47	5.67	.40	1.49	1.67	1.33	1.43
Mazama gouazoubira	17,350	10.44	8.12	.49	1.63	3.07	2.19	2.35

[a]Method of Banse and Mosher 1980.
[b]Method of Western 1983.

used to calculate average production in numbers of animals produced per square kilometer over the course of a year. Values for population densities and rates of increase are for relatively undisturbed sites and for populations growth not limited by resources respectively, so the calculated production values probably would not be attained at most sites.

Production values calculated using equation (3) generally vary inversely with the body mass of the species. This results from the inverse relationships between body mass and average population density (Robinson and Redford 1986a) and between body mass and rates of increase (Robinson and Redford 1986b). For larger-bodied species, the densities and rates of increase of populations are lower and therefore in general so are their production rates. However, there is also an effect of phylogeny, which arises through the effect of phylogeny on rates of increase (Robinson and Redford 1986b). Primates have lower rates of population increase than that predicted from their body mass, while rodents and ungulates have higher rates. This translates into production values: Primates have a much lower maximum production than that expected from their body mass, while rodents and ungulates have a higher maximum production. Both species of peccary have unexpectedly high maximum production values. This effect is evident when production values from our equation are compared to the more general empirical equations derived by Banse and Mosher (1980) and Western (1983), which did not incorporate species-specific variation in rates of population increase. While all production values are within the same order of magnitude, our calculated values for primates are much lower than those indicated by the general models, and our values for rodents and peccary are much higher. For instance, our production value for *Cebus apella* is more than five times lower than that expected from the general Banse and Mosher equation, while our production value for *Tayassu tajacu* is almost six times higher than that predicted from the general equation.

All the maximum production values are based on single values of population density and rate of population increase, but both parameters are highly variable in natural populations. To explore how this variation affects production values, we examined one case, that of the white-lipped peccary *Tayassu pecari* (fig. 27.3) in more detail. Figure 27.4 plots production against population density at four values of λ. Density values varied from one to twelve individuals per square kilometer, the range of variation recorded in our sample of densities. We plotted values of λ from 1.0 to 2.32. When the finite rate of increase of a population is 1.0, the population is stable, and any harvest will decrease the popu-

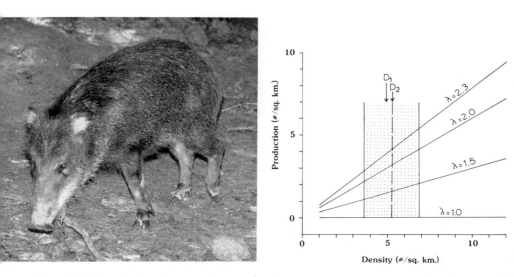

Figure 27.3. The white-lipped peccary (*Tayassu pecari*).

Figure 27.4. Variation in potential production of white-lipped peccary *Tayassu pecari* as it depends on population density and finite rate of population increase (λ). Plotted are the average observed density for this species (D_1), the predicted density (D_2), and the 95% confidence limits for the dietary class.

lation. The finite rate of increase of 2.32 was the maximum possible. Production using these constraints can vary from 0 to about 9 animals per square kilometer. However, we also plot the predicted density for this species and the 95% confidence limits for the dietary class (from Robinson and Redford 1986a). If these limits are taken as likely densities, then production can vary from 0 to a little over 5 animals per square kilometer. Production from equation 3 was 4.16 individuals per square kilometer.

In table 27.2, we present the potential harvest figures for the fourteen species. If harvest is to be sustainable, only a proportion of the number of animals that are produced per square kilometer can be harvested, and that proportion varies with the longevity of the species. Few primates are produced, and only a small fraction can be harvested without seriously reducing the population. Production of rodents is generally high, but in this sample both production and longevity depend strongly on body mass, so harvest falls quickly with increasing body mass. Production of the two peccary is extremely high, and potential harvest is only as low as it is because both species are relatively long-lived. Brocket deer have lower production than the peccary but also lower longevity, so potential harvest is high and comparable to that of the peccary.

If potential harvest is presented as live weight of game that might be harvested per square kilometer, it is evident that the species with the greatest potential for harvest are the medium-sized rodents, the brocket deer, and especially

TABLE 27.2
Calculation of Potential Harvest

	Production (no./km^2)	Age of last reproduction (yr)	Life expectancy	Harvest (no./km^2)	Harvest (kg/km^2)
Primates					
Cebus apella	.88	25	long	.18	.62
Alouatta spp.	1.97	20	long	.39	2.52
Ateles spp.	.80	25	long	.16	1.22
Lagothrix lagothricha	1.19	20	long	.24	2.40
Edentates					
Dasypus novemcinctus	12.98	8	short	5.19	18.40
Rodents					
Sciurus spp.	74.72[a]	<5	very short	44.83	15.52
Myoprocta spp.	7.24[a]	<5	very short	4.34	2.40
Dasyprocta spp.	22.44	10	short	8.98	25.54
Agouti paca	6.56	12	long	1.31	10.78
Ungulates					
Tapirus terrestris	.16	25	long	.03	4.47
Tayassu pecari	4.16	13	long	.83	23.70
Tayassu tajacu	12.03	13	long	2.41	42.22
Mazama americana	1.67	8	short	.67	17.49
Mazama gouazoubira	3.07	7	short	1.23	21.34

[a]Production values for Sciurus and Myoprocta derived from Banse and Mosher's equation.

the peccaries. All of these species have high production and medium to large body masses. The potential harvest of primates by weight is small; production of these species is low and animals are not large bodied.

Discussion

The validity of this harvest model depends on the validity of the various assumptions, the two most important of which are the density dependence of population growth and the proportion of the production that can be taken by the harvest without depleting the standing population. Few field studies have generated data on whether the rate of population increase of neotropical forest species is density dependent. The best published data set concerns a mantled howler monkey (*Alouatta palliata*) population on Barro Colorado Island, Panama, which has been followed since 1932. Following a yellow fever epidemic in 1949, the population was reduced to about 240 animals. Between 1951 and 1959, when the population reached 814 animals, the annual growth rate was 16.7%. Between 1960 and 1967, when the population reached about 1,100, the growth rate had dropped to approximately 4%. During the 1970s, the annual population growth rate averaged 1.5% (Froehlich, Thorington, and Otis 1981). These data indicate a pronounced density dependence, as do unpublished results from a wedge-capped capuchin monkey (*Cebus olivaceus*) population in central Venezuela, but comparable data for other species are not available.

Data on the proportion of production which can be channelled into harvest are also not available. One indirect, and only suggestive, approach is to examine the distribution of weights of hunted animals and compare this to the distribution of weights in a nonhunted population. A concordance between the two distributions would strengthen the argument that hunting was taking animals that would have died anyway and suggest that hunting can take a high proportion of the total production. Natural mortality in large mammals generally follows a U-shaped curve, with high mortality in both young and old animals, but little mortality in juveniles and young adults (Caughley 1977). Hunting mortality of neotropical forest species does not follow the same curve. An example is plotted in figure 27.5, which plots the distribution of capuchin monkey *Cebus apella* weights taken by Aché indians in Paraguay (data from Hill, Kaplan, Hurtado, and Hawkes, pers. comm. 1988). This distribution can be compared to the distribution of natural mortality in an undisturbed population of *Cebus olivaceus* (Robinson 1988). The large fraction of juvenile animals in the hunting distribution suggests that hunting is taking animals that would not necessarily have died. Our estimate that 20% of the production of these long-lived species can be harvested therefore seems appropriate. Comparable data for the shorter-lived species are not available.

The accuracy of the potential harvest values depends on the accuracy of the measurements of body mass, population density, and rate of population in-

Figure 27.5. Distribution by weight
of capuchin monkeys (*Cebus apella*)
hunted by Aché indians in Paraguay
(data from Hill, Kaplan, Hurtado, and
Hawkes, pers. comm. 1988).

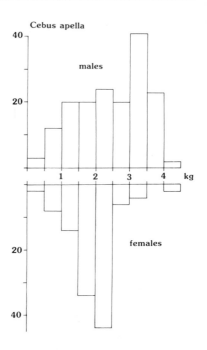

crease. Our body mass measurements (see Robinson and Redford 1986a) were based on a large sample, many of which were collected in the field from harvested populations. Population density estimates, on the other hand, are notoriously inaccurate. Different methodologies generate different results (e.g., Defler and Pintor 1985). The density estimate is usually the largest numerical contribution to our model, so an error in this estimate will generate the largest error in the final harvest value. We used conservative estimates of population density, first taking average values for each species, then deriving a predicted value from the regression of the averages from a number of different species in the same dietary category. Estimates of the rate of population increase were based on estimates of three demographic parameters. The calculation of r_{max} was most sensitive to the age of first reproduction and the annual birth rate of female offspring. Both parameters have been measured for many species in both wild and captive conditions.

The applicability of the results presented in this chapter to a specific site depends on the extent to which body mass, population density, and rate of population increase vary with location. Variation in body mass with area has been documented in a large number of species. For instance, body mass of the mantled howler *Alouatta palliata* varies significantly between the evergreen tropical forest on Barrow Colorado Island, Panama, and the dry tropical forest of Guanacaste province, Costa Rica. At the former, the body mass of fifteen adult females averaged 6,600 g (Thorington, Rudran, and Maek 1979), while at the latter, twenty-four adult females averaged 4,026 g (Glander 1980). Variation in population density has also been well documented. Thirteen density estimates for *Alouatta palliata* averaged 47.6 individuals/km² with a standard deviation of 35.8 individuals/km² and a range from 5.0 to 111.0 individuals/km² (Robinson and Redford 1986a). Some of this variation is undoubtedly the result of inaccuracies in estimation, but much of it probably derives from site-specific variation. Different habitats support different densities of a given species, presumably because they differ in the resources available to animals or in the presence of competing species. Variation in rates of population increase with site are undoubtedly significant but have not been documented.

We can conclude that while data on the characteristics and response to harvest of neotropical forest species are inadequate, the assumptions and estimates in the model are concordant with productivity and harvest information from other ecosystems. A strong caution is indicated however. The potential harvest of these fourteen species indicated by our model is certainly higher than the harvests possible at most sites. Our harvest values incorporate our calculation of maximum productivity. This calculation was based on population density values, which although averages, were generally collected at optimal locations. Most censuses were by field biologists who generally are biased toward locations where animal densities are higher than normal. This calculation also used the *maximum* rates of population increase, and these rates are not expected to be reached in anything except the most optimal habitats.

This model should not be used to generate single-species harvesting schedules of neotropical forest species for a number of reasons. First, the theoretical and practical difficulties of using single-species yield models in even the simpler temperate ecosystems have been demonstrated (Larkin 1977; Beddington and May 1977; Beddington 1980; Rapport, Reiger, and Hutchinson 1985; Pimm 1986). Second, harvesting schedules assume that harvest rates and population densities can be closely monitored and regulated. Data are available on harvest rates at a number of neotropical forest sites (see Redford and Robinson 1987) but in no case have population densities been estimated at the same site. Long-term monitoring and regulation of populations and harvests is probably unrealistic at most sites in Latin America. Third, the approach assumes that wildlife populations could be managed at densities close to those which would produce sustainable yields. In the neotropics those wildlife populations not already protected in reserves, frequently have been hunted to densities far below carrying capacity. For instance, figure 27.6 compares primate densities from lightly hunted areas in Bolivia and Peru to those which have been more heavily hunted. These data from Freese et al. (1982) indicate that densities for many species are much lower than 0.6 K, and that large-bodied species have already been extirpated from hunted areas. Before this approach can be implemented, populations in many areas must be protected and allowed to recover.

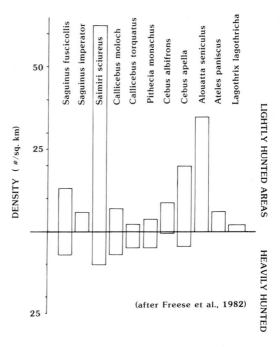

Figure 27.6. Density of primates in Bolivia and Peru in both lightly and heavily hunted areas (after Freese et al. 1982).

What the model can do is to provide a first assessment of the impact of hunting on wildlife populations. It can be used in the absence of detailed information on population densities. Actual harvest data can be quickly collected from human informants and compared to potential harvest values generated by the model. If actual harvest approaches or exceeds potential harvest, surveys of wildlife populations and close monitoring of the harvesting are immediately indicated. Two examples illustrate the approach.

The most complete data set for these purposes has been provided by Bill Vickers in a thorough study of the Siona-Secoya Indians in north-eastern Ecuador. The studied population hunted over an area of approximately 2,500 km², but 93% of hunting man-days were located in a smaller hunting range of 1,150 km², and 81% were located in a core area of 590 km² (Vickers, this volume). Between 1973 and 1975, during the first years of their village's existence, Siona-Secoya hunters annually harvested 662 woolly monkeys (*Lagothrix lagothricha*), 468 white-lipped peccary (*Tayassu pecari*), and 433 collared peccary (*T. tajacu*) (Vickers 1980). Based on trends in hunting yields over 10 years, Vickers (this volume) suggests that the harvest of woolly monkeys is sustainable within the 1,150 km² hunting range but possibly not within the 590 km² core area. He suggests that harvests of both species of peccary are sustainable. Our model generates values that suggest the harvest of woolly monkeys is not sustainable even within the 2,500 km² area (from which a maximum of 600 animals might be harvested under the best possible conditions); the harvest of white-lipped peccary might be sustainable within the 590 km² (a maximum of 490 animals might be harvested); and the harvest of collared peccary probably is sustainable (a maximum of 1,422 animals might be harvested).

In a recent study in the Bolivian Amazon with the Yuqui Indians, Allyn Stearman reported that forty-six *Cebus* monkeys were taken in a hunting area of 314 km² over an 80-day period. This equals an annual harvest of about 210 animals, a number our model indicates could be harvested sustainably only in an area larger than 1,166 km². These figures are a first approximation, but they do suggest that harvest is high and not likely to be at a sustainable level. The model identifies a potential problem and indicates that wildlife populations need to be censused and harvest rates monitored.

Enough data are now available on neotropical forest mammals to begin to assess the impact of hunting. This is only the first step in developing approaches to manage wildlife populations in these forests. Management is essential if humans are to continue to live in and use the forests, and if the species and the biological communities in which they live are to be conserved.

28

Prospects For Wildlife Management in Latin America and the Caribbean

CURTIS H. FREESE AND CARLOS J. SAAVEDRA

Never have the stakes been so high for the discipline of wildlife management in the tropics as they are today and will be for the next several decades. It is in the tropics that most of the world's plant and animal species reside and where most of the world's extinctions will occur in the foreseeable future. It is in the tropics where the socioeconomic potential of wildlife resources is largely unexplored but may be crucial not only for sustainable development, but for the preservation of its rich biotic diversity. And it is in the tropics where, except for perhaps the ocean abyss, the least is known about the biota and ecosystems that are to be managed.

To confront these challenges, wildlife managers in Latin America and the Caribbean face two major tasks of ever increasing importance. One will be to research and manage programs aimed at conserving the biological diversity of the region. Wildlife biologists, working with taxonomists, ecologists, biogeographers, foresters, anthropologists, and other specialists, will need to define the kind of wildland systems and land use practices that will maintain the fullest possible diversity of species, ecosystems, and biological interactions. What distribution, size, and configuration of parks and reserves will be required in a country or region to encompass and maintain its biological diversity? How do we manage parks and reserves to maintain or restore their diversity? What kind of land use practices outside of reserves—in agricultural areas, urban areas, and forest plantations—will favor the maintenance of wildlife populations? How do we gain a better understanding of the sociological side of wildlife management so that management programs respond to local needs and resource use patterns? What is required to make such programs socioeconomically and politically viable?

The other major task is the focus of this book and this concluding chapter. How can wild plant and animal populations (the focus here is animal populations) and the ecosystems in which they are found be managed for the benefit of human populations? Under what circumstances can the neotropical forests, wetlands, and grasslands generate greater socioeconomic returns than the timber, mining, agricultural systems and other forms of development that are replacing them? Where and how is it possible to avoid the either/or scenario, so that the managed landscape provides multiple benefits from wildlife, timber, agriculture, water, tourism, and other sectors, rather than depending on simplified production systems? How do we identify the people who are to benefit from the wildlife resources, and how do we ensure that they become the beneficiaries?

These two tasks, management for maintenance of biological diversity and management for sustainable development, are not unrelated. The survival of many species and ecosystems in Latin America and the Caribbean will require that those species and ecosystems and their products have a utilitarian value. In most cases this will be a crucial incentive for people and governments to maintain the natural or seminatural habitats and associated biological diversity of the region.

In this paper we discuss a series of factors that will strongly influence our future success in addressing these management problems. Our objective is to highlight what we think needs to be done to increase our chances of success.

Ecological Considerations

Nearly all of the ecosystems of Latin America and the Caribbean, except areas of permanent snow cover in the high Andes and a few other extremes, have wildlife resources that could be sustainably exploited for the benefit of local human populations. With the limited financial and personnel resources presently available, what are some of the factors we should consider in judging the importance of different ecosystems and species as we set management priorities?

Some of the less complex ecosystems of Latin America, such as the coniferous forests, Pampas, altiplano and llanos, may offer some of the first well-documented case studies for sustainable wildlife management in the region. The relative simplicity of these systems compared to tropical rainforests may make it easier to study and understand wildlife of interest and to develop sound management practices. It is not surprising that some of the best documented examples of sustainable management come from these ecosystems, including three discussed in this volume, the guanaco (*Lama guanicoe*), capybara (*Hydrochaeris hydrochaeris*), and vicuña (*Vicugna vicugna*) (Franklin; Ojasti; Rabinovich et al. in this volume). Biologically, the lessons learned in these less complex natural systems may be of little application in tropical forest situations. They may, however, serve as important examples to influence public opinion and support about the importance and feasibility of wildlife management programs. We therefore consider such management programs to be particularly important because of the catalytic effect they will have in the near future as models for sustainable use.

Tropical forest wildlife pose the most complex and difficult challenges for the future. Because of the complexity of tropical forest systems, and our relative ignorance about their ecology and functioning, the effects of habitat alteration and manipulation are largely unknown. The responses of target species are equally unpredictable. The diversity of tropical forests suggests that there are hundreds if not thousands of species that may be the subject of management efforts. This diversity of resources is offset by the low harvest rates that many species seem to sustain in nutrient-poor tropical forest systems, such as much of lowland Amazonia. The future success of sustainable wildlife harvesting programs in most tropical forest areas will consequently depend upon the maintenance of low human population densities in these areas (Terborgh, Emmons, and Freese 1986; Taylor 1988). Nevertheless, tropical forests must represent the central, most important challenge for wildlife management in the decades to come. Inappropriate use of tropical forest resources will lead to the loss of thousands of hectares more of forests and thousands of species. It is in tropical forests that wise management can perhaps most benefit the poorest rural colonists and the indigenous people of Latin America.

Wildlife management in Latin America's and the Caribbean's wetlands, including coastal estuaries, freshwater wetlands such as the Pantanal, and the major river systems, also plays a central role in the future of conservation and development in the region. Neotropical wetlands are poorly known in general, and agricultural expansion, shrimp farming, mangrove cutting, pollution, urban sprawl, and other development activities are causing the accelerated loss of major areas (Scott and Carbonell 1986). River systems, particularly the Amazon and Orinoco, are little studied. New species of fish have yet to be described. The dependency of important food fish in the Amazon on fruit fall from floodplain forests (Goulding 1980, 1985) highlights both the complexity of this system and how much we have to learn about it before it can be wisely managed. Although wetlands are especially important for their fisheries, they also support valuable wildlife resources such as capybaras, ducks, crocodilians, and freshwater and marine turtles (see papers in this volume). Because many of these taxa have very broad geographical ranges, and because of their great economic value, their management should be of high priority at the international level, with a strong emphasis on the exchange of technical information concerning research and management results.

The future success of efforts in wildlife management in Latin America and the Caribbean will depend largely on the degree to which research and management programs focus on high-priority species. Some well-developed and -documented cases of successful wildlife management must be established for the concept and practice to gain credibility and acceptance by the resource users, public, politicians, and planners. Glaring gaps exist in the current state of case studies in species management. In any one region there are generally fewer than ten species that stand out as major contributors to local market economies, including direct consumption. In the neotropics, probably no single taxonomic group is a more important source of protein and skins than peccaries (*Tayassu* spp.) (Redford and Robinson 1987). Yet peccary research and management programs in the region are just beginning. The same could be said to varying degrees for the tapir (*Tapirus* spp.), nine-banded armadillo (*Dasypus novemcinctus*), deer (particularly *Mazama* spp.), agoutis (*Agouti paca*), pacas (*Dasyprocta* spp.), and guans (*Penelope* spp.)—all species that rank high in many areas as a source of animal protein (Robinson and Redford 1987). As seen in this volume, research and management efforts are underway for some of these species, but not nearly enough.

Sustainable Wildlife and Wildland Management

The rapid growth and evolution of protected areas and wildland systems in Latin America (Budowski and MacFarland 1984) will demand orders of magnitude greater work in wildlife management if many of these systems are to survive. One task of wildlife management will be to develop habitat and population management techniques that maintain or restore biological diversity and healthy biological systems in both ecologically intact and degraded reserves. The other task, and the major factor that will determine the viability and survival of many, if not most, large protected wildlands, will be to develop systems for sustainable wildlife harvesting and other generators of economic return in these reserves.

Reserves throughout the region are being developed according to variations on the theme of multiple use management (MacKinnon et al. 1986). Furthermore, managers of long-established national parks, seeing the growing threats to these areas, are focusing their attention on community work and alternative management schemes in surrounding buffer zones. For example, most of Mexico's new, large wildland units, such as the Sian Ka'an Biosphere Reserve, are concentrating on managing natural resources that support the socioeconomic development of indigenous and colonist communities within and around the reserves. Spiny lobsters (*Panulirus argus*), for example, are the mainstay of the fishing community of Punta Allen in the Sian Ka'an Reserve. Concern about the sustainability of current harvest levels led to a cooperative research program on the lobsters involving the fishermen, researchers, and reserve managers. A spiny lobster management plan will soon be developed based on this research.

The relatively new wildlife refuge system of Costa Rica includes sustainable wildlife use as an important objective of many of its refuges. The innovative program for harvesting Ridley sea turtle (*Lepidochelys olivacea*) eggs at the Ostional National Wildlife Refuge on Costa Rica's Pacific coast is an excellent case of how a local community can be fully involved in and benefit from the management of a valuable wildlife resource (Cornelius, this volume). Efforts to conserve Costa Rica's Corcovado National Park, which is buffeted by surrounding development pressures, are increasingly focusing on how to sustainably manage forest resources in the Golfo Dulce Forest Reserve around the park. In southern Colombia and adjacent northern Ecuador, work is underway to establish a large, binational biosphere reserve on the Pacific slope of the Andes, where a major goal will be to design schemes of forest management that will fully incorporate the needs of the resident Awá Indians. The 2-million-hectare Pacaya-Samiria National Reserve has been established in northern Amazonian Peru with the objective of sustainably harvesting fisheries and wildlife resources for the benefit of local communities and national markets. Special attention is being given to fish research programs for harvest of the highly esteemed paiche (*Arapaima gigas*) and boquichico (*Prochilodus nigricans*).

Our vision should not be limited to management in and around reserves, for sustainable wildlife management has a potentially significant role in determining the fate of extensive wildlands that exist in private hands and the public domain at large (Freese 1986). Most Amazonian wildlands, for example, are outside of any kind of designated reserve. Thus the future of these tropical rainforests and waters, and the people who inhabit them, will depend in part on how successfully we incorporate wildlife management into the broad array of land use options considered.

A potentially rich field of collaboration that could affect extensive wildland areas exists for wildlife biologists, anthropologists, and Amerindians. The best source of information about wildlife management practices is frequently indigenous peoples, but wildlife biologists and social scientists have only begun to tap this information. The research by Posey (1985) on the sophisticated forest management techniques of the Kayapó Indians of Brazil is an excellent example of the insights that such work may provide. The tens of millions of hectares of primarily tropical forest covered by Amerindian lands may well include some of the most important sites for future wildlife management programs as native peoples practice not only their traditional forms of wildlife management, but in some cases explore ways to market wildlife products for their own economic development (Taylor 1988).

Many wildland reserves and buffer zones are currently supported by the government and local people because they were established on the premise that they will yield resources to help meet basic human needs and for economic development. Conservationists now have an opportunity to demonstrate that this is the case. If, in the next few years, these large tracts of managed wildlands do not begin to produce significant returns in forest and wildlife products for local peoples or the nations' economies, the pressures for spontaneous colonization and rapid mining of natural resources by larger development enterprises will quickly gain the upper hand (Freese 1986; Robinson 1988).

Unfortunately, our ability to manage the resources of tropical systems has not kept pace with the growth of wildland systems created for this purpose. There are consequently very few cases that we can cite in which wildlands are producing the benefits promised. The danger is that managers will try to do too much in attempting to research and manage the broad array of species of potential importance and, as a consequence, will spread themselves too thin and accomplish little. There is a clear need for more dialogue between wildland planners and managers and wildlife biologists if sustainable wildlife management is to be fully and wisely incorporated into wildland development.

At the often theoretical (and rhetorical) level of wildland planning, it is easy to talk about and plan for sustainable use of various wildlife resources in a reserve. However, effective management programs will require management of individual species. As complex as it is to answer all relevant biological and socioeconomic questions on individual species, most wildland reserves in the neotropics would do best to initially focus on just one to three species. Attempts to study and manage more species will dilute too much the limited financial and technical resources available to most areas. One well-managed peccary, fish, or green iguana population will do more for the livelihood of one local community and its consequent support for the reserve than ten poorly managed wildlife populations that lead to unfulfilled promises. Economic return, social acceptance, and management feasibility are equally important criteria in setting species priorities.

We need to ask more frequently what wildlife resources are most important to local people, how they use them, and what they know about them. Local people often are an excellent source of information on the ecology and uses of wildlife. However, priorities for species management are too often determined by the interests of researchers and managers, with insufficient attention given to the utilitarian needs of the local people and market conditions for wildlife products. As a general rule, in the first few years of a wildlife management program more time and money should go into research and management of nonbiological factors than of biological ones (see Lagueux, this volume). Initial research should examine resource use and marketing patterns, but it should also give more attention to developing a mutual understanding and partnership with resource users. The implementation of a wildlife management program will require education and extension work with diverse groups, from local resource users to national conservation organizations. Determining who gets to harvest what wildlife resources, and how, promises to be a very difficult question in Latin America and the Caribbean, especially in large wildland areas where control is already difficult. The "tragedy of the commons," in which resources that are held in common tend to be overexploited, will likely prevail. One of the most vexatious problems concerns how we ensure that local people are included and receive their fair economic share in wildlife management programs.

To address these questions, wildlife professionals will need to broaden the array of people and institutions with whom they work. Perhaps most important will be collaboration with social scientists and workers and rural development agencies, who bring with them years of experience in socioeconomic development issues and additional financial resources. Sustainable wildlife management in the neotropics is a field that can bridge the gap between conservationists and traditional development interests. If development agencies see that wisely managed wildlife populations can provide important benefits to local communities, they can become the single most important ally in the development of wildlife management programs.

More attention must also be given to exploring the proper market conditions for those wildlife products destined for national and international commerce. We need to determine what the market will bear and in some cases undertake market development to foster new uses of wildlife products. Fluctuations in demand from national and international markets must be considered, and for species traded internationally, careful attention must be paid to meeting the requirements of the Convention on International Trade of Wild Species of Fauna and Flora (CITES). Compared to these nonbiological factors, the biological questions of wildlife management will often be the easiest challenges facing natural resource managers in the region. Sociological and marketing issues must receive much more attention than they have to date, and to do this will require a much broader participation by social scientists, economists, and other disciplines.

The future success of multiple use wildlands rests not only on the effectiveness of sustainable wildlife management programs, but also on the ability to integrate wildlife use with an array of other uses. In Latin America and the Caribbean, these other uses are most often timber extraction, tourism, watershed management and the harvest of nonwood plant products for food and medicine. Integration with timber harvesting programs, particularly those involving natural forest management, would seem to be an especially promising area for cooperation (see Johns 1985, for a discussion of some of the issues).

There are at least two major roles for the wildlife researcher and manager in forest management programs. One is to design techniques for enhancing and harvesting wildlife populations in timber production areas. The other is to understand the crucial role of animal pollinators and seed dispersers in forest reproduction and dynamics and to integrate this information into the forest management program. The Yanesha forestry project in the Palcazú Valley of Amazonian Peru, which is testing a rotational strip harvesting system in natural forest, is an example where such collaboration could be particularly useful. Part of the overall forest management strategy there is the harvest of forest wildlife as one additional resource for local people. However, very limited financial resources are currently directed at this important question.

Sustainable Wildlife Use in Human-Dominated Environments

Many tropical wildlife species of socioeconomic importance do well in moderately to highly disturbed habitats. The white-tailed deer (*Odocoileus virginianus*), rock or brown iguana (*Ctenosaura similis*), green iguana (*Iguana iguana*), and opossum (*Didelphis marsupialis*), for example, occupy highly disturbed or modified habitats throughout Central America. Other wildlife species that are often exploited for commercial or subsistence purposes frequently inhabit sites adjacent to areas of human occupation, such as the nesting beaches of sea turtles and wetlands occupied by crocodilians and waterfowl. The importance of these and other species in disturbed habitats will require programs in managing vast, human-occupied areas for wildlife that lie outside of large natural wildlands. Bucher (1987) has proposed such a scheme for the Chaco of northern Argentina, where extraction of wildlife (including tegu lizards, parrots, parakeets, foxes and cats) yielded export revenues of $170 million in 1979.

It is in the primarily agricultural areas that effective wildland management can directly benefit the greatest number of people, and where local people will have a major influence and stake in the outcome of management programs. Where more pristine though fragmented habitats still remain adjacent to degraded agricultural lands, ecological restoration may be the most needed task to once again make these lands productive for wildlife resources. Pilot wildlife management programs in these areas will be important for building public recognition and support for wildlife management and conservation in general.

Wildlife management in human-altered environments will generally require intensive management methods, as in the headstarting and forest restoration techniques for green iguanas in Panama (Werner, this volume) and white-tailed deer reintroduction in Costa Rica (Vaughan and Rodriguez, this volume). Under certain conditions, captive breeding may become an important management option for selected species, as is being done with tegu lizards (*Tegu* spp.) in Argentina (Fitzgerald et al., this volume) and green iguanas in Panama.

Wildlife management can have another significant economic impact in agricultural areas through the control of wildlife that are agricultural pests. Examples of such problems include the giant gopher (*Orthogeomys* spp.) in Central America, which attacks numerous crops, the massive flocks of eared doves (*Zenaida auriculata*) and monk parakeets (*Myiopsitta monachus*) that depredate grain fields in South America; and the occasional jaguar (*Panthera onca*) and puma (*Felis concolor*) that kill livestock. The work of wildlife management is to ensure first that the purported pest is in fact a significant pest, and then, if damages cannot be compensated in some way, find environmentally sound ways to control the pest species.

Several captive management attempts have sprouted throughout the region over the past few decades. More often than not, these efforts have spent relatively large amounts of national and international funds with not-so-promising results. The MAB-UNESCO ecological and behavioral research program of the seventies in Peru for semicaptive and captive management of forest herbivores and turtles is but one example. The misconception that almost anything that breathes and breeds can be profitably raised in a cage, corral, or artificial pond is still widely spread among the new generation of Latin America wildlife students. We believe that there is still far too much emphasis being given to captive breeding by wildlife institutions in the region. Many efforts directed at captive management are wasting valuable time and limited funds that could be better spent on wild populations. As Terborgh, Emmons, and Freese (1986) and Emmons (1987) point out, most wild species are ill suited for domestication and captive management. Furthermore, even the successful captive breeding of wildlife for economic purposes will have little or no significance for the conservation of wild populations, since it provides limited incentive for conserving free-ranging populations or their habitats. We would argue that once a species is being successfully raised in captivity the work belongs to the field of animal husbandry, not wildlife biology.

Project Coordination and Support

If research and management efforts currently underway in Latin American and the Caribbean remain largely uncoordinated and fragmentary, they will yield very little over the next 20 years. As a consequence, wildlife managers will continue to face severe limitations in knowledge about the systems and species they are attempting to manage. Wise decisions will require a combination of science, art, and good luck, with often heavy reliance on the latter. If our limited human and financial resources are not to be squandered, we must consider a multinational effort to establish a priority agenda for wildlife research and management in the region. While politics, nationalism, and the individual needs of countries will inevitably bias priorities toward the scale of individual countries, we should establish priorities for regional work at the level of Central America, Amazonia, the Andes, the Greater Antilles, and other areas. If the white-tailed deer, green iguana, yellow-naped amazon (*Amazona ochrocephala*), spectacled caiman (*Caiman crocodylus*), and marine turtles are priorities for management throughout most of Central America, then one or two research and experimental management projects should be established for each, with the understanding that each project is serving regional needs and that the results are to be fully shared throughout the region. The green iguana management program in Panama (Werner, this volume) perhaps best illustrates this approach, since the project has endeavored to disseminate its results and provide technical assistance to countries throughout Central and South America. Also noteworthy are the recent efforts by the countries of Central America to develop a comprehensive Central American strategy for wildlife conservation (Ponciano 1988). A recent international workshop in Brazil on research priorities and strategies for sustainable use of capybaras, giant Amazon river turtles (*Podocnemis expansa*), and spectacled caiman (FAO 1988) is another indication of the perceived need among wildlife researchers in the region to set joint research agendas, avoid duplication, and exchange scientific and technical information.

More national and international sources of support must be found for research and management activities. The economic austerity measures that almost all countries in the region face, and will continue to face in the foreseeable future, leave little room for significant growth in funding from national sources, unless national research and development priorities are well established. The sooner and more convincingly that the general public and decision makers see the social and economic benefits of sound wildlife management, the sooner and faster national sources of funds for wildlife research and management will be forthcoming.

The tegu lizard program in Argentina illustrates an innovative approach to project funding that should be more widely explored. There is perhaps no better example of having wildlife pay its way than this program, where the skin exporters are making a major financial investment in managing the wildlife resource they depend on. We expect that in the future similar arrangements could be made with exporters of crocodilian hides, live parrots, and other wildlife resources where the exporters or users are organized to the extent that such deals can be negotiated.

The potential for increased support from international sources appears to be greater than ever. Support from nonprofit conservation organizations, such as World Wildlife Fund, The Nature Conservancy, Conservation International, and Wildlife Conservation International, is growing and becoming more diversified. Government agencies such as the U.S. Fish and Wildlife Service, U.S. National Park Service, and Canadian Wildlife Service are beginning to provide significant financial and technical support. Particularly promising is the increased attention that North American and European international assistance agencies are giving to natural resource management and the conservation of biological diversity. The U.S. Agency for International Development, for example, has greatly expanded its financial support to natural resource management and conservation activities in recent years (Brady 1988). Similarly, major private foundations in the United States, Canada, and Europe have recently begun to direct considerable funds toward wildlife and wildland management work in Latin America and the Caribbean. The World Bank and the Interamerican Development Bank are also directing more attention to issues of wildlife and wildland management in their development projects. Goodland (1988) has recently provided an overview of the World Bank's new policies in this area.

The international development agencies and banks control vast financial resources that could be more effectively leveraged to benefit wildlife management programs. Wildlife professionals and institutions in the region and the international conservation community have only begun to capitalize on these opportunities. National and international wildlife institutions must make a concerted effort to increase their knowledge of how these large international agencies work and to think in terms of cost-benefit analysis of wildlife uses. In addition, wildlife institutions in Latin America and the Caribbean must begin to look beyond the limited notion of approaching these agencies only with project proposals in need of funding. The wildlife and related professions can have a greater long-term effect if they work with these organizations to help them draft policies and design programs that will benefit wildlife management over the broad range of multilateral bank activities.

Communication and Information Transfer

The development of wildlife management in Latin America and the Caribbean will require major new efforts by the wildlife profession to improve communication. One of the most urgent needs is a major expansion of technical publications of research and management results so that the wildlife profession is in communication with itself. There is far too much gray literature in the form of reports and unfinished manuscripts stuck away in files never to be seen again, with the result that valuable information is not being shared and wildlife biologists are not benefitting from the experience of others. We estimate that well over half of what is generated from research and management goes unpublished. This paucity of publications reflects the track record of the sciences in general in Latin America, where with 10% of the world's population it contributes only 1% of the world's scientific literature, and 92% of that is from five countries (Chagas et al. 1984).

We believe that there are two primary reasons for this situation in the wildlife sciences. First, there are very few technical journals in which to publish wildlife management articles. Most that do exist appear sporadically and thus are unreliable for getting research published, and they tend to be national in scope and thus seldom reach audiences outside of the country of origin. The recent appearance of the journal *Vida Silvestre Neotropical,* the bulletin *Flora, Fauna y Areas Silvestres,* and more specialized newsletters such as *El Volante Migratorio* have begun to fill this international publication void. Despite the problems facing many national level technical journals, they represent perhaps the only possibility for significantly expanding the number, regularity and quality of technical journals in the region. Some are already of excellent quality and are published regularly; others will require more financial support and attention by capable editors. International distribution of these journals, however, will always be problematic because of currency differences, international mail and costs to subscribers. These factors, in fact, severely limit the distribution of all journals in the region, regardless of origin.

A partial solution to the dearth of technical literature is the creation of documentation centers, such as the Wildlife Management Program of Costa Rica's Universidad Nacional is doing for wildlife management in Central America. The job of such centers is to receive all publications pertinent to the region, and then through a regular newsletter or other means inform professionals throughout the region of the titles of publications received. Individual papers can then be copied and sent at cost to the individual. The development of conservation data centers at several sites throughout Latin America represents another important effort to compile and computerize data so that they are readily retrievable to users. The computerization of the wildlife profession in Latin America may be one of the best mechanisms in the future for enhancing the accessibility and timely exchange of technical information. The plan of the Western Hemisphere Shorebird Reserve Network to donate computers to institutions throughout Latin America that are actively involved in shorebird research and monitoring recognizes the power of this approach. Another option not yet attempted would be the equivalent of the U.S. Fish and Wildlife Service's *Wildlife Review,* but specifically for Latin America and the Caribbean. In this case, a quarterly review would list all papers published on neotropical wildlife, together with the address of the author so that the individual could request a copy directly from the author.

A second reason for the dearth of technical publications is that wildlife biologists in Latin America and the Caribbean are, in general, not trained to prepare scientific papers for publication, nor are they rewarded professionally for publishing. Furthermore, many of the good papers published by Latin American professionals are in English and often appear in journals that are not very accessible to specialists in the region. This is largely because of financial constraints of institutions and individuals to obtain and continue subscriptions to journals abroad. Many qualified Latin American researchers prefer to publish in English because of a sense of status or credibility that it lends to the paper. These conditions should change if we wish to augment the publication of technical and scientific information in the region.

Finally, one of the most timely and effective ways to enhance communication is through individual site visits that enable biologists and managers to directly examine projects of relevance to their work in other countries. Besides the immediate benefit of the exchange of technical information and discussion of ideas, such exchanges generally lead to closer long-term coordination and communication among programs facing similar management questions. While funding is still a limiting factor for these visits, international support is on the rise for research and training programs that favor south-to-south exchange.

Training

The future of wildlife management in Latin America and the Caribbean will be handicapped for at least the next decade, and probably many years beyond, by a shortage of well-trained wildlife biologists and limited training opportunities. The most immediate need is in-service training, that is, training for individuals who already hold research and management positions in wildlife institutions. Most individuals in such positions received their university degrees in basic biology with little or no instruction in wildlife management. Some have since attended perhaps one or two short courses in one area of wildlife management, but that is generally the extent of any formal or semi-formal education they have received on the subject. This situation is exacerbated by the shortage of published information that is available to these individuals.

There are at least three or four wildlife short courses and training workshops, usually international in scope, conducted every year in the region. These cover a range of topics, from iguana management to refuge management to migratory bird research. The number of such training opportunities will need to be greatly expanded if the demand for in-service training is to be met. There are few institutions in the region, however, that have the ability, time, and resources to organize and run such courses. Nevertheless, the number of courses does appear to be increasing, and this growth should be encouraged.

Although short courses offer the chance to provide in-service training to a relatively large numbers of people, such training cannot fully substitute for the more intensive training provided in academic programs. Over the long term, the training needs of Latin America and the Caribbean can be rectified only if we greatly expand the number and quality of university programs in wildlife management and related fields.

What opportunities exist for academic level training in wildlife management for Latin American and Caribbean nationals? While the total numbers are not known, many students receive master's and doctoral level training in the numerous wildlife programs of U.S. and Canadian universities. U.S. and Canadian universities have played and will continue to play a critical role in providing advanced academic training to Latin American and Caribbean wildlife biologists. They offer largely the only option for doctoral level training and a range of options in terms of specialization. U.S. and Canadian universities, both through their staff and libraries, and through cooperative programs with state, federal and other wildlife institutions, offer the student the opportunity to learn from a long and rich history in wildlife management in North America. To the extent that U.S. and Canadian experiences are appropriate and can be adapted to neotropical conditions, we should encourage its dissemination. One word of caution is required. Although we do not have precise numbers, a major risk in such training is that the individual never returns to his or her home country, but remains in the United States or Canada in the more lucrative and intellectually rewarding job market.

Much can be gained by a two-way flow of people and information. U.S., Canadian, and European students and scientists should be encouraged to undertake research on priority wildlife management questions in Latin America and the Caribbean. Foreign investigators can contribute significantly to the overall effort of addressing wildlife management problems, and it further enhances the north-south cross-fertilization of information and ideas. In this regard, national institutions in the region, from the collecting permit office to university biology, anthropology, and forestry departments to wildlife management agencies, should take a more active role in shaping applied research programs and providing incentives to foreign investigators who work in programs of high national priority. Foreign investigators and scholars can frequently provide support for local students to work with them, thereby providing valuable field experience and training.

Highest priority for training must be given to the development of university wildlife programs in Latin America and the Caribbean. Only three universities in the region currently offer an intensive program leading to a masters degree in wildlife management or related fields, and these have developed within the last 2 or 3 years. Several more universities, however, are looking at developing wildlife management curricula. Latin American and Caribbean based programs can, in general, provide academic instruction at a lower cost per student than foreign programs, and they can much more easily focus their programs on regional problems. Training and research activities can be conducted within the proper environmental and socioeconomic context by simply walking out the front door.

Academic programs will need to be developed at two levels: (1) There should be programs, such as those at Costa Rica's National University and Brazil's University of Minas Gerais, that provide master's or doctoral level training. These programs should strive to be international, depending on the student demand from within their respective countries. We cannot expect a rapid increase in the number of these programs over the next decade, and thus they can afford to be highly selective in the students they accept. (2) There should be a reshifting of academic focus in biology departments at the undergraduate level from the classic laboratory biology to field biology and natural resource management. A reorientation of training at the undergraduate level could produce graduates with more capacity to understand and address wildlife and wildland management questions once they enter professional positions as wildland technicians, refuge managers and the like.

The development of wildland management programs in Latin America and the Caribbean cannot proceed without a concomitant expansion of academic training in organismic level biology and ecology and a growth in opportunities for employment and field work in these disciplines. There is a dearth of expertise and work in these sciences in the region. Wildlife management will have a difficult time if wildlife researchers and managers are unable to assign a name to organisms that they encounter or understand very little about the food webs, plant-animal interactions, and productivity of the wildlands they are trying to manage.

Conclusion

The sustainable use of wild plant and animal resources has a potentially major role to play in the success of future development and conservation of biological diversity in Latin America and the Caribbean. Programs of sustainable wildlife use have, until recently, largely fallen outside the interest of national and international natural resource conservation institutions, which had focused on more traditional endangered species conservation and national park development work. National and international development agencies, on the other hand, have generally viewed sustainable wildlife use as too unconventional and of little or no value to the development process. Fortunately, this gap in interest is being closed as both the development and conservation sectors begin to recognize that the sustainable use of wild plants and animals in Latin America and the Caribbean can play a significant role in both socioeconomic development and in the conservation of the region's rich biological heritage. Wildlife management thus has a potentially pivotal role to play in helping to link the interests and needs of both the development and conservation communities. To do so, however, will require a more organized, expanded and assertive participation in the conservation and development arenas by wildlife biologists, social scientists, economists and professionals in other fields.

Contributors

Marcelo Aranda
Instituto de Ecologia
Km. 2.5 Antigua Carretera a Coatepec
91000 Xalapa
Veracruz
Mexico

J. Marcio Ayres
Núcleo de Primatologia
Museu Paraense Emílio Goeldi
Caixa Postal 399
Belém - Pará - 66.040
Brazil

José Luis K. Barreiros
Núcleo de Primatologia
Museu Paraense Emílio Goeldi
Caixa Postal 399
Belém - Pará - 66.040
Brazil

Amie Brautigam
IUCN/SCC Trade Specialist Group
15 Herbert Street
Cambridge CB4 1A9
United Kingdom

Angel F. Capurro
Departamento de Biologia
Facultad de Ciencias Exactas y Naturales
Universidad de Buenos Aires
Pabellón II
Ciudad Universitaria (1428)
Buenos Aires
Argentina

Juan Carlos Castro
Escuela de Biologia
Universidad de Costa Rica
San José
Costa Rica

José Maria Chani
Facultad de Ciencias Naturales e Instituto Miguel Lillo
Universidad Nacional de Tucuman
Miguel Lillo 205
4000 San Miguel de Tucuman
Argentina

Steven E. Cornelius
World Wildlife Fund
1250 Twenty-Fourth St. NW
Washington, DC 20037

Peter Q. Crawshaw Jr.
Department of Wildlife and Range Sciences
118 Newins-Ziegler Hall
University of Florida
Gainesville, FL 32611

Francisco Dallmeier
Smithsonian Institution/M.A.B. Biodiversity Program
National Museum of Natural History
Washington, DC 20560

Oscar E. Donadío
Proyecto Tupinambis
CICUR, Tucuman 1424
8°D, (1050)
Buenos Aires
Argentina

José Manuel V. Fragoso
Department of Wildlife and Range Sciences
118 Newins-Ziegler Hall
University of Florida
Gainesville, FL 32611

Lee A. Fitzgerald
Department of Biology
University of New Mexico
Albuquerque, NM 87131

William L. Franklin
Department of Animal Ecology
Iowa State University
Ames, IA 50011

Curtis H. Freese
World Wildlife Fund
1250 Twenty-Fourth St., NW
Washington, DC 20037

Michael A. Fritz
Department of Animal Ecology
Iowa State University
Ames, IA 50011

Alfred L. Gardner
U.S. Fish and Wildlife Service
National Museum of Natural History
Smithsonian Institution
Washington D.C. 20560

William E. Glanz
Department of Zoology
University of Maine
Orono, ME 04469

Martha J. Groom
Department of Zoology NJ-15
University of Washington
Seattle, WA 98195

Eduardo E. Iñigo-Elias
Department of Wildlife and Range Sciences
118 Newins-Ziegler Hall
University of Florida
Gainesville, FL 32611

Cynthia J. Lagueux
Department of Wildlife and Range Sciences
118 Newins-Ziegler Hall
University of Florida
Gainesville, FL 32611

Deborah de Magalhães Lima
Departamento de História e Antropologia
Universidade Federal do Pará
Campus do Guamá
Belém - Pará - 66.000
Brazil

Mercedes Mata del Valle
Escuela de Ciencias Biologicas
Universidad Nacional de Costa Rica
San José
Costa Rica

Eduardo de Souza Martins
Núcleo de Primatologia
Museu Paraense Emílio Goeldi
Caixa Postal 399
Belém - Pará - 66.040
Brazil

Russell A. Mittermeier
Conservation International
Suite 1000
1015 18th St., NW
Washington, DC 20036

Charles A. Munn
Wildlife Conservation International
New York Zoological Society
Bronx, New York 10460

Juhani Ojasti
Maaherrankatu
S3100 Lappeenranta 10
Finland

Leonor L. Pessina
Centro de Estudios e Investigaciones
Laborales
CONICET, Av. Corrientes 2470
Buenos Aires
Argentina

Robert D. Podolsky
Department of Zoology NJ-15
University of Washington
Seattle, WA 98195

Paul C. Purdy
U.S. Fish and Wildlife Service
Office of Information Transfer
1025 Pennock Place
Ft. Collins, CO 80524

Jorge E. Rabinovich
SPAIDER/SPIDER
Uruguay 263
1015 Buenos Aires
Argentina

Mario A. Ramos
World Wildlife Fund
1250 Twenty-Fourth Street, NW
Washington, DC 20037

Kent H. Redford
Program for Studies in Tropical Conservation
319 Grinter Hall
University of Florida
Gainesville, FL 32611

Douglas C. Robinson
Escuela de Biologia
Universidad de Costa Rica
San José
Costa Rica

John G. Robinson
Wildlife Conservation International
New York Zoological Society
Bronx, NY 10460

Miguel Rodriguez
Costa Rican Wildlife Service
Ministry of Natural Resources, Mines
and Energy
San José
Costa Rica

Carlos J. Saavedra
World Wildlife Fund
1250 Twenty-Fourth Street, NW
Washington, DC 20037

James H. Shaw
School of Biological Sciences
Oklahoma State University
Stillwater, OK 74074

José L. Silva
Fundacion para la Defensa de la Naturaleza
Apartado 70376
Caracas 1071
Venezuela

Nicholas Smythe
Smithsonian Tropical Research Institute
P.O. Box 2072
Balboa
Panama

Stuart D. Strahl
Wildlife Conservation International
New York Zoological Society
Bronx, NY 10460

Jorgen Bent Thomsen
TRAFFIC International
219C Huntingdon Rd
Cambridge CB3 0DL
United Kingdom

John B. Thorbjarnarson
Department of Wildlife and Range Sciences
118 Newins-Ziegler Hall
University of Florida
Gainesville, FL 32611

Roy E. Tomlinson
U.S. Fish and Wildlife Service
Office of Information Transfer
1025 Pennock Place
Ft. Collins, CO 80524

Mario Alvarado Ulloa
Apartment 212
300 North Cedar
Glendale, CA 91206

Christopher Vaughan
Programa Regional de Vida Silvestre
para Mesoamérica y el Caribe
Escuela de Ciencias Ambientales
Universidad Nacional
Heredia
Costa Rica

William T. Vickers
Department of Sociology and Anthropology
Florida International University
Miami, FL 33199

Dagmar I. Werner
Fundacion Pro Iguana
Apartado 1501
Heredia
Costa Rica

References

Ackerman, R. A. 1980. Physiological and ecological aspects of gas exchange by sea turtle eggs. *American Zoologist* 20:575–83.

Acuna, R. A. 1983. El éxito de desarrollo de los huevos de la tortuga marina *Lepidochelys olivacea* (Eschscholtz) en Playa Ostional, Costa Rica. *Brenesia* 21:371–85.

AFA. See American Federation of Aviculturists.

Aguire, A. C. 1976. Distribuição, costumes e exterminio da "avoante" do nordeste, *Zenaida auriculata noronha* Chubb. Rio de Janeiro, Brazil: Academia Brasileira de Ciencias.

Alcedo, C., and N. Saucedo. 1987. El efecto de diferentes densidades de población en el desarrollo de recién nacidos de *Iguana iguana*. B.S. thesis, Department of Biology, Univ. Panama.

Alfaro, A., and J. D. Allen. 1987. *Mamíferos de Costa Rica*. San José, Costa Rica: Tipografía Nacional.

Alho, C. R. J. 1986. *Criação e manejo de capivaras em pequenas propriedades rurais*. Brasilia, Brazil: Empresa Brasileira de Pesquisa Agropecuária.

Alho, C. R. J., Z. M. S. Campos, and H. C. Concalves. 1987a. Ecologia de capivara (*Hydrochaeris hydrochaeris*, Rodentia) do Pantanal. I. Habitats, densidades e tamanho de groupo. *Rev. Brasil. Biol.* 47:87–97.

―――. 1987b. Ecologia de capivara (*Hydrochaeris hydrochaeris*, Rodentia) do Pantanal. II. Atividade, sazonalidade, uso do espaço e manejo. *Rev. Brasil. Biol.* 47:99–110.

Allen, R. 1965. History and results of deer restocking in Alabama. Alabama Department of Conservation.

Alpine, L. 1986. Trends in special interest travel. *Specialty Travel Index* 13:83–84.

Alva, W. 1988. Discovering the new world's richest unlooted tomb. *National Geographic* 174:510–49.

Alvarado, M. 1985. Tasa de éxito de eclosión de nidos naturales de la tortuga marina *Lepidochelys olivacea* (Eschscholtz, 1829) en el Refugio de Fauna Silvestre Ostional, Guanacaste, Costa Rica. Licenciatura thesis, Universidad de Costa Rica, San José.

Alvarez del Toro, M. 1969. Breeding the spectacled caiman (*Caiman crocodilus*) at Tuxtla Gutierrez Zoo. *Int. Zoo Yearbook* 9:35–36.

————. 1974. *Los crocodylia de México*. Instituto Mexicano de Recursos Naturales Renovables, Mexico, D.F.

————. 1980. *Las aves de Chiapas*. Univ. Autónoma de Chiapas, Tuxtla Gtz., Chiapas, México.

Amengual, R. G., G. M. Padilla, J. L. M. Arocha, and C. Rivero Blanco. 1981. *Nuestros animales de caza. Guía para su conservación*. Caracas, Venezuela: Fundación de Educación Ambiental.

American Federation of Aviculturists. 1980. VVND birds destroyed in Miami, exposed shipments traced 33 states. *Watchbird* 71:32–33.

————. 1981. New federal regulations. *Watchbird* 8:27.

————. 1982. Mexican parrots can bring exotic Newcastle disease to U.S. pets and poultry. *Watchbird* 9:10–11.

American Ornithologists' Union. 1973. Bird conservation in middle America. Report of the AOU Conservation Committee 1972–1973. *Auk* 90:877–87.

————. 1983. Checklist of North American birds, ed. 6., Lawrence, Kans.: Allen Press.

Anderson, D. R., and K. P. Burnham. 1976. Population ecology of the mallard. VI. The effect of exploitation on survival. U.S. Department of Interior, Fish and Wildlife Service, Publ. 128.

AOU. *See* American Ornithologists' Union.

Aquino Y. R., and I. Ayala A. 1979. El ronsoco (*Hydrochoerus hydrochaeris*). Fuente de proteína desperdiciada en la cuenca del Tapiche. Ordeloreto, Iquitos, Perú. Unpublished report.

Argentina's trade bans. 1986. *TRAFFIC Bull.* 8:32.

Arnaud, E., and R. Cortez (1976). Aripuanã: Considerações preliminares. *Acta Amazonica* 6(4) Suplemento: 11–31.

Aspelin, P. 1975. External articulation and domestic production: The artifact trade of the Maimaindê of northwestern Mato Grosso, Brazil. Latin American Studies Program Dissertation Series No. 59. Ithaca, N.Y.: Cornell University.

Assaf, A., and O. Cruz Marcano. 1976. Estudio sobre las características físico-químicas de la carne de chigüire. CIEPE, San Felipe, and CONICIT, Caracas, Venezuela. Unpublished report.

Aves International. 1983. Sale list and prices, March.

Avila-Pires, F. D. 1977. Exame da situação atual dos componentes dos ecosistemas e atividades humanas. Pp. 16–27 in *Encontro nacional sôbre conservação da fauna e recursos faunísticos*. Brasilia, Brazil: Inst. Brasil. Desenvolvimento Florestal (IBDF).

Ayarzaguena, J. 1983. Ecología del caimán de anteojos o baba (*Caiman crocodilus* L.) en los Llanos de Venezuela. *Doñana* 10:1–136.

Ayres, J. M. 1981. Observações sobre a ecologia e o comportamento dos cuxiús (*Chiropotes albinasus e Chiropotes satanas, Cebidae*). Belém, Brazil: Grafisa.

Ayres, J. M., and C. Ayres. 1979. Aspectos da caça no alto rio Aripuanã. *Acta Amazonica* 9(2):287–98.

Ayres, M., and M. Ayres, Jr. 1987. *Aplicações estatísticas em Basic*. São Paulo: McGraw-Hill.

Azcárate, T. 1980. Sociobiología y manejo del capibara (*Hydrochoerus hydrochaeris*). *Doñana* 7:1–228.

Baal, F., R. Mittermeier, and M. van Roosmalen. 1988. Primates and protected areas in Suriname. *Oryx* 22:7–14.

Baer, E. 1981. Report of subcommittee on cage and aviary birds. *Watchbird* 7:23–26.

Balee, W. 1985. Ka'apor ritual hunting. *Human Ecology* 13:435–50.

Baker, R. H. 1984. Origin, classification and distribution. Pp. 1–19 in *White-tailed deer: Ecology and management,* ed. L. K. Halls. Harrisburg, Pa.: Stackpole.

Ball, F. 1986. CITES enforcement in Suriname. Nature Conservation Division, Suriname Forest Service, Paramaribo.

Banks, R. C. 1970. Birds imported into the United States in 1968. Special scientific report, Wildlife report No. 136, Washington, D.C.: U.S. Department of Interior, Fish and Wildlife Service.

————. 1976. Wildlife importation into the United States, 1900–1972. Special scientific report, Wildlife report No. 200, Washington, D.C.: U.S. Department of the Interior, Fish and Wildlife Service.

Banks, R. C., and R. B. Clapp. 1972. Birds imported into the United States in 1969. Special scientific report, Wildlife Report no. 148, Washington, D.C.: U.S. Department of Interior, Fish and Wildlife Service.

————. 1973a. Birds imported into the United States in 1970. Special scientific report, Wildlife Report No. 164, Washington, D.C.: U.S. Department of Interior, Fish and Wildlife Service.

————. 1973b. Birds imported into the United States in 1971. Special scientific report, Wildlife Report No. 170, Washington, D.C.: U.S. Department of Interior, Fish and Wildlife Service.

Banks, R. C., M. Clench, and J. Barlow. 1973. Bird collections in the United States and Canada. *Auk* 90:136–70.

Banse, K., and S. Mosher. 1980. Adult body mass and annual production/biomass relationships of field populations. *Ecol. Monogr.* 50:355–79.

Barik, F. 1951. Deer restoration in the southeastern United States. Proc. Southeast Association Game and Fish Commissioners.

Barlow, J. C. 1965. Land mammals of Uruguay: Ecology and zoogeography. Ph.D. diss., Univ. Kansas, Lawrence.

Bean, M. J. 1983. *The evolution of national wildlife law.* New York: Praeger.

Becker, M. 1981. Aspectos de caça em algumas regiões do cerrado de Mato Grosso. *Brasil Florest.* 11:(47)51–63.

Beddington, J. R. 1980. Maximum substainable yield in systems subject to harvesting at more than one trophic level. *Math. Biosc.* 51:261–81.

Beddington, J. R., and R. M. May. 1977. Harvesting natural populations in a randomly fluctuating environment. *Science* 197:463–65.

Beekhuis, J. V. 1981. Tourism in the Caribbean: Impacts on the economic, social and natural environments. *Ambio* 10:325–31.

Benitez A. M. 1986. Laguna El Jocotal, El Salvador: El uso sostenido de las aves acuáticas en beneficio del hombre y la fauna. Unpublished manuscript.

Bennett, A. F., and W. R. Dawson. 1976. Metabolism. Pp. 127–224 in *Biology of the reptilia,* vol. 5, ed. C. Gans and W. R. Dawson. New York: Academic Press.

Bennett, C. F. 1968. *Human influence on the zoogeography of Panama.* Berkeley: Univ. California Press.

Berovides A. V. 1987. Evaluación de los caprómidos de Cuba como recurso natural. *Flora, Fauna y Areas Silvestres* 2:27–29.

Bertoni, J. A. 1985. Estudio de biología y productividad de camélidos sudamericanos en la Puna Jujeña. IDIA no. 429–432: 74–82.

Bertoni, J. A., M. Sánchez Llena, and A. Vorano. 1980. Evaluación del esporal mediante pastoreo con llamas. Memoria Anual de la Estación Experimental del Instituto Argentino de Tecnología Agropecuaria, Salta, Argentina.

Bjorndal, K., ed. 1982. *Biology and conservation of sea turtles*. Washington, D.C.: Smithsonian Institution Press.

Blackard, J. 1971. Restoration of the white-tailed deer in the Southwestern United States. M.S. thesis, Louisiana State Univ., Baton Rouge.

Blankinship, D. R. 1970. White-winged dove nesting colonies in northeastern Mexico. *Trans. North Am. Wildl. Nat. Resour. Conf.* 35:171–82.

Blankinship, D. R., J. G. Teer, and W. H. Kiel, Jr. 1972. Movements and mortality of white-winged doves banded in Tamaulipas, Mexico. *Trans. North Am. Wildl. Nat. Resour. Conf.* 37:312–25.

Blohm, T. 1973. Conveniencia de criar crocodílidos en Venezuela con fines económicos para prevenir su extinción. Proc. del Simposio Int. sobre Fauna Silvestre y Pescas Fluvial y Lacustre Amazónica, Manaus, Brazil.

Bock, B. C. (n.d.). Nesting synchrony and factors influencing hatching success at a green iguana nesting aggregation in Panama. Unpublished manuscript.

———. 1984. Movement patterns relative to nesting site locations in a population of green iguanas (*Iguana iguana*) in Panama. Ph.D. diss., Univ. Tennessee, Knoxville.

Bock, B. C., A. S. Rand, and G. M. Burghardt. 1985. Seasonal migration and nesting site fidelity in the green iguana. Pp. 435–43 in *Migration: Mechanisms and adaptive significance*, ed. M. A. Rankin. Contributions in Marine Science, suppl. 27. Austin: University of Texas.

Bolen, E. G., and M. K. Rylander. 1983. Whistling ducks zoogeography, ecology, anatomy. Spec. Publ. Mus. Tex. Tech. Univ., no. 20. Lubbock, Texas.

Bone, T. G. 1977. Un modelo de simulación para la explotación comercial del chigüire (*Hydrochoerus hydrochoeris*). Thesis, Univ. Central Venezuela, Caracas.

Borrell, J. 1986. The chicken of the trees. *Time Magazine* (Int. Edition), Oct. 27.

Borrero H., J. I. 1967. *Mamíferos Neotropicales*. Univ. del Valle, Cali, Colombia.

Bourne, G. R., and D. R. Osborne. 1978. Black-bellied whistling duck utilization of rice culture habitat. *Interciencia* 3:152–59.

Brack, A., D. Hoces, and J. Sotelo. 1981. Situación actual de la vicuña en el Perú y acciones a ejecutarse para su manejo durante el año 1981. Lima, Perú: Ministerio de Agricultura y Alimentación.

Brady, N. C. 1988. International development and the protection of biological diversity. Pp. 409–18 in *Biodiversity*, ed. E. O. Wilson. Washington, D.C.: National Academy Press.

Brautigam, A., and J. Thomsen. 1988. The Caribbean trade in birds. *World Birdwatch* 10:10.

Brazaitis, P. 1973. The identification of living crocodilians. *Zoologica* 58:59–101.

———. 1986a. Management, reproduction, and growth of *Caiman crocodilus yacare* at the New York Zoological Park. Pp. 389–98 in Proc. of the 7th Working Meeting of the CSG-SSC/IUCN, Caracas, Venezuela.

————. 1986b. An assessment of the current crocodilian hide and product market in the United States. Pp. 379–84 in Proc. of the 7th Working Meeting of the CSG-SSC/ IUCN, Caracas, Venezuela.

Brazaitis, P., and F. W. King. 1984. A guide to the identification and forensic examination of the common caiman (*Caiman crocodilus crocodilus*) and the yacare caiman (*Caiman crocodilus yacare*). Washington, D.C.: U.S. Department of the Interior, Fish and Wildlife Service, workshop training manual.

Bridges, E. L. 1950. *Uttermost part of the earth*. New York: E. P. Dutton and Co.

Broad, S. 1984. The peccary skin trade. *TRAFFIC Bull.* 6:27–28.

————. 1987. International trade in skins of Latin American spotted cats. *TRAFFIC Bull.* 9:56–63.

Brokx, P. 1984. South America. Pp. 525–46 in *White-tailed deer: Ecology and management*, ed. L. K. Halls. Harrisburg, Pa.: Stackpole.

Brookland, J., C. Hora, and N. Carter. 1985. Injury, damage to health and cruel treatment: Present conditions in the shipment of live fauna. Report by the Environmental Investigation Agency. London, England.

Brown, D. E. 1982. Status of the Arizona white-winged dove in Mexico. Ariz. Game Fish Dep. Fed. Aid Proj. W-53-R-31, Special Performance Report.

Bruzual, J., and I. B. Bruzual. 1983. Feeding habits of whistling-ducks in the Calabozo rice fields, Venezuela, during the non-reproductive period. *Wildfowl* 34:20–26.

Buchanan, D., R. Mittermeier, and M. van Roosmalen. 1981. The saki monkeys, genus *Pithecia*. Pp. 391–417 in *Ecology and behavior of neotropical primates*, vol. 1, ed. A. Coimbra-Filho and R. Mittermeier. Rio de Janeiro, Brazil: Brazilian Academy of Sciences.

Bucher, E. H. 1986. Problems and opportunities for wildlife management in natural forests of Argentina. Pp. 601–10 in *Proceedings of the 18th IUFRO World Congress*, IUFRO Secretariat, Schönbrunn-Tirolergarten, Vienna, Austria.

————. 1987. Fauna silvestre chaqueña: Como manejarla? *Flora, Fauna y Areas Silvestres* 1(3):21–24.

Bucher, E. H., and M. B. Martella. 1988. Preliminary Report on the Current Status of *Amazona aestiva* in the Western Chaco, Argentina. *Parrotletter* 1:9–10.

Buckley, P. A., M. S. Foster, E. S. Morton, R. S. Ridgely, and F. G. Buckely. 1985. *Neotropical ornithology*. Ornith. Monogr. no. 36, American Ornithologists' Union, Washington, D.C.

Budowski, G., and C. MacFarland. 1984. Keynote address: the neotropical realm. Pp. 552–60 in *National Parks, Conservation and Development*, ed. J. A. McNeely and K. R. Miller. Washington, D.C.: Smithsonian Institution Press.

Burghardt, G. M., H. W. Greene, and A. S. Rand. 1977. Social behavior of hatchling green iguanas. Life at a reptile rookery. *Science* 195:689–91

Buschbacher, R. J. 1987. Cattle productivity and nutrient fluxes on Amazon pasture. *Biotropica* 19:200–207.

Bustard, H. R. 1971. Crocodiles. Summary of the meeting. IUCN Publ. Series. Suppl. Paper no. 32. Morges, Switzerland.

Cabrera, A., and J. Yepes. 1940. *Mamíferos Sud-Americanos (vida, costumbres y descripción)*. Buenos Aires, Argentina: Historia Natural Ediar, Compañía Argentina de Editores.

Cajal, J. L. 1983. Comentarios sobre el documento: Declaración sobre la Vicuña. Recursos Naturales Renovables, Subsecretaría de Ciencia y Tecnología, Buenos Aires, Argentina.

———. 1985. Densidades. Pp. 147–58, in *Estado actual de las investigaciones sobre camélidos en la República Argentina*, ed. J. Cajal and J. Amaya. Buenos Aires, Argentina: Secretaria de Ciencia y Técnica.

———. 1988. The lesser rhea in the Argentine puna region: Present situation. *Biol. Cons.* 45:81–91.

Cajal, J. L, J. Pujalte, and A. Reca. 1981. La Reserva Provincial de San Guillermo y sus asociaciones ambientales. Buenos Aires, Argentina: Secretaría de Ciencia y Técnica.

———. 1983. Resultados de los censos de camélidos silvestres en las reservas de San Guillermo (San Juan), Laguna Brava (La Rioja) y Laguna Blanca (Catamarca). Report to the XIth Argentine Meeting of Ecology, Córdoba, Argentina.

Callicott, J. B. 1980. Animal liberation: a triangular affair. *Environmental Ethics* 2:311–38.

Campos, L. C. 1986. Distribution, human impact and conservation of flamingos in the high Andes of Bolivia. M.A. thesis, Univ. Florida, Gainesville.

Canin, J., and R. A. Luxmoore. 1985. International trade in sea turtle shell, 1979–1984. Wildlife Trade Monitoring Unit, IUCN.

Carr, A. 1948. Sea turtles on a tropical island. *Fauna* 10:50–55.

———. 1952. *Handbook of turtles: The turtles of the United States, Canada and Baja California*. Ithaca, N.Y.: Comstock Publishing Associates.

Carr, A., M. H. Carr, and A. B. Meylan. 1978. The ecology and migrations of sea turtles. 7. The west Caribbean green turtle colony. *Bull. Am. Mus. Nat. Hist.* 162, article 1.

Carter, N., and D. Currey. 1987. The trade in live wildlife: Mortality and transport conditions. Second Report by the Environmental Investigation Agency, London, England.

Carvalho, C. E. 1986. *A preliminary list of Brazilian fauna sold in Duque de Caxias market, state of Rio de Janeiro*. Rio de Janiero, Brazil: Birdwatchers Club.

Carvalho M. de, J. C. 1967. A conservação da natureza e recursos naturais na Amazônia Brasileira. Pp. 1–44 in *Atas Simp. Biota Amaz.*, vol. 7, ed. H. Lent. Rio de Janeiro, Brazil: Cons. Nac. Pesquisas.

Casler, C., A. R. Rivero, and J. R. Lira. 1981. Los patos (*Dendrocygna*) como causantes de daño en los cultivos de arroz en Venezuela. *Mem. Soc. Cien. Nat. La Salle* 49:105–15.

Castro I., J. C. 1986. Contribución de las tortugas lora solitarias (*Lepidochelys olivacea* Eschscholtz) en el mantenimiento de las poblaciones de esta especie. Licenciatura thesis, Universidad de Costa Rica, San José.

Castro, N., J. Revilla, and M. Neville. 1975–76. Carne de monte como una fuente de proteínas en Iquitos, con referencia especial a monos. *Rev. Forestal del Perú* 6:19–32.

Caufield, C. 1985. *In the rainforest*. London: Cox and Wyman Ltd.

Caughley, G. 1966. Mortality patterns in mammals. *Ecology* 47:906–18.

———. 1970. Eruption of ungulate populations, with emphasis on Himalayan thar in New Zealand. *Ecology* 51:54–72.

———. 1977. *Analysis of vertebrate populations*. New York: Wiley.

———. 1985. Harvesting of wildlife: Past, present, and future. Pp. 3–14 in *Game harvest management,* ed. S. L. Beasom and S. F. Roberson. Kingsville, Texas: Caesar Kleberg Wildlife Research Institute.

Caughley, G., and C. J. Krebs. 1983. Are big mammals simply little mammals writ large? *Oecologia* 59:7–17.

Cei, J. M., and J. A. Scolaro. 1982. Geographic distribution: *Tupinambis rufescens* SSAR. *Herp. Rev.* 13:26.

Chagas, C., P. Garrahan, A. Gómez Puyou, L. de Meis, C. Monge, and R. Villegas. 1984. La ciencia de América Latina: Situación actual y recomendaciones. *Interciencia* 9:316–7.

Chang, A., A. E. Seijas, and D. Figueroa. 1985. Anillado de patos pico rosado, *Dendrocygna autumnalis,* en Venezuela: resultados preliminares. *International Waterfowl Research Bureau,* 31:137–43.

Chapin, M. 1986. The Panamanian iguana renaissance. *Grassroots Development* 10(2):2–7.

Chaves, A. C. 1986 Viabilidad de los huevos de la tortuga marina *Lepidochelys olivacea* (Eschscholtz), en Playa Ostional, Guanacaste, Costa Rica. Licenciatura thesis, Universidad de Costa Rica, San José.

Chávez, L. G. 1984. Determinación de las relaciones hombre fauna silvestre en una zona rural de Quintana Roo. Bol. Tec. no. 94., Ins. Nal. de Investigaciones Forestales (INIF), México, D.F.

Child, G. 1987. The management of crocodiles in Zimbabwe. Pp. 49–62 in *Wildlife Management: Crocodiles and alligators,* ed. G. J. W. Webb, S. C. Manolis, and P. J. Whitehead. Chipping Norton, Australia: Surrey Beatty.

Chivers, D. J. 1974. The siamang in Malaya: A field study of a primate in tropical rainforest. *Contrib. Primatol.* 4:1–335.

Clapp, R. B. 1975. Birds imported into the United States in 1972. Special scientific report, Wildlife no. 193. Washington, D.C.: U.S. Department of Interior, Fish and Wildlife Service.

Clark, C. W. 1976. *Mathematical bioeconomics: the optimal management of renewable natural resources*. New York: Wiley.

Clark, M. M., and B. G. Galef. 1980. Effects of the rearing environment on adrenal weights, sexual development and behavior in gerbils: an examination of Richter's domestication hypothesis. *J. Comp. Physiol. Physchol.* 94:857–63.

———. 1981. Environmental influence on development, behavior and endocrine morphology of gerbils. *Physiol. Behav.* 27:761–64.

Clark, W. R. 1985. *NOLES, user's manual of the Iowa State University VAX*. Unpublished manual, Department of Animal Ecology, Iowa State University, Ames.

Cliffton K., D. O. Cornejo, and R. S. Felger. 1982. Sea turtles of the Pacific coast of Mexico. Pp. 199–209 in *Biology and conservation of sea turtles,* ed. K. S. Bjorndal. Washington, D.C.: Smithsonian Institution Press.

Codazzi, A. 1841. *Resumen de la geografía de Venezuela*. Paris: H. Fournier & Co.

Coe, M. J., D. H. Cummings, and J. Phillipson. 1976. Biomass production of large African herbivores in relation to rainfall and primary production. *Oecologia* 22:341–54.

Coello Hinojosa, F., and J. D. Nations. 1987. Plan maestro de la reserva de producción faunística Cuyabeno, Provincia del Napo, Ecuador. Project report no. 6079, World Wildlife Fund, Washington D.C.

Cohen, E. 1982. Jungle guides in Northern thailand—the dynamics of a marginal role. *Sociolog. Rev.* 30:234–66.

Cohn, J. P. 1987. Nights—and days—of the iguana. *Americas* 39(4):34–39.

Cole, L. C. 1954. The population consequences of life history phenomena. *Q. Rev. Biol.* 29:103–37.

Collar, N. J. 1988. Action plan for conservation of neotropical parrots. In *Second Meeting of the Parrot Specialist Group.* October 13–18, Curitiba, Brazil.

Collett, S. F. 1981. Population characteristics of *Agouti paca* in Colombia. Publ. Mus. Michigan State Univ., Biol. Ser., 5:489–601.

Cook, R., M. White, D. Trainer, and W. Glazener. 1971. Mortality of young white-tailed deer fawns in southern Texas. *J. Wild. Mgmt.* 35:47–56.

Cooke, R. G. 1981. Los hábitos alimentarios de los indígenas precolombinos de Panamá. *Rev. Med. de Panamá* 6:65–89.

Coppens, W. 1983. Los Hoti. Pp. 243–301 in *Los aborígenes de Venezuela,* ed. W. Coppens. Caracas, Venezuela: Texto.

Cordero, G. A., and J. Ojasti. 1981. Comparison of capybara populations of open and forested habitats. *J. Wildl. Mgmt.* 45:267–71.

Cornelius, S. E. 1976. Marine turtle nesting activity at Playa Naranjo, Costa Rica. *Brenesia* 8:1–27.

———. 1982. Status of sea turtles along the Pacific coast of middle America. Pp. 211–19 in *Biology and conservation of sea turtles,* ed. K. S. Bjorndal, Washington, D.C.: Smithsonian Institution Press.

———. 1985. Update on Ostional. *Mar. Turt. Newsletter* 33:5–8.

Cornelius, S. E., and D. C. Robinson. 1981. Abundance, distribution and movements of olive ridley sea turtles in Costa Rica. Final Report to U.S. Fish and Wildlife Service, Endangered Species Office, Albuquerque, N.M.

———. 1982. Abundance, distribution and movements of olive ridley sea turtles in Costa Rica, II. Final Report to U.S. Fish and Wildlife Service, Endangered Species Office, Albuquerque, N.M.

———. 1985. Abundance, distribution and movements of the olive ridley sea turtles in Costa Rica, V. Report to U.S. Fish and Wildlife Service, Endangered Species Office, Albuquerque, N.M.

———. 1986. Post-nesting movements of female olive ridley turtles tagged in Costa Rica. *Vida Silvestre Neotropical* 1:12–23.

Cottam, C., and J. B. Trefethen, eds. 1968. *Whitewings: The life history, status and management of the white-winged dove.* Princeton, N.J.: D. Van Nostrand Co.

Cott, H. B. 1954. The exploitation of wild birds for their eggs. *Ibis* 96:129–49.

Courtenay, W. 1978. The introduction of exotic organisms. Pp. 237–52 in *Wildlife and America,* ed. H. P. Brokaw. Washington, D.C.: Council on Environmental Quality.

Crawford, H. 1984. Habitat management. Pp. 626–46 in *Whitetailed deer: Ecology and management,* ed. L. K. Halls. Harrisburg, Pa.: Stackpole.

Crawley, M. J. 1983. *Herbivory: The dynamics of animal-plant interactions.* Berkeley: Univ. California Press.

Crawshaw, P. G., Jr. 1987. Nesting ecology of the Paraguayan caiman (*Caiman yacare*) in the Pantanal of Mato Grosso, Brazil. M. S. thesis, Univ. Florida, Gainesville.

Crawshaw, P. G., Jr., and G. B. Schaller. 1980. Nesting of the Paraguayan caiman (*Caiman yacare*) in Brazil. *Pap. Avulsos de Zoologia* 33:283–92.

Creed, W., F. Haberland, B. Kohn, and K. McCaffery. 1984. Harvest management: the Wisconsin experience. Pp. 243–60. in *White-tailed deer: Ecology and management*, ed. L. K. Halls. Harrisburg, Pa.: Stackpole.

Croat, T. B. 1978. Flora of Barro Colorado Island. Stanford, Calif.: Stanford Univ. Press.

Cruz, C. A. 1974. *Notas sobre el comportamiento del chigüiro en confinamiento*. Bogotá, Colombia: Instit. Desarr. Rec. Nat. Renov. (INDERENA).

Cruz, G., and M. Espinal. 1985. Informe Nacional de Honduras. First symposium on east Pacific sea turtles. San José, Costa Rica.

Cueto, L. J., and C. F. Ponce. 1985. *Management of vicuña: Its contribution to rural development in the high Andes of Peru*. Conservation Guide no. 11. Rome: Food and Agriculture Organization of the United Nations.

Cunazza P., C. 1980. *El guanaco—importante recurso natural renovable de Magallanes*, 2d ed. Publ. no. 17. Santiago, Chile: Corporación Nacional Forestal, Departemento de Conservación del Medio Ambiente, Ministerio de Agricultura.

———. 1985. Extracción experimental de 100 guanacos en el sector Cameron, Tierra del Fuego. Pp. 100–15, in *Actas de la IV Convención Internacional Sobre Camélidos Sudamericanos*, ed. C. C. Venegas and P. C. Cunazza. Punta Arenas, Chile: Universidad de Magallanes.

———. 1988. Perspectivas de utilización económica de la vicuña y el guanaco en Chile. VI Convención Internacional de Especialistas en Camélidos, Oruro, Bolivia.

Darwin, C. 1845. *Journal of researches into the natural history and geology of the countries visited during the voyage of HMS "Beagle" round the world*. London: Ward, Lock & Co.

Dasmann, R. F. 1964. *Wildlife biology*. New York: Wiley.

———. 1987. The land ethic and the world scene. Pp. 107–14 in *Aldo Leopold: the man and his legacy*, ed. T. Tanner. Ankeny, Ia: Soil Conservation Society of America.

De Fina, A. L. 1976. Datos Agroclimáticos de la Republica Argentina. I.D.I.A. nos. 337–42, 57–186.

De Groot, R. S. 1983. Tourism and conservation in the Galapagos Islands. *Biol. Cons.* 26:291–300.

De Kadt, E. 1979. Social planning for tourism in the developing countries. *Ann. Tourism Res.* 6:36–48.

De la Espriella, R. O. N.d. Proteja y crie la boruga. Bogotá Corporación de Araracuara. Bogotá, Colombia.

De Schauensee, R., and W. H. Phelps. 1978. *A guide to the birds of Venezuela*. Princeton, N.J.: Princeton Univ. Press.

Dean, W. 1985. Forest conservation in southeastern Brazil, 1900 to 1955. *Environ. Rev.* 9:54–69.

Defler, T. R., and D. Pintor. 1985. Censusing primates by transect in a forest of known primate density. *Int. J. Primatol.* 6:243–260.

Defossé, G., and M. Merino. In press. *Structural and dynamic characteristics of grasslands of Northern Patagonia*. Buenos Aires, Argentina: Ed. Breymayer.

Deitz, D. C. 1979. *Behavioral ecology of young American alligators*. Ph.D. diss. Univ. Florida, Gainesville.

Deitz, D. C., and T. C. Hines. 1980. Alligator nesting in north-central Florida. *Copeia,* 1980: 249–58.

Delacour, J., and D. Amadon. 1973. *Curassows and related birds*. New York: American Museum of Natural History.

Delaney, M. J., and D. C. D. Happold. 1979. *Ecology of African mammals*. London: Longman.

Delgado, F. D. 1988. Save the Panamanian macaws: a project of ICBP-Panama. *Parrotletter* 1:12.

Denevan, W. M. 1976. The aboriginal population of Amazonia. Pp. 205–34, in *The native population of the Americas in 1492,* ed. W. M. Denevan. Madison, Wisc.: Univ. Wisconsin Press.

Dennler de la Tour, G. 1954. The guanaco. *Oryx* 2:273–9.

Dessem, D. 1985. Ontogenetic changes in the dentition and diet of *Tupinambis* (Lacertilia: Teiidae). *Copeia* 1985:245–7.

DeSteven, D., and F. E. Putz. 1984. Impact of mammals on early recruitment of a tropical canopy tree, *Dipteryx panamensis*, in Panama. *Oikos* 43:207–16.

DGFFS. See Dirección General de la Flora y Fauna Silvestres.

Diario Oficial de la Federación. 1982. *Ley Federal de Caza*. México, D.F.

———. 1983. Acuerdo que establece el calendario de captura, transporte y aprovechamiento racional de aves canoras y de ornato, correspondiente a la temporada 1983–1984. México, D.F.

———. 1984. Acuerdo que establece el calendario de captura, transporte y aprovechamiento racional de las aves canoras y de ornato, correspondiente a la temporada 1984–1985. México, D.F.

———. 1985. Acuerdo que establece el calendario de captura, transporte y aprovechamiento racional de las aves canoras y de ornato, correspondiente a la temporada 1985–1986. México, D.F.

———. 1986. Acuerdo que establece el calendario de captura, transporte y aprovechamiento racional de aves canoras y de ornato, correspondiente a la temporada 1986–1987. México, D.F.

———. 1987. Acuerdo que establece el calendario de captura, transporte y aprovechamiento racional de las aves canoras y de ornato, correspondiente a la temporada 1987–1988. México, D.F.

———. 1988. Ley General del Equilibrio Ecológico y la Protección al Ambiente. México, D.F.

Dietrich, W. E., D. M. Windsor, and T. Tunne. 1982. Geology, climate, and hydrology of Barro Colorado Island. Pp. 21–46 in *The ecology of a tropical forest,* ed. E. G. Leigh, Jr., A. S. Rand, and D. M. Windsor. Washington, D.C.: Smithsonian Institution Press.

DiMare, M. 1986. Food habits of an insular neotropical white-tailed deer (*Odocoileus virginianus*) population. M.S. thesis, Colorado State Univ., Fort Collins.

Dirección General de la Flora y Fauna Silvestres. 1982. Registro de solicitudes para la exportación de loros, cotorras y pericos en la temporada 1981–1982. SEDUE, México, D.F.

———. 1983. Relación de permisos de captura, para aves canoras y de ornato en la temporada 1982–83. SEDUE, Mexico, D.F.

Domning, D. P. 1982. Commercial exploitation of the manatees *Trichechus* in Brazil c. 1785–1973. *Biol. Cons.* 22:101–26.

Donadío, O. E. 1984. Los lacertilios fósiles de la Provincia de Córdoba (Sauria-Teiidae) y sus relaciones paleoambientales. Pp. 217–23 in *Actas del III Congreso de Paleontología y Bioestratigrafía.* Corrientes, Argentina.

Donadío, O. E., and J. M. Gallardo. 1984. Biología y conservación de las especies del género *Tupinambis* (Squamata, Sauria, Teiidae) en la República Argentina. Revista del Museo Argentino de Ciencias Naturales "Bernardino Rivadavia" e Instituto de Investigación de Ciencias Naturales 13: (11)117–27.

Doughty, R. W. 1975. *Feather fashions and bird preservation.* Berkeley: Univ. California Press.

Doughty, R. W., and N. Myers. 1971. Notes on the Amazon Wildlife Trade. *Envir. Cons.* 3:293–7.

Dourojeanni, M. J. 1974. Impacto de la producción de la fauna silvestre en la economía de la Amazonía Peruana. *Rev. Forest. Perú* 5:15–27.

———. 1978. El manejo integrado de la fauna forestal como fuente de proteínas para la población rural. Eight World Forestry Congr., Jakarta, Indonesia.

Dourojeanni, M. J., R. Hofman, R. Garcia, J. Malleaux, and A. Tovar. 1968. Observaciones preliminares para el manejo de las aves acuáticas del lago Junín, Perú. *Rev. Forest. Perú* 2:3–53.

Downing, R. L. 1980. Vital statistics of animal populations. Pp. 247–67 in *Wildlife management techniques manual, 4th* ed., ed. S. D. Schemnitz. Washington, D.C.: The Wildlife Society.

Duarte, J. C. S., and G. H. Rebêlo. 1985. Carnivore skins held in Brazil. *TRAFFIC Bull.* 7:16–17.

Dubost, G. 1968. Les niches écologiques des forêts tropicales sud-américaines et africaines, sources de convergences remarquables entre rongeurs et artiodactyles. *Terre et Vie* 22:3–28.

Dufour, D. 1983. Nutrition in the northwest Amazon: Household dietary intake and time-energy expenditure. Pp. 329–355 in *Adaptive responses of native Amazonians,* ed. R. B. Hames and W. T. Vickers. New York: Academic Press.

Dugan, B. A. 1982. The mating behavior of the green iguana (*Iguana iguana*). Pp. 320–41 in *Iguanas of the world: Their behavior, ecology and conservation,* ed. G. M. Burghardt and A. S. Rand. Park Ridge, N.J.: Noyes.

Eberhardt, L. L. 1977. Optimal policies for conservation of large mammals, with special reference to marine ecosystems. *Environ. Cons.* 4:205–12.

———. 1981. Population dynamics of the Pribilof fur seals. Pp. 197–220 in *Dynamics of large mammal populations,* ed. C. W. Fowler and T. D. Smith. New York: Wiley-Interscience.

Ehrenfeld, D. 1988. Why put a value on biodiversity? Pp. 212–16 in *Biodiversity,* ed. E. O. Wilson. Washington, D.C.: National Academy of Sciences.

Ehrlich, P., and A. Ehrlich. 1981. *Extinction.* New York: Random House.

Eilers, H. 1985. Protected areas and indigenous peoples. *Cultural Survival Q.* 9:6–9.

Eisenberg, J. F. 1979. Habitat, economy, and society: Some correlations and hypotheses for the neotropical primates. Pp. 215–62 in *Primate ecology and human origins,* ed. I. S. Bernstein and E. O. Smith. New York: Garland STPM Press.

———. 1980. The density and biomass of tropical mammals. Pp. 35–55 in *Conservation biology: An evolutionary-ecological perspective,* ed. M. E. Soulé and B. A. Wilcox. Sunderland, Mass.: Sinauer.

———. 1981. *The mammalian radiations.* Chicago: Univ. Chicago Press.

Eisenberg, J. F., M. A. O'Connell, and P. V. August. 1979. Density, productivity, and distribution of mammals in two Venezuelan habitats. Pp. 187–207 in *Vertebrate ecology in the northern neotropics,* ed. J. F. Eisenberg. Washington, D.C.: Smithsonian Institution Press.

Eisenberg, J. F., and R. Thorington. 1973. A preliminary analysis of a neotropical mammal fauna. *Biotropica* 5(3):150–61.

Eitnier, C. 1980. People and parrots in Mexico. *Watchbird* 7:39–40.

Eltringham, S. K. 1984. *Wildlife resources and economic development.* New York: Wiley.

Eltringham, S. K., and W. J. Jordan. 1981. The vicuña of the Pampa Galeras National Reserve. The conservation issue. Pp. 277–89 in *Problems in management of locally abundant wild animals,* ed. P. A. Jewell and S. Holt. New York: Academic Press.

Emmons, L. H. 1984. Geographic variation in densities and diversities of non-flying mammals in Amazonia. *Biotropica* 16:210–222.

———. 1987. Comparative feeding ecology of felids in a neotropical forest. *Behav. Ecol. Sociobiol.* 20:271–83.

———. 1987. Ecological considerations on the farming of game animals: Capybaras yes, pacas no. *Vida Silvestre Neotropical* 1:54–55.

Enders, R. K. 1935. Mammalian life histories from Barro Colorado Island, Panama. *Bull. Mus. Comp. Zool.* 78: 385–502.

Escobar B., A. 1973. Diagnóstico técnico económico de la explotación comercial del chigüire (*Hydrochoerus hydrochaeris*). Univ. Central Venezuela, Maracay, Venezuela. Unpublished report.

Escobar B., A., and E. Gonzalez-Jimenez. 1976. Estudio de la competencia alimenticia de los herbívoros mayores del Llano inundable con referencia especial al chigüire (*Hydrochoerus hydrochoeris*). *Agron. Tropic.* 26:215–27.

Estrada, H. J. 1966. La ganadería en el Estado Apure. Consejo de Bienestar Rural, Caracas, Venezuela.

Etheridge, R. E. 1982. Checklist of the Iguanine and Malagasy iguanid lizards. Pp. 7–37 in *Iguanas of the world: Their behavior, ecology and conservation,* ed. G. M. Burghardt and A. S. Rand. Park Ridge, N.J.: Noyes.

Evans, W. 1980. Deer transplant report. Alburquerque: New Mexico Department of Game and Fish.

Exotic bird sales soar, and smugglers flock to cash in. 1980. *Wall Street Journal* Jan. 10, 1.

F.A.O. See Food and Agriculture Organization

Fauna Argentina No. 2. *El carpincho.* 1983. Buenos Aires, Argentina: Centro Edit. América Latina.

Fauna Argentina No. 20. *El coipo*. 1983. Buenos Aires, Argentina: Centro Edit. América Latina.

Fauna Argentina No. 30. *La vizcacha*. 1984. Buenos Aires, Argentina: Centro Edit. América Latina.

Fernández, R. 1987. Condición actual del venado cola blanca (*Odocoileus virginianus*) con base en experiencias de caza. Pp. 55–61 in *Actas del Primer Taller Nacional sobre el Venado Cola Blanca del Pacífico Seco, Costa Rica,* ed. V. Solis, M. Rodriguez, and C. Vaughan. Heredia, Costa Rica: Dept. of Publications of the Universidad Nacional.

Fernández de Oviedo, G. 1851–55. *Historia general y natural de las Indias, islas y tierra firme.* Tomo I, Parte II. Madrid: Real Academia de Historia.

Fernandez Gonzales, R. 1980. La metodología del sistema alimentario Mexicano. *Ing. Agron.* 5:4–21.

Ferrario, F. F. 1980. Tourism potential and resource assessment. Pp. 311–20 in *Tourism planning and development issues,* ed. D. E. Hawkins, E. L. Shafer, and J. M. Rovelstad. Washington, D.C.: George Washington Univ.

ffrench, R. 1973. *A guide to the birds of Trinidad and Tobago.* Wynnewood, Pa.: Livingston Publishing.

FIBGE. See Fundação Instituto Brasileiro de Géografia e Estadistica.

Fitch, H. S., and R. W. Henderson. 1977. Age and sex differences, reproduction and conservation of *Iguana iguana.* Milwaukee Public Mus. Contr. Biol. and Geol. 13:1–21.

Fitch, H. S., R. W. Henderson, and D. M. Hillis. 1982. Exploitation of iguanas in Central America. Pp. 397–416 in *Iguanas of the world: Their behavior, ecology and conservation,* ed. G. M. Burghardt and A. S. Rand. Park Ridge, N.J.: Noyes.

Fitter, R. 1986. *Wildlife for man: How and why we should conserve wild species.* London: Collins.

Flamingo eggs smuggled into Chile. 1986. TRAFFIC Bull. 8:53.

Fleagle, J., R. Mittermeier, and A. Skopen. 1981. Differential habitat use by *Cebus apella* and *Saimiri sciureus* in central Surinam. *Primates* 22:361–67.

Flowers, N. M. 1983. Seasonal factors in subsistence, nutrition, and child growth in a central Brazilian community. Pp. 357–90 in *Adaptive responses of native Amazonians,* ed. R. B. Hames and W. T. Vickers. New York: Academic Press.

Food and Agriculture Organization. 1988. Taller sobre estrategias para el manejo y el aprovechamiento racional de capibara, caiman y tortugas de agua dulce. Universidad de São Paulo, Brazil/Oficina Regional de la F.A.O. para América Latina y El Caribe, Santiago, Chile.

Forewaker, J. 1981. *The struggle for land: A political economy of the pioneer frontier in Brazil from 1930 to the present day.* Cambridge Latin American Studies 39. Cambridge: Cambridge University Press.

Forni, F. H. 1981. Laguna Blanca, una comunidad de pastores de llamas en la Puna Catamarqueña. *Boletín CEIL,* no. 7, Buenos Aires, Argentina.

Forni, F. H., and R. Benencia. 1985. Estrategias rurales de reproducción con alta fecundidad; familia troncal y trabajo de migración por relevos. La situacion demográfica de una región subdesarrollada en un país moderno (Santiago del Estero, Argentina). Documento de trabajo No. 15, CEIL, Buenos Aires, Argentina.

Forni, F. H., M. I. Tort, and L. L. Pessina. 1987. El establecimiento de una reserva de vida silvestre en una comunidad de pastores de altura (Laguna Blanca, Depto. de Belén, Catamarca). *Boletín CEIL,* no. 15, 17–27. Buenos Aires, Argentina.

Forshaw, J. 1977. *Parrots of the world.* Neptune, N.J.: T.F.H. Publishers.

———. 1981. *Parrots of the world.* Devon, England: David and Charles.

Foster, R. B., and N. V. L. Brokaw. 1982. Structure and history of the vegetation of Barro Colorado Island. Pp. 67–81 in *The ecology of a tropical forest,* ed. E. G. Leigh, Jr., A. S. Rand, and D. M. Windsor. Washington, D.C.: Smithsonian Institution Press.

Fowler, C. W. 1980. Population models for large mammals. Pp. 297–320 in *Comparative population dynamics of large mammals: a search for management criteria,* ed. C. W. Fowler, W. T. Bunderson, M. B. Cherry, R. J. Ryel, and B. B. Steel. Report MMC-77/20. Washington, D.C.: U.S. Marine Mammal Commission.

———. 1981. Comparative population dynamics in large mammals. Pp. 437–56, in *Dynamics of large mammal populations,* ed. C. W. Fowler and T. D. Smith. New York: Wiley-Interscience.

Fowler, L. E. 1979. Hatching success and nest predation in the green sea turtle, *Chelonia mydas,* at Tortuguero, Costa Rica. *Ecology* 60:946–55.

Fowler, M. 1974. Veterinary aspects of restraint and transportation of wild animals. *Int. Zoo Yearbook* 14:28–33.

Fragoso, J. M. 1983. The ecology and behavior of Baird's tapir in Belize. B. S. thesis, Trent Univ., Peterborough, Ontario, Canada.

———. 1987. The habitat preferences and social structure of tapirs. M.S. thesis, Trent Univ., Peterborough, Ontario, Canada.

Frankel, O. H., and M. E. Soulé. 1981. *Conservation and evolution.* Cambridge: Cambridge University Press.

Franklin, W. L. 1973. High, wild world of the vicuña. *National Geographic* 143:76–91.

———. 1975. Guanacos of Peru. *Oryx* 13:191–202.

———. 1978. Preliminary results: Behavioral ecology of guanaco male groups at Torres del Paine National Park, Chile. Unpublished Earthwatch Field Report.

———. 1982a Round table: Conservation of South American Mammals. Pp. 531–533 in *Mammalian biology in South America,* ed. M. A. Mares and H. H. Genoways. Spec. Publ. Ser., vol. 6. Pittsburgh, Pa.: Pymatuning Laboratory of Ecology, University of Pittsburgh.

———. 1982b. Biology, ecology and relationship to man of the South American camelids. Pp. 457–89, in *Mammalian biology in South America,* ed. M. A. Mares and H. H. Genoways. Spec Publ. Ser., vol. 6. Pittsburgh, Pa.: Pymatuning Laboratory of Ecology, and University of Pittsburgh.

———. 1983. Contrasting socioecologies of South America's wild camelids: The vicuña and guanaco. Pp. 573–629 in *Advances in the study of mammalian behavior,* ed. J. F. Eisenberg and D. Kleiman. Spec. Publ. No. 7. Shippensburg, Pa: American Society of Mammalogists.

Fredin, R. A. 1984. Levels of maximum net productivity in populations of large terrestrial mammals. Pp. 381–87 in *Reproduction in whales, dolphins and porpoises,* ed. W. F. Perrin, R. L. Brownell, Jr., and D. P. De Master. Rep. Int. Whaling Comm., Special Issue 6.

Freese, C. H. 1986. The role of sustainable wildlife use in conservation and development in the tropics. *J. Wash. Acad. Sci.* 76:55–60.

Freese, C. H., P. G. Heltne, N. Castro, and G. Whitesides. 1982. Patterns and determinants of monkey densities in Peru and Bolivia, with notes on distributions. *Int. J. Primatol.* 3:53–90.

Freidmann, H., L. Griscom, and R. T. More. 1950. *Distributional checklist of the birds of Mexico,* Part 1. Pacific Coast Avifauna no. 29.

Fretay, J., and J. Lescure. 1979. Rapport sur l'étude de la protection des tortues marine en Guyane francaise. Notes sur le projet de reserve naturelle de Basse Mana. Ministere de la Culture et de l'Environnement, Paris, France.

Fritz, M. A. 1985. Population dynamics and preliminary estimates of the harvestability of the Patagonian guanaco. M.S. thesis, Iowa State Univ., Ames.

Froehlich, J. W., R. W. Thorington, Jr., and J. S. Otis. 1981. The demography of howler monkeys (*Alouatta palliata*) on Barro Colorado Island, Panama. *Int. J. Primatol.* 2:207–36.

Frost, M. D. 1977. Wildlife management in Belize: Program status and problems. *Wildl. Soc. Bull.* 5:48–51.

Fuerbringer B., J. 1974. El chigüiro, su cría y explotación racional. *Orient. Agroepec.* 99:5–59.

Fuller, K. S. and B. Swift. 1984. *Latin American wildlife trade laws.* Washington, D.C.: World Wildlife Fund—U.S.

———. 1985. *Latin American wildlife trade laws.* 2d ed. Washington, D.C.: TRAFFIC (USA), World Wildlife Fund—U.S.

Fundação Instituto Brasileiro de Géografia e Estadistica. 1983. IX Recenseamento Geral do Brasil—1980. Mão-de-obra, Mato Grosso, Brazil: Censo Demográfico.

Galan, C. 1984. La protección de la cuenca del Río Caroní. Caracas, Venezuela: Editorial Arte.

Galef, B. G. 1970. Aggression and timidity: Responses to novelty in feral Norway rats. *J. Comp. Physiol. Psychol.* 70:370–81.

Garrick, L. D., and J. W. Lang. 1977. Social signals and behaviors of adult alligators and crocodiles. *Am. Zool.* 17:225–39.

Garrido, J. L., R. Mazzanti, and D. A. Garrido. 1988. Distribución y densidades de guanaco en la Patagonia Argentina. VI Convención Internacional de Especialistas en Camélidos, Oruro, Bolivia.

Garza, A. M. 1987. Tráfico de especies en extinción por cientos de millones de dólares. *Excelsior,* July 31, Mexico, D.F.

Gaski, A. 1987. Court indicts three for Mexican bird smuggling. *TRAFFIC* 7:29.

Gaviria G., E. 1980. La fauna silvestre y su aprovechamiento por las comunidades Campa del río Pichis. *Rev. Forest. Perú* 10:192–201.

Geijskes, D. 1954. Het dierlijk voedsel van bosnegers aan de Marowijne. *Vox Guayanae* 1:61–83.

Geist, V. 1988. How markets in wildlife meat and parts, and the sale hunting of privileges, jeopardize wildlife conservation. *Cons. Biol.* 2:15–26.

Gilbert, S. 1983. *U.S. import of neotropical psittacines, 1968–1983.* II Congreso Iberamericano de Ornitología, Xalapa, México. Washington, D.C.: World Wildlife Fund, TRAFFIC (USA).

Gilmore, R. M. 1950. Fauna and ethnozoology of South America. Pp. 345–464 in *Handbook of South American Indians,* vol. 6, ed. J. Steward. Bull. of Bur. Am. Ethnol. 143:1–715.

Glander, K. E. 1980. Reproduction and population growth in free-ranging mantled howling monkeys. *Am. J. Phys. Anthropol.* 53:25–36.

Glanz, W. E. 1982. The terrestrial mammal fauna of Barro Colorado Island: Censuses and long-term changes. Pp. 455–68 in *The ecology of a tropical forest,* ed. E. G. Leigh, Jr., A. S. Rand, and D. M. Windsor. Washington, D.C.: Smithsonian Institution Press.

———. 1984. Food and habitat use by two sympatric *Sciurus* species in central Panama. *J. Mammal.* 65:343–47.

———. In press. Neotropical mammal densities: How unusual is the Barro Colorado Island, Panama, community? in *Four neotropical forests,* ed. A. W. Gentry. New Haven, Conn.: Yale Univ. Press.

Glanz, W. E., R. W. Thorington, Jr., J. Giacalone-Madden, and L. R. Heaney. 1982. Seasonal food use and demographic trends in *Sciurus granatensis.* Pp. 239–52 in *The ecology of a tropical forest,* ed. E. G. Leigh, Jr., A. S. Rand, and D. M. Windsor. Washington, D.C.: Smithsonian Institution Press.

Godoy, J. C. 1963. Evaluación de los recursos naturales de la Argentina: Fauna silvestre. Cons. Fed. Inversiones, Buenos Aires, Argentína.

Goldman, I. 1963. *The Cubeo: Indians of the northwest Amazon.* Urbana: Univ. Illinois Press.

Gómez, F. 1979a. Algunos aspectos sobre la ecología del pato güirirí pico negro (*Dendrocygna viduata* L.) en el llano inundable alto Apure de Venezuela. Trabajo especial de grado. Univ. Central de Venezuela, Carcas, Venezuela.

———. 1979b. Hábitos alimentícios del pato *Dendrocygna viduata* en el llano inundable, alto Apure de Venezuela. *Acta Científica Venezolana* 31:42.

———. 1979c. Crecimiento y desarrollo del pato güirirí pico negro (*Dendrocygna viduata*) en el llano inundable alto Apure, Venezuela. *Acta Científica Venezolana* 31:43.

Gómez, F., and A. T. Cringan. In press. *Biology, conservation and management of waterfowl in Venezuela.* Caracas: FUDENA.

Gómez, F., and M. K. Rylander. 1982. Observations of the feeding ecology and bioenergetics of the white-faced whistling-duck in Venezuela. *Wildfowl* 33:17–21.

Gomez-Nuñez, J. C. 1983. Observaciones sobre la actividad cinegética en Venezuela. *Acta Científica Venezolana* 23(suppl. 1):143.

Gomez-Nuñez, J. C. 1986. Análisis comparativo de las temporadas de caza 1981–1982 y 1982–1983. Informe del Servicio Nacional de Fauna, MARNR, Caracas, Venezuela.

González-Jimenez, E. 1977. The capybara. An indigenous source of meat in tropical America. *World Anim. Rev.* 21:24–30.

———. 1978. Digestive physiology and feeding of capybara (*Hydrochoerus hydrochaeris*). Pp. 163–77 in *Handbook series in nutrition and food,* sect. 9, ed. M. Rechcigl. Cleveland, Ohio: CRC press.

González-Jimenez, E., and J. Ojasti. 1987. Misión de asistencia técnica en el manejo de carpinchos en Argentina. Cons. Nac. Invest. Cient. Tecnol. (CONICIT), Caracas, Venezuela. Unpublished report.

Goodland, R. J. A. 1988. A major new opportunity to finance the preservation of biodiversity. Pp. 437–45 in *Biodiversity,* ed. E. O. Wilson. Washington, D.C.: National Academy Press.

Goodwin, G. 1946. Mammals of Costa Rica. *Bull. Am. Mus. Nat. Hist.* 87: Article 5.

Gorzula, S. J. 1978. An ecological study of *Caiman crocodilus crocodilus* inhabiting savanna lagoons in the Venezuelan Guyana. *Oecologia* 35:21–34.

Gorzula, S. J., and A. C. Seijas. 1989. The common caiman. Pp. 44–61 in *Crocodiles: Their ecology, management, and conservation.* Gland, Switzerland: IUCN

Goulding, W. M. 1980. *The fishes and the forest.* Berkeley: Univ. California Press.

————. 1985. Forest fishes of the Amazon. Pp. 267–76 in *Amazonia,* ed. G. T. Prance and T. E. Lovejoy. Oxford: Pergamon Press.

Gray, P. H. 1980. Wanderlust tourism: Problems of infrastructure. *Ann. Tourism Res.* 8(2):285–90.

Green, D., and F. Ortiz-Crespo. 1982. The status of sea turtle population in the central eastern Pacific. Pp. 221–33 in *Biology and conservation of sea turtles,* ed. K. S. Bjorndal. Washington, D.C.: Smithsonian Institution Press.

Grimwood, I. R. 1968. *Notes on the distribution and status of some Peruvian mammals.* Spec. Publ. 21. New York: New York Zool. Soc.

Groom, M. J. 1986. Recomendaciones sobre el control de los efectos negativos de turismo contra la anidación de aves de la orilla. Technical report to the director general of Forests and Wildlife, Ministerio de Agricultura, Lima, Perú.

————. 1990. Management of ecotourism in Manu National Park: Controlling negative effects on beachnesting birds and other riverine animals. In *Proceedings of First International Symposium on Ecotourism and Resource Conservation,* ed. J. Kuslev and J. Andrews. Washington, D.C.: Association of Wetland Managers.

————. N.d. Sugerencias para un plan de manejo de turismo y el uso humano de las aves de la orilla en el Parque Nacional del Manú. Technical report to the Corporation for the Development of Madre de Dios, Peru. Unpublished manuscript.

Groombridge, B. 1982. *The IUCN Amphibia-Reptilia red data book.* Part 1: *Testudines, Crocodylia, Rhynchocephalia.* Gland, Switzerland: IUCN

Gross, D. R. 1975. Protein capture and cultural development in the Amazon Basin. *Am. Anthropol.* 77:526–49.

Gudynas, E. 1982. Some notes from Uruguay on the behaviour, ecology, and conservation of the macroteiid lizard, *Tupinambis teguixin. Bull. Chicago Herp. Soc.* 16:29–39.

————. 1985. Notas sobre teiidos del Uruguay (Lacertilia: Teiidae), I. Nuevos registros y distribución geográfica de *Tupinambis teguixin, Teius teyou, Cnemidophorus lacertoides* y *Pantodactylus schreibersii.* CIPFE-CED Orione Cont. Biol. Montevideo 12:9–17.

Gumilla, J. S. J. 1741. *El Orinoco llustrado. Historia natural y geografía de este gran río y su caudolosas vertientes.* Madrid: Manuel Fernandez.

Haemig, P. D. 1978. Aztec emperor Auitzoti and the great-tailed grackle. *Biotropica* 10:11–17.

Halffter, G. 1981. The Mapimi Biosphere Reserve: Local participation in conservation and development. *Ambio* 10(2–3):93–96.

Hall, P. M., and D. R. Johnson. 1987. Nesting biology of *Crocodylus novaeguineae* in Lake Murry District, Papua New Guinea. *Herpetologica* 43:249–58.

Halls, L. K., ed. 1984. *White-tailed deer: Ecology and management.* Harrisburg, Pa.: Stackpole.

Hames, R. B. 1979. Comparison of the efficiencies of the shotgun and the bow in neotropical forest hunting. *Human Ecol.* 7:219–52.

Hames, R. B., and W. T. Vickers. 1983. Introduction. Pp. 1–26 in *Adaptive responses of native Amazonians,* ed. R. B. Hames and W. T. Vickers. New York: Academic Press.

Handley, C. O., Jr. 1950. Game mammals of Guatemala. Pp. 141–62 in *A fish and wildlife survey of Guatemala,* ed. G. B. Saunders, A. D. Holloway, and C. Handley, Jr. Spec. Scient. Rep. Wildl. 5. Washington, D.C.: U.S. Dept. of Int., Fish and Wildlife Service.

Hanks, J. 1981. Characteristics of population condition. Pp. 47–73 in *Dynamics of large mammal populations,* ed. C. W. Fowler and T. D. Smith. New York: Wiley.

Hardie, L. 1987. Brazilian macaws get second chance. *TRAFFIC Bull. (USA)* 7:7.

Hardin, G. 1968. The tragedy of the commons. *Science* 162:1243–44.

———. 1985. Filters against folly. New York: Viking Penguin.

Hargrave, L. L. 1970. *Mexican macaws. Comparative osteology and survey of remains from the southwest.* Anthropological papers, no. 20, Univ. Arizona, Tucson.

Harlow, R. F. 1984. Habitat evaluation. Pp. 601–28 in *White-tailed deer: Ecology and management,* ed. L. K. Halls. Harrisburg, Pa.: Stackpole.

Harris, D. M. 1982. The phenology, growth and survival of the green iguana (*Iguana iguana*) in northern Colombia. Pp. 150–61 in *Iguanas of the world: Their behavior, ecology and conservation,* ed. G. M. Burghardt and A. S. Rand. Park Ridge, N.J.: Noyes.

Harris, L. D., and I. H. Kochel. 1981. A decision-making framework for population management. Pp. 221–40 in *Dynamics of large mammal populations,* ed. C. W. Fowler and T. D. Smith. New York: Wiley-Interscience.

Harrison, B. 1974. Animal trade, an international issue. *Int. Zool. Yearbook* 14:3–21.

Hartshorn, G., L. Nicolait, L. Hartshorn, G. Bevier, R. Brightman, J. Cal, A. Cawich, W. Davidson, R. Dubsis, C. Dyer, J. Gibson, W. Hawley, J. Leonard, R. Nicolait, D. Weyer, H. White, C. Wright. 1984. *Belize: Country environmental profile, a field study.* San Jose, Costa Rica: Trejos. Hnos. Sucs.

Hayne, D. H. 1984. Population dynamics and analysis. Pp. 203–10 in *White-tailed deer: Ecology and management,* ed. L. K. Halls. Harrisburg, Pa.: Stackpole.

Haynes, A. M. 1987. Human exploitation of seabirds in Jamaica. *Biol. Cons.* 41:99–124.

Hayssen, V. 1984. Basal metabolic rate and the intrinsic rate of increase: An empirical and theoretical reexamination. *Oecologia* 64: 419–24.

Heckadon, S. 1982. *Colonización y destrucción de bosques en Panamá.* Panamá: Impretex.

———. 1983. *Cuando se acaban los montes.* Panamá: Impretex.

Hemley, G. 1984a. World trade in tegu skins. *TRAFFIC Bull.* 5:60–62.

———. 1984b. Statement on significant trade of Appendix II Species. First Meeting of the Technical Committee of CITES, Brussels, Belgium.

———. 1988. International wildlife trade. Pp. 337–74 in *Audubon wildlife reports,* ed. W. J. Chandler. New York: Academic Press.

Hemley, G., and J. Caldwell. 1986. The crocodile skin trade since 1979. Pp. 398–421 in *Crocodiles*. IUCN Publication. Caracas, Venezuela.

Henderson, R. W. 1974. Aspects of the ecology of the juvenile common iguana (*Iguana iguana*). *Herpetologica* 30:327–32.

Hernández-Camacho, J., and R. W. Cooper. 1976. The nonhuman primates of Colombia. Pp. 35–69 in *Neotropical primates: Field studies and conservation,* ed. R. W. Thorington, Jr., and P. G. Heltne. Washington, D.C.: National Academy of Sciences.

Herrera, E. A. 1986. The behavioural ecology of the capybara, *Hydrochoerus hydrochaeris*. Ph.D. diss., Univ. Oxford.

Hershkovitz, P. 1969. The evolution of mammals on southern continents. *Q. Rev. Biol.* 44:1–70.

Hess, E. 1959. Imprinting. *Science* 130:421–32.

Hesselton, W., and R. Hesselton. 1982. White-tailed deer (*Odocoileus virginianus*). Pp. 878–901 in *Wild mammals of North America: Biology, management and economics,* ed. J. Chapman and G. Feldhamer. Baltimore, Md.: The Johns Hopkins Univ. Press.

Hill, K., and K. Hawkes. 1983. Neotropical hunting among the Aché of eastern Paraguay. Pp. 139–88 in *Adaptive responses of native Amazonians,* ed. R. B. Hames and W. T. Vickers. New York: Academic Press.

Hill, M. D. 1979. TWINSPAN—A FORTRAN program for arranging multivariate data in an ordered two-way table by classification of the individuals and attributes. Ithaca, N.Y.; Cornell Univ.

Hill, R. L., and D. J. Green. 1971. Investigation of the damage by the crab *Ocypode quadrata* to the eggs of the green turtle *Chelonia mydas*. Pp. 11–13 in Bulletin 2 (Suriname turtle notes). Paramaribo, Suriname: The Foundation for Nature Preservation in Suriname (Stinasu).

Hillestad, H. 1984. *Stocking and genetic variability of white-tailed deer in the southeastern United States*. Ph.D. diss., Univ. Georgia, Athens.

Hilty, S. L., and W. L. Brown. 1986. *A guide to the birds of Colombia*. Princeton, N.J.: Princeton Univ. Press.

Hines, T., and C. L. Abercrombie, III. 1987. The management of alligators in Florida. Pp. 43–47 in *Wildlife management: Crocodiles and alligators,* ed. G. J. W. Webb, S. C. Manolis, and P. J. Whitehead. Chipping Norton, Australia: Surrey Beatty.

Hirth, H. F. 1963. Some aspects of the natural history of *Iguana iguana* on a tropical strand. *Ecology* 44(3):613–5.

Hirth, H., F. and A. F. Carr. 1970. The green turtle in the Gulf of Aden and the Seychelles Islands. Verhandlingen der Koninklijke Nederlandse Academia van Wetenschappen, AFD. *Natuurkunde Tweede Reeds* 58:1–48.

Hofmann, R., and D. Otte. 1983. *Consideraciones sobre el manejo de los camélidos silvestres en la Argentina*. Catamarca, Argentina. Unpublished report.

Hofmann, R. K., K. C. Otte, C. F. Ponce, and M. A. Rios. 1983. *El manejo de la vicuña silvestre*. Eschborn, West Germany: Sociedad Alemana de Cooperación Técnica (GTZ).

Holdridge, L. R. 1967. Life zone ecology. San Jose, Costa Rica: Tropical Science Center.

Holdridge, L. R., W. C. Grenke, W. H. Hatheway, T. Liang, and J. A. Tosi, Jr. 1971. *Forest environments in tropical life zones: A pilot study*. Oxford: Pergamon Press.

Hollander, M., and D. A. Wolfe. 1973. *Nonparametric statistical methods.* New York: Wiley.

Hollands, M. 1987. The management of crocodiles in Papua New Guinea. Pp. 73–89 in *Wildlife management: Crocodiles and alligators,* ed. G. J. W. Webb, S. C. Manolis, and P. J. Whitehead. Chipping Norton, Australia: Surrey Beatty.

Hornaday, W. T. 1913. *Our vanishing wildlife.* New York: New York Zool. Soc.

Howard, W. E. 1970. Relationship of wildlife to sheep husbandry in Patagonia, Argentina. *FAO Report* 14: 1–31.

Hughes, D., and J. D. Richard. 1974. The nesting of the Pacific ridley turtle *Lepidochelys olivacea* on Playa Nancite, Costa Rica. *Marine Biology* 24:97–107.

Hughes, G. R. 1974. The sea turtles of southeast Africa. II. The biology of the Tongaland loggerhead turtle *Caretta caretta* L. with comments on the leatherback turtle *Dermochelys coriacea* L. and the green turtle *Chelonia* mydas L. in the study region. Investigational Report 36. Durban, South Africa: Oceanographic Research Institute.

Humbolt, A. B. 1860. *Reise in die Aquinoctial-Gegenden des Neuen Continents.* Stuttgart: J. C. Cottascher Verlag.

Hurlbert, S. H. 1984. Pseudoreplication and the design of ecological field experiments. *Ecol. Monogr.* 54:187–211.

Hurst, G. A., and W. Rosene. 1985. Regulation and restrictions pertaining to bobwhite quail harvests in the southeast. Pp. 301–8 in *Game harvest management,* ed. S. L. Beasom and S. F. Roberson. Kingsville, Texas: Caesar Kleberg Wildlife Research Inst.

Huyghe, M. 1987. Review of CITES implementation in the department of French Guiana. TRAFFIC (Belgium).

Hvidberg-Hansen, H. 1970a. Utilization of the giant otter (*Pterounura brasiliensis Gmelin*) in Peru. FAO Forestry Research and Training Project UNDP/SF no. 116. Unpublished report.

———. 1970b. Utilization of the jaguar (*Panthera onca* Linne 1758) in Peru. FAO Forestry Research and Training Project UNPD/SF no. 116. Unpublished report.

———. 1970c. Utilization of the Amazon otter (*Lutra incarum* Thomas) in Peru. FAO Forestry Research and Training Project UNPD/SF no. 116. Unpublished report.

———. 1970d. Utilization of the capybara (*Hydrochoerus hydrochaeris Linne*) in Peru. FAO Forestry Research and Training Project UNPD/SF/ no. 116. Unpublished report.

———. 1970e. Utilization of the collared peccary (*Tayassu tajacu* Linne) in Peru. FAO Forestry Research and Training Project UNDP/SF no. 116. Unpublished report.

IBGE. See Instituto Brasileiro de Geografica e Estatística.

ICBP. See International Council for Bird Preservation.

Iñigo, E. E. N.d. Explotación de las aves silvestres en México. Memorias del Segundo Congreso Iberoamericano de Ornitología. Diciembre 1983, Xalapa, México. Unpublished manuscript.

———. 1986. Active trade threatens Mexican avifauna. *TRAFFIC (U.S.A.)* 6:6–7.

Iñigo, E. E., J. Ayala, F. Ornelas, J. J. Perez, L. Eguiarte, M. A. Ramos, S. Barrios, and F. Gonzalez. N.d. Psittacine birds in Mexico: a regional report. Second meeting of the Parrot Specialist Group. October 13–18, 1988, Curitiba, Brazil. Unpublished manuscript.

Inskipp, T. P. 1975. *All heaven in a rage: A study into the importation of birds into the United Kingdom*. London: Royal Society for the Protection of Birds.

Inskipp, T., P. S. Broad, and R. Luxmoore. 1988. *Significant trade in wildlife: A review of selected species in CITES appendix II*, Vol. 3: *Birds*. Cambridge, England: IUCN and CITES.

Inskipp, T. P., and A. Gamell. 1979. The extent of world trade in birds and the mortality involved. *ICBP, XIII Bull:* 98–103.

Inskipp, T. P., and G. J. Thomas. 1976. *Airborne birds: A further study in the importation of birds into the United Kingdom*. Royal Society for the Protection of Birds, United Kingdom.

Inskipp, T. P., and S. Wells. 1979. *International trade in wildlife*. London: Earthscan Publications, IIED.

Instituto Brasileiro de Geográfia e Estatística (IBGE). 1977. Geografia do Brasil—Região Centro-Oeste. Rio de Janeiro, Brazil: Fundaçao IBGE.

International Council for Bird Preservation (ICBP). 1983. *Resolutions of the XVIII World Conference*.

International Tourism Reports. 1982. *Peru*. 1988(2):21–36.

International Union for the Conservation of Nature and Natural Resources (IUCN). 1982. *Mammal red data book*. Gland, Switzerland: IUCN.

———. 1988. *1988 IUCN red list of threatened animals*. Gland, Switzerland: IUCN.

———. 1981. IUCN WWF position statement on vicuña. *IUCN Bull*. 12:12–13.

———. 1982. *Directory of neotropical protected areas*. Dublin, Ireland: Tycooly International Publishing.

Iriarte, J. A., and F. M. Jaksić. 1986. The fur trade in Chile: An overview of seventy-five years of export data (1910–1984). *Biol. Conserv*. 38:243–53.

Irurzun, J. 1978. Contribución al conocimiento del clima de la Provincia de Catamarca. Pp. 43–81 in *Geografía de Catamarca*, ed. P. Alberti, et al. Buenos Aires: Sociedad Argentina de Estudios Geográficos. Serie Especial 5, GEA. Argentina.

IUCN. See International Union for the Conservation of Nature and Natural Resources.

Jackson, D. D. 1985. Pursued in the wild for the pet trade, parrots are perched on a risky limb. *Smithsonian* 16:59–66.

Jackson, J. E. 1986. The hare trade in Argentina. *TRAFFIC Bull*. 7:72.

Jackson, J. E., and A. Langguth. 1987. Ecology and status of the pampas deer in the Argentinian pampas and Uruguay. Pp. 402–14 in *Biology and management of the Cervidae*, ed. C. M. Wemmer. Washington, D.C.: Smithsonian Institution Press.

Jahn, L., and J. Trefethen. 1978. Funding wildlife conservation programs. Pp. 456–70 in *Wildlife and America*, ed. H. P. Brokaw. Washington, D.C.: Council on Environmental Quality.

Janzen, D. H. 1982. Wild plant acceptability to a captive Costa Rican Baird's tapir. *Brenesia* 19/20:99–128.

———. 1983a. *Tapirus bairdii*. Pp. 496–97 in *Costa Rican natural history*, ed. D. H. Janzen. Chicago: Univ. Chicago Press.

———. 1983b. Venado, venado cola blanca, white-tailed deer. Pp. 481–83 in *Costa Rican natural history*, ed. D. H. Janzen. Chicago: Univ. Chicago Press.

———. 1986. *Guanacaste National Park: Tropical, ecological, and cultural restoration*. San Jose, Costa Rica: Editorial Universidad Estal a Distancia.

———. 1987. Cambios en al habitat para el venado cola blanca durante los ultimos

10,000 años. Pp. 45–46 in *Actas del Primer Taller Nacional sobre el Venado Cola Blanca (Odocoileus virginianus) del Pacífico Seco, Costa Rica*, ed. V. Solis, M. Rodriguez, and C. Vaughan. Heredia, Costa Rica: Dept. de Publicaciones de la Universidad Nacional.

Jeffreys, T. 1760. *The Natural and Civil History of the French Dominions in North and South America*. London: N.p.

Jenkins, C. L. 1982a. The use of investment incentives for tourism projects in developing countries. *Tourism Mgmt.* 3(2):91–97.

———. 1982b. The effects of scale in tourism projects in developing countries. *Ann. Tourism Res.* 9(2):229–49.

Jenkins, C. L., and B. M. Henry. 1982. Government involvement in tourism in developing countries. *Ann. Tourism Res.* 9(4):499–521.

Jennings, J. 1977. Quarantine stations. *Watchbird* 4:16–19.

Joanen, T., and L. McNease. 1987. The management of alligators in Louisiana, USA. Pp. 33–42 in *Wildlife management: Crocodiles and alligators,* ed. G. J. W. Webb, S. C. Manolis, and P. J. Whitehead. Chipping Norton, Australia: Surrey Beatty.

Johns, A. D. 1983. Ecological effects of selective logging in a West Malaysian rainforest. Ph.D. diss., Univ. Cambridge, Cambridge.

———. 1985. Selective logging and wildlife conservation in tropical rain-forest: Problems and recommendations. *Biol. Cons.* 31:355–75.

———. 1986. Effects of selective logging on the behavioral ecology of West Malaysian primates. *Ecology* 67:684–94.

———. 1987. Continuing problems for Amazon river turtles. *Oryx* 21:25–28.

Johnson, M. S., and D. R. Chaffy. 1972. An inventory of the Chiquibul Forest Reserve, Belize. Land Resources Study no. 14, Land Resources Div., Suributon, England.

Jones, C. G. 1945. Past and present white-wings. *Texas Game and Fish* 3:13–18.

Jorgenson, A., and J. B. Thomsen. 1987. Neotropical parrots imported by the United States, 1981 to 1985. *TRAFFIC (USA)* 7:3–8.

Jorgenson, J. P. 1986. Notes on the ecology and behavior of capybaras in northeastern Colombia. *Vida Silv. Neotrop.* 1:31–40.

Jorgenson, J. P. and A. B. Jorgenson. In press. Imports of CITES-regulated mammals into the United States from Latin America: 1982–1984. In *Latin American mammals: Their conservation, ecology and evolution,* ed. M. A. Mares and H. Genoways.

Jungius, H. 1971. The vicuña in Bolivia: the status of an endangered species, and recommendations for its conservation. *Zeitschrift für Saugetierkunde* 36:129–246.

Kamstra, J. 1983. Habitat preferences, feeding behavior and some conservation considerations of the Baird's tapir in Belize. B. S. thesis, Trent Univ., Peterborough, Ontario, Canada.

Kar, C. S. 1980. Discovery of second mass nesting ground for the Pacific ridley sea turtle in Orissa, India. *Marine Turtle Newsletter* 23:3.

Karr, J. R. 1971. Structure of avian communities in selected Panama and Illinois habitats. *Ecol. Monogr.* 41:207–39.

———. 1982. Avian extinction on Barro Colorado Island, Panama: a reassessment. *Am. Nat.* 119:220–39.

Kerbis, J. 1980. The analysis of faunal remains from the Vidor site. *Vinculos* 6:125–40.

Kilgour, R. 1985. Imprinting in farm animals. In *Ethology of farm animals,* ed. A. F. Fraser. Amsterdam: Elsevier.

Kiltie, R. A. 1980. More on Amazon cultural ecology. *Curr. Anthropol.* 21:541–4.

Kiltie, R. A., and J. Terborgh. 1983. Observations on the behavior of rain forest peccaries in Peru: Why do white-lipped peccaries form herds? *Z. Tierpsychol.* 62:241–55.

King, F. W. 1978. The wildlife trade. Pp. 253–71 in *Wildlife and America,* ed. H. P. Brokaw. Washington, D.C.: Council on Environmental Quality.

———. 1986. Desarrollo de un programa de conservación de los cocodrilos del género *Caiman* en la region central de América del Sur. Unpublished proposal to CITES.

King, F. W., and P. Brazaitis. 1971. Species identification of commercial crocodilian skins. *Sci. Contri. N.Y. Zool. Soc.* 56:15–75.

Koford, C. B. 1957. The vicuña and the puna. *Ecol. Monogr.* 27:153–219.

Krieg, H. 1929. Biologische Reisenstudien in Südamerika. XV. Zur Oekologie de grossen Nagern des Gran Chaco und seiner Grezgebiete. *Z. Morph. Oekol. Tiere* 15:755–85.

Kwapena, N., and M. Bolton. 1982. The national crocodile project in Papua New Guinea. Pp. 315–21 in *Crocodiles.* Gainesville, Fla.: IUCN.

Kyle, R. 1987. Rodents under the carving knife. *New Scientist* 114:58–62.

Lacher, T. E. 1979. Rates of growth in *Kerodon rupestris* and an assessment of its potential as a domesticated food source. *Papeis Avulsos Zool. (S. Paulo)* 33:67–76.

Lamotte, J. 1983. Research on the characteristics of energy flows within natural and man-altered ecosystems. In *Disturbance and ecosystems,* ed. H. A. Mooney and M. Godron. Berlin: Springer-Verlag.

Lander, E. 1974. Observaciones preliminares sobre lapas *Agouti paca* (Linne, 1776) (Rodentia, Agoutidae) en Venezuela. Fac. Agronomia IZA, UCU, Maracay, Venezuela.

Lang, J. W., R. Whitaker, and H. Andrews. 1986. Male parental care in Mugger crocodiles. *Nat. Geogr. Res.* 2:519–25.

Langenau, E., S. R. Kellert, and J. E. Applegate. 1984. Values in management. Pp. 699–720 in *White-tailed deer: Ecology and management,* ed. L. K. Halls. Harrisburg, Pa.: Stackpole.

Larkin, P. A. 1977. An epitaph for the concept of maximum sustained yield. *Trans. Am. Fish. Soc.* 106:1–11.

Lathrap, D. W. 1975. The antiquity and importance of long-distance trade relationships in the moist tropics of Pre-Columbian South America. *World Archaeol.* 5:170–86.

Lavenroth, W. K. 1979. Grassland primary production: North American grasslands in perspective. Pp. 3–24 in *Perspectives in grassland ecology,* ed. N. French. Ecological Studies 32. New York: Springer-Verlag.

Lee, R. B. 1979. *The !Kung San: Men, women, and work in a foraging society.* Cambridge: Cambridge Univ. Press.

Leigh, E. G., Jr. 1982. Introduction. Pp. 11–17 in *The ecology of a tropical forest,* ed. E. G. Leigh, Jr., A. S. Rand, and D. M. Windsor. Washington, D.C.: Smithsonian Institution Press.

Lemke, T. O. 1981. Wildlife management in Colombia: The first ten years. *Wildlife Soc. Bull.* 9:28–36.

Lenselink, J. 1972. De jachtopbrengst in een Surinaams Triodorp. *De Surinaamse Landbouw* 20:37–41.

Leopold, A. S. 1959. *Wildlife of Mexico: The game birds and mammals.* Berkeley: Univ. California Press.

————. 1965. *Fauna silvestre de México.* Mexico City: IMERNAR.

Leslie, P. H. 1945. On the use of matrices in certain population mathematics. *Biometrika* 33:183–212.

Levinson, M. 1987. Cheap thrills. *Int. Wildlife* Sept–Oct. 1987.

Licht, P., and W. R. Moberly. 1965. Thermal requirements of embryonic development in the tropical lizard *Iguana iguana. Copeia* 1965:515–7.

Lizot, J. 1979. On food taboos and Amazonian cultural ecology. *Curr. Anthropol.* 20:150–1.

Lombardero, O. J. 1955. La historia del carpincho. *Diana (Buenos Aires)* 17:60–65.

López, E. 1987. La acción oficial en el control de la utilización del venado cola blanca. Pp. 76–81 in *Actas del Primer Taller Nacional sobre el venado cola blanca (Odocoileus virginianus) del Pacífico Seco, Costa Rica,* ed. V. Solis, M. Rodriguez, and C. Vaughan. Heredia, Costa Rica: Dept. de Publicaciones de la Universidad Nacional.

Lopez, E., and S. E. Cornelius. 1985. Informe nacional de Costa Rica. First symposium on east Pacific sea turtles, San Jose, Costa Rica, 2–6 December 1985.

Lopez Pizarro, E. 1986. Caño Negro national wildlife refuge. Pp. 190–93 in *Gestion de la faune sauvage en forêt neotropicale húmide.* Paris: Cons. Intern. Chasse Conserv. Gibier.

Lorenz, K. 1935. Der Kumpan in der Umwelt dess Vogels. *J. Ornithol.* 83:137–213.

Lott, D. F. 1984. Intraspecific variation in the social system of wild vertebrates. *Behaviour* 88:266–325.

Lovejoy, T. E., R. O. Bierregaard Jr., A. B. Rylands, J. R. Malcolm, C. E. Quintela, L. H. Harper, K. S. Brown, Jr., A. H. Powell, G. V. N. Powell, H. O. R. Schubart, and M. B. Hays. 1986. Edge and other effects of isolation on Amazon forest fragments. Pp. 257–85 in *Conservation biology: The science of scarcity and diversity,* ed. M. E. Soulé. Sunderland, Mass.: Sinauer.

Luxmoore, R. A. 1988. The caiman lizard. *TRAFFIC Bull.* 9:10–81.

Luxmoore, R. A., J. G. Barzdo, S. R. Broad, and D. A. Jones. 1985. *A directory of crocodilian farming operations.* Gland, Switzerland: IUCN.

Lyster, S. 1985. *International wildlife law.* Cambridge: Grotius.

MacKinnon, J., K. MacKinnon, G. Child, and J. Thorsell, comps. 1986. *Managing protected areas in the tropics.* Gland, Switzerland: IUCN.

Madríz, M. 1984. Análisis de la cacería de patos silbadores (*Dendrocygna,* Aves, Anseriformes) en las áreas de cultivo de arroz en Venezuela. *Bol. Soc. Ven. Cien. Nat.* 39:89–105.

Madríz, M. T., N. Márquez, M. Correa, F. Bisbal, and G. Cordero. 1981. Evaluación de la temporada de cacería de patos silbadores *Dendrocygna* (Aves, Antidae), con fines deportivos durante el año 1980 en Venezuela. *Memoria Soc. Cien. Nat. La Salle* 41 (115):117–28.

Magnusson, W. E. 1984. Economics, developing countries and the captive propagation of crocodilians. *Wildl. Soc. Bull.* 12:194–97.

Marcellini. D. L. 1979. Activity patterns and densities of Venezuelan caiman (*Caiman crocodilus*) and pond turtles (*Podocnemis vogli*). Pp. 263–71 in *Vertebrate ecology in the northern neotropics,* ed. J. F. Eisenberg. Washington, D.C.: Smithsonian Institution Press.

Marchinton, L., and D. Hirth. 1984. Behavior. Pp. 129–68 in *White-tailed deer: Ecology and management,* ed. L. K. Halls. Harrisburg, Pa.: Stackpole.

Mares, M. A. 1982. The scope of South American mammalian biology: Perspectives on a decade of research. Pp. 1–26 in *Mammalian biology in South America,* ed. M. A. Mares and H. H. Genoways. Pymatuning Symp. Ecol., Vol. 6. Pittsburgh, Pa.: Univ. of Pittsburgh.

———. 1986. Conservation in South America: Problems, consequences, and solutions. *Science* 233:734–39.

Mares, M. A., and R. A. Ojeda. 1984. Faunal commercialization and conservation in South America. *BioScience* 34:580–84.

Marion, W. R. 1974. Status of the plain chachalaca in south Texas. *Wilson Bull.* 86:200–205.

MARNR. See Ministerio del Ambiente y de los Recursos Naturales Renovables

Marsh, E. G., Jr. 1941. *White-winged dove in Texas.* Texas Game, Fish and Oyster Comm. Typescript.

Marsh, E. G., Jr., and G. B. Saunders. 1942. The status of the white-winged dove in Texas. *Wilson Bull.* 54:145–46.

Marta V., S. 1986. *Evaluación económica de la producción del chigüire en Venezuela 1975–1985.* Ministerio del Ambiente, Caracas. Unpublished report.

Mason, I. L. 1984. Preface in *The evolution of domesticated animals,* ed. I. L. Mason. London: Longman.

Matamoros, Y. 1982a. Notas sobre la biología del tepezcuinte, *Cuniculus paca,* Brisson (Rodentia, Dasyproctidae) en cautiverio. *Brenesia* 19/21:71–82.

———. 1982b. Investigaciones preliminares sobre la reproducción, comportamiento, alimentación y manejo de tepezcuinte (*Cuniculus paca,* Brisson) en cautiverio. Pp. 961–92 in *Zoologia neotropical,* ed. P. J. Salinas. Actas del VIII cong. Latinoamericano de Zoología.

Matamoros, Y., and N. Pashov. 1986. Métodos y técnicas utilizados en la investigación del tepezcuinte (*Agouti paca* sinn. *Cuniculus paca*). *Turrialba* 36:245–262.

Mazzaccaro, A. P. 1980. A study of white-wing dove hunters in south Texas and the Republic of Mexico. Ph.D. diss., Texas A&M Univ., College Station.

McCartney, R. B. 1983. The fulvous tree duck in Louisiana. M. S. thesis, Utah State Univ., Logan.

McCoy, M., and C. Vaughan. 1981. Resultado preliminares del estudio del venado colablanca (*Odocoileus virginianus*) en Costa Rica. Heredia, Costa Rica: Univ. Nacional.

McCullough, D. R. 1979. The George Reserve deer herd: Population ecology of a K-selected species. Ann Arbor: Univ. Michigan Press.

———. 1984. Lessons from the George Reserve, Michigan. Pp. 211–42 in *White-tailed deer: Ecology and management,* ed. L. K. Halls. Harrisburg, Pa.: Stackpole.

McGrath, D. G. 1986. *The animal products trade in the Brazilian Amazon.* Washington, D.C. Unpublished report to WWF-US.

McMahan, L. R. 1986. The international cat trade. Pp. 461–88 in *Cats of the world: Biology, conservation, and management,* ed. S. D. Miller and D. D. Everett. Washington, D.C.: National Wildlife Federation.

McNeely, J. A. 1988. Economics and biological diversity: Developing and using economic incentives to conserve biological resources. Gland, Switzerland: IUCN.

Meanley, B., and A. Meanley. 1959. Observations on the fulvous tree duck in Louisiana. *Wilson Bull.* 71:33–35.

Mech, D. 1984. Predators and predation. Pp. 189–200 in *White-tailed deer: Ecology and management,* ed. L. K. Halls. Harrisburg, Pa.: Stackpole.

Medem, F. 1981. *Los Crocodylia de Sur America.* Vol. 1. Bogotá: Univ. Nac. de Colombia.

———. 1983. *Los Crocodylia de Sur América.* Vol. 2. Bogotá: Univ. Nac. de Colombia.

Meggers, B. J. 1971. *Amazonia: Man and culture in a counterfeit paradise.* Chicago: Aldine-Atherton.

Méndez, E. 1984. Mexico and Central America. Pp. 513–24 in *White-tailed deer: Ecology and management,* ed. L. K. Halls. Harrisburg, Pa.: Stackpole.

El mercado de Sonora y el tráfico ilegal de animales. 1985. *Novedades* (México), 1 December.

Milliken, T., and H. Tolunaga. 1987. *The Japanese sea turtle trade 1970–1986.* Tokyo: TRAFFIC (Japan).

Miller, L. E. 1914. Destruction of the rhea, black-necked swan, herons, and other wildlife in South America. *Bird Lore* 16:259–69.

Miller, S. 1980. Human influences on the distribution and abundance of wild Chilean mammals: Prehistoric–present. Ph.D. diss., Univ. Washington, Seattle.

Miller, S. D., J. Rottmann, and R. D. Taber. 1973. Dwindling and endangered ungulates of Chile: Vicuña, llama, hippocamelus, and pudu. *North Am. Wildl. Nat. Resour. Conf.* 38:55–68.

Miller, S. D., J. Rottmann, K. J. Raedeke, and R. D. Taber. 1983. Endangered mammals in Chile: Status and conservation. *Biolog. Conserv.* 25:335–52.

Minarik [Lagueux], C. 1985. Importancia económica de los huevos de la tortuga golfina (*Lepidochelys olivacea*) en Honduras. Dirección General de Recursos Naturales Renovables (RENARE), Tegucigalpa, Honduras. Unpublished report.

Ministerio de Agricultura y Cria. 1984. *Anuario estadístico agropecuario 1980.* Caracas, Venezuela.

Ministerio del Ambiente y de los Recursos Naturales Renovables (MARNR). N.d. Programa de manejo de la baba (*Caiman crocodilus*). Caracas, Venezuela. Unpublished Manuscript.

Mishra, H. R. 1982. Balancing human need and conservation in Nepal's Royal Chitwan Park. *Ambio* 11:246–51.

Mittermeier, R. 1977. Distribution, synecology and conservation of Surinam monkeys. Ph.D. diss., Harvard University, Cambridge, Mass.

———. 1981. Preliminary observations on habitat utilization and diet in eight Surinam monkeys. *Folia primatol.* 36:1–39.

———. 1982. Conservation of primates in Surinam. *Int. Zoo. Yearbook* 22:59–69.

———. 1983. A synecological study of Surinam monkeys. Pp. 521–34 in *Advances in herpetology and evolutionary biology. Essays in honor of Ernest E. Williams,* ed. A. Rhodin and K. Miyata. Cambridge, Mass.: Museum of Comparative Zoology, Harvard University.

———. 1987. Effects of hunting on rain forest primates. Pp. 109–48 in *Primate conservation on the tropical rain forest,* ed. C. Marsh and R. Mittermeier. New York: Alan R. Liss.

Mittermeier, R., R. Bailey, and A. Coimbra-Filho. 1977. Conservation and status of the Callitrichidae in Brazilian Amazonia, Surinam and French Guiana. Pp. 137–46 in

Biology and conservation of the Callitrichidae, ed. D. Kleiman. Washington, D.C.: Smithsonian Institution Press.

Mittermeier, R., and D. Cheney. 1986. Conservation of primates and their habitats. Pp. 477–490 in *Primate societies,* ed. B. B. Smuts, D. L. Cheney, R. M. Seyfarth, R. W. Wrangham and Thomas T. Struhsaker. Chicago: Univ. Chicago Press.

Mittermeier, R., and A. Coimbra-Filho. 1977. Primate conservation in Brazilian Amazonia. Pp. 117–66 in *Primate conservation,* ed. Prince Ranier of Monaco and G. Bourne. New York: Academic Press.

Mittermeier, R., W. Konstant, H. Ginsberg, M. van Roosmalen, and E. da Silva, Jr. 1983. Further evidence of insect consumption in the bearded saki monkey, *Chiropotes satanas chiropotes. Primates* 24:602–5.

Mittermeier, R., J. Oates, A. Eudey, and J. Thornback. 1986. Primate conservation. Pp. 3–72 in *Comparative primate biology,* vol. 2A: *Behavior, conservation, and ecology,* ed. G. Mitchell and J. Erwin. New York: Alan R. Liss.

Mittermeier, R., and M. J. Plotkin 1986. An action plan for conservation in Suriname. Washington, D.C.: World Wildlife Fund.

Mittermeier, R., and M. van Roosmalen. 1981. Preliminary observations on habitat utilization and diet in eight Suriname monkeys. *Folia Primatol.* 36:1–39.

Moll, D. 1986. The distribution, status and level of exploitation of the freshwater turtle *Dermatemys mawei* in Belize, Central America. *Biol. Cons.* 35:87–96.

Mondolfi, E. 1957. El Chigüire. El Farol (Caracas) 168:38–40.

———. 1972. Mamíferos de caza de Venezuela. La lapa o paca. *Defensa de la Naturaleza* 2:4–16.

Mones, A. 1973. Estudios sobre la familia Hydrochoeridae (Rodentia). I. Introducción e historia taxonómica. *Rev. Brasil. Biol.* 33:277–83.

———. 1980. Estudios sobre la familia Hydrochoeridae (Rodentia). VIII. Sinópsis sobre la situación de la población del carpincho *Hydrochoerus hydrochaeris* (L.) en el Uruguay. *Rev. Fac. Hum. Cienc. (Cienc. Biol.)* 1:101–4.

Mones, A., and J. Ojasti. 1986. *Hydrochoerus hydrochaeris. Mamm. Spec.* no. 264, 1–7.

Morales, J. 1985. Informe nacional de Nicaragua. First symposium on east Pacific sea turtles. San José, Costa Rica. 2–6 December 1985.

Moreira, A., and M. Benitez. 1985. Informe nacional de El Salvador. First symposium on east Pacific sea turtles. San José, Costa Rica. 2–6 December 1985.

Morin, V. 1977. The litigation and update. *Watchbird* 4:32–33.

Moskovits, D. K. 1988. Potential use of *Geochelone* in Amazonia. Unpublished manuscript.

Mossman, S. L., and A. S. Mossman. 1976. Wildlife utilization and game ranching. IUCN Occasional Paper 17. Morges, Switzerland.

Mrosovsky, N. 1983a. *Conserving sea turtles.* London: British Herpetological Society.

———. 1983b. Ecology and nest-site selection of leatherback turtles, *Dermochelys coriacea. Biol. Cons.* 26:47–56.

Mueller, H. 1972. Oekologische und ethologische studien und *Iguana iguana* L. (Reptilia: Iguanidae) in Kolumbien. *Zool. Beitr.,* N.F., 18:109–31.

Munn, C. A. 1988a. Macaw biology in Manu National Park, Peru. *Parrotletter* 1:18–21.

———. 1988b. The real macaws. *Animal Kingdom,* Sept./Oct. 1988:20–32.

Munn, C. A., J. B. Thomsen, and C. Yamashita. 1987. Survey and status of the Hyacinth Macaw (*Anodorhynchus hyacinthinus*) in Brazil, Bolivia, and Paraguay. Lausanne, Switzerland: CITES.

———. 1989. The Hyacinth Macaw. Pp. 404–19 in *Audubon wildlife report 1989*, ed. W. J. Chandler. New York: Academic Press.

Murphy, P. G. 1975. Net primary productivity in tropical terrestrial ecosystems. Pp. 217–31 in *Primary productivity of the biosphere*, ed. H. Leith and R. H. Whittaker. Ecological Studies 14. New York: Springer-Verlag.

Murphy, R. C. 1981. The guano and the anchoveta fishery. Pp. 81–106 in *Resource management and environmental uncertainty: Lessons from coastal updwelling fisheries*, ed. M. H. Glantz and J. D. Thompson. New York: Wiley.

Musters, G. C. 1871. *At home with the Patagonians*. London: John Murray.

Myers, N. 1975. The tourist as an agent for development and wildlife conservation: The case of Kenya. *Int. J. Social Econ.* 2(1):26–42.

———. 1979. *The sinking ark: A new look at the problem of disappearing species*. Oxford: Pergamon Press.

———. 1983. *A wealth of wild species*. Boulder, Colo.: Westview Press.

———. 1986. Tropical deforestation and a mega-extinction spasm. Pp. 394–409 in *Conservation biology: The science of scarcity and diversity*. Sunderland, Mass.: Sinauer.

Nagy, K. A. 1982. Energy requirements of free-living Iguanid lizards. Pp. 49–59 in *Iguanas of the world: Their behavior, ecology and conservation*, ed. G. M. Burghardt and A. S. Rand. Park Ridge, N.J.: Noyes.

Nations, J. D. 1988. Deep ecology meets the developing world. Pp. 79–82 in *Biodiversity*, ed. E. O. Wilson. Washington, D.C.: National Academy of Sciences.

Nations, J. D. and D. Komer. 1983a. Central America's tropical rainforests: Positive steps for survival. *Ambio* 12:231–38.

Nations, J. D., and D. Komer. 1983b. Rainforests and the hamburger society. *Environment* 25:12–19.

Neill, W. T. 1971. The last of the ruling reptiles. New York: Columbia Univ. Press.

Nichols, J. D., and G. M. Haramis. 1980. Inferences regarding survival and recovery rates of winter-banded canvasbacks. *J. Wildl. Mgmt.* 44:164–73.

Nietschmann, B. 1973. *Between Land and Water*. New York: Seminar Press.

———. 1975. Of turtles, arribadas, and people. *Chelonia* 2:6–9.

Nikoletsias, M., and R. K. Lore. 1981. Aggression in domesticated rats reared in a burrow-digging environment. *Aggressive Behav.* 7:245–52.

Nilsson, G. 1981. *The bird business*, 2d ed. Washington, D.C.: Animal Welfare Institute.

———. 1983. *The endangered species handbook*. Washington, D.C.: Animal Welfare Institute.

———. 1985a. *Importation of birds into the United States 1980–1984, vols. I and II*. Washington, D.C.: Animal Welfare Institute.

———. 1985b. Mortality in U.S. bird imports. *TRAFFIC Bull.* 6:72.

Nilsson, G., and D. Mack. 1980. *Macaws: Traded to extinction?* Special Report no. 2:1–136, Washington, D.C.: TRAFFIC (USA).

Nogueira Neto, P. 1973. *A criação de animais indígenas vertebrados. Peixes, anfibios, repteis, aves, mamíferos*. São Paulo, Brazil: Tecnapis.

Nolan, H. J. 1979. Tourist attractions and recreation resources providing for natural and human resources. Pp. 277–82 in *Tourism planning and development issues*, ed. D. E. Hawkins, E. L. Shafer, and J. M. Rovelstad. Washington, D.C.: George Washington Univ.

Norman, D. R. 1986. Man, anacondas, and tegus in eastern Paraguay. M.S. thesis, Tulane University, New Orleans.

―――. 1987. Man and tegu lizards in eastern Paraguay. *Biol. Conserv.* 41:39–56.

Norton, M., and H. Torres. 1980. *Evaluation of ground and trial census work on vicuña on Pampa Galeras, Perú*. Gland, Switzerland: WWF/IUCN. Unpublished report.

Nuevo Freire, C. M. 1982. *La ganadería en la puna de Catamarca*. Santa Rosa, La Pampa, Argentina: Univ. Nac. de la Pampa. Unpublished report.

O'Bryan, M., and D. McCullough. 1985. Survival of black-tailed deer following relocation in California. *J. Wildl.Mgmt.*, 49:115–19.

Ojasti, J. 1973. *Estudio biológico del chigüire o capibara*. Caracas, Venezuela: Fondo Nac. Invest. Agropec.

―――. 1978. The relation between population and production of the capybara. Ph.D. diss., Univ. Georgia, Athens.

―――. 1982. Estudio y manejo racional de la fauna silvestre en Pantanal Matogrossense con especial referencia al capivara y el jacaré. Brasilia, Brazil: IBDF. Unpublished report.

―――. 1984. Hunting and conservation of mammals in Latin America. *Acta Zool. Fenn.* 172:177–81.

―――. 1986. Wildlife management in neotropical moist forests: Overviews and prospects. Pp. 97–119 in *Gestion de la faune sauvage en forêt neotropicale húmide*. Paris: Cons. Intern. Chasse Conserv. Gibier.

Ojasti, J., G. F. Fajardo, and M. Cova O. 1987. Consumo de fauna por una comunidad indígena en el estado Bolívar, Venezuela. Pp. 45–50 in *Actas del 9 Congreso Latinoamericano de Zoología*. Arequipa, Perú.

Ojasti, J., and G. Medina. 1972. The management of capybara in Venezuela. *Trans. North Am. Wildl. Nat. Res. Conf.* 37:268–77.

Ojeda, R. A. and M. A. Mares. 1982. Conservation of South American mammals: Argentina as a paradigm. Pp. 505–21 in *Mammalian biology in South America*, ed. M. A. Mares and H. H. Genoways. Pymatuning Symp. Ecol., vol. 6. Pittsburgh, Pa.: University of Pittsburgh.

―――. 1984. La degradación de los recursos naturales y la fauna silvestre en Argentina. *Interciencia* 9:21–26.

Olswang, J. 1983. Dealers squawk over probe into parrots smuggling. *Los Angeles Times*, August 22.

Oren, D., and F. C. Novaes. 1986. Observations on the golden conure (*Aratinga guarouba*) in northern Brazil. *Biol. Cons.* 36:329–37.

Ortega, I. M. 1985. Social organization and ecology of a migratory guanaco population in southern Patagonia. M.S. thesis, Iowa State Univ., Ames.

Ortega M., H., F. Trevino L., A. Aragon T., and J. Cruces D. 1979. Estudio de la paloma de alas blancas (*Zenaida asiatica asiatica*) durante su época de reproducción en el estado de Tamaulipas—Temporada, 1978. Dir. Gral. Fauna Silvestre, México, D.F. Unpublished report.

Ortíz, F. P. 1983. Despluman al país con la incontrolada exportación de aves. *Proceso* 373:18–21.

Ortiz-Crespo, F. I. 1979. Discovery of an oilbird colony in the western drainage of the Ecuadorian Andes. *Auk* 96:187–89.

Ott, L. 1984. *An introduction to statistical methods and data analysis*. Boston: Duxbury Press.

Ouboter, P. E. and L. R. M. Nanhoe. 1984. An ecological study of *Caiman crocodilus* in northern Surinam. Dept. Anim. Ecol., Catholic Univ. Nijmegen, Nijmegen, Netherlands. Unpublished report.

Overton, S. 1971. Estimating the numbers of animals in wildlife populations. Pp. 403–57 in *Wildlife management techniques, 3d* ed., ed. R. H. Giles. Washington, D.C.: The Wildlife Society.

Pachon Rivera, J. E. 1982. Algunos aspectos relativos a la conservación y manejo de los Crocodylia en Colombia. II. Curso sobre la investigación, manejo y conservación de cocodrilos, Gainesville, Florida: Unpublished report.

Páez, O., R. Rodriguez, O. Aponte, H. Rodriguez, J. Mayo, J. Ochoa, D. Aguero, and F. Freitez. 1981. *El cultivo de arroz*. Publicación técnica divulgativa 7. Araure, Venezuela: Edición Unidad Técnica Estación Experimental.

Páez, R. 1862. *Wild scenes in South America, or Life in the llanos of Venezuela*. New York: Charles Scribner.

País, F. 1955. *Viaje a Laguna Blanca*. Serie de 14 Notas. Catamarca, Argentina: Diario La Unión.

Palmisano, A. W., T. Joanen, and L. L. McNease. 1973. An analysis of Louisiana's 1972 experimental alligator harvest program. Proceedings of the 27th annual conference of the Southeastern Association of Game and Fish Commisioners, Hot Springs, Arkansas.

La paloma de alas blancas en México (*Zenaida asiatica*). Dir. Gral. Fauna Silvestre, Mexico, D.F.

Paolisso, M., and R. Sackett. 1986. Traditional meat procurement strategies among the Irapa-Yukpa of the Venezuela-Colombia border area. *Res. Econ. Anthropol* 7:177–99.

Paredes, R. 1983. Marcaje de hembras anidadoras *Lepidochelys olivacea* en la Estación Biológica Chacocente costa del Pacífico de Nicaragua. Resumen 7. Managua, Nicaragua: Inst. Nic. Rec. Nat. Amb.

Parra, L. 1984. Análisis estadístico de la temporada de caza 1982–1983. Informe del Servicio Nacional de Fauna, MARNR.

Parra L., A. del C. 1986. Uso y manejo tradicional de la fauna silvestre y su relación con otras actividades productivas en San Pedro Jucayan, Oaxaca. Cuadernos de Divulgación, INIREB no. 27, México.

Parra, R., A. Escobar B., and E. Gonzalez-Jimenez. 1978. El chigüire, su potencial biológico y su cría en confinamiento. Pp. 83–94 in *Informe anual IPA*. Maracay, Venezuela: Univ. Central Venezuela.

Parrot Smuggler sentenced. 1988. *TRAFFIC Bull.* 8:7.

Pasquier, R. 1981. Conservation strategies for parrots of the mainland Neotropics. Pp. 7–20 in *Conservation of New World Parrots*, ed. R. F. Pasquier. ICBP Technical Publication no. 1. Washington, D.C.: Smithsonian Institution Press.

Peccary skins seized in Paraguay. 1986. *TRAFFIC Bull.* 8:2.

Pereira, E. M. 1987. Levantamento dos primatas em cativeiro na cidade de Rio Branco, Acre. Licendiado thesis, Universidade Federal do Acre, Rio Branco, Acre, Brazil.

Pereira, N. 1944. A utilizaçao da carne do jacare na Amazonia. *Boletim Geografico* 2:150–2.

Perez, J. J., and L. E. Eguiarte. N.d. Situación actual de tres especies del género *Amazona (A. ochrocephala, A. viridigenalis y A. autumnalis)* en el noreste de México. Unpublished manuscript.

Peterman, R. M. 1977. Graphical evaluation of environmental management options: Examples from a forest-insect pest system. *Ecol. Modelling* 3:133–48.

Phillipson, J. 1975. Rainfall, primary production and "carrying capacity" of Tsavo National Park (East), Kenya. *E. Afr. Wildl. J.* 13:171–201.

Pielou, E. C. 1969. *An introduction to mathematical ecology.* New York: Wiley.

Pierret, P. V, and M. J. Dourojeanni. 1966. La caza y la alimentación humana en las riberas del Río Pachiteca, Perú. *Turrialba* 16:271–77.

———. 1967. Importancia de la caza para la alimentación humana en el curso inferior del Rio Ucayali, Perú. *Revista Forestal de Perú* 1:10–21.

Pigram, J. J. 1980. Environmental implications of tourism development. *Ann. Tourism Res.* 7:554–83.

Pimm, S. L. 1986. Community stability and structure. Pp. 309–29 in *Conservation biology: The science of scarcity and diversity,* ed. M. E. Soulé. Sunderland, Mass.: Sinauer.

Pisano, E. 1974. Estudio ecológico de la región continental sur del area andino-patagónica. II. Contribución a la fitogeografia de la zona del Parque Nacional "Torres del Paine." *Anales Instituto de la Patagonia* 5:59–104.

Plowden, C. 1987a. *The bird trade in Peru. A report on the Peruvian bird trade with emphasis on exports to the United States.* Washington, D.C.: The Humane Society of the United States.

———. 1987b. *The bird trade in Argentina.* Washington, D.C.: The Humane Society of the United States.

Pohl, M., and L. H. Feldman. 1982. The traditional role of women and animals in lowland Maya economy. Pp. 295–311 in *Maya subsistence,* ed. K. V. Flannery. New York: Academic Press.

Polly wants a crackdown. 1988. *The Times* (London), Nov. 14.

Ponce, C. F. 1973. Informe nacional sobre la fauna del Perú. Pp 1–35 in *Simp. Intern. Fauna Silv. Pesca Fluv. Lacustr. Amazónica.* Manaus, Brazil: Ministerio de Agricultura.

Ponce, C. F., ed. 1987. Manejo de fauna silvestre y desarrollo rural. Información sobre siete especies de América Latina y el Caribe. Lima: FAO/PNUMA.

Ponciano, I. 1988. 3a Reunión Contramericana de Jefes de Vida Silvestre, Guatemala, 24–25 de Octubre de 1987. Unpublished report.

Posey, D. A. 1982. The keepers of the forest. *Garden* 6:18–24.

———. 1985. Indigenous management of tropical forest ecosystems: the case of the Kayapó Indians in the Brazilian Amazon. *Agroforestry Sys.* 3:139–58.

Posey, D. A., E. Elisabetsky, A. B. Anderson, M. Campos, A. de O. Rodrigues, and G. M. de la Panha. 1987. *A ciência dos Mēbêngôkre, alternativas contra a destruição.* Belém, Brazil: Museu Paraense Emilio Goeldi.

Prance, G. T., and G. B. Schaller. 1982. Preliminary studies of some vegetation types of the Pantanal, Mato Grosso, Brazil. *Brittonia* 34:228–51.

Presch, W. 1973. A review of the tegus, lizard genus *Tupinambis* (Sauria: Teiidae) from South America. *Copeia* 1973:740–5.

Prescott-Allen, R., and C. Prescott-Allen. 1982. *What's wildlife worth?* Washington, D.C.: International Institute for Environment and Development.

Prichard, H. H. 1902. Field notes upon some of the larger mammals of Patagonia. *Pro. Zool. Society., Lond.* 1:272–7.

———. 1911. *Through the heart of Patagonia*, London: Thomas Nelson.

Pritchard, P. C. H. 1979. *Encyclopedia of turtles*. Hong Kong: T. F. H. Publishers.

———. 1984a. Guest editorial. *Marine Turtle Newsletter* 27:1–2.

———. 1984b. Guest editorial. Ostional management options. *Marine Turtle Newsletter* 31:2–4.

Puig, S. 1986. Ecología poblacional del guanaco (*Lama guanicoe*, Camelidae, Artiodactyla) en la Reserva Provincial de La Payunia, Mendoza. Ph.D. diss., Univ. Buenos Aires, Buenos Aires.

Pujalte, J. C., and A. R. Reca. 1985. Vicuñas y Guanacos. Distribución y ambientes. Pp. 21–49, in *Estado Actual de las Investigaciones sobre Camélidos en la República Argentina*, ed. J. Cajal and J. Amaya. Buenos Aires, Argentina: Secretaria de Ciencia y Técnica.

Purdy, P. C. 1983. Agricultural, industrial and urban development in relation to the eastern white-winged dove. M.S. thesis, Colorado State Univ., Fort Collins.

Purdy, P. C., and R. E. Tomlinson. In press. Agricultural development in relation to the eastern white-winged dove. *Southwest Nat.*

Quiñones, M., and G. Castro. 1975. Aves canoras y de ornato. *Bosques y Fauna* 12:3–9.

Rabinovich, J. E., M. J. Hernandez, and J. L. Cajal. 1985. A simulation model of the management of vicuña populations. *Ecol. Modelling* 30:275–95.

Rabinowitz, A. R. 1986. Jaguar predation on domestic livestock in Belize. *Wildl. Soc. Bull.* 94:170–74.

Rabinowitz, A. R., and B. G. Nottingham, Jr. 1986. Ecology and behaviour of the jaguar (*Panthera onca*) in Belize, Central America. *J. Zool. Lond.* 210:149–59.

Raedeke, K. J. 1978. *El guanaco de Magallanes, Chile. Su distribución y biología.* Corporación Nacional Forestal, Publicacción Tecnica No. 4.

———. 1979. Population dynamics and socioecology of the guanaco (*Lama guanicoe*) of Magallanes, Chile. Ph.D. diss., Univ. Washington, Seattle.

Ramboux, A. 1983. Informe de Guatemala. First western Atlantic turtle symposium, Ad-hoc session on east Pacific turtle research. San José, Costa Rica.

Ramia, M. 1972. Cambios en la vegetación de las sabanas del Hato El Frío, Alto Apure, causados por diques. *Bol. Soc. Ven. Cien. Nat.* 30:57–64.

———. 1974a. Contribución al conocimiento de la ecología de las sabanas del Alto Apure. Ph.D. diss., Univ. Central de Venezuela, Caracas, Venezuela.

———. 1974b. *Plantas de las sabanas llaneras.* Caracas, Venezuela: Monte Avila Editores.

Ramos, M. 1982. *El comercio y la explotación de las aves vivas en México.* Xalapa, Veracruz, México: INIREB, Cuadernos de Divulgación No. 8.

Ramos, M., and E. E. Iñigo. 1985. Comercialización de psittaciformes en México. In *Primer Simposium Internacional sobre Fauna Silvestre,* vol. 2. México, D.F.

Ramos, M., and E. I. Elías. 1985. Comercialización de Psitácidos en México. In *Memoria Primer Simposium Internacional de Fauna Silvestre,* vol. 2. México, D. F.

Rand, A. S. 1968. A nesting aggregation of iguanas. *Copeia* 1968:552–61.

———. 1972. The temperatures of iguana nests and their relation to incubation optima and nesting sites and season. *Herpetologica* 28:252–53.

———. 1984. Clutch size in *Iguana iguana* in central Panama. In *Vertebrate ecology and systematics,* ed. R. A. Siegel, L. E. Hunt, J. L. Knight, L. Malaret, and N. L. Zuschlag. Lawrence: Univ. Kansas Mus. Nat. Hist.

Rand, A. S., and B. A. Dugan. 1980. Iguana egg mortality in the nest. *Copeia* 3:531–34.

———. 1983. Structure of complex iguana nests. *Copeia* 3:705–11.

Rand, A. S., and H. W. Greene. 1982. Latitude and climate in the phenology of reproduction in the green iguana, *Iguana iguana.* Pp. 142–49 in *Iguanas of the world: Their behavior, ecology, and conservation,* ed. G. M. Burghardt and A. S. Rand. Park Ridge, N.J.; Noyes.

Rand, A. S., and W. M. Rand. 1978. Display and dispute settlement in nesting iguanas. Pp. 245–51 in *Behavior and neurology of lizards,* ed. N. Greenberg and P. D. Maclean. Washington, D.C.: National Institutes of Mental Health.

Rand, A. S., and M. H. Robinson. 1969. Predation on iguana nests. *Herpetologica* 25:172–74.

Rapport, D. J., H. A. Reiger, and T. C. Hutchinson. 1985. Ecosystem behavior under stress. *Am. Nat.* 125:617–40.

Rebêlo, G. H., and W. E. Magnusson, 1983. An analysis of the effect of hunting on *Caiman crocodilus* and *Melanosuchus niger* based on the sizes of confiscated skins. *Biol. Conserv* 20:95–104.

Redford, K. H., and J. G. Robinson. 1985. Hunting by indigenous peoples and conservation of game species. *Cultural Survival Quart.* 9:41–44.

———. 1987. The game of choice: Patterns of indian and colonist hunting in the neotropics. *Am. Anthropol.* 89: 650–67.

———. In press. Park size and the conservation of forest mammals in Latin America. In *Latin American Mammals: Their conservation, ecology and evolution,* ed. M. Mares and D. A. Schmidley.

Reichel-Dolmatoff, G. 1971. *Amazonian Cosmos: The sexual and religious symbolism of the Tukano Indians.* Chicago: Univ. Chicago Press.

Rice, E. K. 1988. The palm cockatoo. *Anim. Kingdom* 91:55.

Rice, R. W. 1986. Disturbance in temperate grasslands: Its role as a major ecological factor. Unpublished manuscript.

Richard, J. D. and D. Hughes. 1972. Some observations of sea turtle nesting activity in Costa Rica. *Marine Biology* 16:297–306.

Ridgely, R. S. 1981. The current distribution and status of mainland neotropical parrots. In *Conservation of New World Parrots,* ed. R. F. Pasquier. ICBP Technical Pub. no. 1. Washington, D.C.: Smithsonian Institution Press.

———. 1982. The distribution, status, and conservation of neotropical mainland parrots. Ph.D. diss., Yale University, New Haven, Conn.

Ríos, M., C. I. Ponce, A. Tovar, P. G. Vasquez, and M. Dourojeanni. 1986. *Plan maestro del Parque Nacional del Manú. Sistema Nacional de Unidades de Conservación.* Lima, Perú: Ministerio de Agricultura y Alimentación.

Rios Soto, F., D. Gutierrez, and C. Casler. 1981. Consumo de arroz por los patos (*Dendrocygna*) en los arrozales de Venezuela. *Mem. Soc. Cien. Nat. La Salle.* 46:97–104.

Rivero-Blanco, C. 1974. Hábitos reproductivos de la baba en los llanos de Venezuela, *Natura* 52:24–29.

Rivero-Blanco, C. 1985. Evaluación de algunos aspectos de la temporada de aprovechamiento de la especie baba, *Caiman crocodilus,* de 1985. Caracas, Venezuela: MARNR.

Robinette, W. L., C. M. Loveless, and D. A. Jones. 1974. Field tests of strip census methods. *J. Wildl. Mgmt.,* 38:81–96.

Robinson, D. C. 1983. Las grandes arribadas, sobrevivencia o suicidio? First Western Atlantic Turtle Symposium, Ad-hoc session on east Pacific turtle research. San José, Costa Rica.

Robinson, J. G. 1988. Demography and group structure in wedge-capped capuchin monkeys, (*Cebus olivaceus*). *Behaviour* 104:202–32.

———. 1990. Economic approaches to conservation. *Ecology* 71:410.

Robinson, J. G., and K. H. Redford. 1986a. Body size, diet, and population density of Neotropical forest mammals. *Am. Nat.* 128:665–80.

———. 1986b. Intrinsic rate of natural increase in Neotropical forest mammals: relationship to phylogeny and diet. *Oecologia* 68:516–20.

Robinson, M. H. 1988. Are there alternatives to destruction? Pp. 355–60 in *Biodiversity,* ed. E. O. Wilson. Washington, D.C.: National Academy Press.

Rodriguez, H. 1983. La fauna silvestre en México: Perspectivas de conservación y aprovechamiento. Dir. Gral. de la Fauna y Flora Silvestres. Unpublished manuscript.

———. 1986. México ante la explotación internacional de la fauna silvestre. In *Primer Symposium Internacional sobre Fauna Silvestre.* Mayo 1985, México, D.F.

———. 1987. Condición actual de las poblaciones de venado cola blanca (*Odocoileus virginianus*) en Guanacaste y la Península de Nicoya. San José, Costa Rica: Ministerio de Recursos Naturales, Energía y Minas. Unpublished report.

Rodriguez, M., and V. Solís, 1987. Ciclo reproductivo del venado cola blanca de la Isla San Lucas, Costa Rica. Pp. 31–32 in *Actas del Primer Taller Nacional sobre el Venado Cola Blanca (Odocoileus virginianus) del Pacífico Seco, Costa Rica,* ed. V. Solis, M. Rodriguez, and C. Vaughan. Heredia, Costa Rica: Univ. Nac.

Rodriguez, M., V. Solís, and C. Vaughan. 1987. *Plan de manejo del hato de venado cola blanca de la Isla San Lucas.* Heredia, Costa Rica: Univ. Nac.

Rodriguez, M., and C. Vaughan. 1987. Organización social del venado cola blanca en la Isla San Lucas. Pp. 37–38 in *Actas del Primer Taller nacional sobre el Venado Cola Blanca (Odocoileus virginianus) del Pacífico Seco, Costa Rica,* ed. V. Solís, M. Rodriguez, and C. Vaughan. Heredia, Costa Rica: Univ. Nac.

Rodriguez, R., A. Glade, and E. Nuñez. 1983. *Bases para el manejo de la vicuña en la Provincia de Parinacota. I. Región, Chile.* Documento Trabajo No. 3. Arica, Chile: Corporación Nacional Forestal.

Roe, P. G. 1982. *The cosmic zygote: Cosmology in the Amazon Basin.* New Brunswick, N.J.: Rutgers Univ. Press.

Roet, E., D. Mack, and N. Duplaix. 1981. *Psittacines imported by the United States, October 1979 to June 1980.* TRAFFIC (USA) Special Report no. 7.

————. 1981. Psittacines imported by the United States, October 1979–June 1980. In *Conservation of new world parrots,* ed. R. F. Pasquier. Tech. Publ. no. 1. Morges, Switzerland: ICBP.

Rohter, L. 1987. Mexico becomes hub for wildlife smugglers. *New York Times* July 26, 1, 16.

Romanoff, S. A. 1984. Matses adaptations in the Peruvian Amazon. Ph.D. disser., Columbia Univ., New York.

Rongstad, O., and R. McCabe. 1984. Capture techniques. Pp. 566–686 in *White-tailed deer: Ecology and management,* ed. L. K. Hall. Harrisburg, Pa.: Stackpole.

Roosevelt, A. C. 1980. *Parmana: Prehistoric maize and manioc subsistence along the Amazon and Orinoco.* New York: Academic Press.

Rosales, F. 1985. Informe nacional de Guatemala. First symposium on east pacific sea turtles. San Jose, Costa Rica.

Roseberry, J. L. 1979. Bobwhite population responses to exploitation: Real and simulated. *J. Wildl. Mgmt.* 43:285–305.

Ross, E. B. 1978. Food taboos, diet, and hunting strategy: The adaptation to animals in Amazon cultural ecology. *Curr. Anthropol.* 19:1–16.

Roth, P. N.d. Report on the second half of the project in search of Spix's macaw. Unpublished manuscript.

Ruddle, K. 1970. The hunting technology of the Maraca indians. *Antropologica* 25: 21–63.

Ruddle, K., and J. Wilbert. 1980. Los Yukpa. Pp. 33–124 in *Aborígenes de Venezuela,* ed. W. Coppens. Caracas, Venezuela: Texto.

Ruiz, G. 1979. Fundamentos y programa de manejo para uso público del Parque Nacional del Manú. M.S. thesis, Univ. Nac. Agraria, La Molina, Lima, Perú.

Ruiz, R. A., and A. S. Rand. 1981. Las iguanas y el hombre en Panamá. *Rev. Medica de Panamá* 6(1):118–26.

Saenz, J. 1987. Comportamiento y sobrevivencia de dos poblaciones de venado colablanca (*Odocoileus virginianus*) reintroducidas a un nuevo ambiente. M.S. thesis, Univ. Nac., Heredia, Costa Rica.

Saglio, C. 1979. Tourism for discovery: a project in lower Casamance, Senegal. Pp. 321–35 in *Tourism: Passport to development?* ed. E. DeKadt. Washington, D.C.: World Bank.

SAM. *See* Sistema Alimentario Mexicano.

Sandi, A., E. Sánchez, and M. Yarigaño. 1987. Plan nacional Vicuña. Análisis del plan nacional Vicuña 1965–2013. Plan alternativo. Lima, Perú: Ministerio de Agricultura.

SARH. *See* Secretaría de Agricultura y Recursos Hidráulicos.

Sarmiento, G. 1984. *The ecology of neotropical savannas.* Cambridge, Mass.: Harvard Univ. Press.

Sarmiento, G., and M. Monasterio. 1971. Ecología de las sabanas de América Tropical. I. Análisis macroecológico de los región de Calabozo, Venezuela. *Cuadernos Geográficos* 4:1–126.

Saunders, G. B. 1940. Eastern white-winged dove (*Melopelia asiatica asiatica*) in southeastern Texas. Washington, D.C.: U.S. Fish Wildl. Serv. Unpublished report.

Schaefer, E. 1953. Estudio bio-ecológico comparativo sobre algunos Cracidae del norte y centro de Venezuela. *Bol. Soc. Ven. Cien. Nat.* 15:30–63.

Schaefer, E., and W. H. Phelps. 1954. Las aves del Parque Nacional Henri Pittier (Rancho Grande) y sus funciones ecológicas. *Bol. Soc. Ven. Cien. Nat.* 16: 1–171.

Schaller, G. B. 1983. Mammals and their biomass on a Brazilian ranch. *Arq. Zool. S. Paulo* 31:1–36.

Schaller, G. B., and J. Vasconcelos. 1978. Jaguar predation on capybara. *Zeitschrift für Saugetierkunde* 43:296–301.

Schaller, G. B., and P. G. Crawshaw, Jr. 1980. Movement patterns of jaguar. *Biotropica* 12:161–8.

———. 1981. Social organization in a capybara population. *Säugetierk Mitt.* 29:3–16.

Schulz, J., R. Mittermeier, and H. Reichart. 1977. Wildlife in Surinam. *Oryx* 14:133–44.

Scott, D. A., and M. Carbonell. 1986. *A directory of neotropical wetlands.* IUCN, Cambridge, and IWRB, Slimbridge.

Scott, J. P. 1953. The process of socialization in higher animals. *Proc. Milband Memor. Fund* 29:82–103.

Seago, J. 1974. Responsibilities of an animal catcher. *Int. Zool. Yearbook* 14:39–40.

Seber, G. A. F. 1973. *The estimation of animal abundance.* London: Griffin.

Secretaría de Agricultura y Recursos Hidráulicos (SARH). 1977. Informes estadísticos para los años 1953–1977. Estadistica Agrícola, Dir. Gral. de Distritos de Riego, México.

———. 1978. Características de los distritos y unidades de riego. Dir. Gral. Distritos y Unidades de Riego, México.

———. 1979a. Distritos de Temporal. Representación General de Tamaulipas. Gobierno de Tamaulipas, México.

———. 1979b. Disposiciones del calendario de captura y comercio de aves canoras y de ornato, temporada 1979–1980, México.

Secretaría de Desarrollo Urbano y Ecología (SEDUE). 1983. Ley Federal de Caza. Subsecretaría de Ecología, México.

———. 1985–86. Ley Federal de Caza. Calendarios cinégeticos de las temporadas 1985–86 y 1986–87, México.

———. 1987. Solicitud de permisos para el aprovechamiento de aves canoras y de ornato temporada 1987–1988, México.

SEDUE. *See* Secretaría de Desarrollo Urbano y Ecologia.

Seeger, A. 1982. Native Americans and the conservation of flora and fauna in Brazil. Pp. 177–90 in *Socio-economic effects and constraints in tropical forest management*, ed. E. G. Hallsworth. New York: Wiley.

Seijas, A. E. 1984. Estimaciones poblacionales de babas *Caiman crocodilus* en los Llanos occidentales de Venezuela. Serie Informes Técnicos. Caracas, Venezuela: MARNR.

Seijas, A. E., and S. Ramos. 1980. Características de la dieta de la baba (*Caiman crocodilus*) durante la estación seca en las sabanas moduladas del Estado Apure Venezuela. *Acta Biol. Venezolana* 10:373–89.

Sequeira, W. G. 1985. *La hacienda ganadera en Guanacaste, aspectos económicos y sociales 1850–1900.* San José, Costa Rica: Univ. Estatal de Distancia.

Severinghaus, C. 1949. Tooth development and wear as criteria of age in white-tailed deer. *J. Wildl. Mgmt.* 13:195–216.

SFF. *See* Subsecretaría Forestal y de la Fauna.

Shaw, J. H. 1985. *Introduction to wildlife management.* New York: McGraw-Hill.

Shipley, W. U. 1963. The demonstration in the guinea-pig of a process resembling classical imprinting. *Anim. Behav.* 11:470–4.

Sick, H. N.d. Macaws, parakeets, parrots and allies. Unpublished manuscript.

———. 1985. *Ornitologia Brasileria, uma introduçao.* Brasilia, Brazil: Universidade de Brasilia.

Siegel, S. 1956. *Nonparametric Statistics for Behavioural Sciences.* New York: McGraw-Hill.

Sielfeld K., W. 1983. *Mamíferos Marinos de Chile.* Santiago: Univ. de Chile.

Sielfeld K., W., and Venegas C., C. 1985. Bases para un programa de manejo y explotación de guanacos en Tierra del Fuego, Chile. Pp. 202–11 in *Actas de la IV Convención Internacional Sobre Camélidos Sudamericanos,* ed. C. Venegas C. and C. Cunazza P. Punta Arenas, Chile: Univ. Magallanes.

Silva, J. L., and S. D. Strahl. 1987. Participación Venezolana en el proyecto ecología conductual y conservación de la familia Cracidae en Venezuela. Caracas, Venezuela: FUDENA.

Sims, P. L., and R. T. Coupland. 1979. Producers. Pp. 49–72 in *Grassland ecosystems of the world,* ed. R. T. Coupland. Cambridge: Cambridge University Press.

Sinclair, A. R. E. 1977. *The African buffalo: A study of resource limitation of populations.* Chicago: Univ. Chicago Press.

Singer, P. 1976. *Animal liberation.* New York: Avon Books.

Singh, L. A. K., S. Kar, and B. C. Choudhury. 1986. Indian crocodilians: A 10-year review of management. Pp. 362–71 in *Crocodiles.* IUCN Publication. Caracas, Venezuela: Texto.

Sistema Alimentario Mexicano (SAM). 1980. *La estrategia temporalera del Sistema Alimentario Mexicano y su operación.*

Skins seized in Uruguay. 1986. *TRAFFIC Bull.* 8:32

Sluckin, W. 1968. Imprinting in guinea-pigs. *Nature* 220:1148.

Smith, N. 1983. Enchanted forest. *Nat. Hist.* 92:14–20.

Smith, N. J. H. 1974. Destructive exploitation of the south American river turtle. *Assoc. Pacific Coast Geographers* 36:85–102.

———. 1976a. Spotted cats and the Amazon skin trade. *Oryx* 13:362–71.

———. 1976b. Utilization of game along Brazil's transamazon highway. *Acta Amazonica* 6:455–66.

———. 1978. Human exploitation of terra firme fauna in Amazonia. *Ciencia e Cultura* 30:17–23.

———. 1980. Caimans, capybaras, otters, manatees, and man in Amazonas. *Biol. Cons.* 19:177–87.

Smith, T. D. 1984. Estimating the dolphin population size yielding maximum net production. Pp. 187–90 in *Reproduction in whales, dolphins and porpoises,* ed. W. F. Perrin, R. L. Brownell, Jr., and D. P. DeMaster. *Rep. Int. Whal. Comm.,* Special Issue 6.

Smith, V. 1980. Anthropology and tourism: A science-industry evaluation. *Ann. Tourism Res.* 7(1):13–33.

Smylie, T. 1983. Agents track parrot smugglers. *Fish and Wildlife News,* April–May, 6–7.

————. 1987. American dove take in Mexico tallied. *Fish and Wildlife News*, April–May, 10–11.

Smythe, N. 1983. *Dasyprocta punctata* and *Agouti paca*. Pp. 463–65 in *Costa Rican natural history*, ed. D. H. Janzen. Chicago: Univ. Chicago Press.

————. 1987. The paca (*Cuniculus paca*) as a domestic source of protein for the Neotropical, humid lowlands. *Appl. Anim. Behav. Sci.*, 17:155–70.

Snyder, N. F. R., J. W. Wiley, and C. B. Kepler. 1987. *The parrots of Luguillo: Natural and conservation of the Puerto Rican parrot*. Los Angeles, Calif.: Western Foundation of Vertebrate Zoology.

Sokal, R. R., and F. J. Rolf. 1969. *Biometry*. San Francisco: W. H. Freeman.

————. 1981. *Biometry*, 2d ed. New York: W. H. Freeman.

Solís, V. 1986a. Ecología y comportamiento de las crias de venado cola blanca (*Odocoileus virginianus*) en la Isla San Lucas, Costa Rica. M.S. thesis, Univ. Kansas, Lawrence.

————. 1986b. La alternativa de la educación ambiental. Pp. 63–69 in *Actas del Primer Taller Nacional sobre el Venado Cola Blanca del Pacífico Seco, Costa Rica*, ed. V. Solís, M. Rodriguez, and C. Vaughan. Heredia, Costa Rica: Univ. Nacional.

Solís, V., and M. Rodriguez. 1987. El venado cola blanca en Guanacaste, retrospección histórica. Pp. 15–18 in *Actas del Primer Taller Nacional sobre el Venado Cola Blanca (Odocoileus virginianus) del Pacífico Seco, Costa Rica.*, ed. V. Solís, M. Rodriguez, and C. Vaughan. Heredia, Costa Rica: Univ. Nacional

Solís, V., M. Rodriguez, and C. Vaughan, eds. 1987. *Actas del Primer Taller Nacional Sobre el Venado Cola Blanca (Odocoileus virginianus) del Pacífico Seco, Costa Rica*. Heredia, Costa Rica: Univ. Nac.

Sork, V. L. 1987. Effects of predation and light on seedling establishment in *Gustavia superba*. *Ecology* 68:1341–50.

Sosa-Burgos, L. M. 1981. Comportamiento social del chigüire en relación con su manejo en cautiverio. Bachillerato thesis, Univ. Central Venezuela, Caracas.

South American Handbook. 1989. Bath, England: Mendip Press. Trade and Travel Publications.

Stancyk, S. E. 1982. Non-human predators of sea turtles and their control. Pp. 139–52 in *Biology and conservation of sea turtles,* ed. K. S. Bjorndal. Washington, D.C.: Smithsonian Institution Press.

Statesman's Yearbook. 1987. New York: St. Martin's Press.

Staton, M., and J. R. Dixon. 1975. Studies on the dry season biology of *Caiman crocodilus* from the Venezuelan Llanos. *Mem. Soc. Cienc. Nat. La Salle* 35:237–65.

————. 1977. Breeding biology of the speckled caiman, *Caiman crocodilus crocodilus*, in the Venezuelan Llanos. *U.S. Fish and Wildlife Serv. Rep.* 5:1–21.

Steward, J. H., ed. 1948. *Handbook of South American Indians*. vol. 3: *The tropical forest tribes*. Washington, D.C.: U.S. Government Printing Office.

————. 1949. South American cultures: an interpretative summary. Pp. 669–772 in *The comparative ethnology of South American Indians, handbook of South American Indians,* vol. 5. Washington, D.C.: U.S. Government Printing Office.

Stoney, C. 1987. The day of the iguana. *VITA News*, October 4–8.

Strahl, S. D. In press. Large neotropical forest birds: The need for field research. Memorias, 62da Reunión de la Comisión de Supervivencia de Especies SSC-IUCN. Caracas, Venezuela: Fotoarte Arata/Fudena.

Strahl, S. D., and J. L. Silva. In press. Census methodology for cracid populations. In *II Simposio Internacional sobre la Biología y Conservación de la Familia Cracidae.* Caracas, Venezuela.

Stransky, J. 1984. Hunting the white-tailed. Pp. 739–80 in *White-tailed deer: Ecology and management,* ed. L. K. Halls. Harrisburg, Pa.: Stackpole.

Subsecretaría Forestal y de la Fauna (SFF). 1982. Bases para el control y regulaciones de exportaciones e importaciones de fauna silvestre y sus productos derivados. México.

Sunquist, F. 1984. Cowboys and capybaras. *Int. Wildl.* 14(2):4–9.

Svedeen, K. 1983. Stress: Cage birds' worst enemy. *Watchbird* 9:16–17.

Swanson, P. C. 1950. The Iguana *Iguana iguana* L. *Herpetologica* 6:187–93.

Taylor, K. I. 1988. Deforestation and Indians in Brazilian Amazonia. Pp. 138–44 in *Biodiversity,* ed. E. O. Wilson. Washington, D.C.: National Academy Press.

Taylor, M. K., D. P. DeMaster, F. L. Bunnell, and R. E. Schweinsburg. 1987. Modeling the sustainable harvest of female polar bears. *J. Wildl. Mgmt.* 51:811–20.

Teer, J. G. 1984. Lessons from the Llano Basin, Texas. Pp. 261–90 in *White-tailed deer: Ecology and management,* ed. L. K. Hall. Harrisburg, Pa.: Stackpole.

———. 1987. Aspectos socioeconómicos del venado cola blanca en Texas. Pp. 19–23 in *Actas del Primer Taller Nacional sobre el Venado Cola Blanca (Odocoileus virginianus) del Pacífico Seco, Costa Rica,* ed. V. Solis, M. Rodriguez, and C. Vaughan. Heredia, Costa Rica: Univ. Nac.

Terborgh, J. 1986. Keystone plant resources in the tropical forest. Pp. 330–44 in *Conservation biology,* ed. M. E. Soulé. Sunderland, Mass.: Sinauer.

Terborgh, J., and B. Winter. 1980. Some causes of extinction. Pp. 119–33 in *Conservation biology: An evolutionary-ecological perspective,* ed. M. Soulé and B. Wilcox. Sunderland, Mass.: Sinauer.

Terborgh, J., L. H. Emmons, and C. Freese. 1986. La fauna silvestre de la Amazonia: El despilfarro de un recurso renovable. *Bol. de Lima* 46:77–85.

Terwilliger, V. I. 1978. Natural history of Baird's tapir on Barro Colorado Island, Panama Canal Zone. *Biotropica* 10:211–20.

Thomsen, J. B. 1988. Guyana and Suriname establish quotas on parrot exports. *Parrotletter* 1:11–12.

Thomsen, J. B., and G. Hemley, 1987. Bird trade . . . bird bans. *TRAFFIC (USA)* 7:1, 21–24.

Thomsen, J. B., and C. A. Munn. 1988. *Cyanopsitta spixii:* A nonrecovery report. *Parrotletter* 1:6–7.

Thorbjarnarson, J. 1987. Status, ecology, and conservation of the Orinoco crocodile (*Crocodylus intermedius*) in Venezuela. Fundación para la Defensa de la Naturaleza (FUNDENA) Caracas, Venezuela: Unpublished report.

Thorington, R. W. Jr., R. Rudran, and D. Mack. 1979. Sexual dimorphism in *Alouatta seniculus* and observation on capture techniques. Pp. 97–106 in *Vertebrate ecology in the northern neotropics,* ed. J. F. Eisenberg. Washington, D.C.: Smithsonian Institution Press.

Thresher, P. 1981. The present value of an Amboseli lion. *World Anim. Rev.* 40:30–33.

Tomlinson, R. E. 1987a. Hunter declarations at border ports of doves and pigeons bagged in Mexico during the 1986–87 hunting season. Unpublished report.

———. 1987b. Trip report: White-winged dove nesting colonies in Tamaulipas and Nuevo León, Mexico, June 1987. Unpublished report.

Torres Caona, J. L. 1974. La carne del chigüiro como alimento. *Orient. Agropec* 99:70–75.

Torres, D. 1980. Utilización racional de la nutria. Montevideo, Uruguay. Unpublished report.

Torres, H. 1985. Distribution and conservation of the guanaco. IUCN/SSC South American Camelid Specialist Group Special Report No. 2.

Toufexis, A. 1983. Adventures in the skin trade. *Time* (Dec. 5): 45.

Tovar, A. D. 1969. Man's effect on natural fauna. *Fla. Audubon Soc. Nat. Hist.* 1969:21.

Townsend, C. H. 1925. The Galapagos tortoises in their relation to the whaling industry. A study of old logbooks. *Zoologica* 4:55–99.

TRAFFIC. 1983. U.S. Imports of psittacine species by country of origin, 1968–1982. Draft report.

Trek news. 1987. Vol. 16.

Uhl, C., and G. Parker. 1986. Is a one-quarter pound hamburger worth a half-ton of rainforest? *Interciencia* 11:213.

United States Department of Agriculture (USDA). 1936, 1980. Agricultural statistics. Washington, D.C.: U.S. Government Printing Office.

———. 1979. Quarantine Report Forms "17–13" (Bird Imports from Mexico). Washington, D.C.: U.S. Government Printing Office.

———. 1980a. Smuggled parrots sold at auction. USDA News Feature, May 5.

———. 1980b. Quarantine Report Forms "17–13" (Bird Imports from Mexico). Washington, D.C.: U.S. Government Printing Office.

———. 1981. Quarantine Report Forms "17–13" (Bird Imports from Mexico). Washington, D.C.: U.S. Government Printing Office.

———. 1982. Quarantine Report Forms "17–13" (Bird Imports from Mexico). Washington, D.C.: U.S. Government Printing Office.

———. 1987. Commercial bird importations—Fiscal year 1986. Unpublished report by Wade H. Richie, Animal and Plant Health Inspection Service.

United States Department of Commerce (USDC). 1981. U.S. Imports from Consumption. 1–1.

———. 1982. U.S. Imports from consumption. 1–1.

———. 1986. Tide tables 1987, high and low water predictions, west coast of north and South America including the Hawaiian islands. National Oceanic and Atmospheric Administration (NOAA) National Ocean Service.

United States Fish and Wildlife Service (USFWS). 1983. U.S. CITES Annual Report for 1981: 72–73.

USDA. See United States Department of Agriculture.

Uzzell, P. B. 1950. Status of the white-winged dove in Texas. Texas Game, Fish and Oyster Comm. Unpublished report.

van der Staaij, F. 1975. Jacht in Bigi Poika. Landbouwhogeschool-Wageningen, Centrum voor Landbouwkundig Onderzoek in Suriname, Paramaribo, Surinam. Unpublished report.

van Devender, R. W. 1982. Growth and ecology of spiny-tailed and green iguanas in Costa Rica, with comments on the evolution of herbivory and large body size. Pp. 162–83 in *Iguanas of the world: Their behavior ecology and conservation*, ed. G. M. Burghardt and A. S. Rand. Park Ridge, N.J.: Noyes.

van Roosmalen, M. 1985. Habitat preferences, diet, feeding strategy and social organization of the black spider monkey (*Ateles paniscus paniscus* Linnaeus 1958) in Surinam. *Acta Amazonica* 15 (suppl.).

van Roosmalen, M., R. Mittermeier, and K. Milton. 1981. The bearded sakis, genus *Chiropotes*. Pp. 419–41 in *Ecology and behavior of neotropical primates*, vol I, ed. A. Coimbra-Filho and R. Mittermeier. Rio de Janeiro, Brazil: Brazilian Academy of Sciences.

Vaughan, C. 1983. A report on dense forest habitat for endangered species in Costa Rica. Heredia, Costa Rica: Univ. Nac. Unpublished report.

Vaughan, C., E. Carrillo, and G. Wong. N.d. Consumo de carne de monte en Costa Rica. Unpublished report.

Vaughan, C., and M. Rodriguez. 1986. Comparación de los hábitos alimentarios del coyote (*Canis latrans*) en dos localidades en Costa Rica. *Vida Silvestre Neotropical* 1:6–11.

Vaughan, C., M. Rodriquez, M. DiMare, and J. G. Teer. 1984. Restoration of white-tailed deer in Costa Rica. Heredia, Costa Rica: Univ. Nac. Unpublished report.

Venezuela. 1984. Resolución No. 123 sobre la protección y el aprovechamiento del chigüire. Gaceta Oficial, No. 33134.

Verscheure S., H. E. 1979. Estudio preliminar de utilización del guanaco de Magallanes (*Lama quanicoe* Muller) como recurso natural renovable. M.S. thesis, Universidad de Chile, Santiago.

Vickers, W. T. 1980. An analysis of Amazonian hunting yields as a function of settlement age. Pp. 7–29 in *Working papers on South American Indians,* ed. W. T. Vickers and K. M. Kensinger. Bennington, Vt: Bennington College.

———. 1983. The territorial dimensions of Siona-Secoya and Encabellado adaptation. Pp. 541–78 in *Adaptive responses of native Amazonians,* ed. R. B. Hames and W. T. Vickers, New York: Academic Press.

———. 1988. Game depletion hypothesis of Amazonian adaptation: Data from a native community. *Science* 239:1521–2.

Villalba-Macias, J. S. 1989. South American exports of crocodile skins. Pp. 200–204 in Proc. VIII Working Mtg. IUCN SCC Crocodile Specialist Group. Gland, Switzerland: IUCN.

Waggerman, G., and R. R. George. 1982. Survey, status of the white-winged dove in Texas. Tex. Parks and Wildl. Dept. Austin. Unpublished report.

Wagley, C. 1977. *Welcome of tears: The Tapirape Indians of central Brazil.* New York: Oxford Univ. Press.

Walsh, J., and R. Gannon. 1967. *Time is short and the water rises.* London: Nelson.

Walton, P. 1984. A study of the ecology and behavior of Baird's tapir (*Tapirus bairdii*) in Belize during the months of May, June and July, 1983. B. S. thesis, Univ. Durham, Durham, England.

Weber, A. W. 1987. Socioeconomic factors in the conservation of Afromontane forest reserves. Pp. 205–29 in *Primate conservation in a tropical rainforest,* ed. C. W. Marsh and R. A. Mittermeier. New York: Alan R. Liss.

Weir, B. J. 1974. Reproductive characteristics of hystricomorph rodents. *Symp. Zool. Soc. London* 34:265–301.

Weiser, T. 1988. Llegó ayer procedente de Holanda un cargamento de loros que fué sacado de México de manera ilegal. Uno Más Uno. July 16, 14.

Werner, D. I. 1987. Manejo de la iguana verde en el bosque tropical. *Interciencia* 12:226–9.

———. 1988. The effect of varying water potential on body weight, yolk and fat bodies in neonate green iguanas. *Copeia* 1988:406–11.

Werner, D. I., E. M. Baker, E. Gonzalez, and I. Sosa. 1987. Kinship recognition and grouping in hatchling green iguanas. *Behav. Ecol. Sociobiol.* 21:83–89.

Werner, D. I., and T. J. Miller. 1984. Artificial nests for female green iguanas. *Herp. Rev.* 15(2):57–58.

Werner, D. I., and S. Paton. N.d. Incubation temperature and water potential influence *Iguana iguana* hatchling quality. Unpublished manuscript.

Werner, D. I., and A. S. Rand. 1986. Manejo de la iguana verde en Panamá. *Symp. Cons. Manejo Fauna Silv. Neotrop. (IX CLAZ, Peru):*77–80.

Werner, D. I., and D. I. Rey. 1987. El manejo de la iguana verde. Vol. 1. Biologia. Impretex, Panamá.

Western, D. 1979. Size, life history and ecology in mammals. *Afr. J. Ecol.* 17:185–204.

———. 1982. Amboseli National Park: Human values and the conservation of a savanna ecosystem. Pp. 93–100 in *Proceedings, World Congress on National Parks and Protected Areas,* ed. J. A. McNeely and K. R. Miller. Bali, Indonesia: IUCN.

———. 1983. Production, reproduction and size in mammals. *Oecologia* 59:269–71.

———. 1986. Tourist capacity in East African Parks. *Industry Environment* 9:14–16.

Western, D., and W. Henry. 1979. Economics and conservation in Third World national parks. *BioScience* 29:414–8.

Williams, K. D., and G. Petrides. 1980. Browse use, feeding behavior, and management of the Malayan tapir. *J. Wildl. Mgmt.* 44:489–94.

Wilson, P., and W. L. Franklin. 1985. Male group dynamics and inter-male aggression of guanacos in southern Chile. *Z. Tierpsychol.* 69:305–28.

Witt, C. 1981. Hustlers, rustlers, and just desserts for smugglers. *Watchbird* 7:30–33.

Wolf, E. C. 1987. *On the brink of extinction: conserving the diversity of life.* Worldwatch Paper 78. Washington, D.C.: The Worldwatch Institute.

Woodward, A., and D. David. 1985. A study of the baba (*Caiman crocodilus crocodilus*) population on the Hato Piñero in Venezuela. Unpublished report.

Woody, J. B. 1986. On the dollar value of the Oaxacan ridley fishery. *Marine Turtle Newsletter* 36:6–7.

World fish catch sets record. 1986. *TRAFFIC Bull.* 8:12.

World Resources Institute (WRI). 1987. World Resources 1987: A report by the International Institute for Environment and Development and the World Resources Institute. Washington, D.C.

Ximenez, A. 1978. Sobre el hallazgo de un cráneo de *Hydrochoerus hydrochaeris* (Linné) en la ribera del río San Francisco, Brasil. *Rev. Nordest. Biol.* 1:105–12.

Yamne, T. 1969. *Statistics: an introductory analysis,* 2d ed. New York: Harper & Row.

Yost, J. A., and P. M. Kelley. 1983. Shotguns, blowguns, and spears: the analysis of technological efficiency. Pp. 189–224 in *Adaptive responses of native Amazonians,* ed. R. B. Hames and W. T. Vickers. New York: Academic Press.

Zug, G. R., and A. S. Rand. 1987. Estimation of age in nesting female *Iguana iguana:* Testing skeletochronology in a tropical lizard. *Amphibia-Reptilia* 8:237–50.

Index

The letter *t* following a page number stands for *table;* the letter *f* stands for *figure.*